ISO/IEC 27001:2022 Control A Ologies

KAL, AAJ aur KAL

Dr. Rakhi R Wadhwani
Evita K-Breukel
Sharade Kamalanathan

Become Shakespeare .com

First Published in 2024

Becomeshakespeare.com

One Point Six Technologies Pvt Ltd
Unit no. 26, Grd Floor, A1, Shram Safalya,
Wadala Truck Terminal Road, Near Post Office,
Antop Hill, Mumbai - 400037, India
T: +91 8080226699

ISBN - 978-93-6263-666-9

Acknowledgements

We extend our heartfelt thanks to everyone who helped create this book, especially Merlin, for her constant input and research.

To our beloved readers, we hope to see this book in the hands of people worldwide, from walkers on the street to browsers in bookstores. While this is a great challenge and may not be easily achievable, it is certainly worth attempting.

Take your time, read the book, and strive to reach your highest goals.

Thank you!

Table of Contents

Foreword

Welcome to the indispensable guide on 'ISO/IEC 27001:2022 CONTROL A OLOGIES'. In today's interconnected world, where digital data reigns supreme and cyber threats lurk around every corner, safeguarding information assets has become paramount for organizations of all sizes and sectors. The International Organization for Standardization (ISO) recognized this pressing need and developed the ISO/IEC 27001 standard to provide a comprehensive framework for establishing, implementing, maintaining, and continually improving an Information Security Management System (ISMS).

As technology evolves at an exponential pace, so too must our strategies for protecting sensitive information. ISO/IEC 27001:2022 CONTROL A OLOGIES represents the latest iteration of this vital standard, incorporating the most up-to-date practices and methodologies to address the ever-changing landscape of cybersecurity threats. This book serves as an essential companion for organizations and professionals seeking to navigate the intricacies of ISO 27001:2022 Controls A, offering invaluable insights, practical guidance, and expert commentary to facilitate successful implementation and compliance.

Within these pages, readers will find a wealth of knowledge distilled into clear and concise explanations, covering each control in ISO 27001:2022 Controls A in meticulous detail. From risk assessment and treatment to access control, cryptography, and beyond, this book delves into the core principles and best practices essential for building a robust information security framework. Whether you are a seasoned cybersecurity professional or a newcomer to the field, this book equips you with the tools and expertise needed to safeguard your organization's most precious assets effectively.

I commend the authors for their dedication and expertise in crafting this comprehensive guide, which promises to be an invaluable resource for anyone involved in information security management. By embracing the principles outlined in ISO 27001:2022 Controls A and implementing robust security measures, organizations can mitigate risks, enhance resilience, and instill confidence in their stakeholders.

I trust that this book will serve as a beacon of knowledge, guiding readers towards achieving compliance, bolstering security posture, and ultimately, safeguarding the integrity, confidentiality, and availability of their information assets.

Vikas Madhok
Brig (Retd)
Chief Information Security Officer
Lentra

Preface

As technology continues to shape our lives, the need for cybersecurity has become more crucial than ever before. In this digital era, where threats loom around every virtual corner, drawing inspiration from unexpected sources can provide us with fresh perspectives. The timeless epic of Ramayana and Mahabharata, with its timeless teachings and profound moral lessons, holds invaluable insights for creating a secure cyber world. This article delves into the depths of Ramayana and Mahabharata, unearthing hidden gems of wisdom that can illuminate our path towards a resilient and protected digital landscape.

By drawing upon diverse sources, including ancient epics like the Ramayana, we can enrich our understanding and approach to different aspects of life, including cybersecurity. Let us remember the timeless wisdom of the Ramayana, as we navigate the ever-evolving landscape of cybersecurity, working together to protect our digital assets and ensure a secure and trustworthy online environment.

The timeless wisdom of the Mahabharata offers invaluable lessons for building a secure cyber world. By understanding the importance of preparedness, unity, trust, balancing convenience and security, learning from mistakes, and embracing ethical responsibility, we can mitigate the risks associated with cyber threats. Let us draw inspiration from this ancient epic and apply its teachings to safeguard our digital future. Together, we can create a cyber world that promotes innovation, collaboration, and security for generations to come.

From the principles of resilience, collaboration, and proactive defense, to ethical considerations, continuous learning, and adaptability, the epic provides a rich source of wisdom to fortify the ever-evolving cybersecurity landscape. By embracing these teachings and applying them in practice, cybersecurity professionals can navigate the challenges and secure digital environments with integrity and strategic acumen.

In this book, the authors, are giving away their practical know-how on ISO 27001 security controls. No matter if you are new or experienced in the field, this book teaches you everything you need to know about security controls.

ISO/IEC 27001:2022 CONTROL A OLOGIES is written primarily for beginners to ISO 27001:2022 and for people with moderate knowledge about Annex A of the standard and the 93 security controls that are found in the Annex. It is structured in such a way that someone with no prior experience or knowledge about information security can quickly understand what they are all about; however, if you do have experience with ISO 27001, but feel that you still have gaps in your knowledge, you will also find this book very helpful.

The authors use plain English to explain everything you need to know about security controls in ISO 27001. Also, you will learn everything about the crucial link between risk management and security controls, and get a complete overview of Annex A controls starting from the introduction, structuring of the documentation, and instructions on how to write detailed information security policies, all the way to the requirements for compliance.

So, the purpose of this book is to open a door for you into the world of security controls – it will explain why they are important, how they are structured, how they are selected, how they are related to the security management, and finally the purpose of each control. Once you pick the controls you are particularly interested in, you will know what to search for further, and where to search.

Written in simple language and avoiding the technical jargon, ISO/IEC 27001:2022 CONTROL A OLOGIES is the right book to start learning about the subject.

ISO/IEC 27001:2022 Annexure A

Organizational Controls

A.5.1 Policies for Information Security

Information Security Policies (ISP) is a set of rules enacted by an organization to ensure that all users or networks of the IT structure within the organization's domain abide by the prescriptions regarding the security of data stored digitally within the boundaries the organization stretches its authority. An ISP is governing the protection of information, which is one of the many assets a corporation needs to protect. Putting to work the logical arguments of rationalization, one could say that a policy can be as broad as the creators want it to be: Basically, everything from A to Z in terms of IT security, and even more. Characteristics of good security policies include conciseness, readability, actionability, enforceability, and flexibility. Policies are short and to the point in conveying principles that guide activity within the organization. Policies contain a minimum of specialized vernacular and acronyms; clearly explain any industry specific terms. Employees at all levels will read the security policies to discern how they should act in the best interest of the organization; therefore, the policy should be actionable at every level of executive strategic planning, management of operations, and actual performance of tasks. The policy must allow for determination of compliance with the policy and enforcement of noncompliance. Moreover, policies should potentially apply to the organization for years and not become outdated with the end of life of any product supporting the policy. Any mention of specific product use is in a standard, not a policy. Explanations on how to use products are in procedures, not in policy.

Review information security policies on a regular basis, with no more than 12 months from the last review. Define trigger events for a policy review. The first trigger event is the last review plus 12 months. Other trigger events may include a change in the business environment, like a merger, acquisition, or new business venture. Certainly, new legislation or regulatory reform will prompt policy review. Include a statement of review/revision trigger events in the information security policy. A key question is why capture all this detail in written documentation. Just like a contract, written documentation ensures a meeting of the minds. The organization is working off a common understanding of the expectations and a common understanding of terms. Moreover, the key point is for the organization to capture the policy, standards, procedures, interpretations, and definitions that ensure these details are not just in the minds of a few individuals. It is possible to have excellent security practices in organizations that do not have a single written procedure. Although the practice is good, it is only as good and as enduring as the individual that practices it. The loss of that individual through retirement, resignation, or being hit by the proverbial bus implies a loss (or at least a degradation) of that excellent practice to the organization.

Documentation captures knowledge and promotes the learning organization, where proven good practice by one becomes good practice available to all. Out of carelessness mostly, many organizations without giving much thought choose to download IT policy samples from a website and copy/paste this ready-made material in an attempt to readjust somehow their objectives and policy goals to a mold that is usually crude and has to broad-spectrum protection. Understandably, if the fit is not quite right, the dress would eventually slip off. A high-grade ISP can make the difference between a growing business and a successful one. Improved efficiency, increased productivity, clarity of the objectives each entity has, understanding what IT and data should be secured and why identifying the type and levels of security required, and defining the applicable information security best practices are enough reasons to back up this statement. To put a period to this topic in simple terms, let's say that if you want to lead a prosperous organization/company in today's digital era, you certainly need to have a good information security policy. The initial process in developing an information security policy is to identify which laws, regulations, and information security drivers are applicable to your organization.

- Perform a high-level gap analysis of each regulatory requirement and driver that is applicable to determine where policy is needed.
- Develop a prioritized action plan that will help you organize your efforts.
- Prepare a summary document of the impact that the information security policy or policies will have on the organization. The document should:
    - Describe the policy
    - Communicate the reason or business justification for the policy, as well as the risks and negative impact of not implementing the policy
    - Identify regulatory, technical, cultural, and organizational dependencies for implementation of the policy
    - Identify milestones and possible roadblocks of implementation, compliance, and enforcement
    - Identify impacted stakeholders
- Develop the policy in collaboration with other key stakeholders at your organization.
- Ensure the policy is vetted by impacted subject matter experts and business owners, including information security, legal counsel, human resources, and any other applicable steering committees.
- Review resources such as the standards and regulations that address specific requirements.
- Publish, communicate, train, and implement.

A.5.1 Policies for Information Security – A linkage with Ancient Era

Lakshman Rekha and the Importance of Security Policies

While going in search of Lord Ram, Lakshman draws a line around their dwelling in order to ensure the safety of Mata Sita. He then instructs Mata Sita not to cross this line until they return. However, Mata Sita fails to obey Lakshman's orders and falls prey to the wicked plans of King Ravana. The Lakshman Rekha is similar to the security policies within an organization. The idea of defining the security policies is to strategize how the internal data and devices can be secured from external threats. However, when there are no proper security policies or when the existing policies are not followed properly, the possibility of facing a cyber-attack increase.

Control:

Information security policy and topic-specific policies should be defined, approved by management, published, communicated to and acknowledged by relevant personnel and relevant interested parties, and reviewed at planned intervals and if significant changes occur.

Purpose:

To ensure continuing suitability, adequacy, effectiveness of management direction and support for information security in accordance with business, legal, statutory, regulatory and contractual requirements.

Guidelines:

At the highest level, the organization should define an "information security policy" which is approved by top management and which sets out the organization's approach to managing its information security. The information security policy should take into consideration requirements derived from:

- Business strategy and requirements;
- Regulations, legislation and contracts;
- The current and projected information security risks and threats.

The information security policy should contain statements concerning:

- Definition of information security;

- Information security objectives or the framework for setting information security objectives;
- Principles to guide all activities relating to information security;
- Commitment to satisfy applicable requirements related to information security;
- Commitment to continual improvement of the information security management system;
- Assignment of responsibilities for information security management to defined roles;
- Procedures for handling exemptions and exceptions.

Top management should approve any changes to the information security policy. At a lower level, the information security policy should be supported by topic-specific policies as needed, to further mandate the implementation of information security controls. Topic-specific policies are typically structured to address the needs of certain target groups within an organization or to cover certain security areas. Topic-specific policies should be aligned with and complementary to the information security policy of the organization.

Examples of such topics include:

- Access Control;
- Physical and Environmental Security;
- Asset Management;
- Information Transfer;
- Secure configuration and handling of user endpoint devices;
- Networking Security;
- Information Security Incident Management;
- Backup;
- Cryptography and Key Management;
- Information Classification and Handling;
- Management of Technical Vulnerabilities;
- Secure Development.

The responsibility for the development, review and approval of the topic-specific policies should be allocated to relevant personnel based on their appropriate level of authority and technical competency. The review should include assessing opportunities for improvement of the organization's information security policy and topic-specific policies and managing information security in response to changes to:

- The organization's business strategy;
- The organization's technical environment;
- Regulations, statutes, legislation and contracts;
- Information security risks;
- The current and projected information security threat environment;
- Lessons learned from information security events and incidents.

The review of information security policy and topic-specific policies should take the results of management reviews and audits into account. Review and update of other related policies should be considered when one policy is changed to maintain consistency. The information security policy and topic-specific policies should be communicated to relevant personnel and interested parties in a form that is relevant, accessible and understandable to the intended reader. Recipients of the policies should be required to acknowledge they understand and agree to comply with the policies where applicable. The organization can determine the formats and names of these policy documents that meet the organization's needs. In some organizations, the information security policy and topic-specific policies can be in a single document. The organization can name these topic-specific policies as standards, directives, policies or others.

If the information security policy or any topic-specific policy is distributed outside the organization, care should be taken not to improperly disclose confidential information.

Differences between Information Security Policy and Topic-Specific Policy:

	Information Security Policy	**Topic-specific policy**
Level of Detail:	General or High-Level	Specific and Detailed

Documented and formally approved by:	Top Management	Appropriate Level of Management Topic-Specific Policies can vary across organizations.

A Formal Approach to Establish Policy:

The adoption of one or more information security policies is the first step that the organization takes to express its commitment to the protection of their information resources and the information entrusted to them by their customers and partners. The policy statement should clearly communicate the organization's beliefs, goals, and objectives for information security.

The information security policy also provides the organization's leaders with an opportunity to set a clear plan for information security, describe its role in supporting the missions of the organization, and its commitment to comply with relevant laws and regulations. The policy should be brief, clear to understand, enforceable, and focused on desired behaviors and outcomes, and most importantly, balanced in affording security while enabling and preserving productivity.

An overarching information security policy document is often drafted through a consensus-building process with solicitation and feedback from all identified stakeholders. Once approved and published, its effective communication and periodic reviewing and updating ensure that the policy stated intent and corresponding expectations are consistent and relevant over time to reflect changes in technology, laws, business practices, and other factors.

Prior to starting the policy development process, it is important to understand the difference between policies, procedures, guidelines, and standards. Organizational policies are typically broad, short statements that reflect the philosophies, attitudes, or values of an organization related to a specific issue. Procedures are more detailed and generally mandatory, describing how to accomplish a task or reach a goal. Guidelines sometimes referred to as best practices, contain information about how to accomplish a task or reach a specific goal, but may not be mandatory. Standards establish a rule from a recognized authority, with no deviation allowed.

Difference between Policy, Standard, Guidelines, Procedure, and Checklist:

- **Policy:** A Policy is typically a document that outlines specific requirements or rules that must be met. In the information/network security realm, policies are usually point specific, covering a single area. Policies are statements that reflect the philosophies, attitudes, or values of an organization related to a specific issue. They are generally represented in a paragraph or perhaps two but not pages. They might say "what" but not "how". Checklists, procedures, standards, and guidelines all must implement, reflect, and support the applicable policy or policies. The entire set of statements is sometimes considered to be the "Policy."
- **Standard:** A standard is typically a collection of system-specific or procedural-specific requirements that must be met by everyone. Standards are statements dictating the state of affairs or action in a particular circumstance. They establish a rule from a recognized authority, with no deviation allowed.
- **Guideline:** A guideline is typically a collection of system-specific or procedural-specific "suggestions" for best practice. They are not requirements to be met but are strongly recommended. Effective security policies make frequent references to standards and guidelines that exist within an organization. Guidelines contain information about how to accomplish some tasks or reach a specific goal. The more explanatory text is usually involved.
- **Procedures:** Procedures contain one or more sentences describing how to accomplish a task or reach a goal - i.e., directive statements. The specified actions are generally mandatory for a specific situation. The more explanatory text is usually involved. A sequence is not necessary but sometimes is important.
- **Checklists:** Checklists contain one or more statements dictating how to accomplish a task - i.e., "commands". The items are applicable to immediate circumstances and mandatory in that situation. They are typically immediately at hand and written in simple language with no amplifying text. The sequence is always important. Flowcharts are also used as a method for conveying similar information.

Some organization has developed a "policy on policies" that provide an organizational statement and set of procedures about how policies are formatted, who develops them, and how they get approved. The benefit of a formal approach is that it makes policy development consistent and recognizes policy development and policy approval authorities. The formal approach can contain the following stages:

1. Identify issues,
2. Conduct analysis,
3. Draft Language,
4. Get Approvals,
5. Determine Distribution/Education,
6. Solicit Evaluation and Review, and
7. Plan Measurement and Compliance.

Stages 1 and 2 are considered "Pre-Development"

Stages 3-5 are part of "Development"

Stages 6 and 7 are "Maintenance"

First, issue identification contains a proactive component and is designed to build upon a security risk analysis, including the identification of existing information or data security policies. Second, the identification of the policy owner, policy path, and team to develop the policy is critical to ensuring the ultimate success of the security policy.

There are mixed views about whether or not to include legal counsel as part of the policy drafting team or whether they should be a part of a subsequent review process to determine the legal sufficiency of policy documents. There is a danger that security policy could become too legalistic or written in terms too complex for users or employees. On the other hand, lawyers should be knowledgeable about security requirements under Federal or state law. Third, drafting language and getting approvals is a strategic and political process at most organizations. Because of the urgency of computer and network security for the organizations, it may be more expedient to issue "guidelines" or "interim policies and procedures" to protect assets and ensure legal compliance while using shared governance processes for formal review and adoption of organizational policy. Fourth, increasing education and awareness of security issues and corresponding policies and procedures is critical. A policy that no one knows about or worse yet a policy that is not followed can do more harm than good. Finally, the maintenance stage underscores the importance of regularly evaluating security policies to ensure that they are effective and evolve as technology changes.

Policy Elements:

If the goal of organizational policies is to direct individual behavior and guide organizational decisions, then the effectiveness of formal policy statements will depend upon their readability and usefulness. Many organizations suffer from the lack of a common and consistent approach or format to writing organizational policies. The outline below suggests some common elements that should be included in any security policies.

1. **Rationale or Purpose**. The rationale or purpose statement expresses "why" the policy is being written. The rationale or purpose may also contain or cross reference "background" materials or more explanatory details regarding legal, regulatory, or other factors that led to the development of the policy.

2. **Policy Statement.** The policy statement should be a concise statement of "what" the policy is intended to accomplish. The policy should only be a one or two sentence description of general organization intent with respect to the specific topic of the policy. The policy statement should be general enough to provide some flexibility and accommodation to periodic changes in technology.
3. **Scope of Policy.** The scope of the policy can set important parameters such as to whom will the policy apply (e.g., faculty, staff, customers, vendors, and guests) and to what (e.g., paper and electronic records, information and computer assets, etc.)
4. **Procedures.** The procedures will detail "how" the policy statement will be attained. Procedures may include information on how to report computer security incidents. Procedures may also describe enforcement provisions or methods for appeal. Procedures are sometimes provided in a separate document or left for local determination to provide greater flexibility for updates as well as local control.
5. **Roles and Responsibilities.** The procedures may contain details about who is responsible for what. The policy should also identify who is responsible for enforcement or compliance and who will provide interpretations in the event of the need for clarification or when there is a dispute.
6. **Definitions**. Policies should be precise and easy to understand. Sometimes terms will need to be defined to clarify meaning. However, the policy should attempt to convey messages in simple yet precise terms; excessive definitions may make a policy document unreadable or subject it to greater scrutiny.
7. **References.** It is possible that there are other policies or organizational documents that complement, supplement, or help explain the provisions contained within the current policy. References to other policies or organizational documents and citations to statutory or regulatory items can improve the usefulness of the policy.

If a policy is a statement of intent, then a policy for information security can be defined as a formal high-level statement that embodies the course of action adopted by an organization regarding the use and safeguarding of the organizational information resources. The policy statement should clearly communicate the institution's beliefs, goals, and objectives for information security.

To be effective an information security policy must:

1. Require compliance
2. Be Implementable
3. Be Enforceable
4. Be Brief and Easy to Understand
5. Balance Protection with Productivity

Also, the information security policy should:

1. State why the policy is needed (i.e., business reasons)
2. Exemplify the organization's commitment to information security
3. Express leadership support for the role of information security in the carrying out of the organization's missions,
4. Focus on desired behaviors (e.g., acceptable use) and outcomes
5. Define roles and responsibilities
6. Outline the standards and procedures to be followed.

A careful balance must be reached to ensure that the policy enhances organizational security by providing enough detail that community members understand their expected role and contribution but not so much detail that the organization is exposed to unnecessary risk.

Policies for Information Security:

There are a number of methods that can be used as a foundation for an organization's information security policy framework. Choosing the right policy framework is all about what will work best for the organization and its missions. The organization should consider the following when selecting a framework for its information security policy:

- What works for the organization?
- What has not worked before?
- What fits the organization's culture?

- What regulatory requirements must be met?
- What are the organizational drivers?
- What future technology is on the organization's roadmap?
- What resources (staff, budget, skillsets) are needed to obtain the desired outcomes?

It is important to keep in mind that one of the main goals of an information security policy is to issue directives. The difficult part is deciding on the appropriate level of control to exert. The appropriate level should be informed by the following facts control to exert. The appropriate level should be informed by the following facts:

- If policies are too restrictive or hard to implement, people will find ways to circumvent the controls.
- Technical controls are not always possible or, at times, desirable.
- Ensure that directives are 'top-down', i.e., fully supported by top management.

Organizational Drivers

Since most information security practitioners would agree that it is impossible to protect everything the same way all the time, organizations should identify the business and technical drivers that will guide the creation and implementation of the information security policy as well as assist in its vetting, approval, and socialization. These drivers can be high-level statements that convey the organization's priorities and direction and help stakeholders make the right decisions regarding what standards to require, what technology to deploy, and how to build the architecture required to implement the policy.

The information security CIA triad exemplifies the highest-level driver, to preserve the confidentiality, integrity, and availability of organizational information resources. More specific examples include:

1. Uniquely identify and authenticate all users and entities affiliated with the organization
2. Provide users with the least access required to perform their job function

3. Adopt information security industry standards where appropriate
4. Implement mitigating controls proactively and based on risk and cost of risk mitigation
5. Identify what information the organization maintains, where is it located, and who owns is responsible for it
6. Classify the organizational data and safeguard it based on risk
7. Balance the business needs to offer and deploy new applications and services against the security risks it might pose to the organization

Review of Information Security Policy:

Most organizations will have a documented periodic policy review process in place (e.g., annually) to ensure that policies are kept up to date and relevant. In some cases, a policy manager would be the individual who would determine the need for a new policy or the update to an existing policy. In a small organization, the role of policy manager may be played by the Business Owner (e.g., the Chief Information Security Officer may be the owner/manager of the information security policy.)

Policy Review and Update Drivers:

The information security policy owner or manager will review and update the policy at the required intervals or when external or internal drivers require the review and update of the policy. The following are the most common drivers that would prompt a review of the institution's information security policy.

1. Changes in Federal or State laws and regulations
2. Changes in technology (e.g., increased use of mobile devices on campus)
3. Major information security project deployments (e.g., deployment of Mobile Device Management (MDM))
4. Audit findings
5. Policy format changes (e.g., new policy management function and process)
6. Increased reliance on third-party service providers (e.g., outsourcing, cloud)

7. New business practices (e.g., online education, telecommuting, telemedicine)

Policy Review and Update Process

The process to review and update the information security policy should include the following steps:

1. Document needed changes
2. Make changes to a draft version of the policy
3. Are the changes significant or alter the intent of the original policy?
4. If yes, ensure the changes are vetted by impacted subject matter experts and business owners, information security, legal counsel, human resources if applicable, any other applicable steering committee
5. Publish, communicate, train, and implement

A.5.2 Information Security Roles and Responsibilities

All information security and its responsibilities need to be defined and approved by the management. The responsibilities can be general (e.g., protecting information) or specific (e.g., the responsibility for accessing particular permissions). Consideration should be given to the ownership of information assets or groups of assets when identifying responsibilities. Access to information security should be granted to relevant staff members for e.g.; CEOs, Business Owners, General Manager; HR managers; and Internal auditors. The auditor will be looking to gain confidence that the organization has made clear who is responsible for, and what is adequate according to the size and nature of the organization. For smaller organizations, it is generally unrealistic to have full-time roles associated with these roles and responsibilities. To protect information security one can, choose relevant authority within the organization to-hold the responsibility and implementing the process.

A.5.2 Information Security Roles and Responsibilities – A linkage with Ancient Era

Collaboration and Teamwork

Lord Ram's journey in the Ramayana is filled with allies and companions who assist Him in his mission. Similarly, in cybersecurity collaboration and teamwork are crucial. It takes the collective effort of individuals, security professionals, organizations and governments to combat cyber threats effectively. The Ramayana emphasizes the importance of building alliances, trust and working together to achieve a common goal, which can be applied to the cybersecurity domain.

Control:

Information security roles and responsibilities should be defined and allocated according to the organization needs.

Purpose:

To establish a defined, approved and understood structure for the implementation, operation and management of information security within the organization.

Guidance:

Allocation of information security roles and responsibilities should be done in accordance with the information security policy and topic-specific policies. The organization should define and manage responsibilities for:

- Protection of information and other associated assets;
- Carrying out specific information security processes;
- Information security risk management activities and in particular acceptance of;
- Residual risks (e.g., to risk owners);
- All personnel using an organization's information and other associated assets.

These responsibilities should be supplemented, where necessary, with more detailed guidance for specific sites and information processing facilities. Individuals with allocated information security responsibilities can assign security tasks to others. However, they remain accountable and should determine that any delegated tasks have been correctly performed.

Each security area for which individuals are responsible should be defined, documented and communicated. Authorization levels should be defined and documented. Individuals who take on a specific information security role should be competent in the knowledge and skills required by the role and should be supported to keep up to date with developments related to the role and required in order to fulfill the responsibilities of the role.

Other Information:

Many organizations appoint an information security manager to take overall responsibility for the development and implementation of information security and to support the identification of risks and mitigating controls. However, responsibility for resourcing and implementing the controls often remains with individual managers.

One common practice is to appoint an owner for each asset who then becomes responsible for its day-to-day protection. Depending on the size and resourcing of an organization, information security can be covered by dedicated roles or duties carried out in addition to existing roles.

Information security is the responsibility of everyone at the organization.

It is important to establish roles and responsibilities for staff, managers, and contractors/vendors so that everyone knows what is expected of them when handling information. Some examples of the business roles which are likely to have some information security relevance include; Departmental Heads; Business Process Owners; Facilities Manager; HR Manager; and Internal Auditor. Leadership is also very important, and many institutions have at least one person who is primarily responsible for organizing the information security program. Typically, this is a CISO, ISO, Director of Information Security, although the title may vary depending on the organization. As such, clarifying specific information security responsibilities within existing job roles is important e.g., the Operations Director or CEO might also be the equivalent of the CISO, with overarching responsibility for all of the ISMS. The CTO might own all the technology related information assets etc. No matter what title is selected, there should be someone at the organization who can provide a high level of decision-making support to leadership when considering information security issues and solutions. It is also important to establish data ownership and data handling roles (e.g., data owners, stewards, custodians, and users). The auditor will be looking to gain assurance that the organization has made clear who is responsible for what in an adequate and proportionate manner according to the size and nature of the organization.

Here are some of the vital IT security roles and the responsibilities associated with them. Don't be surprised that sometimes, different roles share some responsibilities.

Information Security Board of Review

The Information Security Board of Review (ISBR) may appoint administrative authority whose role is to provide oversight and direction regarding information systems security and privacy assurance campus-wide. In collaboration with the Chief Information Officer, the ISBR's specific oversight responsibilities include the following:

1. Oversee the development, implementation, and maintenance of a strategic information systems security plan.
2. Oversee the development, implementation, and enforcement of

information systems security policy and related recommended guidelines, operating procedures, and technical standards.

3. Oversee the process of handling requested policy exceptions.
4. Advise the management on related risk issues and recommend appropriate actions in support of the risk management programs.

Chief Information Security Officer (CISO)

A CISO is the one whose task is to oversee corporate security strategy. The typical CISO's responsibilities include:

1. Planning long-term security strategy
2. Planning and implementing data loss prevention measures
3. Managing access
4. Ensuring that the organization implements proper safeguards to meet compliance requirements
5. Investigating any incidents and preventing them in the future
6. Assessing security risk
7. Arranging security awareness training

Security and Information Compliance Officers

The Security and Information Compliance Officers may oversee the development and implementation of the ISP. Specific responsibilities can include:

1. To ensure related compliance requirements are addressed, e.g., privacy, security, and administrative regulations associated with federal and state laws.
2. To ensure appropriate risk mitigation and control processes for security incidents as required.
3. To document and disseminate information security policies, procedures, and guidelines.
4. To coordinate the development and implementation of a information security training and awareness program.

5. To coordinate a response to actual or suspected breaches in the confidentiality, integrity or availability of information assets.

Data Owner

A Data Owner is an individual or group or people who have been officially designated as accountable for specific data that is transmitted, used, and stored on a system or systems within a department, location or administrative unit. The role of the data custodians is to provide direct authority and control over the management and use of specific information. Responsibilities of a Data Owner include the following:

1. Ensure compliance with organizational polices and all regulatory requirements. Data Owners need to understand whether or not any organizational policies govern their information assets. Data Owners are responsible for having an understanding of legal and contractual obligations surrounding information assets within their functional areas.
2. Assign an appropriate classification to information assets. All information assets are to be classified based upon its level of sensitivity, value and criticality to the organization.
3. Determine appropriate criteria for obtaining access to sensitive information assets. A Data Owner is accountable for who has access to information assets within their functional areas. This does not imply that a Data Owner is responsible for day-to-day provisioning of access. Provisioning access is the responsibility of a Data Custodian.
4. A Data Owner may decide to review and authorize each access request individually or may define a set of rules that determine who is eligible for access based on business function, support role, etc. Access must be granted based on the principles of least privilege as well as separation of duties. A Data Custodian should document these rules in a manner that allows little or no room for interpretation.
5. Approve standards and procedures related to management of information assets. While it is the responsibility of the Data Custodian to develop and implement operational procedures, it is the Data Owner's responsibility to review and approve these standards and procedures. A Data Owner should consider the classification of the

data and associated risk tolerance when reviewing and approving these standards and procedures. For example, high risk and/or highly sensitive data may warrant more comprehensive documentation and, similarly, a more formal review and approval process.

6. Understand how information assets are stored, processed, and transmitted. Understanding and documenting how information assets are being stored, processed and transmitted is the first step toward safeguarding that data. Without this knowledge, it is difficult to implement or validate safeguards in an effective manner. One method of performing this assessment is to create a data flow diagram for a subset of data that illustrates the system(s) storing the data, how the data is being processed and how the data traverses the network. Data flow diagrams can also illustrate security controls as they are implemented. Regardless of approach, documentation should exist and be made available to the appropriate Data Owner.
7. Implement appropriate physical and technical safeguards to protect the confidentiality, integrity and availability of information assets. Data Custodians should work with Data Owners to gain a better understanding of these requirements. Data Custodians should also document what security controls have been implemented and where gaps exist in current controls. This documentation should be made available to the appropriate Data Owner.
8. Document and disseminate administrative and operational procedures to ensure consistent storage, processing and transmission of information assets. Documenting administrative and operational procedures goes hand in hand with understanding how data is stored, processed and transmitted. Data Custodians should document as many repeatable processes as possible. This will help ensure that information assets are handled in a consistent manner and will also help ensure that safeguards are being effectively leveraged.
9. Provision and de-provision access as authorized by the Data Owner. Data Custodians are responsible for provisioning and de-provisioning access based on criteria established by the appropriate Data Owner.
10. Understand and report security risks and how they impact the confidentiality, integrity and availability of information assets. Data Custodians need to have a thorough understanding of security

risks impacting their information assets. For example, storing or transmitting sensitive data in an unencrypted form is a security risk. Protecting access to data using a weak password and/or not patching vulnerabilities in a system or application are both examples of security risks.

11. Security risks need to be documented and reviewed with the appropriate Data Owner so that he or she can determine whether greater resources need to be devoted to mitigating these risks. Information Technology department can assist Data Custodians with gaining a better understanding of their security risks.

Data Users

All users have a critical role in the effort to protect and maintain information systems and data. For the purpose of information security, a Data User is any employee, contractor or third-party provider of the who is authorized to access Information Systems and/or information assets. Responsibilities of data users include the following:

1. Adhere to policies, guidelines and procedures pertaining to the protection of information assets.
2. Users are also required to follow all specific policies, guidelines, and procedures established with which they are associated and that have provided them with access privileges.
3. Report actual or suspected security and/or policy violations or breaches to IT. During the course of day-to-day operations, users may come across a situation where they feel the security of information assets might be at risk. For example, a user comes across sensitive information on a website that he or she feels shouldn't be accessible. If this happens, it is the users responsibly to report the situation.

Application Security Engineer

The job of an application security engineer has two major aspects. Firstly, you will need to help developers to create more secure apps. Secondly, you'll need to control third-party apps used by your organization and ensure their safety. Some of the typical responsibilities and tasks include:

1. Configuring technical security controls

2. Conducting an app risk assessment
3. Whitelisting/blacklisting apps
4. Performing penetration testing

For application security engineers, it's vital to control SaaS apps and the risks related to them. Risky and insecure apps should be blacklisted. To automate the job and remain time efficient, application security engineer will probably need specialized software that helps with application security assessment and whitelisting/blacklisting.

Data Protection Officer (DPO)

Having a DPO may be one of the compliance requirements. A DPO must be appointed in organizations working with large-scale systematic monitoring or processing of sensitive data. Officers oversee corporate data protection measures and their effectiveness. A specialist, appointed to the DPO role, controls whether corporate security is of a sufficient level to meet compliance requirements, and recommends security upgrades if needed. That's why an in-depth understanding of data security and compliance are essential skills. The DPO orchestrates, manages, and supervises all the activities that are aimed at protecting users' data and communicates the status to both internal and external parties. This includes:

1. Creating an effective step-by-step privacy program
2. Supervising the entire implementation process of the program at all stages
3. Assuring that all the data processes are being conducted
4. Reporting to the management, stakeholders, and all the parties involved on how the implementation process goes
5. Reporting to the management on the potential threats to data security and general integrity, and what can be done to eliminate them
6. Educating employees on the matters of data privacy and data protection
7. Training staff that is directly related to or involved in the data collection, processing, or storing

8. Keeping track of and recording all the operations that involve users' personal data and the reasons for these operations to take place
9. Auditing the data processes to assess their performance and address possible problems proactively
10. Reporting on the progress of the implementation and maintenance of the data privacy program in the organization to the authorities, stakeholders, and public/customers
11. Being a connective link between the organization and data subjects (users/customers). Communicating with data subjects on how their data are being handled, what rights do they have, and addressing all their requests concerning their data
12. Communicating with supervisors and being a connecting link between the organization and authorities

Network Security Engineer

A network security engineer's job is to protect corporate networks from data breaches, human error, or cyberattacks. Engineers are responsible for:

1. Configuring network security settings
2. Performing penetration testing
3. Developing and implementing sufficient measures to detect cyber threats
4. Implementing network security policies
5. Installing and maintaining security software like firewalls or backups
6. Also, a deep understanding of cloud security may be required.

Security Administrator

An IT security admin is a role that includes a wide range of skills and responsibilities to manage the protection of the organization's data. Some of the most common admin's responsibilities include:

1. Managing access
2. Ensuring that data migration is secure
3. Configuring security software

4. Monitoring data behavior for abnormal activities
5. Implementing security policies
6. Testing organization's systems to locate potential risks and vulnerabilities
7. Reporting security statuses and incidents (if any)
8. Using software tools to automate some of the tasks

An admin's role is more significant than it may seem at first glance. An admin has to keep the whole organization's security landscape in mind and ensure that even the tiniest processes are executed correctly. After all, even one careless click may be enough to initiate a cyberattack.

Security Analyst

This role is related to protecting corporate information against cyber-attacks and insider threats. Generally, an analyst has to determine potential risks and vulnerabilities inside the system, so a deep understanding of data security threats and ways to prevent them is a must. As a security analyst, your responsibilities will include:

1. Analyzing and configuring corporate systems to improve their security
2. Analyzing data loss prevention measures
3. Looking for system vulnerabilities and ways to fix them
4. Monitoring data behavior for abnormal activities
5. Verifying security, availability, and confidentiality of corporate data
6. Also, the security analyst's role requires an understanding of white hat hacking to design more advanced protection against cyberattacks. Analysts often work together with security architects.

Security Architect

A security architect is one of the senior-level IT security positions. An architect is focused on creating a secure-by-design environment. Generally, an architect's responsibilities include:

1. Assessing the system's security controls and processes to find potential security gaps
2. Planning changes and upgrades for corporate IT infrastructure

3. Maintaining system integrity
4. Implementing insider threat control measures
5. Choosing new security software if needed
6. Implementing disaster recovery measures
7. Analyzing previous incidents and creating an incident response plan
8. Analyzing the costs and benefits of security solutions

Of course, the exact scope of your tasks as an architect will vary depending on each organization's unique infrastructure and needs. Often, an architect needs to assess corporate systems for meeting security compliance standards to decide what changes are needed to become compliant.

Security Specialist

An IT security specialist is a person responsible for keeping corporate data safe. Security specialists maintain and upgrade systems and procedures to prevent data loss or leakage. Depending on a specific environment, an information security specialist will have a stronger focus on cloud, network, application, database or device security. In some cases, especially in small businesses, an IT security specialist is an all-rounder with responsibilities combining many cyber security roles at the same time. That's why a security specialist must have strong IT skills and a deep understanding of both software and hardware—and, of course, an ability to locate potential vulnerabilities and fix them.

A.5.3 Segregation of Duties

The purpose of segregation of duties in ISO 27001 is to ensure that a single point of compromise does not have significant impacts on the business. Conflicts can occur when two or more employees have similar or different responsibilities towards a particular task. When this happens, the employees may end up doing the same thing twice, or doing different things that cancel out each other's efforts. This wastes corporate resources and reduces productivity, which affects both the organization's bottom line and morale. In order to make sure that your organization does not suffer from this problem, it is important to understand what conflicting areas of responsibilities are, why they happen and how you can prevent them from occurring in your organization. For the most part, this means separating duties so that different people handle different roles in the organization.

Conflicting duties and areas of responsibility must be segregated in order to reduce the opportunities for unauthorized or unintentional modification or misuse of any of the organization's assets. The risk being that if a single post is responsible for highly privileged actions and is not monitored or controlled, then compromise of that role could result in disastrous impacts to the organization. The organization needs to ask itself whether or not the segregation of duties been considered and implemented where appropriate. To be compliant with this requirement, the organization must be able to demonstrate that highly privileged role functions and conflicting duties/areas of responsibility are sufficiently segregated. A two-man rule might be appropriate in certain circumstances, in others it may be appropriate to provide an extra layer of authorization before a task can be carried out supported by enhanced monitoring of user operations. This provides a defense in depth approach and means that any unauthorized activity can be tracked, monitored and alerted upon.

A.5.3 Segregation of Duties – A linkage with Ancient Era

Ram Setu – the Principle of Distributed Responsibilities and Checks and Balances

In the story of Ram Setu, Lord Ram builds a bridge (Setu) with the help of His army of moneys to reach Lanka and rescue His wife Mata Sita from the demon King Ravana. The construction of the bridge required teamwork, coordination, and division of labor among various characters like Hanuman, Surgriv, and the Vanar Army. Similarly, in the context of business or organizational operations, segregation of duties is a fundamental principle of internal controls. It involves dividing tasks and responsibilities among different individuals to prevent fraud, errors or misuse of resources. By segregating duties, no single individual has complete control over a critical process or transaction from beginning to end, thus reducing the risk of misconduct or errors going undetected. Just as in the construction of Ram Setu where each character had specific roles and responsibilities, in organizations, segregation of duties ensures that different individuals are responsible for different aspects of a process, providing a system of checks and balances.

Control

Conflicting duties and conflicting areas of responsibility should be segregated.

Purpose

To reduce the risk of fraud, error and bypassing of information security controls.

Guidance

Segregation of duties and areas of responsibility aims to separate conflicting duties between different individuals in order to prevent one individual from executing potential conflicting duties on their own. The organization should determine which duties and areas of responsibility need to be segregated. The following are examples of activities that can require segregation:

- Initiating, Approving and Executing a change;
- Requesting, Approving and Implementing access rights;
- Designing, Implementing and Reviewing code;
- Developing Software and Administering production systems;
- Using and Administering applications;
- Using Applications and Administering Databases;
- Designing, Auditing and Assuring information security controls.

The possibility of collusion should be considered in designing the segregation controls. Small organizations can find segregation of duties difficult to achieve, but the principle should be applied as far as is possible and practicable. Whenever it is difficult to segregate, other controls should be considered, such as monitoring of activities, audit trails and management supervision. Care should be taken when using role-based access control systems to ensure that persons are not granted conflicting roles. When there is a large number of roles, the organization should consider using automated tools to identify conflicts and facilitate their removal. Roles should be carefully defined and provisioned to minimize access problems if a role is removed or reassigned.

Segregation of duties reduces the risk of intentional manipulation or error and increases the element of checking. Functions that should be separated include those of authorization, execution, custody, and recording and, in the case of a computer-based accounting system, systems development, and daily operations. Segregation of duties is the concept of having more than one person required to complete a task. This is a best practice, especially in cases where sensitive data is being handled. This is seemingly obvious, but often difficult to do in practice. Essentially try to eliminate processes or situations where someone can access, change or use information assets without detection.

Segregation of duties is a control put in place by many organizations to mitigate the risk of an insider threat or accidental employee mistakes. Sometimes this isn't practical or possible, but the institution should be aware of the risks of a single person having too much access. Ideally, critical processes or activities should be split up between multiple people. Segregation of duties refers to practices where the knowledge and/or privileges needed to complete a process are broken up and divided among multiple users so that no single one is capable of performing or controlling it by himself.

The main reason to apply segregation of duties is to prevent the perpetration and concealment of fraud and error in the normal course of the activities. Extremely lean processes increase the risk of wrongdoing by concentrating means and opportunity (access to and privileges over the process). By implementing segregation of duties, an organization minimizes the risk by splitting knowledge and privileges. However, the benefits of segregation of duties to security must be balanced with the increased cost/effort required. By using the ISO 27001 requirements for risk assessment, an organization can identify the most vulnerable and the most mission-critical elements of the business to which segregation of duties will represent real added value to the business and other interested parties.

The principles that can be applicable to segregation of duties are:

- Sequential separation,
- Individual separation,
- Spatial separation,
- Factorial separation.

These principles can be used in isolation or together, depending upon the security an organization requires to protect its processes.

Sometimes the segregation of duties is impractical because the organization is too small to designate functions to different persons. In other cases, breaking down tasks can reduce business efficiency and increase costs, complexity, and staffing requirements. In these situations, compensating controls should be in place to ensure that even without segregation of duties the identified risks are properly handled.

A.5.4 Management Responsibilities

Management Responsibilities covers the need for management to ensure that all personnel stick to all the information security topic-specific policies and procedures as defined in the established information security policy of the organization. An effective information security policy should be tailored to the specific needs of an organization and supported by senior management to ensure appropriate allocation of resources. It communicates the overarching principles on how management would like employees to handle sensitive data and how the organization will protect its information assets. IT is often derived from laws, regulations and best practices that must be adhered to by the organization. Information security policies are usually created by an organization's senior management, with input from its IT security staff. Policies should also include a framework for defining roles and responsibilities and a timeline for periodic review.

A.5.4 Management Responsibilities – A linkage with Ancient Era

Lord Hanuman's Devotion

Lord Hanuman, a devoted ally of Lord Ram, plays a critical role in the Ramayana by using these extraordinary abilities to assist Lord Ram in various ways. Lord Hanuman's unwavering loyalty and dedication can be compared to cybersecurity professionals who tirelessly work to protect systems and data from cyber threats. Just as Lord Hanuman's devotion helped Lord Ram in overcoming obstacles, cybersecurity professional's expertise and commitment are vital in identifying vulnerabilities, mitigating risks, and ensuring the overall security of digital environments.

Control

Management should require all personnel to apply information security in accordance with the established information security policy, topic-specific policies and procedures of the organization.

Purpose

To ensure management understand their role in information security and undertake actions aiming to ensure all personnel are aware of and fulfil their information security responsibilities.

Guidance:

Management should demonstrate support of the information security policy, topic-specific policies, procedures and information security controls. Management responsibilities should include ensuring that personnel:

- Are properly briefed on their information security roles and responsibilities prior to being granted access to the organization's information and other associated assets.
- Are provided with guidelines which state the information security expectations of their role within the organization.
- Are mandated to fulfil the information security policy and topic-specific policies of the organization.
- Achieve a level of awareness of information security relevant to their roles and responsibilities within the organization.
- Compliance with the terms and conditions of employment, contract or agreement, including the organization's information security policy and appropriate methods of working.
- Continue to have the appropriate information security skills and qualifications through ongoing professional education.
- Where practicable, are provided with a confidential channel for reporting violations of information security policy, topic-specific policies or procedures for information security ("whistleblowing"). This can allow for anonymous reporting or have provisions to ensure that knowledge of the identity of the reporter is known only to those who need to deal with such reports.
- Are provided with adequate resources and project planning time for implementing the organization's security-related processes and controls.

Management should require employees, contractors and third-party users to apply security controls in accordance with established policies and procedures of the organization. Management should define responsibilities for general personnel, including contractors and volunteers, in relation to implementing or maintaining security in line with the organization's policies. It must also specify responsibilities for the protection of particular assets, including critical infrastructure, or for the execution of particular security processes or activities. They must also communicate the requirement for personnel to report security events and incidents (actual or perceived) and uphold the requirement to report other security risks that are identified. Management may note that the personal circumstances of personnel such as financial problems, changes in their behavior or lifestyle, recurring absences and evidence of stressful situations or illness may give rise to security implications in the workplace. Control includes:

- Appropriately informing all employees, contractors, and third-party users of their information security roles and responsibilities, prior to granting access to sensitive information or information systems.
- Providing all employees, contractors, and third parties with guidelines/ rules that state the security control expectations of their roles within the organization.
- Achieving an appropriate level of awareness of security controls among all employees, contractors, and third parties, relevant to their roles and responsibilities, and an appropriate level of skills and qualifications, sufficient to execute those security controls.
- Assuring the conformity to the terms and conditions of employment related to security.
- Motivating adherence to the security policies of the organization, such as with an appropriate sanctions policy; and
- Mitigating the risks of a failure to adhere to policies, by ensuring that all persons have appropriately limited access to the organization's information and information facilities.

The Information Security Management (ISM) is responsible for establishing and maintaining a corporate wide information security management program to ensure that information assets are adequately protected. The management must be responsible for identifying, evaluating and reporting on information security risks in a manner that meets compliance and regulatory requirements, and aligns with and supports the risk posture of the enterprise. The ISM must have a visionary leader with sound knowledge of business management and a working knowledge of information security technologies. The ISM must work with business units to implement practices that meet define policies and standards for information security. They must oversee a variety of IT relate risk management activities.

The ISM's responsibilities are composed of a variety of activities, including very tactical, operational and strategic activities in support of the ISM's program initiatives, such as:

Strategic Support and Management

- Develop, implement and monitor a strategic, comprehensive enterprise information security and IT risk management program to ensure that the integrity, confidentiality and availability of information is owned, controlled or processed by the organization.
- Manage the enterprise's information security organization, consisting of direct reports and indirect reports (such as individuals in business continuity and IT operations). This includes hiring, training, staff development, performance management and annual performance reviews.
- Facilitate information security governance through the implementation of a hierarchical governance program, including the formation of an information security steering committee or advisory board.
- Develop, maintain and publish up-to-date information security policies, standard and guidelines. Oversee the approval, training, and dissemination of security policies and practices.
- Create, communicate and implement a risk-based process for vendor risk management, including the assessment and treatment for risks that may result from partners, consultants and other service providers.
- Develop and manage information security budgets and monitor them for variances.
- Create and manage information security and risk management awareness training programs for all employees, contractors and approved system users.
- Work directly with the business units to facilitate IT risk assessment and risk management processes, and work with stakeholders throughout the enterprise on identifying acceptable levels of residual risk.

- Provide regular reporting on the current status of the information security program to enterprise risk teams, senior business leaders and the board of directors as part of a strategic enterprise risk management program.
- Create a framework for roles and responsibilities with regard to information ownership, classification, accountability and protection.
- Develop and enhance an information security management framework.
- Provide strategic risk guidance for IT projects, including the evaluation and recommendation of technical controls.
- Liaise with the enterprise architecture team to ensure alignment between the security and enterprise architectures, thus coordinating the strategic planning implicit in these architectures.
- Coordinate information security and risk management projects with resources from the IT organization and business unit teams.
- Ensure that security programs comply with relevant laws, regulations and policies to minimize or eliminate risk and audit findings.
- Define and facilitate the information security risk assessment process, including the reporting and oversight of treatment efforts to address negative findings.
- Manage security incidents and events to protect corporate IT assets, including intellectual property, regulated data and the organization's reputation.
- Monitor the external threat environment for emerging threats and advise relevant stakeholders on the appropriate courses of action.
- Develop and oversee effective disaster recovery policies and standards to align with enterprise business continuity management program goals. Coordinate the development of implementation plans and procedures to ensure that business critical services are recovered in the event of a security event. Provide direction, support and in-house consulting in these areas.
- Facilitate a metrics and reporting framework to measure the efficiency and effectiveness of the program, facilitate appropriate resource allocation, and increase the maturity of the security.

- Understand and interact with related disciplines through committees to ensure the consistent application of policies and standards across all technology projects, systems and services, including, but not limited to, privacy, risk management, compliance and business continuity management.

Security Liaison

- Liaise among the information security team and corporate compliance, audit, legal and HR management teams as required.
- Liaise with external agencies, such as law enforcement and other advisory bodies as necessary, to ensure that the organization maintains a strong security posture.
- Assist resource owners and IT staff in understanding and responding to security audit failures reported by auditors.
- Work as a liaison with vendors and the legal and purchasing departments to establish mutually acceptable contracts and service-level agreements.
- Manage security issues and incidents and participate in problem and change management forums. Ensuring timely reporting and adequate participation in investigation for ICT security incidents, with CERT and/or Law Enforcement agencies as applicable.
- Work with various stakeholders to identify information asset owners to classify data and systems as part of a control framework implementation.
- Work with the IT and business stakeholders to define metrics and reporting strategies that effectively communicate successes and progress of the security program.

Architecture/Engineering Support

- Consult with IT and security staff to ensure that security is factored into the evaluation, selection, installation and configuration of hardware, applications and software.
- Recommend and coordinate the implementation of technical controls to support and enforce defined security policies.
- Research, evaluate, design, test, recommend or plan the implementation

of new or updated information security hardware or software, and analyze its impact on the existing environment; provide technical and managerial expertise for the administration of security tools.

- Work with the enterprise architecture team to ensure that there is a convergence of business, technical and security requirements; liaise with IT management to align existing technical installed base and skills with future architectural requirements.
- Develop a strong working relationship with the security engineering team to develop and implement controls and configurations aligned with security policies and legal, regulatory and audit requirements.

Operational Support

- Coordinate, measure and report on the technical aspects of security management.
- Manage outsourced vendors that provide information security functions for compliance with contracted service-level agreements.
- Manage and coordinate operational components of incident management, including detection, response and reporting.
- Maintain a knowledgebase comprising a technical reference library, security advisories and alerts, information on security trends and practices, and laws and regulations.
- Manage the day-to-day activities of threat and vulnerability management, identify risk tolerances, recommend treatment plans and communicate information about residual risk.
- Ensure audit trails, system logs and other monitoring data sources are reviewed periodically and comply with policies and audit requirements.
- Design, coordinate and oversee security-testing procedures to verify the security of systems, networks and applications, and manage the remediation of identified risks.

A.5.5 Contact with Authorities

Communication with the appropriate authorities must be kept open at all times. Processes should be put in place to define when and with whom officials should communicate and how identified information security violations will be reported as soon as possible by organizations. Maintaining these connections may also be required in information security to assist incident management or business continuity and contingency planning operations. Contacts with regulatory authorities are also beneficial in predicting and planning for any changes in the rules or regulations that the organization must enforce. Organization can consider to contact with their data protection regulator that is likely mandated in law, utility companies for power and water, health and safety if relevant, fire departments for business continuity and incident management, perhaps the telecoms provider for routing if lines go down. Organization are going to have to ensure that:

- Organization identify and document what authorities apply to them;
- In what circumstances organization would contact them;
- How information security incidents should be reported, if relevant;
- Understand what expectations these authorities have, if any;
- Include relevant contact steps in organization incident management processes;
- Include relevant contact steps in organization business continuity and disaster recovery processes.

A.5.5 Contact with Authorities – A linkage with Ancient Era

Building Strong Partnerships

The Mahabharata highlights the importance of building alliances and seeking assistance when needed. Similarly, in the cyber world, forging strong partnerships with cybersecurity experts, collaborating with industry peers and seeking guidance from authorities can enhance security measures. Sharing knowledge, experience, and resources can help build a collective defense against cyber threats.

Control

The organization should establish and maintain contact with relevant authorities.

Purpose

To ensure appropriate flow of information takes place with respect to information security between the organization and relevant legal, regulatory and supervisory authorities.

Guidance

The organization should specify when and by whom authorities (e.g., law enforcement, regulatory bodies, supervisory authorities) should be contacted and how identified information security incidents should be reported in a timely manner. Contacts with authorities should also be used to facilitate the understanding about the current and upcoming expectations of these authorities (e.g., applicable information security regulations).

Other Information

Organizations under attack can request authorities to take action against the attack source. Maintaining such contacts can be a requirement to support information security incident management or the contingency planning and business continuity processes. Contacts with regulatory bodies are also useful to anticipate and prepare for upcoming changes in relevant laws or regulations that affect the organization. Contacts with other authorities include utilities, emergency services, electricity suppliers and health and safety, telecommunication providers and water suppliers.

The organization needs to maintain useful contact information with appropriate authorities. The purpose is to ensure appropriate flow of information take place with respect to information security between the organization and relevant legal, regulatory and supervisory authorities. An appropriate forum for dialogue and cooperation between the organization and relevant legal, regulatory and supervisory authorities must be in place. It covers the requirement, purpose and implementation instructions on how to identify and report information security events in a timely way, as well as who and how to contact in the event of an incident. Where attacks stem from the internet various authorities and providers may need to be called to action in order to divert/suppress/mitigate the threat. This will help with business continuity and security incident management. The objective is to identify which stakeholders would need to be contacted in the event of a security event. It is important that organization have already identified these stakeholders before an incident occurs. A protocol for engagement with law enforcement can be a part of the security incident response plan or a broader crisis management procedure for the organization. The plan should be clear about which situations require working with law enforcement, such as when laws are broken. The plan should also clearly state who contacts authorities and under what circumstances. Contact with Authorities means that the organization should establish and implement informal communication with authorities concerning information security issues, including:

- Ongoing communication with relevant authorities to ensure that the organization is aware of current threats and vulnerabilities.
- Informing relevant authorities of vulnerabilities discovered in the organization's products, services or systems.
- Receiving information from relevant authorities about threats and vulnerabilities.

The main objective of control is to establish the organization's relationship with law enforcement agencies as it relates to managing information security risks. To meet the requirements, it is expected that if an information security incident is discovered, the organization should specify when and by which authorities should be notified, as well as how identified information security incidents are to be reported in a timely manner. The exchange of information with authorities should also be used to gain a better knowledge of the existing and forthcoming expectations of these agencies (e.g., applicable information security regulations). This requirement is designed to ensure that the organization has a coherent strategy for its relationship with law enforcement agencies and that it has identified the most appropriate point of contact in these agencies.

Contacts with regulatory bodies are also useful to anticipate and prepare for upcoming changes in relevant laws or regulations that affect the organization. Appropriate contacts with relevant authorities must be maintained and the legal responsibilities for contacting authorities such as the Police, the Information Commissioner's Office or other regulatory bodies should always be continued particularly relevant to utilities, telecoms, banking organizations and the emergency services. Where attacks stem from the internet various authorities and providers may need to be called to action in order to divert/suppress/mitigate the threat. All authorities can be listed and retained in an appropriately shared and access-controlled repository.

The ISMS coordinator can keep records up to date and identify which and when contact is made by the appropriate relationship owner with specific contact circumstances, and the nature of the information provided. It should clearly identify who is responsible for contacting authorities, which authorities should be contacted (e.g., which region/country), and in what cases this needs to happen. Specification of the manner and timing in which breaches shall be communicated to external authorities so as to ensure appropriate reporting.

A.5.6 Contact with Special Interest Groups

Most organizations today have some sort of relationship with special interest groups. They may be a customer group, supplier group, or a group that has some influence in the organization. The purpose is to ensure appropriate flow of information takes place with respect to information security among these special interest groups. A special interest group may be defined as an association of persons or organizations with an interest in, or working in, a certain field of expertise, where members cooperate/ work to solve issues, generate solutions, and acquire knowledge. In our situation, this area of expertise would be information security. Organization must identify and document any professional associations, forums or interest groups they are part of or can be part of. Specialist forums, professional groups and even the government are examples of a special interest group. Organization are involved in getting knowledge about best practice, are up to date with current best practices, that organization get early warnings of alerts, advisories and patches being a part of special interest group. It can show that organization got specialist information security advice and share and exchange information.

A.5.6 Contact with Special Interest Groups – A linkage with Ancient Era

The Power of Unity

The Mahabharata teaches us the power of unity through the alliance of the Pandavas. Similarly, collaboration is crucial in the realm of cybersecurity. Organizations, Governments, and Individuals must come together to share knowledge, best practices, and threat intelligence. By fostering, a united front, we can create stronger defense against cyber threats and prevent them from causing significant harm.

Control

The organization should establish and maintain contact with special interest groups or other specialist security forums and professional associations.

Purpose

To ensure appropriate flow of information takes place with respect to information security.

Guidance

Membership in special interest groups or forums should be considered as a means to:

- Improve knowledge about best practices and stay up to date with relevant security information;
- Ensure the understanding of the information security environment is current;
- Receive early warnings of alerts, advisories and patches pertaining to attacks and vulnerabilities;
- Gain access to specialist information security advice;
- Share and exchange information about new technologies, products, services,
- Threats or vulnerabilities;
- Provide suitable liaison points when dealing with information security incidents.

Other Information

Information sharing agreements can be established to improve cooperation and coordination of security issues. Such agreements should identify requirements for the protection of confidential information.

An ISMS is only as good as its ability to keep up with the requirements of the business and provide adequate protection against the risks the organization is exposed to. To accomplish this, information about the environment must be evaluated constantly, but who will do this? Moreover, where can this information be found? The truth is that no one in your organization, not even dedicated teams, can do that by themselves. With the use of critical information getting broader and broader (e.g., by the use of teleworking, virtual teams, etc.), IT demands became more complex, and ISMS and security needs along with it. This means that the level of effort required to cover information related to every single security aspect of your organization would make the costs prohibitive. But organization still have to monitor this information. So, how to do it? Fortunately, ISO 27001 suggests an alternative: contact with special interest groups, control A.5.6 of Annex A of the standard.

In a general way, organization can define a special interest group as an association of individuals or organizations with interest in, or acting in a specific area of knowledge, where members cooperate/work to solve problems, produce solutions, and develop knowledge. In our case, this area of knowledge would be information security.

An organization's ISMS needs to keep up with business requirements and organizational risks. To cover these issues, the A.6.1.4 control from Annex A suggests the following issues for the organization to identify a special interest group to help you:

- **Best practices adopted by the market:** policies, procedures, guidelines, and checklists that organization can adapt for their organization's needs.
- **Market and security trends related to the industry:** laws and regulations, customers' requirements, suppliers' situations your organization has to be aware of or comply with.
- **News and alerts about threats, vulnerabilities, attacks, and patches:** organization need these to check their defenses because it is better to learn from others' mistakes and misfortunes than your own, isn't it?
- **News related to new technologies and products:** what can the organization use to improve their security, or to achieve the same level with reduced costs and/or effort?
- **Specialized consultancy:** organization may not have the expertise, or time, to make the solution or resolve the problem by themselves, so who can help them?
- **Specialized support to handle information security incidents** (e.g., other organizations, police, government security agencies, etc.): when organization have a problem and need help to resolve it, who can help them?

The government as a special interest group is a unique case, because of its access to additional resources (like police, emergency services, firefighters, etc.), and, depending on the legal requirements of each country, its involvement is mandatory. Some of these issues organization can identify for free (accessing the public content on the Internet, signing up for a regular newsletter, or identifying the person/job title to be in contact with a professional association or state agency), and some organization have to pay for (consultant or support services). However, in the latter case, it would be recommended to establish contact with potential suppliers through the defined procurement process.

Since the information organization will be working with could have a great impact on your ISMS, organization should be careful about which special interest groups they interact with, considering:

1. **The quality of the information provided**: Not all of them have precise or updated information.
2. **The availability of the information**: What is the update frequency of the information? If the source organization use takes too much time to update its info, your organization could be exposed to a problem or risk for a longer period.
3. **The legitimacy of the source**: Not all of them are authorized representatives of the one responsible for the information (e.g., manufacturers have specific forums to communicate with their clients or to provide patches). Another case is if security peers recognize the group as a reliable source of information.

In the cases where organization have to send or receive information, be sure to verify whether there is an agreement about how the shared information will be protected. Appropriate contacts with special interest groups or other specialist security forums and professional associations must be maintained. IS owners can keep appropriate contacts with Special Interest Groups or other specialist security forums and professional associations maintained. Contact details, business cards, membership certificates, diaries of meetings etc. can provide evidence of professional contacts, particularly for information risk, security and compliance specialists. Valid contact details embedded within incident response, business continuity and disaster recovery plans provide further evidence of this control, along with notes or reports from previous incidents concerning the contacts made. In the cases where you have to send or receive information, be sure to verify whether there is an agreement about how the shared information will be protected.

A.5.7 Threat Intelligence

Threat intelligence is information gathered from a range of sources about current or potential attacks against an organization. The purpose is to ensure that organizations are aware of their threat environment so that they can put in place a mechanism to collect and analyze these threats and determine the proper actions that can be taken to protect their information security. The information is analyzed, refined and organized and then used to minimize and mitigate information security risks. Organizations embrace threat intelligence to ensure that a) they are properly prepared to deal with today's threat landscape and b) their controls and other investments are well selected and performing as planned. Data is collected, processed, and analyzed to understand a threat actor's motives, targets, and attack behaviors. Threat intelligence enables us to make faster, more informed, data-backed security decisions and change their behavior from reactive to proactive in the fight against threat actors. The main purpose of threat intelligence is to show organizations the various risks they face from external threats. Threat intelligence includes in-depth information and context about specific threats, such as who is attacking, their capabilities and motivation, and the indicators of compromise.

With this information, organizations can make informed decisions about how to defend against the most damaging attacks. In a security context, intelligence is information that provides an organization with decision support and possibly a strategic advantage.

Threat intelligence is a part of a bigger security intelligence strategy. It includes information related to protecting an organization from external and inside threats, as well as the processes, policies and tools used to gather and analyze that information.

Threat intelligence provides better insight into the threat landscape and threat actors, along with their latest tactics, techniques and procedures. It enables organizations to be proactive in configuring its security controls to detect and prevent advanced attacks and zero-day threats. Many of these adjustments can be automated so security stays aligned with the latest intelligence in real time.

A.5.7 Threat Intelligence – A linkage with Ancient Era

Sugriva's Alliance and Threat Intelligence Sharing

Sugriva, the King of the Vanar's, forms an alliance with Lord Ram to defeat King Ravan. This can be compared to the practice of Threat Intelligence sharing in cybersecurity. Threat Intelligence sharing involves collaborating and exchanging information about cyber threats and vulnerabilities among organizations, security researchers, and government agencies. Sugriva's alliance with Lord Ram exemplifies the power of collective knowledge and co-operating to identify and combat evolving cyber threats effectively.

Ravan's Spies and Intrusion Detection Systems

In the Ramayana, King Ravan deploys spies in the form of his followers to gather intelligence and monitor the activities of Lord Ram's army. This can be associated with the use of Intrusion Detection Systems (IDS) in cybersecurity. IDS are security tools that monitor network traffic, identify potential threats or unauthorized activities and alert administrators to take appropriate actions. King Ravan's spies highlight the need for proactive detection and monitoring of potential intrusions in the digital realm.

Control

Information relating to information security threats should be collected and analyzed to produce threat intelligence.

Purpose

To provide awareness of the organization's threat environment so that the appropriate mitigation actions can be taken.

Guidance

Information about existing or emerging threats is collected and analyzed in order to:

- Facilitate informed actions to prevent the threats from causing harm to the organization;
- Reduce the impact of such threats.

Threat intelligence can be divided into four layers, which should all be considered:

- Strategic threat intelligence,
- Tactical threat intelligence,

- Technical threat intelligence
- Operational threat intelligence.

Threat intelligence should be:

- Relevant;
- Insightful;
- Contextual, to provide situational awareness;
- Actionable.

Threat intelligence activities should include:

- Establishing objectives for threat intelligence production;
- Identifying, vetting and selecting internal and external information sources that are necessary and appropriate to provide information required for the production of threat intelligence;
- Collecting information from selected sources, which can be internal and external;
- Processing information collected to prepare it for analysis;
- Analyzing information to understand how it relates and is meaningful to the organization;
- Communicating and sharing it to relevant individuals in a format that can be understood.

Threat intelligence should be analyzed and later used:

- By implementing processes to include information gathered from threat intelligence sources into the organization's information security risk management processes;
- As additional input to technical preventive and detective controls like firewalls, intrusion detection system, or anti malware solutions;
- As input to the information security test processes and techniques.

The organization should share threat intelligence with other organizations on a mutual basis in order to improve overall threat intelligence.

Other Information

Organizations can use threat intelligence to prevent, detect, or respond to threats. Organizations can produce threat intelligence, but more typically receive and make use of threat intelligence produced by other sources. Threat intelligence is often provided by independent providers or advisors, government agencies or collaborative threat intelligence groups. The effectiveness of controls such as 5.25, 8.7, 8.16 or 8.23, depends on the quality of available threat intelligence.

Threat intelligence is used to inform decisions and actions to present these threats causing harm to the organization and reduce the impact of such threats. It requires an organization to collect and analyze information relating to information security threats and use that information take mitigation action. Threat intelligence is used to prevent, detect or respond to threats. Organization can either produce their own threat intelligence or make use of threat intelligence produced by others. It is often provided by independent providers and advisors which can include government sources and more than likely products and services will spring up around this new control to offer it as a service, at a cost . The organization have to ensure that:

1. Objectives for threat intelligence production are established
2. Internal and external sources of information are identified, selected and vetted where necessary and appropriate
3. Information is collected from selected sources
4. Information is then prepared for analysis for example by formatting or translating it
5. Information is analyzed to understand how it relates to you
6. Communication and sharing of information are done to relevant in people in a way they will understand it
7. Conduct periodic reviews of your threat environment (e.g., by reviewing reports from government agencies, other organizations and/or industry associations)
8. Analyze current events and past incidents to determine possible new attack vectors and trends
9. And most of all, create defenses that can be used to mitigate the effect of threat to the organization's information security.

When implementing threat intelligence, organization are analyzing and using information and including it in the risk management process. It can be used as input to inform how to implement and configure technical controls and adapting information security tests and techniques based on it. An organization must know what its threat environment is in order to ensure that it has the right controls in place; that it is able to respond and recover appropriately if something adverse were to happen; and that its security posture is appropriate for its threat environment.

There are four varieties of threat intelligence: strategic, tactical, technical and operational. All four are essential to build a comprehensive threat assessment.

- **Strategic Threat Intelligence**. This analysis summarizes potential security attacks and the possible consequences for nontechnical audiences and stakeholders, as well as decision-makers.
- **Tactical Threat Intelligence**. Tactical intelligence provides information about the tactics, techniques and procedures that threat actors use.
- **Technical Threat Intelligence**. This information focuses on signs that indicate an attack is starting. These signs include reconnaissance, weaponization and delivery.
- **Operational Threat Intelligence**. With this approach, information is collected from a variety of sources, including chat rooms, social media, antivirus logs and past events. It is used to anticipate the nature and timing of future attacks. Data mining and machine learning are often used to automate the processing of hundreds of thousands of data points across multiple languages.

Focusing on strategic, tactical, technical and operational threat intelligence will help organizations improve their awareness and visibility of the threat environment looming outside their organization. In doing so, it looks to encourage better collection and analysis of information surrounding outsider threats as it enables organizations to better understand what they are up against and take the appropriate steps to protect from and mitigate such threats. The organizations should demonstrate that how they are: collecting and analyzing threat intelligence, actioning insights derived from that analysis, incorporating threat intelligence into their ISMS.

Combined, these actions determine how effectively organizations are using threat intelligence while encouraging them to reach a certain standard that requires them to be more informed, better protected, and better equipped to adjust their security posture in line with threat insights. For example, when choosing a new intrusion detection system, organizations should consider how threats against them are likely to manifest. All implemented protections should detect and target those threats, including the tactics used by their likely adversaries. This way, threat intelligence adds to the risk understanding and allows businesses to choose solutions that actually resolve the problems they are likely to encounter.

There are numerous tools that can help organizations collect data and apply threat intelligence within existing security operations. Threat intelligence services also provide organizations with information related to potential attack sources relevant to their businesses; some also offer consultation services.

A.5.8 Information Security in Project Management

For a project manager, a bad week might go something like this:

- You open your email and see that one of your technical resources has inadvertently forwarded a network diagram to a competitor of your client.
- You're rolling out server builds during a weekend Go-Live and you realize your inventory spreadsheet is corrupted.
- You're about to walk into a meeting with your project sponsor and discover the laptop where you've stored the presentation you've been working on for three days has bluescreened.

Each scenario represents a security failure, a failure to maintain the CIA triad of Information Security: Confidentiality, Integrity, Availability. Project managers have special interests in all three components of the CIA triad. IT projects warrant special consideration for maintaining confidentiality. The business case for any IT project will include strategic business goals whether the project delivers an exciting new technology or a mundane but essential upgrade to maintain enterprise productivity. IT project documentation also frequently includes intimate details of network and systems architecture that presents an attractive target for industrial espionage and hackers. Failed changes to IT systems can also impact availability and integrity. Special attention to backups, back-out plans, and security risks early in the project will pay big dividends when project rollout leaves little time to consider how to undo the changes made during a Go-Live or react to an unexpected risk occurrence that may cause systems to go down, or cause data loss, corruption or breach. Project managers should develop plans to mitigate risks to the project documentation and methodology itself.

A good week for a project manager might look something like this:

- You open your email and see that one of your technical resources has flagged an email containing a network diagram as confidential, preventing it from being forwarded to a competitor of your client.
- You're rolling out server builds during a weekend Go-Live and you realize your inventory spreadsheet is corrupted. Your change window gives you time to retrieve a pristine copy of the inventory from

backup, verified with your document versioning system, and your team completes the builds successfully.

- You're about to walk into a meeting with your project sponsor and discover the laptop where you've stored the presentation you've been working on for three days has bluescreened.

Information security is to be addressed in project management regardless of the type of project.

- Understand what is "PROJECT" for your organization.
- Understand the business & security purpose of the PROJECT.
- Understand end to end project flow from the respective owner.
- Define security baseline for a particular project; Complete the Project; verify security baseline (project risk management)

The need for project management skills within the practice of information security may not at first be self-evident. It is emphasized that information security is a process, not a project. However, each element of an information security program must be managed as a project, even if the overall program is perpetually ongoing. This implies, among other things, that the security of the information is present in any establishment of the organization, being a pillar of the same, and serving as cross support to the entire organization. Project management involves identifying and controlling the resources applied to the project as well as measuring progress and adjusting the process as progress is made toward the goal. It is, in fact, a continuous series or chain of projects, each link in this chain could be a specific project, and each of these projects would be guided by the SDLC. These managed processes include the monitoring of the external and internal environments during incident response, ongoing risk assessments of routine operations, and continuous vulnerability assessment and vulnerability repair. These activities are called operations and are ongoing.

- Clear definition of project constraints,
- Establishing measures of performance and creation of project milestones simplifies project monitoring,
- Early identification of deviations in quality, time, or budget enables early correction.

Successful project management relies on careful and realistic project planning coupled with aggressive, proactive control. The project success may be defined differently in each organization, but in general, a project has deemed a success when:

- It is completed on time or early.
- It comes in at or below the expenditures planned for in the baseline budget.
- It meets all specifications outlined in the approved project definition, and the deliverables are accepted by the end-user and/or assigning entity.

To lead information security projects, some organizations assign technically skilled IT or information security experts; others assign an experienced project and general managers. Some organizations use both approaches simultaneously. Regardless of the approach, the goal is the same: to have all elements of the information security program completed with quality deliverables, on a timely basis, and within budget.

It is not the same to say that we are going to establish a methodology to manage projects in the field of information security, as to say that we are going to establish a methodology to treat the security of information in project management.

A.5.8 Information Security in Project Management – A linkage with Ancient Era

Story of Abhimanyu – lies in the importance of proper planning, preparedness, and defense mechanisms against potential risks and challenges

Abhimanyu, possessed exceptional skills in warfare despite his young age. During the battle of Kurukshetra, he was tasked with breaking the Chakravyuha, a formidable and intricate military formation. Abhimanyu knew how to penetrate the formation but was unaware of how to exit it, as he had only partially heard the strategy from his mother's womb. Despite his bravery and skill, he ultimately fell victim to the lack of complete knowledge about navigating the formation's complexities. Similarly, in project management, security encompasses the protection of project assets, data and resources against various threats, including risks to CIA. Security measures in project management involve risk assessment, access controls, data encryption, and contingency planning to mitigate potential vulnerabilities and safeguard project objectives. Just as Abhimanyu's partial knowledge of breaking the Chakravyuha led to his vulnerability, incomplete understanding or inadequate security measures in project management can expose projects to risks and vulnerabilities that may compromise their success.

Control

Information security should be integrated into project management.

Purpose

To ensure information security risks related to projects and deliverables are effectively addressed in project management throughout the project life cycle.

Guidance

Information security should be integrated into project management to ensure information security risks are addressed as part of the project management. This can be applied to any type of project regardless of its complexity, size, duration, discipline or application area. The project management in use should require that:

- Information security risks are assessed and treated at an early stage and periodically as part of project risks throughout the project life cycle;
- Information security requirements are addressed in the early stages of projects;
- Information security risks associated with the execution of projects are considered and treated throughout the project life cycle;
- Progress on information security risk treatment is reviewed and effectiveness of the treatment is evaluated and tested.

The appropriateness of the information security considerations and activities should be followed up at predefined stages by suitable persons or governance bodies, such as the project steering committee. Responsibilities and authorities for information security relevant to the project should be defined and allocated to specified roles. Information security requirements for products or services to be delivered by the project should be determined using various methods, including deriving compliance requirements from information security policy, topic-specific policies and regulations. Further information security requirements can be derived from activities such as threat modelling, incident reviews, use of vulnerability thresholds or contingency planning, thus ensuring that the architecture and design of information systems are protected against known threats based on the operational environment. Information security requirements should be determined for all types of projects, not only ICT development projects. The following should also be considered when determining these requirements:

- What information is involved (information determination), what are the corresponding information security needs (classification) and the potential negative business impact which can result from lack of adequate security;
- The required protection needs of information and other associated assets involved, particularly in terms of confidentiality, integrity and availability;
- The level of confidence or assurance required towards the claimed identity of entities in order to derive the authentication requirements;
- Access provisioning and authorization processes, for customers and other potential business users as well as for privileged or technical users such as relevant project members, potential operation staff or external suppliers;
- Informing users of their duties and responsibilities;
- Requirements derived from business processes;
- Requirements mandated by other information security controls;
- Compliance with the legal, statutory, regulatory and contractual environment in which the organization operates;
- Level of confidence or assurance required for third parties to meet the organization's information security policy and topic-specific policies including relevant security clauses in any agreements or contracts.

Other Information

The project development approach, such as waterfall or agile life cycle, should support information security in a structured way that can be adapted to suit the assessed severity of the information security risks, based on the character of the project. Early consideration of information security requirements for the product or service (e.g., at the planning and design stages), can lead to more effective and cost-efficient solutions for quality and information security. ISO 21500 and ISO 21502 provide guidance on concepts and processes of project management that are important for the performance of projects. ISO/IEC 27005 provides guidance on the use of risk management processes to identify controls to meet information security requirements.

The operation of each organization is determined by the constant execution of projects in the short, medium, and long term. But security is something that is usually forgotten in projects. However, in some organizations, mainly large companies, that have included the information security in their projects as just one more activity (for example, running a risk assessment, focused on information security, at the beginning of any project to identify threats/vulnerabilities and risks). And this is basically what ISO 27001 requests in Annex A.6.1.5 Information security in project management: Information security shall be addressed in project management, regardless of the type of the project. All projects basically need resources, activities to develop, and established time objectives. Information security can be integrated into project management activities in several ways:

- Include information security objectives in project objectives.
- Perform a risk assessment in an early stage of the project.
- Carry out treatment of the identified risks and implement security measures
- Make the information security policy an indispensable part of all stages of the project

It's particularly important to include information security in project activities for those projects, e.g., which deal with or target integrity, availability, and confidentiality of the information. To make security a higher priority, project teams or managers need to implement or address the following:

Secure Development Policy (SDP): Secure development is a requirement to build up a secure service, architecture, software and system. Within a secure development policy, the following aspects should be put into consideration:

- Security of the development environment;
- Guidance on the security in the Project life cycle;
- Secure coding guidelines for each programming language used;
- Security requirements in the design phase;
- Security checkpoints within the project milestones;
- Secure repositories; version control, access control
- Developers' capability of avoiding, finding and fixing vulnerabilities.

An organization Information Security Governance Team needs to create or document Secure Development Policy. If there were no formal documented policy, then organization personnel at any level would have no guidance on how to make decisions during entire project life cycle. This helps employees to initiate actions and take responsibility without constant reference to management, increase the accountability of business or organizations and its staff. In reality, however, the existence of policy provides many benefits provided they are written well and kept up to date. This policy needs to be reviewed at least once in a year or update in case of any changes in policy. After review and changes (if any), this should be approved by Chief Information Security Officer (CISO) or Department Heads only.

Standard Operating Procedures (SOP): Operating procedures shall be documented and made available to all developers/users who need them. The SOP should be in place so that Project Team should know the security requirements on each and every phase during project phases of the life cycle. All step-by-step instructions should be incorporated into the document with the individual's roles & responsibilities. The approved procedure is documented in a format that is easy to follow and reduces the chance of errors being made. The idea behind it is to reduce the possibility of human error and to provide guidelines for employees to follow.

Segregation of development, testing and production environments: Development, testing and production environment shall be separated to reduce risks and threats of unauthorized access or changes to the operational environment. The intent of this requirement is to ensure that development/test functions are separated from production functions. In environments where one individual performs multiple roles, duties should be assigned such that no one individual has end-to-end control of a process without an independent checkpoint. Reducing the number of personnel with access to the production environment minimizes risk and helps ensure that access is limited to those individuals with a business need to know. Organization IT Services or Technology team is responsible for the segregation of all environments and access control as per business needs. Network team recommends separate VLAN for the environments and the Server team is responsible for Server deployment in Data Center or Server Room. Security processes such as Change Management, Secure guidelines as per standard operating environment to be followed as per Industry best practices.

Protection from Malware: This is software that is specifically designed to gain access or damage a computer without the knowledge of the owner. There are various types of malwares including spyware, key loggers, true viruses, worms, or any type of malicious code that infiltrates a computer. Generally, the software is considered malware based on the intent of the creator rather than its actual features. Malware creation is on the rise due to the sheer volume of new types created daily and the lure of money that can be made through organized Internet crime. The malware was originally created as experiments and pranks but eventually led to vandalism and destruction of targeted machines. Today, much of malware is created for profit through forced advertising (adware), stealing sensitive or confidential information (spyware), and spreading email spam. During the Project Life Cycle, we need to ensure that information and information processing facilities are protected against malware. Detection, prevention and recovery controls shall be implemented to protect against malware.

Change Management: A proper Change Management Process should be followed in case of any changes during development up to till production. Threats may occur sometime in case of false changes are made without any testing or staging. The development environment requires a level of security commensurate with the planned security level of the software product being produced. Appropriate controls and configuration management of the development artefacts are essential. There may be specific tools required, such as for static code analysis, to aid the production or testing of secure software. Change is a necessary part of the overall SDLC process. Organization responsible team should write a change management plan, leaders intentionally design a process that helps everyone know what needs to change, why it needs to change, and how to go about making the change take place smoothly.

Risk Assessment: Security Risks, threats and vulnerabilities are the potential attackers and are described in terms of (employee, business partner, contractor or supplier) with an objective (financial gain, project code, organization's IPR or obtaining proprietary corporate information, disabling essential business systems), and with a set of resources (personnel, a computing software, tools, hardware, skill, knowledge of internal systems). A risk assessment explores how a component could be exploited by the identified threats and vulnerabilities (i.e., what could go wrong) and analyzes the possible responses to such attacks. The response options for risk are to (a) mitigate (reduce the probability of the event, reduce impact, improve recovery), (b) transfer (insurance, contracted agreements), (c) ignore (for low impact and highly unlikely threats), or (d) avoid, which may require changes in requirements. The factors involved with a risk assessment that is done early in the development process are predominantly business rather than technical. Project management needs to ensure stakeholder participation in such activities. The attack patterns would be rather abstract for a preliminary system risk assessment and would become more detailed as the software architecture and detailed design are created. Risk management process to be followed by the organization where Information Security experts need to identify, assess, and prioritize the risks followed by coordinated and economical application of resources to minimize, monitor, and control the probability and/or impact of unfortunate events or to maximize the realization of opportunities.

Activities required to complete deliverables: Regulatory or contractual compliance may require a demonstration that the software provides the necessary controls for accessing the information. Security governance typically increases the complexity of meeting security requirements.

Regulatory compliance, Contractual compliance, requirements are set by Customers only and vendors or suppliers should adhere to those guidelines. Delivering "Secure" software requires demonstrating that the desired level of assurance has been achieved. While demonstrating that a system provides the required functionality is an essential aspect of software assurance, software security assurance depends more on demonstrating what a system does not do. An improper input leads to a system failure or enables an attacker to bypass authentication. The production of such an assurance case must be planned and managed. An assurance case provides an argument for how the software meets an identified threat. That argument typically is based on assumptions about how the software behaves under certain operating conditions. Hence, an early step in building an assurance case is to provide evidence that software behavior satisfies the assumptions of the assurance argument. The production of an assurance case is an incremental activity. The assurance case should describe the architecture's role for meeting security requirements, and the architectural risk assessment and analysis should provide evidence that the architecture satisfies those requirements. Syntactic analysis of the source code reduces the probability of coding errors that might lead to a security vulnerability. Risk-based testing can target the components and interfaces that are most likely to lead to a system compromise.

Restrictions on software/tools installation: Procedures shall be implemented to control the installation of tools/software's on development, testing and production systems. The organization should define and enforce strict policy on which types of software users may install. The principle of least privilege should be applied. If granted certain privileges, users may have the ability to install the software. The organization should identify what types of software installations are permitted and what types of installations are prohibited. These privileges should be granted having regard to the roles of the users concerned. Uncontrolled installation of software on computing devices can lead to introducing vulnerabilities and then to information leakage, loss of integrity or other information security incidents, or to violation of intellectual property rights.

Note: Software licensing agreements that are such that organizations may become liable for licensing for client software on workstations owned privately by employees or external party users;

System and application (code level) access control: Access to information and application system functions should be restricted in accordance with the access control policy. Restrictions to access should be based on individual business application requirements and in accordance with the defined access control policy. The following should be considered in order to support access restriction requirements

- Providing menus to control access to application system functions
- Controlling which data can be accessed by a particular user
- Controlling the access rights of users, e.g., read, write, delete and execute
- Controlling the access rights of other applications
- Limiting the information contained in outputs
- Providing physical or logical access controls for the isolation of sensitive applications, application data, or systems.
- Secure log-on procedures

Use of secret authentication information/source code: Users should be required to follow the secure coding guidelines/practices in the use of secret authentication information. All users should be advised to:

- Keep secret code/authentication information confidential, ensuring that it is not divulged to any other parties, including people of authority.
- Avoid keeping a source code/important records information, unless this can be stored securely and the method of storing has been approved.
- Change secret authentication information whenever there is any indication of its possible compromise.
- When passwords are used as secret authentication information, select quality passwords with sufficient minimum length.
- Ensure proper protection of passwords when passwords are used as secret authentication.
- Information in automated log-on procedures and are stored.

- Not use the same secret authentication information for business and non-business purposes.

Facilities and Staffing: Security expertise on most projects is limited and may be an internal or a contracted service. The allocation of that resource is often difficult to even when security activity is limited to networks, authentication, and access control, but when security has to be incorporated into application development, that expertise is spread much thinner. An increase in the level of assurance can significantly affect both the security and software engineering expertise required. For this discussion, we divide security expertise into two categories. One category consists of knowledge of security functions such as the specification and implementation of access control, authentication, and encryption functions. Such security functionality may be encapsulated in the system infrastructure. The second category of expertise consists of the skills to identify and mitigate exploitable system vulnerabilities. Historically, a significant number of the vulnerabilities that lead to a security failure were created by application errors and not by failures with the security infrastructure. Vulnerabilities may be in the least exercised parts of the system and depend on pathological aspects of the interface. Such vulnerabilities may be missed by application development teams, who normally concentrate on the core functionality. The security functionality for authentication, authorization, and encryption is typically composed of commercially supplied components that can be tailored for a specific operating environment. Those components must have the required assurance level. It would not be surprising to find the security knowledge associated with the first category to be concentrated within a few teams. The security specialists associated with that infrastructure should be aware of the security issues associated with development and project management. Unfortunately, application development teams rarely have the necessary security expertise. The resources in the second security knowledge category must be spread across multiple development efforts Tasks such as risk assessments, code reviews, threat modeling, vulnerability assessment, require security expertise. On the other hand, there are security improvement practices that can be implemented without requiring extensive security experience. For example, although security knowledge may be necessary to configure a tool for the static analysis of the source code, the use of such a tool does not require a security background. Testing provides a second example. Penetration testing is often part of an acceptance test or certification process. Penetration testing might be implemented by what is called a red team: security experts who attempt to breach the system defenses.

Project and Product Risks: Poor management of requirements scope is another frequent cause for project failure. Scope management is particularly important where the learning curve is a necessity because of the immaturity of the business usage or the supporting technology. Business integration requirements are pushing the connectivity of networked information systems beyond an organization's IT systems. Meeting business requirements may depend on using relatively new protocols such as those for Web Services. Those protocols are currently a moving target, as they continue to be revised to reflect the experiences of early adopters. Best practices in this context have short lives, and the lack of well-defined and proven practices adversely affects planning. Plans for these circumstances might include a prototype or use of an iterative or incremental approach. Security mechanisms that mitigate a specific risk may create additional ones.

Security integrated into project management methodology: The Project Management Institute defines a project as an interactively elaborated endeavor and security should be considered within each project management process or stage. Security checkpoints built into the project during several key processes will ensure progress toward the desired security end state at the project closure. The best opportunity to ensure secure project delivery exists in the early stages of the project during initiating and planning. Beginning with the end in mind, i.e., the delivery of a security system will avoid costly scope, budget and schedule impacts.

- **Develop Project Charter:** The true business value of a security solution is the amount of risk mitigation provided compared to the cost of solution implementation and maintenance. Project Managers can make a convincing case that security dollars will accomplish more if security is baked into the project from the outset, rather than applied as a Band-Aid to pass an audit during operational handoff, or worse, spent to recover from damage after a security incident. A security impact analysis as part of a larger cost-benefit analysis should be executed during the initiation phase of every IT project to make a sound financial decision. Security can be considered part of the larger Cost of Quality of the project. Large organizations may have a project methodology that requires a security stage gate to be passed; small organizations may need to simply assign a capable reviewer to examine the project proposal at critical points in the project, especially prior to committing funds to the project.

- **Identify Stakeholders:** A Standard Interest vs. Influence Stakeholder analysis matrix focused specifically on security considerations may be revealing. Identify the organizational security office, and find out if they have security sign-off on deliverables for your project. Analyze your sponsor's security attitude, especially if you anticipate the budget is inadequate for security. You may need to move key players higher on the security interest scale, including your project sponsor, technical teams and operations staff. Depending on the formality of the sponsoring organization, the PM may assign a standard list of security roles to project team members. Involving operations staff early in the project and soliciting their input on security requirements during planning will minimize the risk of last-minute security fixes as the system rolls into production.
- **Plan Communications:** The bulk of a Project Managements' work during the executing stage of a project has to do with communications. A communications plan should include not only the method, frequency and audience for communications but may also consider guidelines and technical standards for a wide variety of communication channels:
    - Secure project document sharing that uses adequate encryption and access control for data transfers and storage.
    - Telephone conference calls, including the requirement to password, protect the meetings and/or use the roll call feature of the conferencing provider to ensure only those invited are on the line and periodically changing meeting passcode, especially when a project closes.
    - Distribution of meeting minutes and other project documents via email, including the availability of an encryption mechanism like PGP for sensitive emails.

  - Instant messaging via a provider that meets organization's security standards.
  - Guidelines regarding forwarding work-related email to personal cell phones and what information is acceptable to be left in voice mailboxes and in auto-responders.
  - Desktop or application sharing/video conferencing via an approved provider.
  - Regular backups to guard against data loss due to computer crashes or user error.
  - Guidelines for use of social media.

- **Develop Project Team:** Perhaps the most likely risk during project execution is inadvertent data leakage via one of the myriads of communication channels project managers utilize every day: email, phone, VOIP, IM, numerous options for document sharing, and the newest threat to information security, social media. The ideal defense against inadvertent data leakage is a project team that is aware of the risk and uses secure information systems intelligently. To achieve that, security training may be needed. A review of the communications plan at a team kickoff meeting can set expectations. Periodic reviews of the plan will remind team members of their critical role in project security.
- **Plan Risk Management:** Of the project management processes, "Plan Risk Management" often gets less attention than, say, "Create Work Breakdown Structure" or "Estimate Costs," but information security, and ultimately project management, are fundamentally about risk management. Risk management attempts to qualify and quantify potential impacts and choose effective mitigation strategies. Qualitatively, organizations may have particular risks they tend to avoid. Quantifying security risk is even more challenging and numerous models and techniques are available. Technical experts designing an IT system will likely use more sophisticated techniques for risk analysis than the project manager will use to manage risks to the project, but both aspects of risk management are essential to successful project delivery. Each IT security risk to a project may require custom estimates. Four factors are most important in determining the likelihood that a breach of private consumer data will result in

litigation: data type, breach cause, evidence of misuse and size of the incident. These four general factors may also be useful for evaluating the impact of a breach for other types of IT data. More valuable data such as account names and passwords or network details will have a higher impact than publicly available email addresses. Information stolen by bad actors will likely have a higher impact than information inadvertently misdirected. Information that is actively misused will have a higher impact than information stolen with no evidence of intent to misuse. And the loss of larger amounts of data will be higher impact than smaller amounts of data.

- **Secure Communications:** Communication is at the heart of project management and every communication channel carries the risk of exposing confidential data. An email sent to the wrong person or worse, distribution list, a team member that stores project documents with an insecure cloud provider, a smartphone lost on the bus, a laptop left in a hotel room. Something as simple as neglecting to sanitize internal document meta-data before forwarding to external customers runs the risk of exposing confidential information. IT project records are a rich source of valuable documents and due to the temporary and fast-moving nature of project work, access controls and records systems may not be maintained after the project closes and the team moves on. Industrial espionage targets blue chip companies and small and mid-sized businesses have also been targeted, especially as easy targets for banking fraud, so no organization is immune to the threat.
- **Authentication and Password Management:** 100% of breaches by Advanced Persistent Threat "bad actors" involve stolen credentials. APT groups are large, well-organized, and well-funded, sometimes by national military organizations. Their mission is to methodically gather broad categories of intellectual property like business plans, email addresses and contact lists of organizational leadership, technology blueprints, and proprietary manufacturing processes. Attackers frequently steal data to make reconnaissance faster, like network infrastructure data and sysadmin guides. In particular, VPN configuration files, systems documentation, and network documentation like firewall configuration files are specifically targeted during reconnaissance. Nearly every aspect of a hacked computer

and a user's online life can be and has been commoditized. The argument that "no one would be interested in my data" has been thoroughly debunked. Hackers market lists of stolen credentials for online retailers by the gigabyte. Credentials for critical systems are a prized commodity. LinkedIn, Yahoo and Twitter are just a few of the many sites which have been high-profile victims of password-stealing attacks. Passwords that are reused on a variety of sites and are never changed are a big security risk.

- **Access Management:** Members of the project team should have the access they need and only the access they need to systems. In the name of speed, credentials are sometimes handed out fast and loose. Defining and documenting a clear system for on-boarding and off-boarding personnel will not only improve the efficiency of these processes but also ensure credentials are current. Team member access rights need to be reviewed and updated periodically. If people leave the project or organization, access should be revoked.
    - Document and use secure onboarding and off-boarding procedures.
    - Schedule periodic reviews of access permissions.
- **Encryption:** Encryption protects sensitive and valuable data at rest and in motion by transforming plain text into a coded form referred to as cypher text. Encryption is an almost invisible part of many communications protocols, including web browsing, email, instant messaging, VoIP. Encryption can be especially valuable for the storage of data as another layer of protection against data theft or breaches on cloud infrastructure or mobile devices. The ease and convenience of cloud storage bring new challenges, including inadvertent data leakage during storage or transfer or even through deliberate data harvesting by the cloud provider, and challenges for the availability of project records. It's a mistake to choose a cloud vendor based solely on the quality of service and price if their privacy and security standards are not adequate. It has been reported that many organizations had experienced a breach of outsourced consumer data. The vendor should provide verifiable evidence that data is secure on their infrastructures like security certifications that require audits of their practices with

respect to NIST and FISMA standards by accredited organizations like Logyx and Veris group, or via STAR or FedRAMP certifications. Project Manager must make sure that they are familiar with and understand the disaster recovery provisions, privacy terms and conditions, and long-term financial viability of the cloud provider before storing project records in the cloud. Cloud storage providers like Microsoft and Amazon have responded to being hacked by improving their default security configuration. However, even strong encryption is only as secure as the password(s) used to unlock the encryption. Data on mobile devices like laptops and smartphones should be secured with encryption plus strong authentication since they are frequently lost or stolen.

  - Protect data in the cloud or on mobile devices with encryption.
  - Enforce strong authentication policies for accessing encrypted data.
  - Transmit data only with secure protocols.

- **Wireless Attacks:** Employees on road will undoubtedly have been faced with the question of whether connecting to a hotel, airport or coffee shop wireless connection is "safe." Connecting to an open wireless network provides a fast attack surface, including the possibility of bad actors potentially intercepting transmitted information, compromising the computer or smart device, or harvesting passwords or information about secure corporate VPN or wireless systems due to unsecured behaviour of the wireless card. Handhelds like smartphones hold and transmit rapidly increasing amounts of data and deserve special scrutiny since they are easily and frequently lost or stolen and have in many cases minimal built-in provisions for security. If they do not conform to organization security policies for passwords, encryption and virus protection they should not have access to organization data, including email and voice messaging. The most common cause of data breaches due to smartphones is a lost device.

  - Require a secure configuration and security measures for all devices accessing internal data, especially smartphones and laptops.
  - Restrict end-user administrative permissions.

- Avoid using unsecured wireless networks. If using unsecured networks is unavoidable, use a VPN or another secure tunnel to access all data.
- Keep smartphone software up-to-date by enabling automatic updates.
- Backup smartphone data periodically to avoid losing data, especially contacts, if the device is lost, stolen or damaged.

- **Physical Security:** If your employer or client has locations in several countries, it is likely they are an attractive target for intellectual property theft or industrial espionage. Any work-related information on your laptop or smartphone will require special consideration for maintaining the confidentiality of that information. Physical security for project records should include not only physical access to the electronic systems that store data such as laptops but also physical access to printouts and paper filing systems. Recycling bin, printer and fax output trays and filing cabinets all need to be covered by the security policy. Sensitive documents should never be left unattended in insecure locations and should be shredded with cross-cut shredders when disposed of. Commercial software can now digitally reassemble most documents shredded on popular and inexpensive strip shredders
  - Secure hard copies of data in file cabinets, on fax machines, in printer trays and in wastebaskets/shredders.
  - Use security cables. Educate travelers about the risks of theft and data leakage.
- **Secure Deliverables:** Requirements gathering is a critical stage for project security. Security requirements should consider the sponsoring organization's security policy and regulatory environment. The PMBOK notes that security requirements may impact project costs via the scope baseline and procurement. Requirements elicitation is often not straight-forward; security requirements elicitation maybe even less well-defined. A systematic approach may help to achieve a consistent, complete set of security requirements.
- **Monitor and Control Risks - Change Control:** Information security is often identified only with hackers and malware, but basic system

availability is impacted by a much broader category of events, including planned and even routine system changes. Project Managers tend to leave technical change management to their technical teams. However, technical change management presents risks to information security availability and integrity and project managers should be familiar with its risks and mitigation of those risks. If a system goes down during a Go-Live event and adequate time has not been reserved to back out changes, the availability of the system to support business functions is compromised. A good change control plan will include enough time to make all changes and complete testing, plus enough time to roll back all changes if the system doesn't pass operational or functional tests at a scheduled checkpoint(s). Similarly, information integrity is at risk if adequate measures aren't in place to backup and then restore data from backup during the change window if necessary. Changes should be evaluated on a risk matrix, based on impact urgency, risk, benefits, and costs, and managed to minimize impacts to business needs. Change windows should have longer lead times and be larger for higher-risk changes.

- **Verify Deliverables:** Operations may expect the project delivery team to deliver an inherently secure system, while the project delivery team may expect security to be the responsibility of operations management after the system is handed off. Consideration should be given to when and how security concerns are most efficiently and effectively addressed in the total system life cycle, not just during project delivery. Ownership of security should rest with the project manager to the extent that the initial system setup is securable. An organization can either incorporate security guidance into its general project management processes or react to security failures. If security has been included in requirements gathering with input from the operations team, operational hand-off will be organized around verifying security deliverables as specified and transferring ownership rather than reacting to security problems identified by operations staff as the system is being put into production. Operational Acceptance Testing checklists for non-functional components of a system (i.e., quality attributes such as performance, availability, and reliability) like backup/recovery, maintenance, and security can guide the hand-off and ensure that operations staff have the documentation and verified configurations they need to support the system.

- **Document Lessons Learned:** In the excitement of a completed project and the usual pressure to move on to a new one, it may be often overlooked, but capturing lessons learned is an important part of building Organizational Process Assets and your security expertise as a project manager. Lessons learned can be one of the most effective ways to motivate secure behaviors and to establish a culture of security in your organization over the long-term. Any security experiences, risks, or threats that materialized or not should be noted in the risk register and documented for future project evaluation and planning.

A.5.9 Inventory of Information and other Associated Assets

An asset is defined as "Any item of economic value owned by an individual or corporation". An information asset management has a long history in business continuity planning (BCP), disaster recovery (DR), and incident response planning. The first step in any of those processes involves identifying critical systems, networks, databases, applications, data flows and other components that need protection. If organization do not know what needs protection or where it resides, then organization cannot plan for how to protect it. Asset and data management is based on the idea that it is important to identify, track, classify, and assign ownership for the most important assets in the organization to ensure they are adequately protected. Tracking inventory of IT hardware is the simplest example of asset management. The control requires taking an inventory of all information and other associated assets, classifying them into distinct categories, identifying their owners, and documenting the controls that are or should be in place. This is a crucial step toward ensuring that all information assets are adequately protected. An inventory of information and other associated assets is a list of everything an organization stores, processes, or transmits. It also includes the location and security controls for each item. The goal is to identify every single piece of data. This is a list of information assets that an organization owns, including fixed assets such as property and equipment, as well as intangible assets such as personal data. Creating such an inventory is essential for managing assets and, by extension, mitigating against information security risks. This can be used to identify gaps in the information security program and identify vulnerabilities during the risk assessments that could lead to a breach. It can also be used as evidence during compliance audits that organization have done due diligence in identifying sensitive data, which helps avoid fines and penalties. The inventory of information assets should also include details of who owns each asset and who manages it. It should also include information about the value of each item in the inventory and how critical it is to the success of the organization's business operations. It is important that inventories are kept up-to-date so that they reflect changes within the organization.

A.5.9 Inventory of Information and other Associated Assets – A linkage with Ancient Era

Importance of Project Valuable Assets

In the Ramayana, Mata Sita represents an invaluable asset for Lord Ram, and Her abduction by King Ravan highlights the importance of protecting what is valuable to us. Similarly, in the cyber world, organizations and individuals possess valuable digital assets like sensitive data, intellectual property, financial information etc. the Ramayana serves as a reminder to safeguard these assets and take necessary measures to protect them from cyber threats.

Control

An inventory of information and other associated assets, including owners, should be developed and maintained.

Purpose

To identify the organization's information and other associated assets in order to preserve their information security and assign appropriate ownership.

Guidance

Inventory

The organization should identify its information and other associated assets and determine their importance in terms of information security. Documentation should be maintained in dedicated or existing inventories as appropriate. The inventory of information and other associated assets should be accurate, up to date, consistent and aligned with other inventories. Options for ensuring accuracy of an inventory of information and other associated assets include:

- Conducting regular reviews of identified information and other associated assets against the asset inventory.
- Automatically enforcing an inventory update in the process of installing, changing or removing an asset.

The location of an asset should be included in the inventory as appropriate. The inventory does not need to be a single list of information and other associated assets. Considering that the inventory should be maintained by the relevant functions, it can be seen as a set of dynamic inventories, such as inventories for information assets, hardware, software, virtual machines (VMs), facilities, personnel, competence, capabilities and records. Each asset should be classified in accordance with the classification of the information associated to that asset. The granularity of the inventory of information and other associated assets should be at a level appropriate for the needs of the organization. Sometimes specific instances of assets in the information life cycle are not feasible to be documented due to the nature of the asset. An example of a short-lived asset is a VM instance whose life cycle can be of short duration.

Ownership

For the identified information and other associated assets, ownership of the asset should be assigned to an individual or a group and the classification should be identified. A process to ensure timely assignment of asset ownership should be implemented. Ownership should be assigned when assets are created or when assets are transferred to the organization. Asset ownership should be reassigned as necessary when current asset owners leave or change job roles.

Owner Duties

The asset owner should be responsible for the proper management of an asset over the whole asset life cycle, ensuring that:

1. Information and other associated assets are inventoried;
2. Information and other associated assets are appropriately classified and protected;
3. The classification is reviewed periodically;
4. Components supporting technology assets are listed and linked;
5. Requirements for the acceptable use of information and other associated assets are established;
6. Access restrictions correspond with the classification and that they are effective and are reviewed periodically;
7. Information and other associated assets, when deleted or disposed, are handled in a secure manner and removed from the inventory;

8. They are involved in the identification and management of risks associated with their asset;
9. They support personnel who have the roles and responsibilities of managing their information.

Other Information

Inventories of information and other associated assets are often necessary to ensure the effective protection of information and can be required for other purposes, such as health and safety, insurance or financial reasons. Inventories of information and other associated assets also support risk management, audit activities, vulnerability management, incident response and recovery planning. Tasks and responsibilities can be delegated, but the person or group who delegated them remains accountable. It can be useful to designate groups of information and other associated assets which act together to provide a particular service. In this case, the owner of this service is accountable for the delivery of the service, including the operation of its assets. See ISO/IEC 19770-1 for additional information on information technology (IT) asset management. See ISO 55001 for additional information on asset management.

An organization should identify assets relevant in the life cycle of information and document their importance. The life cycle of information should include creation, processing, storage, transmission, deletion and destruction. Documentation should be maintained in dedicated or existing inventories as appropriate. The asset inventory should be accurate, up to date, consistent and aligned with other inventories. For each of the identified assets, ownership of the asset should be assigned and the classification should be identified. Inventories of assets help to ensure that effective protection takes place, and may also be required for other purposes. ISO provides examples of assets that might need to be considered by the organization when identifying assets. The process of compiling an inventory of assets is an important prerequisite of risk management. Individuals, as well as other entities having approved management responsibility for the asset life cycle, qualify to be assigned as asset owners. A process to ensure timely assignment of asset ownership is usually implemented. Ownership should be assigned when assets are created or when assets are transferred to the organization.

The identified owner can be either an individual or an entity who has approved management responsibility for controlling the whole life cycle of an asset. The identified owner does not necessarily have any property rights to the asset. Routine tasks may be delegated e.g., to a custodian looking after the assets on a daily basis, but the responsibility remains with the owner. In complex information systems, it may be useful to designate groups of assets that act together to provide a particular service. In this case, the owner of this service is accountable for the delivery of the service, including the operation of its assets.

In order to effectively manage an organization's assets, organization must first understand what assets they have and where the organization keeps them. Supporting assets should be included in the inventory. All assets should be accounted for and have an owner. If improperly managed, assets can become liabilities.

1. **Categorize assets**. Begin by defining distinct categories of the types of assets in the organization. Each category should have its own inventory or classification structure based on the assets that category may contain. (Category: Data Center Hardware)
2. **Create a list of assets for each category**. Creating a list of an institution's assets and their corresponding locations is the beginning of asset inventory. Often, the process of doing so helps identify additional assets that previously had not been considered. (Category: Data Center Hardware; Asset: Core Network Switches)
3. **Add a location for each asset.** The location could be a brick-and-mortar physical location such as a classroom, data center or office. It could also be collaborative research materials on a file share or financial information stored in a database. (Category: Data Center Hardware; Asset: Core Network Switches; Location: Room no 001)

Because assets can be many things and serve multiple functions, there will likely be more than one inventory process or system used to capture the range of assets that exist in an organization. Make sure organization connect with other areas to see what form of hardware inventory already exists. Don't start from zero. Each inventory system should not unnecessarily duplicate other inventories that may exist.

Asset Responsibility/Ownership

Once organization have begun to capture an inventory of the potential assets and their locations, start identifying the responsible person for each asset. An owner is a person, or persons or department, that has been given formal responsibility for the security of an asset. The owner is responsible for securing the asset during the life cycle of the asset. At this juncture in the exercise, it is important to understand the distinction between the term "owner" and "custodian" of assets. The custodian is responsible for ensuring that the asset is managed appropriately over its life cycle, in accordance with rules set by the asset owner. The custodian is often a subject matter expert or "owner" of the business process for a particular information asset. An owner of an information asset, Data Owners if they have direct operational responsibility for the management of one or more types of data. The owner of the assets should be able to identify acceptable uses or provide information on which policy governs its acceptable use. Work with the responsible owner, if need be, on acceptable uses. The acceptable uses should include items such as who assumes the risk of loss, gives access to the asset and how a critical asset is kept functional during or after a loss. Policies governing the use, preservation, and destruction of hardware may originate from the asset management office. Many organizations also find it helpful to document expectations for the acceptable and responsible use of information technology assets in an Acceptable and Responsible Use Policies

Physical and Environmental Asset Importance

Gaining a clear understanding of the relative importance of each asset when compared to other organizational assets is an essential step if organization are to adequately protect their assets. The importance of an asset can be measured by its business value and security classification or label. Create a rating system for the asset. It can be as simple as (highest to lowest)

1. Critical is always available and protected
2. Very Important this asset is available and protected
3. Important if this asset is available and protected
4. Good if this asset is available with minimal protection

A.5.10 Acceptable Use of Information and Other Associated Assets

This control states that the rules for the acceptable use and procedures for handling information and other associated assets should be identified, documented and implemented. There must be a clear guideline of how users should behave when working with information assets, to ensure confidentiality, integrity and availability of the organization's information security assets. Acceptable use of information and other associated assets means using information assets in ways that do not put at risk the availability, reliability, or integrity of data, services or resources. It also means using them in ways that do not violate laws or the organization's policies. The Acceptable Use of Information Assets applies to all members of an organization and assets owned or operated by the organization. It applies to all uses of information assets for any purpose, including commercial. The following are examples of information assets, but not limited to:

- **Hardware:** computers, mobile devices, phones and fax machines.
- **Software:** operating systems, applications (including Web-based apps), utilities, firmware and programming languages.
- **Data:** structured data in relational databases, flat files and No SQL data; unstructured data such as text documents, spreadsheets, images, video and audio files; records in any format.
- **Networks:** wired and wireless networks; telecommunications systems; voice over IP services.
- **Services:** cloud services, email accounts and other hosted services.
- **People:** employees, contractors, vendors, suppliers.

A.5.10 Acceptable use of Information and other Associated Assets – A linkage with Ancient Era

Draupadi Vastra Haran (Disrobing of Draupadi) – provides insights into the misuse of power, dignity, and assets, highlighting the consequences of such actions.

- Duryodhana, Duhshasana, and other Kauravas, driven by jealousy and arrogance, attempt to dishonor Draupadi by stripping her of her clothing in a public assembly. This act symbolizes the abuse of power and the disregard for the dignity and rights of others. It underscores how assets, including clothing, can be used as tools for humiliation and oppression when wielded by individuals devoid of righteousness and ethics.

Control

Rules for the acceptable use and procedures for handling information and other associated assets should be identified, documented and implemented.

Purpose

To ensure information and other associated assets are appropriately protected, used and handled.

Guidance

Personnel and external party users using or having access to the organization's information and other associated assets should be made aware of the information security requirements for protecting and handling the organization's information and other associated assets. They should be responsible for their use of any information processing facilities.

The organization should establish a topic-specific policy on the acceptable use of information and other associated assets and communicate it to anyone who uses or handles information and other associated assets. The topic-specific policy on acceptable use should provide clear direction on how individuals are expected to use information and other associated assets. The topic-specific policy should state:

1. Expected and unacceptable behaviors of individuals from an information security perspective;
2. Permitted and prohibited use of information and other associated assets;
3. Monitoring activities being performed by the organization.

Acceptable use procedures should be drawn up for the full information life cycle in accordance with its classification and determined risks. The following items should be considered:

1. Access restrictions supporting the protection requirements for each level of classification;
2. Maintenance of a record of the authorized users of information and other associated assets;
3. Protection of temporary or permanent copies of information to a level consistent with the protection of the original information;
4. Storage of assets associated with information in accordance with manufacturers' specifications;
5. Clear marking of all copies of storage media (electronic or physical) for the attention of the authorized recipient;
6. Authorization of disposal of information and other associated assets and supported deletion method.

Other Information

It can be the case that the assets concerned do not directly belong to the organization, such as public cloud services. The use of such third-party assets and any assets of the organization associated with such external assets should be identified as applicable and controlled, for example, through agreements with cloud service providers. Care should also be taken when a collaborative working environment is used.

After going through the asset inventory, categorization, and ownership identification, ensure there are documented policies regarding the acceptable use of assets. Define, and document, the rules that clarify the acceptable uses of assets associated with information and information processing facilities. It is important, once the rules are clarified, that appropriate controls are implemented and the security requirements are communicated. Target the communication of security requirements to employees and, if appropriate, third parties who may use these assets. Asset owners should be responsible and accountable, even if the owner has delegated responsibility, for their use of facilities and resources. The control was designed to ensure that policies, procedures and technical controls are in place to prevent users from inappropriately accessing, using or disclosing information assets. This control aims to provide a framework for organizations to ensure that information and other assets are appropriately protected, used and handled. This includes ensuring that the policies and procedures exist at all levels within the organization, as well as ensuring that those policies and procedures are consistently enforced. Organization have put in place the various requirements related to how they protect IT assets including:

1. The protection of information in storage, processing and transit.
2. The protection and appropriate use of IT equipment.
3. The use of appropriate authentication services to control access to information systems.
4. The processing of information within an organization only by users with appropriate authorization.
5. The allocation of information-related responsibilities to specific individuals or roles.
6. The education and training of users regarding their security responsibilities.

Organization will need to develop procedures for handling assets associated with their information and information processing facilities. It is important that organization asset handling procedures respect and reflect how they have classified it. Ensure that

1. Information is handled and protected according to its classification. This includes sharing with external entities.
2. There are procedures to control classified information.
3. Information is stored, processed, transmitted and copied according to its classification. Copies should get the same protections.
4. Access restrictions are designed for each level of classification. Restrictions must meet protection requirements.
5. There is a formal record of the authorized recipients of the assets. Specify who the authorized recipient should be. Label media copies appropriately.

All of the above bullet points can be incorporated into one procedural access handling document. Remember, keep it simple so others will be able to understand and comply with the requirements. Hold a session with information and physical asset owners so they can help define the requirements. It's important everyone feels ownership of this process.

A.5.11 Return of Assets

Both staff and external stakeholders must return all of the organizational assets in their possession upon termination of their job, contract or agreement. This control states that personnel and other interested parties as appropriate should return all the organization's assets in their possession upon change or termination of their employment, contract or agreement. Information assets can include physical documents, digital files and databases, software programs, and even intangible items like trade secrets and intellectual property. Information assets can have value in a variety of ways. They may contain personally identifying information (PII) about customers, employees or other stakeholders that could be used by bad actors for financial gain or identity theft. They could contain sensitive information about organization's finances, research or operations that would provide a competitive advantage to your competitors if they were able to get their hands on it. This is why it is important that staff and contractors whose business are terminated with organizations are compelled to return all such assets in their possession. The termination process must be legally concluded with the return of all tangible and electronic assets previously assigned, owned or entrusted to the organization. This means that the organization must have a written policy that defines clear rules for returning assets upon termination. Organizations must also have personnel that will confirm receipt of returned assets, and ensure that assets are properly inventoried and accounted for. When an employee or external user buys the equipment of the organization or uses his/her own personal equipment, it is important to follow protocols to ensure that all relevant information is transmitted to the organization and safely removed from the equipment. In situations where an employee or external user is aware that this information is necessary for ongoing operations, it should be reported and transmitted to the organization. During the notice period of termination, unauthorized copying of sensitive information by terminated staff should be monitored by the organization.

A.5.11 Return of Assets – A linkage with Ancient Era

Lord Ram's ring to Mata Sita by Lord Hanuman – lies in the themes of loyalty, devotion, and the rightful restoration of belongings.

- **Loyalty and Devotion:** Lord Hanuman, a devoted follower of Lord Ram, undertakes a perilous journey to Lanka to find Mata Sita, who has been abducted by King Ravana. His unwavering loyalty and devotion to Lord Ram drive him to search tirelessly for Mata Sita and eventually locate her in King Ravana's kingdom.

- **Recovery of Assets:** During His search for Mata Sita, Lord Hanuman encounters her in captivity in Lanka. To reassure Mata Sita of Lord Ram's imminent rescue mission, Lord Hanuman presents her with Lord Ram's ring. This ring serves as a symbolic asset, representing Lord Ram's commitment and love for Mata Sita.
- **Restoration of Belongings:** Lord Hanuman's return of Lord Ram's ring to Mata Sita signifies the restoration of a valuable asset and, more importantly, the restoration of hope and trust.

Overall, the return of Lord Ram's ring to Mata Sita by Lord Hanuman underscore's themes of loyalty, devotion, and the rightful restoration of assets.

Control

Personnel and other interested parties as appropriate should return all the organization's assets in their possession upon change or termination of their employment, contract or agreement.

Purpose

To protect the organization's assets as part of the process of changing or terminating employment, contract or agreement.

Guidance

The change or termination process should be formalized to include the return of all previously issued physical and electronic assets owned by or entrusted to the organization. In cases where personnel and other interested parties purchase the organization's equipment or use their own personal equipment, procedures should be followed to ensure that all relevant information is traced and transferred to the organization and securely deleted from the equipment. In cases where personnel and other interested parties have knowledge that is important to ongoing operations, that information should be documented and transferred to the organization. During the notice period and thereafter, the organization should prevent unauthorized copying of relevant information by personnel under notice of termination. The organization should clearly identify and document all information and other associated assets to be returned which can include:

- User Endpoint Devices
- Portable Storage Devices
- Specialist Equipment
- Authentication Hardware
- Physical Copies of Information.

Other Information

It can be difficult to return information held on assets which are not owned by the organization. In such cases, it is necessary to restrict the use of information using other information security controls such as access rights management or use of cryptography. This is designed to protect the organization's assets as part of the process of changing or terminating employment, contract or agreement. The intent of this control is to prevent authorized individuals from retaining assets that belong to the organization. When employees and contractors leave your organization, you have to make sure that they don't take any sensitive data with them. Organization do that by identifying any potential threats and monitoring the user's activities before their departure. This control is to ensure that the individual does not have access to the IT systems and networks when they are terminated. Organizations should establish a formal termination process which ensures that individuals are not able to gain access to any IT systems after their departure from the organization. This can be done by revoking all permissions, disabling accounts and removing access from building premises. Procedures should be in place to ensure that employees, contractors, and other relevant parties return all organizational assets that are no longer required for business purposes or are due for replacement. Organizations may also want to perform a final check of the individual's work area to ensure that all sensitive information has been returned.

For example:

- Upon separation, organization-owned equipment is collected.
- Contractors return equipment and information at the end of their contract.

All employees and external party users are expected to return any organizational and information assets upon termination of their employment, contract or agreement. As such it must be an obligation for employees and external users to return all the assets and these obligations would be expected in the relevant agreements with staff, contractors and others. A solid, documented process is also required to ensure that the return of assets is appropriately managed and can be evidenced for each person or supplier that goes through it. Where assets are not returned according to the process, unless otherwise agreed and documented as part of the exit process, the non-return should be logged as a security incident and followed-up. The return of assets procedure is never fool proof and this also underlines the need for periodic audit of assets to ensure their continued protection. In order to meet the requirements, the change or termination process should be formalized to include the return of all previously issued physical and electronic assets owned by or entrusted to the organization. The process should also ensure that any and all access rights, accounts, digital certificates and passwords are removed. This formalization is especially important in cases where a change or termination occurs unexpectedly, such as death or resignation, in order to prevent unauthorized access to organization assets which could lead to a data breach. The process should ensure that all assets are accounted for, and that they have all been returned/disposed of in a secure manner.

This can be achieved through a formal checklist containing all necessary items to be returned/disposed of and completed by the user upon termination, along with any necessary signatures confirming that the assets have been returned/disposed of successfully. It is critical that organizations protect their information on the equipment of employees when their employment is terminated. Make sure all relevant information that will be needed by the institution is preserved, but all information on the asset is erased. Develop an employee exit checklist that addresses the return of all institutional assets, physical or information, before the employee's last day. There are, of course, emergency situations dealing with immediate termination that may not lend themselves to a measured checklist. Create a simple checklist for those instances as well. Get to know a resource in HR area and work with that resource to incorporate physical and electronic assets at termination. As stated before, assets can be a variety of items. Employee knowledge is also an information asset to the organization. Preserve their relevant knowledge, document, before the individual leaves the organization, and ensure that knowledge is in the organization's possession. Once again, use the checklist to incorporate this aspect of asset return. A sample may include:

1. The employee has returned all computing equipment to IT.
2. IT will preserve the information on the equipment by copying to an external drive or employee group shared file server. Preserved information will be given to the employee's supervisor.
3. The employee has transferred all organization information from his/her personal equipment and given that to their supervisor.
4. Employee rights to information assets have been terminated as of this date.
5. Employee knowledge transfer has occurred.

Don't forget about the contractors, consultants, or any other external third party upon termination of contract or agreement. The same rules apply. Organization may wish to have a separate asset security checklist for all external agents and ensure this information is part of their contract or agreement.

A.5.12 Classification of Information and A.5.13 Labeling of Information

Information classification is a process in which organizations assess the data that they hold and the level of protection it should be given. Organizations usually classify information in terms of confidentiality – i.e., who is granted access to view it. Data Classification or Information Classification is the process of classifying corporate information into significant categories to ensure critical data is protected. A typical system contains four levels of classification:

1. Confidential
2. Restricted
3. Internal
4. Public

The levels shouldn't be based on employees' seniority but on the information that's necessary to perform certain job functions. Organization just need to follow simple steps:

- **Enter organization assets into an inventory:** The first step is to collate all information into an inventory (or asset register). You should also note who is responsible for it (who owns it) and what format it's in (electronic documents, databases, paper documents, storage media, etc.).
- **Classification:** Next, classify the information. Asset owners are responsible for this, but it's a good idea for senior management to provide guidelines based on the results of the organization's ISMS risk assessment. Information that would be affected by more significant risks should usually be given a higher level of confidentiality. But be careful, because this isn't always the case. There will be instances where sensitive information must be made available to a broader set of employees for them to do their job. The information may well pose a threat if it's confidentiality is compromised, but the organization must make it widely available in order to function.
- **Labeling:** Once information has been classified, the asset owner must create a system for labeling it. You'll need different processes

for information that's stored digitally and physically, but it should be consistent and clear.

A 5.12 Classification of Information

A.5.12 Classification of Information – A linkage with Ancient Era

The Story of Hanuman crossing the river highlights the importance of strategy, problem-solving, and adaptability in achieving goals.

- **Information Assessment:** Lord Hanuman crossing the river, he encounters the problem of not knowing his own strength. He had forgotten his divine capabilities due to a curse. Similarly, in information classification, understanding the nature and significance of different pieces of information is crucial for effective decision-making.
- **Strategic Planning:** Lord Hanuman, faced with the challenge of crossing the river to reach Lanka, strategically evaluates his options. He eventually realizes his own strength and decides to leap across the ocean. Similarly, in information classification, strategizing involves categorizing information based on its relevance, importance, and potential impact on decision-making processes.
- **Adaptability:** Lord Hanuman adapts to the situation by harnessing his inner strength and overcoming the limitations imposed by the curse. He demonstrates flexibility and resourcefulness in finding a solution to the obstacle he faces. Similarly, in information classification, being adaptable allows individuals or organizations to adjust their approach based on new insights or changing circumstances.
- **Risk Assessment:** Before making the leap, Lord Hanuman assesses the risks involved in his decision. He weighs the potential challenges and consequences but ultimately decides to proceed with determination and courage. Similarly, in information classification, understanding the risks associated with different types of information helps in making informed decisions and mitigating potential negative outcomes.
- **Goal Achievement:** Lord Hanuman's successful crossing of the river signifies the attainment of his objective despite the challenges he encounters. It emphasizes perseverance, determination, and the ability to overcome obstacles in pursuit of a goal. Similarly, effective

information classification facilitates goal achievement by providing clarity, direction, and actionable insights.

The story of Lord Hanuman crossing the river exemplifies key principles relevant to information classification, including strategic planning, adaptability, risk assessment, and goal achievement. It highlights the importance of discernment, problem-solving, and perseverance in navigating challenges and achieving desired outcomes.

Control

Information should be classified according to the information security needs of the organization based on confidentiality, integrity, availability and relevant interested party requirements.

Purpose

To ensure identification and understanding of protection needs of information in accordance with its importance to the organization.

Guidance

The organization should establish a topic-specific policy on information classification and communicate it to all relevant interested parties. The organization should take into account requirements for CIA in the classification scheme.

Classifications and associated protective controls for information should take account of business needs for sharing or restricting information, for protecting integrity of information and for assuring availability, as well as legal requirements concerning the CIA of the information. Assets other than information can also be classified in compliance with classification of information, which is stored in, processed by or otherwise handled or protected by the asset. Owners of information should be accountable for their classification. The classification scheme should include conventions for classification and criteria for review of the classification over time. Results of classification should be updated in accordance with changes of the value, sensitivity and criticality of information through their life cycle.

The scheme should be aligned to the topic-specific policy on access control and should be able to address specific business needs of the organization. The classification can be determined by the level of impact that the information's compromise would have for the organization. Each level defined in the scheme should be given a name that makes sense in the context of the classification scheme's application. The scheme should be consistent across the whole organization and included in its procedures so that everyone classifies information and applicable other associated assets in the same way. In this manner, everyone has a common understanding of protection requirements and applies appropriate protection. The classification schemes used within the organization can be different from the schemes used by other organizations, even if the names for levels are similar.

In addition, information moving between organizations can vary in classification depending on its context in each organization, even if their classification schemes are identical. Therefore, agreements with other organizations that include information sharing should include procedures to identify the classification of that information and to interpret the classification levels from other organizations. Correspondence between different schemes can be determined by looking for equivalence in the associated handling and protection methods.

Other Information

Classification provides people who deal with information with a concise indication of how to handle and protect it. Creating groups of information with similar protection needs and specifying information security procedures that apply to all the information in each group facilitates this. This approach reduces the need for case-by-case risk assessment and custom design of controls. Information can cease to be sensitive or critical after a certain period of time. For example, when the information has been made public, it no longer has confidentiality requirements but can still require protection for its integrity and availability properties. These aspects should be taken into account, as over-classification can lead to the implementation of unnecessary controls resulting in additional expense or, on the contrary, under-classification can lead to insufficient controls to protect the information from compromise. As an example, an information confidentiality classification scheme can be based on four levels as follows:

- Disclosure causes no harm;

- Disclosure causes minor reputation damage or minor operational impact;
- Disclosure has a significant short-term impact on operations or business objectives;
- Disclosure has a serious impact on long term business objectives or puts the survival of the organization at risk.

A.5.13 Labelling of Information – A linkage with Ancient Era

Lord Krishna's Life – Principles of Identity, Ownership, and Spiritual Significance

- **Identity and Ownership**: In Lord Krishna's life, various objects and entities are labeled with symbolic significance. For example, his divine flute represents enchanting music and spiritual longing, while his peacock feather denotes beauty and grace. Similarly, in the classification of assets, labeling helps establish identity, ownership, and attributes associated with each asset, facilitating their management and utilization.
- **Symbolism and Representation**: Lord Krishna's life is filled with symbolism, where each object or entity represents deeper spiritual meanings. For instance, the Sudarshan Chakra symbolizes divine protection and justice, while the Kaustubha Gem represents auspiciousness and divine favor. Likewise, in asset labeling, symbols and labels are used to represent the nature, purpose, and value of each asset, conveying its significance and role within a context.
- **Management and Stewardship**: Lord Krishna's role as a divine leader and ruler involves the management and stewardship of assets for the welfare of society and the preservation of dharma (righteousness). He utilizes His assets, such as His divine weapons and resources, to uphold justice, protect devotees, and restore balance in the world. Asset labeling facilitates effective management and stewardship by providing clarity, accountability, and organization in asset allocation and usage.

Control

An appropriate set of procedures for information labeling should be developed and implemented in accordance with the information classification scheme adopted by the organization.

Purpose

To facilitate the communication of classification of information and support automation of information processing and management.

Guidance

Procedures for information labeling should cover information and other associated assets in all formats. The labeling should reflect the classification scheme established in 5.12. The labels should be easily recognizable. The procedures should give guidance on where and how labels are attached in consideration of how the information is accessed or the assets are handled depending on the types of storage media. The procedures can define:

- Cases where labeling is omitted;
- How to label information sent by or stored on electronic or physical means, or any other format;
- How to handle cases where labeling is not possible.

Examples of labeling techniques include:

- Physical Labels;
- Headers and Footers;
- Metadata;
- Watermarking;
- Rubber-Stamps.

Digital information should utilize metadata in order to identify, manage and control information, especially with regard to confidentiality. Metadata should also enable efficient and correct searching for information. Metadata should facilitate systems to interact and make decisions based on the associated classification labels. The procedures should describe how to attach metadata to information, what labels to use and how data should be handled, in line with the organization's information model and ICT architecture. Relevant additional metadata should be added by systems when they process information depending on its information security properties. Personnel and other interested parties should be made aware of labeling procedures. All personnel should be provided with the necessary training to ensure that information is correctly labelled and handled accordingly. Output from systems containing information that is classified as being sensitive or critical should carry an appropriate classification label.

Other Information

Labeling of classified information is a key requirement for information sharing. Other useful metadata that can be attached to the information is which organizational process created the information and at what time. Labeling of information and other associated assets can sometimes have negative effects. Classified assets can be easier to identify by malicious actors for potential misuse. Some systems do not label individual files or database records with their classification but protect all information at the highest level of classification of any of the information that it contains or is permitted to contain. It is usual in such systems to determine and then label information when it is exported.

Businesses handle vast amounts of data every day however, not all data is equally important, and some pieces will require more protection than others. Such sensitive and important information needs to be protected from vulnerabilities to security threats. That is why information classification is so important. It helps to determine which information needs special protection and how to label and classify data. A well-planned data classification system makes important information easy to manipulate and track, besides making data easier to locate and retrieve. The most common reasons why information classification is of particular importance are:

1. **Efficiency** – on a basic level, businesses that have their information classified are able to manage and deliver day-to-day operations more efficiently. Data can be easily located and retrieved; changes easily traced.
2. **Security** – protecting sensitive information is the main idea behind information classification. It is a useful tactic to classify information in order to facilitate appropriate security responses according to the type of information being retrieved, transmitted, or copied. Data

encryption, data storage in safe servers with strong firewalls, and compliance with data protection standards can help immensely to protect against outside threats. Besides, there can be inside threats that are equally dangerous – like intentional data theft, accidental data breaches. Hence it is very important to restrict information and prevent threats.

3. **Safety** – information classification helps create security awareness throughout the organization. The responsibility of protection of information lies with everyone handling the information. The system ensures that employees understand the value of the information they work with and safeguard that information.
4. **Compliance** – information classification in information security helps organizations label information as sensitive, protect it against threats, and help comply with regulations. Organizations can easily implement standards to classify information.

To implement a robust classification of information scheme, organizations should adopt a topic-specific approach, understand each business unit's needs for information, and determine the level of sensitivity and criticality of information. The organizations must take into account the following criteria when implementing a classification scheme:

- Establish a topic-specific policy and address the specific business needs. The classification scheme and levels should take specific business needs into account.
- Take into account business needs for sharing and use of information and the need for availability. If organization assign an information asset to a classification category that is unnecessarily higher, this may bring the risk of disruption to critical business functions by restricting access to and use of information. Therefore, organization should strive to find a balance between specific business needs for availability and use of information and the requirements for confidentiality and integrity of that information.
- Consider legal obligations. Some laws may impose stricter obligations to ensure confidentiality, integrity and availability of information. When assigning information assets to categories, legal obligations should take priority over organization own classification.

- Take a risk-based approach and consider the potential impact of a compromise. Each type of information has a different level of criticality to each business's operations and has a different level of sensitivity depending on the context. In implementing classification of information scheme, organizations should ask what impact would the compromise of integrity, availability and confidentiality of this information have on the organization?
- Regularly review and update the classification. The value, criticality and sensitivity of information is not static and can change throughout the life cycle of the information. Therefore, organization need to regularly review each classification and make necessary updates.
- Consult with other organizations you share information with and address any differences. There is no one way to classify information and each organization can have different names, levels and criteria when it comes to classification of information schemes. These differences may lead to risks when the two organizations exchange information assets with each other. Therefore, organization need to put in place an agreement with their counterpart to ensure that there is consistency in classification of information and interpretation of classification levels.
- Organizational-level consistency. Each department within the organization should have a common understanding of classification levels and procedures so that classifications are consistent across the entire organization.

The valuable data every organization needs to be protected commensurate with how it is classified. Customers, employees, and vendors entrust the organization with a give data set and there is an implied bargain that the data so entrusted will be protected from any use or disclosure other than as agreed to when the data was given. To do this, each organization has to govern the data it uses so that it will be received, made, used, stored, shared, or destroyed in a purposeful manner that recognizes the pact to protect data in its's daily mission. Areas to consider in a data governance program include:

- Sensitivity Level;
- Retention Period;

- Data Utilization;
- Data Back-up;
- Management of Storage Media;
- Electronic Data Transfers;
- Disposal of Media.

Information assets may not be equally important, nor equally sensitive or confidential in nature, nor require the same care in handling. One common method of ascertaining the importance of assets is data classification. Information assets should be classified according to their need for security protection and labeled accordingly. To begin to start with federal or state laws, regulations, rules, or organizational policies that require certain information assets to be protected. Implement a classification metric.

Different assets have different impacts on the continuity and reputation of the organization. Once organization have determined the importance of various organizational assets, the process of determining how best to protect them can be put in place. Many methods are employed to protect assets, ranging from policies to technical security controls. Additionally, assets must be protected throughout their life cycle, from creation or purchase through final disposal or long-term storage. Protection measures range from addressing purchasing controls to managing access by appropriate personnel to ensuring adequate physical security for assets throughout their lifetime. Some organization has established Data Stewardship policies to help ensure responsibilities for protecting data are effectively accomplished. Other organizations conduct regular security assessments of assets considered to be critical for the functioning of an organization. They may also address asset protection through physical security measures, or through background checks for newly hired and continuing personnel.

Labeling of Information

Labeling of Information is a procedure that enables organizations to put their information classification scheme into practice by attaching classification labels to relevant information assets. Once organization have classification scheme in place then the information and assets will be labelled accordingly. Organization will have to:

- Implement procedures for information labelling
- Cover information and other associated assets in all formats

It is good practice to consider where labeling is omitted such as the case of non-confidential information so that we can reduce the workload on people. The written and defined procedures should give guidance on where and how labels are attached and the different types of storage media. Organization will look at how to label information sent by or stored on physical, electronic devices and because the standard likes to catch everything, on what it helpfully calls 'any other format'. Nothing like future proofing for the unknowns.

Of course, there may be situations where labeling is not possible, and this is fine, as long as the organization have covered how to handle those cases. How organization handles it may be to tag it with meta data or put in place some other compensating controls such as having an exception list and managing it via risk management. Once the labeling processes and procedures has been defined and documented, train staff on how to use and follow them and be able to evidence the process.

Control 5.13 addresses how organizations should develop, implement and manage a robust information labeling procedure based on the classification scheme adopted through Control 5.12. It identifies four specific steps that organizations should implement to carry out labeling of information.

Develop and implement an Information Labeling Procedure: Organizations should develop an organization-wide Information Labeling Procedure that adheres to the information classification scheme created in accordance with Control 5.12. Furthermore, 5.13 requires that this procedure be extended to all information assets, regardless of whether it is in digital or paper format and that the labels must be easy to recognize. While there is no limit to what this procedure document can contain, the Control 5.13 states that the Procedures should at least include the following:

- Description of the methods to attach labels to information assets depending on the storage medium and how the data is accessed.
- Where the labels are to be attached for each type of information asset?
- Which information assets will not be labelled, if any?

- Description of measures for cases where it is not possible to label certain types of information due to technical, legal or contractual limitations.
- The rules on how the labeling of information transmitted to internal or external parties should be handled.
- For digital assets, the procedure must explain how the metadata should be inserted.
- Names of labels to be used for all assets.

Provide adequate training to staff on how to adhere to the labeling procedure: The procedure for labeling of information can be effective only to the extent that personnel and other relevant stakeholders are well-informed about how to correctly label information and how to deal with labelled information assets. Therefore, organizations should provide staff and other relevant parties with training on the procedure.

Use metadata for labeling of digital information assets: Control 5.13 requires the use of metadata for labeling of digital information assets. Furthermore, it notes that the metadata should be deployed in a way that makes it easy and efficient to identify and search for information and also in a way that streamlines the decision-making process between systems related to labelled information.

Take extra measures to label sensitive data that may outflow of the system: Considering the risks involved in outward transfer of sensitive data from systems, 5.13 recommends organizations to label these information assets with those most appropriate to the level of criticality and sensitivity of the information concerned.

Now the standard starts to stray into implementation territory with its guidance on metadata. Metadata has its place but we have to look at the appropriateness of the control to our risk and our organization. Remember that the annex controls are guidance for consideration and organization do not have to implement them, only consider them, so if metadata is not appropriate that is fine, just note it down and manage it via risk management process, accepting the risk. Where it does apply and makes sense then look at metadata to identify, manage and control information, especially in relation to confidentiality. Metadata searching for example is going to be reliant on specific technologies and implementations. If organization are using metadata then the procedures are going to describe how to attach metadata to information, what labels to use and how data should be handled.

Organization may already have property control of assets where items over a certain dollar amount are automatically tagged with a unique, usually numeric, identifier by Property Control. If not, create on. Use the newly created inventory of assets to assign a unique identifier to each one. Prepare labels that are easy to recognize and sturdy, and attach them to a visible place on the equipment. Make sure organization clarify when labels should not be used on equipment. This could be based on the dollar amount or the level of risk organization have assigned to the asset. Information needs labeling as well. Develop information labeling procedures based on the data classification schema, developed previously. Metadata is a common type of information label. Do be careful how organization will manage the information labeled as restricted or confidential. Because of the labeling, be careful how organization will manage restricted/sensitive or confidential information. It is much easier to steal or misuse when the assets are easy to identify.

Information classifications and labeling help prioritize data protection efforts to increase data security and regulatory compliance. Among its benefits are improved user productivity and decision making and reduced costs by eliminating data that's not needed.

- **Rediscovery of business**: Identification of information is the beginning step in information classification. Organizations, therefore, need to actively discover information that is generated, stored, and accessed by departments within the organization. This information discovery basically leads to rediscovering the business. This allows decision-makers to review how information is empowering the business or possibly functioning ineffectively.
- **Raises awareness of cyber risk**: Information security teams connect face to face with business owners to discuss information security and how it could impact their business. Thus, owners have a direct contact point where to reach if they have questions or need help regarding managing cyber risks or incidents. Awareness of cyber threats and information security management rises to realistic levels, prompting

the issue to be discussed and accepted at all levels throughout the organization.

- **Optimize risk and resources**: Defining information classification improves risk and information classification resources, leading to efficient and effective protection of information. By classifying data based on sensitivity and level of business impact, businesses are informing which information must be protected with high priority, thereby deciding where to spend the information security budgets.
- **Limit dissemination**: Well-defined information classification is controlled by laws and regulations, thereby allowing businesses to restrict their dissemination on a need-to-know basis. This reduces the chances of data theft or loss, which helps to minimize penalties charged due to non-compliance.

A.5.14 Information Transfer

This control requires organizations to put in place appropriate rules, procedures, and/or agreements to maintain the security of data when it is shared within an organization or when transmitted to third parties. When information is transferred to internal or external parties, it creates a heightened risk to the confidentiality, integrity, availability, and security of information transmitted. This control gives requirements that organizations must satisfy to maintain the security of data when it is shared internally or when it flows out of the organization to third parties. This control suggests that the organization should have controls in place to ensure that incidents such as interception, unauthorized access, misrouting, modification, and destruction are avoided. It further includes the concept of non-repudiation, which simply means that a person(s) doing something wrong should not be able to walk away by neglecting their actions; therefore, it is recommended that organizations should have proper rules, procedures and agreements in place while transferring any type of information both in physical and digital form. This control considers three types of information transfer, namely, Physical, Electronic and Verbal. It further provides details regarding how each of these methods should be handled, and the required steps to take.

A.5.14 Information Transfer – A linkage with Ancient Era

Shivaji Maharaj Life and Leadership

- **Strategic Communication:** Shivaji Maharaj was known for his strategic communication skills, which played a crucial role in his military campaigns and governance. He maintained a vast network of spies, messengers, and informants to gather intelligence, relay orders, and coordinate movements across his kingdom. Effective information transfer allowed him to stay informed about enemy activities, respond swiftly to threats, and maintain control over his territories.
- **Code of Secrecy:** Shivaji Maharaj understood the importance of secrecy and discretion in warfare and governance. He devised codes and ciphers to encrypt sensitive communications and protect valuable information from falling into enemy hands. The meticulous management of information transfer helped him maintain strategic

advantage and outmaneuver his adversaries during times of conflict and political intrigue.

- **Propaganda and Public Relations:** Shivaji Maharaj employed propaganda and public relations strategies to rally support for his cause and legitimize his rule. He disseminated narratives of valor, justice, and Hindu resurgence through oral traditions, literature, and folk songs, shaping public perceptions and garnering popular acclaim for his resistance against Mughal and Adil Shahi dominance. Information transfer played a pivotal role in shaping collective consciousness and fostering a sense of identity and solidarity among his subjects.
- **Legacy of Communication Infrastructure:** Shivaji Maharaj's reign witnessed significant investments in communication infrastructure, including roads, forts, and administrative centers, which facilitated efficient information transfer and governance across his expanding empire. His visionary leadership in infrastructure development laid the foundation for economic prosperity, cultural exchange, and social cohesion in the Maratha heartland for centuries to come.
- **Inspiration for Modern Leadership**: Shivaji Maharaj's strategic acumen, resilience, and commitment to justice continue to inspire leaders and strategists in contemporary contexts. His emphasis on effective communication, intelligence gathering, and decentralized governance resonates with principles of leadership and statecraft in an era marked by rapid globalization, technological innovation, and geopolitical uncertainty.

Control

Information transfer rules, procedures, or agreements should be in place for all types of transfer facilities within the organization and between the organization and other parties.

Purpose

To maintain the security of information transferred within an organization and with any external interested party.

Guidance

General

The organization should establish and communicate a topic-specific policy on information transfer to all relevant interested parties. Rules, procedures and agreements to protect information in transit should reflect the classification of the information involved. Where information is transferred between the organization and third parties, transfer agreements should be established and maintained to protect information in all forms in transit. Information transfer can happen through electronic transfer, physical storage media transfer and verbal transfer. For all types of information transfer, rules, procedures and agreements should include:

- Controls designed to protect transferred information from interception, unauthorized access, copying, modification, misrouting, destruction and denial of service, including levels of access control commensurate with the classification of the information involved and any special controls that are required to protect sensitive information, such as use of cryptographic techniques;
- Controls to ensure traceability and non-repudiation, including maintaining a chain of custody for information while in transit;
- Identification of appropriate contacts related to the transfer including information owners, risk owners, security officers and information custodians, as applicable;
- Responsibilities and liabilities in the event of information security incidents, such as loss of physical storage media or data;
- Use of an agreed labeling system for sensitive or critical information, ensuring that the meaning of the labels is immediately understood and that the information is appropriately protected;
- Reliability and availability of the transfer service;
- The topic-specific policy or guidelines on acceptable use of information transfer facilities;
- Retention and disposal guidelines for all business records, including messages; NOTE Local legislation and regulations can exist regarding retention and disposal of business records.
- The consideration of any other relevant legal, statutory, regulatory and contractual requirements related to transfer of information.

The control's main objective to maintain the security of any information received or sent on the networks. In order to protect the transferees by using all types of communication facilities, official transfer policies, procedures and controls should be developed. So, any entity could not alter, detect or manipulate the originality of the information.

The information transfer aspect includes the following controls:

- Information transfer can happen using different communication channels and for that purpose, organization should define the acceptable use of all these communication tools, what kind of information should be transferred, and how these communication channels will be protected. These policies and procedures should be communicated to the relevant personnel.
- Agreements on information transfer: in some cases, when organization transfers sensitive information to third parties, formal agreements should be signed. These agreements can include elements such as rules for labelling the information, usage of cryptography, defining access controls, defining responsibilities for managing security incidents, etc.
- Electronic messaging: meaning protection of the information involved in electronic messaging, by defining which public services are allowed to be used.
- Confidentiality and non-disclosure agreements: one way of protecting sensitive organization data is by using legal means through confidentiality statements and nondisclosure agreements. These should be signed by both employees and external parties.

This section is significant because it covers the controls for communicating information inside and outside the organization, which is an essential activity of all organizations operating in today's information age. Communications security is also critical because the confidentiality, availability, and integrity of the information might be endangered during transit.

Clear policies and procedures that govern the transfer of information between individuals both within and outside the organization should be established. Be sure to consider all possible methods of communication, including face-to-face, e-mail, voice, fax, and video, when drafting your policies. General policies about information transfer should include guidelines for acceptable use, and more specific procedures can be established to ensure secure transfer using approved methods. Make sure users are aware of the limitations of each system. In addition to establishing policies, technical controls should be implemented, when feasible, to protect the confidentiality, integrity, and availability of the information being transferred. Most anti-virus and anti-malware solutions have tools that can scan e-mails in real-time, and encrypting important e-mails can be done for free or implemented enterprise-wide. These controls can provide the first line of defense against infection and/or compromise. It is still important, however, to discuss information transfer as a part of the organization's information security awareness program. Educating your users about not communicating confidential information over insecure channels, state and organizational retention guidelines, and the dangers of e-mail auto-forwarding, among other topics, can go a long way toward ensuring that organization systems and data remain secure. Formal transfer policies, procedures, and controls must be in place to protect the transfer of information through the use of all types of communication facilities. Whatever type of communication facility is in use, it is important to understand the security risks involved in relation to the confidentiality, integrity, and availability of the information and this will need to take into account the type, nature, amount, and sensitivity or classification of the information being transferred. It is especially important to implement such policies and procedures when information is being transferred out of or into the organization from third parties. Different but complementary controls may be required to protect information being transferred from interception, copying, modification, misrouting, and destruction and should be considered holistically when identifying which controls are to be selected.

Information may be transferred digitally or physically and agreements must address the secure transfer of business information between the organization and any external parties. Formal transfer policies procedures and technical controls should be selected, implemented, operated, monitored, audited, and reviewed to ensure ongoing effective security protection. Often, communications and transfer systems and procedures are put in place, without a real understanding of the risks involved which therefore creates vulnerabilities and possible compromise. ISO 27002 touches on implementation considerations including consideration of notifications, traceability, escrow, identification standards, the chain of custody, cryptography, access control, and others. If the organization has a business that needs to transfer information to a third party, then the organization should enter into an official agreement with them in order to preserve the security of that information. These agreements generally set minimum standards for protecting the data, and may also establish the limits of liability for both parties in the event of a breach or other unauthorized disclosure of data. If the data being transferred is considered HIPAA protected then the two parties must enter into a Business Associate Agreement (BAA). BAA's are required to include clauses covering data security data disclosure, and data destruction, among others. Similarly, if the data is considered highly sensitive, then the organization may require additional data security provisions, similar to those found in a BAA, for such a contract.

Information transfer agreements may also include the following: agreed-upon cryptographic standards for encrypting data in transit and at rest, and chain of custody for physical transfer. For example, any agreement between the organization and a company that provides off-site backup storage for your critical systems and data should include clauses that cover minimum standards for the protection of your data in transit from one location to the other (e.g., are the tapes secured in a locked box? Who has the key?), and procedures for identifying and authorizing individuals from one organization or the other.

The organization must develop rules, procedures, and agreements, including a topic-specific information transfer policy, that provides data in transit with a level of protection appropriate to the classification assigned to that information. The level of protection should match the level of criticality and sensitivity of information transmitted. The organizations must sign transfer agreements with recipient third parties to guarantee secure transmission of data. It lists the elements that must be included in all rules, procedures, and agreements for all types of transfers in general:

- Organizations must define controls appropriate to the level of classification of the information to protect the information in transit from unauthorized access, modification, interception, copying, destruction, and denial-of-service attacks;
- An organization must keep control over the chain of custody while

it is in transit and must define and implement controls to ensure traceability of information;

- Relevant parties involved in the transfer of information should be defined and their contact details should be provided. This may include information owners and security officers;
- Allocation of liabilities in case a data breach occurs;
- Using a labeling system;
- Ensuring the availability of the transfer service;
- Creating topic-specific guidelines on the information transfer methods;
- Guidelines for storage and deletion of all business records, including messages;
- Analysis of the impact any applicable laws, regulations, or other obligations may have over the transfer.

Electronic messaging includes e-mail, peer-to-peer file transfer, social network-based communications and more. The organization should consider introducing a policy that governs the authorized use of these mediums; at a minimum, such a policy should establish the authority to represent your organization in an official capacity on the Internet. Also, because the organization is unable to apply technical controls to third-party electronic messaging mediums - Twitter, Facebook, et. al. - there is no way to quantify or improve their level of security in order to effectively secure a confidential message travelling across one of these mediums. The solution to this problem is to clearly state in the policy that organization-related business is only to be communicated and/or conducted using approved, secured methods. Any information that is involved in any form of electronic messaging needs to be appropriately protected. Put in simple terms, when using electronic messaging, it should be protected to ensure no unauthorized access can be gained. The organization should create a policy which sets out which forms of electronic messaging should be used for the different types of information being transferred. Considerations will also need to be made for voice & fax communications transfer, and physical transfer. This should align with access controls and other secure authentication policies and log-on procedures. Rules, procedures and agreements should also consider the following items when using electronic communication facilities for information transfer:

- Detection of and protection against malware that can be transmitted through the use of electronic communications;
- Protection of communicated sensitive electronic information that is in the form of an attachment;
- Prevention against sending documents and messages in communications to the wrong address or number;
- Obtaining approval prior to using external public services such as instant messaging, social networking, file sharing or cloud storage;
- Stronger levels of authentication when transferring information via publicly accessible networks;
- Restrictions associated with electronic communication facilities (e.g., preventing automatic forwarding of electronic mail to external mail addresses);
- Advising personnel and other interested parties not to send short message service (SMS) or instant messages with critical information since these can be read in public places (and therefore by unauthorized persons) or stored in devices not adequately protected;
- Advising personnel and other interested parties about the problems of using fax machines or services, namely:
    - Unauthorized access to built-in message stores to retrieve messages;
    - Deliberate or accidental programming of machines to send messages to specific numbers.

Physical storage media transfer:

When transferring physical storage media (including paper), rules, procedures and agreements should also include:

- Responsibilities for controlling and notifying transmission, dispatch and receipt;
- Ensuring correct addressing and transportation of the message;
- Packaging that protects the contents from any physical damage likely

to arise during transit and in accordance with any manufacturers' specifications;

- A list of authorized reliable couriers agreed by management;
- Courier identification standards;
- Depending on the classification level of the information in the storage media to be transported, use tamper evident or tamper-resistant controls;
- Procedures to verify the identification of couriers;
- Approved list of third parties providing transportation or courier services depending on the classification of the information;
- Keeping logs for identifying the content of the storage media, the protection applied as well as recording the list of authorized recipients, the times of transfer to the transit custodians and receipt at the destination.

Verbal transfer:

To protect verbal transfer of information, personnel and other interested parties should be reminded that they should:

- Not have confidential verbal conversations in public places or over insecure communication channels since these can be overheard by unauthorized persons;
- Not leave messages containing confidential information on answering machines or voice messages since these can be replayed by unauthorized persons, stored on communal systems or stored incorrectly as a result of misdialing;
- Be screened to the appropriate level to listen to the conversation;
- Ensure that appropriate room controls are implemented;
- Begin any sensitive conversations with a disclaimer so those present know the classification level and any handling requirements of what they are about to hear.

A.5.15 Access Control

Access control is the process of granting authorized users the right to use a service while preventing access to non-authorized users. Access control is a security technique that regulates who or what can view or use resources in a computing environment. It is a fundamental concept in security that minimizes risk to the business or organization. The Access Control addresses requirements to control access to information assets and information processing facilities. The controls are focused on the protection against accidental damage or loss, overheating, threats, etc. This requires a documented control policy and procedures, registration, removal, and review of user access rights, and the control over privileged utilities and restriction of access to program source code. It provides the following value:

- Controlled access to services ensures that the organization is able to maintain more effectively the confidentiality of its information.
- Employees have the right level of access to execute their jobs effectively.
- There is less likelihood of errors being made in data entry or in the use of a critical service by an unskilled user.
- The ability to audit the use of services and to trace the abuse of services.
- The ability more easily revokes access rights when needed - an important security consideration.
- Maybe needed for regulatory compliance.

There are two types of access control: physical and logical. Physical access control limits access to campuses, buildings, rooms and physical IT assets. Logical access control limits connections to computer networks, system files and data. To secure a facility, organizations use electronic access control systems that rely on user credentials, access card readers, auditing and reports to track employee access to restricted business locations and proprietary areas, such as data centers. Some of these systems incorporate access control panels to restrict entry to rooms and buildings, as well as alarms and lockdown capabilities, to prevent unauthorized access or operations. Logical access control systems perform identification, authentication and authorization of users and entities by evaluating required login credentials that can include passwords, personal identification numbers, biometric scans, security tokens or other authentication factors. Multifactor authentication (MFA), which requires two or more authentication factors, is often an important part of a layered defense to protect access control systems.

A.5.15 Information Transfer – A linkage with Ancient Era

Lord Hanuman in Lanka

- **Infiltration and Reconnaissance:** Lord Hanuman's journey to Lanka involves strategic planning and reconnaissance, akin to an infiltration mission. He carefully observes the layout of the city, assesses the strengths and weaknesses of the enemy, and gathers crucial information about Mata Sita's whereabouts. Similarly, in access control, there is a focus on understanding the layout and vulnerabilities of a system or facility to enhance security measures.
- **Overcoming Obstacles:** Lord Hanuman encounters various obstacles while navigating through Lanka, including enemy forces, geographical barriers, and magical defenses. His determination, agility, and divine powers enable him to overcome these challenges and continue his mission. Similarly, in access control scenarios, security measures are designed to deter and overcome potential threats or intrusions.
- **Deception and Subterfuge:** Lord Hanuman employs deception and subterfuge to achieve his objectives, such as disguising himself as a Brahmin to enter the city unnoticed. This aspect of the story underscores the importance of clever tactics and disguise in bypassing security measures. In access control, there is a constant need to anticipate and counteract deceptive tactics employed by intruders.
- **Gaining Access to Restricted Areas:** Lord Hanuman eventually gains access to King Ravana's palace, where he finds Mata Sita imprisoned. This feat highlights the significance of breaching restricted areas or high-security zones, which may be protected by multiple layers of access control measures. Lord Hanuman's success in reaching Mata Sita illustrates the potential vulnerabilities within even the most fortified environments.

- **Rescue and Liberation:** Ultimately, Lord Hanuman's mission culminates in the liberation of Mata Sita and the eventual defeat of King Ravana, symbolizing the triumph of righteousness over evil. This aspect of the story resonates with the broader goal of access control, which is to safeguard individuals, assets, and information from potential harm or exploitation.

Control

Rules to control physical and logical access to information and other associated assets should be established and implemented based on business and information security requirements.

Purpose

To ensure authorized access and to prevent unauthorized access to information and other associated assets.

Guidance

Owners of information and other associated assets should determine information security and business requirements related to access control. A topic-specific policy on access control should be defined which takes account of these requirements and should be communicated to all relevant interested parties. These requirements and the topic-specific policy should consider the following:

- Determine what entities require access to certain pieces of information and/or assets. This can be achieved by keeping an accurate record of job roles and data access requirements, that is in line with the organizational structure.
- The integrity and security of all relevant applications. A formal risk assessment could be carried out to examine the security characteristics of individual applications.
- Physical access controls. This can be demonstrated by a robust set of building and room access controls, including managed entry systems, security perimeters and visitor procedures, where appropriate.
- A organization-wide "need to know" principle, when it comes to information distribution, security and categorization by adhering to

strict best-practice policies that do not offer blanket access to data across an organizational chart.

- Ensure restrictions to privileged access rights. Data access privileges above and beyond that of a standard user need to be closely monitored and audited.
- Adherence to any prevailing pieces of legislation, sector-specific regulatory guidelines or contractual obligations related to data access by tailoring Access Control policies in accordance with any external obligations they have with regards to data, asset and resource access.
- Oversight of potential conflicts of duty. Policies should include controls that eliminate an individual's ability to compromise a broader Access Control function, based on their own levels of access.
- The three main functions of an Access Control Policy - requests, authorizations and administration - should be addressed in isolation. Access Control policies need to acknowledge that whilst Access Control is a self-contained function, it's made up of a number of individual steps that carry their own set of requirements on a topic-by-topic basis.
- Access requests should be conducted in a structured, formal manner. Organizations should implement an authorization process that requires formal, documented approval from an appropriate member of staff.
- Ongoing management of access rights. Data integrity and security perimeters need to be maintained through a continual cycle of periodic audits, HR oversight and job-specific changes.

Maintaining adequate logs, and controlling access to them. Organization should collect and store data on access events alongside safeguarding against unauthorized access to security event logs, and operate with a comprehensive set of incident management procedures.

Access control rules should be implemented by defining and mapping appropriate access rights and restrictions to the relevant entities. An entity can represent a human user as well as a technical or logical item. To simplify the access control management, specific roles can be assigned to entity groups. The following should be taken into account when defining and implementing access control rules:

- Consistency between the access rights and information classification;
- Consistency between the access rights and the physical perimeter security needs and requirements;
- Considering all types of available connections in distributed environments so entities are only provided with access to information and other associated assets, including networks and network services, that they are authorized to use;
- Considering how elements or factors relevant to dynamic access control can be reflected.

Other Information

There are often overarching principles used in the context of access control. Two of the most frequently used principles are:

- Need-to-Know: an entity is only granted access to the information which that entity requires in order to perform its tasks;
- Need-to-Use: an entity is only assigned access to information technology infrastructure where a clear need is present.

Care should be taken when specifying access control rules to consider:

- Establishing rules based on the premise of least privilege, "Everything is generally forbidden unless expressly permitted", rather than the weaker rule, "Everything is generally permitted unless expressly forbidden";
- Changes in information labels that are initiated automatically by information processing facilities and those initiated at the discretion of a user;
- Changes in user permissions that are initiated automatically by the information system and those initiated by an administrator;
- When to define and regularly review the approval. Access control rules should be supported by documented procedures and defined responsibilities.

There are several ways to implement access control, such as MAC (mandatory access control), DAC (discretionary access control), RBAC (role-based access control) and ABAC (attribute-based access control). Access control rules can also contain dynamic elements. Access control rules can be implemented in different granularity, ranging from covering whole networks or systems to specific data fields and can also consider properties such as user location or the type of network connection that is used for access. These principles and how granular access control is defined can have a significant cost impact. Stronger rules and more granularity typically led to higher cost. Business requirements and risk considerations should be used to define which access control rules are applied and which granularity is required.

Access Control governs the ways in which human and non-human entities on any given networks are granted access to data, IT resources and applications. It relies upon managerial staff from various parts of an organization maintaining a thorough understanding of who needs access to what resources, access rights are ultimately a maintenance function that are controlled by staff with administrative rights over any given network. The ownership should rest with a member senior management with overarching technical authority across an organization's domains, subdomains applications, resources and assets, such as a Head of IT. This control mentions four different types of access control, but not limited to, which can be broadly classified as follows:

- **Mandatory Access Control (MAC)**: Access is centrally managed by a sole security authority. This is a security model in which the system administrator defines the rules that govern access to resource objects. These rules are often based on conditions, such as time of day or location. It is not uncommon to use some form of both rule-based access control and RBAC to enforce access policies and procedures.
- **Discretionary Access Control (DAC)**: The opposite method to MAC, where object owners are able to pass on privileges to other users. This is an access control method in which owners or administrators of the protected system, data or resource set the policies defining who or what is authorized to access the resource. Many of these systems enable administrators to limit the propagation of access rights. A common criticism of DAC systems is a lack of centralized control.

- **Role-based Access Control (RBAC)**: The most common type of commercial access control, based around predefined job functions and privileges. This is a widely used access control mechanism that restricts access to computer resources based on individuals or groups with defined business functions rather than the identities of individual users. The role-based security model relies on a complex structure of role assignments, role authorizations and role permissions developed using role engineering to regulate employee access to systems. RBAC systems can be used to enforce MAC and DAC frameworks.
- **Attribute-based Access Control (ABAC)**: Access rights are granted to users through the use of policies which combine attributes together. This is a methodology that manages access rights by evaluating a set of rules, policies and relationships using the attributes of users, systems and environmental conditions.

Access Control Policy

Access Control policies should clearly communicate the organization's business requirements regarding the identification of users, access to organizational information resources, user access rights, and special access privileges and restrictions. The following could comprise the core of an organizational access control policy framework.

- Roles and responsibilities
  - Need-to-Know: Access only to information needed to perform assigned tasks.
  - Need-to-Use: Access only to information resources needed to perform assigned tasks
  - Access levels and privileges by role
  - Periodic review and removal of access levels and privileges
  - Segregation of duties for requesting, authorizing, and reviewing access levels and privileges
- What is required to identify users?
  - The requirement for vetting users in person
  - A requirement to archive records concerning user identification and credentials

- What criteria are used to determine the types of credentials used?
- What criteria are used to determine the level of access to applications and services?
    - Identification of roles with privileged access
    - Contractual obligations for limiting access granted to vendors and partners
- What is required from identity providers and from service providers?
    - The requirement to identify the security requirements of applications – both, purchased and developed internally
    - The requirement to determine the Level of Authentication (LOA) required to access a service based on risk

Data owners shall determine, approve and assign the level of access to organizational systems and data based on the responsibilities, job functions, reporting or outreach requirements based on the confidentiality of the data and to the restrictions imposed by federal, state and organizational rules and regulations.

Access Control Program

As data, access, and networks continue to expand, organizations have an ever-increasing need to manage identities and access. The optimum solution for this function may be a well-planned and organization-wide Access Management Program. In its simplest form, Access Management ensures that only the right people can access the right services at the right time. However, within a complex organization, establishing an Access Management Program is not an easy task. Many stakeholders, technology areas, policies, and processes must work together for a scalable and robust Program. In addition, governance plays a key role in the success of any Access Management Program and implementation.

Activities of access control

Access control is integrated into an organization's IT environment. It can involve identity management and access management systems. These systems provide access control software, a user database and management tools for access control policies, auditing and enforcement. When a user is added to an access management system, system administrators use an automated provisioning system to set up permissions based on access control frameworks, job responsibilities and workflows. The best practice of least privilege restricts access to only resources that employees require to perform their immediate job functions. The steps for access control can be:

- **Requesting Access**: Access can be requested using one or any number of mechanisms, e.g.
    - A standard request
    - A request for change
    - A service request
    - Executing a pre-authorized script or option
    - Rules for requesting access are normally documented as part of the service catalogue
- **Verification**: It needs to verify every request for access to a service from two perspectives:
    - That the user requesting access is who they say they are
    - That they have a legitimate requirement for that service
- **Providing Rights**: It does not decide who has access to which services. It only executes the policies and regulations defined. It enforces decisions to restrict to provide access, rather than making the decision. As soon as a user is verified, it will provide that user with the rights to use the requested service. In most cases, this will result in a request to every team or department involved in supporting that service to take the necessary action. Ideally, these tasks should be automated.
- **Monitoring Identity Status**: As users work in the organization, their roles change as do their needs to access services. It should understand and document the typical user lifecycle for each type of user and use it to automate the process. Access Control tools should provide features that enable a user to be moved from one state to another or from one group to another, easily and with an audit trail.
    - **Job Changes**: In this case, the user will possibly need access to different or additional services.

- **Promotions or Demotions**: The user will probably use the same set of services, but will need access to different levels of functionality or data.
- **Transfers**: In this situation, the user may need access to exactly the same set of services, but in a different region with different working practices and different sets of data.
- **Resignation**: Access needs to be completely removed.
- **Death**: Access needs to be completely removed.
- **Retirement**: In many organizations, an employee who retires may still have access to a limited set of services, including benefits systems or systems that allow them to purchase organization products at a reduced rate, alumni information, etc.
- **Disciplinary Action**: In some cases, the organization will require a temporary restriction to prevent the user from accessing some or all of the services that they would normally have access to. There should be a feature in the process and tools to do this, rather than having to delete and reinstate the user's access rights.
- **Dismissals**: Where an employee or contractor is dismissed, or where legal action is taken against a customer, access should be revoked immediately. In addition, access management, working together with information security management, should take active measures to prevent and detect malicious action against the organization from that user.

- **Logging and Tracking Access**: Access management should not only respond to requests. It is also responsible for ensuring that the rights that they have provided are being properly used. Information security management plays a vital role in detecting unauthorized access and comparing it with the rights that were provided by access management. Access management may also be required to provide a record of access for specific services during forensic investigations. If a user is suspected of breaches of policy, inappropriate use of resources, or fraudulent use of data, access management may be required to provide evidence of dates, time, and even content of that user's access to specific services.

- **Removing or Restricting Rights**: Just as access management provides rights to use a service, it is also responsible for revoking those rights. Again, this is not a decision that it makes on its own. Access management will execute the decisions and policies made during service strategy and design and also decisions made by managers within the organization.

Challenges of access control

Many of the challenges of access control stem from the highly distributed nature of modern IT. It is difficult to keep track of constantly evolving assets because they are spread out both physically and logically. Specific examples of challenges include the following:

- Dynamically managing distributed IT environments;
- Password fatigue;
- Compliance visibility through consistent reporting;
- Centralizing user directories and avoiding application-specific silos; and
- Data governance and visibility through consistent reporting.

Many traditional access control strategies, which worked well in static environments where a organization's computing assets were help on premises, are ineffective in today's dispersed IT environments. Modern IT environments consist of multiple cloud-based and hybrid implementations, which spreads assets out over physical locations and over a variety of unique devices, and require dynamic access control strategies. Organizations often struggle to understand the difference between authentication and authorization. Authentication is the process of verifying individuals are who they say they are using biometric identification and MFA. The distributed nature of assets gives organizations many avenues for authenticating an individual. Authorization is the act of giving individuals the correct data access based on their authenticated identity. One example of where authorization often falls short is if an individual leaves a job but still has access to that organization's assets. This creates security holes because the asset the individual used for work. One solution to this problem is strict monitoring and reporting on who has access to protected resources so, when a change occurs, it can be immediately identified and access control lists and permissions can be updated to reflect the change. Another often overlooked challenge of access control is user experience. If an access management technology is difficult to use, employees may use it incorrectly or circumvent it entirely, creating security holes and compliance gaps. If a reporting or monitoring application is difficult to use, the reporting may be compromised due to an employee mistake, which would result in a security gap because an important permissions change or security vulnerability went unreported.

A.5.16 Identity Management

Identity management is the organizational process for ensuring individuals have the appropriate access to technology resources. This includes the identification, authentication and authorization of a person, or persons, to have access to applications, systems or networks. This is done by associating user rights and restrictions with established identities. Identities are used by computer networks to identify an entity's underlying ability to access a predetermined set of hardware and software resources. IT deals with the approval, registration and administration, defined as the 'full life cycle', of human and non-human identities on any given network. The purpose is to identify who (users, groups of users) or what (applications, systems and devices) is accessing data or IT assets at any given time, and how those identities are granted access rights across the network. It maintains risk by acting as the main perimeter for all associated information security and cyber security operations, as well as the primary mode governance that dictates an organization's Identity and Access Management framework. Identity management includes authenticating users and determining whether they're allowed access to particular systems. Identity Management is focused on Authentication, while Access Management is aimed at Authorization.

A.5.16 Identity Management – A linkage with Ancient Era

Vali and False Positives

Vali, a powerful King Vanar in the Ramayana, is mistakenly shot by Lord Ram due to a case of mistaken identity. This can be compared to the occurrence of false positives in cybersecurity. False positives are instances where a security system mistakenly identifies legitimate activities as malicious or unauthorized. Vali's story reminds us of the importance of refining security systems to minimize false positives and avoid unnecessary disruptions or harm to legitimate users of systems.

Control

The full life cycle of identities should be managed.

Purpose

To allow for the unique identification of individuals and systems accessing the organization's information and other associated assets and to enable appropriate assignment of access rights.

Guidance

The processes used in the context of identity management should ensure that:

- Where identities are assigned to a person, only that specific person is allowed to authenticate with and/or use that identity, when accessing network resources. IT policies need to clearly stipulate that users are not to share login information, or allow other users to roam the network using any identity other than the one they've been assigned.
- Sometimes it may be necessary to assign an identity to multiple people – also known as a 'shared identity'. This approach should be used sparingly, and only to satisfy an explicit set of operational requirements. Organizations should treat the registration of shared identities as a separate procedure to single user identities, with a dedicated approval workflow.
- So-called 'non-human' entities should be considered differently to user-based identities at the point of registration. As with shared identities, non-human identities should in turn have their own approval and registration process that acknowledges the underlying difference between assigning an identity to a person, and granting one to an asset, application or device.
- Identities that are no longer required should be disabled by a network administrator, or removed entirely, as is required. IT staff should carry out regular audits that list identities in order of use, and identify which entities (human or non-human) are able to be suspended or deleted. HR staff should include identity management in their off-boarding procedures, and inform IT staff of leavers in a timely manner.
- Duplicate identities should be avoided at all costs. Firms should adhere to a 'one entity, one identity' rule across the board. IT staff should remain vigilant when assigning roles across a network, and ensure that entities aren't granted access rights based on multiple identities.
- Adequate records should be kept of all 'significant events' regarding identity management and authentication information. The term

'significant event' can be interpreted in various ways, but on a basic level organization need to ensure that their governance procedures include identity registration documentation, robust change request protocols with an appropriate approval's procedure, and the ability to produce a comprehensive list of assigned identities at any given time.

The organization should have a supporting process in place to handle changes to information related to user identities. These processes can include re-verification of trusted documents related to a person. When using identities provided or issued by third parties, the organization should ensure the third-party identities provide the required trust level and any associated risks are known and sufficiently treated. This can include controls related to the third parties as well as controls related to associated authentication information.

Other Information

Providing or revoking access to information and other associated assets is usually a multi-step procedure:

1. Confirming the business requirements for an identity to be established;
2. Verifying the identity of an entity before allocating them a logical identity;
3. Establishing an identity;
4. Configuring and activating the identity. This also includes configuration and initial setup of related authentication services;
5. Providing or revoking specific access rights to the identity, based on appropriate authorization or entitlement decisions.

Identities are the things that identify users, systems, services and are their virtual representation allowing access to data and resources. They can be managed, allocated and used to control, monitor and report on what people and systems do and are doing. The control is achieved through a combination of ensuring that identity-based procedures are clearly articulated in policy documents, and monitoring day-to-day adherence among staff. The ownership should be directed towards IT staff who have been assigned Global Administrator rights (or equivalent for non-Windows based infrastructure). Whilst there are other built-in roles that allow users to administer identities, ownership should rest with the individual who has ultimate responsibility for an organization's entire network, including all subdomains and Active Directory tenants.

The main goal of identity management is to ensure only authenticated users are granted access to the specific applications, systems or IT environments for which they are authorized. This includes control over user provisioning and the process of on boarding new users such as employees, partners, clients and other stakeholders. Identity Management also includes control over the process of authorizing system or network permissions for existing users and the off boarding of users who are no longer authorized to access organization systems. ID management determines whether a user has access to systems and sets the level of access and permissions a user has on a particular system. Identity Governance, the policies and processes that guide how roles and user access should be administered across a business environment, is an important aspect of identity management. Identity Governance is key to successfully managing role-based access management systems. Identity Management is an important part of the Information Security, as it is linked to both the security and productivity of the organization. In many organizations, users are granted more access privileges than they need to perform their functions. Attackers can take advantage of compromised user credentials to gain access to organizations' network and data. Using identity management, organizations can safeguard their corporate assets against many threats including hacking, ransomware, phishing and other malware attacks. Identity management systems add an additional layer of protection by ensuring user access policies and rules are applied consistently across an organization.

The step involved in Identify Management is

1. Implement an approval process for creating, revoking or deleting of identities.
2. Confirm the business requirement for creating an identity.
3. Verify the identity of an entity before creating the virtual representation.
4. Create the identity.
5. Configure the identity and activate it.

Considerations when implementing Identity Management:

1. **One person one ID**: Where an identity is assigned to an individual then it should be unique to that individual so we know what that individual did if things go wrong and we can control what the individual has access to and can do.
2. **Many persons one ID**: The standard wants one individual to one ID but it does allow for many people using one ID where they are required for business, operational needs and have appropriate documentation.
3. **Non-Human IDs**: The organization will implement an approval process for system and non-human identities. It is recommended to perform periodic review of all service accounts to make sure they are needed still and perhaps alternating with a check on the configuration of the ID and what it can do.
4. **Remove old IDs**: The organization will have a starter, leaver, mover process hopefully where HR will inform if someone has left so the ID can be removed. The organization will also have regular access reviews to verify who and what has access to what so that the organization can mop up where the HR process has failed.

Logging

The standard wants records of significant events on the use and management of identities. Logging and monitoring of identities and administrative actions is a must.

A.5.17 Authentication Information

Authentication information such as passwords, encryption keys, and card chips are the gateway to information systems that host sensitive information assets. Poor management or improper allocation of authentication information may result in unauthorized access to information systems and in loss of confidentiality, availability, and integrity of sensitive information assets. Research shows that 30% of all data breaches occur as a result of weak passwords or poor password management practices. Therefore, organizations should have a robust authentication information management process in place to allocate, manage and protect authentication information. Organizations must properly allocate and manage authentication information, eliminate risks of failure in the authentication process and prevent security risks that may arise due to compromise of authentication information. Authentication management is an important practice for an organization. One of the most effective methods of information security breaches is the circumvention of the authentication process. Therefore, it is crucial that organization considers aspects such as:

- Non-Guessable, Unique Password and Personal Identification Number (PINs) generated automatically.
- Procedure to identify and verify the temporary and permanent authentication methods.
- Authentication information transferred to a secure location using a secure manner.
- Dodgy authentication devices and methods to be removed from the system.

It is beneficial for the organization to record the details of authentication methods in a well-structured document. Identifying the responsibilities of the users and all relevant authentication methods.

A.5.17 Authentication Information – A linkage with Ancient Era

Mata Sita and the importance of Authentication

While Lord Hanuman visits Mata Sita in the Ashoka Vatika, She requests that He describes the characteristics of Lord Ram. Further, She also inspects the ring that Lord Hanuman presents. This shows the importance of authentication. Multi-Factor Authentication is highly essential to ensure the identify of every user. This will help organizations keep malicious actors at bay. The Zero-Trust framework highly recommends organizations enforce MFA for authentication purposes.

Mata Sita's Agni Pariksha and Authentication

In the Ramayana, Mata Sita undergoes the Agni Pariksha (a trial by fire) to prove Her purity and loyalty to Lord Ram. This can be compared to authentication mechanisms in cybersecurity. Authentication is the process of verifying the identity of an individual or system before granting access to resources. Just as Mata Sita's Agni Pariksha confirmed Her identity and loyalty, authentication methods like passwords, biometrics, two-factor authentication, and digital certificates ensure that only authorized users gain access to digital systems and data.

Control

Allocation and management of authentication information should be controlled by a management process, including advising personnel on the appropriate handling of authentication information.

Purpose

To ensure proper entity authentication and prevent failures of authentication processes.

Guidance

Allocation of Authentication Information

The allocation and management process should ensure that:

- Personal passwords or personal identification numbers (PINs) generated automatically during enrollment processes as temporary secret authentication information are non-guessable and unique for each person, and that users are required to change them after the first use;
- Procedures are established to verify the identity of a user prior to providing new, replacement or temporary authentication information;
- Authentication information, including temporary authentication information, is transmitted to users in a secure manner and the use of unprotected electronic mail messages for this purpose is avoided;

- Users acknowledge receipt of authentication information;
- Default authentication information as predefined or provided by vendors is changed immediately following installation of systems or software;
- Records of significant events concerning allocation and management of authentication information are kept and their confidentiality is granted, and that the record-keeping method is approved.

User Responsibilities

Any person having access to or using authentication information should be advised to ensure that:

- Secret authentication information such as passwords are kept confidential. Personal secret authentication information is not to be shared with anyone. Secret authentication information used in the context of identities linked to multiple users or linked to non-personal entities are solely shared with authorized persons;
- Affected or compromised authentication information is changed immediately upon notification of or any other indication of a compromise;
- When passwords are used as authentication information, strong passwords according to best practice recommendations are selected, for example:
    - Passwords are not based on anything somebody else can easily guess or obtain using person-related information;
    - Passwords are not based on dictionary words or combinations thereof;
    - Use easy to remember passphrases and try to include alphanumerical and special characters;
    - Passwords have a minimum length;
- The same passwords are not used across distinct services and systems;
- The obligation to follow these rules is also included in terms and conditions of employment.

Password Management System

When passwords are used as authentication information, the password management system should:

1. Allow users to select and change their own passwords and include a confirmation procedure to address input errors;
2. Enforce strong passwords according to good practice recommendations of 'User Responsibilities';
3. Force users to change their passwords at first login;
4. Enforce password changes as necessary, for example after a security incident, or upon termination or change of employment when a user has known passwords for identities that remain active;
5. Prevent re-use of previous passwords;
6. Prevent the use of commonly-used passwords and compromised usernames, password combinations from hacked systems;
7. Not display passwords on the screen when being entered;
8. Store and transmit passwords in protected form. Password encryption and hashing should be performed according to approved cryptographic techniques for passwords.

Other Information

Passwords or passphrases are a commonly used type of authentication information and are a common means of verifying a user's identity. Other types of authentication information are cryptographic keys, data stored on hardware tokens that produce authentication codes and biometric data such as iris scans or fingerprints. Additional information can be found in the ISO series. Requiring frequent change of passwords can be problematic because users can get annoyed by the frequent changes, forget new passwords, note them down in unsafe places, or choose unsafe passwords. Provision of Single Sign On (SSO) or other authentication management tools reduces the amount of authentication information that users are required to protect and can thereby increase the effectiveness of this control. However, these tools can also increase the impact of disclosure of authentication information. Some applications require user passwords to be assigned by an independent authority.

Guidance on allocation of Authentication Information

Secret authentication information is a gateway to access valuable assets. It typically includes passwords, encryption keys etc. so needs to be controlled through a formal management process and needs to be kept confidential to the user. This is usually tied into employment contracts, disciplinary processes and supplier obligations if sharing with external parties. Procedures should be established to verify the identity of a user prior to providing new, replacement or temporary secret authentication information. Any default secret authentication information provided as part of a new system use should be changed as soon as possible. Organizations should comply with the requirements for allocation and management of authentication information as per the recommendations mentioned in the Allocation of Authentication Information under Guidance section.

Guidance on User Responsibilities

Making sure that users follow the policies and will therefore tie in with Human Resource Security for contracts, user education for awareness and compliance. These include: keep any secret authentication information confidential; avoid keeping a record of it that can be accessed by unauthorized parties; change it whenever there is any suggestion of possible compromise; select quality passwords with sufficient minimum length and strength to follow broader password policy controls. Users who can access to and use authentication information should be instructed to comply with the following:

- Users must maintain the confidentiality of secret authentication information such as passwords and should not share such secret information with anyone else. When multiple users are involved in the use of authentication information or the information is linked to non-personal entities, the authentication information should not be disclosed to unauthorized persons.
- Users must change their passwords immediately if the confidentiality of their passwords are compromised.
- Users should select hard-to-guess strong passwords by following industry best practices. For instance:
    - Passwords should not be selected based on personal information that is easy to obtain, such as names or dates of birth.

  - Passwords should not be created based on anything that can be easily guessed.
  - Passwords should not include dictionary words or combinations of these words.
  - Alphanumeric and special characters should be used in the password.
  - There should be a minimum length for passwords.
  - Users should not use the same password for different services.
- Organizations should include the requirements for creation and use of passwords in their employment contracts with their employees.

Users should be made aware of their responsibilities towards protecting their issued credentials, choosing strong passwords and keeping them confidential, and preventing the unauthorized disclosure of sensitive information under their care. The following can be included in the organization's Acceptable Use of Information Security Policy.

- Systems should be locked when left unattended. Users shall:
  - Access data in order to comply with the duties of their role or job duties on a need-to-know basis.
  - Not attempt to access data or programs contained on systems for which they do not have authorization or consent.
  - Not share their computer/network account, password, personal identification number (PIN), digital certificate, security token, or any other device used for identification and authorization purposes.
  - Not share digital certificate passwords used for digital signatures.
  - Not circumvent password entry through the use of auto logon, application "remember password" features, embedded scripts or hard-coded passwords in client software.
  - Password-protect their desktops/laptops when left unattended

Guidance on Password Management Systems

The purpose of a password management system is to ensure quality passwords meet the required level and are consistently applied. Password generation and management systems provide a good way of centralizing the provisioning of access and they serve to reduce the risk of people using the same login for everything. As with any control mechanism, password generation and management systems need to be carefully implemented to ensure adequate and proportionate levels of protection. Wherever possible users should be able to choose their own passwords as this makes them easier to remember than machine-generated ones, however, it needs to be up to a certain level of strength. There are lots of conflicting views on password management systems and password policies so we encourage organizations to look at the frequently changing best practices and adopt approaches based on the risk appetite and culture of the organization. Organizations should comply with the recommendations as mentioned in the Password Management System under Guidance section when establishing a password management system.

Furthermore, organizations should perform hashing and encryption techniques in accordance with the authorized cryptography methods for passwords. It is important to realize that people will share their passwords unless the organization will provide them with some other method of allowing specific individuals to access information in their accounts. For instance, individuals in upper management often ask an administrative assistant to check their e-mail. Also, when people go on vacation, they may need to give someone temporary access to data on their computers, in the e-mail, and on other systems. Password sharing policies should be put in place along with solutions that provide needed functionality with accountability for the shared resource.

What is a Strong Password?

The strength of a password is determined by some restrictions - like minimum length, password age, use of multiple types and special characters, and reuse restrictions - which determines the average number of guesses an attacker must try to guess the password and ease with which the attacker can test the validity of the guessed password.

To Change or Not to Change Password? How Often?

Again, there are as many answers to these questions as there are information security professionals. The argument for changing passwords regularly is that the longer a password remains the same and the more often the same password is used, then it is more likely that the password will be discovered or compromised. Also, the benefit of an "expiration date" on a password is that it limits the amount of time a lost or compromised password can be used by an unauthorized party. The more secure or sensitive information resources, the more frequently passwords should be changed. Conversely, the argument against changing passwords regularly is that strong passwords are reasonably secure and they take longer time and more effort to guess thus making them less likely to be discovered or compromised. Also, it may not be as easy to come up with easy to remember a strong password every 30 or 60 days. Even though there is no "right" or "perfect" answer, the following points are worth considering:

1. Password policy should be based on risk, vulnerabilities, and deployed safeguards;
2. The period of time between changes should be determined by the required strength of the passwords being used;
3. Password changes make it harder for users to use the same password for multiple services (i.e., forces password "diversity");
4. Periodic password changes, especially when done as a routine, could limit successful phishing attempts since users would know when it is time to change passwords and when it is not.

Password Management Problems: By no means a comprehensive list

- Need (and failure) to remember multiple passwords.
- Need (and failure) to remember strong passwords.
- The frequency of password change.
- Coming up with easy to remember but difficult to hack passwords multiple times per year.
- Need to replicate password changes to multiple devices or applications.
- The sophistication of social engineering and "phishing" attacks.

Passphrases

A passphrase is just a different way of thinking about a "secret" or "something you know". The main difference is that a passphrase is longer.

While a usual password is 8 to 10 characters long, a passphrase can be twice as long. Compared to passwords, a passphrase is generally stronger because it is more memorable than passwords thus reducing the need to write them down, they make some types of brute force attacks impractical since they are much longer than passwords, and they make phrase or quote dictionary attacks almost impossible if the passphrase is well constructed.

Guidance

In addition to passwords, there are other types of authentication information such as cryptographic keys, smart cards and biometric data such as fingerprints. Considering that frequent change of passwords might be cumbersome and annoying for users, organizations may consider implementing alternative methods such as single sign-on or password vaults. However, it should be noted that these alternative methods may expose authentication information to higher risk of unauthorized disclosure.

A.5.18 Access Rights

Every employee within the organization will need to have access to certain computers, databases, information systems, and applications to perform their tasks. While HR personnel may need access to sensitive data of employees, the finance department may rely on accessing and using databases containing employee salary details. However, these access rights should be provided, modified, and revoked in line with the organization's access control policy and its access controls so that it can prevent unauthorized access to, modification of, and destruction of information assets. This control deals with how organizations should assign, modify and revoke access rights taking into account business requirements. While provisioning of access rights to critical information seems to be the first of a user stepping into the system, it is recommended to review, modify, and if necessary, delete the access right of the user in a long run. This is a common mistake of organizations that do not or forget to review and modify users' access rights, which facilitates the ground for numerous information security incidents to happen. For instance, disgruntled employees degrading from a higher position to a lower position in an organization could cause damage to critical information that they have access to using their escalated access rights. Similarly, an attacker might target sensitive information of the organization utilizing a person with a lower position but escalated access rights within the organization. Therefore, access rights provisioning, reviewing, modifying, and deleting within the access control policy is a considerable aspect of the organization.

A.5.18 Access Rights – A linkage with Ancient Era

Lord Hanuman in Lanka

- **Infiltration and Reconnaissance:** Lord Hanuman's journey to Lanka involves strategic planning and reconnaissance, akin to an infiltration mission. He carefully observes the layout of the city, assesses the strengths and weaknesses of the enemy, and gathers crucial information about Mata Sita's whereabouts. Similarly, in access control, there is a focus on understanding the layout and vulnerabilities of a system or facility to enhance security measures.
- **Overcoming Obstacles:** Lord Hanuman encounters various obstacles

while navigating through Lanka, including enemy forces, geographical barriers, and magical defenses. His determination, agility, and divine powers enable him to overcome these challenges and continue His mission. Similarly, in access control scenarios, security measures are designed to deter and overcome potential threats or intrusions.

- **Deception and Subterfuge:** Lord Hanuman employs deception and subterfuge to achieve His objectives, such as disguising Himself as a Brahmin to enter the city unnoticed. This aspect of the story underscores the importance of clever tactics and disguise in bypassing security measures. In access control, there is a constant need to anticipate and counteract deceptive tactics employed by intruders.
- **Gaining Access to Restricted Areas:** Lord Hanuman eventually gains access to King Ravan's palace, where He finds Mata Sita imprisoned. This feat highlights the significance of breaching restricted areas or high-security zones, which may be protected by multiple layers of access control measures. Lord Hanuman's success in reaching Mata Sita illustrates the potential vulnerabilities within even the most fortified environments.
- **Rescue and Liberation:** Ultimately, Lord Hanuman's mission culminates in the liberation of Mata Sita and the eventual defeat of King Ravan, symbolizing the triumph of righteousness over evil. This aspect of the story resonates with the broader goal of access control, which is to safeguard individuals, assets, and information from potential harm or exploitation.

Control

Access rights to information and other associated assets should be provisioned, reviewed, modified and removed in accordance with the organization's topic-specific policy on and rules for access control.

Purpose

To ensure access to information and other associated assets is defined and authorized according to the business requirements.

Guidance

Provision and revocation of access rights

A process must be implemented to assign or revoke access rights for all user types to all systems and services. It's the set of processes for managing user attributes and policies that determine a user's access rights to an information resource. In other words, what user attributes, job functions, and organizational affiliations can serve as the basis for access authorization decisions. Users should be granted the least privilege, the most restrictive set of permissions or access rights, needed to perform assigned work tasks. Two common problems are an excessive privilege and creeping privilege. The former happens when a user has more access or permissions than the assigned work tasks and/or role requires. The latter happens when a user account accumulates privileges over time as roles and assigned work tasks to change. Both problems are addressed by periodic review of user access rights. Management of administrative privileges is particularly important since very common cyber-attack techniques take advantage of unmanaged administrative privileges. Another common attack involves domain administration privileges in Windows environments potentially giving an attacker significant control over numerous devices and access to the data they contain.

User access should always be business led and access based around the requirements of the business. Organizations should incorporate the rules and controls into the process for assignment and revocation of access rights to an authenticated individual as mentioned in the Guidance section - Provision and revocation of access rights. The provisioning process for assigning or revoking physical and logical access rights granted to an entity's authenticated identity should include:

- Obtaining authorization from the owner of the information and other associated assets for the use of the information and other associated assets. Separate approval for access rights by management can also be appropriate;
- Considering the business requirements and the organization's topic-specific policy and rules on access control;
- Considering segregation of duties, including segregating the roles of approval and implementation of the access rights and separation of conflicting roles;
- Ensuring access rights are removed when someone does not need to access the information and other associated assets, in particular

ensuring access rights of users who have left the organization are removed in a timely fashion;

- Considering giving temporary access rights for a limited time period and revoking them at the expiration date, in particular for temporary personnel or temporary access required by personnel;
- Verifying that the level of access granted is in accordance with the topic-specific policies on access control and is consistent with other information security requirements such as segregation of duties;
- Ensuring that access rights are activated (e.g., by service providers) only after authorization procedures are successfully completed;
- Maintaining a central record of access rights granted to a user identifier to access information and other associated assets;
- Modifying access rights of users who have changed roles or jobs; removing or adjusting physical and logical access rights, which can be done by removal, revocation or replacement of keys, authentication information, identification cards or subscriptions;
- Maintaining a record of changes to users' logical and physical access rights.

Review of Access Rights

Some data, due to its nature or confidentiality requirements, may be restricted from general access by users and may require additional levels of formal approval before being made available. Users are granted access to these data on a need-to-know basis - when there are justified work-related reasons for access or need to know. An important characteristic of need-to-know access is the access is granted for a limited period of time. When the reasons for access are no longer valid, access to the data is (or should be) revoked. Least privilege and need-to-know access underscore the importance of the periodic review of user accounts and their corresponding access rights. Dormant user accounts - active user accounts that show no activity for very long periods of time - poses an unnecessary risk for unauthorized access to confidential data. The periodic review of user accounts and corresponding access rights with system owners, disabling user accounts after a preset period of inactivity, purging them after a longer period of inactivity are all good practices to ensure that a system does not contain old, unused user accounts and to mitigate risk. Asset owners must review users' access rights at regular intervals, both around individual change (on-boarding, change of role and exit) as well broader audits of the systems access. Authorizations for privileged access rights should be reviewed at more frequent intervals given their higher risk nature. This ties in with for internal audits and should be done at least annually or when major changes take place. Regular reviews of physical and logical access rights should consider the following:

- Users' access rights after any change within the same organization (e.g., job change, promotion, demotion) or termination of employment;
- Authorizations for privileged access rights.

Consideration before change or termination of employment

Before an employee is promoted or demoted within the same organization or when his/her employment is terminated, his/her access rights to information processing systems should be evaluated and modified by taking into account the following risk factors:

- Whether the termination process is initiated by the employee or by the organization and the reason for termination.
- Current responsibilities of the employee within the organization.
- Criticality and value of information assets accessible to the employee.

Other Information

Consideration should be given to establishing user access roles based on business requirements that summarize a number of access rights into typical user access profiles. Access requests and reviews of access rights are easier managed at the level of such roles than at the level of particular rights. Consideration should be given to including clauses in personnel contracts and service contracts that specify sanctions if unauthorized access is attempted by personnel. In cases of management-initiated termination, disgruntled personnel or external party users can deliberately corrupt information or sabotage information processing facilities. In cases of persons resigning or being dismissed, they can be tempted to collect information for future use. Cloning is an efficient way for organizations to assign access to users. However, it should be done with care based on distinct roles identified by the organization rather than just cloning an identity with all associated access rights. Cloning has an inherent risk of resulting in excessive access rights to information and other associated assets.

All staff has a broad constituency with varying degrees of affiliation with the organization. One thing in common among all staff is that all require access to some type of organizational information for a determined period of time – they all become users. At a high level, organizations can divide users into two groups based on their type of affiliation with the organization:

- **Formal Affiliation**: These are users whose affiliation to the organization is established by some kind of contract or agreement. Users in this group include staff members, employees, vendors, clients, and management.
- **Casual Affiliation**: These are users whose affiliation to the organization is transitory, periodic, mostly informational and not established by a contract or agreement. Users in this group include guests, retirees, the relative of employees, visitors for the website, etc.

Organization must establish and implement appropriate procedures and controls to assign, modify and revoke access rights to information systems in compliance with the organization's access control policy and its access controls. An Information Security Officer should be responsible to establish, implement and review appropriate rules, processes, and controls for provision, modification and revocation of access rights to information systems. When assigning, modifying, and revoking access rights, the Information Security Officer should consider business needs and should closely work with information asset owners to ensure that rules and processes are adhered to.

Supplementary Guidance

Organizations should consider establishing user access roles based on their business requirements. These roles should include the types and number of access rights to be granted to each user group. Creating such roles will make it easier to manage and review access requests and rights. Organizations should include contractual provisions for unauthorized access and sanctions for such access in their employment/service contracts with their staff. Organizations should be cautious against disgruntled employees who are laid off by the management because they may damage information systems on purpose. If organizations decide to use the cloning techniques to grant access rights, they should perform it on the basis of distinct roles established by the organization. It should be noted that cloning comes with the inherent risk of granting excessive access rights.

A.5.19 Information Security in Supplier Relationships

External suppliers are a vital component of business operations. Suppliers may have access to a wide range of information from the supported organization. Once shared with a supplier, direct control of this information is lost, regardless of sensitivity or value. As a result, appropriate technical and contractual controls and mitigation processes must be established with all external suppliers. One essential control would be to ensure the existence of a data-sharing agreement that clearly delineates roles and responsibilities. Some data privacy regulations may have specific data sharing requirements that must be met. The contracting organization should understand that the management of external providers is a life cycle. Part of this cycle is a process to monitor and continuously assess provider performance and compliance. A variety of tools may be used to assess and validate external supplier data protection practices. In almost all cases, some mitigation will be contractual and requires extensive documentation. In addition to protecting information handled and used by external suppliers, the organization must also assess service availability. If business-critical data or functions are supported by an external entity, then the provider's disaster recovery processes are integral to the recovery processes of the hiring entity. Agreements regarding the return of data in the event of contract termination or unexpected closure should also be considered within the life cycle. This control is about information security in supplier relationships. The objective here is the protection of the organization's valuable assets that are accessible to or affected by suppliers. The organization must also consider other key relationships here too, for example, partners if they are not suppliers but also have an impact on the organization assets that might not simply be covered by a contract alone. This is an important part of the ISMS especially. Let's understand those requirements and what they mean in a bit more depth now. The contracting organization should understand that the management of external providers is a life cycle. Part of this cycle is a process to monitor and continuously assess provider performance and compliance. A variety of tools may be used to assess and validate external supplier data protection practices. In almost all cases, some mitigation will be contractual and requires extensive documentation. In addition to protecting information handled and used by external suppliers, the organization must also assess service availability. If business-critical data or functions are supported by an external entity, then the provider's disaster recovery processes are integral to the recovery processes of the hiring entity. Agreements regarding the return of data in the event of contract termination or unexpected closure should also be considered within the life cycle.

A.5.19 Information Security in Supplier Relationship – A linkage with Ancient Era

Vanar Sena – Importance of Collaboration, Coordination, Mutual Trust in Safeguarding Sensitive Information

- **Collaborative Defense:** The Vanar Sena, led by Lord Hanuman, plays a crucial role in assisting Lord Ram in his quest to rescue Mata Sita. Similarly, in Supplier Relationships, collaboration is essential for ensuring information security. Companies and their suppliers must work together as a cohesive unit to identify potential vulnerabilities, implement security measures, and respond effectively to security threats. Just as the Vanar Sena collaborated with Lord Ram to achieve their common goal, companies and suppliers must collaborate to defend against cybersecurity risks.
- **Specialized Skills and Expertise:** The members of the Vanar Sena possess diverse skills and expertise that complement each other, allowing them to overcome various challenges. Similarly, suppliers often bring specialized knowledge and capabilities to the table, enhancing the overall security posture of the partnership. Whether it's expertise in cybersecurity protocols, data encryption, or threat detection, suppliers can contribute valuable insights and resources to strengthen information security defenses. Just as the Vanar Sena's unique abilities were instrumental in overcoming obstacles, suppliers' specialized skills can bolster companies' defenses against cyber threats.
- **Trust and Loyalty:** The Vanar Sena's unwavering loyalty to Lord Ram and their trust in His leadership are central themes. Similarly, trust and loyalty are foundational elements of secure supplier relationships. Companies must trust their suppliers to handle sensitive information responsibly and adhere to security protocols. In turn, suppliers must demonstrate loyalty by prioritizing the security and confidentiality of

their clients' data. Just as the Vanar Sena trusted Lord Ram to lead them to victory, companies rely on their suppliers to uphold their end of the security partnership.

- **Effective Communication and Coordination:** The success of the Vanar Sena in the Ramayana is attributed in part to their effective communication and coordination. Similarly, in supplier relationships, clear communication and coordination are essential for ensuring that security measures are implemented consistently and that any security incidents are promptly addressed. By maintaining open lines of communication and establishing clear protocols for sharing information and responding to threats, companies and their suppliers can enhance their collective ability to protect sensitive data. Just as the Vanar Sena coordinated their efforts to achieve their objectives, companies and suppliers must collaborate closely to safeguard against cyber threats.

Control

Processes and procedures should be defined and implemented to manage the information security risks associated with the use of supplier's products or services.

Purpose

To maintain an agreed level of information security in supplier relationships.

Guidance

The organization should establish and communicate a topic-specific policy on supplier relationships to all relevant interested parties. The organization should identify and implement processes and procedures to address security risks associated with the use of products and services provided by suppliers. This should also apply to the organization's use of resources of cloud service providers. These processes and procedures should include those to be implemented by the organization, as well as those the organization requires the supplier to implement for the commencement of use of a supplier's products or services or for the termination of use of a supplier's products and services, such as:

- Identifying and documenting the types of suppliers which can affect the confidentiality, integrity and availability of the organization's information;

- Establishing how to evaluate and select suppliers according to the sensitivity of information, products and services;
- Evaluating and selecting supplier's products or services that have adequate information security controls and reviewing them; in particular, accuracy and completeness of controls implemented by the supplier that ensure integrity of the supplier's information and information processing and hence the organization's information security;
- Defining the organization's information, ICT services and the physical infrastructure that suppliers can access, monitor, control or use;
- Defining the types of ICT infrastructure components and services provided by suppliers which can affect the confidentiality, integrity and availability of the organization's information;
- Assessing and managing the information security risks associated with:
    - The suppliers' use of the organization's information and other associated assets, including risks originating from potential malicious supplier personnel;
    - Malfunctioning or vulnerabilities of the products or services provided by the suppliers;
- Monitoring compliance with established information security requirements for each type of supplier and type of access, including third-party review and product validation;
- Mitigating non-compliance of a supplier, whether this was detected through monitoring or by other means;
- Handling incidents and contingencies associated with supplier products and services including responsibilities of both the organization and suppliers;
- Resilience and, if necessary, recovery and contingency measures to ensure the availability of the supplier's information and information processing and hence the availability of the organization's information;

- Awareness and training for the organization's personnel interacting with supplier personnel regarding appropriate rules of engagement, topic-specific policies, processes and procedures and behavior based on the type of supplier and the level of supplier access to the organization's systems and information;
- Managing the necessary transfer of information, other associated assets and anything else that needs to be changed and ensuring that information security is maintained throughout the transfer period;
- Requirements to ensure a secure termination of the supplier relationship, including:
    - De-provisioning of access rights;
    - Information handling;
    - Determining ownership of intellectual property developed during the engagement;
    - Information portability in case of change of supplier or in sourcing;
    - Records management;
    - Return of assets;
    - Secure disposal of information and other associated assets;
    - Ongoing confidentiality requirements;
- Level of personnel security and physical security expected from supplier's personnel and facilities.

The procedures for continuing information processing in the event that the supplier becomes unable to supply its products or services should be considered to avoid any delay in arranging replacement products or services by identifying an alternative supplier in advance or always using alternative suppliers.

Other Information

In cases where it is not possible for an organization to place requirements on a supplier, the organization should:

- Consider the guidance given in this control in making decisions about choosing a supplier and its product or service;

- Implement compensating controls as necessary based on a risk assessment.

Information can be put at risk by suppliers with inadequate information security management. Controls should be determined and applied to manage the supplier's access to information and other associated assets. For example, if there is a special need for confidentiality of the information, non-disclosure agreements or cryptographic techniques can be used. Another example is personal data protection risks when the supplier agreement involves transfer of, or access to, information across borders. The organization needs to be aware that the legal or contractual responsibility for protecting information remains with the organization. Risks can also be caused by inadequate controls of ICT infrastructure components or services provided by suppliers. Malfunctioning or vulnerable components or services can cause information security breaches in the organization or to another entity. See ISO 27036-2 for more detail.

Suppliers are used for two main reasons; the organization wants them to do work that they have chosen not to do internally themselves, or the organization can't easily do the work as well or as cost effectively as the suppliers. The organization should identify and require information security controls that specifically address external parties gaining authorized access to the organization's information in the policy. The controls should also specify processes and procedures that should be followed, either when third-party contractors work within the organization or when there are service provider/hosting arrangements. Suppliers should be managed throughout the life cycle of a relationship with them–from initially reviewing their contracts and security methods to monitoring their SLAs and performance agreements once they are engaged to perform services and/or provide solutions. Access control, especially for sensitive information must be accurately defined, managed, and monitored. Awareness training for both the organization's staff and supplier staff that handle or interact with this data must be addressed. Finally, service transitions should be documented and include procedures for secure data transfers and availability as the relationship changes during the lifecycle. Many (but not all) supplier relationships will involve cloud computing services and processes, which should be carefully considered as a part of Supplier Relationship Management. One essential control that the organization can implement is the development of a checklist to assess contractual cloud service providers. If regulated and/or sensitive data is being put out in the cloud, then the organization should consider obtaining formal written assurances from cloud service providers, including the regular submission of independent assessments and/or audits. The organization should always consider asking these cloud service providers for a copy of a report which focuses strictly on reviewing controls related to the confidentiality, integrity, and availability of information and systems. The organization has seen a move from consumer-level adoption of cloud services to enterprise deployment of full-scale cloud storage and collaboration platforms. Enterprise services can now offer the convenience of cloud storage and collaboration services with single sign-on through the organization's identity management system, integration with other services, and contractual assurances of privacy, security, and uptime. The deployment of enterprise cloud storage and collaboration services has introduced new opportunities for how documents are conceived, completed, and submitted. This technology provides the opportunity for employees to bring their work wherever they go, access it instantly, and collaborate with colleagues in a private and secure digital environment.

The supplier should be agreed with the documented information security requirements which relates to the risk of access by suppliers to organization assets. If any organization wants to provide access to its supplier, the risk assessment should be done. The organization must identify and involve required security information controls. These could include the following:

1. Identification and reporting of supplier forms, e.g., IT services, financial services etc. which are accessible to the organization;
2. Controls over the accuracy and completeness of information transmitted by either party;
3. Resilience and, if necessary, recovery and contingency plans to ensure the availability by all parties of information or processing;
4. Training in awareness of applicable policies, processes and procedures for the organization staff involved in acquisitions;
5. Training in awareness of how the organization's staff interacts with supplier staff on appropriate rules of engagement and behavior

based on provider type and level of supplier access to the system and information of the organization;

6. A legal contract must be signed by both parties to maintain the integrity of the relationship.

There are many important things to consider in the approach to supplier selection and management but one size does not fit all and some suppliers will be more important than others. As such the organization controls and policies should reflect that too and segmentation of the supply chain is sensible. These range from those who are business-critical to other vendors who have no material impact on your organization. Some suppliers are also more powerful than their customers (imagine telling Amazon what to do if the organization is using their AWS services for hosting) so it's pointless having controls in place that the suppliers will not adhere to. Therefore, reliance on their standard policies, controls, and agreements are more likely, meaning the supplier selection and risk management becomes even more important. In order to take a more forward approach to information security in the supply chain with the more strategic (high value/higher risk) suppliers, organizations should also avoid binary 'comply or die' risk transferring practices e.g., awful contracts preventing good collaboration. Instead, we recommend they develop more close working relationships with those suppliers where high value information and assets are at risk, or they are adding to your information assets in some (positive) way. This is likely to lead to improved working relationships, and therefore deliver better business results too. A good policy describes the supplier segmentation, selection, management, exit, how information assets around suppliers are controlled in order to mitigate the associated risks, yet still enable the business goals and objectives to be achieved. Smart organizations will wrap their information security policy for suppliers into a broader relationship framework and avoid just concentrating on security per se, looking to the other aspects as well. An organization may want suppliers to access and contribute to certain high-value information assets (e.g., software code development, accounting payroll information). They would therefore need to have clear agreements of exactly what access they are allowing them, so they can control the security around it. This is especially important with more and more information management, processing, and technology services being outsourced. That means having a place to show management of the relationship is happening; contracts, contacts, incidents, relationship activity, and risk management, etc. Where the supplier is also intimately involved in the organization, but may not have its own certified ISMS, then ensuring the supplier staff is educated and aware of security, trained on your policies, etc. is also worth demonstrating compliance around.

Compliance with this control involves adhering to what's known as a 'topic-specific' approach to information security in supplier relationships. Topic-specific approaches encourage organizations to create supplier-related policies that are tailored towards individual business functions, rather than adhering to a blanket supplier management policy that applies to any and all third-party relationships across an organization's commercial operation. The organization must implement policies and procedures that not only govern the organization's use of supplier resources and cloud platforms, but also form the basis of how they expect their suppliers to conduct themselves prior to and throughout the term of the commercial relationship. It can be viewed as the essential qualifying document that dictates how information security governance is handled over the course of a supplier contract.

A.5.20 Addressing Information Security within Supplier Agreements

Any suppliers that view, process, store, communicate or provide IT infrastructure component information for the organization should be defined and agreed with all applicable information security requirements. This control governs how an organization forms a contractual relationship with a supplier, based on their security requirements and the type of suppliers they deal with. Supplier agreements should be defined and recorded so that the organization and the supplier do not misinterpret the obligations of the two parties to meet the applicable information security requirements. This clause explains about defining and accepting the obligations as well as record them securely under a relevant documented policy. This policy may consist of all the roles and responsibility and limit of accessing the information security of the supplier. It also gives exclusive right to the organization to audit the supplier and its sub-contractors. In the ISO 27001 supplier register, the organization records whether they have a contract that covers the products or services that they are buying. To implement this, the organization would also have a local copy of the contract that they could get access to and they would check that the contract includes information security requirements. The organization always want to have an in-date contract that meets the requirements of this clause before we go for ISO 27001 certification audit.

A.5.20 Addressing Information Security within Supplier Agreements – A linkage with Ancient Era

Vanar Sena – Establishing Clear Expectations, Fostering Collaboration, and Ensuring Mutual Accountability

- **Clear Security Requirements:** Just as Lord Ram provided clear instructions to the Vanar Sena, companies must outline specific security requirements within supplier agreements. This includes detailing encryption standards, access controls, data handling procedures, and compliance with relevant regulations. Clear expectations ensure that both parties understand their responsibilities regarding information security.
- **Collaborative Risk Management:** The Vanar Sena succeeded through teamwork and coordination. Similarly, companies and suppliers should

collaborate on risk management efforts. This involves conducting joint risk assessments, sharing threat intelligence, and identifying vulnerabilities in the supply chain. By working together, both parties can better understand and mitigate potential security threats.

- **Continuous Monitoring and Improvement:** Like Lord Ram's vigilance over the Vanar Sena's progress, continuous monitoring is crucial in information security. Supplier agreements should include provisions for ongoing monitoring of security controls and performance metrics. Regular audits and assessments can help identify areas for improvement and ensure compliance with agreed-upon security standards.
- **Incident Response Planning:** Lord Ram and the Vanar Sena were prepared to respond to unforeseen challenges. Similarly, supplier agreements should outline procedures for handling security incidents. This includes reporting requirements, escalation procedures, and collaboration on incident response efforts. Having a well-defined incident response plan helps minimize the impact of security breaches and ensures a coordinated response.
- **Training and Awareness:** Just as Lord Ram provided guidance and leadership to the Vanar Sena, companies should invest in training and awareness programs for their suppliers. Educating suppliers on security best practices, policies, and procedures enhances their ability to safeguard sensitive information. Training should be ongoing to keep suppliers informed about evolving threats and security requirements.
- **Mutual Trust and Accountability:** Trust was fundamental to the success of the Vanar Sena, and is similarly crucial in supplier relationships. Supplier agreements should foster trust and accountability by clearly defining each party's responsibilities and consequences for non-compliance. Building a trusting relationship encourages open communication and collaboration, essential for effective information security management.
- **Regular Review and Revision:** Like Lord Ram's periodic assessments of the Vanar Sena's progress, supplier agreements should undergo regular review and revision. As technology evolves and new threats emerge, agreements may need updates to address changing security

requirements. Regular review ensures that agreements remain effective in mitigating current risks and supporting business objectives.

Control

Relevant information security requirements should be established and agreed with each supplier based on the type of supplier relationship.

Purpose

To maintain an agreed level of information security in supplier relationships.

Guidance

Supplier agreements should be established and documented to ensure that there is clear understanding between the organization and the supplier regarding both parties' obligations to fulfill relevant information security requirements. The following terms can be considered for inclusion in the agreements in order to satisfy the identified information security requirements:

- Description of the information to be provided or accessed and methods of providing or accessing the information.
- Classification of information according to the organization's classification scheme.
- Mapping between the organization's own classification scheme and the classification scheme of the supplier.
- Legal, statutory, regulatory and contractual requirements, including data protection, handling of personally identifiable information (PII), intellectual property rights and copyright and a description of how it will be ensured that they are met.
- Obligation of each contractual party to implement an agreed set of controls, including access control, performance review, monitoring, reporting and auditing, and the supplier's obligations to comply with the organization's information security requirements.
- Rules of acceptable use of information and other associated assets, including unacceptable use if necessary.
- Procedures or conditions for authorization and removal of the

authorization for the use of the organization's information and other associated assets by supplier personnel.

- Information security requirements regarding the supplier's ICT infrastructure; in particular, minimum information security requirements for each type of information and type of access to serve as the basis for individual supplier agreements based on the organization's business needs and risk criteria.
- Indemnities and remediation for failure of contractor to meet requirements.
- Incident management requirements and procedures.
- Training and awareness requirements for specific procedures and information security requirements.
- Relevant provisions for sub-contracting, including the controls that need to be implemented, such as agreement on the use of sub-suppliers.
- Relevant contacts, including a contact person for information security issues.
- Any screening requirements, where legally permissible, for the supplier's personnel, including responsibilities for conducting the screening and notification procedures if screening has not been completed or if the results give cause for doubt or concern.
- The evidence and assurance mechanisms of third-party attestations for relevant information security requirements related to the supplier processes and an independent report on effectiveness of controls.
- Right to audit the supplier processes and controls related to the agreement.
- Supplier's obligation to periodically deliver a report on the effectiveness of controls and agreement on timely correction of relevant issues raised in the report.
- Defect resolution and conflict resolution processes.
- Providing backup aligned with the organization's needs.
- Ensuring the availability of an alternate facility not subject to the same

threats as the primary facility and considerations for fall back controls in the event primary controls fail.

- Having a change management process that ensures advance notification to the organization and the possibility for the organization of not accepting changes.
- Physical security controls commensurate with the information classification.
- Information transfer controls to protect the information during physical transfer or logical transmission.
- Termination clauses upon conclusion of the agreement including records management, return of assets, secure disposal of information and other associated assets, and any ongoing confidentiality obligations.
- Provision of a method of securely destroying the organization's information stored by the supplier as soon as it is no longer required.
- Ensuring, at the end of the contract, handover support to another supplier or to the organization itself.

The organization should establish and maintain a register of agreements with external parties to keep track of where their information is going. The organization should also regularly review, validate and update their agreements with external parties to ensure they are still required and fit for purpose with relevant information security clauses.

Other Information

The agreements can vary considerably for different organizations and among the different types of suppliers. Therefore, care should be taken to include all relevant requirements for addressing information security risks.

All relevant information security requirements must be in place with each supplier that has access to or can impact the organization's information or assets that process it. Again, this should not be a one size fits all – take a risk-based approach around the different types of suppliers involved and work they do. Working with suppliers that already meet the majority of the organization's information security needs for the services they provide and have a good track record of addressing information security concerns responsibly is a very good idea – as it will make all of these processes much easier. In simple terms, look for suppliers that already have achieved an independent ISO 27001 certification or equivalent themselves. It is also important to ensure that the suppliers are being kept informed and engaged with any changes to the ISMS or specifically engaged around the parts that affect their services. The auditor will want to see this evidenced – so, by keeping a record of this in your supplier onboarding projects or annual reviews it will be easy to do so. Things to include in the supply scope and agreements generally include: the work and its scope; information at risk and classification; legal and regulatory requirements; reporting and reviews; non-disclosure; IPR; incident management; specific policies to comply with if important to the agreement; obligations on subcontractors; screening on staff etc. A good standard contract will deal with these points but as above, sometimes it might not be required, and could be way over the top for the type of supply, or it might not be possible to force a supplier to follow your idea of good practice. Be risk centered in the approach. An organization may want suppliers to access and contribute to certain high value information assets and therefore would need to have clear agreements of exactly what access they are allowing them, so they can control the security around it. This is especially important with more and more information management, processing, and technology services being outsourced. Where the supplier is also intimately involved in the organization, but may not have its own certified ISMS, then ensuring the supplier staff is educated and aware of security, trained on your policies, etc. is also worth demonstrating compliance around.

Supplier agreements should be established and documented to ensure there is no misunderstanding regarding both parties' obligations to fulfill relevant security, legal, and/or regulatory requirements. Organizations are increasingly using outsourced services. While sensitive data processes and services might be outsourced, responsibility for the associated risk remains with the organization. Supplier agreements should include (as appropriate) clear and concise information regarding:

- The types of data being accessed and methods of access;
- Definitions of data ownership and disposition throughout the service lifecycle;
- The organization's data classification requirements as it applies to the supplier;

- Definition of acceptable uses for the data handled by the supplier;
- Establishment of security incident notification requirements;
- Processes and procedures for monitoring compliance with the contract requirements;
- A "right to audit" the supplier or regular access to external assessments;
- Conflict and defect resolution;
- The required screening, training or other obligations of the suppliers' staff;
- The use of subcontractors to provide services and the extension of security requirements to them.

It is important to address the risk early in the procurement phase of the relationship with external parties so that roles, responsibilities, and expectations can be clearly defined in agreements or contracts. This control explicitly states that both parties should exit the process with a "clear understanding" of their information security obligations to one another. A clear description should be provided detailing the information that needs to be accessed in any way, and how that information is going to be accessed. The organization should classify the information to be accessed in accordance with its published classification scheme. Adequate consideration should be given to the supplier-side classification scheme, and how that relates to the organization's classification of information. Both parties' rights should be categorized into four main areas – legal, statutory, regulatory and contractual. Within these four areas, various obligations should be clearly outlined, as is standard in commercial agreements, including accessing PII, intellectual property rights and copyright stipulations. The agreement should also cover how each of these key areas will be addressed in turn. Each party should be obligated to enact a series of concurrent controls that monitor, assess and manage information security risk levels such as access control policies, contractual reviews, systems monitoring, reporting and periodic auditing. In addition, the agreement should clearly outline the need for supplier personnel to adhere to an organization's information security standards. There should be a clear understanding of what constitutes both acceptable and unacceptable use of information, and physical and virtual assets from either party. Procedures should be put in place that deal with the levels of authorization required for supplier-side personnel to access or view an organization's information. Information security should be considered alongside the supplier's own ICT infrastructure, and how that relates to the type of information that the organization has provided access to, the risk criteria and the organization's base set of business requirements. Consideration should be given to what courses of action the organization is able to take in the event of a breach of contract on the part of the supplier, or failure to comply with individual stipulations. The agreement should clearly outline a mutual Incident Management procedure that clearly stipulates what needs to happen when problems arise, particularly concerning how the incident is communicated between both parties. Personnel from both parties should be given adequate awareness training on key areas of the agreement, specifically concerning key risk areas such as Incident Management and the provision of access to information. Adequate attention should be given to the use of subcontractors. If the supplier is permitted to use subcontractors, the organizations should take steps to ensure that any such individuals or companies are aligned with the same set of information security requirements as the supplier. Where it's legally possible and operationally relevant, organizations should consider how supplier personnel are screened prior to interacting with their information, and how screening is recorded and reported to the organization, including non-screened personnel and areas for concern. Organizations should stipulate the need for third-party attestations that verify the supplier's ability to fulfill organizational information security requirements, including independent reports and third-party audits. Organizations should have the contractual right to assess and audit a supplier's procedures. Suppliers should have an obligation to deliver reports (at varying intervals) that cover the effectiveness of their own processes and procedures, and how they intend to address any issues raised in such a report. The agreement should take steps to ensure the timely and thorough resolution of any defects or conflicts that take place during the course of the relationship. Where relevant, the supplier should operate with a robust policy, in line with the organization's needs, that covers off three main considerations:

1. Backup type (full server, file and folder etc., incremental etc.)
2. Backup frequency (daily, weekly etc.)

3. Backup location and source media (onsite, offsite)

Data resilience should be achieved by operating with a disaster recovery location that is separate from the supplier's main ICT site, and is not subject to the same level of risk. The supplier should operate with a comprehensive change management policy that gives advance notification to the organization of any changes that may affect information security, and provide the organization with the ability to reject such changes. Physical security controls should be enacted that are relevant to the kind of information they are permitted to access. When the need arises to transfer information between assets, sites, servers or storage locations, the supplier should ensure that data and assets are protected from loss, damage or corruption throughout the process. The agreement should outline a comprehensive list of actions to be taken by either party in the event of termination, including but not limited to:

- Asset disposal and/or relocation
- Information deletion
- Return of IP
- Removal of access rights
- Ongoing confidentiality obligations

The supplier should outline precisely how it intends to destroy/ permanently delete the organization's information the moment it is no longer required i.e., in the event of a termination. If, at the end of a contract, the need arises to handover support and/or services to another provider not listed on the agreement, steps are taken to ensure that the process results in zero business interruption. To ensure that the benefits of outsourcing operations outweigh the risks of including providers in the scenario, contracts should be written properly, and ISO 27001 requires an organization to consider security clauses in contracts. Some examples of security clauses are:

- **Right to Audit**: clause ensuring the organization has the right to audit and test the security controls periodically, or upon significant changes to the relationship.
- **Notification about Security Breaches**: clause requiring the provider to inform the organization in a timely manner regarding any security

breaches that may impact the organization's business. Generally, this clause is related to data breach notification laws that affect either the organization or the provider, or both.

- **Adherence to Security Practices**: clause requiring the provider to adhere to the organization's security practices, and to communicate any situations where this adherence is not achievable, helping to prevent security gaps or conflicts that could impair security performance.
- **Response Time to Vulnerabilities**: clause requiring the provider to provide, in a timely manner, proper treatment for known vulnerabilities that may impact the organization's business.
- **Demonstration of Compliance**: clause requiring the provider to provide independent evidence that its operations and controls comply with contractual requirements.
- **Management of Supplier's Supply Chain Risks**: clause requiring the provider to ensure, within its own supply chain, the fulfillment of the same security clauses applied to the provider.
- **Communication of Changes**: clause requiring the provider to inform the organization in a timely manner regarding changes in its environment that may impact the organization's business.
- **Maintenance of Service Levels**: clause requiring the provider to inform the organization regarding its plans to ensure service levels in normal conditions and during disruptive events, on either the organizations or the provider's premises.

The organization should note this is not a definitive list and other clauses may arise from risk assessments, and that all contractual clauses should be reviewed by legal personnel to ensure proper wording and application. To define which clauses to apply, you should focus on each supplier's risks, by means of surveys, questionnaires, and gathering of controls documentation during supplier selection. To help you manage information on multiple suppliers, you can use criteria like:

- Categorizing suppliers based on what they do for the organization
- Prioritizing suppliers based on information the organization share with them, or information they may have access to.

A.5.21 Managing Information Security in the ICT Supply Chain

Information and Communications Technology (ICT) is integral for the daily operations and functionality of the organization. From cell phones to cloud storage to satellite connectivity, the ICT supply chain encompasses the entire life cycle of hardware, software, and services and a diverse array of entities, including third-party vendors, suppliers, service providers, and end users. However, the globally-distributed and interconnected nature of ICT also means that compromise of vulnerabilities in the supply chain can have cascading impacts on organization Information Security. Vulnerabilities in supply chains either developed intentionally for malicious intent or unintentionally through poor security practices can enable data and intellectual property theft, loss of confidence in the integrity of the system, or exploitation to cause system or network failure. Compounding the risk associated with supply chains is that vulnerabilities may be introduced during any phase of the ICT life cycle: design, development and production, distribution, acquisition, deployment, maintenance, and disposal. These vulnerabilities include malicious software and hardware; counterfeit components; and poor product designs, manufacturing processes, and maintenance procedures.

Processes and procedures should be defined and implemented to manage the information security risks associated with the ICT products and services supply chain.

A.5.21 Managing Information Security in the ICT Supply Chain – A linkage with Ancient Era

Vanar Sena

- **Strategic Organization:** Just as Lord Ram strategically organized the Vanar Sena to achieve his objectives, organizations need to strategically organize their ICT supply chain. This involves identifying key stakeholders, defining roles and responsibilities, and creating a structured framework for managing security throughout the supply chain.
- **Risk Assessment and Mitigation:** Lord Ram conducted risk assessments to identify potential threats and vulnerabilities to the Vanar Sena. Similarly, organizations must assess risks within the ICT

supply chain and mitigation strategies should be implemented to reduce these risks.

- **Supplier Management:** Lord Ram carefully selected and managed members of the Vanar Sena based on their skills and capabilities. Similarly, organizations must carefully select and manage suppliers in the ICT supply chain which includes evaluating suppliers' security practices, ensuring compliance with relevant regulations and standards, and monitoring their performance to ensure they meet security requirements.
- **Establishing Security Standards:** Lord Ram provided clear instructions and standards for the Vanar Sena to follow. Likewise, organizations must establish clear security standards and protocols for the ICT supply chain which includes defining minimum security requirements, specifying security controls, and ensuring that suppliers adhere to these standards through contractual agreements.
- **Collaborative Security Efforts:** The success of the Vanar Sena depended on collaboration and teamwork. Similarly, managing information security in the ICT supply chain requires collaboration between organizations and their suppliers. This involves sharing threat intelligence, conducting joint risk assessments, and coordinating security efforts to address vulnerabilities collectively.
- **Continuous Monitoring and Improvement:** Lord Ram continuously monitored the progress of the Vanar Sena and made adjustments as needed. Similarly, organizations must continuously monitor the security posture of the ICT supply chain and implement improvements where necessary, which includes regular security assessments, monitoring for emerging threats, and updating security measures to address evolving risks.
- **Incident Response Planning:** Lord Ram and the Vanar Sena were prepared to respond to unexpected challenges during their mission. Similarly, organizations must have robust incident response plans in place to address security incidents within the ICT supply chain effectively. This involves defining response procedures, establishing communication protocols, and conducting regular drills to ensure readiness.

- **Training and Awareness**: Lord Ram provided guidance and leadership to the Vanar Sena through training and guidance. Similarly, organizations should invest in training and awareness programs to educate suppliers and employees about information security best practices. This helps ensure that all stakeholders understand their roles and responsibilities in maintaining security within the ICT supply chain.

Control

Processes and procedures should be defined and implemented to manage the information security risks associated with the ICT products and services supply chain.

Purpose

To maintain an agreed level of information security in supplier relationships.

Guidance

The following topics should be considered to address information security within ICT supply chain security in addition to the general information security requirements for supplier relationships:

- Defining information security requirements to apply to ICT product or service acquisition;
- Requiring that ICT services suppliers propagate the organization's security requirements throughout the supply chain if they subcontract for parts of the ICT service provided to the organization;
- Requiring that ICT products suppliers propagate appropriate security practices throughout the supply chain if these products include components purchased or acquired from other suppliers or other entities;
- Requesting that ICT products suppliers provide information describing the software components used in products;
- Requesting that ICT products suppliers provide information describing the implemented security functions of their product and the configuration required for its secure operation;
- Implementing a monitoring process and acceptable methods for

validating that delivered ICT products and services comply with stated security requirements;

- Implementing a process for identifying and documenting product or service components that are critical for maintaining functionality and therefore require increased attention, scrutiny and further follow up required when built outside of the organization especially if the supplier outsources aspects of product or service components to other suppliers;
- Obtaining assurance that critical components and their origin can be traced throughout the supply chain;
- Obtaining assurance that the delivered ICT products are functioning as expected without any unexpected or unwanted features;
- Implementing processes to ensure that components from suppliers are genuine and unaltered from their specification. Monitoring for out of specification performance can be an indicator of tampering or counterfeits. Prevention and detection of tampering should be implemented during multiple stages in the system development life cycle, including design, development, integration, operations and maintenance;
- Obtaining assurance that ICT products achieve required security levels;
- Defining rules for sharing of information regarding the supply chain and any potential issues and compromises among the organization and suppliers;
- Implementing specific processes for managing ICT component life cycle and availability and associated security risks. This includes managing the risks of components no longer being available due to suppliers no longer being in business or suppliers no longer providing these components due to technology advancements. Identification of an alternative supplier and the process to transfer software and competence to the alternative supplier should be considered.

Other Information

The specific ICT supply chain risk management practices are built on top of general information security, quality, project management and system engineering practices but do not replace them. Organizations are advised to work with suppliers to understand the ICT supply chain and any matters that have an important effect on the products and services being provided. The organization can influence ICT supply chain information security practices by making clear in agreements with their suppliers the matters that should be addressed by other suppliers in the ICT supply chain. ICT should be acquired from reputable sources. The reliability of software and hardware is a matter of quality control. While it is generally not possible for an organization to inspect the quality control systems of its vendors, it can make reliable judgments based on the reputation of the vendor. Examples of ICT supply chains are:

- Cloud services provisioning, where the cloud service provider relies on the software developers, telecommunication service providers, hardware providers;
- IoT, where the service involves the device manufacturers, the cloud service providers, the developers for mobile and web applications, the vendor of software libraries;
- Hosting services, where the provider relies on external service desks including first, second and third support levels.

See ISO 27036-3 for more details including risk assessment guidance. Software identification (SWID) tags can also help to achieve better information security in the supply chain, by providing information about software provenance. See ISO 19770-2 for more details.

This control is focused on the information and communication technology supply chain that may need something in addition or instead of the standard approach. ISO advocates numerous areas for implementation and whilst these are all good, some pragmatism is needed as well. The organization should again recognize its size compared to some of the very large providers that it will sometimes be working with e.g., data centers & hosting services, banks, etc., therefore potentially limiting its ability to influence practices further into the supply chain. The organization should consider carefully what risks there may be based upon the type of information and communication technology services that are being provided. Agreements with suppliers should include requirements to address the information security risks associated with information and communications technology services and product supply chains. This section is largely physical in nature and defines additional points to include in supplier agreements, specifically related to their use of technology, both hardware, and software. There should be a process to identify a product or service that is a critical capability and require increased scrutiny. This is especially true for components built outside the supplier organization. The ability to trace origins and compliance with security requirements is integral in ensuring both integrity and availability. Finally, the organization should address the risks of a component or service becoming unavailable or no longer supported. Supplier agreements include requirements to reduce the security risks connected with the IT services and the product supply chain. This means that if there's a possibility of a data breach, the supplier and contractor will have to get in touch. Suppliers are required to describe how they dealt with minor risks, as well as how they assured the risk was eradicated, even if it is a small risk. Controlling supplier relations effectively requires using crucial services to track the supply chain's history and its point of origin.

Given the expansion of cross-platform on-premise and cloud services over the last decade, it deals with the supply of both hardware and software-related components and services (both on-premise and cloud-based), and rarely draws a distinction between the two. As well as the relationship between the supplier and the organization, several controls also deal with a supplier's obligations when sub-contracting elements of the supply chain to third-party organizations. Organizations should draft a clear set of information security standards that apply to their individual needs, to set clear expectations on how suppliers should conduct themselves when delivering ICT products and services. If the ICT supplier sub-contracts any element of the supply chain, the supplier should take measures to ensure that contractors and their personnel are fully conversant with the organization's unique information security standards. If the need arises to acquire components (physical or virtual) purchased from a third party, the supplier should disseminate the organization's security requirements to any vendors or suppliers they themselves use. Suppliers should be asked to provide information on the nature and function of the software components they use to deliver a service to the organization. Organizations should identify the underlying security functions of any product or service supplied, and how to operate said product or service in a way that doesn't compromise on information security. Organizations shouldn't take risk levels for granted, and draft procedures that ensure any products or services that a supplier delivers are of a secure nature and compliant with accepted industry standards. Methods may include certification checks, internal testing and supporting compliance documentation. When receiving a product or service, organizations should adhere to a process of first identifying then recording any elements that are deemed to be essential to maintaining core functionality – especially if those components have originated from a sub-contractor/outsourced agreement. Suppliers should be able to provide concrete assurances that "critical components" benefit from a thorough audit log that traces their movement throughout the ICT supply chain, from creation through to delivery. As ICT products and services are delivered, organizations should seek categorical assurance that said products and services are not only operating within scope, but do not contain any additional features which may present a collateral security risk. Component specifications are key to ensuring that an organization understands the hardware and software components it's introducing onto its network. Suppliers should consider antitampering measures throughout the development life cycle, and organizations should require stipulations which verify components as legitimate upon delivery. Assurances should be sought to confirm that ICT products are in alignment with industry-standard and/or sector-specific security requirements, as relevant to each product. Common methods for achieving this include achieving a minimum level of formal security certification, or adhering to a set of internationally recognized information standards per product. Organizations should take steps to ensure that suppliers are aware of their obligations when sharing information and/or data concerning the mutual supply chain operation, including acknowledging any potential conflicts or problems that may arise between both parties, and how to deal with them at source. Organizations need to draft procedures that manage risk when operating with unavailable, unsupported or legacy components, wherever they reside. Where components have fallen into one of these categories, organizations should be able to adapt accordingly and identify alternatives.

Protecting organization's information in a digitally-connected world requires understanding not only organization's immediate supply chain, but also the extended supply chains of third-party vendors, service providers, and customers. These essential steps will assist the organization in managing supply chain risks.

1. **Identify the people**: Build a team of representatives from various roles and functions of the organization. Ensure personnel at all levels are well-trained in the security procedures of their role or function.
2. **Manage security and compliance**: Document the set of policies and procedures that address security, integrity, resilience, and quality. Ensure they are based on industry standards and best practices.
3. **Assess the components**: Build a list of ICT components that the organization procures to enable your business. Know which internal systems are relied upon for critical information or functions, and which systems have remote access capability that must be protected to prevent unauthorized access.
4. **Know the supply chain and suppliers**: Identify the suppliers and, when possible, the suppliers' sources.
5. **Verify assurance of third-parties**: Verify that the suppliers maintain an adequate security culture to appropriately address the risks that concern the organization. Establish the protocols the organization will use to assess the supply chain practices of their suppliers.
6. **Evaluate risk associated with ITC supply**: Determine the frequency with which to review the risk, incorporate feedback, and make changes to the risk assessment. This may also include auditing suppliers against practices and protocols established by the organization.

A.5.22 Monitoring, Review and Change Management of Supplier Services

The objective is to maintain an agreed level of information security and service delivery in line with supplier agreements. Once operations of service providers have started, ensuring that the services delivered conform to the specifications of third-party contracts are important. This can include everything from availability levels of the service to something more granular, such as examining the security controls the service provider agreed to in the contract. If there is a great level of dependency upon third-party service providers, checking into service capabilities, plans for handling information security incidents or service disruptions, and business continuity testing may be warranted. Systematic monitoring and reviews of services and controls are also recommended, including scrutinizing service reports provided by the third-party to ensure the information is sufficient and relevant. As business or information technology requirements are modified, this may also require a change in the provision of third-party services, and procedures should be in place to handle any new requirements. Additionally, modifications may also call for a review of existing information security controls to ensure they are adequate.

A.5.22 Monitoring, Review and Change Management of Supplier Services – A linkage with Ancient Era

Vanar Sena

- **Continuous Monitoring:** Just as Lord Ram kept a close eye on the activities of the Vanar Sena, organizations need to continuously monitor the performance and activities of their suppliers within the ICT supply chain. This involves tracking service levels, compliance with security requirements, and any emerging risks or issues that may affect information security.
- **Performance Review:** Lord Ram periodically reviewed the progress and performance of the Vanar Sena to ensure they were meeting their objectives. Similarly, organizations should conduct regular performance reviews of their suppliers to evaluate their effectiveness in delivering services and maintaining security standards. This

includes assessing key performance indicators, identifying areas for improvement, and providing feedback to suppliers.

- **Change Management:** When changes were necessary within the Vanar Sena, such as adjustments to strategy or tactics, Lord Ram managed these changes effectively. Similarly, organizations must have robust change management processes in place to address changes in supplier services within the ICT supply chain. This involves assessing the impact of changes on information security, communicating effectively with stakeholders, and implementing changes in a controlled manner to minimize disruption.
- **Risk Assessment and Mitigation:** Lord Ram conducted risk assessments to identify potential threats and vulnerabilities to the Vanar Sena. Likewise, organizations must assess risks associated with changes in supplier services within the ICT supply chain. This includes evaluating the potential impact on information security, implementing mitigation measures to address identified risks, and monitoring the effectiveness of these measures over time.
- **Communication and Collaboration:** Effective communication and collaboration were essential for managing the Vanar Sena in the Ramayana. Similarly, organizations must maintain open lines of communication and collaboration with their suppliers within the ICT supply chain. This involves sharing information about changes, discussing potential impacts on security, and working together to address any challenges or concerns that arise.
- **Documentation and Documentation:** Lord Ram kept detailed records and documentation of the activities and decisions of the Vanar Sena. Likewise, organizations should maintain comprehensive documentation of their interactions with suppliers within the ICT supply chain. This includes documenting agreements, changes, performance reviews, and any incidents or issues that occur, providing a clear audit trail for future reference.

Control

The organization should regularly monitor, review, evaluate and manage change in supplier information security practices and service delivery.

Purpose

To maintain an agreed level of information security and service delivery in line with supplier agreements.

Guidance

Monitoring, review and change management of supplier services should ensure the information security terms and conditions of the agreements are complied with, information security incidents and problems are managed properly and changes in supplier services or business status do not affect service delivery. This should involve a process to manage the relationship between the organization and the supplier to:

- Monitor service performance levels to verify compliance with the agreements;
- Monitor changes made by suppliers including:
    - Enhancements to the current services offered;
    - Development of any new applications and systems;
    - Modifications or updates of the supplier's policies and procedures;
    - New or changed controls to resolve information security incidents and to improve information security;
- Monitor changes in supplier services including:
    - Changes and enhancement to networks;
    - Use of new technologies;
    - Adoption of new products or newer versions or releases;
    - New development tools and environments;
    - Changes to physical location of service facilities;
    - Change of sub-suppliers;
    - Sub-contracting to another supplier;
- Review service reports produced by the supplier and arrange regular progress meetings as required by the agreements;
- Conduct audits of suppliers and sub-suppliers, in conjunction with

review of independent auditor's reports, if available and follow-up on issues identified;

- Provide information about information security incidents and review this information as required by the agreements and any supporting guidelines and procedures;
- Review supplier audit trails and records of information security events, operational problems, failures, tracing of faults and disruptions related to the service delivered;
- Respond to and manage any identified information security events or incidents;
- Identify information security vulnerabilities and manage them;
- Review information security aspects of the supplier's relationships with its own suppliers;
- Ensure that the supplier maintains sufficient service capability together with workable plans designed to ensure that agreed service continuity levels are maintained following major service failures or disaster ensure that suppliers assign responsibilities for reviewing compliance and enforcing the requirements of the agreements;
- Evaluate regularly that the suppliers maintain adequate information security levels.

The responsibility for managing supplier relationships should be assigned to a designated individual or team. Sufficient technical skills and resources should be made available to monitor that the requirements of the agreement, in particular the information security requirements, are being met. Appropriate actions should be taken when deficiencies in the service delivery are observed.

Other Information

See ISO/IEC 27036-3 for more detail.

This control describes how organizations regularly monitor, review their supplier service delivery. Conducting reviews and monitoring is best done based on the information at risk. The organization should aim to conduct its reviews in line with the proposed segmentation of suppliers in order to therefore optimize their resources and make sure that they focus effort on monitoring & reviewing where it will have the most impact. Sometimes there is a need for pragmatism, you are not necessarily going to get an audit, human relationship review, and dedicated service improvements with AWS if you are a very small organization. You could, however, check their annually published SOC II reports and security certifications remain fit for your purpose. Evidence of monitoring should be completed based on the power, risks, and value, thus allowing auditor to be able to see that it has been completed and that any necessary changes have been managed through a formal change control process. The organization cannot overlook the need to manage the risk to their information assets that are accessed, processed, communicated to, or managed by external parties. The service provider should be continuously monitored to assure that services provided are meeting the terms of the contract and security is maintained. There should be an ongoing review of service reports, a process to address concerns and issues, and periodic audits. This section also encompasses documentation and procedures for handling security incidents, including incident reporting, mitigation, and subsequent reviews. Finally, service capability levels must be monitored to ensure that the service provider continues to meet the contract terms and needs of the business. In addition to regular review and monitoring of the services provided, the contracting organization should:

- Conduct audits of suppliers in conjunction with outside assessments;
- Require the supplier to promptly notify regarding security incidents;
- Provide regular audit trails and records for security events;
- Have a conflict resolution process that can be invoked if requirements are not met.

Organizations need to take steps to ensure that employees who are responsible for managing SLAs and supplier relationships have the requisite levels of skill and technical resources to be able to adequately assess supplier performance, and information security standards are not being breached.

Some external parties provide independent audits based on the Statement on Standard for Attestation Engagements which focuses on the design of controls and their operating effectiveness. When independent audit opinions are not available, the organization might choose to evaluate the risk themselves. Monitoring can mean different things to different people. It can simply mean to assess, to watch, to keep track of, or to check, usually, with a special purpose. It does not mean or implies to verify or even to test.

Actually, monitoring is more of a spectrum that ranges from just "keeping an eye" in the low end to requiring a site audit in the high end. Given the availability of resources at the organization of higher education, verification could be an impractical and significantly costly requirement if applied to all or most suppliers effective monitoring of suppliers requires a process or methodology in place that defines the approach to take based on the risk of the supplier or engagement, activities should be more stringent and closer to the high end of the spectrum as risk increases or when exceptional situations warrant them. The organizational policy may refer to instances in which the sharing of sensitive data will result in a significant risk. Again, "significant" can mean a number of things but, ultimately, depends on the organization's risk management practices and risk tolerance. Supplier monitoring include a requirement to perform a site audit, or results of a Statement on Standards for Attestation Engagements audit, or results of an audit performed by an independent auditor. What should an organization do to monitor compliance with agreement requirements in most cases? Define the incremental risk to the organization when engaging a supplier as well as defining a due diligence process for mitigating those risks, third-party risk from remote access, data transmission and offsite storage. Consider the following as an outline for a contract monitoring process:

During System/Application/Process Implementation

- Identify the individual(s) responsible for monitoring the relationship with the supplier.
- During project status meetings:
  - Assess and review status reports regarding progress made in the implementation of the security requirements included in the contract and/or statement of work.
  - Identify new areas or security requirements that may arise from changes in scope.
- If applicable, perform or request audit of vendor security practices and

procedures and/or perform a penetration test. It may be necessary to include a legal review by general counsel, as well.

- During final test and prior to sign-off
  - Test system/application/process security functionality required in the contract.
  - Review progress reports and determine if all security requirements included in the contract and/or statement of work were completed.
- If applicable, perform application scan.

Post Implementation

- Follow up with system/application/process owner.
  - Require the owner to perform a risk assessment based on policy.
  - Review with the owner the risk assessment results. Any concerns? Any problems? Any unknowns that need to be addressed with the vendor?
- Follow up with the supplier. Access logs available? Any pending items resolved? Are things on their end as expected? Any owner concerns? Risk assessment identified deficiencies?
- Based on risk (annually or bi-annually), resubmit third-party information security risk assessment to assess what has changed, what needs closer scrutiny, or identify inconsistencies with previous assessments.
- Establish a working relationship with your supplier.
- Participate in supplier's product improvement committee. What changes are been considered? How would they impact the organization's risk and security postures?
- Review security incidents involving the system/application/process. Are these due to non-compliance?
- If applicable, based on the contract, require subsequent assurance tests.

For currently established suppliers, assess their risk, and start with the steps listed in the Post Implementation section above as needed. It is important to keep in mind that supplier monitoring is the last step of a cascading progression. The initial identification of process and data impacted as well as initial security requirements are used to formulate purchasing requirements. The answers to the requirements are used to evaluate potential suppliers and refine security requirements. The evaluation and risk assessment of finalists refine the security requirements that will, in turn, be added as the language to the contract or statement of work. And, finally, it is the final contract and corresponding risk level that determine the appropriate supplier monitoring approach.

A good control describes how any changes to the provision of services by suppliers, including maintaining and improving existing information security policies, procedures, and controls, are managed. It takes into account the criticality of business information, the nature of the change, the supplier type/s affected, the systems and processes involved, and a re-assessment of risks. Changes to supplier's services should also take into account the intimacy of the relationship and the organization's ability to influence or control change in the supplier. All technology systems are undergoing a continuous upgrade, change, and repair. Changes to service provisions by suppliers should be managed and documented, taking into account the sensitivity of information and services and re-assessment of risks. The contracting organization should determine how to integrate its change management process with that of the supplier. Items to consider include:

1. Service Enhancements
2. Bug Fixes
3. Use of New Technology
4. New Development Tools
5. Enhanced Security Measures
6. Change of Subcontractor
7. Change of Physical Sites

Where possible, supplier changes should be integrated with the contracting organization's change management processes.

A.5.23 Information Security for use of Cloud Services

Modern enterprises have swiftly adopted cloud-based services for their business operations. If they haven't done so already, they're rapidly integrating such services. ISO defines Cloud services as "One or more capabilities offered via cloud computing invoked using a defined interface." and Cloud Computing as "Paradigm for enabling network access to a scalable and elastic pool of shareable physical or virtual resources with self-service provisioning and administration on-demand." Organizations place their trust in cloud providers to ensure a secure environment. Unfortunately, that approach has numerous problems, namely that cloud providers don't always know the risk associated with a customer's systems and data. They don't have visibility into other components in the customer's ecosystem and the security requirements of those components. Failing to take ownership of cloud security is a serious downfall that could lead organizations to suffer data loss, system breaches and devastating attacks. This control provides guidance and references for acquiring, using, managing, and exiting third-party cloud services. This control requires an organization to define the roles and responsibilities of the cloud service provider and understand who is responsible for what. When organizations opt for cloud services, such engagements can involve shared responsibilities for information security. This results in a collaborative effort between the cloud service customer and the cloud service provider. The roles and responsibilities of both parties must be defined clearly. A cloud service customer does not have negotiation powers, as cloud service agreements are pre-defined and offered in a 'take it-or leave it' manner. For all possible cloud services an organization has availed, it must review relevant contracts to understand the distribution of risks related to cloud services between the service provider and the customer.

A.5.23 Information Security for Use of Cloud Services – A linkage with Ancient Era

Cloud Services and Lord Ram's Bow and Arrow – symbolizes Strength, Precision, and Protection.

- **Strength and Protection:** Just as Lord Ram's bow symbolizes strength and protection; cloud services should provide a robust security infrastructure to protect data from unauthorized access and cyber threats. This includes implementing encryption mechanisms to safeguard data both in transit and at rest, as well as deploying firewalls and intrusion detection systems to defend against external attacks.

- **Precision and Accuracy:** Lord Ram's skill with the bow represents precision and accuracy, essential qualities in information security. Similarly, cloud service providers must ensure that access controls are finely tuned to allow authorized users to access only the data and resources they need, while preventing unauthorized access or data breaches. This involves implementing identity and access management solutions, multi-factor authentication, and role-based access controls to enforce security policies effectively.
- **Reliability and Consistency:** Lord Ram's bow is depicted as reliable and consistent, always ready to defend against threats. Similarly, cloud service providers must ensure the reliability and availability of their services to prevent downtime and data loss. This includes implementing redundant infrastructure, disaster recovery plans, and regular backups to maintain data integrity and continuity of operations.
- **Adaptability and Flexibility:** Lord Ram's ability to use different arrows for various purposes highlights adaptability and flexibility, crucial traits in information security for cloud services. Cloud providers should offer a range of security features and customization options to meet the diverse needs of their customers. This includes providing configurable security controls, compliance frameworks, and security-as-a-service offerings to adapt to evolving threats and regulatory requirements.
- **Continuous Improvement:** Lord Ram's proficiency with the bow reflects continuous improvement and mastery over time. Similarly, cloud service providers must continuously monitor and update their security measures to address emerging threats and vulnerabilities. This involves conducting regular security assessments, patch management, and security training to enhance the overall security posture of their cloud services.

Control

Processes for acquisition, use, management and exit from cloud services should be established in accordance with the organization's information security requirements.

Purpose

To specify and manage information security for the use of cloud services.

Guidance

The organization should establish and communicate topic-specific policy on the use of cloud services to all relevant interested parties. The organization should define and communicate how it intends to manage information security risks associated with the use of cloud services. It can be an extension or part of the existing approach for how an organization manages services provided by external parties. The use of cloud services can involve shared responsibility for information security and collaborative effort between the cloud service provider and the organization acting as the cloud service customer. It is essential that the responsibilities for both the cloud service provider and the organization, acting as the cloud service customer, are defined and implemented appropriately. The organization should define:

- All relevant information security requirements associated with the use of the cloud services;
- Cloud service selection criteria and scope of cloud service usage;
- Roles and responsibilities related to the use and management of cloud services;
- Which information security controls are managed by the cloud service provider and which are managed by the organization as the cloud service customer;
- How to obtain and utilize information security capabilities provided by the cloud service provider;
- How to obtain assurance on information security controls implemented by cloud service providers;
- How to manage controls, interfaces and changes in services when an organization uses multiple cloud services, particularly from different cloud service providers;
- Procedures for handling information security incidents that occur in relation to the use of cloud services;

- Its approach for monitoring, reviewing and evaluating the ongoing use of cloud services to manage information security risks;
- How to change or stop the use of cloud services including exit strategies for cloud services.

Cloud service agreements are often pre-defined and not open to negotiation. For all cloud services, the organization should review cloud service agreements with the cloud service provider(s). A cloud service agreement should address the confidentiality, integrity, availability and information handling requirements of the organization, with appropriate cloud service level objectives and cloud service qualitative objectives. The organization should also undertake relevant risk assessments to identify the risks associated with using the cloud service. Any residual risks connected to the use of the cloud service should be clearly identified and accepted by the appropriate management of the organization. An agreement between the cloud service provider and the organization, acting as the cloud service customer, should include the following provisions for the protection of the organization's data and availability of services:

- Providing solutions based on industry accepted standards for architecture and infrastructure;
- Managing access controls of the cloud service to meet the requirements of the organization;
- Implementing malware monitoring and protection solutions;
- Processing and storing the organization's sensitive information in approved locations or within or subject to a particular jurisdiction;
- Providing dedicated support in the event of an information security incident in the cloud service environment;
- Ensuring that the organization's information security requirements are met in the event of cloud services being further sub-contracted to an external supplier;
- Supporting the organization in gathering digital evidence, taking into consideration laws and regulations for digital evidence across different jurisdictions;
- Providing appropriate support and availability of services for an

appropriate time frame when the organization wants to exit from the cloud service;

- Providing required backup of data and configuration information and securely managing backups as applicable, based on the capabilities of the cloud service provider used by the organization, acting as the cloud service customer;
- Providing and returning information such as configuration files, source code and data that are owned by the organization, acting as the cloud service customer, when requested during the service provision or at termination of service.

The organization, acting as the cloud service customer, should consider whether the agreement should require cloud service providers to provide advance notification prior to any substantive customer impacting changes being made to the way the service is delivered to the organization, including:

- Changes to the technical infrastructure that affect or change the cloud service offering;
- Processing or storing information in a new geographical or legal jurisdiction;
- Use of peer cloud service providers or other sub-contractors.

The organization using cloud services should maintain close contact with its cloud service providers. These contacts enable mutual exchange of information about information security for the use of the cloud services including a mechanism for both cloud service provider and the organization, acting as the cloud service customer, to monitor each service characteristic and report failures to the commitments contained in the agreements.

Other Information

This control considers cloud security from the perspective of the cloud service customer. Additional information relating to cloud services can be found in ISO 17788, ISO 17789 and ISO 22123-1. Specifics related to cloud portability in support of exit strategies can be found in ISO 19941. Specifics related to information security and public cloud services are described in ISO 27017. Specifics related to PII protection in public clouds acting as PII processor are described in ISO 27018. Supplier relationships for cloud services are covered by ISO 27036-4 and cloud service agreements and their contents are dealt with in the ISO 19086 series, with security and privacy specifically covered by ISO 19086-4.

This control outlines the processes that are required for the acquisition, use, management of and exit from cloud services, in relation to the organization's unique information security requirements. When an organization avails of a cloud service, the service provider signs an agreement with the organization that specifies the nature of service, terms and conditions, and service level agreements, among other important information. This agreement must specify the controls for which the service provider is responsible and the controls for which the organization is responsible. It should also include roles and responsibilities related to the usage of cloud services, along with detailed information on using, changing, or stopping cloud services. It allows organizations to first specify then subsequently manage and administer information security concepts as related to cloud services, in their capacity as a "cloud services customer". It contains a host of procedures that encompass many distinct elements of an organization's operation. Compliance involves adhering to what's known as a 'topic-specific' approach to cloud services and information security. Given the variety of cloud services on offer, topic-specific approaches encourage organizations to create cloud services policies that are tailored towards individual business functions, rather than adhering to a blanket policy that applies to information security and cloud services across the board. Adherence to control is a collaborative effort between the organization and their cloud service partner. Control should also be closely aligned with information management in the supply chain and the management of supplier services. However, an organization chooses to operate, this control should not be taken in isolation and should complement existing efforts to manage supplier relationships. With information security at the forefront, the organization should define:

- Any relevant security requirements or concerns involved in the use of a cloud platform;
- The criteria involved in selecting a cloud services provider, and how their services are to be used;

- Granular description of roles and relevant responsibilities that govern how cloud services are to be used across the organization;
- Precisely which information security areas are controlled by the cloud service provider, and those that fall under the remit of the organization themselves;
- The best ways in which to first collate then utilize any information security-related service components provided by the cloud service platform;
- How to obtain categorical assurances on any information security-related controls enacted by the cloud service provider;
- The steps that need to be taken in order to manage changes, communication and controls across multiple distinct cloud platforms, and not always from the same supplier;
- Incident Management procedures that are solely concerned with the provision of cloud services;
- How the organization expects to manage its ongoing use and/or wholesale adoption of cloud platforms, in-line with their broader information security obligations;
- A strategy for the cessation or amendment of cloud services, either on a supplier-by- supplier basis, or through the process of cloud to on-premise migration.

In addition to the potential for data breaches and lack of visibility, the most common cloud security challenges are:

- Misconfigurations and inadequate change controls;
- Lack of cloud security architecture and strategy;
- Insufficient identity, credential, access and key management;
- Account hijacking;
- Insecure interfaces and APIs; and
- Abuse and nefarious use of cloud services.

The fallout from the cloud attack is often exponential. To prevent cloud attack, the organization can:

- Vet and oversee potential providers;

- Inspect provider security model;
- Deploy enhanced authentication, such as multifactor authentication, where possible;
- Encrypt data in motion and at rest in the cloud;
- Patch consistently;
- Utilize manual and automatic methods to discover and inventory cloud assets;
- Manage access.

Steps to Create Cloud Security Policy

Step 1: Account for Relevant Laws: Organization must adhere to some privacy or compliance regulation. All cloud-based activities must conform to legal obligations.

Step 2: Assess the Security Controls of the Cloud Vendor: Different providers offer different levels of security control. Inspect Provider's security practices and form solutions that align with the offering.

Step 3: Assign Roles and Access Rights: Specify clear roles for personnel and set their access to applications and data. Give employees access only to the assets they need to perform their tasks. Additionally, define how the organization logs and reviews access.

Step 4: Protect Data: Determine how to protect organization data. Most businesses choose to encrypt all sensitive data moving through the cloud and the Internet. The policy must document security rules for internal and external data stores.

Step 5: Defend the Endpoints: A single infected endpoint can lead to data breaches in multiple clouds. Therefore, there must be a set clear rules surrounding connections with the cloud to avoid this issue.

Step 6: Define Responses: A policy must not only cover prevention. Consider ideal ways for teams to handle data breaches, outline reporting processes, and specify forensic functions. It also helps to establish protocols for disaster recovery.

Step 7: Ensure Good Integrations: Integrate properly multiple safety solutions. Poorly combined solutions create vulnerabilities, so find a way to integrate and leverage the organization's security devices.

Step 8: Perform Security Audits: Conduct regular reviews and upgrade components to remain ahead of the latest threats. Also, perform routine checks of the vendor's SLAs.

A.5.24 Information Security Incident Management Planning and Preparation, A.5.25 Assessment and Decision on Information Security Events, A.5.26 Response to Information Security Incidents, A.5.27 Learning from Information Security Incidents, A.5.28 Collection of Evidence

Software complexity, near-universal worldwide connectivity, and the criminals determined to profit from these factors make information security incidents inevitable. The goal of an effective information security incident management strategy is a balance of driving the impact of the incidents down while processing incidents as efficiently as possible. Good incident management will also help with the prevention of future incidents. How this plays out is to develop a program that prepares for incidents. From a management perspective, it involves the identification of resources needed for incident handling, as well as developing and communicating the formal detection and reporting processes. An effective security program includes important aspects of detecting, reporting, and responding to adverse security events as well as weaknesses that may lead to events if they are not appropriately addressed.

Effective incident response in many organizations other than IT, involve having trained personnel equipped and ready for response. Having trained individuals ready to respond with advance preparation is the first task. Designing an effective means of the detection of incidents is also essential and this often consists of trained users and administrators, together with technical controls. Effective, appropriate communication at all levels of an organization is essential for limiting the impact of security events, using formal detection and reporting processes. All members of the community should be trained and comfortable regarding procedures for reporting failures, weaknesses, and suspected incidents; methods to recognize and detect problems with security protections; as well as how to escalate reporting appropriately. In addition, technical controls must be implemented for the automated detection of security events, coupled with as near real-time reporting as possible, to investigate and initiate immediate responses to problems. For new IT systems, often the best time to develop automated detection of security events is when the preventive security controls are being architected. Confirmation of an adverse security event is an inevitable outcome in any organization. A formal management procedure and policy for incident response, including roles and responsibilities for each aspect of the response, is essential. Aspects include funding and cost models, analysis, containment, and recovery responsibilities, decision-making authority for notifications; legal and/or law enforcement involvement; forensic investigations; responsibility for after-incident debriefing; and policy, procedure, and process improvements. No matter the extent of the defenses, it is inevitable that information security incidents will occur. For this reason, establishing, periodically assessing, and continually improving incident management processes and capabilities is very important. If you are just getting started in this area of your security program, then the following areas are very useful stepping stones that are covered in this chapter:

- Define what constitutes an information security incident and review how varied incidents can be classified.
- Consider what constitutes an information security incident that requires special handling (vs. common security events). Review incident classification schemes that allow for aligning handling procedures to potential impacts and risks.
- Identify and establish essential roles and procedures needed for effective incident management.
- Evaluate the technical and operational capabilities of your organization to detect and respond to security incidents. Consider how senior management support can be gained to formalize effective incident management processes. Formulate procedures and workflow for effectively addressing incidents throughout the life cycle.
- Create effective communication, coordination, and reporting plans for a broad spectrum of incidents including data breach events.
- Identify key partners and stakeholders and levels of communication and engagement. Review the legal and contractual communication requirements associated with data types that may be involved in Information Security Incidents.
- Adapt and learn from security incidents and strive for continual improvement by identifying and planning for training needs and enhancement of response capabilities.

The reality of security incidents, breaches, and loss of data has become all too familiar to a growing number of organizations. Efforts to be prepared need to be engaged prior to these episodes occurring through a comprehensive approach involving on-premise, qualified team construction, vendor participation, appropriate insurance or retainers, and organizational counsel. The best reaction to an information security incident is being proactive and the worst is proceeding without caution, expertise, and proper guidance. If qualified personnel does not exist on staff, external assistance needs to be contracted and ready to employ. Without previous agreements, even qualified vendors may have difficulties meeting your required timeline. Proceeding without a consistent, fully-developed response plan can lead to lost evidence, data, and inability to verify loss and recovery leading to a false sense of containment and resolution of the event. The incident management plan should be clear, concise describing the steps to be taken, resources utilized and their respective roles, and the timelines under which the tasks are to be performed. The getting started section included articles, papers, presentations, sample policies flowcharts, and checklists to help an organization get the process started. The remainder of this document provides resources and processes to help ensure that a proper and complete assessment, analysis, containment, and response are in order.

A 5.24 Information security incident management planning and preparation

A.5.24 Information Security Incident Management Planning and Preparation – A linkage with Ancient Era

- **The Consequences of Negligence:** The Ramayana teaches lessons about the consequences of negligence and taking security lightly. The episode of Lord Hanuman brings the city of Lanka highlights the vulnerability of a seemingly impenetrable fortress. In cybersecurity, neglecting security measures or understanding the potential risks can lead to significant breaches and damage. The Ramayana serves as a reminder to remain vigilant and proactive in ensuring the security of digital systems and data.
- **Jayatu's Sacrifice and Incident Response:** Jatayu tries to rescue Mata Sita from King Ravan but is ultimately mortally wounded. His sacrifice

demonstrates His commitment to protecting the righteous cause which can be linked to incident response in cybersecurity. Incident response involves swiftly and effectively responding to cybersecurity incidents, such as data breaches or network compromises. Jatayu's sacrifice signifies the importance of prompt action, preparedness and resilience in mitigating the impact of cyber incidents and protecting valuable assets.

- **Lord Hanuman's Strategic Planning and Incident Response:** Lord Hanuman, meticulously plans and executes His mission to locate and rescue Mata Sita. Incident response involves developing a well-defined plan, identifying and containing cybersecurity incidents, and restoring normal operations. Lord Hanuman's strategic planning, agility, and quick thinking reflect the qualities required in effective incident response, emphasizing the importance of preparedness and swift action in mitigating cyber threats.
- **The Dangers of Impulsivity:** The Mahabharata portrays the consequences of impulsive actions, such as when Duryodhana's hasty decision led to disastrous outcomes. Similarly, in the digital world, impulsive behavior can lead to security breaches. Clicking on suspicious links, downloading unknown files, or sharing sensitive information without verification can expose individuals and organizations to cyber risks. Patience, Critical Thinking, and Exercising Caution are essential to maintain a secure cyber world.
- **Incident Response and Recovery:** The Mahabharata teaches us the importance of effective incident response and recovery strategies. Similarly, in the world of cybersecurity, having a well-defined plan for responding to security incidents and recovering from potential breaches is essential. This includes timely identification of incidents, containment of the damage, and swift recovery to ensure minimal disruption and loss.
- **Lord Krishna's Role in the Kurukshetra War:** Highlights the importance of Crisis Management and Incident Response in Cybersecurity. Organizations must establish effective incident response plans, conduct regular drills and simulations, and have well-defined processes to handle cybersecurity incidents promptly and efficiently. Develop effective Crisis Management and Incident Response capabilities in

Cybersecurity. During the Kurukshetra war, Lord Krishna played a key role in managing crisis and responding to critical situations. He provided guidance, resolved conflicts and made strategic decisions to ensure the Pandava's victory.

Control

The organization should plan and prepare for managing information security incidents by defining, establishing and communicating information security incident management processes, roles and responsibilities.

Purpose

To ensure quick, effective, consistent and orderly response to information security incidents, including communication on information security events.

Guidelines

Roles and Responsibilities

The organization should establish appropriate information security incident management processes. Roles and responsibilities to carry out the incident management procedures should be determined and effectively communicated to the relevant internal and external interested parties.

The following should be considered:

- Establishing a common method for reporting information security events including point of contact;
- Establishing an incident management process to provide the organization with capability for managing information security incidents including administration, documentation, detection, triage, prioritization, analysis, communication and coordinating interested parties;
- Establishing an incident response process to provide the organization with capability for assessing, responding to and learning from information security incidents;
- Only allowing competent personnel to handle the issues related to information security incidents within the organization. Such personnel

should be provided with procedure documentation and periodic training;

- Establishing a process to identify required training, certification and ongoing professional development for incident response personnel.

Incident Management Procedures

The objectives for information security incident management should be agreed with management and it should be ensured that those responsible for information security incident management understand the organization's priorities for handling information security incidents including resolution time frame based on potential consequences and severity. Incident management procedures should be implemented to meet these objectives and priorities. Management should ensure that an information security incident management plan is created considering different scenarios and procedures are developed and implemented for the following activities:

- Evaluation of information security events according to criteria for what constitutes an information security incident;
- Monitoring, detecting, classifying, analyzing and reporting of information security events and incidents, by human or automatic means;
- Managing information security incidents to conclusion, including response and escalation according to the type and the category of the incident, possible activation of crisis management and activation of continuity plans, controlled recovery from an incident and communication to internal and external interested parties;
- Coordination with internal and external interested parties such as authorities, external interest groups and forums, suppliers and clients;
- Logging incident management activities;
- Handling of evidence;
- Root cause analysis or post-mortem procedures;
- Identification of lessons learned and any improvements to the incident management procedures or information security controls in general that are required.

Reporting Procedures

Reporting procedures should include:

- Actions to be taken in case of an information security event;
- Use of incident forms to support personnel to perform all necessary actions when reporting information security incidents;
- Suitable feedback processes to ensure that those persons reporting information security events are notified, to the extent possible, of outcomes after the issue has been addressed and closed;
- Creation of incident reports.

Any external requirements on reporting of incidents to relevant interested parties within the defined time frame should be considered when implementing incident management procedures.

Other Information

Information security incidents can transcend organizational and national boundaries. To respond to such incidents, it is beneficial to coordinate, response and share information about these incidents with external organizations as appropriate. Detailed guidance on information security incident management is provided in the ISO/IEC 27035 series.

Preparation involves the identification of resources needed for incident handling and having trained individuals ready to respond, and developing and communicating a formal detection and reporting process. Effective, appropriate communication at all levels of an organization is essential for limiting the impact of security events. The policy can have the following components:

1. Statement of Management Commitment;
2. Purpose and Objectives of the Policy;
3. Scope of the Policy;
4. Definition of Computer Security Incidents and their consequences within the Context of the Organization;
5. Prioritization or Severity Ratings of Incidents;

6. Performance Measures;
7. Reporting and Contact Resources.

Organizational structure and delineation of roles, responsibilities, and levels of authority should include the authority of the incident response team to confiscate or disconnect equipment, monitor suspicious activity, and the requirements for reporting certain types of incidents.

Prioritization of incidents is an important element, as are escalation procedures. Interestingly, incident priorities differ between organizations depending on their culture and other policies, and there are certain types of incidents that one organization may tolerate while another may not. In addition, policies are required to outline permitted monitoring of system and network activities, and under specific circumstances. It is also advisable to have policies that specify who can access data relating to an incident under what circumstances and what auditing is required to document the access. Separate policies should be considered describing the data retention of non-incident-related log data and data preserved during the investigation of an incident. The term forensic is used to describe a characteristic of evidence that satisfies its suitability for admission as fact and its ability to persuade based on proof. Once you have decided what types of data you are going to maintain, it is prudent to take steps to preserve their integrity and document their location, format, and any other associated details. Documenting the location of important data sources, and outlining how these data can be accessed and interpreted, will help use the data efficiently when necessary. Marking the location of important data sources on a network topology map is a useful way to summarize this information graphically, facilitating evidence gathering during high-pressure incidents. This type of graphical view of data sources on a network can also be useful for finding gaps in coverage and developing better approaches to monitoring system activities and preserving existing data. In addition to preparing data sources for incidents, it is also important to be operationally prepared for incidents. This involves purchasing the necessary equipment and training at least one individual to handle incidents and use tools for recovering and examining data.

A. 5.25 Assessment of and decision on Information Security Events

Control

The organization should assess information security events and decide if they are to be categorized as information security incidents.

Purpose

To ensure effective categorization and prioritization of information security events.

Guidance

A categorization and prioritization scheme of information security incidents should be agreed for the identification of the consequences and priority of an incident. The scheme should include the criteria to categorize events as information security incidents. The point of contact should assess each information security event using the agreed scheme. Personnel responsible for coordinating and responding to information security incidents should perform the assessment and make a decision on information security events. Results of the assessment and decision should be recorded in detail for the purpose of future reference and verification.

Other Information

The ISO/IEC 27035 series provides further guidance on incident management.

The point of contact should assess each information security event using the agreed information security event and incident classification scale and decide whether the event should be classified as an information security incident. Classification and prioritization of incidents can help to identify the impact and extent of an incident. In cases where the organization has an Information Security Incident Response Team (ISIRT), the assessment and decision can be forwarded to the ISIRT for confirmation or reassessment. Results of the assessment and decision should be recorded in detail for the purpose of future reference and verification.

A formal management procedure and policy for incident response, including roles and responsibilities for each aspect of the response, is essential. Aspects to document include funding and cost models; analysis, containment, and recovery responsibilities; decision-making authority for notifications; legal and/or law enforcement involvement; forensic investigations; responsibility for after-incident debriefing; and policy, procedure, and process improvements. The primary goals of security incident response are to determine the cause and effect of incidents, including any sanctions which may be appropriate and any new preventive measures that may need to implement, as well as to restore the affected infrastructure to an operational state in a timely manner. The general activities or stages to an effective response and improvement are described in the table below.

Stages	**Activities**
Identification and Prioritization of incident, and performing a timely assessment of the situation	• Determine the scope/impact. The number of users affected, or a number of devices or segments of the network should be considered. Is a single user or account involved? • Assess the severity. What is the sensitivity of the data involved? What is the criticality of the service, or system, or application? What is the potential for damage or liability? Is there potential for harm? • Assess the urgency of the event. Is it an active problem, threat, or event-in-progress? Was the problem discovered after the fact? Is the intrusion “dormant”, or completed? Does this involve the use of an account rather than a system? Is this involving the safety or privacy of individuals?
Containment of the event	• Does the system need to be removed from the network? Does active memory need to be imaged or captured? • Are there user accounts or system-level accounts that need to be disabled or changed? Are there sessions that need to be dropped?

Stages	Activities
Investigation of what occurred and how (includes "root cause" analysis)	• An incident tracking record needs to be created. If deemed necessary, due to the scope, seriousness, or complexity of the incident, an incident notes log should also be created. • Gathering and preserving relevant information should be conducted by trained security personnel. • Evaluation of evidence commences. It may be a "forensic" caliber assessment, or a less comprehensive analysis, depending on the type of incident and organization's policies. Decisions with respect to the appropriate resolution and response should be discussed with decisionmakers and key stakeholders.
Response (Effect)	• Eradication of the problem and associated changes to the system need to be applied. This includes technical actions such as operating system and application software install new or changed firewall rules, custom configurations applied, databases created, backup data restored, accounts created and access controls applied. • Recovery to a fully operational state always follows appropriate testing or assurance of the system integrity and stability. Effective customer service includes regular communications with stakeholders who may be anxious for recovery. • Outcomes, including possible sanctions, should be determined. Sanctions, if they are deemed appropriate to the response, maybe internal, such as disciplinary action, or they may be external, such as referral to law enforcement.

Stages	Activities
Follow Up (Improvements)	• After incident debriefing. It is important to review the process and how it could have been better after an incident is closed. This is especially valid for new types of incidents, and particularly severe or costly incidents. • Consider policy and process changes. Were any procedures missing, communications unclear, or stakeholders that were not appropriately considered? Did the technical staff have appropriate resources (information as well as equipment) to perform the analysis and/or the recovery? • Consider controls improvements, leading to prevention. What can we do to ensure this does not happen again? What improvements can we implement to make our response and recovery timelier?

A.5.26 Response to Information Security Incidents

Control

Information security incidents should be responded to in accordance with the documented procedures.

Purpose

To ensure efficient and effective response to information security incidents.

Guidance

The organization should establish and communicate procedures on information security incident response to all relevant interested parties. Information security incidents should be responded to by a designated team with the required competency.

The response should include the following:

- Containment, if the consequences of the incident can spread, the systems affected by the incident;

- Collecting evidence as soon as possible after the occurrence;
- Escalation, as required including crisis management activities and possibly invoking business continuity plans;
- Ensuring that all involved response activities are properly logged for later analysis;
- Communicating the existence of the information security incident or any relevant details thereof to all relevant internal and external interested parties following the need-to-know principle;
- Coordinating with internal and external parties such as authorities, external interest groups and forums, suppliers and clients to improve response effectiveness and help to minimize consequences for other organizations;
- Once the incident has been successfully addressed, formally closing and recording it;
- Conducting information security forensic analysis, as required;
- Performing post-incident analysis to identify root cause. Ensure it is documented and communicated according to defined procedures;
- Identifying and managing information security vulnerabilities and weaknesses including those related to controls which have caused, contributed to or failed to prevent the incident.

Other Information

The ISO/IEC 27035 series provides further guidance on incident management.

It is always good to assign owners, be clear on actions and timescales, and as with everything for ISO 27001, retain the information for audit purposes. The individual placed in charge of dealing with the security event will be responsible for restoring a normal level of security.

In many cases, a more in-depth evaluation of the incident and circumstances is warranted. It may be to determine if confidential information was involved in, or stored on, the system in question. It may also be an effort to determine the vulnerability or action that enabled the incident to occur. This is typically where a forensic evaluation comes into play. Unfortunately, in some cases, an incident will involve or expose confidential information, such as Personally Identifiable Information (PII) that is protected by law, other policy, or local practices. When this occurs, there is often some sort of requirement in the response stage for notification to affected persons.

A.5.27 Learning from Information Security Incidents

Control

Knowledge gained from information security incidents should be used to strengthen and improve the information security controls.

Purpose

To reduce the likelihood or consequences of future incidents.

Guidance

The organization should establish procedures to quantify and monitor the types, volumes and costs of information security incidents. The information gained from the evaluation of information security incidents should be used to:

- Enhance the incident management plan including incident scenarios and procedures.
- Identify recurring or serious incidents and their causes to update the organization's information security risk assessment and determine and implement necessary additional controls to reduce the likelihood or consequences of future similar incidents. Mechanisms to enable that include collecting, quantifying and monitoring information about incident types, volumes and costs.
- Enhance user awareness and training by providing examples of what can happen, how to respond to such incidents and how to avoid them in the future.

Other Information

There should be mechanisms in place to enable the types, volumes, and costs of information security incidents to be quantified and monitored. The information gained from the evaluation of information security incidents should be used to identify recurring or high-impact incidents. The evaluation of information security incidents may indicate the need for enhanced or additional controls to limit the frequency, damage, and cost of future occurrences, or to be taken into account in the security policy review process. With due care of confidentiality aspects, anecdotes from actual information security incidents can be used in user awareness training as examples of what could happen, how to respond to such incidents, and how to avoid them in the future.

This is an important control, and your policy needs to demonstrate that knowledge gained from analyzing and resolving information security incidents will be used to help reduce the likelihood or impact of any future incidents. As part of the commitment to continuous service improvement, you should ensure that you learn from the lessons of any security incident to therefore help evolve and adapt the ISMS to meet the changing landscape that is worked in. Once an incident has been resolved, it should be placed into a status of review and learning, where the lead responder for that incident will discuss any changes required to the processes of the ISMS policies as a result. Any relevant recommendations should then be put to the ISMS Board for further discussion. Once the review and learning have been completed, updates have been made to the policies as required, the relevant staff must be notified and re-trained if required, and the cycle of information security awareness and education continues. The purpose of metrics here is to identify the major causes and sources of incidents, to measure the damage caused by incidents, and to observe trends in both. Some useful incident measures to consider are:

- The number of detected but unsuccessful intrusion attempts to compare with the number of successful ones.
- The damage/losses caused by disruptive incidents, to help develop plans for reducing outages and the staff hours spent responding to incidents.
- Reductions in downtime of the network or critical systems.
- Metrics for any special security initiatives such as alarms or monitoring of systems, to help in assessing their effectiveness.

A. 5.28 Collection of evidence

Control

The organization should establish and implement procedures for the identification, collection, acquisition and preservation of evidence related to information security events.

Purpose

To ensure a consistent and effective management of evidence related to information security incidents for the purposes of disciplinary and legal actions.

Guidance

Internal procedures should be developed and followed when dealing with evidence related to information security events for the purposes of disciplinary and legal actions. The requirements of different jurisdictions should be considered to maximize chances of admission across the relevant jurisdictions.

In general, these procedures for the management of evidence should provide instructions for the identification, collection, acquisition and preservation of evidence in accordance with different types of storage media, devices and status of devices. Evidence typically needs to be collected in a manner that is admissible in the appropriate national courts of law or another disciplinary forum. It should be possible to show that:

- Records are complete and have not been tampered with in any way;
- Copies of electronic evidence are probably identical to the originals;
- Any information system from which evidence has been gathered was operating correctly at the time the evidence was recorded.

Where available, certification or other relevant means of qualification of personnel and tools should be sought, so as to strengthen the value of the preserved evidence. Digital evidence can transcend organizational or jurisdictional boundaries. In such cases, it should be ensured that the organization is entitled to collect the required information as digital evidence.

Other Information

When an information security event is first detected, it is not always obvious whether or not the event will result in court action. Therefore, the danger exists that necessary evidence is destroyed intentionally or accidentally before the seriousness of the incident is realized. It is advisable to involve legal advice or law enforcement early in any contemplated legal action and take advice on the evidence required.

ISO/IEC 27037 provides definitions and guidelines for identification, collection, acquisition and preservation of digital evidence. The ISO/IEC 27050 series deals with electronic discovery, which involves the processing of electronically stored information as evidence.

Internal procedures should be developed and followed when dealing with the evidence for the purposes of disciplinary and legal action. In general, these procedures for evidence should provide processes of identification, collection, acquisition, and preservation of evidence in accordance with different types of media, devices, and status of devices. The procedures should take account of:

1. Chain of Custody;
2. Safety of Evidence;
3. Safety of Personnel;
4. Roles and Responsibilities of Personnel involved;
5. Competency of Personnel;
6. Documentation;
7. Briefing.

Where available, certification or other relevant means of qualification of personnel and tools should be sought, so as to strengthen the value of the preserved evidence. Forensic evidence may transcend organizational or jurisdictional boundaries. In such cases, it should be ensured that the organization is entitled to collect the required information as forensic evidence. The requirements of different jurisdictions should also be considered to maximize the chances of admission across the relevant jurisdictions.

The organization has to define and apply controls for the identification, collection, acquisition, and preservation of information, which can be used as evidence, especially if there are criminal or civil proceedings likely to happen from the incident. Where the organization suspects or knows that a security incident may result in legal or disciplinary action, they should carry out the collection of evidence carefully, ensure a good chain of custody and avoid any threat of being caught out by poor management. It's sensible to tie information security incident management clearly to disciplinary procedures too. Everyone should know to take precautions whilst also being clear on the consequences for those who fail to take it seriously.

Recommended Tools and Resources for Incident Handlers

- **Incident Handler Communications and Facilities:**
    - Contact information including after hours (on-call) information
    - Incident reporting mechanisms
    - Pagers and/or cell phones
    - Encryption software
    - Secure storage location/area
    - Work area
- **Incident Analysis Hardware and Software:**
    - Computer forensic workstations and/or backup devices, laptops
    - Spare devices
    - Blank media, cables, housings, converters, and write blockers
    - Portable printer
    - Packet sniffers and protocol analyzers
    - Computer forensic software
    - Removable media
    - Evidence gathering accessories
- **Incident Analysis Resources:**
    - Port lists
    - OS documentation
    - Network diagrams
    - Lists of critical assets
    - Baselines
    - Cryptographic hashes of critical files
- **Incident Mitigation Resources:**
    - Media
    - Security patches
    - Backup images

A.5.29 Information Security during Disruption

Organizations are vulnerable to a variety of natural and man-made emergencies, disasters, and hazards. Recognizing that not all events can be prevented and some risks may be deemed acceptable, proper planning is essential to maintain or restore services when an unexpected or unavoidable event disrupts normal operations. Business Continuity Planning includes the identification of vulnerabilities, priorities, dependencies, and measures for developing plans to facilitate continuity and recovery before, during, and after such a disruption. Comprehensive business continuity plans are designed and implemented to ensure continuity of operations under abnormal conditions. Plans promote the readiness of organizations for rapid recovery in the face of adverse events or conditions, minimize the impact of such circumstances, and provide means to facilitate functioning during and after emergencies. The development process is usually based on a single framework, and involves key individuals in the functional areas. Plans are based on a risk assessment and business impact analysis and include a process for regular maintenance, including training, testing/drills, and updates. In addition, information security and privacy should be integrated within plans.

Measures must be taken to ensure the integrity, security, accuracy, and privacy of all systems and data. Such measures include adherence to all governmental regulations and directives. As major disasters have brought acute awareness to the organization, the management recognizes the need for extensive planning and coordination to assure preparedness by developing, testing, and refining plans to handle all types of disruptions to normal services. Use the following steps to get started with a business continuity plan:

- Obtain commitment and authority from organization leadership. High-level support is essential for building the cross-functional teams that are needed to prepare and deploy the plan.
- Establish a planning team for each business unit.
- Perform a risk assessment in each unit.
- Identify critical resources such as People, Places, Systems, Other, etc.
- Determine continuity and recovery strategies within each unit.
- Train students, faculty, and staff on what to do in case of a disaster.

- Test system recovery procedures. Generate scenarios and simulate them with tabletop exercises.
- Create a communication plan.
- Review the business continuity plan annually.

A well-prepared organization should develop a plan addressing all key services and their administration, delivery, and support. The organization should be considering or embarking on the development of a plan, including commitments, procedures, technologies, resources, methodologies, and communications essential to planning development, support, and deployment.

A.5.29 Information Security During Disruption – A linkage with Ancient Era

The Kurukshetra War – A legendary battle

- **Physical Security Measures:** During ancient wars like the Kurukshetra War, physical security of information was crucial. Important messages, documents or artifacts would have been physically guarded, often by trusted individuals or a select group of warriors. Access to sensitive information would have been restricted to those with clearance.
- **Cipher Systems:** While the ancient world didn't have modern encryption techniques, they did employ various cipher systems. These included simple substitution ciphers or more complex methods like transposition ciphers. These were used to encode messages, making them unintelligible to anyone who intercepted them without the corresponding key.
- **Limited Communication Channels:** Communication channels during the Kurukshetra War were limited compared to today's standards. Messengers on foot or horseback were likely the primary means of communication. These messengers would have been selected for their trustworthiness and often traveled through less frequented routes to avoid interception.
- **Verbal Communication:** In situations where written communication was risky, verbal communication would have been relied upon. However, even verbal communication would have been cautious, with sensitive information only shared with those deemed trustworthy.

- **Strategic Disinformation:** Just as in modern warfare, disinformation might have been strategically. False messages or misleading information could have been planted to confuse or mislead the enemy. This tactic is evident in the various strategies employed by both sides in the Mahabharata.
- **Importance of Trust and Loyalty:** Ultimately, trust and loyalty, were perhaps the most critical components of information security during ancient wars warriors, advisors, and messengers needed to be fiercely loyal to their leaders and their cause to ensure that sensitive information remained secure.

Control

The organization should plan how to maintain information security at an appropriate level during disruption.

Purpose

To protect information and other associated assets during disruption.

Guidance

The organization should determine its requirements for adapting information security controls during disruption. Information security requirements should be included in the business continuity management processes. Plans should be developed, implemented, tested, reviewed and evaluated to maintain or restore the security of information of critical business processes following interruption or failure. Security of information should be restored at the required level and in the required time frames. According to the information security continuity requirements, the organization should establish, document, implement and maintain:

- Information security controls, supporting systems and tools within business continuity and ICT continuity plans;
- Processes, procedures and implement changes to maintain existing information security controls during an adverse situation;

Compensating controls for information security controls that cannot be maintained during disruption.

Other Information

In the context of business continuity and ICT continuity planning, it can be necessary to adapt the information security requirements depending on the type of disruption, compared to normal operational conditions. As part of the business impact analysis and risk assessment performed within business continuity management, the consequences of loss of confidentiality and integrity of information should be considered and prioritized in addition to the need for maintaining availability. Information on business continuity management systems can be found in ISO 22301 and ISO 22313. Further guidance on business impact analysis (BIA) can be found in ISO/TS 22317.

The objective of this control is information security continuity should be embedded in the organization's business continuity management systems. The organization should determine its requirements for information security and the continuity of information security management in adverse situations. An organization should determine whether the continuity of information security is captured within the business continuity management process or within the disaster recovery management process. Information security requirements should be determined when planning for business continuity and disaster recovery. In the absence of formal business continuity and disaster recovery planning, information security management should assume that information security requirements remain the same in adverse situations, compared to normal operational conditions. Alternatively, an organization could perform a business impact analysis for information security aspects to determine the information security requirements applicable to adverse situations. In order to reduce the time and effort of an 'additional' business impact analysis for information security, it is recommended to capture information security aspects within the normal business continuity management or disaster recovery management business impact analysis. This implies that the information security continuity requirements are explicitly formulated in the business continuity management or disaster recovery management processes.

The organization should establish, document, implement and maintain processes, procedures, and controls to ensure the required level of continuity for information security during an adverse situation. An organization should ensure that:

1. An adequate management structure is in place to prepare for, mitigate and respond to a disruptive event using personnel with the necessary authority, experience and competence;
2. Incident response personnel with the necessary responsibility, authority, and competence to manage an incident and maintain information security are nominated;
3. Documented plans, response, and recovery procedures are developed and approved, detailing how the organization will manage a disruptive event and will maintain its information security to a predetermined level, based on management-approved information security continuity objectives.

Within the context of business continuity or disaster recovery, specific processes and procedures may have been defined. Information that is handled within these processes and procedures or within dedicated information systems to support them should be protected. Therefore, an organization should involve information security specialists when establishing, implementing, and maintaining business continuity or disaster recovery processes and procedures. Information security controls that have been implemented should continue to operate during an adverse situation. If security controls are not able to continue to secure information, other controls should be established, implemented, and maintained to maintain an acceptable level of information security.

The organization should verify the established and implemented information security continuity controls at regular intervals in order to ensure that they are valid and effective during adverse situations. Organizational, technical, procedural, and process changes, whether in an operational or continuity context, can lead to changes in information security continuity requirements. In such cases, the continuity of processes, procedures, and controls for information security should be reviewed against these changed requirements. Organizations should verify their information security management continuity by:

1. Exercising and testing the functionality of information security

continuity processes, procedures, and controls to ensure that they are consistent with the information security continuity objectives;

2. Exercising and testing the knowledge and routine to operate information security continuity processes, procedures, and controls to ensure that their performance is consistent with the information security continuity objectives;
3. Reviewing the validity and effectiveness of information security continuity measures when information systems, information security processes, procedures, and controls or business continuity management/disaster recovery management processes and solutions change.

The verification of information security continuity controls is different from general information security testing and verification and should be performed outside the testing of changes. If possible, it is preferable to integrate verification of information security continuity controls with the organization's business continuity or disaster recovery tests.

The organization must determine its requirements for information security and the continuity of information security management in adverse situations. The best ISMS will already have broader Annex A controls that mitigate against a need to implement a disaster recovery process or business continuity plan. Despite that effort, more significant disruptive incidents may still happen so planning for them is important. Having considered the various events and scenarios that need to be planned for, the organization can then document the plan in whatever detail is required to demonstrate it understands those issues and the steps required to address them. The organization needs to establish, document, implement and maintain processes, procedures, and controls to ensure the required level of continuity for information security during a disruptive situation. Once requirements have been identified, the organization must implement policies, procedures, and other physical or technical controls that are adequate and proportionate in order to meet those requirements. Description of the responsibilities, activities, owners, timescales, mitigating work to be undertaken. A management structure and relevant escalation trigger points should be identified to ensure that if and when an event increases in severity the relevant escalation to the appropriate authority is made effectively and in a timely manner.

It should also be made clear when there is a return to business as usual and any BCP processes stop. The organization must verify the established and implemented information security continuity controls at regular intervals in order to ensure that they are valid and effective during these situations. The controls implemented for information security continuity must be tested, reviewed, and evaluated periodically to ensure they are maintained against changes in the business, technologies, and risk levels. The auditor will want to see that there is evidence of; periodic testing of plans and controls; logs of plan invocations and the actions taken through to resolution and lessons learned, and periodic review and change management to ensure that plans are maintained against change.

Business Continuity Plans are an integral part of all organized information security activities. The plans are a well-reasoned, step-by-step approach to determine how, when, where, who, and what will be needed should a disruption of normal operations occur and the plan must address the continuity of security and privacy under less-than-ideal circumstances. Below are some references to further describe the intent of such plans.

Planning Information Security Continuity: Information security must be an integral part/element of all organizational policies, procedures, and practices including business continuity management system. Business continuity plans must recognize the need to strictly adhere to organizational security and privacy policies and regulations, even while the organization is functioning during extraordinary conditions. Good business continuity plans should be built in accordance with strong organizational security and privacy policies as well as state and federal regulations. This will allow important security and privacy practices to continue to be practiced, even during and after a disruptive event. Such practices should be elements of all planning, implementation, testing, and evaluation efforts.

Organization Commitment: Obtain Commitment and Authority from Organization Leadership: A plan should begin with an organization-wide commitment to develop, staff, and support efforts that will be activated when circumstances clearly indicate that business has been or will be disrupted for more than a brief or acceptable time. A plan is not intended to address routine disruptions such as planned or routine maintenance. On the contrary, well-developed and tested plans are essential during and after catastrophic events that preclude the resumption of normal business functioning within well-defined time frames. Begin the planning process by obtaining the buy-in from the executive level of the organization. This high-level mandate establishes the ability, authority, and support to build the cross-functional teams needed for the preparation and the deployment of the plan, facilities and resources, necessary redundancy of services and resources, and commitment from units for ongoing participation. Organizational support for business continuity should include funding for plan development, staffing, training, testing, updating, deployment, and transitioning to normal operations. Developing a plan forces priorities to be identified and implemented and identifies which risks are acceptable and which must be addressed. And when possible, additional components of a plan should be implemented.

Framework and Planning Cycle: Having a framework assures a defined structure for the planning process, the development of a plan, priorities, and dependencies within a plan, testing of a plan, procedures for maintaining and updating the plan, and responsibilities of individuals and units before, during, and after the activation of a business continuity plan. Choose a framework to be used as the basis for the plan which includes: Create the plan, Train the participants, Perform drills, Do post mortems on the drills, Review the plan, Revise the plan

Who Should be Involved and in What Role – Establish a Planning Team for Each Business Unit: At its core, business continuity management is a well-coordinated, well-tested, cross functional effort. Representatives from each functional area or business unit are responsible for the identification, prioritization, documentation, and updating of their aspects of the plans, covered services, and facilities. Remember to include academic and their support areas in the list of units to be included. Members of a business continuity team are responsible for the compilation and integration of all input from each functional area into the overall plan. Team coordinators are responsible for the overall coordination of the plan, its deployment, and its refinement. They must be good, dependable managers with strong leadership and problem-solving skills, capable of keeping the effort organized according to procedures, yet able to be creative when things don't go as planned.

Scope of the Plan: A Business Continuity Plan cannot be unlimited in scope, so it's important to define the comprehensiveness of the plan:

whether it covers contingencies for all major potential threats or a subset of these disruptions. Defining the scope does not negate the concept that BCP should broadly account for any business disruption. It's a practical measure acknowledging that the continuity planning process is impacted by budgetary restraints.

Business Continuity and Risk Management - Perform a Risk Assessment in Each Unit: It is important to determine the impact of risks on the functioning of the organization under normal operating conditions as well as under the extraordinary conditions during which a business continuity plan will be activated. In Business Continuity Management, it is important to determine what activities are vulnerable under what conditions, what measures should be taken to reduce risk and at what cost, what risks are acceptable, and what measures should be taken to facilitate functioning during and immediately after incidents that disrupt normal operations of the organization.

Business Impact Analysis - Identify Critical Resources: A Business Impact Analysis (BIA) identifies the organization's critical services and resources and the Maximum Tolerable Downtime (MTD) for these critical services. The BIA must identify vulnerabilities, threats, and risks and prioritize the order of events for the restoration of key business processes. The BIA is distinguished from Risk Assessment in that it defines the window of time available to restore services. First determine the organization's key functions and resources that must be continuously available, during and immediately after major disruptive events. Business units must identify their key resources, prioritize them, and assess the risks to determine how long these key resources can be unavailable and factors that impact that duration. Each unit must perform a risk assessment to identify measures to be taken to reduce risks as well as identify acceptable risks where the cost of mitigation is higher than the cost of the consequence. Each unit must also assess the priority of resources and services. This prioritization should be identified by the unit itself. Alternate resources may be identified for use should the primary resources become unavailable or inaccessible. The results of the business impact analysis are input to the development of the business continuity plan.

Documentation: All required information pertaining to the plan, key resources, facilities, management structure, priorities/dependencies, documentation, and personnel should be kept in secure locations. This information should also be made available to key personnel who will be responsible for coordinating continuity efforts during and after the incident or event. Documentation will assist others in performing the required tasks. Emergency templates for all functions included in the plan should include a summary of business impact analysis data, required resources for the application to run, dependencies on other applications and resources, vendor contacts, people who should be kept apprised of the status of the recovery, and the list of key individuals and how to reach them.

Contact Information: The inability to contact key team members can hamper the most well-designed plan. Contact information must include all means for reaching people at all times. This list must include alternate people should a key individual be unavailable or unreachable. Contact information must be kept current at all times and include alternative means such as home and cell phone numbers, alternate email addresses, and social networking, text, and Twitter contact information.

Checklists: Checklists should be created to document the inventory of everything kept in designated physical, remote, virtual, and/or cloud locations for coordinating efforts, contact information, documentation, resources/systems, backup power, communications equipment, food, water, vendor contacts, etc.

Keep Track of Activities: While testing a plan or during an actual deployment, remember to keep track of who is doing what. This can be done via conference calls, texting, alternative websites, and actual staff reporting in to track all activities as well as make sure that people are safe and getting sufficient food, water, and rest. Communication may be difficult, but it is essential.

Personnel: People are the key elements of the plan. Being able to communicate during a crisis may not be easy due to loss or overloading of infrastructure. Continuity plan leaders or coordinators should be good leaders and managers, capable of keeping the effort organized according to procedures, yet able to be creative when things don't go as planned. Have at least two people scheduled at all times as team coordinators for the continuity effort. Never have a single point of failure! Team coordinators should be involved in the monthly assessment of the resources and facilities.

Establish a substitution procedure for team coordinators should one be unavailable due to schedule conflicts, illness, or vacations. Substitution should be communicated carefully to avoid confusion. Because people are key, it is important to care for their needs as the organization is heavily dependent on their skills and ability to perform.

Communication: Being able to communicate during a crisis is essential. Stakeholders such as employees, customers, and vendors need to know what is happening as well as what they can/cannot do. Relatives of employees want to know about the safety of individuals in the organization. Employees involved in continuity need to know how, when, and where they should report. Continuity plan personnel need to communicate with campus executives on the status of services and resources. Everyone needs to know what they should/should not do and when circumstances are expected to change. Determine alternative means for communication. "Normal" communication means and data feeds for supplying such information such as phone numbers may not be available. Plans should include alternative technologies for communicating and the availability of key data. Social networking sites should be considered as an alternative means of communication, but not necessarily as a primary method. Power losses may result in disruption of services. Other failures have equally disruptive consequences. During 9/11 in New York City, dial tone was lost, cell service was spotty and overloaded, and most internet access was disrupted due to the loss of the carriers. No services were maintained during Hurricane Katrina. Super Storm Sandy presented major disruptions to infrastructure (electricity, natural gas, communications, roads), routine and emergency services, life/safety services, housing, deliveries (food/water/fuel), and facilities. Many of its impacts are still being experienced today. Identify alternative means for contacting individuals needed to manage the process and to provide continuity services. Consider digital signage, landlines, or speakers in locations where cell signals are weak/unavailable, CATV, text messaging, social media, and new technologies as they proliferate in the classroom, residential, administrative, and service buildings. People need to know what the emergency is, how to react, and what to expect in order to prevent a bad situation from becoming worse. No information, or worse, bad information can transition a bad situation into a crisis. Emergency responders must be contacted, know if/when they are needed, what roles they will play, and where you want them to perform tasks. Remember, people are the key component to business continuity, and communication with and among them is absolutely necessary. Communication is also a life/safety concern for the community, not just for first responders. Timely consistent communications are essential before, during, or after natural disasters, weather/natural disasters, lockdowns, and any event that impacts the life/safety of individuals and the availability of services and facilities. It is also important to be able to determine who is ok after an incident. A preset, known means for communication is essential.

Training, Maintaining, and Re-assessing Business Continuity Plans: Business continuity plans must include managed, organized procedures for the development of procedures to assure the continuity of operations under extraordinary circumstances including the maintenance of measures to assure the privacy and security of its information resources. It includes training individuals with responsibilities for the plan's implementation, having regular reviews and updates to keep the plan correct, and testing the plan to evaluate its feasibility, thoroughness, and effectiveness even under the most unusual of circumstances while maintaining the privacy and security of its information resources. Training of all plan coordinators and key personnel should take place at least once a year. Training should include: The process, expectations of individuals, applications and resources, priorities, contact information and methods, procedures, documentation, facilities, and schedules. At least once a year a drill should be conducted. This can be a table-top exercise or a "live" test. At the conclusion of the drill, a review of responses and actions should be completed to determine the next steps such as modifications to the plan, additional training, and further testing. In addition to drills to test the plan, its components/procedures, and its people, it is critical to test all methods of emergency communication with members of the organizations. Organizations should have multiple methods for contacting members in the event of an emergency or urgent change in regular functions. Employees, customers, contractors, and suppliers should be enrolled in an emergency communication alert list, including all cell phones which would likely be used for text messages. Data collected should not be limited to campus supplied phones and email addresses. All information collected will only be used in the event of an emergency and should not be shared outside the organization. Everyone should be prompted at least semi-annually to review/update their data. Drills should be scheduled at least quarterly to test this emergency alert system. Events in the last year can demonstrate the necessity for such emergency alert systems using personal communication devices as well as other technologies.

Document and Review Activities - Review the Business Continuity Plan Annually: Business Continuity plans are living documents that must change and evolve to reflect organizational changes. To be effective, plans must be continually revised and improved to be in alignment with the current environment. A review should be conducted at least annually to document all organizational changes that will impact the plan including:

- Information gleaned from recent incidents;
- Information gleaned from plan training and testing;
- Changes in the Business Impact Analysis;
- Implementation of new equipment and technology;
- Organizational restructuring;
- Major additions or changes to facilities.

A.5.30 ICT Readiness for Business Continuity

Information and Communication Technology (ICT) has become an integral part of many of the activities which are elements of the critical infrastructures in all organizational sectors, whether public, private or voluntary. The proliferation of the Internet and other electronic networking services, and today's capabilities of systems and applications, has also meant that organizations have become ever more reliant on reliable, safe and secure ICT infrastructures. Meanwhile, the need for business continuity, including incident preparedness, disaster recovery planning, and emergency response and management, has been recognized. Failures of ICT services, including the occurrence of security issues such as systems intrusion and malware infections, will impact the continuity of business operations. Thus, managing ICT and related continuity and other security aspects form a key part of business continuity requirements. Furthermore, in the majority of cases, the critical business functions that require business continuity are usually dependent upon ICT. This dependence means that disruptions to ICT can constitute strategic risks to the reputation of the organization and its ability to operate. ICT readiness is an essential component for many organizations in the implementation of business continuity and information security. It is critical to develop and implement a readiness plan for ICT services to help ensure business continuity. As a result, effective business continuity is frequently dependent upon effective ICT readiness to ensure that the organization's objectives can continue to be met in times of disruptions. This is particularly important as the consequences of disruptions to ICT often have the added complication of being invisible and/or difficult to detect. In order for an organization to achieve ICT Readiness for Business Continuity, it needs to put in place a systematic process to prevent, predict and manage ICT disruption and incidents which have the potential to disrupt ICT services.

A.5.30 ICT Readiness for Business Continuity – A linkage with Ancient Era

The Kurukshetra War – The Importance of Preparedness.

Just as Arjuna, prepared himself for the battle, we must be proactive in fortifying our digital defenses.

- **Communication Infrastructure:** In modern Business Continuity

Planning, having robust communication infrastructure is vital. Similarly, in ancient warfare, communication channels were established through means and these channels ensured that critical information could be transmitted swiftly to maintain strategic coordination.

- **Backup Systems:** ICT readiness involves having backup systems in place to ensure continuity in the event of system failures or disruptions. In the Kurukshetra War, warriors were often deployed in formations, with backups and reserves strategically positioned to fill gaps or replace fallen soldiers. This ensured the continuity of battle strategies despite losses.
- **Data Security and Encryption:** Just as modern businesses employ encryption and other security measures to protect sensitive data, ancient civilizations utilized encryption techniques to safeguard messages during warfare. Although the methods were rudimentary compared to modern encryption algorithms, the principle of encoding information to prevent unauthorized access remains similar.
- **Redundancy Planning:** Modern ICT readiness often involves redundancy planning, where multiple systems or facilities are in place to ensure continuity of operations. Similarly, in the Kurukshetra War, military leaders often devised backup plans and alternative strategies to adapt to changing battlefield conditions or unforeseen events.
- **Risk Assessment and Mitigation:** ICT readiness includes assessing potential risks to business operations and implementing measures to mitigate them. Similarly, military commanders in ancient times would have assessed various risks and formulated strategies to minimize vulnerabilities and maximize chances of success.
- **Training and Preparedness:** Just as employees in modern businesses undergo training for disaster response and business continuity procedures, warriors in ancient civilizations underwent rigorous training in combat techniques, strategy, and tactics. This training ensured that they were prepared to execute their roles effectively even in chaotic and challenging circumstances.
- **Adaptability and Flexibility:** ICT readiness emphasizes the importance of adaptability and flexibility to respond to unexpected disruptions. Similarly, in the Kurukshetra War, military leaders had to adapt their

strategies based on evolving battlefield conditions, unexpected maneuvers by the enemy, or changes in alliances.

Control

ICT readiness should be planned, implemented, maintained and tested based on business continuity objectives and ICT continuity requirements.

Purpose

To ensure the availability of the organization's information and other associated assets during disruption.

Guidance

ICT readiness for business continuity is an important component in business continuity management and information security management to ensure that the organization's objectives can continue to be met during disruption. The ICT continuity requirements are the outcome of the business impact analysis (BIA). The BIA process should use impact types and criteria to assess the impacts overtime resulting from the disruption of business activities that deliver products and services. The magnitude and duration of the resulting impact should be used to identify prioritized activities which should be assigned a Recovery Time Objective (RTO). The BIA should then determine which resources are needed to support prioritized activities. An RTO should also be specified for these resources. A subset of these resources should include ICT services.

The BIA involving ICT services can be expanded to define performance and capacity requirements of ICT systems and Recovery Point Objectives (RPO) of information required to support activities during disruption. Based on the outputs from the BIA and risk assessment involving ICT services, the organization should identify and select ICT continuity strategies that consider options for before, during and after disruption.

The business continuity strategies can comprise one or more solutions. Based on the strategies, plans should be developed, implemented and tested to meet the required availability level of ICT services and in the required time frames following interruption to, or failure of, critical processes. The organization should ensure that:

- An adequate organizational structure is in place to prepare for, mitigate and respond to a disruption supported by personnel with the necessary responsibility, authority and competence.

- ICT continuity plans, including response and recovery procedures detailing how the organization is planning to manage an ICT service disruption, are:
    - Regularly evaluated through exercises and tests;
    - Approved by management;
- ICT continuity plans include the following ICT continuity information:
    - Performance and capacity specifications to meet the business continuity requirements and objectives as specified in the BIA;
    - RTO of each prioritized ICT service and the procedures for restoring those components;
    - RPO of the prioritized ICT resources defined as information and the procedures for restoring the information.

Other Information

Managing ICT continuity forms a key part of business continuity requirements concerning availability to be able to:

- Respond and recover from disruption to ICT services regardless of the cause.
- Ensure continuity of prioritized activities are supported by the required ICT services.
- Respond before a disruption to ICT services occurs, and upon detection of at least one incident that can result in a disruption to ICT services.

Further guidance on ICT readiness for business continuity can be found in ISO/IEC 27031. Further guidance on business continuity management systems can be found in ISO 22301 and ISO 22313. Further guidance on BIA can be found in ISO/TS 22317.

"ICT Readiness for Business Continuity" defines the business continuity management requirements for information security in much more specific terms. The control includes the availability requirements based on the results of the Business Impact Analysis (BIA). Two key elements of disaster recovery are addressed. When assessing the Business Impact Analysis, the following points must be considered:

- **Recovery Time Objective (RTO)** – How long can a business process/ system be down? The Recovery Time Objective is the time taken from the moment of damage until business processes are fully restored (recovery of: Infrastructure – Data – Reprocessing of data – Resumption of activities) may elapse. The time period can vary from 0 minutes (systems must be available immediately) to several days (in some cases weeks).
- **Recovery Point Objective (RPO)** – How much data loss can be accepted? The Recovery Point Objective is the time period between two backups, i.e., how much data/transactions can be lost between the last backup and the system failure. If no data loss is acceptable, the RPO is 0 seconds.

Based on the results of the BIA, contingency strategies are to be defined for the ICT resources with contingency options before during and after interruptions. Based on these strategies, contingency plans are to be developed, implemented and tested. In doing so, it is required that the organization implement an adequate organizational structure to deal with business interruptions, have ICT contingency plans that are regularly tested and approved by management, have ICT plans that include performance and capacity specifications to meet the requirements from the BIA, as well as RTOs and RPOs.

ICT Readiness for Business Continuity can be achieved by:

- **Protect** - Protecting the ICT environment from environmental failures, hardware failures, operations errors, malicious attack and natural disasters is critical to maintaining the desired levels of system availability for an organization.
- **Detect** - Detecting incidents at the earliest opportunity minimizes the impact to services, reduces the recovery efforts and preserves the quality of service.
- **React** - Reacting to an incident in the most appropriate manner leads to a more efficient recovery and minimizes any downtime. Reacting poorly can result in a minor incident escalating into something more serious.

- **Recover** - Identifying and implementing the appropriate recovery strategy will ensure the timely resumption of services and maintain the integrity of data. Understanding the recovery priorities allows the most critical services to be reinstated first. Services of a less-critical nature may be reinstated at a later time or, in some circumstances, not at all.
- **Operate** - Operating in disaster recovery mode until return to normal is possible may require some time and necessitate "scaling up" disaster recovery operations to support increasing business volumes that need to be serviced over time.
- **Return** - Devising a strategy for every IT continuity plan allows an organization to migrate back from disaster recovery mode to a position in which it can support normal business.

ICT Readiness for Business Continuity supports Business Continuity Management by ensuring that the ICT services are as resilient as appropriate and can be recovered to pre-determined levels within timescales required and agreed by the organization. This control enables an organization to measure its ICT continuity, security and hence readiness to survive a disaster in a consistent and recognized manner. ICT readiness encompasses preparing the organization's ICT, plus the associated processes and people, against unforeseeable events that could change the risk environment and impact ICT and business continuity. It also helps in leveraging and streamlining resources among business continuity, disaster recovery, emergency response and ICT security incident response and management activities. ICT readiness reduces the impact of information security incidents on the organization. ICT readiness is important for business continuity purposes because:

- ICT is prevalent and many organizations are highly dependent on ICT supporting critical business processes;
- ICT also supports incident, business continuity, disaster and emergency response, and related management processes;
- Business continuity planning is incomplete without adequately considering and protecting ICT availability and continuity.

Processes and procedures created through control should be drafted following a thorough BIA, that considers how an organization needs to react when experiencing operational disruption. A BIA should make use of differing impact types and organization-specific variables to gauge how business continuity will be affected, should any or all products and services be rendered unavailable or inoperable, due to any level of disruption. Organizations should use two key variables to formulate an agreed-upon RTO, that sets clear goals for resumption of normal operations:

- The magnitude of the disruption
- The type of disruption experienced

Within their BIA, organizations should be able to specify precisely what ICT services and functions are required to achieve recovery, including individual performance and capacity requirements. Organizations should undergo a risk assessment that evaluates their ICT systems and forms the basis of an ICT continuity strategy (or strategies) that bolsters recovery prior to, during and following a period of disruption. Once a strategy has been agreed, specific processes and plans should be put in place to ensure that ICT services are resilient and adequate enough to contribute towards recovery of critical processes and systems, before, during and after disruption. Within the scope of ICT continuity plans, it outlines three main guidance points:

- ICT incidents often require quick decisions to be made relating to information security by senior members of staff, in order to expedite recovery.
- Organizations need to maintain a robust chain of command that includes competent individuals with the ability to make authoritative decisions on technical matters related to business continuity and RTO adherence.
- Organizational structures need to be up to date and widely communicated, to facilitate adequate communication and speed up recovery times.

ICT continuity plans should be given a great deal of attention, including regular testing and evaluations, and approval by senior management. Organizations should conduct test runs to gauge their effectiveness, and measure key metrics such as response and resolution times. ICT continuity plans should contain the following information:

- Performance and capacity requirements of any systems or processes used in recovery efforts;
- A clear RTO for each ICT service in question, and how the organization aims to restore them;
- A recovery point objective (RPO) is designated for each ICT resource, and procedures are created that ensure information is able to be restored.

The benefits of ICT readiness for business continuity:

- Understands the risks to continuity of ICT services and their vulnerabilities;
- Identifies the potential impacts of disruption to ICT services;
- Encourages improved collaboration between its business managers and its ICT service providers;
- Develops and enhances competence in its ICT staff by demonstrating credible responses through exercising ICT continuity plans and testing IRBC arrangements;
- Provides assurance to top management that it can depend upon predetermined levels of ICT services and receive adequate support and communications in the event of a disruption;
- Provides assurance to top management that information security is properly preserved, ensuring adherence to information security policies;
- Provides additional confidence in the business continuity strategy through linking investment in IT solutions to business needs and ensuring that ICT services are protected at an appropriate level given their importance to the organization.

A.5.31 Legal, Statutory, Regulatory and Contractual Requirements

Organizations are subject to numerous laws, regulations, and contractual obligations that specify requirements related to the appropriate management and protection of diverse information sets. Understanding and maintaining compliance with these different requirements is sometimes a difficult road. Laws, regulations and contractual requirements form a large part of an organization's information security responsibilities. Organizations should have a clear understanding of their obligations at any one time and be prepared to adapt their information security practices in accordance with their role as a responsible data handler. The path to establishing compliance takes a complete look at the areas in which your organization has responsibilities, whether legal, regulatory, contractual, or self-imposed. Important elements to consider when developing a plan for compliance include the following:

- Awareness of relevant regulations/laws;
- Awareness of relevant policies;
- Awareness of relevant contractual agreements;
- Awareness of relevant standards or best practices;
- Management of organizational records;
- Awareness of how records are managed by your organization;
- Approach to complying with each item;
- Awareness of internal and/or external audit activities

Organizations should keep in mind their legal, statutory, regulatory and contractual requirements when:

- Drafting and/or amending their information security procedures and internal policy documents;
- Designing, amending or implementing information security controls;
- Categorizing information when considering their broader information security requirements, either for organizational purposes or related to their relationships with a third party;
- Undergoing risk assessments relating to information security

activities, including internal roles and responsibilities relating to an organizational structure;

- Establishing the nature of a supplier relationship, and their contractual obligations throughout the supply of products and services.

A.5.31 Legal, Statutory, Regulatory and Contractual Requirements – A linkage with Ancient Era

The Information Technology (IT Act) - Modern legal framework that governs various aspects of Electronic Transactions, Cybersecurity and Digital Governance in India.

- **Legal Recognition of Electronic Records:** The IT Act provides legal recognition to Electronic Records and Digital Signatures. Similarly, in the Ramayana, there are instances where written messages or agreements are considered legally binding. For example, the exile of Lord Ram is triggered by a promise made by King Dasharatha to Queen Kaikeyi, which is recorded in writing and considered irrevocable.
- **Cybersecurity and Data Protection:** The IT Act includes provisions for safeguarding sensitive personal data and protecting against cybercrimes. In the Ramayana, there are parallels where characters take precautions to protect sensitive information. For instance, Lord Hanuman discreetly enters Lanka to gather intelligence about Mata Sita's whereabouts, ensuring that his mission remains covert and his findings are protected from interception.
- **Electronic Commerce and Contracts:** The IT Act facilitates electronic commerce by providing legal validity to electronic contracts and transactions. Similarly, in the Ramayana, there are instances where agreements and contracts are made verbally or in writing, establishing legal obligations between parties. For example, when Lord Ram allies with various tribes and kingdoms to build an army to rescue Mata Sita, these alliances are akin to contractual agreements for mutual cooperation.
- **Authentication and Digital Signatures:** The IT Act recognizes digital signatures as a means of authentication in electronic transactions. In the Ramayana, characters often use symbols, tokens, or seals as a form of authentication or identification. For instance, Lord Ram presents

His signet ring to Lord Hanuman as a token of His authority and trust when sending him on a mission to find Mata Sita.

- **Electronic Evidence and Legal Proceedings:** The IT Act governs the admissibility of electronic evidence in legal proceedings. Similarly, in the Ramayana, there are instances where verbal testimony, written records, or divine revelations serve as evidence in legal disputes or trials. For example, when Mata Sita undergoes the trial by fire (Agni Pariksha) to prove Her chastity, it serves as evidence of Her purity and fidelity to Lord Ram.

Control

Legal, statutory, regulatory and contractual requirements relevant to information security and the organization's approach to meet these requirements should be identified, documented and kept up to date.

Purpose

To ensure compliance with legal, statutory, regulatory and contractual requirements related to information security.

Guidance

General

External requirements including legal, statutory, regulatory or contractual requirements should be taken into consideration when:

- Developing information security policies and procedures;
- Designing, implementing or changing information security controls;
- Classifying information and other associated assets as part of the process for setting information security requirements for internal needs or for supplier agreements.
- Performing information security risk assessments and determining information security risk treatment activities.
- Determining processes along with related roles and responsibilities relating to information security.
- Determining suppliers' contractual requirements relevant to the organization and the scope of supply of products and services.

Legislation and Regulations

The organization should:

- Identify all legislation and regulations relevant to the organization's information security in order to be aware of the requirements for their type of business;
- Take into consideration compliance in all relevant countries, if the organization:
    - Conducts business in other countries;
    - Uses products and services from other countries where laws and regulations can affect the organization;
    - Transfers information across jurisdictional borders where laws and regulations can affect the organization;
- Review the identified legislation and regulation regularly in order to keep up to date with the changes and identify new legislation;
- Define and document the specific processes and individual responsibilities to meet these requirements.

Cryptography

Cryptographic controls should be used in compliance with all relevant agreements, laws, and regulations. A good control describes how cryptographic controls are used in compliance with all relevant agreements, legislation, and regulations. The use of cryptographic technologies is subject to legislation and regulation in many territories, and it is important that an organization understands those that are applicable and implements controls and awareness programs that ensure compliance with such requirements. This is especially true when cryptography is transported or used in territories other than the organizations or user's normal place of residence or operation. Trans-border import/export laws may include requirements relating to cryptographic technologies or usage. The auditor will be looking to see that considerations for the appropriate regulation of cryptographic controls have been made and relevant controls and awareness program implemented to ensure compliance. As such, the whole concept of encryption and cryptography usually involves specific legal requirements and a considerable amount of topic-specific regulatory guidance that need to be adhered to. Compliance with the relevant agreements, laws and regulations relating to the following items should be taken into consideration:

- Restrictions on import or export of computer hardware and software for performing cryptographic functions;
- Restrictions on import or export of computer hardware and software which is designed to have cryptographic functions added to it;
- Restrictions on the usage of cryptography;
- Mandatory or discretionary methods of access by the countries' authorities to encrypted information;
- Validity of digital signatures, seals and certificates.

It is recommended to seek legal advice when ensuring compliance with relevant legislation and regulations, especially when encrypted information or cryptography tools are moved across jurisdictional borders.

Contracts

Contractual requirements related to information security should include those stated in: Contracts with clients, suppliers, insurance contracts.

All relevant legislative statutory, regulatory, contractual requirements and the organization's approach to meet these requirements should be explicitly identified, documented and kept up to date for each information system and the organization. The specific controls and individual responsibilities to meet these requirements should also be defined and documented. Managers should identify all legislation applicable to their organization in order to meet the requirements for their type of business. If the organization conducts business in other countries, managers should consider compliance in all relevant countries. Organizations should "define and document" internal processes and responsibilities that allow them to:

- Identify, analyze and understand their legislative and regulatory obligations relating to information security, including periodic reviews of legislation and regulations;
- Ensure that they remain compliant across all legislative and regulatory environments in whatever countries they operate in. This extends to

the use of products and services that originate outside of the country they usually operate in.

The objective is to avoid breaches of legal, statutory, regulatory or contractual obligations related to information security and of any security requirements. The goal here is to help outline effective practices for identifying compliance obligations, as well as the roles and responsibilities, activities and controls needed to manage all of the organization's legal, contractual, and records management requirements. A good control describes how all relevant legislative statutory, regulatory, contractual requirements and the organization's approach to meet these requirements should be explicitly identified, documented and kept up to date for each information system and the organization. The identification of the relevant legislation, regulation and contractual requirements are likely to include engagement with legal experts, regulatory bodies and contract managers. The auditor will be looking to see how the organization has identified and recorded its legal, regulatory and contractual obligations; the responsibilities for meeting such requirements and any necessary policies, procedures and other controls required for meeting the controls. Additionally, they will look to see that this register is maintained on a regular basis against any relevant change, especially in legislation across common areas that they would expect any organization to be impacted by. Legal requirements need to be explicitly identified and recognized and a plan in place for meeting applicable requirements. To meet this part of compliance, controls should be developed which:

- Identify the person(s) responsible for ascertaining the legal requirements. Those requirements should then be placed against the other controls that exist in some sort of matrix which shows controls in place to meet the requirements. Each state has breach laws, personal information protection laws, social security protections laws, or other laws related to technology furnished at the organization. Each state must be taken as its own legal island and an organization must know if any of the following impact or enhance security efforts.
- Identify the person(s) responsible for reviewing contracts to determine any information security requirements, whether they are requirements of the organization or requirements of the vendor. Those requirements

should then be placed against the other controls that exist in some sort of matrix which shows controls in place to meet the requirements.

Every contract that involves organizational data must be documented and any controls specified in that contract must also be documented. It is crucial to know what your contractual responsibilities are so that you can look at the physical and technical controls you have in place and determine if they are adequate for the assumed contractual liability. In instances where contracting parties have access to organizational data, you want to be sure that you can audit the contractual controls and protections that the other party has agreed to follow. The initial process in developing compliance initiatives is to identify which laws, regulations, and policies are applicable to the organization. To that end, confer with your legal and/or audit departments, and review the most common federal and state data protection laws.

- Identify key stakeholders and/or partners across the organization who regularly deal with organizational compliance issues;
- Perform a high-level gap analysis of each compliance requirement that is applicable to determine where progress needs to be made;
- Develop a prioritized action plan that will help you organize your efforts;
- Develop a policy, standard, roles, and responsibilities, and/or procedures in collaboration with other key stakeholders at your organization;
- Familiarize yourself with common standards and regulations that address specific requirements;
- Determine whether Governance, Risk, and Compliance (GRC) solutions can assist you with managing compliance.

A.5.32 Intellectual Property Rights

According to ISO, Intellectual Property Rights (IPR) is defined as "legal rights associated with intellectual property" and intellectual property is defined as "result of intellectual activities that is eligible for protection by law".

Intellectual property rights include copyright and related rights, trademarks, geographical indications, industrial design rights, patents, layout-designs of integrated circuits and protection of undisclosed information. Intellectual property can include inventions, scientific discoveries, literary, scientific, or artistic works, symbols, designs, names, and images used in commerce, industrial designs, performances, recordings, broadcasts and other creative and industrial works.

This control describes the steps organizations need to take to ensure compliance with IPR, including using proprietary software purchased, subscribed to, or leased from a third party. This control focuses more on obligations towards third parties whose IPR are covered by licence agreements, data sharing agreements, etc. rather than as an IP holder. It is a preventive control that maintains risk by enforcing procedures that ensure that the business remains compliant with any prevailing IP or copyright requirements, including mitigating the risk that employees will not adhere to their own obligations. "Legal, statutory, regulatory or contractual" agreements often place restrictions on the use of proprietary software, including restrictions on copying, extracting, or reverse engineering the source code.

A.5.32 Intellectual Property Rights – A linkage with Ancient Era

Intellectual Property Rights encompass legal rights that protect creations of the mind

- **Authorship and Attribution:** The Ramayana, traditionally attributed to the Sage Valmiki, highlights the importance of authorship and attribution in creative works. Sage Valmiki is revered as the original composer of the epic, and his name is associated with its creation. This aligns with the modern notion of recognizing and attributing authorship to creators, which is a fundamental aspect of copyright law.

- **Cultural Heritage and Folklore:** The Ramayana is not just a literary work but also a cultural heritage that has been passed down through generations. In modern IP discourse, there's a growing recognition of the rights of indigenous peoples and communities over traditional cultural expressions and folklore. Similarly, the Ramayana represents a rich repository of cultural heritage that is valued and preserved by various communities.
- **Derivative Works and Adaptations:** The Ramayana has inspired countless adaptations, retellings, and interpretations across different mediums, including literature, art, theater, dance, and film. While modern copyright law governs the creation of derivative works and adaptations based on original works, the Ramayana serves as a prime example of how cultural narratives evolve and adapt over time through creative reinterpretations.
- **Moral Rights and Integrity:** Moral rights, a component of copyright law, protect the integrity and reputation of authors by allowing them to control how their works are used and attributed. Similarly, Ramayana is regarded with reverence, and there's a sense of moral responsibility associated with its portrayal and interpretation. Artists and storytellers often adhere to certain ethical considerations when representing characters and events from the epic.
- **Traditional Knowledge and Innovation:** The Ramayana contains a wealth of traditional knowledge, wisdom, and philosophical insights that have influenced Indian culture and thought for centuries. In contemporary discussions on IP, there's increasing recognition of the importance of protecting traditional knowledge and fostering innovation while respecting the rights and interests of indigenous communities.

Control

The organization should implement appropriate procedures to protect intellectual property rights.

Purpose

To ensure compliance with legal, statutory, regulatory and contractual requirements related to intellectual property rights and use of proprietary products.

Guidance

The following guidelines should be considered to protect any material that can be considered intellectual property:

- Defining and communicating a topic-specific policy on protection of IPR;
- Publishing procedures for IPR compliance that define compliant use of software and information products;
- Acquiring software only through known and reputable sources, to ensure that copyright is not infringed upon;
- Maintaining appropriate asset registers and identifying all assets with requirements to protect intellectual property rights;
- Maintaining proof and evidence of ownership of licenses, manuals, etc.;
- Ensuring that any maximum number of users or resources permitted within the license is not exceeded;
- Carrying out reviews to ensure that only authorized software and licensed products are installed;
- Providing procedures for maintaining appropriate license conditions;
- Providing procedures for disposing of or transferring software to others;
- Complying with terms and conditions for software and information obtained from public networks and outside sources;
- Not duplicating, converting to another format or extracting from commercial recordings other than permitted by copyright law or the applicable licenses;
- Not copying, in full or in part, standards, books, articles, reports or other documents, other than permitted by copyright law or the applicable licenses.

Other Information

IPR include software or document copyright, design rights, trademarks, patents and source code licenses. Proprietary software products are usually supplied under a license agreement that specifies license terms and conditions. See the ISO/IEC 19770 series for details about IT asset management.

Data can be acquired from outside sources. It is generally the case that such data is obtained under the terms of a data sharing agreement or similar legal instrument. Such data sharing agreements should make it clear what processing is permitted for the acquired data. It is also advisable that the provenance of the data is clearly stated. See ISO/IEC 23751:1 for details about data sharing agreements. Legal, statutory, regulatory and contractual requirements can place restrictions on the copying of proprietary material. In particular, they can require that only material that is developed by the organization or that is licensed or provided by the developer to the organization, can be used. Copyright infringement can lead to legal action, which can involve fines and criminal proceedings. Aside from the organization needing to comply with its obligations towards third party IPR, the risks of personnel and third parties failing to uphold the organization's own IPR should also be managed.

IPR are a dominant issue at any organizations. Organizations may have many different types of research and proprietary information that can be protected via these rights. These rights are also attached to the different technologies that the organization might buy or license from others (and the rights are then protected via contract provisions). Copyright and/or IP infringement can lead to severe financial and legal consequences for any organization that willfully or unwittingly breaches an agreement. This should be given adequate consideration in order to avoid any unnecessary business interruptions or information security incidents. A good control describes how the appropriate procedures ensure compliance with legislative, regulatory and contractual requirements related to IPR rights and use of proprietary software products. Policies, processes and technical controls are likely to be needed for both of these aspects. Within asset registers and acceptable use policies it is likely that IPR considerations will need to be made. Controls to ensure that only authorized and licensed software are in use within the organization should include regular inspection and audit. The auditor will want to see that registers of licenses owned by the organization for use of others' software and other assets are being kept and updated. The auditor will also be looking at how the organization protects its own IPR, which might include: data loss and prevention controls; policies and awareness program targeting user education; or non-disclosure and confidentiality agreements that continue post termination of employment. Appropriate controls to identify and protect intellectual property include:

- An IPR compliance policy;
- Ensuring proper use of software and other technology licenses;
- Education and awareness on respecting IPR;
- Keeping track of IP assets.

A.5.33 Protection of Records

ISO defines record as "information created, received and maintained as evidence and as an asset by a organization or person, in pursuit of legal obligations or in the transaction of business." Records, within the scope of IS, are another term for the data and information an organization retains and/or uses to carry out its day to day business activities, including but not limited to individual events, transactions, work processes, activities, functions. Organization has an obligation to ensure that any record it has including but not limited to any persons, financial information or areas of operations kept safe and secure, and internal procedures remain compliant with all prevailing requirements. This control deals with the protection of records against loss, destruction, falsification, unauthorized access, unauthorized release or publication.

A.5.33 Protection of Records – A linkage with Ancient Era

- **Preservation of Manuscripts:** In ancient times, written records were meticulously preserved on manuscripts. The Ramayana itself is believed to have been transmitted orally for generations before being penned down by the Sage Valmiki. This act of preserving the epic in written form ensured its survival and dissemination over millennia.
- **Guardianship of Sacred Texts:** Throughout history, sacred texts like the Ramayana were considered invaluable treasures and were guarded with utmost care. Temples and monasteries served as repositories for such texts, and priests or scholars were entrusted with their protection. These custodians were responsible for ensuring the integrity and safety of the records.
- **Transmission of Knowledge:** The Ramayana, like other ancient texts, played a crucial role in the transmission of knowledge, culture, and values across generations. Sages, scholars, and storytellers were tasked with passing down these records orally or through written copies to ensure that the wisdom contained within them was preserved and disseminated.
- **Cultural Memory and Identity:** The Ramayana served as more than just a historical record; it was a foundational text that shaped the cultural identity of ancient Indian society. The characters, events, and teachings contained within the epic were woven into the fabric of

society, influencing art, literature, religion, and philosophy. Protecting the integrity of the Ramayana meant safeguarding the cultural memory and identity of the people.

- **Symbolic Protection:** In the Ramayana, certain characters or artifacts symbolize the protection of knowledge and righteousness. For example, Lord Hanuman is often depicted as the guardian of dharma and is tasked with protecting Mata Sita, symbolizing the safeguarding of virtue and knowledge.

Control

Records should be protected from loss, destruction, falsification, unauthorized access and unauthorized release.

Purpose

To ensure compliance with legal, statutory, regulatory and contractual requirements, as well as community or societal expectations related to the protection and availability of records.

Guidance

The organization should take the following steps to protect the authenticity, reliability, integrity and usability of records, as their business context and requirements for their management change over time:

- Issue guidelines on the storage, handling chain of custody and disposal of records, which includes prevention of manipulation of records. These guidelines should be aligned with the organization's topic-specific policy on records management and other records requirements;
- Draw up a retention schedule defining records and the period of time for which they should be retained.
- An inventory of main information sources should be maintained.

The system of storage and handling should ensure identification of records and of their retention period taking into consideration national or regional legislation or regulations, as well as community or societal expectations, if applicable. This system should permit appropriate destruction of records after that period if they are not needed by the organization.

When deciding on protection of specific organizational records, their corresponding information security classification, based on the organization's classification scheme, should be considered. Records should be categorized into record types, each with details of retention periods and type of allowable storage media which can be physical or electronic. Data storage systems should be chosen such that required records can be retrieved in an acceptable time frame and format, depending on the requirements to be fulfilled. Where electronic storage media are chosen, procedures to ensure the ability to access records throughout the retention period should be established to safeguard against loss due to future technology change. Any related cryptographic keys and programs associated with encrypted archives or digital signatures, should also be retained to enable decryption of the records for the length of time the records are retained.

Storage and handling procedures should be implemented in accordance with recommendations provided by manufacturers of storage media. Consideration should be given to the possibility of deterioration of media used for storage of records.

Other Information

Any set of information, regardless of its structure or form, can be managed as a record. This includes information in the form of a document, a collection of data or other types of digital or analogue information which are created, captured and managed in the course of business. In the management of records, metadata is data describing the context, content and structure of records, as well as their management over time and is an essential component of any record. It can be necessary to retain some records securely to meet legal, statutory, regulatory or contractual requirements, as well as to support essential business activities. National law or regulation can set the time period and data content for information retention.

A good control describes how records are protected from loss, destruction, falsification, unauthorized access and unauthorized release, in accordance with the legislator, regulatory, contractual and business requirements. Different types of record will likely require different levels and methods of protection. It is especially important to understand how long records must, should or could be kept for and what technical or physical issues might affect these over time, bearing in mind that some legislation might trump others for retention and protection. The auditor will be checking to see that considerations for the protection of records have been made based on business requirements, legal, regulatory and contractual obligations.

An established record is valuable if it is authentic, reliable, usable, and well-maintained integrity. Regardless of the format of data, whether it is on paper or digital, it requires protection. Evidently, there are pros and cons to both formats of data-keeping. While paper documents are less susceptible to issues such as non-availability and tampering; issues such as consumption of storage, transport, and physical damage are common vulnerabilities of paper-based documents. On the other hand, digital records are flexible, amendable, easily movable, and so forth. Nonetheless, digital records are susceptible to attacks capable of compromising confidentiality, integrity, and availability of digital records. Moreover, digital records require to be safe while at rest, in transit, and in processing, which in a sense makes them more susceptible to cyber-attacks. An organization should establish, implement, and communicate record-keeping policies and procedures. Some organizations might prefer to have the whole subject in a separate document, while others keep it as a part of the information security policy. A better practice is to establish a label handling and transfer policy/procedure. An organization's needs are fluid when it comes to the amount and type of records that are required to do business from one day to the next. Records can be categorized as:

- Authenticity;
- Reliability;
- Integrity;
- Useability.

Within the scope of these attributes, organizations must draft and publish guidelines that deal with four main functions, alongside topic-specific policies that caters to the underlying nature of the records in question:

- Record Storage;
- Record Handling Chain of Custody;
- Record Disposal;
- Preventing Manipulation.

It must maintain a functional records retention schedule that clearly outlines the length of time that records of differing types should be retained, relating to their individual business function. It must create storage and handling procedures that take into account:

- Any prevailing laws that deal with commercial record keeping;
- "Community and Societal" expectations of how an organization should handle its records.

It implements procedures that destroy records in a safe and appropriate manner the moment they're not needed after leaving the retention period and classify records for protection based on their security risk, and various types, including (but not limited to):

- Accounting Records;
- Business Transactions;
- Personnel Records;
- Legal Records.

It must ensure that any storage procedures cater for an acceptable time frame for retrieval, should the organization be asked to produce them by a third party, or for internal use. Where electronic media is used to store records, consider and mitigate the possibility of access to or retrieval of records being inhibited by technological amendments, including the retention of cryptographic information and adhere to manufacturer guidelines when storing or handling records on or via electronic media, including adequate consideration for the natural deterioration of said media.

ISO has a separate standard, ISO 15489 "Information and Documentation - Records Management." This standard goes into greater detail about how an organization recognizes the context in which records are created, received, used, stored, and destroyed as an implicit part of the data governance process. This "records management" function may be placed anywhere in organizations, and sometimes it is part of an organization's IT structure. Organization's policies and guidelines on retention, storage, handling, and disposal of records should be reviewed. Oftentimes this will require a security control to ensure that these policies and guidelines are carried out properly. Policies that protect records from loss, destruction, or falsification. The related classification based on the organization's classification scheme is to be taken into account when determining whether to secure relevant organizational documents.

Categorized records in the following types of records, such as accounting records, database records, transaction records, audit logs, and operating procedures, should include details on retention periods and the type of media permitted for storage, such as paper, microfiche, magnetic, optical. Any associated encryption keys and programs related to encrypted or digital signatures must also be stored so that records are decrypted for a period of time during which records are kept. The possibility of media deterioration used for record storage should be taken into consideration. In accordance with the manufacturer's recommendations, storage and handling procedures should be implemented. When electronic storage media are selected, protocols should be developed in order to protect against loss due to potential technical changes to ensure access for data over the retention period. Data storage systems should be assigned so that the data required can be recovered, depending on the requirements to be fulfilled, in a time and format acceptable. The storage and handling system should, if appropriate, ensure that records and their retention periods are known as specified in national or regional laws. After that period, if records are not required by the organization, this system should allow appropriate destruction.

A.5.34 Privacy and Protection of PII

According to ISO, Personally Identifiable Information (PII) is defined as "any information that (a) can be used to establish a link between the information and the natural person to whom such information relates, or (b) is or can be directly or indirectly linked to a natural person." The "natural person" in the definition is the PII principal. To determine whether a PII principal is identifiable, account should be taken of all the means which can reasonably be used by the privacy stakeholder holding the data, or by any other party, to establish the link between the set of PII and the natural person. A public cloud PII processor is typically not in a position to know explicitly whether information it processes falls into any specified category unless this is made transparent by the cloud service customer. ISO defines PII principal as "natural person to whom the PII relates". Depending on the jurisdiction and the particular PII protection and privacy legislation, the synonym "data subject" can also be used instead of the term "PII principal". PII is any representation of information that permits the identity of an individual to whom the information applies to be reasonably inferred by either direct or indirect means. PII directly identifies an individual or identify specific individuals in conjunction with other data elements, i.e., indirect identification. Additionally, information permitting the physical or online contacting of a specific individual is the same as PII. This information can be maintained in either paper, electronic or other media. The loss of PII can result in substantial harm to individuals, including identity theft or other fraudulent use of the information.

A.5.34 Privacy Protection of PII – A linkage with Ancient Era

- **Seclusion and Privacy of Characters:** Throughout the Ramayana, characters often seek seclusion or privacy to discuss personal matters or engage in introspection. For example, Mata Sita retreats to the forest when she feels distressed, seeking solitude and privacy to reflect on Her situation. This illustrates the natural inclination of individuals to safeguard their personal thoughts and emotions in private settings.
- **Confidential Conversations:** There are several instances in the Ramayana where characters engage in confidential conversations, revealing personal information or discussing sensitive matters in private. For instance, Lord Ram confides in His trusted advisors or discusses matters of state in secluded chambers, away from

public scrutiny. This underscores the importance of maintaining confidentiality and trust in interpersonal communications.

- **Respect for Personal Boundaries:** The Ramayana emphasizes the importance of respecting personal boundaries and privacy rights. Characters like Mata Sita or King Ravan expresses their desire for privacy, and their boundaries are respected by others. This reflects a cultural norm of honoring individual autonomy and privacy within interpersonal relationships.
- **Information Security:** While not explicitly stated, certain incidents in the Ramayana highlight the consequences of information security breaches. For example, the abduction of Mata Sita by King Ravan exposes Her to potential harm due to the unauthorized access and misuse of Her personal information. This underscores the importance of safeguarding sensitive data and preventing unauthorized access in order to protect individuals from harm.
- **Trust and Confidentiality:** Trust and Confidentiality play significant roles in the Ramayana, as characters rely on trusted allies to safeguard their secrets and personal information. For example, Lord Ram entrusts Lord Hanuman with the task of locating Mata Sita, demonstrating His trust in Lord Hanuman's discretion and loyalty. This emphasizes the importance of trust in maintaining confidentiality and protecting personal information from unauthorized disclosure.

Control

The organization should identify and meet the requirements regarding the preservation of privacy and protection of PII according to applicable laws and regulations and contractual requirements.

Purpose

To ensure compliance with legal, statutory, regulatory and contractual requirements related to the information security aspects of the protection of PII.

Guidance

The organization should establish and communicate a topic-specific policy on privacy and protection of PII to all relevant interested parties.

The organization should develop and implement procedures for the preservation of privacy and protection of PII. These procedures should be communicated to all relevant interested parties involved in the processing of PII. Compliance with these procedures and all relevant legislation and regulations concerning the preservation of privacy and protection of PII requires appropriate roles, responsibilities and controls. Often this is best achieved by the appointment of a person responsible, such as a Privacy Officer, who should provide guidance to personnel, service providers and other interested parties on their individual responsibilities and the specific procedures that should be followed. Responsibility for handling PII should be dealt with taking into consideration relevant legislation and regulations. Appropriate technical and organizational measures to protect PII should be implemented.

Other Information

A number of countries have introduced legislation placing controls on the collection, processing, transmission and deletion of PII. Depending on the respective national legislation, such controls can impose duties on those collecting, processing and disseminating PII and can also restrict the authority to transfer PII to other countries. ISO 29100 provides a high-level framework for the protection of PII within ICT systems. Further information on privacy information management systems can be found in ISO 27701. Specific information regarding privacy information management for public clouds acting as PII processors can be found in ISO 27018. ISO 29134 provides guidelines for privacy impact assessment (PIA) and gives an example of the structure and content of a PIA report. Compared with ISO 27005, this is focused on PII processing and relevant to those organizations that process PII. This can help identify privacy risks and possible mitigation to reduce these risks to acceptable levels.

PII forms a key part of an organization's data governance strategy, and carries a number of unique regulatory, legislative and contractual risks. A good control describes how privacy and protection of PII is assured for relevant legislation and regulation. Any information handled that contains PII is likely to be subject to the obligations of legislation and regulation. PII is especially likely to have high requirements for confidentiality and integrity, and in some cases availability as well. This control deals with PII in three distinct ways: Preservation, Privacy, Protection. Under some legislation some types of PII are defined as additionally "sensitive" and require further controls to ensure compliance. It is important that awareness campaigns are used with staff and stakeholders to ensure a repeated understanding of individual responsibility for protecting PII and privacy. Organizations should treat PII as a topic-specific business function, and develop policies that are unique to their organization, and the categories of PII that are most common to their day-to-day operation. First and foremost, the organization should draft, develop and implement a series of policies that cater to the preservation, privacy and protection of PII, and ensure these are communicated to and used by all employees that process PII – not just those who are obligated to deal with it as part of their job roles. PII needs to be managed in a structured, clear and concise manner. To achieve this control asks organizations to draft policies that consider individual roles, responsibilities and data controls throughout their organization. The easiest and most efficient way to achieve this is to adopt a top-down approach that features a Privacy Officer, whose job it is to provide guidance to employees and third-party organizations on the subject of PII, and offer advice to senior management on how to remain compliant with the organization's obligations. Alongside regulatory, legislative and contractual guidelines, an organization should also implement technical and operational measures that deal with the practical handling of PII as it's stored by and flows through the business. The auditor will be looking to see how PII is handled, if the appropriate controls have been implemented, are being monitored, reviewed and where necessary improved. They will also be looking to check that handling requirements are being met and audited suitably. Smart organizations will tie these audits up alongside their ISO 27001 audits and avoid duplication or gaps.

As organizations continuously collect, store and distribute PII and other sensitive data, employees, administrators and third-party contractors need to understand the repercussions of mishandled data and be held accountable. It is the responsibility of the individual employee to protect data to which they have access. Employee having access to personal information must respect the confidentiality of such information, and refrain from any conduct that would indicate a careless or negligent attitude toward such information. Only individuals who have a "need to know" in their official capacity shall have access to such systems of records. Predictive analytics and artificial intelligence (AI) are in use at organizations to sift through large data sets so that any data stored is compliant with all PII rules. Additionally, organizations establishing procedures for access control can prevent inadvertent disclosure of PII. Other best practices include using strong encryption, secure passwords, and two-factor (2FA) and multifactor authentication (MFA). Other recommendations for protecting PII are:

1. Encouraging employees to practice good data backup procedures;
2. Safeguard information to which their employees have access at all times;
3. Obtain management's written approval prior to taking any sensitive information away from the office. The manager's approval must identify the business necessity for removing such information from the facility;
4. Safely destroying or removing old media with sensitive data;
5. Installing software, application and mobile updates;
6. Using secure wireless networks, rather than public Wi-Fi; and
7. Using Virtual Private Networks (VPNs).

A.5.35 Independent Review of Information Security, A.5.36 Compliance with Policies, Rules, and Standards for Information Security

A good control describes the organization's approach to managing information security and its implementation is reviewed independently at planned intervals or when significant changes occur. Ensure that information security compliance requirements are effectively addressed and maintained over time. In order to meet compliance requirements, it is necessary to continually review compliance methods, systems, and processes of departments that are affected by various policies, regulatory requirements, and laws to ensure that their approach to compliance is effective. It is good to get an independent review of security risks and controls to ensure impartiality and objectivity as well as benefit from fresh eyes. That doesn't mean it has to be external, just benefit from another colleague reviewing policies in addition to the main author/administrator. These reviews should be carried out at planned, regular intervals (at least annually) and when any significant, security-relevant changes occur. The auditor will be looking for both regular independent security review and review when significant changes occur, as well as take confidence there is a plan for regular reviews. They will also require evidence that reviews have been carried out and any issues or improvements identified in the reviews are appropriately managed.

A.5.35 Independent Review of Information Security

A.5.35 Independent Review of Information Security – A linkage with Ancient Era

- **Surveillance and Reconnaissance:** In the Ramayana, there are instances where characters engage in surveillance and reconnaissance activities to gather information about their enemies. For example, Lord Hanuman's reconnaissance mission to Lanka serves as a form of information gathering and assessment of the enemy's security measures. This can be seen as an early form of independent review aimed at evaluating the strength of the enemy's defenses.
- **Strategic Planning and Risk Assessment:** Throughout the epic, various characters engage in strategic planning and risk assessment

to mitigate potential threats. Lord Ram and His allies strategize on how to breach the enemy's defenses, anticipating potential risks and vulnerabilities. This proactive approach can be linked to the process of conducting independent reviews of information security practices to identify weaknesses and vulnerabilities before they are exploited by adversaries.

- **Trust and Verification:** In the Ramayana, characters often rely on trusted allies to verify information and assess the reliability of intelligence reports. For example, Lord Ram trusts Lord Hanuman to verify Mata Sita's whereabouts in Lanka and gather accurate information about Her well-being. This demonstrates the importance of trust and verification in ensuring the accuracy and integrity of information, which are fundamental aspects of independent reviews of information security practices.
- **Lessons Learned and Continuous Improvement:** As the epic unfolds, characters learn from their experiences and adapt their strategies accordingly. They analyze past failures and successes to improve their future actions. Similarly, independent reviews of information security often involve analyzing past incidents and vulnerabilities to identify areas for improvement and implement corrective measures to enhance security posture.
- **Accountability and Oversight:** While not explicitly stated, the Ramayana underscores the importance of accountability and oversight in ensuring the effectiveness of security measures. Leaders like Lord Ram and Lord Hanuman are held accountable for their decisions and actions, and their leadership is subject to scrutiny by their peers and allies. This can be seen as a form of oversight akin to the independent review process, where security practices are evaluated and scrutinized to ensure compliance with established standards and protocols.

Control

The organization's approach to managing information security and its implementation including people, processes and technologies should be reviewed independently at planned intervals, or when significant changes occur.

Purpose

To ensure the continuing suitability, adequacy and effectiveness of the organization's approach to managing information security.

Guidance

The organization should have processes to conduct independent reviews. Management should plan and initiate periodic independent reviews. The reviews should include assessing opportunities for improvement and the need for changes to the approach to information security, including the information security policy, topic-specific policies and other controls. Such reviews should be carried out by individuals independent of the area under review. Individuals carrying out these reviews should have the appropriate competence. The results of the independent reviews should be reported to the management who initiated the reviews and, if appropriate, to top management. These records should be maintained. If the independent reviews identify that the organization's approach and implementation to managing information security is inadequate, management should initiate corrective actions. In addition to the periodic independent reviews, the organization should consider conducting independent reviews when:

- Laws and regulations which affect the organization change;
- Significant incidents occur;
- The organization starts a new business or changes a current business;
- The organization starts to use a new product or service, or changes the use of a current product or service;
- The organization changes the information security controls and procedures significantly.

Other Information

ISO/IEC 27007 and ISO/IEC TS 27008 provide guidance for carrying out independent reviews.

The overarching aim is for management to create and implement processes that cater for independent reviews of their information security practices. An independent review is necessary to ensure the continuing suitability, adequacy and effectiveness of organization's approach to managing information security. The review should include assessing opportunities for improvement and the need for changes to the approach to security, including the policy and control objectives. Individuals carrying out these reviews should have the appropriate skills and experience. The results of the independent review should be recorded and reported to the management who initiated the review. These records should be maintained. Reviews should focus on any changes that are required to improve an organization's approach to information security, including:

- The Information Security Policy.
- Topic-Specific Policies.
- Related Controls.

If the independent review identifies inadequacies in the approach or implementation of information security, management should consider corrective actions. The organization that seeking for ISO 27001 certification (ISMS) must maintain a 'Master List of Independent Information Security Reviewers'. For each independent review, the certified ISO 27001 organization chooses reviewer(s) from its 'Master List of Independent Information Security Reviewers' and gets the review done. Reports submitted by the independent reviewers shall be discussed immediately with the top management and the concerned department within the organization, and, necessary corrective and/or preventive actions are taken. The outcome of independent review and actions taken would be discussed in the subsequent management review as well.

Alongside periodic reviews, it may be necessary to initiate ad-hoc reviews. These reviews can be justified across 5 key areas:

- Any laws, guidelines or regulations are amended which affect the organization's information security operation;
- Major incidents occur that have an impact on information security;
- A new business is created, or major changes are enacted to the current business;
- The organization adopts a new product or service that has information security implications, or makes underlying changes to a current product or service;
- Major changes are made to the organization's bank of information security controls, policies and procedures.

The objective of independent review is to ensure that information security is implemented and operated in accordance with the organizational policies and procedures. It is important to have unbiased reviews of information security organization programs and initiatives on a recurring basis in order to measure and ensure effectiveness. Often, these reviews are carried out by multiple parties: internal audit departments, external auditors, and assessments performed by contractors or consultants. It is also important that individuals performing reviews and assessments are qualified to do so. The primary objective of independent reviews is to measure effectiveness and ensure continuous improvements are made. In the event that the organization does not have an internal audit function, you may be able to develop a cooperative agreement with another organization or hire a consulting firm to conduct an audit and/or assessment of specific areas you need to have assessed. Note: For some organizations, an independent review may include representatives from legal counsel, an executive leadership team, and/or a system office.

A 5.36 Compliance with Policies, Rules and Standards for Information Security

A.5.36 Compliance with Policies, Rules, and Standards for Information Security – A linkage with Ancient Era

- **Royal Decrees and Commands:** Throughout the epic, kings and rulers issue decrees and commands that establish policies and rules governing the conduct of their subjects. These decrees often include directives related to information security, such as the protection of classified information or the dissemination of sensitive intelligence. For example, King Dasharatha's orders to maintain secrecy regarding Lord Ram's exile can be interpreted as a form of information security policy aimed at safeguarding sensitive information.
- **Confidentiality and Discretion:** Characters in the Ramayana demonstrate a commitment to confidentiality and discretion when handling sensitive information. For instance, Lord Ram instructs Lord Hanuman to discreetly gather intelligence about Mata Sita's whereabouts in Lanka, emphasizing the importance of maintaining confidentiality to avoid alerting the enemy. This reflects a form of adherence to information security standards aimed at protecting classified information from unauthorized disclosure.
- **Trust and Loyalty:** Trust and Loyalty play significant roles in ensuring compliance with information security policies and rules. Characters like Lord Hanuman and Vibhishana are trusted allies who demonstrate unwavering loyalty to Lord Ram, adhering to His directives and upholding information security standards. Their loyalty ensures that sensitive information is safeguarded and shared only with trusted individuals, minimizing the risk of leaks or breaches.
- **Strategic Planning and Risk Management:** Leaders in the Ramayana engage in strategic planning and risk management to mitigate potential threats to information security. For example, Lord Ram and His allies devise elaborate strategies to infiltrate enemy territories, anticipating potential risks and vulnerabilities. This proactive approach to risk management reflects a commitment to complying with information security standards and protecting sensitive information from exploitation by adversaries.

- **Consequences of Non-Compliance:** The Ramayana also illustrates the consequences of non-compliance with information security policies and rules. Characters who disregard confidentiality or betray trust face severe repercussions for their actions. For instance, spies who divulge sensitive information to the enemy are punished for their betrayal, underscoring the importance of compliance with information security standards and the consequences of failing to uphold them.

Control

Compliance with the organization's information security policy, topic specific policies, rules and standards should be regularly reviewed.

Purpose

To ensure that information security is implemented and operated in accordance with the organization's information security policy, topic-specific policies, rules and standards.

Guidance

Managers, Service Providers or Information Owners should identify how to review that information security requirements defined in the information security policy, topic specific policies, rules, standards and other applicable regulations are met. Automatic measurement and reporting tools should be considered for efficient regular review. If any non-compliance is found as a result of the review, managers should:

- Identify the causes of the non-compliance;
- Evaluate the need for corrective actions to achieve compliance;
- Implement appropriate corrective actions;
- Review corrective actions taken to verify its effectiveness and identify any deficiencies or weaknesses.

Results of reviews and corrective actions carried out by Managers, Service Providers or Information Owners should be recorded and these records should be maintained. Managers should report the results to the persons carrying out independent reviews when an independent review takes place in the area of their responsibility. Corrective actions should be completed in a timely manner as appropriate to the risk. If not completed by the next scheduled review, progress should at least be addressed at that review.

Department Managers have a compliance responsibility to make sure that applicable security procedures related to their area of control are implemented and performed correctly to achieve compliance with internal security policies and standards. Department Managers are responsible for all initial and recurring security incident policy training of workforce members, and for enforcing computer and data security policies and standards. Managers should identify how to review and assess that information security requirements defined in policies, standards and other applicable regulations are met. If any non-compliance is found as a result of the review, managers should:

1. Identify the causes of the non-compliance;
2. Evaluate the need for actions to achieve compliance;
3. Implement appropriate corrective action;
4. Review the corrective action taken to verify its effectiveness and identify any deficiencies or weaknesses.

Results of reviews and corrective actions carried out by managers should be recorded and these records should be maintained. Managers should report the results to the persons carrying out independent reviews when an independent review takes place in the area of their responsibility

Many organizations are considering the implementation of Governance, Risk, and Compliance (GRC) solutions to automate compliance reviews and reporting, as well as assisting with determining corrective actions that need to be managed. ISMS managers should regularly review the compliance of information processing and procedures within their area of responsibility. For efficient routine analysis, automated measuring and reporting tools should be considered. If any failure to comply results from the review are detected, managers should:

1. Identify the reasons of failure to comply;
2. Assess the need for compliance measures;
3. Implement effective remedial measures;
4. Review the steps taken to verify their efficiency and recognize any deficiencies or vulnerabilities.

Details of the managers' assessments and disciplinary measures should be reported and documented. If an independent review takes place within its area of responsibility, administrators will report the findings to individuals conducting independent reviews Policies are only effective if they are enforced and compliance is tested and reviewed on a regular periodic basis. It is usually the responsibility of the line management to ensure that their subordinate staff complies with organizational policies and controls but this should be complemented by occasional independent review and audit. Where noncompliance is identified, it should be logged and managed, identifying why it occurred, how often it is occurring and the need for any improvement actions either relating to the control or to the awareness, education, or training of the user that caused the noncompliance.

The auditor will be looking to see that both:

- Proactive preventative policies, controls, and awareness programs are in place, implemented, and effective;
- Reactive compliance monitoring, review, and audit are also in place.

They will also be looking to see that there is evidence of how improvements are made over time to ensure an improvement in compliance levels or maintenance if compliance is already at the acceptable level.

This dovetails into the main requirements of ISO 27001 for 9 and 10 around internal audits, management reviews, improvements, and non-conformity too. Staff awareness and engagement is also important to tie into this part for compliance confidence. Technical compliance should be reviewed, either by IT or as part of an independent review, preferably with the assistance of automated tools, which generate technical reports for subsequent interpretation by a technical specialist. Alternatively, manual reviews by an experienced system engineer could be performed. If penetration tests or vulnerability assessments are used, caution should be exercised as such activities could lead to a compromise of the security of the system. Such tests should be planned, documented and repeatable. Any technical compliance review should only be carried out by competent, authorized persons or under the supervision of such persons. Information systems should be regularly reviewed for compliance with the organization's information security policies and standards. Automated tools are normally used to check systems and networks for technical compliance and these should be identified and implemented as appropriate. Where tools such as these are used, it is necessary to restrict their use to a few authorized personnel as to possible and to carefully control and coordinate when they are used to prevent compromise of system availability and integrity. Adequate levels of compliance testing will be dependent on business requirements and risk levels, and the auditor will expect to see evidence of these considerations being made. They will also expect to be able to inspect testing schedules and records.

A.5.37 Documented Operating Procedures

Documented procedures for operating information processing and communications facility activities should be prepared including computer start-up and closing down, backup, maintenance of equipment, media handling, computer room and mail management, and safety. Operating procedures must be documented and readily available to the teams for which they have relevance. These procedures should cover methods that reduce the likelihood of introducing or enhancing risks due to accidental or ill-advised changes. Before authoring documentation, it is often very important to identify up-front who the intended audience is. It is very important that operating procedures be treated as formal documents that are maintained and managed with version and approval processes and controls in place. As technology and systems infrastructure changes, it is an absolute certainty that operational procedures will become out of date or inaccurate. By adopting formal documentation and review processes, organization can help reduce the likelihood of outdated procedures that bring forth their own risks, such as, loss of availability, failure of data integrity, and breaches of confidentiality. This control deals with the concept of information security as an operational activity, with its constituent elements being carried out and/or managed by one or more individuals. and outlines a series of operational procedures that ensure an organization's information security facility remains efficient and secure, and in line with their documented requirements.

A.5.37 Documented Operating Procedures – A linkage with Ancient Era

Construction of the Bridge – Ram Setu

- **Strategic Planning and Organization**: The construction of Ram Setu involved meticulous planning and organization. Lord Ram, along with His trusted advisors and generals, likely developed a strategic plan outlining the steps needed to build the bridge. While not explicitly documented in writing, these plans would have been communicated orally and followed as operational procedures by the various teams involved in the construction.
- **Allocation of Tasks and Resources:** A project of such magnitude would have required the allocation of tasks and resources to different teams

and individuals. Lord Ram and His commanders would have assigned specific roles to each group, such as gathering materials, transporting them to the construction site, and actually building the bridge.

- **Construction Techniques and Methods:** The construction of Ram Setu likely involved specific techniques and methods passed down through generations of engineers and builders. While not explicitly documented in written form, these construction practices would have been part of the documented operating procedures communicated orally from experienced craftsmen to the laborers involved in the project.
- **Quality Control and Inspection:** As the construction progressed, there would have been measures in place to ensure quality control and inspection of the bridge. Lord Ram or His appointed officials may have overseen the construction process, ensuring that the bridge was being built according to specifications and standards. Any deviations from the documented operating procedures may have been addressed promptly to maintain the integrity of the project.
- **Safety Protocols and Risk Management:** Given the challenging nature of the construction site and the potential risks involved, safety protocols and risk management strategies would have been implemented. Teams would have been instructed on safety procedures to prevent accidents and injuries. Lord Hanuman, with His strength and agility, may have played a crucial role in mitigating risks and ensuring the safety of the workers, in accordance with the documented operating procedures.

Control

Operating procedures for information processing facilities should be documented and made available to personnel who need them.

Purpose

To ensure the correct and secure operation of information processing facilities.

Guidance

Documented procedures should be prepared for the organization's operational activities associated with information security. The operating procedures should specify:

- The responsible individuals;
- The secure installation and configuration of systems;
- Processing and handling of information, both automated and manual;
- Backup and resilience;
- Scheduling requirements, including inter dependencies with other systems;
- Instructions for handling errors or other exceptional conditions which can arise during job execution;
- Support and escalation contacts including external support contacts in the event of unexpected operational or technical difficulties;
- Storage media handling instructions;
- System restart and recovery procedures for use in the event of system failure;
- The management of audit trail and system log information and video monitoring systems;
- Monitoring procedures such as capacity, performance and security;
- Maintenance instructions.

Documented operating procedures should be reviewed and updated when needed. Changes to documented operating procedures should be authorized. Where technically feasible, information systems should be managed consistently, using the same procedures, tools and utilities.

Operating procedures must be documented and then made available to all users who need them. Documented operating procedures help to ensure consistent and effective operation of systems for new staff or changing resources, and can often be critical for disaster recovery, business continuity and for when staff availability is compromised. Where information systems are "cloud-based" traditional operational activities such as system start-up, shut-down, backup etc. become less relevant and may often be outsourced to a cloud provider. In more traditional computing environments and architectures operating procedures are much more likely to be required. It is important that documents are maintained in a correct and current state and should therefore be subject to formal change management and periodic review procedures, as the auditor will be specifically looking to see this.

Similarly, if procedures are evolving or regularly changing the organization may want to have procedures that can be easily and quickly updated too. Again, if lots of new resource is being added and the area has risk and complexity around it, then more depth to the procedures may be needed. The areas of the business that need to be considered for documented procedures should be where your information assets are at risk through incorrect operation, which of course will be identified as part of the risk assessment. That might include software development, IT management, through to financial accounting, customer management, consulting or manufacturing work etc. depending on the nature of the business.

What should be documented?

The decision on what areas deserve documentation must be informed by an understanding of organizational risks including issues that have previously been observed. However, a good list of items to consider include the following items, but not limited to:

1. Configuration and build procedures for servers, networking equipment, and desktops;
2. Automated and Manual Information Processing;
3. Backup Procedures;
4. System Scheduling Dependencies;
5. Error Handling;
6. Change Management Processes;
7. Capacity Management & Planning Processes;
8. Support and Escalation procedures;
9. System Restart and Recovery;
10. Special Output;
11. Logging & Monitoring Procedures;
12. Any individuals responsible – both incumbents and new operators;

13. A set of guidelines that maintain security during the installation and subsequent configuration of any related business systems;
14. How information is processed throughout the activity;
15. BCP/DR plans and implications, in the event of data loss or a major event;
16. Linked dependencies with any other systems, including scheduling;
17. A clear procedure for dealing with "handling errors" or miscellaneous events that have the potential to occur;
18. A full list of personnel to be contacted in the event of any disruption, including clear escalation procedures;
19. How to operate any relevant storage media associated with the activity;
20. How to reboot and recover from a system failure;
21. Audit trail logging, including all associated event and system logs;
22. Video monitoring systems that monitor onsite activities;
23. A robust set of monitoring procedures that cater to the operational capacity, performance potential and security of said activity;
24. How the activity should be maintained, in order to be kept at optimal performance levels.

All of the above procedures should be subject to periodic and/or ad-hoc reviews, as an when required, with all changes being ratified and approved by Management in a timely manner to safeguard information security activity across the organization. Procedures and documented procedures for system operations should be treated as managerial authorized formal documents and alterations. Where technically feasible, IT system should be consistently administered using the same procedures, tools, and utilities.

People Controls

A.6.1 Screening

Appropriate background verification checks, also known as "screening" or "clearance", for all candidates for employment, contractor status, or third-party user status, should be carried out. Prior to employment screening is the process of verifying information that job candidates supply on their resumes and job applications. It may also be referred to by other names, such as:

- Background Checks;
- Criminal Background Checks;
- Background Screening.

This type of background check is usually initiated to see if a prospective employee is trustworthy enough to protect confidential or sensitive information, or manage the financial resources of a business. They may also be used to try to determine if job candidates have any criminal tendencies or character flaws that might limit their effectiveness or hurt the employer in other ways, such as endangering the staff or tarnishing the organization's reputation. Most employers conduct a prior to employment screening of job applicants. However, all or part of the screening process is usually outsourced to private third-party organizations that specialize in this type of background check. An employment background check verifies the employee's past employment details, criminal records, and/or financial records. This is usually the final step in the recruitment cycle and it ensures that the hiring decision made by the employers are sound and appropriate. Control includes checks that are:

- Commensurate with the organization's business needs, and with relevant legal, regulatory, certificatory requirements;
- Take into account the classification/sensitivity of the information to be accessed, and the perceived risks;
- Take into account all privacy, protection of personal data and other relevant employment legislation; and
- Include, where appropriate, components such as identity verification, character references, CV verification, criminal and credit checks.

A.6.1 Screening – A linkage with Ancient Era

Ethical Responsibility

- **Identification and Verification:** When Lord Ram first encounters Lord Hanuman, He doesn't immediately recognize Him as the devout devotee and faithful servant that He is. Instead, He sees Lord Hanuman in the guise of a diminutive monkey. In modern terms, this initial encounter could be seen as a form of screening where Lord Ram needs to identify and verify Lord Hanuman's identity before establishing trust and rapport.
- **Testing Loyalty and Devotion:** After their initial encounter, Lord Ram tests Lord Hanuman's loyalty and devotion by assigning Him various tasks. For example, He asks Lord Hanuman to leap across the ocean to search for Mata Sita. This can be interpreted as a form of screening to assess Lord Hanuman's commitment and capability to serve Lord Ram's cause.
- **Building Trust through Actions:** As Lord Hanuman demonstrates His unwavering loyalty, bravery, and intelligence through His actions, Lord Ram gradually begins to trust Him. This trust is further solidified as Lord Hanuman successfully locates Mata Sita and delivers Lord Ram's message to Her. In modern screening processes, trust is often established through a series of actions and validations of character and capability.
- **Establishing Communication Channels:** Communication plays a crucial role in building trust and collaboration between Lord Ram and Lord Hanuman. Through their interactions, they establish clear communication channels, allowing them to convey their intentions, concerns, and objectives effectively. This effective communication is essential in modern screening processes to ensure mutual understanding and alignment of goals.
- **Mutual Respect and Partnership:** As the story progresses, Lord Ram and Lord Hanuman develop a deep mutual respect and partnership based on trust, loyalty, and shared values. This partnership becomes instrumental in their quest to defeat King Ravan and rescue Mata Sita. In modern screening contexts, mutual respect and partnership are also key factors in establishing successful collaborations and relationships.

Control

Background verification checks on all candidates to become personnel should be carried out prior to joining the organization and on an ongoing basis taking into consideration applicable laws, regulations and ethics and be proportional to the business requirements, the classification of the information to be accessed and the perceived risks.

Purpose

To ensure all personnel are eligible and suitable for the roles for which they are considered and remain eligible and suitable during their employment.

Guidance

A screening process should be performed for all personnel including full-time, parttime and temporary staff. Where these individuals are contracted through suppliers of services, screening requirements should be included in the contractual agreements between the organization and the suppliers. Information on all candidates being considered for positions within the organization should be collected and handled taking into consideration any appropriate legislation existing in the relevant jurisdiction. In some jurisdictions, the organization can be legally required to inform the candidates beforehand about the screening activities. Verification should take into consideration all relevant privacy, PII protection and employment-based legislation and should, where permitted, include the following:

- Availability of satisfactory references;
- A verification for completeness and accuracy of the applicant's curriculum vitae;
- Confirmation of claimed academic and professional qualifications;
- Independent identity verification;
- More detailed verification, such as credit review or review of criminal records if the candidate takes on a critical role.

When an individual is hired for a specific information security role, the organization should make sure the candidate:

- Has the necessary competence to perform the security role;
- Can be trusted to take on the role, especially if the role is critical for the organization.

Where a job, either on initial appointment or on promotion, involves the person having access to information processing facilities and, in particular, if these involve handling confidential/restricted/sensitive information the organization should also consider further, more detailed verifications. Procedures should define criteria and limitations for verification reviews (e.g., who is eligible to screen people and how, when and why verification reviews are carried out). In situations where verification cannot be completed in a timely manner, mitigating controls should be implemented until the review has been finished, for example:

- Delayed on boarding;
- Delayed deployment of corporate assets;
- On boarding with reduced access;
- Termination of employment.

Verification checks should be repeated periodically to confirm ongoing suitability of personnel, depending on the criticality of a person's role.

Prior to employment screening involves gathering all the information required to make a good hire. This includes identifying candidates that meet predetermined job qualifications and verifying the information they provide. The prior to employment screening process spans from application review to the final hiring decision. Throughout that time, candidates are screened for the following items:

- Relevant skills and abilities required to be successful in the position;
- Personality traits;
- Cultural fit;
- Educational experience;
- Professional experience;
- History of drug abuse;
- Criminal history.

When the time comes to make an offer, thorough prior to employment screening leaves the organzation confident that they've selected the most qualified candidate and the best fit for the organization. Employment background verification involves reviewing a potential candidate's past employment records, personal information, and financial data to confirm the authenticity of their claims. The verification ensures that the candidate can be trusted with sensitive information and will be able to execute their tasks responsibly. Hence, the organization will be able to make an informed decision based on the background verification. Employee background screenings adds a layer of security in the hiring process, filtering the most dependable candidates from the lot. Additionally, these checks offer the following benefits:

- Improvement in staff quality;
- Lower risk of workplace violence;
- Reduction employee attrition;
- Identifying qualified employees for the technical work;
- Better organization culture and environment;

Employers must be mindful of the following things when conducting employment background screening :

- Identify the legislation and laws that require you to conduct the background verification;
- Inform the candidate that their candidature in the organization is subject to police verification;
- Seek the candidate's approval for the background check;
- Keep the candidate's information and background check results private and confidential.

The employment background screening is a tedious process involving the following steps:

- Selection of the applicant by the hiring department;
- Contingent offer made to the applicant by the hiring department;
- Acceptance of the offer letter by the applicant;
- The hiring department submits an employment background check request;
- The human resource department approves the request;
- Instructions are sent to the employment background check agency or are done in house;
- The agency/HR conducts the background check and submits the results.

Types of Prior to Employment Screening

There are actually a number of different types of pre-employment screening, and employers will often use more than one.

- **Criminal Records Checks:** Criminal record checks will often include a combination of records derived from multiple sources. They can be done at county, state, federal, or even international levels. Companies can commonly access this data from just online databases. Using those databases to check criminal records is referred to as screen-scraping. This process can sometimes turn up charges against job applicants that are very old or have been dismissed. The general consensus is that the most effective method of getting an accurate picture of a job candidate is to have real people looking through hard copies of records, in order to ensure that they are getting information about the correct person and the true outcome of all criminal cases. Prior to employment screening services are offered by government agencies to employers who want information about driving or criminal records. It's possible that checking criminal records will protect a organization in any negligent hiring lawsuits.
- **Drug Testing:** Drug testing is probably one of the most common screenings that employers use to ensure that job candidates will be productive employees and as a preventative measure against injuries in the workplace. Drug tests identify illegal substances potential employees may have ingested or been exposed to. It must be done in strict compliance with laws of the state where the business is located.
- **Motor Vehicle Records Screening:** Records of license suspensions, accidents, convictions, violation or any disciplinary actions may be verified. Companies whose employees operate motor vehicles in the course of their work, such as trucking, delivery or sales, are most likely to require this type of prior to employment screening.
- **Employment Verification:** Employers verify previous employment listed on resumes and job applications using this type of prior to employment screening. It is also used to check the accuracy of date of employment, job title, and other related details. However, some of the employers which job candidates list on their resume or application may have policies which limit what type of information they will provide

about a former employee. Another important screening element is to verify that a job applicant is eligible to work in the said country.

- **Supervisor/Reference Interviews:** Employers will sometimes want to interview references or former supervisors, in order to evaluate the ability of a candidate to perform the job in question. In these cases, the employers will usually be required to provide written permission from the applicant before anyone will speak with them.
- **Education Verification:** Particularly for entry-level employees, employers like to verify a job applicant's degree, academic performance or major. These reports will verify the dates students attended the academic institution, which fields were studied, the degree earned, grade point averages, and the date of graduation.
- **Licensing and Professional Certification Verification:** Companies will always want to verify that their employees have any licenses that are required for their work. This would include attorneys, medical personnel, engineers, accountants, real estate agents, and more. The pre-employment screening will reveal whether a license is valid, the expiration date, and whether the applicant has been the subject of any type of disciplinary action.

Should Social-Media Be Utilized for Prior to employment screening?

Using social media as a form or prior to employment screening is a controversial issue. While you may be able to tell a lot about a potential employee by looking at their Instagram, Twitter, or Facebook account, doing so may result in legal issues for a organization. There are pros and cons to a business considering social media checks, but it is not yet typically included in standard background screening.

A firm's screening procedures for the appointment or employment of officers and employees must ensure that an individual is not appointed or employed unless:

- For a higher-impact individual: the firm is satisfied that the individual has the appropriate character, knowledge, skills and abilities to act honestly, reasonably and independently; or
- For any other individual: the firm is satisfied about the individual's integrity.

A.6.2 Terms and Conditions of Employment

Security responsibilities must be addressed at the recruitment stage, included in contracts, and monitored during an individual's employment. Candidates must be adequately screened commensurate to the sensitivity of the information being handled. If necessary, all employees and third-party users should sign a confidentiality (nondisclosure) agreement. Prior to hiring or contracting employees or companies, security roles and responsibilities should be clearly articulated in job descriptions or well defined in contract terms and conditions. These roles and responsibilities should be defined in accordance with the organization's security policies. Careful attention should be paid to the validation of references and the appropriate level of background checks as determined by the security roles and responsibilities of the position or contract.

Consideration should be given that the receipt of affirmative references and the successful completion of a background check at a level commensurate with the position's roles and responsibilities be a condition of hire. The purpose of this section is to introduce the security controls for people who work for the organization. These controls are really important because the statistics worldwide show that people working for the companies represent the biggest threat to information security. The most common ways of implementing these security controls are:

- Documenting a human resource management procedure, although it is not a mandatory document;
- Signing contracts with employees and other contractors that include information security clauses;
- Regularly training people on security issues and continual awareness-raising campaigns;
- Introducing a disciplinary process, for all employees who have committed information security breaches.

The objective of this category is to ensure that employees, contractors, and third-party users understand their responsibilities, and are suitable for the roles for which they are considered, in order to reduce the risk of theft, fraud, or misuse of facilities. Security roles and responsibilities of employees, contractors, and third-party users should be defined and documented in accordance with the organization's information security policy. Control includes requirements to:

- Act in accordance with the organization's information security policy, including the execution of processes or activities particular to the individual.

A.6.2 Terms and Conditions – A linkage with Ancient Era

The Kurukshetra War

- **Rules of Engagement:** Before the war began, both sides agreed to certain rules of engagement to ensure a fair and honorable conflict. These rules included not attacking unarmed opponents, refraining from fighting after sunset, and adhering to the principles of dharma in battle. While not written down as formal terms and conditions, these rules were understood and upheld by both sides as part of the ethical conduct of warfare.

- **Alliances and Treaties:** Throughout the epic, various alliances and treaties are formed between different factions involved in the war. These alliances often come with certain conditions and terms, such as mutual defense agreements or promises of support in exchange for territory or resources. The terms of these alliances were typically verbal agreements or understood through customary practices rather than formal written contracts.

- **Code of Conduct:** Both sides in the Kurukshetra War followed certain codes of conduct and ethical principles governing their actions on the battlefield. These codes included concepts such as valor, chivalry, and adherence to one's duty. While not explicitly stated as terms and conditions, these codes guided the behavior of warriors and leaders during the war.

- **Consequences of Violating Agreements:** In the Mahabharata, there are consequences for violating agreements and betraying trust. For example, the violation of rules of engagement or the betrayal of alliances often leads to condemnation and repercussions for the offending party. These consequences serve as a form of informal enforcement of the terms and conditions governing the conduct of the war.

Control

The employment contractual agreements should state the personnel's and the organization's responsibilities for information security.

Purpose

To ensure personnel understand their information security responsibilities for the roles for which they are considered.

Guidance

- The contractual obligations for personnel should take into consideration the organization's information security policy and relevant topic-specific policies. In addition, the following points can be clarified and stated:
  - Information about the scope of access and other privileges the person will have, with respect to the organization's information and information processing facilities;
  - Information about the person's responsibilities, under legal-regulatory-certificatory requirements and organizational policies, specified in that or other signed agreements;
  - As appropriate, information about responsibilities for classification of information and management of organizational information facilities that the person may use;
  - As appropriate, information about the handling of sensitive information, both internal to the organization and that received from or transferred to outside parties;
  - Information about responsibilities that extend outside the organization's boundaries (e.g., for mobile devices and teleworking);
  - Information about the organization's responsibilities for the handling of information related to the person him/herself, generated in the course of employment, contractor or other third-party relationship;
  - Actions that can be anticipated, under the organization's disciplinary process, as a consequence of failure to observe security requirements.

Information security roles and responsibilities should be communicated to candidates during the pre-employment process. The organization should ensure that personnel agree to terms and conditions concerning information security. These terms and conditions should be appropriate to the nature and extent of access they will have to the organization's assets associated with information systems and services. The terms and conditions concerning information security should be reviewed when laws, regulations, the information security policy or topic-specific policies change. Where appropriate, responsibilities contained within the terms and conditions of employment should continue for a defined period after the end of the employment.

Other Information

A code of conduct can be used to state personnel's information security responsibilities regarding confidentiality, PII protection, ethics, appropriate use of the organization's information and other associated assets, as well as reputable practices expected by the organization. An external party, with which supplier personnel are associated, can be required to enter into contractual agreements on behalf of the contracted individual. If the organization is not a legal entity and does not have employees, the equivalent of contractual agreement and terms and conditions can be considered in line with the guidance of this control.

Employees, contractors, and third-party users should agree to and sign a statement of rights and responsibilities for their affiliation with the organization, including rights and responsibilities with respect to information security. The organization should define security roles and responsibilities in accordance with its information security policy. The organization must ensure that information security policies are readily accessible and formally communicated to all personnel on a periodic basis. All employees including contractors, temporary staff, board, and/or committee members should sign confidentiality or non-disclosure agreements as part of their initial terms and conditions of employment. Such agreements should give notice to users of the organization's policies, rights, obligations, and responsibilities in relation to access to information assets. This controls talks about the need for contractual agreement to inform any new employee about their responsibility as well as that of the organization towards information security. What this means is that employees should know about the organization's information security policy, as well as the roles and responsibilities of people who work with information security in the organization. This can be done by having personnel sign an employment contract or something similar. Such a contractual agreement will typically outline the general requirements for protecting information assets, including physical security, environmental controls, access controls and contingency planning as well as a confidentiality agreement. Information security obligations should be explicitly stated in contracts with both employees and contractors. Insist that all parties involved are aware of and familiar with NDAs, legal rights and duties, data processing, and the use of third-party information. It is critical that disciplinary measures are guided by certain policies within the organization. The contractual agreement with employees and contractors must state their and the organization's responsibilities for information security. These agreements are a good place to put key information security general and individual responsibilities as they carry legal weight - meaning they are backed up by the law. This is also very important as regards to compliance obligation. They should reference and cover a whole range of control areas including overall compliance with the ISMS as well as more specifically acceptable use, IPR ownership, return of assets etc.

Confidentiality, non-disclosure, and/or contractual agreements should also be reviewed when there are changes to terms of employment or contract, particularly when employees are due to leave the organization or contracts are due to expire. The organization should ensure that that all personnel employed are adequately bound to the confidentiality and non-disclosure requirements. Punitive and/or remedial action(s) to be taken if the employee disregards security requirements should also be clearly described in the terms and conditions. Such measures must be aligned with a formally documented disciplinary process. Casual staff and third-party users not already covered by an existing contract should also be required to sign a confidentiality agreement prior to being given access to information processing facilities or information assets. The organization must establish agreements with equipment repairers to safeguard the confidentiality of information on equipment undergoing repair.

This control may also include the provision of an organizational code of conduct or code of ethics to the employee, contractor, or third party. It may also include a requirement to sign, prior to being given access or other privileges to information or information processing facilities, a separate confidentiality or non-disclosure agreement; and/or acceptable use of assets agreement.

Code Of Conduct

Code of Conduct should include clear instructions for safeguarding sensitive information. The organization should provide every employee with a copy of this policy and require every new hire to sign an agreement to abide by the code of conduct. Over time the organization might need to update or amend this document to accommodate the implementation of new processes or procedures. HR representatives are responsible for ensuring that employees are made aware of such changes.

A.6.3 Information Security Awareness, Education and Training

This control aims to ensure that employees, contractors, and third-party users are aware of information security threats and concerns, of their responsibilities and liabilities, and are equipped to support organizational security policy in the course of their normal work and to reduce the risk of human error. It covers the need for employees of an organization to receive appropriate information security awareness, education, and training, plus regular updates of the organization's information security policy, especially as it applies to their job function.

Employee Orientation for new employees: All new employees should participate in new employee orientation workshops or be provided with pertinent information including security policies and procedures and potential disciplinary processes/actions for any security breaches. Additionally, new employees should be required to sign an acknowledgment indicating that they read and understand the organization's acceptable use policy, the organization's security policies, and any non-disclosures (if applicable). All managers and supervisors should be expected to emphasize the importance of security to their employees. Organizations should provide relevant information security information delivered on a defined schedule (annually, bi-annually, etc.) appropriate to the employee's job roles and responsibilities. All employees should be required to take general training on basic information security practices and/or acknowledge their basic understanding of the organization's security policies and procedures. The main benefit of information security awareness training is protection from attacks on digital systems or a data breach. Preventing such incidents is critical because a successful cyber-attack can financially cripple an organization and significantly harm its brand reputation.

A.6.3 Information Security Awareness, Education and Training – A linkage with Ancient Era

- **The Power of Deception and Social Engineering:** The Ramayana, narrates instances where characters, such a King Ravan and Maricha, use deception tactics to manipulate others. Similarly, cyber-attackers often employ social engineering techniques, such as Phishing, to deceive individuals and gain unauthorized access to their systems or sensitive information. By studying the tricks and consequences depicted in the Ramayana, one can develop an understanding of how deception can be used and how to be cautious against such tactics in the digital realm.

- **The Golden Deer and Social Engineering:** In the Ramayana, King Ravan disguises himself as a golden deer to lure Lord Ram and Lakshman away from their heritage, creating an opportunity for him to abduct Mata Sita. This can be compared to Social Engineering tactics used by the cyber-attackers who often send deception emails or messages to trick individuals into revealing sensitive information or clicking on malicious links. Just as Lord Ram and Lakshman fell victim to the deception of the golden deer, individuals can unknowingly fall prey to social engineering attacks, emphasizing the need for awareness and caution in the digital world.
- **Insider Threats and Trust: The Story of Shakuni's Influence:** In the Mahabharata, Shakuni, the material uncle of the Kaurav's, manipulated his nephews into engaging in unethical practices and conspiracies against the Pandav's. His influence on the Kaurav's led to various incidents, including the infamous game of dice that triggered the Kurukshetra war. This story highlights the potential risks posed by Insider Threats within the organizations. Insider Threats can arise from employees with malicious intent, negligence, or vulnerability to manipulation. Cybersecurity professionals should implement Strict Access Controls, Monitor User Activities, and Establish Mechanism to detect and mitigate Insider Threats.
- **Continuous Learning and Adaptability - Lord Krishna's role as a Problem Solver:** Throughout the Mahabharata, Lord Krishna exhibited a remarkable ability to solve problems, address challenges and adapt to changing circumstances whether it is in battle war or the king court. He was always there with Pandav's to solve the problem and guide them. This story emphasizes the importance of continuous learning and adaptability in cybersecurity. Professionals should stay updated with the latest threats, technologies, and industry practices, while also cultivating a mindset of adaptability to navigate evolving cybersecurity landscapes.
- **Lessons from Vibhishan and Insider Threats:** Vibhishan realizes the

error of his ways and switches sides to support Lord Ram. His betrayal of King Ravan highlights the concept of insider threats in cybersecurity. Insider Threats refer to individuals within an organization who misuse their unauthorized access to cause harm or compromise security. Vibhishan's transformation reminds us of the importance of insider threat detection and prevention measures in organizations, such as monitoring user activities, implementing access controls, and fostering a culture of security awareness.

Control

Personnel of the organization and relevant interested parties should receive appropriate information security awareness, education and training and regular updates of the organization's information security policy, topic-specific policies and procedures, as relevant for their job function.

Purpose

To ensure personnel and relevant interested parties are aware of and fulfill their information security responsibilities.

Guidance

General

An information security awareness, education and training programme should be established in line with the organization's information security policy, topic-specific policies and relevant procedures on information security, taking into consideration the organization's information to be protected and the information security controls that have been implemented to protect the information. Information security awareness, education and training should take place periodically. Initial awareness, education and training can apply to new personnel and to those who transfer to new positions or roles with substantially different information security requirements. Personnel's understanding should be assessed at the end of an awareness, education or training activity to test knowledge transfer and the effectiveness of the awareness, education and training programme.

Awareness

An information security awareness programme should aim to make personnel aware of their responsibilities for information security and the means by which those responsibilities are discharged. The awareness programme should be planned taking into consideration the roles of personnel in the organization, including internal and external personnel. The activities in the awareness programme should be scheduled over time, preferably regularly, so that the activities are repeated and cover new personnel. It should also be built on lessons learnt from information security incidents.

The awareness programme should include a number of awareness-raising activities via appropriate physical or virtual channels such as campaigns, booklets, posters, newsletters, websites, information sessions, briefings, e-learning modules and e-mails.

Information security awareness should cover general aspects such as:

1. Management's commitment to information security throughout the organization;
2. Familiarity and compliance needs concerning applicable information security rules and obligations, taking into account information security policy and topic-specific policies, standards, laws, statutes, regulations, contracts and agreements;
3. Personnel accountability for one's own actions and inaction, and general responsibilities towards securing or protecting information belonging to the organization and interested parties;
4. Basic information security procedures and baseline controls;
5. Contact points and resources for additional information and advice on information security matters, including further information security awareness materials.

Education and Training

The organization should identify, prepare and implement an appropriate training plan for technical teams whose roles require specific skill sets and expertise. Technical teams should have the skills for configuring and maintaining the required security level for devices, systems, applications and services. If there are missing skills, the organization should take action and acquire them. The education and training programme should consider different forms [e.g., lectures or self-studies, being mentored by expert staff or consultants (on-the-job training), rotating staff members to follow different activities, recruiting already skilled people and hiring consultants]. It can use different means of delivery including classroom-based, distance learning, web-based, self-paced and others. Technical personnel should keep their knowledge up to date by subscribing to newsletters and magazines or by attending conferences and events aimed at technical and professional improvement.

Other Information

When composing an awareness programme, it is important not only to focus on the 'what' and 'how', but also the 'why', when possible. It is important that personnel understand the aim of information security and the potential effect, positive and negative, on the organization of their own behavior. Information security awareness, education and training can be part of, or conducted in collaboration with, other activities, for example general information management, ICT, security, privacy or safety training.

All employees of the organization, and, where relevant, contractors and third-party users, should receive appropriate awareness training in and regular updates of organizational policies and procedures relevant to their job functions. Information security awareness, education, and training is the process of informing users about the importance of information security and encouraging them to improve their own computer security habits. Users must be made aware of the security risks that can come from their activities and how they can protect themselves against these risks. Information security awareness, education, and training is critical components of any organization's success. It is critical that all employees understand the importance of information security and how it impacts everyone. The more employees understand how to protect themselves from cyber threats, the more secure your organization will be. The organization must ensure that information security awareness programs inform personnel of the existence and availability of current versions of the information security policy, standards, and procedures. The organization must ensure that employee information security awareness and procedures are reinforced by regular updates. Security reminder messages should be posted in secured areas and/or regularly communicated to personnel according to the intended audience and/or classification of the notifications. A copy of the information security policies should be issued to all new personnel as they join and to all existing personnel.

Personnel should be made aware of the security classifications of the information assets that they use, and that they handle them appropriately. Some of the control includes:

1. A formal induction process that includes information security training, prior to being granted access to information or information systems;
2. Ongoing training in security control requirements, legal-regulatory-certificate responsibilities, and correct procedures generally, suitable to each person's rules and responsibilities; and
3. Periodic reminders that cover both general security topics and specific issues of relevance to the organization given its history of security incidents; and
4. Other appropriate efforts to raise and maintain awareness of security issues.

In crafting a good security awareness training program, companies should emphasize to employees the criticality of protecting the organization and provide an overview of the corresponding corporate policies and procedures that cover how to work securely and who to contact if they discover a potential threat. They should also tailor the program to reach employees of all levels at different stages of their employment to keep information security a top priority and prevent any employee, whether brand new or decades in, from endangering the organization. An effective training program should reach workers with varying degrees of technical aptitude and knowledge with different learning styles.

It should be multifaceted, with a collection of lessons and learning opportunities so it engages everyone in the organization, regardless of their knowledge levels and learning styles. Additionally, a comprehensive program has role-based content, delivering instructional material tailored to the needs of an employee's role and even material tailored to third-party stakeholders, such as business partners and contract workers, to ensure those individuals don't put the organization at risk.

The training content should range from written material to interactive online learning to gamification sessions so employees can access information in formats they learn best, whether it's audio, visual, etc. Content should include lessons with varying degrees of complexity so employees can access the most relevant information according to their roles. Follow-up and ongoing messaging remind employees of the organization's security policies; delivers short refreshers on how to identify and avoid security risks and violations, as well as how to handle possible security problems; and alerts them to any emerging threats. Measuring and reporting employees involvement in training programs, as well as the effectiveness of the organization's awareness training, help identify any weaknesses in the program and areas in need of strengthening. A good training program typically has a mix of the following:

- Formal education, such as structured lessons and mandatory instruction;
- Informational learning opportunities, such as weekly emails containing tips, policy updates and security news updates;
- Experiential sessions and even gamification, where employees are required to work through simulations and scenarios to test their understanding and reinforce their training so they're better prepared to handle real-world security challenges; and
- Security champions, employees who have become particularly skilled at understanding security and are willing to teach and promote security best practices among their colleagues.

The security awareness training program should be comprehensive, starting with rudimentary lessons and moving up to advanced materials. It should also include an assessment process to help organizations identify employees's level of security awareness and subsequently create a learning pathway for them. Additionally, organizational leaders need to consider that different roles within the organization face different risks and threats while developing the training program. For example, an entry-level employee with limited access to sensitive data and core IT systems likely encounters fewer risky scenarios than a high-level executive who works with the organization's proprietary information and financial systems or a senior IT employee who is authorized to work on the core technologies that enable the business. Larger organizations with significant HR departments may be able to develop and deliver their own awareness training program or at least supplement it with outside resources. Many organizations choose to outsource most or all of the training, however, considering this the most effective and efficient way to implement necessary education for its employees. Either way, organizational leaders should have mechanisms to measure whether the training is effective at both the enterprise level and at the individual employee level.

Experts agree awareness and training should be ongoing within the organization. Ongoing training helps employees build a security mindset, helping them stay diligent, and gives organizations opportunities to educate employees on new policies and procedures and alert them to the new and evolving threats and risks they may face. To best achieve this, organizations should establish a schedule to determine what training to deliver to what employees and how frequently training must occur. Security awareness training should ideally take place when a new employee joins the organization as part of a mandatory onboarding process. When assessments, evaluations or testing indicate a lapse in best practices, organizations should consider mandatory training for the whole enterprise or for individual employees. Many organizations opt to use a learning management system to make training content easily and readily available to employees.

A.6.4 Disciplinary Process

Disciplinary Process talks about the need for organizations to put in place some form of disciplinary process to serve as a deterrent so that personnel will not commit information security violations. Information security violation is a breach of the rules or laws governing the proper handling of information. Information security policies are established by organizations to protect confidential, proprietary and personal data. Information security policies also include computer security policies that help ensure the safety and integrity of data stored on computers. Information security violations include but are not restricted to:

- Browsing computer or paper records without appropriate authorization and a legitimate business reason;
- Information lost or compromised;
- Loss or theft of equipment containing organizational information;
- Repeated incidents of unattended or lost smart cards;
- Using unencrypted memory sticks;
- Using customer or employee personal data or information without appropriate authorization and a legitimate business reason;
- Disclosing customer or employee personal data or information without appropriate authorization and legitimate business reason;
- Disclosing computer passwords;
- Sending the information insecurely outside the organization;
- Sending sensitive personal data or identifiable personal information to the wrong person or customer;
- Unauthorized disclosure of organizational information to third parties.

This disciplinary process should be formally communicated and a suitable penalty designed for employees and other relevant interested parties who commit a violation. If an employee violates an organization's information security policy, he or she could be subject to disciplinary action or termination from employment. In some cases, a organization may choose not to terminate an employee who breaks its computer usage policy, but instead take other appropriate measures to prevent future violations of organization policy.

A.6.4 Disciplinary Process – A linkage with Ancient Era

Mata Sita Abduction

- **Violation of Security Protocol**: Mata Sita's abduction can be seen as a breach of security protocol. In a modern organizational setting, security protocols are established to protect assets and personnel. King Ravan's actions in forcibly taking Mata Sita against Her will, can be interpreted as a violation of these protocols, leading to consequences.
- **Investigation and Accountability:** Following the abduction, Lord Ram and His allies conduct an investigation to determine the circumstances of Mata Sita's disappearance and hold accountable those responsible. In a disciplinary process, there is often an investigation phase to gather evidence and determine culpability before taking corrective action.
- **Imposition of Sanctions:** In response to Mata Sita's abduction, Lord Ram mobilizes His allies and resources to confront King Ravan and rescue Mata Sita. This can be likened to imposing sanctions or corrective measures in a disciplinary process to address the violation and restore order.
- **Rehabilitation and Reconciliation:** After the rescue of Mata Sita and the defeat of King Ravan, there is a process of rehabilitation and reconciliation. Lord Ram welcomes Mata Sita back into His fold but also subjects Her to a trial by fire (Agni Pariksha) to prove Her purity and dispel any doubts. This can be seen as a form of reconciliation and restoration of trust, albeit through a culturally specific ritual.
- **Learning and Improvement:** The Vastra Haran incident serves as a learning opportunity for the characters in the Ramayana, highlighting the importance of vigilance, adherence to protocols, and the consequences of security lapses. Similarly, in organizational discipline, incidents of misconduct or security breaches often prompt reviews and improvements to prevent future occurrences.

Lanka Dahan

- **Violation of Ethical Standards:** King Ravan's actions, including his abduction of Mata Sita and his refusal to return Her despite multiple warnings, can be seen as a violation of ethical standards. In a modern organization, such actions might lead to disciplinary measures due to their unethical nature.

- **Investigation and Accountability:** Prior to the burning of Lanka, Lord Ram and His allies engage in discussions and deliberations to determine the appropriate course of action. This can be linked to an investigation phase in a disciplinary process, where evidence is gathered and accountability is established before taking action.
- **Decision-Making and Leadership:** Lord Ram, as the leader, makes the decision to burn Lanka as a strategic and punitive measure against King Ravan. This decision reflects His authority and leadership in the situation, which is akin to the role of management in disciplinary processes within organizations.
- **Execution of Disciplinary Action**: The burning of Lanka can be interpreted as a form of disciplinary action or consequence for King Ravan's actions. It serves as a decisive and forceful response to King Ravan's defiance and wrongdoing, demonstrating the consequences of unethical behavior.
- **Restorative Justice and Rehabilitation**: Following the burning of Lanka, there is a process of reconciliation and restoration. Lord Ram, after defeating King Ravan, restores order and justice by installing Vibhishana as the new ruler of Lanka. This can be seen as a form of restorative justice and rehabilitation, where stability is restored after disciplinary action has been taken.
- **Learning and Improvement:** The burning of Lanka serves as a lesson for characters in the Ramayana, highlighting the consequences of unethical behavior and the importance of adhering to moral principles. Similarly, in modern organizations, disciplinary actions often prompt reflection and learning, leading to improvements in behavior and practices.

Control

A disciplinary process should be formalized and communicated to take actions against personnel and other relevant interested parties who have committed an information security policy violation.

Purpose

To ensure personnel and other relevant interested parties understand the consequences of information security policy violation, to deter and appropriately deal with personnel and other relevant interested parties who committed the violation.

Guidance

The disciplinary process should not be initiated without prior verification that an information security policy violation has occurred. The formal disciplinary process should provide for a graduated response that takes into consideration factors such as:

- The nature and gravity of the breach and its consequences;
- Whether the offence was intentional or unintentional;
- Whether or not this is a first or repeated offence;
- Whether or not the violator was properly trained.

The response should take into consideration relevant legal, statutory, regulatory, contractual and business requirements as well as other factors as required. The disciplinary process should also be used as a deterrent to prevent personnel and other relevant interested parties from violating the information security policy, topic specific policies and procedures for information security. Deliberate information security policy violations can require immediate actions.

Other Information

Where possible, the identity of individuals subject to disciplinary action should be protected in line with applicable requirements. When individuals demonstrate excellent behavior with regard to information security, they can be rewarded to promote information security and encourage good behavior. There should be a formal disciplinary process for employees who have committed a security breach. A security breach happens where there has been a deliberate attempt, whether successful or not, to compromise organizational assets such as information, people, IT, premises, or any accident resulting in loss of assets. A formal disciplinary process must be established by the organization in relation to employees who have violated the organization's security policies and procedures and, for retention of evidence. Disciplinary processes should aim to be a deterrent to employees who might otherwise be inclined to disregard security policies and procedures. Where appropriate, discipline should be in line with the relevant employment act conditions. For employees not covered under this, discipline should be in line with contract terms and conditions. Where it is formally stated that some activity is not allowed, but informally action is not generally taken against the activity (e.g., banning the distribution of jokes via e-mail), any subsequent disciplinary action that is taken in this regard may be subject to legal challenge and may, therefore, be unenforceable. Disciplinary action should accurately reflect the nature of the breach of policy. Minor infringements are to be expected and should be dealt with through cautions and user security awareness education. Repeated minor infringements may be symptomatic of an inappropriate policy or control, and should entail a re-assessment of its suitability. Repeated minor infringements not due to an inappropriate policy or control, or a major breach of security, maybe more suitably dealt with by formal sanctions such as termination of temporary or permanent access or legal action. The nature of appropriate disciplinary action should be determined by the workforce management function, in consultation with security officers and with legal officers if legal action is contemplated. Control includes:

- A reasonable evidentiary standard to initiate investigations;
- Appropriate investigatory processes, including specification of roles and responsibilities, standards for the collection of evidence and chain of custody of evidence;
- Disciplinary proceedings that observe reasonable requirements for due process and quality of evidence;
- A reasonable evidentiary standard to determine fault, that ensures correct and fair treatment for persons suspected of a breach;
- Sanctions that appropriately take into consideration factors such as the nature and gravity of the breach, its impact on operations, whether it is a first or repeat offence, whether or not the violator was appropriately trained, whether or not the violator exercised due care or exhibited negligence;
- An overall process that functions both as deterrent and sanction.

A.6.5 Responsibilities after Termination or Change of Employment

This control covers the need for organizations to define the information security duties and responsibilities that remain valid should personnel stop work or move to a new department. These duties and responsibilities should be communicated to the employee as well as any other relevant party. To prevent unauthorized access to sensitive information, access must be revoked immediately upon termination/separation of an employee with access to such information. This also includes the return of any assets of the organization that was held by the employee. To protect the organization's interests as part of the process of changing or terminating employment. This Annex says that, if the termination happened for any employee, they are legally bound to maintain the information security. Employees should sign a Return of Property form policy where they return all the properties of the organization. This is not just about the exit and termination, it's about confidentiality. The organization must advise the employee that they don't have access to information asset and must be kept confidential.

A.6.5 Responsibilities after Termination or Change of Employment – A linkage with Ancient Era

Exile of Lord Ram:

Lord Ram is unjustly banished from the kingdom due to the manipulation of His stepmother, Queen Kaikeyi, who seeks the throne for her own son, Bharat. Despite being rightful heir, Prince Ram willingly accepts the exile to fulfil His father's promise. Just as Prince Ram accepted this change in circumstances with grace and dignity, individuals facing termination or a change in employment should handle the situation professionally, accepting the reality and focusing on the next steps.

Control:

Information security responsibilities and duties that remain valid after termination or change of employment should be defined, enforced and communicated to relevant personnel and other interested parties.

Purpose:

To protect the organization's interests as part of the process of changing or terminating employment or contracts.

Guidelines:

The process for managing termination or change of employment should define which information security responsibilities and duties should remain valid after termination or change. This can include confidentiality of information, intellectual property and other knowledge obtained, as well as responsibilities contained within any other confidentiality agreement. Responsibilities and duties still remain valid after termination of employment or contract should be contained in the individual's terms and conditions of employment, contract or agreement. Other contracts or agreements that continue for a defined period after the end of the individual's employment can also contain information security responsibilities. Changes of responsibility or employment should be managed as the termination of the current responsibility or employment combined with the initiation of the new responsibility or employment. Information security roles and responsibilities held by any individual who leaves or changes job roles should be identified and transferred to another individual. A process should be established for the communication of the changes and of operating procedures to personnel, other interested parties and relevant contact persons. The process for the termination or change of employment should also be applied to external personnel when a termination occurs of personnel, the contract or the job with the organization, or when there is a change of the job within the organization.

Other Information

In many organizations, the HR function is generally responsible for the overall termination process and works together with the supervising manager of the employee transitioning to manage the information security aspects of the relevant procedures. In the case of personnel provided through an external party, this termination process is undertaken by the external party in accordance with the contract between the organization and the external party.

Termination or Change of Employment

This control should be implemented when an employee or contractor leaves the organization, or the contract is terminated before it expires. The purpose of this control is to protect the organization's information security interests as part of the process of changing or terminating employment or contracts. This control can also work to protect against the risk of employees who have access to sensitive information and processes, misusing their position for personal gain or malicious intent, particularly after they have left the organization or job role. Control aims to protect the organization's information security interests as part of the process of changing or terminating employment or contracts. This includes employees, contractors and third parties who have access to the organization sensitive information. Implementing the control means assessing whether any individuals who have access to the organization sensitive personal data are leaving the organization and whether it is necessary to take steps to ensure that they do not retain and continue to access the sensitive personal data after their departure. If organization finds that someone is leaving and there is a risk that sensitive personal data may be disclosed, then the organization must take reasonable steps before they leave, or as soon as possible after they have left, so this does not happen. In order to meet the requirements, the terms and conditions of an individual's employment, contract, or agreement should specify any information security responsibilities and duties that remain in effect after the end of the relationship. Information security duties may also be included in other contracts or agreements that extend beyond the end of an employee's employment.

To ensure that employees, contractors, and third-party employees exit the organization, or change employment responsibilities within the organization, in an orderly manner. Responsibilities for performing employment termination or change of employment should be clearly defined and assigned. The organization must implement and maintain a procedure or set of procedures to effectively manage departing employees or the withdrawal of assigned responsibilities for employees, contractors, and other third-party users. The procedure must also be included for the withdrawal of assigned responsibilities resulting from a change in employment status for employees, contractors, and other third-party users. The organization should ensure that important knowledge or operational skills have been transferred to other resources prior to the departure of the employee and/or contractor. Control includes:

- Changes of responsibilities and duties within the organization are processed as a termination and re-hire, using standard controls for those processes unless otherwise indicated;
- Other employees, contractors, and third parties are appropriately informed of a person's changed status; and
- Any post-employment responsibilities are specified in the terms and conditions of employment, or a contractor's or third party's contract;

Return of Assets

All employees, contractors, and third parties should return all of the organization's assets in their possession upon termination of the employment relationship or contract. The organization must establish procedures and processes to transfer official information contained on personal devices/assets to organization-owned information assets. Such procedures shall include a provision for the secure erasure of all official information that is stored on the personal device. Assets must be sanitized, secured and those assets not required must be safely disposed of. Control includes:

- Formalization of the process for return;
- Inclusion in this requirement of the organization's hardware, software and data of any kind; and
- Where the employee, contractor or third party use personal equipment, secure erasure of software and data belonging to the organization.

Removal of Access Rights

Access rights to information and information systems should be removed upon termination of the employment or contractual relationship. The organization must have an established and logged procedure for the withdrawal and/or modification of access rights for departing employees, contractors, and third-party users. Control includes:

- Changes of employment or contractual status include removal of all rights associated with prior roles and duties, and creation of rights appropriate to the new roles and duties;

- Removal or reduction of access rights prior to the termination, where risks indicate this step to be appropriate.

A.6.6 Confidentiality or Non-Disclosure Agreements

A Non-Dsclosure Agreement (NDA), also known as a confidentiality agreement, is a legally binding contract in which one party usually the organization agrees to give a second party confidential information about its business or products and the second party agrees not to share this information with anyone else for a specified period of time. NDAs are used to protect sensitive information and intellectual property (IP) by outlining in detail what information must remain private and what information can be shared or released to the public. NDAs are typically signed at the beginning of a business relationship. The information covered by a NDA can be unlimited, ranging from test results to system specifications to customer lists and sales figures. If the NDA is broken and information is leaked, it is considered a breach of contract.

Key elements of a NDA include but not limited to:

- Identification of the participants;
- Definition of what is considered to be confidential;
- Duration of the confidentiality commitment;
- Exclusions from confidential protection;
- Statement of the appropriate use of the information to be disclosed;
- Miscellaneous provisions;
- Terms of agreements;
- Consequences of violating a NDA.

A.6.6 Confidentiality or Non-Disclosure Agreements – A linkage with Ancient Era

- **Mata Sita's disguise in the Ashoka Grove:** After being abducted by King Ravan and imprisoned in the Ashoka Grove in Lanka, Mata Sita maintains Her identity in secrecy. Despite King Ravan's persistent attempts to extract information from Her, She remains tight-lipped about Her true identity and Her relationship with Lord Ram. This can be linked to the obligation of individuals under NDA to keep sensitive information confidential, even in the face of pressure or coercion.
- **Hanuman's Reconnaissance Mission:** When Lord Hanuman is sent by Lord Ram to locate Mata Sita, He enters Lanka in disguise and gathers

crucial information about Her whereabouts without revealing His true identity or the purpose of His mission. Lord Hanuman's discretion and ability to gather intelligence covertly demonstrate a parallel to the confidentiality expected under NDA, where individuals are required to handle sensitive information with care and refrain from disclosing it to unauthorized parties.

Control

Confidentiality or non-disclosure agreements reflecting the organization's needs for the protection of information should be identified, documented, regularly reviewed and signed by personnel and other relevant interested parties.

Purpose

To maintain confidentiality of information accessible by personnel or external parties.

Guidance

Confidentiality or NDA should address the requirement to protect confidential information using legally enforceable terms and are applicable to interested parties and personnel of the organization. Based on an organization's information security requirements, the terms in the agreements should be determined by taking into consideration the type of information that will be handled, its classification level, its use and the permissible access by the other party. To identify requirements for confidentiality or nondisclosure agreements, the following elements should be considered:

- A definition of the information to be protected;
- The expected duration of an agreement, including cases where it can be necessary to maintain confidentiality indefinitely or until the information becomes publicly available;
- The required actions when an agreement is terminated;
- The responsibilities and actions of signatories to avoid unauthorized information disclosure;
- The ownership of information, trade secrets and intellectual property, and how this relates to the protection of confidential information;

- The permitted use of confidential information and rights of the signatory to use the information;
- The right to audit and monitor activities that involve confidential information for highly sensitive circumstances;
- The process for notification and reporting of unauthorized disclosure or confidential information leakage;
- The terms for information to be returned or destroyed at agreement termination;
- The expected actions to be taken in the case of non-compliance with the agreement.

The organization should take into consideration the compliance with confidentiality and NDA for the jurisdiction to which they apply. Requirements for confidentiality and NDA should be reviewed periodically and when changes occur that influence these requirements.

Other Information

Confidentiality and NDA protect the organization's information and inform signatories of their responsibility to protect, use and disclose information in a responsible and authorized manner. Confidentiality or NDA are legally enforceable documents designed to protect the organization's confidential information and intellectual property. These agreements, signed by the organization and its employees and/or third parties, establish the responsibilities of all parties to ensure that no one discloses sensitive data in an unauthorized manner. These agreements can be used in a wide range of situations, including:

- **Employment:** A confidentiality agreement may be part of the employment contract for a new employee. The agreement ensures that the employee does not disclose any confidential information about the organization, its products or services, employees or vendors. NDA are also used by businesses to prevent their employees from disclosing sensitive information after they leave their jobs.
- **Business Transactions**: Confidentiality agreements are often included in business transactions and the purpose of these agreements is to prevent both parties from disclosing any confidential information obtained during the transaction.

- **Partnerships**: Confidentiality agreements are often used in business transactions when one party wants to protect its existing relationships with customers or suppliers from being disclosed to a new partner.
- **Partnerships** often include confidentiality clauses as part of their partnership agreement so each partner agrees not to disclose any confidential information obtained during their partnership.

Confidentiality agreements are entered into by individuals and businesses alike. They have many purposes, such as:

- Protecting trade secrets and proprietary information from competitors who might otherwise use it against them;
- Preventing an employee from sharing sensitive organization information with another organization; and
- Protecting intellectual property (IP) rights like patents and copyrights.

A good control describes how the requirements for confidentiality or NDA that reflect the organization's needs for the protection of information must be identified, regularly reviewed and documented. As such the organization needs to ensure that any information that needs to be protected, is done so through the use of confidentiality and NDA. Agreements are usually specific to the organization and should be developed with its control needs in mind following the risk analysis work. Standard agreements for confidentiality and non-disclosure that may warrant consideration here include:

- General non-disclosure and mutual NDA;
- Customer agreements using standard terms and conditions, expressing confidentiality within the context of the use of products sold and any complimentary services outlined in a related order form;
- Associate/supplier/partner agreements used for small suppliers and independent service providers who the organization use for delivery of services;
- Employment-related terms;
- Privacy Policies.

A.6.7 Remote Working

Remote working is a practice in which an employee works at a location, usually, but not always, one's home, that is remote from the actual business facility at which he/she is employed. Under this arrangement, the employee maintains close contact with colleagues, and supervisors via various forms of computer, internet, and communication technology. Remote working is an increasingly popular work option in many businesses and industries, and its usage is expected to increase in the future, boosted by new innovations in computer and communication technology.

This desire to spend more time at home and avoid long commutes is touted as a key factor in making telecommuting an attractive benefit. Finally, new technologies have made working from home a viable alternative. With the advent of high-speed modems, fax machines, voice mail, powerful personal computers, electronic mail and the like, workers can now perform their jobs without losing touch with employers and customers.

Advantages of Remote Working

Both employers and employees have found remote working to be a mutually beneficial arrangement in many instances. Proponents cite several positive factors in particular:

- **Happier Employees**: Teleworking arrangements can help workers realize a general improvement in their personal "quality of life." They avoid long, stressful commutes, thus gaining more time for pleasurable activities and more flexibility for changeable tasks like a child and eldercare.
- **Increased Retention of Valued Employees:** Many businesses lose employees when those employees undergo significant life changes, such as starting a family or relocating to another region or state because of a spouse's career. Teleworking is one way in which a business may be able to continue to utilize the services of an otherwise unavailable employee.
- **Increased Employee Productivity**: Business studies and anecdotal evidence both suggest that employees are often much more productive at home, where "drop-in" interruptions and meetings are not distractions. Instead, the teleworker can focus on the job at hand.

Of course, productivity at home is directly related to the employee's level of self-discipline and abilities.

- **Cost Savings**: Businesses can often gain significant savings in facilities costs like office space and parking space requirements when employees telecommute.

Disadvantages of Remote Working

But while telecommuting programs have been highly successful for many businesses of all shapes, sizes, and industry orientations, there are potential pitfalls associated with them. Commonly cited drawbacks include the following:

- **Lack of Oversight**: Direct supervision of teleworkers is not possible.
- **Diminished Productivity**: Some people are unable to be productive at-home work settings, either because of family distractions or their own limited capacity to focus on tasks when more pleasurable activities beckon.
- **Security Problems**: Procedures should be implemented to allow employee access while keeping out unwanted intruders. This includes periodically updated password protection and informing employees concerning the need for remote access security.
- **Isolation**: Partial teleworking arrangements, in which the employee spends a portion of each week (1-3 days) in the office and the remainder working from home, can sometimes be an effective means of addressing this problem.
- **Erosion of Organization Culture and/or Departmental Morale**: Many businesses include certain employees who have a major positive impact on the prevailing office environment. When these employees enter into telecommuting programs, their absence is often deeply felt by the employees left behind. In some cases, this departure from the organization's everyday operations can even have a deleterious effect on the operation's overall culture.
- **Loss of "brainstorming" ability**: The informal bouncing around of ideas is difficult, or even impossible, without the face-to-face contact of a shared workplace.
- **Perceived Damage to Career**: A common perception among

employees of businesses that embrace remote working options is that telecommuters are placed at a disadvantage in terms of career advancement and opportunity.

- **Legal Vulnerability**: Some analysts have expressed concern that some employer liability issues regarding telecommuting practices have yet to be completely settled. They cite issues such as employer liability for home-office accidents under common law; applicability of the employer's insurance coverage when they work at home; and responsibility for equipment located in the home as particular concerns.

A.6.7 Remote Working – A linkage with Ancient Era

Lord Hanuman crossing the ocean to Lanka:

- **Adaptation to Challenges**: Lord Hanuman faced the challenge of crossing a vast ocean to reach Lanka. Similarly, remote workers may encounter various challenges, such as communication barriers, time zone differences, or technical issues. Like Lord Hanuman, they need to adapt to these challenges and find creative solutions to overcome them, whether it's through effective use of technology or adjusting their work schedules.
- **Resourcefulness:** Lord Hanuman didn't have a conventional means of crossing the ocean, so he utilized his extraordinary abilities and the resources available to him. Remote workers similarly need to be resourceful, making use of available tools and technologies to accomplish their tasks and stay connected with their team members despite physical distance.
- **Independence and Self-Reliance:** Lord Hanuman embarked on His mission alone, demonstrating a high degree of independence and self-reliance. Similarly, remote workers often need to work autonomously, managing their tasks and responsibilities without direct supervision. Like Lord Hanuman, they must be self-motivated and proactive in their approach to work.
- **Communication and Collaboration:** Despite being on a solo mission, Lord Hanuman maintained communication with His allies, such as Lord Ram and Sugriv, through His messenger role. In remote working,

effective communication and collaboration are crucial for staying connected with team members and ensuring alignment on goals and tasks. Lord Hanuman's role as a messenger emphasizes the importance of clear and timely communication in remote work settings.

- **Determination and Focus:** Lord Hanuman remained focused and determined in His mission to find Mata Sita, despite facing obstacles and challenges along the way. Similarly, remote workers need to maintain focus and determination in achieving their goals, even when working outside of a traditional office environment.
- **Delegation and Trust:** Lord Ram demonstrates the importance of delegating tasks and trusting his allies to carry out their responsibilities. When Lord Ram tasks Lord Hanuman with the mission to find Mata Sita, He entrusts him with a critical mission, confident in Lord Hanuman's abilities and loyalty. Likewise, in remote work environments, managers need to trust their team members to fulfill their roles and responsibilities, even when they are not physically present.
- **Supporting Remote Teams:** Just as Lord Ram provides guidance and support to His allies during their missions, leaders in remote work settings must offer support and resources to ensure their teams can succeed. This includes providing access to necessary tools and technology, offering clear communication and direction, and fostering a supportive work culture where team members feel valued and motivated.

Control

Security measures should be implemented when personnel are working remotely to protect information accessed, processed or stored outside the organization's premises.

Purpose

To ensure the security of information when personnel are working remotely.

Guidance

Remote working occurs whenever personnel of the organization work from a location outside of the organization's premises, accessing information whether in hard copy or electronically via ICT equipment. Remote working environments include those referred to as "teleworking", "telecommuting", "flexible workplace", "virtual work environments" and "remote maintenance".

NOTE: It is possible that not all the recommendations in this guidance can be applied due to local legislation and regulations in different jurisdictions. Organizations allowing remote working activities should issue a topic-specific policy on remote working that defines the relevant conditions and restrictions. Where deemed applicable, the following matters should be considered:

- The existing or proposed physical security of the remote working site, taking into account the physical security of the location and the local environment, including the different jurisdictions where personnel are located;
- Rules and security mechanisms for the remote physical environment such as lockable filing cabinets, secure transportation between locations and rules for remote access, clear desk, printing and disposal of information and other associated assets, and information security event reporting;
- The expected physical remote working environments;
- The communications security requirements, taking into account the need for remote access to the organization's systems, the sensitivity of the information to be accessed and passed over the communication link and the sensitivity of the systems and applications;
- The use of remote access such as virtual desktop access that supports processing and storage of information on privately owned equipment;
- The threat of unauthorized access to information or resources from other persons at the remote working site;
- The threat of unauthorized access to information or resources from other persons in public places;
- The use of home networks and public networks, and requirements or restrictions on the configuration of wireless network services;
- Use of security measures, such as firewalls and protection against malware;

- Secure mechanisms for deploying and initializing systems remotely;
- Secure mechanisms for authentication and enablement of access privileges takin into consideration the vulnerability of single-factor authentication mechanisms where remote access to the organization's network is allowed.

The guidelines and measures to be considered should include:

- The provision of suitable equipment and storage furniture for the remote working activities, where the use of privately-owned equipment that is not under the control of the organization is not allowed;
- A definition of the work permitted, the classification of information that can be held and the internal systems and services that the remote worker is authorized to access;
- The provision of training for those working remotely and those providing support.
- This should include how to conduct business in a secure manner while working remotely;
- The provision of suitable communication equipment, including methods for securing remote access;
- Physical security;
- Rules and guidance on family and visitor access to equipment and information;
- The provision of hardware and software support and maintenance;
- The provision of insurance;
- The procedures for backup and business continuity;
- Audit and security monitoring;
- Revocation of authority and access rights and the return of equipment when the remote working activities are terminated.

Establishing Remote Working

Allowing employees to work away from the office is becoming a common practice in the way to do business today. The ability to work remotely is seen as both a source of incentive for an employee's productivity and cost savings for organizations, not to mention the possibility for the organization to reach the right professional it wants in any part of the world. But, this scenario of information outside the direct control of the organization also poses significant risks to information security that should be handled properly. The characteristics of teleworking is:

- The worker is outside of the organization's environment;
- Information and communication technologies are used to stay linked to the office.

Considering this, we can have these possible scenarios for teleworking:

- People are working from home or from a place that neither is their home or the organization;
- People are using fixed or mobile device;
- People are using public or private communication networks.

Knowing these scenarios is critical to identify the most probable situations that can put your information at risk. From the scenarios previously presented, an information security risk assessment could raise the following risks:

- An employee's family or friends can use the device accessing the organization's systems and see sensitive information;
- Hard copy material used at the remote worksite can be lost or stolen;
- The device itself can be lost or stolen;
- A device lost or stolen can be used to gain unauthorized access to the organization's systems;
- Information can be intercepted during transmission between the organization and the device;
- An outdated device can be compromised and used to invade the organization's systems;
- Information could be copied and extracted from the organization's environment without anyone knowing. The communication channel can be intercepted and used to invade the organization's environment.

It's important to note that, although all devices are at risk of being lost or stolen, the nature of mobile devices increases this risk. An organization can establish the rules for the implementation of safeguards to protect information accessed, processed, or stored outside the organization, such as:

- Who may work remotely?
- Which services are available for teleworkers?
- Which information can be accessed by remote working?
- Which access controls shall be applied before access to information and resources is granted?
- How devices and remote sites should be configured, protected, and used?

Additionally, by implementing an information security awareness, education, and training program based on control A.7.2.2, an organization can structure its efforts to enhance the security of its remote employees by instructing them to take safety precautions related to opening emails, setting strong passwords on their devices, and making clear that information compromise related to a lack of caution could result in disciplinary proceedings and even legal action. No matter in what industry you work, at some point your organization, or at least part of it, will start relying on remote working.

The connectivity provided by information and communication technologies not only allows employees to work from anywhere, increasing productivity and improving response time, but also enables organizations to count on trained professionals from anywhere in the world. But, by exposing organization infrastructure, systems, and information in this way, an organization needs to take precautions for the high risks involved, and with the help of the requirements of ISO 27001 for information security risk management, and the security controls of its Annex A, this task can become less complex and allow organization to take full advantage of teleworking with the least risk.

Implementing a Remote Working Program

- **Identify a Remote Working Coordinator:** If the organization plan to implement remote working with 10 or more employees, it is recommended to identify one employee as the remote working coordinator. This person should manage the overall remote working program to help improve the quality and effectiveness of the organization's program. The remote working coordinator, typically an individual in HR team, is responsible for organizing remote working schedules, arranging proper equipment for each remote worker, tracking program progress and promoting the benefits of remote working among employees.

- **Establish a Remote Working Committee:** The first action for the remote working coordinator is to establish a planning committee composed of representatives from HR, legal, information technology and management. This group can help establish program goals, objectives, written policies and procedures and develop an implementation plan and schedule with milestones. The remote working committee should be responsible for determining the three most important elements of the organization's program: policy, training and evaluation.
- **Create a Remote Working Policy:** Good communication is the essential element of a successful remote working program and all employees should know the program's guidelines and expectations. The remote working policy should define program parameters, including which positions are best suited for remote working. Additionally, the policy should include necessary forms or documentation, including a remote working contract/agreement.
- **Train Employees and Managers:** Since remote working typically involves a cultural change within the organization, each employee and manager should receive training on the remote working policy, procedures and techniques for managing remote workers. Discuss work schedules, communication methods, required technology, success strategies and proper organization to ensure all employees are fully aware of what is expected of them when working remotely.
- **Determining who should do Remote Working:** One of the major challenges for supervisors is determining who is a candidate for remote working. This can be a difficult task, as managers may experience employees who want to do remote working, but are not the best candidate to do so. Managers also may be concerned that if one person is allowed to do remote working, all employees will want to do remote working.
- **Employee Suitability:** A good starting point is to review all positions

and employees within your organization and determine which have the most potential as teleworkers. The best way to determine who is best suited for a remote working situation is to determine certain criteria to be eligible for remote working, and then evaluate each employee's working style against these criteria. Those employees who are highly focused, self-sufficient, flexible, have great organization skills and enjoy the solitude of working at home may be the most adaptable to remote working. The decision process to grant employees the option to remote working could be facilitated by completing a "screening" form that both managers and employees can review and complete together. This process can help the employee understand why he or she may not be a suitable candidate for remote working. This form should allow a manager to rate an employee on characteristics that lead to success in remote working.

- **Job Suitability:** In addition to determining if an employee possesses the right skills to handle a remote working arrangement, managers also need to consider the position or job this person has within the organization. Initially, a particular position may not appear to be compatible with a remote working arrangement; however, if the position is broken down into individual tasks, you may be able to identify tasks that could be accomplished in a remote working setting.
- **Breaking the Cultural Barriers:** A remote working program challenges management traditions, as it fundamentally changes how a manager should think about supervising employees. With teleworkers, managers should evaluate an employee's performance by results, not by physical presence. However, this type of management style brings forth issues of employee trust and empowerment, two key elements of a strong working relationship. Maintain a sense of control even when people are out of sight. Develop increased level of trust and use trust as a purposeful tool. Use technology for staying in touch with remote workers. Rethink and redesign the way certain jobs are performed. Plan further in advance for meetings and other team activities. Focus objectives and expectations on short-term, project-based goals. Adopt location-independent ways of measuring performance and results. Transition teamwork toward more electronic-based collaboration. Trust remote workers at all times and demonstrate this

trust by assigning challenging projects once the employee delivers a strong performance. For example, but not limited to:

- Include remote works in surveys and evaluations;
- Manager must try teleworking yourself when they have the opportunity. It will help increase personal effectiveness and improve understanding of the pros and cons of teleworking;
- Consider remote worker's point of view in all situations. Understand the time frames involved in completing tasks and the resources required to complete them;
- Involve remote workers when setting work goals and objectives;
- Delegate assignments fairly among teleworkers and non-teleworkers;
- Include remote workers in day-to-day activities. Be aware of your remote workers' attitudes and involvement to ensure they don't feel isolated from the main office;
- Encourage informal communication within your team to keep remote workers and co-workers in touch and up-to-date. Consider establishing a "virtual water cooler" via a shared e-mail folder or organizational Intranet;
- Communicate on a regular basis with all technology methods, including phone, email, instant messaging and online meetings;
- Be flexible and open to increasing the frequency of remote working if it is working well for the employee;
- Keep an open mind about remote working. Be flexible with the program's policies and procedures in case they need to be adjusted for any reason.

- **Choosing the Right Remote working Tools:** Before launching a remote work program, an organization should determine a teleworker's technology needs in order to be just as sufficient working remotely as he or she would be in the main office. There are several technology options to help implement remote work, some of which you are already familiar with and others you may need to research further before making the right decision. The inherent technology needs for a teleworker include the following, but not limited to:

- Computer
- Internet Connectivity (high-speed broadband is best)
- E-mail Program
- Telephone
- Fax machine
- Collaboration Software

In looking at these necessities, few allow for quality interaction between an employer and remote worker, and they do not address the "myths" or concerns that managers have when considering remote work. Management's highest concern is the fear of having less control over employees who work from home, and not being able to reach a teleworker when you need them. Both of these concerns, among others, can be addressed with a collaboration software program.

- **Consider Collaboration:** By equipping each remote worker and office worker with high-speed Internet, a web camera, headset and collaboration software, managers can get in touch with remote workers at all times and in return, teleworkers can contact managers, employees, vendors and clients. An effective and useful tool, a collaboration program should include such features as real-time video, telephone quality audio and presence detection systems to allow better interaction between the main office and teleworkers. Additionally, a collaboration tool should have more in-depth interactive components of its system to help the teleworker further engage in activities occurring at the main office. Such components include instant messaging, joint editing, white boarding, live view, chat and secure file sharing/storing. Using a combination of communication methods, such as online meetings, e-mail, fax and phone, will provide a comprehensive Remote Working program.
- **Select a Collaboration Tool:** After establishing specific policies, procedures and measurement methods for the remote working program, organization should next select the right technology. The most interactive and secure method for communications with

teleworkers is a collaboration software program that is designed specifically for the industry and organization structure. The following questions can help organization select a collaboration tool that best meets the organization's teleworking needs:

- Does the collaboration solution offer everything a teleworker needs to work effectively from home?
- Are all the necessary services integrated into one package or would organization need to consider other alternatives?
- Will the solution maintain total privacy and confidentiality of video, audio and data?
- Does the system use a high level of encryption methods?
- How does the provider protect the data and where is it stored?
- Does the system operate through firewalls?
- Is security included in the overall price of the solution, or is it an add-on cost?
- Is education and training about how and when to use the service readily available and/or customized for the teleworker?
- What type of support will be available to the teleworker? Is the support included, or must you pay for telephone calls to client services?
- What are the contractual arrangements? Does the provider offer one price for multiple participants, sometimes called "seats"?

The organization find the best solutions for remote working, but also find ways to save costs on implementing the program. To minimize technology expenses, look for a collaboration program that allows you to purchase "seats," which means you can purchase licenses for a group of participants rather than having to pay for each minute you are online using the program for a meeting.

- **Ensuring Security at Home:** Oftentimes, organizations overlook the potential security risks when allowing an employee to work from home. While office may have security measures in place, employee's home may not. The Computer Security Institute, a San Francisco-based association of information security, recently conducted its

10th annual "Computer Crime and Security Survey." According to the survey, large corporations and government agencies acknowledged more than $130 million of financial losses due to computer breaches. Therefore, it is imperative to consider technology tools that provide stringent security standards to ensure the organization's information is not compromised from a teleworker's computer.

- **Protect E-mail Systems:** E-mail can still be an effective, easy and paperless way to communicate, but organizations need to understand the threats to security when relying solely on e-mail for communications. For remote working purposes, the e-mail system should be fully encrypted to avoid security breaches. Additionally, it is helpful to have a junk e-mail folder and virus detection to protect the systems against any potential e-mail viruses. Highly confidential information, such as financials, salary data, strategic plans or budgets, should not be transmitted via unprotected e-mail methods opt instead for an encrypted method of sharing and storing sensitive information.
- **Secure Online Meetings:** A collaboration software program provides organizations with a cost-effective method for transferring important files over a secure channel. While most products have security as an add on, others build strong security specifics within the tool to provide better protection. All components of a collaboration tool should be protected with the strongest levels of encryption. Some of the security factors you should look for include, but not limited to:
    - Lock-tight password protection;
    - Comprehensive encryption system using Advanced Encryption Standard (AES) Public Key Encryption;
    - Encrypted file storage.
- **Stay in Control:** Perhaps the most effective way to protect sensitive files is by having the control. Any form of communication, and specifically a collaboration tool, should provide the organization with the control to grant employees access to certain information. A collaboration product should let the organization designate which of the employees has access and to what files, and it should handle details surrounding need-to-know and right-to-know permissions.
- **Secure Networks and Applications:** Lastly, the organization should

consider ways to secure both the network; the organization is transmitting information with and the application being used to communicate. This is especially important for teleworkers who use a wireless network, as the security implications with a Wi-Fi network are still being discovered and the vulnerabilities are endless. Acting as two security layers, if the network is breached and you have a secure application, the hacker can only get access to encrypted files, which prevents the hacker from reaching any confidential information.

- **Launching the Program:** Initially, managers will feel somewhat overwhelmed with the changes and challenges in launching a remote working program. When initiating a remote working arrangement, managers need to help employees adapt to this culture change in the beginning stages of implementation. Share information about the program as it is developed, and ensure that employees receive training on the organization's remote working policies, procedures and any new technologies that need to be utilized on a daily basis. Once all employees are given an opportunity to review the remote working program and decide if they would like to participate or not, then the organization should move into launching the program.
- **Maintain Balance:** Once a remote working program is underway, it is important to emphasize equality between remote workers and office workers. Be sure to communicate frequently with employees in the main office and those who are working remotely to maintain a cohesive team. While managers can maintain communications with conference calls and e-mails, if the organization has a collaboration program, they can also touch base via instant messaging and online meetings. Managers could host regular staff meetings via online, which allows the teleworker to stay involved and included without having to commute to the office. This is especially important if the organization has employees working in another city, state or even overseas, as it would be very costly to transport them to the main office for each staff meeting. Additionally, an online meeting allows the teleworker to not only hear other participants in the meeting but also see everyone in the meeting, allowing for more quality interaction with managers and employees.
- **Set Expectations:** Before beginning a remote working program,

managers should clearly define expectations from an employee's performance before he or she begins working remotely. Focus on results, such as accomplishments, products, or services provided to measure their performance since it will be difficult to observe activities, behaviors or demonstrated competencies. Performance plans also should include standards that are measurable, observable and at least verifiable. Whether an employee works at the main office or at home, they should know what they are supposed to do, and how well they are supposed to do it, in order to ensure successful performance.

- **Monitor Performance:** Monitoring performance includes measuring performance and providing feedback. In a remote working situation, measuring the results of employees' efforts rather than their activities can be more efficient and effective. Quantity, quality, timeliness, and cost-effectiveness are four general measures that should be considered at all times for all employees, whether they work from home or in the office. After establishing performance measures, communicate where an employee stands on performance frequently. Since remote workers are not in the office to receive quick, informal feedback, make a conscious effort to send an instant message to remote workers so they know they are doing a good job.
- **Evaluate the Program:** In order to measure the success of the remote working program, the remote working committee should develop an evaluation plan before implementation. This plan should be based on quantifiable program goals and objectives to measure and compare results. When evaluating the organization's remote working program, it is recommended to first analyze the key issues that affect the organization. While you also can evaluate external issues impacted by remote working, these factors are usually evaluated through a community effort by a consortium of interested organizations. There are several measurement strategies managers might want to include in the evaluation plan. Also, conduct pre- and post- measurements on the remote workers alone, analyzing performance before and after they begin working remotely. To evaluate productivity, develop various levels of performance to measure each employee. Identify quantifiable tasks and determine which can be accomplished in an

office setting and which can take place via remote working. Similar to measuring costs, it is important to take enough time to evaluate satisfaction with the program.

- **Security Issues for Remote Working:** Remote working is the use of telecommunications to create an "office" away from the established office. The telecommuting office could be in an employee's house, a hotel room or conference centre, any site an employee travels to, or a telecommuting center. The telecommuter's office may or may not have the full computer functionality of the established office. Teleworking is becoming accepted as the way to do business. However, opening up corporate systems to dial-in and other forms of access presents three significant security risks.
    - The first risk is that intruders will be able to access corporate systems without having to be on site. Hackers armed with war dialers, electronic eavesdroppers at conference sites, or shoulder surfers watching employees enter IDs and passwords are all very real threats in today's environment. In addition to intruders whose goal may be mischief, hacking is attractive to people trying to steal or misuse corporate information. Electronic access to records is often more anonymous than trying to bribe employees or gain physical access;
    - The second risk of telecommuting, closely related to the first, is that corporate information can be read, and potentially modified, while it is in transit;
    - Telecommuting also presents organizations with more pedestrian risks. These include the risk of losing corporate information and resources when they are outside the protective shell of the organization.
- **Security Issues for Protecting Internal Systems:** In planning for the security of remote working, the first step is to examine what type of access is needed? What systems and data do employees need? What is the sensitivity of these systems and data? Do they need system administrator privileges? Do they need to share files with other employees? Is the data confidential? From a security perspective, the critical determinations are:

- What would happen if an intruder gained the same access as the employee?
- What would happen if an intruder were able to use the employee's account, but gain more access than authorized for that user?

If the answer to either of these questions is "uh-oh," then security is important.

- **Firewalls/Secure Gateways:** A secure gateway, often called a firewall, blocks or filters access between two networks, often between a private network and a larger more public network such as the Internet or public switched network. For telecommuting, the trick is to decide what to make available to telecommuting employees using public networks, what degree to ensure that only authorized users can get to the internal network, and how to ensure that the secure gateway works properly? If possible, it can be more secure to put all the resources needed by telecommuting employees outside of a secure gateway. However, this is only possible if employees do not need access to corporate databases. However, most telecommuting employees will need more access. For traveling employees, this may be limited to needing email. There are many firewall implementations that use an email proxy to allow access to the files on a protected system without having to directly access that system. Once again, many telecommuting employees will need more access. They need access to internal resources. The employees may need to use a variety of resources such as LAN applications, mainframe applications, run client software, use TCP/IP services. A secure gateway, or series of gateways, can be used to divide internal resources based on the access needs of telecommuters. For example, computers with high-risk organizational data may be separated by the router from systems with a lower level of risk. A series of routers can be used to further restrict access to the highest-risk systems. For some situations, current firewall technology can be used to give virtual access by using proxies. In addition, the current firewall can use IP filtering to permit access to only certain types of resources. However, for many organizations, the primary security function of the secure gateway is to provide robust authentication of users. Secure gateways may also provide additional auditing and session monitoring. The gateway can perform an intrusion detection function. For example, the secure gateway could monitor a session for keystrokes which may indicate someone trying to exceed access.

- **Robust Authentication:** For most organizations, robust authentication should be required if access is given to internal systems. However, many organizations should require robust authentication even for the email if it is relied on to discuss business decisions. Robust authentication can increase security in two significant ways: 1) It can require the user to possess a token in addition to a password or PIN and 2) it can provide one-time passwords. Tokens when used with PINs provide significantly more security than passwords. For a hacker or other would-be impersonator to pretend to be someone else, the impersonator must have both a valid token and the corresponding PIN. This is much more difficult than obtaining a valid password and user ID combination.

  Robust authentication can also create one-time passwords. Electronic monitoring or observing a user type in a password is not a threat with one-time passwords because each time a user is authenticated to the computer, a different "password" is used. Most commercial robust authentication systems use smart tokens. The user provides a PIN which unlocks the token and then uses the token to create a one-time password. However, it is possible to use software-only one-time password schemes.

  Telecommuting employees who directly access internal systems should be robust authenticated and should be routed to specific computer systems. The combination of routing and robust authentication can greatly increase security and reduce the cost associated with robust authentication by limiting it to employees with the greatest access.

- **Port Protection Devices:** A port protection device (PPD) is fitted to a communications port of a host computer and authorizes access to the port itself, prior to and independent of the computer's own access control functions. A PPD can be a separate device in the communications stream or it may be incorporated into a communications device. PPDs typically require a separate authenticator, such as a password, in order to access the communications port. One of the most common PPDs is the dial-back modem. A typical dial-back modem sequence follows:

a user calls the dial-back modem and enters a password. The modem hangs upon the user and performs a table lookup for the password provided. If the password is found, the modem places a return call to the user to initiate the session. The return call itself also helps to protect against the use of lost or compromised accounts. This is, however, not always the case. Malicious hackers can use such advance functions as call forwarding to reroute calls.

- **Security Issues for Data Transfer:** In addition to intruders possibly gaining access to internal systems, it is also possible to eavesdrop on an entire session. Eavesdropping is not technically difficult if there is physical access to cable or wire used for communication or logical access to switching equipment. If a telecommuting employee will be transferring data for which someone would go to the trouble of eavesdropping to get, then encryption may be necessary. Another scenario when eavesdropping is more likely is if an employee is at a large conference or other location where an eavesdropper may set up equipment in hopes of hearing something useful. Some conferences offer equipment to attendees to use to check email, transfer files, etc. This is useful to attendees since they do not need to provide laptops; however, this could be a target for electronic eavesdropping. Software or hardware-based encryption provides strong protection against electronic eavesdropping. However, it is more expensive than robust authentication. It is most useful if highly confidential data needs to be transmitted or if even moderately confidential data will be transmitted in a high-threat area. It is, however, unlikely that employees will always know when they are in a high threat area. It is incumbent on management to train employees.
- **Security Issues for Telecommuting from Home:** Many employees telecommute from home, which raises an additional set of issues. Some of these concerns relate to whether employees are using their own computers or using computers supplied to them by the organization.
- **Home Data Storage Integrity and Confidentiality:** Other members of the employee's household may wish to use the computer used for telecommuting. Children, spouses, or other household members may inadvertently corrupt files, introduce viruses or snoop. Organizations can take several approaches:

- **Employee Accountability**. Some organizations may choose not to have specific rules forbidding household members from using PCs, but hold the employee responsible for the integrity and confidentiality of the data. Obviously, this is not a good choice if the data is highly confidential.
- **Removable Hard Drives**. If corporate data is stored on a removable media, then the risk is greatly reduced.
- **Data Encryption**. Corporate data can be kept encrypted on the hard disk. This will protect its confidentiality and will detect changes to files.
- **Dedicated Use**. If an organization requires this, it should recognize that it is difficult to enforce.

- **Home System Availability:** In addition to the possibility of a home computer breaking or being stolen, it may not be compatible with office configurations. This may complicate set up, software support, troubleshooting, or repair. It is in the best interest of the organization to ensure that policy covers all these situations.
- **Security Issues for Telecommuting Centers:** Telecommuting centres, normally located in outlying suburbs, are another choice for organizations. From a security perspective, they may offer hardware for encryption, removable hard drives, and increased availability. However, by concentrating telecommuters, they may make themselves a more attractive target for eavesdropping. At a minimum, organizations should require robust authentication from telecommuting centre. If communications encryption is supported by the centre, the netizen should be aware that data may not be encrypted while it is inside the centre. The encryption may occur at a modem pool.

Remote Working - The Threats

With the increased freedom afforded us by teleworking there also comes increased information risk. The risk may be considered in two layers - the risk at the remote PC and the risk at the corporate network.

- **Exposure of Remote PC on the Net:** The remote worker's PC cannot be protected by the organization at all times. When not connected to the office network, the teleworker's PC will be used for web surfing, new software will be installed, old software reconfigured, e-mail attachments opened and Internet files downloaded. Hence, the system build is clearly not compliant with the corporate standard, which raises questions on the effectiveness of any security software running on the remote PC, and the risk of virus infection is increased. There is also the risk of physical access to corporate information stored on the remote PC. A corporate PC is situated within the office premises, where it is generally protected by multiple layers of building access controls, 24-hour on-site security personnel and surveillance equipment. On the other hand, the remote PC is likely to have only one layer of physical access control and is unlikely to have 24-hour on-site protection or surveillance. The risk of the PC and/or the information it contains being stolen or otherwise exposed is hence increased. All of this activity is generally restricted by the organization security policy but this cannot be enforced on a private PC. Hence, when the user next logs in to the office, the damage may already have been done – information may already have been accessed directly from the remote PC, and/or a compromised/infected PC becomes part of the office network.

- **Exposure of Corporate Resources on the Internet:** Consider the nature of the access required by a remote worker. The aim is to allow them to work from home as effectively as they might in the office. Hence, they need access to the data available in the office environment. This may require mapping network drives to the remote PC, access to confidential databases, intranet web servers, or corporate applications. Ordinarily, these services would never be made available outside the corporate network. In fact, the teleworker's remote PC effectively becomes part of the corporate network but it sits outside the traditional network perimeter and information defenses. Hence, by extending the network to the remote worker's home via the Internet, the risk of these services being exposed on the Internet is increased. The exposure may be direct or indirect – direct to the Internet by presenting service interfaces at the corporate network perimeter and transmission of corporate information over public lines, or indirect by use of the remote PC to bridge between the Internet and the corporate network. Direct exposure can be mitigated by strong identification, authentication and authorization at the corporate firewall or DMZ and the use of encryption technology to protect data integrity and confidentiality. Indirect exposure can be mitigated by protecting the remote PC by deploying standard security measures on the PC but, as discussed above, the security status of the remote PC cannot be guaranteed and hence the corporate network must be protected against a compromised remote PC. Hence, the teleworker's activity could be monitored even if the hacker is locked out of the system while it is connected to the corporate network.

Mitigating the Threats

As demonstrated, there are some very real security issues to be considered around teleworking. These issues are wide-ranging, the accidental introduction of viruses to the office environment; increased exposure to Internet attacks; even acting as a backdoor into the heart of the corporate network. To protect against these issues security must be taken seriously by the teleworker and his or her organization. The remote PC must be protected against the Internet and the corporate network should be protected from the remote PC. This final section discusses the vital areas which must be tackled in protecting the teleworker and the organization.

Security Policy

- **Who may work remotely**: identify the roles/jobs which may be considered for teleworking.
- **Services available to remote workers**: the types of network and application services which may be provided to remote workers.
- **Information Restrictions:** are there classified information types which should not be made available to remote workers?
- **Identification/Authentication/Authorization**: how should teleworkers be identified, authenticated and authorized before accessing corporate resources.
- **Equipment and Software Specifications:** are there any specific equipment or software products which must be deployed on the teleworker's PC?
- **Integrity and Confidentiality**: consider how the connection to the remote PC should be protected and how data on the machine should be protected.

- **Maintenance Guidelines**: how should the remote worker's PC configuration be protected, updated and monitored?
- **User Guidelines**: clarify the user's role in protecting corporate resources.
- **User Education**: ensure that users understand the possible information risks associated with remote working, how those risks are addressed, and the user's role in minimizing the risks.
- **User Education:** User education is essential. Users must understand that teleworking does entail genuine security risks and that they have a role to play in protecting corporate resources from attack, damage or loss. It is also to their own benefit that they understand the risks to their own PC and private data of their behavior while accessing the web in their own time, and how to mitigate those risks.
- **Protect the Remote PC:** The remote PC must be protected from the Internet and corporate information stored locally should be protected from prying eyes.
- **Firewalls:** The corporate perimeter defenses need to be extended to bring the remote PC within the perimeter should be installed on the remote PC. However, there are several issues around the effectiveness of the firewall. The firewall software must be properly maintained and the firewall must be correctly configured. Bear in mind that the remote PC probably belongs to the user and hence he or she has full administrator access to the machine – the system configuration may change regularly which could leave the firewall disabled. Hence, you should consider implementing an automated audit process when the user logs into the corporate network. This audit should check that the software is operational, correctly configured and that patches have been applied. If necessary, patches should be applied before allowing the user to continue. The firewall product should preferably be capable of monitoring and blocking all network traffic from applications that have not been specifically authorized to access the network/Internet. The user's education should include an understanding of the role played by the firewall and how important it is that the firewall is running correctly. The user should be encouraged to have the firewall running whenever they are connected to the Internet, even when not connected to the corporate network. This will help to protect

the user's own files and ultimately protects corporate resources. A home firewall is an essential precaution on the remote PC. However, designing a standard configuration which is maximally effective for every home PC is essentially impossible. The manual configuration could be considered but this could prove time-consuming and expensive if it is to be handled by qualified personnel, while most end users do not have the experience to handle this unaided. Hence, it should not be assumed that the remote firewall is fireproof. Multiple layers of security will be required – strength in depth is the key.

- **Virus Protection:** Anti-virus software is an essential measure on any web user's PC, whether or not they remote working. As per the firewall, the anti-virus product must be properly maintained, the software must be patched as and when necessary, the virus definition files must be regularly updated, and the software must be configured correctly. It should be configured for automatic scanning of e-mails and files opened. Entire system scans should be performed at regular intervals. Again, it is possible that the software could be disabled as a result of user action. Hence, consider performing an automatic audit of the virus software at login, ensuring that the software is running, that definition files are up to date and that patches have been applied. If possible, check the time of the last system scan. New definition files or patches should be applied and the last system scan should be confirmed as recent before the user is allowed to continue. The user's education should include an understanding of the importance of the antivirus software and the correct operation of the product. Teach good practice in the handling of downloads and attachments. The user should be encouraged to keep the product operational at all times, whether connected to the Internet or not. However, it is always possible that a virus will be missed by the software and the remote PC will be infected anyway, spreading to the corporate network at the next login. To counter this possibility, consider running anti-virus software in the DMZ back at the office.
- **Data Protection:** If corporate data will be stored on the remote PC, then it should be protected by encryption software. There are packages that will encrypt disk partitions or individual files as required. If the data will be stored on removable media, then not only should it

be encrypted but it should also be removed from the PC and locked away when not in use. Information can be lost due to hardware or media failures and hence backups should be kept. Since the typical home PC is unlikely to have an automated backup network-attached, the teleworker should be careful to make backups as required. Also, information security is about availability. Information stored on the remote PC is not likely to be available from the office. For these reasons, it is preferable that corporate information should be stored on the corporate network and not at home.

Protect Corporate Resources from the Internet: If the remote PC is compromised by a hacker and/or infected by a virus, then the corporate network is at risk. Alternatively, the link between the remote PC and the office could be compromised directly. Hence, precautions should be taken to control the PC's access to corporate resources and to monitor the contents of the traffic.

- **Identify, Authenticate and Authorize Remote Connections:** It is vital that only authorized personnel are able to access corporate resources remotely. All attempts to connect to corporate services should be captured within the DMZ until the source of the connection has been identified and authenticated. Strong authentication technology should be employed. At the least, this should be strong passwords – i.e., of appropriate length, not easily guessed, and containing nonalphanumeric characters. These requirements should be enforced automatically. One-time password technologies make it almost impossible for the hacker to steal a usable password, and hence these technologies are far preferable. Typical one-time password technologies involve the use of a password combined with a passcode. The passcode is generated using an electronic token and is based on a hash generated from the current time or from a randomly generated challenge provided by the corporate authentication server. Since the hacker does not have access to the token he or she cannot reply with the correct passcode and hence cannot be authenticated. Once identified and authenticated the user should be permitted access only to services and resources for which they have been authorized. This is particularly important in order to protect against the possibility of a hacker compromising the remote PC and posing as the authenticated user. Ideally, each individual service/resource request will be authorized separately, rather than simply allowing access to an area of the corporate network. It is only if the user's access rights are understood at this level of detail that the inappropriate behavior of a hacker might be effectively identified.

- **Protect the Remote Link:** The remote link should be protected against surveillance and interference by the use of VPN tunnel technology. VPN creates a secure link between the remote host and corporate DMZ. Data confidentiality is protected by encrypting the payload of the TCP/IP packets in transit. Data integrity is ensured by including a hash of the payload in the header. Source and target IP addresses on the private networks are also protected. Since no unauthorized party can read or interfere with the payload, we effectively have a secure tunnel through the public network. The use of VPN's is becoming very popular as a solution for secure teleworking communications. However, it should be remembered that the VPN only protects the data in transit and is not an entire solution in its own right. It is essential to protect against unauthorized VPN connections to the corporate network and to monitor/authorize remote behavior via the VPN connection in case it has been hijacked. The configuration of the VPN client on the remote PC is also essential. In particular, the risk of bridging between the Internet and the corporate network can be minimized by configuring the VPN to disable access to the Internet while connected to the corporate network. In this mode, while VPN is active, the PC's default route is to the VPN server at the office and the Internet is not visible. Similarly, communications services on the PC are not made available on the Internet.
- **Protect Corporate Resources from the Remote PC**
    - **Monitor Traffic and Behavior:** VPN technology is a powerful tool to ensure the confidentiality of data on the remote link. However, if the user's PC is compromised, then the VPN tunnel allows the cracker, posing as the authenticated user, direct access to the corporate information network, and may actually be effective in disguising the cracker's behavior. Hence, it is important that the VPN is terminated within a DMZ. The external firewall, facing the Internet, will authenticate and authorize the connection to the

telecommuter's machine. However, data packets are encrypted within the VPN and hence the cracker's activities are disguised at this firewall. Beyond the end of the VPN, network-based IDS should be deployed before the internal firewall in order to monitor the user's activity. This should watch for unusual or inappropriate behavior, such as network activity out with the user's typical working hours, uploading or downloading of large amounts of data, or the use of network scanning tools. The use of SSL to access the corporate intranet over VPN should also be considered carefully. Since SSL is encrypted "end-to-end", it may be used to hide a cracker's activity. Hence, the use of web proxies should be considered. The proxy should be located within the DMZ, and the IDS should monitor the intranet traffic. So, the teleworker's network traffic should be scanned for viruses within the DMZ. This will help to protect the office network from any virus which may have slipped past the scanners on the remote PC.

- **Restrict Remote Service Functionality at Source:** In some cases, there is no better protection than to prevent access to a service or resource altogether. Any such application or information should be carefully segregated from the remote access systems by appropriate use of access control and authorization systems, network firewalls and IDS. Some degree of control over the movement of data to and from the corporate network can also be provided by thin client technology.
- **Refuse Remote Access if necessary:** Bear in mind that it may be necessary to completely refuse remote access. This may a blanket ban across the entire firm. Or simply a restriction on the job roles which may request remote access – e.g., individuals handling cash transfers cannot use remote access, and so on. The key to making this decision, as ever, is to weigh the benefits of remote access against the perceived risks and impact.

A.6.8 Information Security Event Reporting

Information security event reporting can be defined as the process of documenting incidents, breaches and other events related to cyber threats that occur within an organization for the purposes of analyzing them for future prevention and detection. Information security events should be reported through appropriate management channels as quickly as possible. In addition to recording these events, it's also important to analyze them in order to develop strategies for preventing future incidents from happening. Information security event reporting is important because without it, you won't have any way of knowing if your network has been hacked or if there are any other potential threats facing your organization. Without this knowledge, you won't know how to prevent future attacks from occurring again or even if there have been previous attacks that need addressing. Information security events are a critical part of any organization's response to an incident. The speed with which you can respond to an incident is often critical for both protecting your business and limiting the impact on customers and other stakeholders.

A.6.8 Information Security Event Reporting – A linkage with Ancient Era

Lord Hanuman's mission in Lanka:

- **Awareness and Vigilance**: Just as information security professionals remain vigilant to detect any potential threats or breaches, Lord Hanuman displayed keen awareness during his reconnaissance mission in Lanka. He carefully observed the surroundings, gathering intelligence about Mata Sita's whereabouts and King Ravan's defenses. This parallels the need for individuals involved in information security to maintain a constant watch for any signs of suspicious activity or vulnerabilities in their systems.
- **Timely Reporting:** Lord Hanuman's mission involved gathering critical information and reporting it back to Lord Ram and His allies in a timely manner. Similarly, in information security, it's essential to report any security incidents or breaches promptly to relevant stakeholders to facilitate a swift response and mitigation efforts. Lord Hanuman's role as a messenger underscores the importance of timely reporting to ensure effective incident response.

- **Accuracy and Detail:** Lord Hanuman ensured that the information He conveyed to Lord Ram and His allies was accurate and detailed, providing insights into Mata Sita's location, King Ravan's strength, and Lanka's layout. Similarly, in information security event reporting, it's crucial to provide accurate and comprehensive details about the nature and severity of security incidents or breaches to facilitate appropriate actions and decision-making by stakeholders.
- **Confidentiality and Trust:** Lord Hanuman maintained confidentiality and trustworthiness in his role as a messenger, ensuring that sensitive information about Lord Ram's plans or strategies was not compromised. Similarly, in information security, event reporting often involves handling sensitive or confidential information, and individuals entrusted with this responsibility must adhere to strict confidentiality protocols to prevent unauthorized disclosure or misuse of information.
- **Coordination and Collaboration:** Lord Hanuman's mission required coordination and collaboration with allies such as Sugriv and Vibhishan to gather intelligence and plan the rescue of Mata Sita. Similarly, effective information security event reporting often involves collaboration between different teams or departments, such as IT Security, Incident Response, and Management, to coordinate efforts and address security incidents in a unified manner.

Control

The organization should provide a mechanism for personnel to report observed or suspected information security events through appropriate channels in a timely manner.

Purpose

To support timely, consistent and effective reporting of information security events that can be identified by personnel.

Guidance

All personnel and users should be made aware of their responsibility to report information security events as quickly as possible in order to prevent or minimize the effect of information security incidents. They should also be aware of the procedure for reporting information security events and the point of contact to which the events should be reported.

The reporting mechanism should be as easy, accessible and available as possible. Information security events include incidents, breaches and vulnerabilities. Situations to be considered for information security event reporting include:

- Ineffective Information Security Controls;
- Breach of Information Confidentiality, Integrity or Availability Expectations;
- Human Errors;
- Non-Compliance with the Information Security Policy, Topic-Specific Policies or Applicable Standards;
- Breaches of Physical Security Measures;
- System Changes that have not gone through the Change Management Process;
- Malfunctions or other anomalous system behavior of software or hardware;
- Access Violations;
- Vulnerabilities;
- Suspected Malware Infection.

Personnel and users should be advised not to attempt to prove suspected information security vulnerabilities. Testing vulnerabilities can be interpreted as a potential misuse of the system and can also cause damage to the information system or service, and it can corrupt or obscure digital evidence. Ultimately, this can result in legal liability for the individual performing the testing.

Designing an effective means of the detection of incidents is also essential, using both trained users and trained system administrators, and various technical controls. All members of the community should be trained regarding procedures for reporting failures, weaknesses, and suspected incidents methods to recognize and detect problems with security protections how to escalate reporting appropriately.

In addition, technical controls must be implemented for the automated detection of security events, coupled with as near real-time reporting as possible, to investigate and initiate immediate responses to problems.

For new IT systems, often the best time to develop automated detection of security events is when the preventive security controls are being developed and implemented. The most fundamental approaches to detecting intrusions are to monitor server logs for signs of unauthorized access, to monitor firewall or router logs for abnormal events, and to monitor network performance for spikes in traffic. Since intruders can alter or destroy local logs, a best practice is to take the precaution of sending logs to a remote log server. This includes a combination of host-level and network-level detections, which when used together provide the most powerful system for detecting problems. The purpose of Information Security Event Reporting is to support timely, consistent and effective reporting of information security events that can be identified by personnel. This is to ensure that information security events are reported in a timely manner and that the information is recorded accurately to support incident response activities and other security management responsibilities.

Information security event reporting is the process of documenting and logging information security events that occur in an organization. It recommends that organizations need to have an information security event reporting program, which will facilitate the process of receiving, assessing and responding to reports of incidents which have a potential impact on information security for the purposes of detecting incidents and mitigating adverse effects. This control is designed to:

- Support timely, consistent and effective reporting of information security events that can be identified by personnel;
- Proactively detect unauthorized access or misuse of information systems;
- Facilitate Incident Response Planning;
- Provide a foundation for continuous monitoring activities;
- Regular review of incidents and trends in order to identify problems before they become major incidents.

The following are some of the basic requirements for the control:

All personnel and users should be made aware of their responsibility to report information security events as quickly as possible in order to prevent or minimize the effect of information security incidents. The organization shall have a documented point of contact for reporting information security incidents to appropriate parties. The reporting mechanism should be as easy, accessible and available as possible. The organization shall maintain documentation of information security events, including incident reports, event logs, change requests, problem reports and system documentation. Situations to be considered for information security event reporting are mentioned above.

It is also important to point out here that it is not the place of the personnel reporting to test the vulnerability or effectiveness of the information security event. This can lead to legal liabilities for the employee and so should be left for qualified personnel to handle.

Even if an organization installs a network intrusion detection system or other monitoring systems, the resulting alerts can quickly overload personnel. An effective approach is to use analysis tools to help manage intrusion detection systems and summarize the data. Even when log summarization is used, maintaining and monitoring intrusion detection systems can require resources and technical skills that are beyond some organization's means. A less expensive alternative to developing your own IDS capabilities is to collaborate with other higher education institutions, helping each other deploy intrusion detection systems and even having a single person monitoring all systems, or to contract for the service with your ISP. Two major weaknesses of network IDS are that they cannot detect attacks in encrypted traffic and they cannot determine what is occurring within a targeted compromised host. Host-based intrusion detection systems (HIDS) can address both of these issues and can be used to monitor systems processes, file system changes, and log files for suspicious activities. Many commercial endpoint security offerings now include HIDS functionality, and servers can utilize open-source monitoring tools. Communicating security alerts through an interface that system administrators use to monitor the status and performance of their systems increases the likelihood that they will notice problems quickly.

Physical Controls

A.7.1 Physical Security Perimeters

Physical perimeter security can be defined as systems and technologies that protect people and assets within a facility and its grounds by blocking unauthorized physical intrusions across the perimeter. Achieving effective perimeter security requires the creation of layers to defend and deter potential attackers. The term physical security refers to measures taken to protect systems, buildings, and related supporting infrastructure against threats associated with their physical environment. Physical security perimeters are used to identify the physical boundaries of a building or area and control access to it. Physical security perimeters may include fences, walls, gates and other barriers that prevent unauthorized access by people or vehicles. In addition to physical barriers, electronic surveillance equipment such as closed-circuit television cameras can be used to monitor activity outside the facility. Physical Security Perimeters provide a first line of defense against intruders who might try to enter your computer system through the network cable or wireless connection in an organization. They are often used in conjunction with other types of information security controls such as identity management, access control and intrusion detection systems. The organization must establish secure areas that protect the valuable information and information assets only authorized people can access. This is also related to the risk assessment and risk appetite for an organization.

The best, most viable physical security strategies make use of both technology and specialized hardware to achieve its safety goals. You will need to protect your assets from intruders, internal threats, cyberattacks, accidents and natural disasters, which in turn requires a mix of technology and in-person monitoring that requires careful planning and placement of security staff and other tactics. For your preventive measures and countermeasures to be effective, you also need to introduce a security perimeter, the size and scope of which may vary depending on your specific needs and possible threats to your facility. Physical security bundles many needs together, so make sure you consider your space as a whole, not as separate parts.

A.7.1 Physical Security Perimeters – A linkage with Ancient Era

Lord Hanuman crossing the ocean to Lanka:

- **Identification of Boundaries:** Just as physical security perimeters define the boundaries of a protected area, Lanka's shoreline served as a natural boundary that Lord Hanuman needed to cross to reach the inner sanctum where Mata Sita was held captive. Understanding and crossing these boundaries required strategic planning and execution.
- **Obstacle Detection and Management:** Lord Hanuman encountered various obstacles while crossing the ocean, including rough waters, sea creatures, and aerial attacks from King Ravan's forces. Similarly, physical security perimeters may face challenges such as natural terrain features, structural barriers, or technological deterrents that need to be identified and managed to ensure successful protection.
- **Surveillance and Reconnaissance:** Before crossing into Lanka, Lord Hanuman conducted reconnaissance to gather intelligence about the enemy's defenses and the layout of the land. Similarly, physical security perimeters rely on surveillance measures such as cameras, sensors, and patrols to monitor activities and detect potential threats along the perimeter.
- **Access Control:** Once Lord Hanuman breached Lanka's perimeter, He faced additional layers of security as He navigated through the city to find Mata Sita. Similarly, physical security perimeters often incorporate access control measures such as fences, gates, guards, and checkpoints to regulate entry and prevent unauthorized access to protected areas.
- **Response to Intrusions:** As Lord Hanuman penetrated deeper into Lanka, He encountered resistance from King Ravan's forces, requiring Him to adapt and respond to threats swiftly. Likewise, physical security perimeters must have response protocols in place to address intrusions or breaches effectively, including procedures for alerting authorities, mobilizing security personnel, and implementing containment measures.
- **Coordination and Communication:** Throughout His mission, Lord Hanuman maintained communication with Lord Ram and His allies, providing updates on His progress and seeking guidance when needed.

Similarly, effective physical security perimeters rely on coordination and communication between security personnel, management, and other stakeholders to ensure a cohesive and timely response to security threats or incidents.

Control

Security perimeters should be defined and used to protect areas that contain information and other associated assets.

Purpose

To prevent unauthorized physical access, damage and interference to the organization's information and other associated assets.

Guidance

Implementing this control may also cover the unauthorized use of facility space, equipment and supplies in order to protect information and other associated assets. The following guidelines should be considered and implemented where appropriate for physical security perimeters:

- Defining security perimeters and the siting and strength of each of the perimeters in accordance with the information security requirements related to the assets within the perimeter;
- Having physically sound perimeters for a building or site containing information processing facilities. The exterior roofs, walls, ceilings and flooring of the site should be of solid construction and all external doors should be suitably protected against unauthorized access with control mechanisms. Doors and windows should be locked when unattended and external protection should be considered for windows, particularly at ground level; ventilation points should also be considered;
- Alarming, monitoring and testing all fire doors on a security perimeter in conjunction with the walls to establish the required level of resistance in accordance with suitable standards. They should operate in a fail-safe manner.

Other Information

Physical protection can be achieved by creating one or more physical barriers around the organization's premises and information processing facilities. A secure area can be a lockable office or several rooms surrounded by a continuous internal physical security barrier. Additional barriers and perimeters to control physical access can be necessary between areas with different security requirements inside the security perimeter. The organization should consider having physical security measures that can be strengthened during increased threat situations.

Physical security manages and protects resources in the form of administrative, technical, and physical controls. Access control systems, intrusion detection systems, and auditing systems are examples of technical controls. Some examples of administrative controls are site location, facility design, building construction, emergency response, and employee controls. Physical control examples include types of building materials, perimeter security including fencing and locks, and guards.

Deterrence, Denial, Detection then Delays are the controls used for securing the environment. Attempts to obtain physical resources should be deterred through the use of fences, gates, and guards around the perimeter. Locked doors and vaults protecting physical assets through denial. Physical Intrusion detection systems (IDS) and alarms are the next lines of defense and notify first respondents if a breach is detected. If attackers reach their target, security measures such as a cable lock on a computer must delay the suspect from acquiring assets until guards or police arrival.

An organization must demonstrate that it has adequate physical security perimeters in place to prevent unauthorized physical access to information and other associated assets. This includes preventing:

1. Unauthorized entry to buildings, rooms or areas containing information assets;
2. Unauthorized removal of assets from premises;
3. Unauthorized use of assets on premises; and
4. Unauthorized access to electronic communications equipment.

Physical security perimeters can be implemented through the following two categories:

- **Physical Access Control**: Provides controls over the entry into facilities and buildings, as well as the movement within them. These controls include locking doors, using alarms on doors, using fences or barriers around facilities, etc.

- **Hardware Security**: Provides controls over physical equipment used by an organization to process data such as printers and scanners that may contain sensitive information.

Physical and environmental safeguards are often overlooked but are very important in protecting information. Physical security over past decades has become increasingly more difficult for organizations. Technology and computer environments now allow more compromises to occur due to increased vulnerabilities. USB hard drives, laptops, tablets, and smartphones allow for information to be lost or stolen because of portability and mobile access. In the early days of computers, they were large mainframe computers only used by a few people and were secured in locked rooms. Today, desks are filled with desktop computers and mobile laptops that have access to organization data from across the enterprise. Protecting data, networks, and systems has become difficult to implement with mobile users able to take their computers out of the facilities. Fraud, vandalism, sabotage, accidents, and theft are increasing costs for organizations since the environments are becoming more "complex and dynamic". Physical security becomes tougher to manage as technology increases with complexity, and more vulnerabilities are enabled. Buildings and rooms that house information and information technology systems must be afforded appropriate protection to avoid damage or unauthorized access to information and systems. In addition, the equipment housing this information must be physically protected. Equipment theft is of primary concern, but other issues should be considered, such as damage or loss caused by fire, flood, and sensitivity to temperature extra. Physical and environmental security programs define the various measures or controls that protect organizations from loss of connectivity and availability of computer processing caused by theft, fire, flood, intentional destruction, unintentional damage, mechanical equipment failure, and power failures. Physical security measures should be sufficient to deal with foreseeable threats and should be tested periodically for their effectiveness and functionality.

- Determine which managers are responsible for planning, funding, and operations of the physical security of the Data Center;
- Review best practices and standards that can assist with evaluating physical security controls;
- Establish a baseline by conducting a physical security controls gap assessment that will include the following as they relate to your campus Data Center:
    - Environmental Controls;
    - Natural Disaster Controls;
    - Supporting Utility Controls;
    - Physical Protection and Access Controls;
    - System Reliability;
    - Physical Security Awareness and Training;
    - Contingency Plans.
- Determine whether an appropriate investment in physical security equipment has been made and if these controls have been tested and function correctly;
- Provide responsible managers guidance in handling risks;
- Maintain a secure repository of physical and environmental security controls and policies and establish timelines for their evaluation, update, and modification;
- Create a team of physical security auditors, outside of the management staff, to periodically assess the effectiveness of the measures taken and provide feedback on their usefulness and functionality.

A.7.2 Physical Entry

Entry controls and access points are a crucial part of any building's security system. They're what makes it possible for you to get in and out of your building without compromising its safety, and they can also prevent unauthorized or unwanted people from entering. Entry controls are the devices that allow you access into a building through doors or gates, such as keypads, card readers, biometric scanners and fobs. They can also include other features such as locking mechanisms for doors and gates, as well as turnstiles or revolving doors. An access point is an electronic device that provides security in large commercial buildings. It uses Radio Frequency Identification (RFID) technology to track all movement in and out of the facility. The access point transmits data back to headquarters so that security personnel can monitor when someone enters or leaves the facility and which areas they are accessing while they are there. Secure areas need to be protected by the appropriate entry controls to ensure only authorized personnel are allowed access. As a really basic example, only those employees who have been given the alarm access code and received a key can access the office. More risk averse organizations and or those with more sensitive information at threat might go much deeper with policies that include biometrics and scanning solutions too. Entry controls will need to be selected and implemented based on the nature and location of the area being protected, and the ability to implement such controls if for example, the location is not owned by the organization. The processes for granting access through the entry controls need to be robust, tested and monitored and may also need to be logged and audited. The control of visitors will also be especially important and the processes related to such should be considered. Extra consideration should be given to access being granted to areas in which sensitive or classified information is being processed or stored. Whilst areas containing key IT infrastructure equipment in particular need to be protected to a greater extent and access limited to only those that really need to be there. The auditor will expect to see that appropriate controls are in place as well as regularly tested and monitored.

Once you have identified physical security perimeters, you must implement entry controls to govern who can move between secure areas of the premises. The most common example of this will be keycodes issued to employees so that they can enter the office, but physical entry controls can take many forms. Organizations should select controls based on the nature and location of the area being protected. As a rule, the strength of the control should reflect the sensitivity of the data being stored. By contrast, highly classified data might require multiple security controls or ones that are less likely to be compromised, such as biometric and scanning solutions. Additionally, organizations might have multiple levels of security within their premises.

A.7.2 Physical Entry – A linkage with Ancient Era

Lakshman Rekha:

- **Barrier and Boundary:** Lakshman draws a line, known as Lakshman Rekha, around the hut where Mata Sita is staying to protect Her during Lord Ram's absence. This line serves as a physical barrier and boundary, similar to security perimeters or fences used in physical security to demarcate protected areas and control access.
- **Access Control:** Lakshman instructs Mata Sita not to cross the Lakshman Rekha, emphasizing the importance of controlling access to the protected area. Similarly, physical security measures often involve access control mechanisms such as gates, guards, or barriers to regulate entry and prevent unauthorized access to restricted areas.
- **Deterrence and Warning:** Lakshman warns Mata Sita and others about the consequences of crossing the Lakshman Rekha, indicating the deterrent effect of physical barriers and boundaries in discouraging unauthorized entry or intrusion. Similarly, physical security measures often include warning signs, alarms, or visual cues to deter potential intruders and alert individuals to restricted areas.
- **Monitoring and Enforcement:** Lakshman remains vigilant and monitors the Lakshman Rekha to ensure compliance with his instructions. Similarly, physical security perimeters may involve surveillance measures such as cameras, sensors, or patrols to monitor activities and enforce access control policies effectively.
- **Response to Intrusion:** When King Ravan, disguised as a sage, tricks Mata Sita into crossing the Lakshman Rekha, Lakshman responds swiftly to the intrusion by confronting and challenging him. Similarly,

physical security protocols include response procedures to address intrusions or breaches, including alerting authorities, mobilizing security personnel, and implementing containment measures.

- **Coordination and Communication:** Lakshman communicates the importance of respecting the Lakshman Rekha to Sita and others, emphasizing the need for coordination and communication in enforcing security measures and ensuring compliance with access control policies.

Control

Secure areas should be protected by appropriate entry controls and access points.

Purpose

To ensure only authorized physical access to the organization's information and other associated assets occurs.

Guidance

General

Access points such as delivery and loading areas and other points where unauthorized persons can enter the premises should be controlled and, if possible, isolated from information processing facilities to avoid unauthorized access. The following guidelines should be considered:

- Restricting access to sites and buildings to authorized personnel only. The process for the management of access rights to physical areas should include the provision, periodical review, update and revocation of authorization;
- Securely maintaining and monitoring a physical logbook or electronic audit trail of all access and protecting all logs and sensitive authentication information;
- Establishing and implementing a process and technical mechanisms for the management of access to areas where information is processed or stored;
- Setting up a reception area monitored by personnel, or other means to control physical access to the site or building;

- Inspecting and examining personal belongings of personnel and interested parties upon entry and exit. Note local legislation and regulations can exist regarding the possibility of inspecting personal belongings;
- Requiring all personnel and interested parties to wear some form of visible identification and to immediately notify security personnel if they encounter unescorted visitors and anyone not wearing visible identification. Easily distinguishable badges should be considered to better identify permanent employees, suppliers and visitors;
- Granting supplier personnel restricted access to secure areas or information processing facilities only when required. This access should be authorized and monitored;
- Giving special attention to physical access security in the case of buildings holding assets for multiple organizations;
- Designing physical security measures so that they can be strengthened when the likelihood of physical incidents increases;
- Securing other entry points such as emergency exits from unauthorized access;
- Setting up a key management process to ensure the management of the physical keys or authentication information and to ensure a log book or annual key audit and that access to physical keys or authentication information is controlled.

Visitors

The following guidelines should be considered, but not limited to:

- Authenticating the identity of visitors by an appropriate means;
- Recording the date and time of entry and departure of visitors;
- Only granting access for visitors for specific, authorized purposes and with instructions on the security requirements of the area and on emergency procedures;
- Supervising all visitors, unless an explicit exception is granted.

Delivery and loading areas and incoming material

The following guidelines should be considered, but not limited to:

- Restricting access to delivery and loading areas from outside of the building to identified and authorized personnel;
- Designing the delivery and loading areas so that deliveries can be loaded and unloaded without delivery personnel gaining unauthorized access to other parts of the building;
- Securing the external doors of delivery and loading areas when doors to restricted areas are opened;
- Inspecting and examining incoming deliveries for explosives, chemicals or other hazardous materials before they are moved from delivery and loading areas;
- Registering incoming deliveries in accordance with asset management procedures on entry to the site;
- Physically segregating incoming and outgoing shipments, where possible;
- Inspecting incoming deliveries for evidence of tampering on the way. If tampering is discovered, it should be immediately reported to security personnel.

The organization must ensure that only authorized physical access to the organization's information and other associated assets occurs. Physical security is of primary importance when protecting the confidentiality, integrity, and availability of information assets. This control is primarily concerned with protecting information and other associated assets from unauthorized access, theft or loss. To this end, appropriate entry controls and access points must be in place to ensure that only authorized individuals can access secure areas. These controls should be designed so that they provide a reasonable assurance that physical access is restricted to authorized persons and that these persons are in fact who they claim to be. This includes the use of locks and keys, security guards, monitoring systems and other barriers around entrances and access points. Access control systems such as passwords, card keys or biometric devices may also be used to control access to sensitive areas in the facility should also be deployed. Upon entry and departure, visitors should be registered and supervised, without prior authorization. Only approved personnel should be granted access, and guidelines should be provided regarding the region's safety and emergency procedures. A suitable method should be used to verify visitors' identities. Suitable access controls should be introduced to areas where information is handled or stored, such as a two-factor authentication system that uses an access card and a PIN. Maintaining and monitoring an audit trail of all access records in a physical logbook or electronically. Employees, contractors, and external parties should all wear some kind of visible identification and tell security personnel immediately if they meet persons who are not escorted or who do not have identification. Employees outside of the organization who require external support should only have limited access to secure areas or confidential information processing facilities; access authority should be provided and monitoring should be carried out. It is necessary to review, update, and revoke access privileges to protected areas periodically. Whenever necessary.

- **Administrative Controls**
    - **The Site and Facility Considerations:** All sites should have automated controls in place to protect the physical environment. The first line of defense must be administrative, technical and physical controls. The last line of defense should always be employees. Limiting human interaction with attackers reduces the risk of injury. These controls must be at the center when applying and sustaining physical security to protect people, IT infrastructure and operations. Controls must be utilized so that attackers have an opposition to stop or delay them.
    - **Facility Plan:** The facility plan uses critical path analysis which is a systematic approach that identifies relationships between processes, operations, and applications. An example could be a organization web server that needs access to the internet, power, climate control, computer hardware, storage location. In this example, resources that require securing are identified. Additionally, dependencies and interactions that support the business functions are reduced to only the mandatory ones because the processes, operations, and applications were identified. Critical path analysis is the first stage in securing the IT infrastructure. IT infrastructure includes computers, servers, networking equipment, water, electricity, climate control, and buildings. Using current and future technologies, such as operating systems or mobile

devices simultaneously is important. Current solutions improve, and new ones emerge as technologies involved. It is necessary to strategize how the older legacy systems and the new systems will merge together. The integration of old and new systems is called technology convergence. An organization could potentially have multiple systems doing the same function as technologies change, creating inefficiencies and risk to the organization as it can be difficult to differentiate which system performs a particular task. In some cases, such as an e-commerce website, multiple servers are required to run in parallel, so there is not a single point of failure. Another example could be the intrusion alarm system, fax, and phone line utilizing a single phone line cable. One phone line that different systems connect to is a single point of failure and if an attacker compromised the line at one location, none of these systems would work. Having separate phone lines ran to each system would lower the risk of all three losing their connection at the same time. Parties including management, employees, and especially safety and security personnel, should contribute to the site plan. Management should be in the planning process so they can make sure funds are available for the project. Employee safety concerns should be addressed during the creation of the facility plan. Security staff can point out important aspects of physical security. Security goals for the business and the facility are supported further when their knowledge is used to help make the site plan.

- **Site Location:** Geographical location, price, and size are factors that involve thought when purchasing a site location. Security requirements should always be the primary concern when determining a location. Buying an existing facility or building a new one also needs to be considered. Site physical security involves deliberation of situational awareness. It is important to take into account that looting, riots, vandalism, and break-ins can occur. Other things to consider before determining a site's visibility, including the terrain around the building, facility markings, signs, neighbors, and area population. Accessibility to the site is important. Road access, traffic, and distance to train stations, freeways, and airports are important aspects. Building facilities susceptible to these accounts should be avoided. Geographical areas prevalent in natural disasters are not ideal site locations. These threats cannot be avoided because natural disasters are not predictable. The IT staff, emergency personnel, management, and disaster recovery team must be prepared and equipped to handle natural disasters. Disaster recovery plans contained within the business continuity plan is the overarching plan that lists the details necessary to recover from a tragedy.

- **Securing Data:** Data centers and server rooms that house IT or communications equipment must be off-limits to unauthorized individuals. These rooms have to be locked down to prevent attacks. These rooms should be protected and have limited access to those employees that require access to job duties. The more human-incompatible these rooms are, the less likely attacks are executed. Oxygen displacement, extremely dim lighting, cold temperatures and hard to maneuver due to little space are methods used in creating a human inhospitable environment. These data center rooms store mission-critical equipment and should be located in the middle of the facility and not in the basement, ground or top floors.

- **Physical Controls**

  Facilities need physical access controls in place that control, monitor and manage access. Categorizing building sections should be restricted, private or public. Different access control levels are needed to restrict zones that each employee may enter depending on their role. Many mechanisms exist that enable control and isolation access privileges at facilities. These mechanisms are intended to discourage and detect access from unauthorized individuals.

  - **Perimeter Security:** Man traps, gates, fences, and turnstiles are used outside of the facility to create an additional layer of security before accessing the building. Fences distinguish clear boundaries between protected and public areas. Materials used to create fences vary in types and strengths. Protected assets dictate the necessary security levels of the fences. Types of fences include electrically charged, barbed wire, heat, motion or laser detection, concrete, and painted stripes on the ground. Gates are entry and exit points through a fence. To be an effective deterrent, gates must offer the same level of protection equal to the fence; otherwise, malicious people have the opportunity to circumvent the fence and use the gate as the point of intrusion. Construction of gates should consist of hardened hinges, locking mechanisms, and closing devices. Gates should be limited in number to consolidate resources needed to secure them. Dogs or surveillance cameras should monitor gates when guards are not present. Turnstiles are a type of gate that allows only one person to enter. They must provide the same protection level as the fence they are connected. Turnstiles operate by rotating in one direction like a revolving door and allow one individual to leave or enter the premises at a time. Mantraps are small rooms that prevent individuals from tailgating. The design of man traps only allows one person may enter at a time. The idea is to trap the person trying to gain access by locking them inside until proof of identity is confirmed. If the individual has permission to enter, the inside door opens allowing entry. This is a security control measure that delays unauthorized people from entering the facility until security or police officers arrive.

- **Badges:** Proof of identity is necessary for verifying if a person is an employee or visitor. These cards come in the forms of name tags, badges, and identification (ID) cards. Badges can also be smart cards that integrate with access control systems. Pictures, RFID tags, magnetic strips, computer chips, and employee information are frequently included to help security validate the employee.

- **Motion Detectors:** Motion detectors offer different technology options depending on necessity. They are used as intrusion detection devices and work in combination with alarm systems. Infrared motion detectors observe changes in infrared light patterns. Heat-based motion detectors sense changes in heat levels. Wave pattern motion detectors use ultrasonic or microwave frequencies that monitor changes in reflected patterns. Capacitance motion detectors monitor for changes in electrical or magnetic fields. Photoelectric motion detectors look for changes in light and are used in rooms that have little to no light. Passive audio motion detectors listen for unusual sounds.

- **Intrusion Alarms:** Alarms monitor various sensors and detectors. These devices are door and window contacts, glass break detectors, motion detectors, water sensors, and so on. Status changes in the devices trigger the alarm. In hardwired systems, alarms notice the changes in status by the device by creating wiring short. Types of alarms are deterrent, repellant, and notification. Deterrent alarms attempt to make it more difficult for attackers to get to major resources by closing doors and activating locks. Repellant alarms utilize loud sirens and bright lights in the attempt to force attackers off the site. Notification alarms send alarm signals through dial-up modems, internet access or GSM means. The siren output may be silenced or audible depending on if the organization is trying to catch criminals in the act.

- **Technical Controls**

  The main focus of technical controls is access control because it is one of the most compromised areas of security. Smart cards are a technical control that can allow physical access into a building or secured room and securely log in to organization networks and computers. Multiple layers of defense are needed for overlap to protect from attackers gaining direct access to organization resources. Intrusion detection systems are technical controls that are essential because they detect an intrusion. Detection is a must because it notifies the security event. Awareness of the event allows the organization to respond and contain the incident. Audit trails and access logs must be continually monitored. They enable the organization to locate where breaches are occurring and how often. This information helps the security team reduce vulnerabilities.

  - **Smart Cards:** Token cards have microchips and integrated circuits built into the cards that process data. Microchips and integrated circuits enable the smart card to do two-factor authentication. This authentication control helps keeps unauthorized attackers or employees from accessing rooms they are not permitted to enter. Employee information is saved on the chip to help identify and authenticate the person. Two-factor authentication also protects computers, servers and data centers from unauthorized individuals. Access will not be granted with possession of the card alone. A form of biometrics (something you are) or a PIN or password (something you know) must be entered to unlock the card to authenticate the user. Access token smart cards come in two types, contact and contactless. Contact smart cards have a contact point on the front of the card for data transfer. When the card is inserted, fingers from the device make a connection with chip contact points. The connection to the chip powers it and enables communication with the host device. Contactless smart cards use an antenna that communicates with electromagnetic waves. The electromagnetic signal provides power for the smart card and communicates with the card readers. Access token cards are thought to be impervious to tampering methods; however, these cards are not hackerproof. Security is provided through the complexity of the smart token. The smart token only allows the card to be read after the correct PIN is entered. Encryption methods keep malicious people from acquiring the data stored in the microchips. Smart cards also have the ability to delete data stored on it the card detects tampering. Cost is a disadvantage of smart card technology. It is expensive to create smart cards and purchase cards, readers. Smart cards are basically small computers and carry the same risks. As technology evolves, storage capacity and the ability to separate "security critical computations" inside the smart cards. Smart cards can store keys used with encryption systems which helps security. The self-contained circuits and storage, permit the card to use encryption algorithms. The encryption algorithms allow for protected authorization that can be applied enterprise-wide.

- **Proximity Readers and RFID:** Access control systems use proximity readers to scan cards and determines if it has authorized access to enter the facility or area. Access control systems evaluate the permissions stored within the chip sent via radio frequency identification RFID. This technology utilizes the use of transmitters (for sending) and responders (for receiving). In physical access control, the use of proximity readers and access control cards that contain passive tags are used. Passive tags are powered from the proximity of readers through an electromagnetic field generated by the card reader. A signal is sent to the reader when a card is swiped. The door unlocks once the signal is received and verified. Active tags contain batteries to self-power the RFID tag. Active tags have a battery power source built-in that allows them to transmit signals further than passive tags. However, the cost of these is significantly higher, and their life is limited because of battery life. These are typically used to track high-value items. Readers can track movements and locate items when connected to the network and detection systems. If an asset is removed from certain areas, the organization can have the access control system trigger an alarm.

- **Intrusion Detection, Guards and CCTV:** If the equipment is relocated without approval, Intrusion Detection Systems (IDS) can monitor and notify of unauthorized entries. IDS are essential to security because the systems can send a warning if a specific event occurs or if access was attempted at an unusual time. Guards are a significant part of an IDS because they are more adaptable than other security aspects. Security officers may be fixed at one location or make rounds patrolling the campus. While making rounds, guards can verify the doors and windows are locked, and vaults are protected. Guards may be accountable for watching IDS and CCTVs and can react to suspicious activity. They can call for backup or local police to help capture a suspect if necessary. CCTV or surveillance systems utilize cameras and recording equipment to provide visual protection. In areas that cameras monitor, having enough light in the right areas is essential. It might be too dim for the camera to capture decent video quality necessary to prosecute or identify persons of interest without enough light. Cameras can be a fixed lens or a zoom lens. In monitoring something that is stationary, you would want to use the right type of fixed lens depending on the distance and width you are monitoring. Fixed lenses are available in wide, narrow or wide-angle. The zoom lens is recommended when viewing a target that might need an enlarged view. Another type of camera is a pan, tilt, zoom camera. These are dome style cameras that have the ability to move in all directions as well as zoom in. PTZ cameras are best for tracking suspects because the camera automatically detects and follows a suspect. PTZ cameras can auto-track moving objects through mechanical or application methods. Cameras that use software applications have the ability to change targets and can filter out images that are stationary, saving bandwidth and storage.

- **Auditing Physical Access:** Auditing physical access control systems require the use of logs and audit trails to surmise where and when a person gained false entry into the facility or attempted to break-in. The software and auditing tools are detectives, not preventive. Consistent monitoring of audit trails and access logs are needed to act swiftly. The system has no value if the organization does not respond or response time is limited. Management needs to know when there are incidents so they can make security decisions. Adding additional resources to particular areas or at certain times might be necessary to protect the environment. Access logs and audit trails must include the date and time that the incident occurred. These logs should capture all failed access attempts, the person's employee information, and the location where the attacker tried to gain entry.

Access points such as delivery and loading areas and other points where unauthorized persons could enter the premises shall be controlled and, if possible, isolated from information processing facilities to avoid unauthorized access. For some organizations, delivery/loading areas are either not available or not controlled by the organization. However, where the organization can control or influence these areas, it is important that risks are identified and assessed and appropriate controls are therefore implemented. The auditor will inspect the delivery and loading protection to assure there are appropriate controls relating to the control of incoming materials and the control of outgoing materials. Although, the level of assurance around delivery and loading relative to the assessed risk levels that the auditor will be looking for will depend on the availability and ownership of such facilities. There should be complete control of all the access points where necessary. The information stored within the building should be secured and consider as a legal responsibility. Examples of these controls may include;

- Docks away from the main office building;
- Security Guards, CCTV monitoring and recording;
- Procedures to prevent external and internal access.

A.7.3 Securing Offices Rooms and Facilities

Security of offices, rooms and facilities may seem easy and obvious, but it is worth considering and regularly reviewing who should have access, when and how. Some of the things that often get missed are: Who can see or even hear into the office from outside and what to do about it? Is access updated when staff leave or transfer so no longer need access to this particular room? Do visitors need to be escorted in this area and so, are they? And are staff vigilant about challenging and reporting people they do not recognize? For rooms that are shared with others, policies would also include the protection and or removal of valuable assets when it is not occupied by the organization, ranging from laptops, through to information posted on whiteboards, flip charts etc. The external auditor will be inspecting the security controls for offices, rooms and facilities and checking to see that there is evidence of adequate, risk-based control implementation, operation and review on a periodic basis.

A.7.3 Securing Offices Rooms and Facilities – A linkage with Ancient Era

Abhimanyu Chakravyuh:

- **Access Control Measures:** In the Mahabharata, Abhimanyu possesses knowledge about how to penetrate the Chakravyuh formation, a complex military strategy. Similarly, securing office rooms and facilities involves implementing access control measures to regulate entry and prevent unauthorized access.
- **Training and Education:** Abhimanyu learned the technique of entering the Chakravyuh while still in his mother's womb, but he did not learn how to exit it. Similarly, employees may receive training on accessing certain rooms or facilities in the office, but they may not always be educated on proper exit procedures or security protocols.
- **Vulnerability to Exploitation:** Abhimanyu's knowledge of entering the Chakravyuh is exploited by his enemies who take advantage of his lack of knowledge about exiting the formation. Similarly, employees with access to secure areas in the office may inadvertently pose security risks if they are not adequately trained or if proper exit strategies are not in place.

- **Security Breaches:** Abhimanyu's situation highlights the potential consequences of a security breach when unauthorized individuals gain access to restricted areas. In office security, breaches can lead to theft, data breaches, or sabotage, emphasizing the importance of implementing robust security measures to prevent unauthorized access.
- **Response and Mitigation:** In the Mahabharata, Abhimanyu's allies respond to his predicament by attempting to rescue him and counter the enemy forces. Similarly, in office security, it's essential to have response and mitigation strategies in place to address security breaches effectively, including alerting authorities, implementing containment measures, and restoring normal operations.
- **Continuous Improvement:** Abhimanyu's story serves as a lesson about the importance of continuous improvement in security strategies. After his tragic death, his allies learn from the experience and develop better tactics to counter similar threats in the future. Likewise, in office security, it's crucial to continually assess and improve security measures to adapt to evolving threats and vulnerabilities.

Control

Physical security for offices, rooms and facilities should be designed and implemented.

Purpose

To prevent unauthorized physical access, damage and interference to the organization's information and other associated assets in offices, rooms and facilities.

Guidance

The following guidelines should be considered to secure offices, rooms and facilities:

- Siting critical facilities to avoid access by the public;
- Where applicable, ensuring buildings are unobtrusive and give minimum indication of their purpose, with no obvious signs, outside or inside the building, identifying the presence of information processing activities;

- Configuring facilities to prevent confidential information or activities from being visible and audible from the outside. Electromagnetic shielding should also be considered as appropriate;
- Not making directories, internal telephone books and online accessible maps identifying locations of confidential information processing facilities readily available to any unauthorized person.

Physical security is a critical element of information security. Information security is the protection of information and information systems from unauthorized access, use, disclosure, disruption, modification, or destruction. Physical security refers to protective measures taken to safeguard personnel, facilities, equipment and other assets against natural or man-made hazards by reducing risks related to burglary, sabotage, terrorism and other criminal acts. The first step in physical security for information sensitive locations is determining if you have one. Information sensitive locations are rooms, offices and facilities, where there are computers that contain sensitive data or where there are people who have access to sensitive data. Physical security can include:

- **Locks and Keys:** Locking doors, windows and cupboards; using security seals on laptops and mobile devices; password protection for computers; encryption for sensitive data.
- **CCTV:** CCTV cameras are an excellent way of monitoring activity around premises or in specific areas of a building.
- **Intruder Alarms**: These can be activated by movement, heat or sound and are used to alert you to intruders or people who shouldn't be in a particular area.

The purpose is to prevent unauthorized physical access, damage and interference to the organization's information and other associated assets in offices, rooms and facilities and is to reduce the level of risk of unauthorized physical access to offices, rooms, and facilities, to an acceptable level by:

- Preventing unauthorized physical access to offices, rooms and facilities by persons other than authorized personnel;
- Prevent damage or interference with the organization's information and other associated assets inside offices, rooms and facilities;

- Ensuring that any information security sensitive areas are unobtrusive to make it hard for people to determine their purpose;
- Minimizing the risk of theft or loss of property within offices, rooms and facilities;
- Ensuring that people who have authorized physical access are identified;
- Where possible, CCTV or other monitoring devices should be used to provide security surveillance over key areas such as entrances/exits.

It applies to all buildings used by the organization for offices or administrative functions. It also applies to rooms where confidential information is stored or processed, including meeting rooms where sensitive discussions take place. It does not apply to reception areas or other public areas of an organization's premises unless they are used for administrative purposes. It specifies that rooms and facilities must be secured. The following security measures can be taken to ensure that rooms and facilities are secure, but not limited to:

- Siting critical facilities to avoid access by the public;
- Where applicable, ensuring buildings are unobtrusive and give minimum indication of their purpose, with no obvious signs, outside or inside the building, identifying the presence of information processing activities;
- Configuring facilities to prevent confidential information or activities from being visible and audible from the outside;
- Not making directories, internal telephone books and online accessible maps identifying locations of confidential information processing facilities readily available to any unauthorized person.

Some step companies can take to secure office rooms and facilities, but not limited to:

- A physical security perimeter;
- Physical entry controls;
- Secure offices, rooms and facilities;
- Protection against external and environmental threats;

- Secure area protection;
- Physical security for public access, delivery and loading areas;
- The walls, ceilings and floor of any secure area should be of the same strength. If someone can access a secure area via, a false ceiling you will be non-compliant;
- The most sensitive assets should be stored in the most secure areas. Using the "onion technique", each perimeter "layer" should house progressively more sensitive assets;
- Ban mobile phone and camera use in secure areas;
- Prohibit lone working in secure areas;
- Don't co-store other assets in secure areas;
- Ensure delivery and loading areas don't give direct access to secure areas;
- Install a welcome desk where all visitors are required to report first;
- Have security guards challenge unknown persons;
- Monitor spaces around the perimeter with CCTV or security patrols;

A.7.4 Physical Security Monitoring

This control deals with the implementation of appropriate surveillance systems to prevent unauthorized access by intruders to sensitive physical premises. Physical security monitoring is designed to protect buildings, and safeguard the equipment inside. In short, they keep unwanted people out, and give access to authorized individuals. While network and cyber security are important, preventing physical security breaches and threats is key to keeping your technology and data safe, as well as any staff or faculty that have access to the building. Without physical security plans in place, your office or building is left open to criminal activity, and liable for types of physical security threats including theft, vandalism, fraud, and even accidents. Physical security monitoring requires organizations to detect and prevent external and internal intruders who enter into restricted physical areas without permission by putting in place suitable surveillance tools. These surveillance tools constantly monitor and record access-restricted areas and protect organization against risks that may arise as a result of unauthorized access, including but not limited to:

- Theft of sensitive data;
- Loss of information assets;
- Financial damage;
- Theft of removable media assets for malicious use;
- Infection of IT assets with a malware;
- Ransomware attacks that may be carried out by an intruder.

From landscaping elements and natural surveillance, to encrypted key cards or mobile credentials, to lock down capabilities and emergency mustering, there are many different components to preventing all different types of physical security threats in the modern workplace.

A.7.4 Physical Security Monitoring – A linkage with Ancient Era

Vigilance and Surveillance

The character of Krishna in the Mahabharata was known for His vigilance and ability to anticipate threats. Similarly, maintaining constant vigilance and employing robust surveillance mechanisms are key to identifying and mitigating cyber threats. Advanced monitoring systems, intrusion detection tools, and threat intelligence platforms can help organizations detect and respond to potential breaches in real-time.

Control

Premises should be continuously monitored for unauthorized physical access.

Purpose

To detect and deter unauthorized physical access.

Guidance

Physical premises should be monitored by surveillance systems, which can include guards, intruder alarms, video monitoring systems such as CCTV and physical security information management software either managed internally or by a monitoring service provider. Access to buildings that house critical systems should be continuously monitored to detect unauthorized access or suspicious behavior by:

- Installing video monitoring systems such as closed-circuit television to view and record access to sensitive areas within and outside an organization's premises;
- Installing, according to relevant applicable standards, and periodically testing contact, sound or motion detectors to trigger an intruder alarm such as:
    - Installing contact detectors that trigger an alarm when a contact is made or broken in any place where a contact can be made or broken to be used as a panic alarm;
    - Motion detectors based on infra-red technology which trigger an alarm when an object passes through their field of view;
    - Installing sensors sensitive to the sound of breaking glass which can be used to trigger an alarm to alert security personnel;
- Using those alarms to cover all external doors and accessible windows. Unoccupied areas should be alarmed at all times; cover should also be provided for other areas.

The design of monitoring systems should be kept confidential because disclosure can facilitate undetected breakins. Monitoring systems should be protected from unauthorized access in order to prevent surveillance information, such as video feeds, from being accessed by unauthorized persons or systems being disabled remotely. The alarm system control panel should be placed in an alarmed zone and, for safety alarms, in a place that allows an easy exit route for the person who sets the alarm. The control panel and the detectors should have tamper proof mechanisms. The system should regularly be tested to ensure that it is working as intended, particularly if its components are battery powered. Any monitoring and recording mechanism should be used taking into consideration local laws and regulations including data protection and PII protection legislation, especially regarding the monitoring of personnel and recorded video retention periods.

In the built environment, we often think of physical security control examples like locks, gates, and guards. While these are effective, there are many additional and often forgotten layers to physical security for offices that can help keep all your assets protected. A comprehensive physical security plan combines both technology and specialized hardware, and should include countermeasures against intrusion such as:

- Site Design and Layout;
- Environmental Components;
- Emergency Response Readiness;
- Training;
- Access Control;
- Intrusion Detection;
- Power and Fire Protection;

Organizations are to implement these three steps at a minimum to detect and deter unauthorized access to facilities that host critical information assets:

- **Step 1: Put in place a video monitoring system**

  Organizations should have a video surveillance system in place to continuously monitor access to restricted areas which hosts critical information assets. Furthermore, this surveillance system should keep a record of all entries into the physical premises.

- **Step 2: Install detectors to set off an alarm**

  Trigger an alarm when an intruder accesses physical premises enables the security team to respond quickly to security breaches. Furthermore, it can also be effective at deterring the intruder. Organizations should use motion, sound, and contact detectors that set off an alarm when an unusual activity within the physical premises is detected. In particular:

  - A contact detector should be installed and it should set off an alarm when an unknown object/individual gets in contact with an object or breaks contact with an object;
  - Motion detectors can be programmed to start an alarm when the movement of an object is detected within their range of view;
  - Sound detectors such as break glass detectors can be activated when a sound is detected.

- **Step 3: Configuration of alarms to protect all internal premises**

  The third compliance step requires the configuration of the alarm system to ensure that all sensitive areas are within the range of the alarm system so that there is no vulnerability that can be exploited. The top 5 most common threats your physical security system should protect against are:

  - Theft and Burglary;
  - Vandalism;
  - Natural Disasters;
  - Terrorism or Sabotage;
  - Violence in the Workplace.

  Depending on where your building is located, and what type of industry you're in, some of these threats may be more important for you to consider. For example, if your building or workplace is in a busy public area, vandalism and theft are more likely to occur. If your building houses a government agency or large data storage servers, terrorism may be higher on your list of concerns. Before updating a physical security system, it's important to understand the different roles technology and barriers play in your strategy. The smartest security strategies take a layered approach, adding physical security controls. This means building a complete system with strong physical security components to protect against the leading threats to your organization. The four main security technology components are:

- **Deterrence:** These are the physical security measures that keep people out or away from the space. Deterrent security components can be a physical barrier, such as a wall, door, or Turnstile. Technology can also fall into this category. Access control systems and video security cameras deter unauthorized individuals from attempting to access the building, too.
- **Detection:** Detection components of your physical security system help identify a potential security event or intruder. Sensors, alarms, and automatic notifications are all examples of physical security detection.
- **Delay:** There are certain security systems that are designed to slow intruders down as they attempt to enter a facility or building. Access control, such as requiring a key card or mobile credential, is one method of delay. Smart physical security strategies have multiple ways to delay intruders, which makes it easier to mitigate a breach before too much damage is caused.
- **Response:** These are the components that are in place once a breach or intrusion occurs. Examples of physical security response include communication systems, building lock downs, and contacting emergency services or first responders.

Together, these physical security components work to stop unwanted individuals from accessing spaces they shouldn't, and notify the necessary teams to respond quickly and appropriately. The organization physical security plans should address each of the components above, detailing the technology and processes the organization will use to ensure total protection and safety. Before implementing physical security measures in the building or workplace, it's important to determine the potential risks and weaknesses in the current security. Detection is of the utmost importance in physical security. While it is impossible to prevent all intrusions or physical security breaches, having the right tools in place to detect and deal with intrusions minimizes the disruption to the business in the long run. To locate potential risk areas in the facility, first consider all the public entry points. Where people can enter and exit from the facility, there is always a potential security risk. Baseline physical security control procedures, such as proper access control measures at key entry points, will help the organization manage who is coming and going, and can alert for potential intrusions. Once inside the facility, the organization will want to look at how data or sensitive information is being secured and stored. Does the organization have server rooms that need added protection? Are desktop computers locked down and kept secure when nobody is in the office? Do employees have laptops that they take home with them each night? Even USB drives or a disgruntled employee can become major threats in the workplace. List out all the potential risks in the building, and then design security plans to mitigate the potential for criminal activity. Take a look at these physical security examples to see how the right policies can prevent common threats and vulnerabilities in the organization.

- Restrict access to IT and server rooms, and anywhere laptops or computers are left unattended;
- Use highly secure access credentials that are difficult to clone, fully trackable, and unique to each individual;
- Require multi-factor authentication (MFA) to unlock a door or access the building;
- Structure permissions to employ least-privilege access throughout the physical infrastructure;
- Eliminate redundancies across teams and processes for faster incident response;
- Integrate all building and security systems for a more complete view of security and data trends;
- Set up automated security alerts to monitor and identify suspicious activity in real time.

Physical security planning is an essential step in securing the office building. Use this guideline to create a physical security plan that addresses your unique concerns and risks, and strengthens your security posturing.

- Identify the scope of your physical security plans. This should include the types of employees the policies apply to, and how records will be collected and documented.

- Determine who is responsible for implementing your physical security plans, as well as the key decision-makers for making adjustments or changes to the plan.
- Include the different physical security technology components your policy will cover.
- State the types of physical security controls your policy will employ. Include any physical access control systems, permission levels, and types of credentials you plan on using.
- List out key access points, and how you plan to keep them secure.
- Define your monitoring and detection systems. What types of video surveillance, sensors, and alarms will your physical security policies include? Identify who will be responsible for monitoring the systems, and which processes will be automated.
- Outline all incident response policies. Your physical security planning needs to address how your teams will respond to different threats and emergencies.
- Scope out how to handle visitors, vendors, and contractors to ensure your physical security policies are not violated.
- Create a cybersecurity policy for handling physical security technology data and records. Include your policies for encryption, vulnerability testing, hardware security, and employee training.
- Address how physical security policies are communicated to the team, and who requires access to the plan.

Here's a quick overview of the best practices for implementing physical security for buildings, but not limited to:

- Install perimeter security to prevent intrusion. Physical barriers like fencing and landscaping help establish private property, and deter people from entering the premises;
- Use access control systems to provide the next layer of security and keep unwanted people out of the building;
- Integrate your access control with other physical security systems

like video surveillance and user management platforms to fortify your security;

- Employ cyber and physical security convergence for more efficient security management and operations;
- Regularly test your physical security measures to ensure you're protected against the newest physical security threats and vulnerabilities;
- Always communicate any changes to your physical security system with your team.

A.7.5 Protecting against Physical and Environmental Threats

Physical security for information systems refers to the prevention methods put into place that aim to stop people entering a physical premises that will give them access to information. Environmental controls are mechanisms put in place that will ensure the protection of your organization's information and resources from any environmental impact.

Physical controls are important because the organization does not want just anybody having access to their information. In order to implement effective physical controls, organization must review the physical building the organization is set up in, and any other buildings that employees may work from or information be held. Organization may also need to review any hosts of the product or service, ensure the host of their service is protected. Organization then need to record this information down, and review it regularly to ensure it is always secure. Environmental controls are important for information security because if there is a failure in environmental controls, there could be a threat of loss of important information or data.

This clause centers on protecting the inevitable attacks on the organizations. These attacks can be environmental, or a cyber threat that steals organizational information, or the private data of customers and/or suppliers. Natural disasters like floods, earthquakes, and fires are inevitable events. Organizations must include procedures and policies to deal with these threats. This pandemic has made organizations aware of the fact they need to proceed with remote working; some may work where the risk is high, and this needs to be identified by the management team. This could be addressed by identifying the risk around the business areas. Understanding location and what is in the immediate vicinity is critical to identifying potential risks. It is required under this standard, physical and environmental threats are recognized and controlled by the organization well.

Appropriate environmental threat protection controls are necessary to limit the impact that either human-made or environmental threats may have on an organization's operations, systems, personnel, or data availability. If not appropriately addressed, the lack of these controls can have a negative impact on an organization's ability to maintain the delivery of their products or services. Organizations must be enabled to measure the potential adverse effects of environmental and physical threats and to mitigate and/or eliminate these effects by putting in place appropriate measures. Threats to information assets are not merely digital: An organization's critical physical infrastructure hosting information assets are also exposed to environmental and physical threats that may result in loss, destruction, theft and compromise of information assets and sensitive data. These threats may include natural events such as earthquakes, floods and wildfires. They may also include man-made disasters such as civil unrest and criminal activities. Organizations can assess, identify and mitigate risks to critical physical infrastructure due to physical and environmental threats.

A.7.5 Protecting Against Physical and Environmental Threats – A linkage with Ancient Era

- **Natural Hazards:** Throughout their journey, Lord Ram, Mata Sita, and Lakshman encounter various natural hazards such as dense forests, rugged terrain, and extreme weather conditions. Their experiences highlight the importance of being prepared for environmental threats by carrying appropriate supplies, maintaining physical fitness, and having survival skills to navigate through challenging landscapes.
- **Enemy Attacks:** Lord Ram's allies, including the Vanar's and Sugriv's army, face enemy attacks from demons and other adversaries loyal to King Ravan. This highlights the importance of being prepared for physical confrontations and having defensive strategies in place to protect against hostile forces. Training in combat skills, fortifying defenses, and coordinating with allies are crucial for defending against enemy attacks.
- **Environmental Disasters:** In addition to natural hazards, the characters in the Ramayana also face environmental disasters such as floods and storms. These events emphasize the importance of disaster preparedness and resilience in the face of environmental threats. Building structures that can withstand natural disasters, having evacuation plans, and establishing emergency response teams are essential for mitigating the impact of environmental disasters.

Control

Protection against physical and environmental threats, such as natural disasters and other intentional or unintentional physical threats to infrastructure should be designed and implemented.

Purpose

To prevent or reduce the consequences of events originating from physical and environmental threats.

Guidance

Risk assessments to identify the potential consequences of physical and environmental threats should be performed prior to beginning critical operations at a physical site, and at regular intervals. Necessary safeguards should be implemented and changes to threats should be monitored. Specialist advice should be obtained on how to manage risks arising from physical and environmental threats such as fire, flood, earthquake, explosion, civil unrest, toxic waste, environmental emissions and other forms of natural disaster or disaster caused by human beings. Physical premises location and construction should take account of, but not limited to:

- Local topography, such as appropriate elevation, bodies of water and tectonic fault lines;
- Urban threats, such as locations with a high profile for attracting political unrest, criminal activity or terrorist attacks.

Based on risk assessment results, relevant physical and environmental threats should be identified and appropriate controls considered.

Other Information

Safes or other forms of secure storage facilities can protect information stored therein against disasters. Organizations can consider the concepts of crime prevention through environmental design when designing the controls to secure their environment and reduce urban threats. This control relates primarily to natural disasters and infrastructural damage. Threats include weather events, such as floods, fires and heavy snowfall, as well as man-made incidents, including property damage and sabotage. The external and environmental threats that an organization is most likely to face will depend on its location, on a macro and micro level. The key to compliance is to identify the likelihood and probability of external and environmental risks occurring, and to treat them appropriately. Some risks will be unavoidable or prohibitively expensive to eradicate, so organizations should focus on ways to mitigate the risk. Other times, there will be potentially devastating risks that can be addressed with simple fixes.

Physical protection against the damage from fires, floods, earthquakes, explosions, civil unrest, and other forms of environmental or human-made disasters should be implemented to protect organization. These protective controls are generally defined and documented in a Physical Security Policy that is made available to all appropriate personnel. Once defined, these controls can be used to not only protect information systems and personnel, but also address the risk treatment or risk mitigation of findings identified by the organization's risk assessment. Smoke or heat activated fire detectors and alarms should be installed. Organizations should ensure these detectors and alarms are continuously operating effectively. Detectors should not be located near air conditioning vents or intake ducts that can disperse smoke, thus preventing the triggering of alarms. Fire authorities should be automatically notified when a fire alarm is activated. Appropriate fire suppression systems, such as sprinklers, should be implemented throughout your facilities and within secure areas containing information systems. These suppression systems should be automated for any facilities or areas that are not staffed continuously. Fire suppression and detection devices or systems that are supported by independent energy sources should be implemented and maintained. Maintenance logs should be kept up to date to demonstrate these physical security devices are regularly maintained. Water or moisture detection devices should be located in dropped ceilings and within raised floors to detect water leaks or possible flooding. Information systems should be protected from damage resulting from water leaks by ensuring that master shutoff valves are installed, accessible, and working properly. Master shutoff valves should be clearly marked, and their location should be known by all key personnel.

A three-step process to identify and eliminate risks due to physical and environment threats:

- **Step 1: Complete a Risk assessment**

  Organizations should conduct a risk assessment to identify potential physical and environmental disasters that may occur on each specific physical premise and then measure the effects likely to arise due to the identified physical and environmental threats. Considering that each physical premise and infrastructure therein will be subject to different environmental conditions and physical risk factors, the type of threat and the level of risk identified will vary by each premise and its location. Another critical requirement is that this risk assessment should be carried out before launch of operations on a physical premise.

- **Step 2: Identify and Implement Controls**

  Based on the type of threat and the level of risk identified in the first step, organizations should put in place appropriate controls taking into account the likely consequences of the environmental and physical threats. To illustrate, examples of controls that can be put in place for the following threats:

  - **Fire:** Organizations should deploy systems to trigger alarms when a fire is detected or to activate fire suppression systems capable of protecting storage media and information systems from damage.
  - **Flooding:** Systems should be deployed and configured to detect flooding in areas where information assets are stored. Furthermore, tools such as water pumps should be ready to be used in case of flooding.
  - **Electrical Surges:** Servers and critical information management systems should be maintained and protected against electrical outages.
  - **Explosives and Weapons:** Organizations should carry out random audits and inspections on all individuals, items and vehicles entering into premises that hosts critical infrastructure.

- **Step 3: Monitoring**

  Considering that the type of threats and the level of risks may change over time, organizations should continuously monitor the risk assessments and reconsider the controls they implemented if needed.

The four specific considerations that organizations should take into account.

- **Consultation With Experts:** Each specific type of environmental and physical threat, whether it is toxic waste, earthquake or fire, is unique in terms of its nature, the risks it presents and counter-measures it requires. Therefore, organizations should seek for expert advice on how to identify eliminate and/or mitigate risks arising out of these threats.
- **Choice of Location for Premises:** Taking into account the local topography, water levels and tectonic movements of the potential location for premises can help identify and eliminate risks early on. Furthermore, organizations should consider the risks of man-made disasters in the chosen urban area such as political unrest and criminal activity.
- **Extra Layer of Security:** In addition to the specific controls implemented, secure information storage methods such as safes can add an extra layer of security against disasters such as fire and flooding.
- **Crime Prevention Through Environmental Design:** Organizations can consider this concept when implementing controls to enhance the security of premises. This method can be used to eliminate urban threats such as criminal activities, civil unrest and terrorism.

Incidents are always a question of when, not if. By actual business trends, technical and administrative controls may catch more attention from security practitioners, but they can never forget that those controls ultimately rely on physical assets that must be protected as well, in many cases with superior levels of reliability. In addition to hardware and software, construction measures can be incorporated that reduce the likelihood of compromise, like:

- **Location**: By knowing the previous history of a place, an organization can avoid those subjects to natural events like earthquakes, floods, and hurricanes, or activities like criminal actions and vandalism. If it does not have other options, at least it can prepare the site/facility to deal with those kinds of situations.
- **Walls:** Reinforced walls and treatments to protect them against agents

like fire, water, and chemicals can help minimize or delay the effects of those agents over an organization's assets.

- **Entrances:** Windows and doors represent a dilemma, since they should consider reinforcement against unauthorized access as well as facilitate people's exit in case of emergency. For other not-so-obvious entrance points, they should consider measures to prevent both people and animals from sneaking into the site or gaining access to the cabling or piping.
- **External Services:** No organization is fully autonomous, and that means they depend on some external services like energy, communications, public transport, and, in case of accidents and disaster, emergency services. An organization should consider its needs for locations accessible by multiple routes and providers.
- **Natural Surveillance:** See and be seen is a key factor for threat mitigation, and landscaping obstructions may cause points of vulnerability. While thinking about site surroundings, try to ensure there is a clear view of people, to make threatening activities easier to spot. Low solid fences, high tree foliage and points of observation are good examples.
- **Natural Access Control**: Use the natural landscape to direct traffic flow. Entrances sided by low hills offer more protection than those sided by flat terrain. A single entrance is better than multiple. Colored lines signaling routes are another alternative to make users naturally find their way in and out and increase opportunities to spot and discourage suspicious behavior.
- **Territorial Reinforcement:** And though spaces can be welcoming, they should be well defined and possess clear boundaries. In this way the organization can change the way people use the areas, through unconscious rules that help prevent or spot undesirable behavior. Subtle changes in layout and signaling are good examples of territorial reinforcement.
- **Other elements** that can be considered are traffic calming, transition zones, maintenance, and lighting.

Prevention and Protection

Physical security needs to conform to the standards in force concerning both fire and environmental risks. Next, organizations should define sensitive areas which must be protected in a specific way because they shelter vital data or critical infrastructures; a sort of high-level inventory dedicated to security. The protection of sensitive areas must be based on a prioritization of which risks to combat first. A recovery plan should be put in place and tested, including the protection of all IT infrastructure. For all types of risk, the approach should be the same:

- Define the perimeter;
- Introduce preventive (to avoid the disaster) and protective (to protect the installation in case the disaster occurs) measures;
- Test and evaluate these measures regularly.

To protect against all of these risks, approaches may vary depending on the situation. Below are some basic protective measures which are required for most cases:

To Guard Against:	Protective Measure:
Electrical Failure	• Electronic Protection/Controls • Redundancy
Fire	• Detection and Fire Protection • Decentralized Back-ups • Redundancy
Flooding	• Location of computer rooms outside risk areas • Flood detection system • Elevation of computer equipment • Use of hermetic tubes for wiring • Compartmentalized flooring • Decentralized back-ups, dry archives

To Guard Against:	Protective Measure:
Theft, Intrusion, Espionage	• Restricted Physical Access • Tracking of Visitors • Alarm Systems
Sabotage	• Redundancy • Decentralized back-ups • Restricted Physical Access
Hardware Malfunctions	• Regulation of Temperature

A.7.6 Working in Secure Areas

Secure areas are areas within buildings or facilities where personnel work with sensitive information or assets. Secure areas are sites where sensitive information is handled or housed. This means that anywhere IT equipment or personnel are sheltered qualifies as a secure area. The purpose of physical security processes is to ensure that information is protected from physical threats and this includes both physical and digital assets. Organizations must put in place appropriate security measures that apply to all personnel working in secure areas so that they cannot access, use, modify, destruct, damage, or interfere with information assets or information facilities without authorization. Housing sensitive information assets in secure areas such as secure server rooms and implementing strict access controls is not sufficient to maintain the security of these assets. Employees with access to secure rooms may, deliberately or negligently, cause damage to the hardware equipment and digital assets stored in secure areas or access, use, destruct these information assets and facilities without permission.

A.7.6 Working in Secure Areas – A linkage with Ancient Era

- **Concealment and Camouflage:** Duryodhana hides himself in the lake to escape from his enemies during the battle. Similarly, working in secure areas often involves the need for concealment and camouflage, where individuals may need to blend in or remain inconspicuous to avoid detection by unauthorized personnel.
- **Secure Access Points:** Duryodhana's ability to hide in the lake implies that the area was not easily accessible to his enemies. Similarly, secure areas in workplaces are often protected by restricted access points, such as locked doors, security checkpoints, or biometric scanners, to prevent unauthorized entry and ensure the safety of individuals within.
- **Covert Operations:** Duryodhana's act of hiding in the lake can be seen as a form of covert operation to evade, capture or attack. Similarly, working in secure areas may involve engaging in covert operations or sensitive tasks that require discretion and confidentiality to protect classified information or assets.
- **Surveillance and Monitoring:** Duryodhana's enemies may have

employed surveillance and monitoring techniques to locate him while he was hiding in the lake. Similarly, secure areas in workplaces are often equipped with surveillance cameras, sensors, or patrols to monitor activities and detect any unauthorized individuals or security breaches.

- **Response and Containment:** Duryodhana's enemies likely implemented response and containment measures to capture or neutralize him once his location was discovered. Similarly, working in secure areas requires having response and containment protocols in place to address security incidents or breaches effectively, including alerting authorities, mobilizing security personnel, and implementing containment measures.
- **Risk Management:** Duryodhana's decision to hide in the lake carries risks, as he may be vulnerable to detection or attack by his enemies. Similarly, working in secure areas involves managing risks associated with potential threats or vulnerabilities to ensure the safety and security of individuals and assets within the area.

Control

Security measures for working in secure areas should be designed and implemented.

Purpose

To protect information and other associated assets in secure areas from damage and unauthorized interference by personnel working in these areas.

Guidance

The security measures for working in secure areas should apply to all personnel and cover all activities taking place in the secure area. The following guidelines should be considered:

- Making personnel aware only of the existence of, or activities within, a secure area on a need-to- know basis;
- Avoiding unsupervised work in secure areas both for safety reasons and to reduce chances for malicious activities;
- Physically locking and periodically inspecting vacant secure areas; not

allowing photographic, video, audio or other recording equipment, such as cameras in user endpoint devices, unless authorized;

- Appropriately controlling the carrying and use of user endpoint devices in secure areas;
- Posting emergency procedures in a readily visible or accessible manner.

The security measures should cover all personnel working in secure areas and should apply to all activities carried out in these areas. While the type and degree of security measures implemented may vary depending on the level of risk to specific information assets, organizations should adhere to:

- Organizations should inform their personnel about the existence of secure areas and about the specific operations conducted in these areas on a need-to-know basis;
- No personnel should be allowed to carry out any unsupervised activity in the designated secure areas;
- Unoccupied secure areas should be locked and should be subject to periodic inspections;
- Use of recording equipment, including those used to record audio, video, and photos, should be subject to strict authorization procedures;
- Carriage and use of end-point user devices in secure areas should be subject to strict controls;
- Emergency procedures should be displayed in a place easily accessible to all personnel working in secure areas;
- Writing an operational requirement;
- The principle of locating them in spaces where the vulnerabilities are at their lowest;
- The concept of multiple layers, following the principles of deter, detect, delay etc.;
- The following three central pillars of barriers, access control and detection;
- The successful implementation of procedural controls to ensure security integrity;

- A physical security perimeter;
- Physical entry controls;
- Secure offices, rooms and facilities;
- Protection against external and environmental threats;
- Secure area protection;
- Physical security for public access, delivery and loading areas.

A.7.7 Clear Desk and Clear Screen

When an employee leaves his/her workstation unattended, sensitive information contained in digital and physical materials on his workspace will be exposed to a heightened risk of unauthorized access, loss of confidentiality, and damage. The clean desk and clear screen policy refers to practices that ensure sensitive information - both in digital and physical format, and assets are not left unprotected at personal and public workspace when they are not in use, or when someone leaves his workstation, either for a short time or at the end of the day. A clear screen policy directs all your organization's employees to lock their computers when leaving their desk and to log off when leaving for an extended period of time. This ensures that the contents of the computer screen are protected from prying eyes and the computer is protected from unauthorized use. A clear screen policy and a clean desk policy work hand-in-hand to safeguard the organization's information. With the popularity of open plan offices and sharing computer workstations, there is a greater need to safeguard the organization's information. In addition, a clean desk and clear screen policy should be adopted because of the benefits it can provide to the organization.

- **Prevent Prying Eyes**: Computers that are left logged on and unattended pose as a tempting target for prying eyes.
- **Prevent Unauthorized Access**: A clear screen policy not only prevents curious passerby's from observing information they should not have access to, it also prevents unauthorized access.

A.7.7 Clear Desk and Clear Screen - A linkage with Ancient Era

- **Cleanliness and Order:** In the forest exile, Lord Ram, Mata Sita, and Lakshman maintain a clean and organized living space despite the challenging conditions. This emphasis on cleanliness reflects the idea of maintaining a "clear desk" in modern workplaces, where clutter-free environments promote productivity and focus.
- **Focus and Concentration:** Lord Hanuman's single-minded determination to find Mata Sita and Lord Ram's steadfast commitment to righteousness exemplify the importance of maintaining a "clear screen" in one's mind, free from unnecessary distractions or clutter, to achieve objectives effectively.

- **Preparation and Readiness:** Lord Ram meticulously plans His approach to rescuing Mata Sita from King Ravan's captivity, considering various factors and potential challenges. This preparation aligns with the idea of maintaining a "clear desk and clear screen" in the workplace, where organized and focused individuals are better equipped to handle tasks efficiently and respond to unexpected developments.
- **Discipline and Self-Control:** Lakshman's unwavering dedication to protecting Lord Ram and Mata Sita demonstrates disciplined focus and commitment. Similarly, maintaining a "clear desk and clear screen" in the workplace requires discipline and self-control to resist distractions and maintain productivity.

Control

Clear desk rules for papers and removable storage media and clear screen rules for information processing facilities should be defined and appropriately enforced.

Purpose

To reduce the risks of unauthorized access, loss of and damage to information on desks, screens and in other accessible locations during and outside normal working hours.

Guidance

The organization should establish and communicate a topic-specific policy on clear desk and clear screen to all relevant interested parties. The following guidelines should be considered:

- Locking away sensitive or critical business information when not required, especially when the office is vacated;
- Protecting user endpoint devices by key locks or other security means when not in use or unattended;
- Leaving user endpoint devices logged off or protected with a screen and keyboard;
- Locking mechanism controlled by a user authentication mechanism when unattended. All computers and systems should be configured with a timeout or automatic logout feature;

- Making the originator collect outputs from printers or multi-function devices immediately. The use of printers with an authentication function, so the originators are the only ones who can get their printouts and only when standing next to the printer;
- Securely storing documents and removable storage media containing sensitive information and, when no longer required, discarding them using secure disposal mechanisms;
- Establishing and communicating rules and guidance for the configuration of popups on screens (e.g., turning off the new email and messaging pop-ups, if possible, during presentations, screen sharing or in a public area);
- Clearing sensitive or critical information on whiteboards and other types of display when no longer required;
- Being aware of the classification of the information;
- Ensuring that restricted information is not kept on the screen when not needed;
- Knowing where the mobile and portable storage devices are at all times.

The organization should have procedures in place when vacating facilities including conducting a final sweep prior to leaving to ensure the organization's assets are not left behind.

Organizations should create and enforce a topic-specific policy that sets out clear desk and clear screen rules. A clear screen policy is simple and practical to implement. Employees should already be accustomed to logging off and/or shutting down their computer when leaving for the day, but few may lock their computers when leaving their desks, especially for short breaks. A clear screen policy is most difficult to enforce in its infancy. However, once the organization stresses the importance of having a clear screen policy, employees will eventually make it into a habit. A clear screen policy should be in writing and communicated to all employees, especially during introductory and refresher training. Have all employees sign the document for approval. Organizations should take into account when establishing and enforcing clear desk and clear screen rules by following the recommendations mentioned in the Guidance section.

When an organization vacates a facility, physical and digital materials previously stored in that facility should be securely removed so that sensitive information is not left insecure. Therefore, organizations need to establish procedures to vacate facilities so that all sensitive information assets housed in that facility are securely disposed of. These procedures may include carrying out a final sweep so that no sensitive information is left unprotected.

A.7.8 Equipment Siting and Protection

Equipment needs to be sited and protected to reduce the risks from environmental threats and hazards, and against unauthorized access. The siting of equipment will be determined by a number of factors including the size and nature of the equipment, it's proposed use and accessibility and environmental requirements. Those responsible for siting equipment must conduct a risk assessment and apply the following wherever possible in line with the risk levels. It addresses how organizations can eliminate and mitigate risks arising out of physical and environmental threats to equipment hosting information assets. Physical and environmental threats to IT equipment may also compromise the availability, confidentiality, and integrity of information assets. The equipment should be located in a safe location where conditions are met for proper operation. Therefore, it is important to set humidity and temperature sensors, and to control conditions in order to allow the equipment to operate properly. When talking about working conditions, remember that the equipment is prepared to work under certain conditions, and many computers/servers are prepared to shut down automatically at the moment that these conditions are not met. They do this mainly to prevent damage to the equipment, which consequently, implies an interruption to your business. Here it is also important that the equipment be sited in a safe location to minimize unnecessary access, and for this, you can use different work areas, protecting them with physical access control. And, it is also important that the information processing facilities handling sensitive data be positioned carefully. When it comes to the protection of physical equipment, on the other hand, to maintain an adequate environment, it also tends to be a good practice to establish a norm that employees do not eat, smoke, or drink in the vicinity of the equipment.

A.7.8 Equipment Siting and Protection – A linkage with Ancient Era

- **Protection of Valuables:** Throughout the Ramayana epic, characters possess valuable equipment such as weapons, chariots, and divine artifacts. These items are often crucial for achieving their goals and overcoming obstacles. For example, Lord Ram's bow, the divine weapon bestowed upon Him by Lord Shiva, plays a significant role in His quest to rescue Mata Sita. The careful protection and siting of such valuable equipment ensure that they remain accessible and effective when needed.

- **Strategic Positioning:** Characters in the Ramayana often strategically position themselves and their equipment to gain tactical advantages in battles or confrontations. For instance, during the defense of the bridge to Lanka, Lord Ram strategically positions His army and equipment to repel King Ravan's forces effectively. This strategic siting ensures that resources are deployed optimally to defend against threats and achieve strategic objectives.
- **Fortification and Defense:** In the Ramayana, characters fortify their positions and protect their equipment from enemy attacks. For example, when constructing the bridge to Lanka, Lord Ram's army employs various defensive measures to protect themselves and their equipment from King Ravan's forces. This emphasis on fortification and defense highlights the importance of ensuring the safety and security of equipment in hostile environments.
- **Divine Protection:** In addition to conventional methods of protection, characters in the Ramayana often rely on divine intervention to safeguard their equipment from harm. For example, Lord Ram's bow is not only a powerful weapon but also imbued with divine protection, ensuring its resilience against enemy attacks. This divine protection serves as an additional layer of security for important equipment in the epic.
- **Resource Management:** Characters in the Ramayana demonstrate prudent resource management practices, ensuring that equipment is utilized efficiently and effectively. For example, when constructing the bridge to Lanka, Lord Ram's army carefully manages their resources to ensure that they have an adequate supply of materials and equipment for the task at hand. This efficient management of resources ensures the successful completion of their objectives.

Control

Equipment should be sited securely and protected.

Purpose

To reduce the risks from physical and environmental threats, and from unauthorized access and damage.

Guidance

The following guidelines should be considered to protect equipment:

- Siting equipment to minimize unnecessary access into work areas and to avoid unauthorized access;
- Carefully positioning information processing facilities handling sensitive data to reduce the risk of information being viewed by unauthorized persons during their use;
- Adopting controls to minimize the risk of potential physical and environmental threats;
- Establishing guidelines for eating, drinking and smoking in proximity to information processing facilities;
- Monitoring environmental conditions for conditions which can adversely affect the operation of information processing facilities;
- Applying lightning protection to all buildings and fitting lightning protection filters to all incoming power and communications lines;
- Considering the use of special protection methods for equipment in industrial environments;
- Protecting equipment processing confidential information to minimize the risk of information leakage due to electromagnetic emanation;
- Physically separating information processing facilities managed by the organization from those not managed by the organization.

Physical security must be in place to control physical access to restricted areas and facilities containing covered devices. Covered devices such as server, hardware, desktop computers and storage media should be locked behind cabinets or tied down to physical restraints that prevent unauthorized removal from restricted area. Access to areas containing covered device should be granted to personnel with a need-to-know based on job function. Restricted areas should display signs to give clear indication that access is for authorized personnel only. Facilities containing covered device should give minimum indication of their purpose, with no obvious signs identifying the presence of covered data or related functions. Physical access control devices such as key card reader, doors and cabinet locks, should be tested prior to use and on a periodic basis (e.g., annually). Resource proprietors and custodians should produce physical or electronic audit trails to record all personnel's physical access to restricted area for the purpose of security incident investigation. Inventory of who has access to physical access control devices should be regularly reviewed and any inappropriate access identified during the review should be removed promptly.

Advice to Protect your Equipment

- Keep doors and windows locked;
- Keep sensitive hard copy records locked away if possible;
- Fit an intruder alarm, with unique codes for each employee;
- Fit bars or shutters to vulnerable windows;
- Use CCTV to deter intruders and record incidences of criminal activity;
- Consider using computer locking cables on individual desktop machines and laptops;
- Keep a fire extinguisher suitable for use with electrical equipment, near your computer;
- Take care how you dispose of packaging that might advertise that you have new equipment;
- Consult with your insurance organization or local crime prevention officer for additional security advice.

Advice for Servers & IT infrastructure

- Keep servers and network equipment in a locked room and control access to it;
- Server and networking racks and cabinets can also be protected by individual locks;
- Disable unused network ports;
- Locate equipment to minimize risks from fire, flooding and theft;
- Keep a fire extinguisher suitable for use with electrical equipment, near your IT equipment.

Advice on Visitors to your Business

- Be vigilant about granting access to any visitors, and escort them where appropriate;

- Vet contractors and support personnel;
- Restrict access to sensitive areas, such as server rooms or HR records;
- Encourage staff to challenge unescorted strangers in secure areas.

Limit the Impact of a Theft or Loss

- Make a note of all IT equipment serial numbers to enable reporting if stolen;
- Security mark computers and other high-value items;
- Keep printed photographic records of all equipment and lock them away safely;
- Never store passwords on computers;
- Ensure computer equipment is adequately insured;
- Back up data.

A.7.9 Security of Assets Off-Premises

When devices containing information assets are taken out of an organization's premises, they will be exposed to higher risks of damage, loss, destruction, theft, or compromise. This is because physical security controls implemented within an organization's facilities will not be effective, leaving the assets taken off-site vulnerable to threats such as physical risks and unauthorized access by malicious parties. For example, employees working off-site can take corporate computers containing sensitive information out of business premises, work at a coffee house or a hotel lobby, connect to an insecure public Wi-Fi and leave their devices unattended. All of these present risks to the security, confidentiality, integrity, and availability of information hosted on these devices. Organizations are to establish and apply procedures and controls that cover all devices owned by or used on behalf of the organization. Furthermore, the creation of an asset inventory and upper management's approval of the use of personal devices is essential to the effective protection of off-site devices.

Security controls need to be applied to off-site assets, taking into account the different risks involved with working outside the organization's premises. Considerations should be made and risk assessments carried out for assets that are taken off site, either routinely or by exception. Controls will likely include a mixture of: Technical controls such as access control policies, password management, encryption; Physical controls such as locks might also be considered too; alongside policy and process controls such as instruction to never leave assets unattended in public view. It is particularly important to review security incident trends relating to off-site assets. The auditor will expect to see evidence of this risk assessment taking place and the proportionate controls selected according to the evaluated risk levels. They will also expect to see evidence of policy compliance.

A.7.9 Security of Assets Off-Premises – A linkage with Ancient Era

- **Protection of Exile:** After being banished from Ayodhya, Lord Ram, Mata Sita, and Lakshman are forced to leave the kingdom and reside in the forest. This exile represents a situation where valuable assets (in this case, the kingdom itself and its rightful rulers) are vulnerable and need protection while being off-premises. Despite being away from the kingdom, Lord Ram takes measures to ensure the security of Ayodhya's interests by entrusting the administration to His younger brother Bharata.

- **Safekeeping of Valuables:** During their exile, Lord Ram and His companions carry valuable possessions with them, such as Lord Ram's divine bow and other weapons. These items hold immense significance and are essential for their protection and survival in the forest. Lord Ram ensures the security of these assets by keeping them close and guarded, even though they are off-premises from their rightful place in Ayodhya.
- **Safe Passage of Messengers:** Throughout the Ramayana, messengers play a crucial role in communication between characters who are often located in different places. Whether it's Lord Hanuman's journey to Lanka to find Mata Sita or emissaries sent to allies for assistance, ensuring the security of these messengers while they are off-premises becomes essential. Lord Ram and His allies take precautions to safeguard the messengers and ensure the successful completion of their missions
- **Protection of Allies:** Lord Ram forms alliances with various allies during His quest to rescue Mata Sita and defeat King Ravan. These allies often provide support and resources from their own territories, which are off-premises from Lord Ram's immediate location. Ensuring the security of these allies and their assets becomes crucial for maintaining trust and cooperation in the pursuit of common goals.
- **Safe Return of Captives:** After the war with King Ravan, Lord Ram ensures the safe return of Mata Sita and other captives from Lanka to Ayodhya. This process involves ensuring the security of the captives while they are off-premises, especially during their journey through unfamiliar territories. Lord Ram takes measures to protect them and ensure their safe return to their rightful place in Ayodhya.

Control

Off-site assets should be protected.

Purpose

To prevent loss, damage, theft or compromise of off-site devices and interruption to the organization's operations.

Guidance

Any device used outside the organization's premises which stores or processes information, including devices owned by the organization and devices owned privately and used on behalf of the organization [bring your own device (BYOD)] needs protection. The use of these devices should be authorized by management. The following guidelines should be considered for the protection of devices which store or process information outside the organization's premises, but not limited to:

- Not leaving equipment and storage media taken off premises unattended in public and unsecured places;
- Observing manufacturers' instructions for protecting equipment at all times;
- When off-premises equipment is transferred among different individuals or interested parties, maintaining a log that defines the chain of custody for the equipment including at least names and organizations of those who are responsible for the equipment. Information that does not need to be transferred with the asset should be securely deleted before the transfer;
- Where necessary and practical, requiring authorization for equipment and media to be removed from the organization's premises and keeping a record of such removals in order to maintain an audit trail;
- Protecting against viewing information on a device on public transport, and the risks associated with shoulder surfing;
- Implementing location tracking and ability for remote wiping of devices.

Permanent installation of equipment outside the organization's premises [such as antennas and automated teller machines (ATMs)] can be subject to higher risk of damage, theft or eavesdropping. These risks can vary considerably between locations and should be taken into account in determining the most appropriate measures. The following guidelines should be considered when siting this equipment outside of the organization's premises:

- Physical security monitoring;
- Protecting against physical and environmental threats;
- Physical access and tamper proofing controls;
- Logical access controls.

It may be difficult to maintain the same level of security controls for information systems or other assets when they are taken off-premises. Controls in place while systems are connected to the organization's network may not be enforceable when working off of the network. Physical security controls are very likely to be significantly different as well. These risks may be further magnified if personnel are not well trained on security best practices and acceptable use requirements. Computers, peripherals, paperwork, reports, software, or other information assets belonging to the organization should not be taken off site without prior authorization. Records should be maintained for all information assets that are taken off site. These records should be updated once a timely return of the equipment or other information assets has been completed. The asset inventory of the organization is likely the most convenient place to document what assets have been taken off-site, by whom, and when they are scheduled to be returned. Information asset security controls should be applied to offsite equipment that are comparable to on-site controls. The different risks associated with working outside the organization's premises should be considered. Particular attention should be given to protecting equipment during business or personal travel. Full-disk encryption should be deployed on all laptops. Information assets remain the property of the organization even when they are off-premises. Personnel should be trained that these assets should not be used by family members or friends. This unauthorized use may introduce not only technical risks, but also potential risks to the confidentiality of data contained on devices due to improper viewing of information by unauthorized audiences. All the employees need to be responsible, and held accountable, for all actions performed on or with the information assets that are presently assigned to them. When equipment goes off the premises, it is not only important to establish that its content is encrypted, the employees who take equipment out of the facility must also ensure its physical safety at all times, with special attention in public places, and take care not to let it become damaged. These same measures should also apply if the employee works from home. Organizations can maintain the security of equipment containing information assets by preventing specific risks by following the recommendations in the Guidance section.

Advice for Laptop, Tablet & Smartphone Users

- Employees should keep mobile devices with them at all times. When unattended they should keep them hidden or physically locked away. They should also be carried in hand baggage on an aircraft or coach;
- Laptops, tablets and smartphones should never be left on a vehicle seat. Even when the driver is in the vehicle, their device could be vulnerable when stationary;
- Employees with tablets and smartphones should do their best not to have them on display when out and about owing to the increasing trend of snatch robberies, sometimes involving physical violence;
- Ensure your employees use padded bags to carry their laptops and, where feasible, tablets. Many laptops are broken simply by dropping them.

A.7.10 Storage Media

The objective of this control is to prevent unauthorized disclosure, modification, removal or destruction of information stored on media. In computers, a storage media are physical devices that receives and retains electronic data for applications and users and makes data available for retrieval. It might be inside a computer or other device or attached to a system externally, either directly or over a network. The singular form of this term is storage medium. Storage media comes in many different forms, among them:

- **Hard Disk Drives:** It contains metal platters coated with a magnetic layer. The platters usually spin continuously when a computer is on, storing data in different sectors on the magnetic disk.
- **RAID:** It works by placing data on multiple disks and balancing input/output (I/O) operations across those disks.
- **Flash Memory**: Here data is written to microchips, making storage operations much faster than traditional disks.
- **Solid State Drives (SSD)**: SSDs is both network-based storage, such as NAS and SAN, and Direct Attached Storage (DAS).
- **USB Flash Drives**: A USB flash drive is a type of removable storage medium that attaches to a server or other device through a USB port.
- **Optical Disc**: Optical disc technology uses lasers to write and read data.
- **Tape**: Tape was a dominant backup storage medium until the 1990s but was gradually pushed aside by magnetic disk.

Use of storage media devices such as SSDs, USB sticks, external drives, and mobile phones are vital to many critical information processing operations such as data back-up, data storage, and information transfer. However, the storage of sensitive and critical information on these devices introduces risks to the integrity, confidentiality, and availability of information assets. These risks may include loss or theft of storage media containing sensitive information, propagation of malware into all corporate computing networks via the storage media, and failure and degradation of storage media devices used for data back-up. This control addresses how organizations can establish appropriate procedures, policies, and controls to maintain the security of storage media throughout its life cycle, from its acquisition to its disposal.

A.7.10 Storage Media – A linkage with Ancient Era

Protection of Valuables

In the Ramayana, the protection of treasure is often depicted as crucial, especially when considering valuable possessions like divine weapons, jewels, and other priceless artifacts.

- **Storage Media as a Vault:** In the modern digital age, storage media act as virtual vaults where valuable data is stored and protected. Similarly, in the Ramayana, various characters and kingdoms employ physical fortifications, strongholds, and magical barriers to safeguard their treasures. For instance, the kingdom of Lanka, ruled by King Ravan, is depicted as heavily fortified to protect its riches and precious possessions.
- **Data Encryption and Magical Protections:** Just as modern encryption techniques are used to secure data stored in digital formats, the Ramayana features instances of magical protections placed on treasures. For example, King Ravan's palace is said to be guarded by mystical defenses to prevent unauthorized access.
- **Backup and Redundancy:** In the realm of data storage, redundancy and backup systems are essential for ensuring data integrity and availability. Similarly, in the Ramayana, characters take measures to safeguard treasures by creating duplicates or hiding them in secure locations. For instance, Lord Ram's divine bow, the Pinaka, is kept in a secure place until it's time for Mata Sita's Swayamvara.
- **Guardianship and Custodianship:** In both contexts, the protection of treasure involves the appointment of guardians or custodians responsible for its safekeeping. In the Ramayana, characters like Lord Hanuman, Jatayu, and Vibhishan serve as guardians of valuable possessions, ensuring their protection against adversaries.
- **Threat Mitigation and Defense Strategies:** Just as modern security protocols are employed to mitigate threats to data, characters in the Ramayana devise defense strategies to protect treasures from

being stolen or destroyed. These strategies may include surveillance, fortification, and preemptive action against potential threats.

Control

Storage media should be managed through their lifecycle of acquisition, use, transportation and disposal in accordance with the organization's classification scheme and handling requirements.

Purpose

To ensure only authorized disclosure, modification, removal or destruction of information on storage media.

Guidance

Removable Storage Media

The following guidelines for the management of removable storage media should be considered:

- Establishing a topic-specific policy on the management of removable storage media and communicating such topic-specific policy to anyone who uses or handles removable storage media;
- Where necessary and practical, requiring authorization for storage media to be removed from the organization and keeping a record of such removals in order to maintain an audit trail;
- Storing all storage media in a safe, secure environment according to their information classification and protecting them against environmental threats, in accordance with manufacturers' specifications;
- If information confidentiality or integrity are important considerations, using cryptographic techniques to protect information on removable storage media;
- To mitigate the risk of storage media degrading while stored information is still needed, transferring the information to fresh storage media before becoming unreadable;
- Storing multiple copies of valuable information on separate storage media to further reduce the risk of coincidental information damage or loss;

- Considering the registration of removable storage media to limit the chance for information loss;
- Only enabling removable storage media ports if there is an organizational reason for their use;
- Where there is a need to use removable storage media, monitoring the transfer of information to such storage media;
- Information can be vulnerable to unauthorized access, misuse or corruption during physical transport, for instance when sending storage media via the postal service or via courier;
- In this control, media also includes paper documents. When transferring physical storage media, apply security measures in control for information transfer.

Secure Reuse or Disposal

Procedures for the secure reuse or disposal of storage media should be established to minimize the risk of confidential information leakage to unauthorized persons. The procedures for secure reuse or disposal of storage media containing confidential information should be proportional to the sensitivity of that information. The following items should be considered:

- If storage media containing confidential information need to be reused within the organization, securely deleting data or formatting the storage media before reuse;
- Disposing of storage media containing confidential information securely when not needed anymore;
- Having procedures in place to identify the items that can require secure disposal;
- Many organizations offer collection and disposal services for storage media. Care should be taken in selecting a suitable external party supplier with adequate controls and experience;
- Logging the disposal of sensitive items in order to maintain an audit trail;
- When accumulating storage media for disposal, giving consideration

to the aggregation effect, which can cause a large quantity of non-sensitive information to become sensitive.

A risk assessment should be performed on damaged devices containing sensitive data to determine whether the items should be physically destroyed rather than sent for repair or discarded.

Other Information

When confidential information on storage media is not encrypted, additional physical protection of the storage media should be considered.

This control enables organizations to eliminate and mitigate risks of unauthorized access to, use, deletion, modification, and transfer of sensitive information hosted on storage media devices by setting out procedures for the handling of storage media across its entire lifecycle. It applies both to digital and physical storage media such as storage of information on physical files. It requires organizations to create and implement appropriate procedures, technical controls, and organization-wide policies on the use of storage media based on the organization's own classification scheme and its data handling requirements such as legal and contractual obligations. Procedures must be put in place for the management of removable media in accordance with the classification scheme. General use of removable media must be risk assessed and it may be necessary to carry out use-specific risk assessments beyond that too. Removable media should only be allowed if there is a justified business reason. If no longer required, the contents of any re-usable media should be made unrecoverable and securely destroyed or erased. All media should be stored in a safe, secure environment, in accordance with manufacturers' specifications and additional techniques like cryptography considered where appropriate. Where necessary and practical, authorization should be required for media removed from the organization, and a record kept in order to maintain an audit trail.

When no longer required media must be disposed of securely by following documented procedures. These procedures minimize the risk of confidential information leakage to unauthorized parties. The procedures should be proportional to the sensitivity of the information being disposed. Things that should be considered include; whether or not the media contains confidential information; and having procedures in place which help identify the items which might require secure disposal.

Any media containing information needs to be protected against unauthorized access, misuse or corruption during transportation. The following should be considered to protect media when being transported: reliable transport or couriers should be used, perhaps a list of authorized couriers should be agreed with management; packaging should be sufficient in order to protect the contents from any physical damage during transit; and logs should be kept, identifying the content of the media and the protection applied. It should also be noted that when confidential information on media is not encrypted, additional physical protection of the media should be considered.

Equipment, information or software taken off-site needs management too. That might be controlled with some form of check in-out process or more simply associated to an employee as part of their role and managed in accordance with their terms and conditions of employment. In the ever-mobile working world, some assets such as mobile devices, may be routinely removed from organizational premises to facilitate mobile or home working. Where assets are not designed to be routinely removed from site or if they are of a sensitive, highly classified, valuable or fragile nature then processes should be in place to request and authorize removal and to check return of the assets. Consideration for limiting the length of time assets are allowed to be removed for should be made and should be risk based. The auditor will be looking to see that these risk assessments have been carried out for when non-routine removal of assets occurs and for policies that determine what is and isn't routine.

Management of Removable Media

Integrate necessary controls to manage media items, whether tapes, disks, flash disks, or removable hard drives, CDs, DVDs, or printed media, to ensure the integrity and confidentiality of organization data. Guidelines should be developed and implemented to ensure that media are used, maintained, and transported in a safe and controlled manner. Handling and storage should correspond with the sensitivity of the information on the media. Procedures to erase media if no longer needed, to ensure information is not leaked, are also important. While removable storage media is essential to many business operations and they are commonly used by most personnel, they present the highest degree of risk to the sensitive information. The organizations should adhere to for the management of removable storage media throughout its life cycle as per the Guidance - Removable Storage Media section

Secure Reuse or Disposal

Procedures for handling classified information should cover the appropriate means of its destruction and disposal. Serious breaches of confidentiality occur when apparently worthless disks, tapes, or paper files are dumped without proper regard to their destruction. Procedures for handling and storage of sensitive information, together with audit trails and records, are important. Accountability should be introduced and data classification and risk assessments performed, to ensure that necessary controls are applied to protect sensitive data. Appropriate access controls should be implemented to protect information from unauthorized disclosure or usage. Systems are also vulnerable to the unauthorized use of system documentation; much of this type of information should be regarded and handled as confidential. Security procedures, operating manuals, and operations records all come into this category. It provides separate guidance on secure reuse and disposal of storage media so that organizations can mitigate and eliminate risks to the compromise of the confidentiality of information. The organizations should define and apply procedures for the reuse and disposal of storage media, taking into account the sensitivity level of information contained in the storage media as per the Guidance - Secure Reuse or Disposal section.

A.7.11 Supporting Utilities

Failure or disruptions of utilities such as electricity, gas, water, or cooling needed for proper and continuous functioning of information processing facilities may result in compromise of information assets or may intercept business continuity. For example, the failure of air conditioning equipment in a data centre may lead to a sudden rise in temperature when the data centre is hit by a heatwave. This may cause servers hosting website and/ or customer data to shut down, and thus result in loss of availability of data and disruptions to business operations. Organizations can eliminate risks to the availability and integrity of information assets due to the failure of supporting utilities such as gas, cooling, telecommunications, water, and electricity by putting in place appropriate measures that protect supporting utilities against failures and disruptions such as power outages. Organization must identify risks to the continuous operations of supporting utilities and implementation of appropriate measures and controls to ensure that availability and integrity of information assets are not affected by failures of these utilities. The equipment needs to be safeguarded against threats relating to utility failures including power outages from fallen lines or blown transformers or loss of wireless connectivity. Most of these incidents will affect the temporary availability of the information systems. Although some threats are genuinely unforeseeable. Consider having a backup plan that involves a generator or dual routing access and power supplies.

A.7.11 Supporting Utilities – A linkage with Ancient Era

- **Lord Hanuman as a Supporting Utility:** Lord Hanuman plays a critical role as a loyal ally and messenger to Lord Ram. He possesses extraordinary abilities, including the power to fly and change in size at will. Similarly, supporting utilities in modern contexts empower users by providing them with tools and capabilities to accomplish tasks efficiently. Just as Lord Hanuman aids Lord Ram in His quest to rescue Mata Sita, supporting utilities aid users in navigating digital tasks and challenges.
- **Jatayu as a Security Utility:** Jatayu attempts to rescue Mata Sita from King Ravan clutches but is ultimately defeated. His courageous effort to protect Mata Sita symbolizes the importance of security in the face of adversity. In the digital realm, security utilities like antivirus

software, firewalls, and encryption tools serve to protect users' data and devices from threats. Like Jatayu's valiant defense of Mata Sita, these utilities act as guardians against malicious entitities and intrusions.

- **Vibhishana as a Consulting Utility:** Vibhishana defects to Lord Ram's side recognizing the righteousness of His cause. He offers valuable advice and strategic insights to Lord Ram, contributing to the eventual victory over King Ravan. Similarly, consulting utilities, such as productivity apps, project management software, and knowledge bases, provide users with guidance and expertise to make informed decisions and achieve their goals effectively.
- **Divine Weapons as Performance Utility:** In the Ramayana, Divine Weapons like Lord Ram's bow and arrow, as well as Lord Hanuman's mace, are instrumental in defeating adversaries and overcoming obstacles. These weapons symbolize power, precision and efficacy in combat. Likewise, performance utilities in modern computing, such as optimization tools, task managers, and debugging software, enhance the efficiency and effectiveness of digital operations. They enable users to execute tasks swiftly and accurately, akin to the swift strikes of divine weapons in the epic battles of the Ramayana.
- **Lord Krishna as a Supporting Utility:** Lord Krishna, serves as guide, advisor and charioteer to Arjuna. He provides strategic counsel, moral guidance, and divine intervention when needed. Similarly, supporting utilities in modern contexts, such as personal assistants, virtual mentors, and AI-driven decision-making tools, empower users by offering insights, recommendations, and assistance in navigating complex tasks and decisions.
- **Bhishma Pitamah as a Legacy Utility:** Bhishma Pitamah, embodies principles of duty, honor, and sacrifice. Despite His loyalty to His Kingdom, He remains bound by His vow of celibacy and allegiance to the throne. His legacy serves as a guiding principle for future generations. Similarly, legacy utilities in modern technology, such as version control systems, code repositories, and archival tools, preserve and maintain historical data, knowledge, and contributions for future reference and continuity.
- **Drona as a Training Utility:** Dronacharya, imparts martial training and

skills to His disciples. He challenges them to excel in warfare and hone their abilities through rigorous discipline and practice. Similarly, training utilities in modern contexts, such as e-learning platforms, simulation software, and skill development applications, provide users with educational resources, interactive exercises, and hands-on training to acquire new skills and knowledge.

- **Vidur as an Advisory Utility:** Vidur, offers sagacious counsel and moral guidance to the Karu dynasty. His insights and warnings often go unheeded, but His wisdom remains invaluable. Similarly, advisory utilities in modern technology, such as financial advisors, risk management software, and analytics platforms, offer users data-driven insights, recommendations, and forecasts to inform decision making and mitigate risks.

Control

Information processing facilities should be protected from power failures and other disruptions caused by failures in supporting utilities.

Purpose

To prevent loss, damage or compromise of information and other associated assets, or interruption to the organization's operations due to failure and disruption of supporting utilities.

Guidance

Organizations depend on utilities (e.g., electricity, telecommunications, water supply, gas, sewage, ventilation and air conditioning) to support their information processing facilities. Therefore, the organization should take into account following to comply with the requirements:

- Organizations should conform to the manufacturer's instructions when configuring, using, and maintaining the devices used to control the utilities.
- Utilities should be audited to ensure that they are fit to fulfil business growth objectives and they operate with other utilities without any issue.
- All equipment supporting the utilities should go through regular

inspections and testing so that there is no disruption or failure of their proper functioning.

- Depending on the level of risk to the information assets and business continuity, an alarm system can be established for malfunctioning equipment supporting the utilities.
- To minimize the risk, utilities should have multiple feeds with separate physical routing.
- The network connected to the equipment supporting utilities should be segregated from the network connected to IT facilities.
- Equipment supporting the utilities should be allowed to connect to the internet only if it is strictly necessary and this connection should be established in a secure manner.

Emergency lighting and communications should be provided. Emergency switches and valves to cut off power, water, gas or other utilities should be located near emergency exits or equipment rooms. Emergency contact details should be recorded and available to personnel in the event of an outage.

Other Information

Additional redundancy for network connectivity can be obtained by means of multiple routes from more than one utility provider.

Organizations should take the necessary steps to help ensure the potential operational impact associated with supporting utility failures is limited. The clear risk associated with not addressing supporting utility controls is the potential unplanned outages that affect business operations. All supporting utilities, such as electricity, natural gas, water supplies, sewage, and heating ventilation and air conditioning (HVAC), should be adequate for the systems, as well as personnel, they are supporting. Supporting utilities also need to be able to support any new infrastructure devices or other new equipment planned for implementation as the organization grows. A suitable electrical supply should be provided that meets power requirements defined by equipment manufacturers. An Uninterruptible Power Supply (UPS) should be implemented to support the orderly shutdown for equipment that supports critical business operations. UPS devices and generators should be regularly checked to ensure they have adequate capacity. Testing of these devices should be performed in accordance with the recommendations of the respective manufacturer or vendor. Emergency lighting should be installed and regularly tested to ensure it is operating correctly in case of a power failure. Emergency lighting should cover all emergency exits and planned evacuation routes within each of the organization's facilities. Emergency power-off switches should be located near emergency exits in data centers and equipment rooms to facilitate a rapid power down in case of an emergency. These devices should be maintained, prominently marked, and protected from accidental activation. It seems obvious that the equipment must be connected to a power outlet, and in many cases, there is a UPS and/or a generator that can provide power if the main energy supplier fails. But often companies have never tried their alternative energy supply, or do not know the capacity. Therefore, it is not only important to establish an alternative, but it is also important to define a maintenance plan and define the tasks that will be performed. And, it is highly recommended that organization generate a report with results.

Some of the cause for disruption in information processing facilities are, but not limited to:

1. **Cybercrime**: Because cybercrime has become the second most common cause of unplanned disruption, security must be addressed at every level. Defending against attacks is only half of the battle. Cyberthreats, including phishing and ransomware attacks, are among the most dangerous causes of disruption. Cyber attackers can exploit the weaknesses within your organization and get access to your sensitive data, exposing vital information and endangering your business.
2. **Human Error:** Regular and thorough training for staff should be a top priority. To reduce errors and ensure desired outcomes, you may also document method-of-process (MOP) techniques for carrying out complicated activities. Only qualified experts should monitor, maintain and manage the power and infrastructure to minimize downtime.
3. **Weather:** Natural catastrophes are unavoidable, but taking preventative precautions before something happens can help you avoid severe damage. Regularly test your disaster recovery plan and backup diesel generators.

4. **Generators:** Even though generator failures account for only 6% of faults, they are still essential to check and switch gears regularly. You must make use of N+1 redundancy and perform preventative maintenance.
5. **Insufficient Backup Power:** The most common reason for disruption is power loss. Power outages can happen at any time. Due to this possibility, data centers typically have additional power sources in case their primary one is interrupted. The most commonly used backup power sources are generators and batteries. However, issues arise when operators do not run power failure tests or replace batteries often enough. Without taking the necessary preventative steps, your backup power may not be available when you need it.
6. **Cooling Failures:** Because information processing facilities generate an incredible amount of heat, effective cooling solutions are vital to preventing equipment from overheating or suffering from shortened life spans. If your cooling solutions don't work as intended, it may experience erratic temperatures, it could be freezing one minute and sizzling the next. Failing to implement backup cooling procedures and properly maintain the ones you currently have can cause productivity to take a hit.

After highlighting those supporting utilities such as water supply, electricity, communications, sewage, and air conditioning is vital to the operations carried out in information processing facilities. Organizations should take into account to comply with the requirements as mentioned in the Guidance section.

Emergency Procedures: Organizations should determine an emergency contact person and record his/her contact details. These details should be provided to all personnel in the event a failure or disruption occurs. Emergency switches and valves to halt utilities such as water, gas, and electricity should be placed near the emergency exits. Emergency lighting and communications should be ready to be used in case an emergency arises.

Network Connectivity: Organizations can consider having additional routes from alternative service providers to increase network connectivity so that failures or disruptions of supporting utilities are prevented.

A.7.12 Cabling Security

Most modern technologies would not function properly without cables such as fiber, network, or power cables. Cabling is more than just your CAT6e or CAT7 data cabling or your fibre, ISO27001 wants you to also consider power as well. Anything that is carrying data or that is supporting information services needs to be considered and protected from interception, interference, or damage. While cables are essential to the transmission of information assets, and to the provision of information services, they expose risks to the availability and confidentiality of information assets and also to continuity of business operations. These risks may arise from damage to, interception, or interference with these cables. Furthermore, personnel with access to these cables may accidentally cause damage. Cabling security needs to be considered to reduce risks related to eavesdropping and data theft which is increased if the organization uses a cable supplier. Attackers can tap into the cables, interfere with operations or steal data. Controls such as hiding the cables, protecting them in covers, monitoring for interference or using multiple lines for specific high-risk departments.

Organizations aims to achieve two distinct purposes:

- Protecting information assets carried via cables against unauthorized access, use, damage, or destruction by implementing appropriate measures;
- Ensuring the continuity of business operations by maintaining the security of cables that carry information assets, power, and electricity.

A.7.12 Cabling Security – A linkage with Ancient Era

Lord Hanuman's Tail

- **Protection and Resilience:** Just as cabling security measures protect network infrastructure from threats and vulnerabilities, Lord Hanuman's tail represents a protective barrier against external dangers. Both serve to safeguard valuable assets and ensure the continuity of operations in the face of adversity.
- **Adaptability and Flexibility:** Lord Hanuman's ability to alter the size and strength of His tail mirrors the flexibility and adaptability required in maintaining secure network connections. Cabling security

measures must be scalable and adaptable to accommodate evolving technological needs and emerging threats.

- **Symbolism of Strength and Loyalty:** Lord Hanuman's unwavering devotion to Lord Ram symbolizes loyalty, commitment, and courage. Similarly, cabling security practices embody the commitment to safeguarding data integrity and confidentiality, reflecting the strength and dedication of those responsible for maintaining secure networks.

Control

Cables carrying power, data or supporting information services should be protected from interception, interference or damage.

Purpose

To prevent loss, damage, theft or compromise of information and other associated assets and interruption to the organization's operations related to power and communications cabling.

Guidance

The following guidelines for cabling security should be considered:

- Power and telecommunications lines into information processing facilities being underground where possible, or subject to adequate alternative protection, such as floor cable protector and utility pole; if cables are underground, protecting them from accidental cuts;
- Segregating power cables from communications cables to prevent interference;
- For sensitive or critical systems, further controls to consider include:
    - Installation of armored conduit and locked rooms or boxes and alarms at inspection and termination points;
    - Use of electromagnetic shielding to protect the cables;
    - Periodical technical sweeps and physical inspections to detect unauthorized devices being attached to the cables;
    - Controlled access to patch panels and cable rooms;
    - Use of fiber-optic cables;
- Labeling cables at each end with sufficient source and destination

details to enable the physical identification and inspection of the cable.

Specialist advice should be sought on how to manage risks arising from cabling incidents or malfunctions.

Other Information

Sometimes power and telecommunications cabling are shared resources for more than one organization occupying co-located premises.

Power and telecommunications cabling carrying data or supporting information services needs to be protected from interception, interference or damage. If power and network cables are not sited and protected adequately it is possible that an attacker may be able to intercept or disrupt communications or shut down power provision. Wherever possible, network and power cables should be underground or otherwise protected and separated in order to protect against interference. Depending on the sensitivity or classification of data it may be necessary to separate communications cables for different levels and additionally inspect termination points for authorized devices. The auditor will be visually inspecting the cables and if they are relevant to the level of classification/ risk request evidence of visual inspection. Organizations take into account the following criteria for compliance:

- Telecommunications and power cables connected to the information processing facilities should be placed underground to the extent it is feasible. Furthermore, cables laid down in the underground should be protected against accidental cuts through suitable techniques such as armored conduits. If placing the cables underground is not possible, organizations can consider implementing alternative protective measures such as floor cable protectors and utility poles.
- Power and communications cables should be segregated to eliminate the risk of interference.
- Considering that cables connected to critical information systems present higher risks to the sensitive information assets and to business operations, organizations should consider putting in place the following controls:

  - Using armored conduit, installing locked rooms and boxes, and setting up alarm systems both at inspection and terminal points.
  - Applying electromagnetic shielding technique to prevent damage to cables.
  - Cables should be subject to inspections at regular intervals and to technical sweeps to ensure that no unauthorized device is connected to the cables.
  - Establishing access control procedures and measures for access to cable rooms and patch panels.
  - Using fiber-optic cables.
- The source and destination details of each cable should be labelled at both the starting and endpoints of the cable so that the cable can be easily identified and inspected.

Furthermore, organizations are also advised to seek expert advice on how to manage risks that may arise from cable malfunctioning. Last but not the least, organizations should consider the risks related to the use of communications and power cables by more than one organization when they are on shared premises.

Structured IT cabling is the design and installation of a cabling system that will support multiple hardware uses both today and any additional hardware added in the future. It is the foundation of network infrastructure and enables all data transmission and telephone service done through computer. Every business has some sort of structured cabling network, but they vary in size, organization, and capability. No matter how large your business is, having a seamlessly functional structured cabling network will save you and your employees a lot of trouble. Here are the top 4 reasons that structured cabling networks are critical for IT security.

- **Compliance and Security:** IT infrastructure is essentially the nucleus of the organization. It is where servers, switches, routers are located and every piece of hardware is connected to them by various cabling. If these cables are not labeled and organized well it is very difficult to know what they are connected to. It will also be difficult to tell if an unauthorized person has made changes to the organization physical network. Having photos of cabling network on file for reference so it can be easy to identify changes and potentially identify why someone has made those changes. It is the simplest way to tell if someone is tampering with the network from a physical standpoint.

- **Faster Speeds and Reliability:** One of the most important things to any business is network stability and speed. There is nothing more frustrating that being on an important virtual meeting and having latency issues or drop-offs. Having a highly functional structured cabling network enables the employees to have trustworthy connection to the internet, and speed with locating important files stored on the network. If you have ever tried searching for a specific file and had to wait an extended period of time for it to be located, you may have some issues with your physical cabling system.
- **More Effective Support and Troubleshooting:** Technology by nature is ever changing and evolving and with this comes issues that need to be addressed. If the structured cabling network is poorly installed, organized, or labeled the support team will have a much tougher time identifying the issues. This can lead to longer wait times to getting back to the task at hand, and even the need to reach out to third-parties for help.
- **Cost Saving:** Structured cabling network can save time and money. As mentioned above, it is the nucleus of the organization and should be invested in on the front end, so the organization does not have to spend more money down the road to fix or even reinstall the entire network. If employees are unable to be productive due to latency issues, drop-offs, and lost files and the support team needs to spend twice as much time locating the issue and the lost files, then the organization are losing money.

Power and telecommunications cabling that is in place to support information system or transfer data should be protected from interception, interference, or damage. The organization should use clearly identifiable cable markings to minimize potential handling errors. Physical access to information system distribution and transmission lines should be controlled within the organization's facilities. Physical network ports throughout the facilities should be disabled when there is not a continuous need for them to be active. Having a live network port outlet, with no additional technical controls, could potentially provide a hacker or other bad actor direct access into organization's networks. Depending on the size of the organization and the number of information systems in use, cabling security controls may require a notable time investment to implement correctly. It is highly recommended to spend the time that is necessary to ensure cables are labeled and neatly organized to prevent unintentional, unforced errors. A short-term project to address cabling today, will help prevent countless issues tomorrow.

A.7.13 Equipment Maintenance

IT equipment such as servers, laptops, network devices, and printers are vital to many information processing operations such as storage, use, and transfer of information assets. However, if this equipment is not maintained taking into account product specifications and environmental risks, it may degrade in quality and performance. This lack of maintenance may result in the compromise of availability, integrity, and confidentiality of information assets stored on this equipment. For example, if an organisation fails to perform regular maintenance on server hardware, it may not recognize that the disk space is full. This may result in loss of data transmitted to or out of the server. Furthermore, employees or external service providers may gain access to IT equipment as part of the maintenance procedure and this may also present risks to the confidentiality of sensitive information. For instance, an external maintenance service provider may gain access to sensitive information stored on laptops or install malware into devices. The organisation can establish and implement appropriate procedures and measures for the proper maintenance of equipment so that the information assets stored on this equipment are not compromised.

- Maintenance is considered as the set of all actions which have as an objective to retain an item in, or restore to, a state in which it can perform the required function. The actions include the combination of all technical and related administrative, managerial, and supervisory actions such as tests, measurements, replacements, adjustment and repairs. Maintenance is distinguished as:
  - Preventive, which aims in retaining the system's capabilities before the occurrence of any problem.
  - Corrective, which aims in restoring the defective item(s) to the required state.
  - Adaptive, which focus in adjusting an equipment to properly interface with a changing environment.
  - Perfective, which refers to enhancements to the product in order to either add new capabilities or modify existing functions.

A.7.13 Equipment Maintenance – A linkage with Ancient Era

- **Precision and Accuracy:** Just as regular maintenance ensures that a bow and arrow remain precise and accurate in hitting their target, meticulous attention to detail and continuous improvement in skills and knowledge are essential for success in any endeavor. Regular practice, learning, and refinement contribute to maintaining sharpness and effectiveness in achieving goals.

- **Reliability and Consistency:** Proper maintenance of weapons ensures their reliability and consistency in performance. Similarly, in life, consistency and reliability are key to building trust and credibility. Regular self-care, mental well-being practices, and personal development efforts contribute to maintaining one's reliability and consistency in various roles and responsibilities.
- **Longevity and Durability:** Weapons, like bows and arrows, require regular maintenance to prolong their lifespan and durability. Similarly, investing in self-care, health maintenance, and personal development activities ensures one's longevity and endurance in facing life's challenges. Taking proactive steps to preserve physical, mental, and emotional well-being contributes to long-term resilience and sustainability.
- **Prevention of Malfunction and Failure:** Regular maintenance helps prevent malfunctions and failures in weapons, reducing the risk of accidents or mishaps during critical moments. Likewise, practicing self-awareness, stress management, and conflict resolution techniques helps prevent personal breakdowns or crisis, enabling individuals to navigate challenges effectively and avoid potential setbacks.
- **Adaptation and Improvement:** Maintenance of weapons involves adapting to changing conditions, making necessary adjustments, and incorporating improvements to enhance performance. Similarly, in life, embracing change, learning from experiences, and seeking continuous improvement contribute to personal growth and development. Flexibility, adaptability, and a willingness to evolve are essential for success in dynamic environments.

Control

Equipment should be maintained correctly to ensure availability, integrity and confidentiality of information.

Purpose

To prevent loss, damage, theft or compromise of information and other associated assets and interruption to the organization's operations caused by lack of maintenance.

Guidance

The following guidelines for equipment maintenance should be considered:

- Maintaining equipment in accordance with the supplier's recommended service frequency and specifications;
- Implementing and monitoring of a maintenance program by the organization;
- Only authorized maintenance personnel carrying out repairs and maintenance on equipment;
- Keeping records of all suspected or actual faults, and of all preventive and corrective maintenance;
- Implementing appropriate controls when equipment is scheduled for maintenance, taking into account whether this maintenance is performed by personnel on site or external to the organization, subjecting the maintenance personnel to a suitable confidentiality agreement;
- Supervising maintenance personnel when carrying out maintenance on site;
- Authorizing and controlling access for remote maintenance;
- Applying security measures for assets off-premises if equipment containing information is taken off premises for maintenance;
- Complying with all maintenance requirements imposed by insurance;
- Before putting equipment back into operation after maintenance, inspecting it to ensure that the equipment has not been tampered with and is functioning properly;
- Applying measures for secure disposal or re-use of equipment if it is determined that equipment is to be disposed of.

Other Information

Equipment includes technical components of information processing facilities, uninterruptible power supply (UPS) and batteries, power generators, power alternators and converters, physical intrusion detection systems and alarms, smoke detectors, fire extinguishers, air conditioning and lifts.

The organizations are to put in place necessary technical measures and procedures to carry out proper maintenance activities on equipment used to store information assets. These measures and procedures provide assurance that information assets are not lost or damaged, and they are not exposed to the risk of compromise such as unauthorized access. The organization must create a list of equipment, carrying out a risk assessment based on environmental factors and product specifications and establishing and implementing suitable procedures and measures for proper maintenance. The following are considered equipment, but not limited to:

- Technical components of information processing facilities;
- Batteries;
- Fire extinguishers;
- Lifts;
- Power converters;
- Air conditioners;
- Similar assets.

The organization to consider the following specific recommendations:

- Maintenance procedures should conform to the equipment manufacturer's specifications such as recommended service frequency;
- Organizations should establish and apply a maintenance program for all equipment;
- Only the authorized personnel or third parties should be allowed to perform maintenance activities or repairs on equipment;
- Organizations should create and maintain a record of all equipment malfunctioning and faults. Furthermore, this record should also include all maintenance activities carried out on equipment;
- Organizations should apply suitable measures during the performance

of maintenance, considering whether the maintenance is performed by an employee or a third-party service provider. Furthermore, the relevant personnel should sign a confidentiality agreement;

- Personnel performing the maintenance work should be supervised at all times;
- Remote maintenance work should be subject to strict access and authorization procedures;
- If equipment is taken out of premises for maintenance work, organizations should apply appropriate security measures;
- Organizations should adhere to all requirements imposed by insurance providers on how to carry out maintenance;
- Organizations should inspect equipment that went through maintenance work to ensure that it is not tampered with and functions properly;
- If the equipment will be disposed of or reused, organizations should establish and implement suitable measures and procedures.

Steps to carry out Maintenance

- **Preparing:** Since the organization may possess information systems and tools purchased from different vendors in a long time period, an efficient record keeping of the systems in hand is essential for maintenance management; hence performing a hardware, software and telecommunications inventory is the first step of an efficient maintenance program. Appropriate maintenance of the records and transaction monitoring result to keeping the information up-to-date, which in turn allows statistical data extraction to be used as input to further consideration about system maintainability, sustainability and related costs. For record keeping, simple techniques like spreadsheets and custom databases may be used; for efficient monitoring of complex systems an integrated asset management tool is required. A data preservation survey must be conducted, indicating volumes, importance and retention period of data, which in turn results to decisions about data retention periods, backups and requirements on availability and security. Finally, simple and consistent processes must be defined for issues reporting and restoring activities.

- **Obtain a good and detailed system documentation:** A well-documented system is very important, especially for software maintenance. Furthermore, an updated documentation, reflecting the changes derived from the maintenance activities, should be provided for future purposes. Good documentation aims in providing structured instead of unstructured maintenance:
    - Unstructured maintenance wades straight into the source code and makes changes based on that alone
    - Structured maintenance examines and modifies the original design, and then reworks the code to match it
    - Clearly structured maintenance is a more reliable and a more efficient process. Unfortunately, it's not possible without detailed design documentation.
- **Prioritizing needs:** Maintenance costs are a significant part of the system's total life cycle costs. Therefore, revision of the business non-functional requirements for each part of the system is essential before signing any new maintenance contract in order to keep organization's costs within affordable barriers.
- **Contracting:** Maintenance contracts may be signed with the equipment providers who supplied the equipment system or third parties who are in possession of the appropriate infrastructure. Increasing the number of contracts and contractors increases complexity and may cause administrative problems; hence it is advisable to review and consolidate maintenance contracts regularly, possibly achieving significant cost reductions as well.
- **Hardware Inventory includes:**
    - Enterprise Level Servers, Disk Storage Equipment;
    - Distributed Servers, Disk Storage and Network Communications Equipment;
    - Local Desktop Devices, Laptops, Cell Phones, PDA's, etc.;
    - UPS, Generators, Emergency Power Systems;
    - Associated Maintenance Agreements;
    - System Documentation.

- **Software Inventory includes:**
    - Verification of the type of license and transferability;
    - Enterprise level commercial-off-the-shelf (COTS) software licenses, installation media and documentation;
    - Custom developed software, configuration management libraries and procedures, binary images, documentation and all project related material;
    - Distributed COTS software licenses, installation media and documentation;
    - Local COTS software licenses, installation media and documentation;
    - Software and Associated Maintenance Agreements;
    - Transfer to New Department or Local Entity;
    - System Documentation;
    - Version Control;
    - Configuration Management.
- **Telecommunications Inventory includes:**
    - Network Equipment, Maintenance Agreements and Circuits;
    - PBX, Switches;
    - Racks and Other Peripherals;
    - Circuits, Service Providers, Maintenance and Monitoring Contracts;
    - Point-to-Point Connections;
    - Impact on internal and external entities if services are terminated.
- **Scheduling:** Maintenance activities scheduling takes place only for preventive maintenance, which is performed during planned outage periods. Preventive maintenance has the following objectives:
    - Keeping equipment and facilities in satisfactory operating condition by providing for systematic inspection, detection, and

correction of incident failures either before they occur or before they develop into major defects.

- Maintenance, including tests, measurements, adjustments, and parts replacement, performed specifically to prevent faults from occurring.

- **Monitoring:** Maintenance Activities must be monitored. Related transaction data serve in the calculation of the penalties (if applicable), tracing of the costs etc., whereas statistical data contribute to decisions about system maintainability, sustainability or upgrade needs.

A.7.14 Secure Disposal or Reuse of Equipment

Organizations must ensure that the process for the disposal or re-use of equipment is strictly controlled. The improper disposal or re-use of any information system, system component, or storage device could potentially impact the confidentiality of data by inadvertently making it available to unauthorized audiences. This could easily result in a reportable security incident or data breach. All media should be disposed of safely and securely when it is no longer needed. This should be performed using formally documented procedures to ensure that any protected or otherwise sensitive data has been completely removed or securely overwritten prior to media disposal. Information systems or other devices that contain sensitive or protected information should be physically destroyed or the information must be destroyed, deleted, or overwritten using techniques to make the original information non-retrievable. These techniques must remove the original data permanently, rather than using the standard delete or disk formatting functions. It is highly recommended that your organization holds all devices or media scheduled for destruction locally until the materials are destroyed or shredded onsite by an approved internal process or external provider. All items of equipment including storage media should be verified to ensure that any sensitive data and licensed software has been removed or securely overwritten prior to disposal or re-use. This is another area of common vulnerability where many incidents have arisen from poor disposal or re-use practices. If equipment is being disposed of that contained sensitive information, it is critical that data bearing devices and components are either physically destroyed or securely wiped using appropriate tools and technologies. If equipment is going to be re-used it is important that any previous data and potentially installed software is securely "wiped" and the device returned to a known "clean" state. Depending on the level of sensitivity of data contained on equipment being destroyed it may be necessary to ensure physical destruction and this should be done using a process that can be fully audited.

A.7.14 Secure Disposal or Reuse of Equipment – A linkage with Ancient Era

Secure Disposal or Reuse of Equipment:

In the Mahabharata, the Kurukshetra War results in massive destruction and loss of life. The aftermath of the war necessitates decisions regarding the disposition of equipment and resources.

- **Post-War Reconstruction:** After the Kurukshetra War, efforts were made to rebuild and reconcile the warring factions. The secure disposal or reuse of equipment symbolize the process of rebuilding and repurposing resources for constructive purposes, emphasizing the importance of reconciliation, forgiveness, and collective healing.
- **Lessons Learned:** The aftermath of the Kurukshetra War serves as a profound lesson in dharma and the consequences of actions. The secure disposal or reuse of equipment symbolizes the process of reflection and learning from past experiences to avoid repeating mistakes, highlighting the themes of personal growth and transformation.

Control

Items of equipment containing storage media should be verified to ensure that any sensitive data and licensed software has been removed or securely overwritten prior to disposal or re-use.

Purpose

To prevent leakage of information from equipment to be disposed or re-used.

Guidelines

Equipment should be verified to ensure whether or not storage media is contained prior to disposal or re-use. Storage media containing confidential or copyrighted information should be physically destroyed or the information should be destroyed, deleted or overwritten using techniques to make the original information non-retrievable rather than using the standard delete function. Labels and markings identifying the organization or indicating the classification, owner, system or network, should be removed prior to disposal, including reselling or donating to charity. The organization should consider the removal of security controls such as access controls or surveillance equipment at the end of lease or when moving out of premises. This depends on factors such as:

- Its lease agreement to return the facility to original condition;
- Minimizing the risk of leaving systems with sensitive information on them for the next tenant;
- The ability to reuse the controls at the next facility.

Other Information

Damaged equipment containing storage media can require a risk assessment to determine whether the items should be physically destroyed rather than sent for repair or discarded. Information can be compromised through careless disposal or re-use of equipment. In addition to secure disk deletion, full-disk encryption reduces the risk of disclosure of confidential information when equipment is disposed of or redeployed, provided that:

- The encryption process is sufficiently strong and covers the entire disk;
- The cryptographic keys are long enough to resist brute force attacks;
- The cryptographic keys are themselves kept confidential.

Techniques for securely overwriting storage media differ according to the storage media technology and the classification level of the information on the storage media. Overwriting tools should be reviewed to make sure that they are applicable to the technology of the storage media.

IT equipment should be maintained properly and disposed of securely. Information stored in equipment being disposed of, redistributed, or sold must be securely removed to prevent the disclosure of the information to unauthorized parties. All equipment containing storage media should be checked to ensure that sensitive data and licensed software have been removed or securely overwritten prior to secure disposal. All equipment has a life cycle, after which it is necessary to get rid of it. Be careful with this point: remember that the organization's information is stored on computers/servers, and it can remain there even if you believe you have removed it. Therefore, to avoid possible leakage of information in computers that are reused or eliminated, you should safely dispose of the information through software, or physically destroy the hard drive that contains the information. If you want to add an additional layer of security, you can encrypt the information before destroying it, in this way, in the hypothetical case that someone could recover the information through some mechanism, they would then have to decrypt it. Organizations should take following into account for compliance:

- **A proactive approach should be adopted**: Before disposal takes place or the equipment is made available for reuse, organizations must confirm whether the equipment contains any information assets and licensed software and should ensure that such information or software is permanently deleted.
- **Physical destruction or irretrievable deletion of information**: The two methods by which the information contained in equipment can be securely and permanently removed:
    - Equipment hosting storage media devices that contain information should be physically destroyed.
    - Information stored on the equipment should be erased, overwritten, or destroyed in a non-retrievable manner so that malicious parties cannot access information.
- **Removal of all labels and markings:** Components of the equipment and the information contained in it can have labels and markings that identify the organization or that disclose the name of the asset owner, network, or information classification level assigned. All these labels and markings should be irretrievably destroyed.
- **Removal of Controls:** Taking into account the following conditions, organizations may choose to uninstall all security controls such as access restrictions or surveillance systems when they vacate facilities:
    - The terms of the lease agreement related to conditions on which it needs to be returned;
    - Eliminating and mitigating the risk of unauthorized access to sensitive information by the next tenant;
    - Whether the existing controls can be reused at the next facility.
- **Damaged Equipment:** When damaged equipment containing information is sent to repair, it may be exposed to the risk of unauthorized access by third parties. Organizations should carry out a risk assessment taking into account the level of sensitivity of the information and consider if destroying the equipment is a more viable option than repair.

- **Full-Disk Encryption:** While the full-disk encryption technique greatly minimizes risks to the confidentiality of information, it should adhere to the following standards:
    - Encryption is robust and it covers all parts of the disk, including slack space;
    - Cryptographic keys should be long enough to prevent brute force attacks;
    - Organizations should maintain the confidentiality of cryptographic keys. The encryption key should not be stored on the same disk.
- **Overwriting Tools:** Organizations should choose an overwriting technique taking into account the following criteria:
    - Level of information classification assigned to the information asset;
    - Type of storage media on which the information is stored.

An important input for media disposal is information classification. A lot of companies classify their information, because not all media have the same information, and not all of the information has the same value for the business. For example, there is a big difference between a USB pen drive containing a PDF file with a presentation of the business (which can be considered public information), and a USB pen drive containing the organization's database of clients (which can be considered confidential). If the information is public, organization can share it in the public domain, because there is not a risk of confidential information leakage. But, if the information is not public (confidential, restricted, internal), organization need to store and dispose of it in a secure way, because it can carry a risk of confidential information leakage, which can destroy the business, as well as showing noncompliance with legal regulations.

Besides handling confidential information securely, there are other reasons for secure asset and media disposal. They may appear to be simple activities, since organization generally only dispose of things that they deem no longer needed or not valuable. However, thinking about environmental recycling activities, organization can see that what is worthless to someone can be highly valuable to someone else. The same applies to information. Some piece of information organization consider not valuable can lead a competitor to gain a business advantage, a criminal to explore an organization's weaknesses or, worse, cause damage to a customer or person's life by using personal or private information to commit a crime posing as those persons. No less important, in some cases clients and potential business partners ask for a hard drive destruction certificate. Equipment containing storage media shall be verified to ensure it is free of sensitive information prior to disposal or re-use. As other forms of control, secure disposal should be supported by an organizational policy.

1. **Disposal procedures should be proportional to the information classification level:** The higher the classification, the greater assurance that information cannot be retrieved after disposal. Shredding or incineration of the media, or data overwritten, are examples of good practices.
2. **Clear identification of information that will require secure disposal:** By the use of watermark, or colored border, it is easier for someone to identify the information that should be securely disposed.
3. **Dispose media mixing different types**: The greater the mix of different items the harder is to recover a specific media, and more secure.
4. **Control access to accumulated media for disposal:** A large quantity of non-sensitive information together can make it possible to retrieve sensitive information. Think about defining a short accumulation period or small storage volume to execute the disposal procedures.
5. **Keep traceability of sensitive disposed items:** To ensure the items were properly disposed, you should keep log information listing, at a minimum, who performed the procedure, when, and what method was used.
6. **Equipment verification prior to disposal or re-use:** You should verify whether or not storage media is contained within the equipment. The organization could use a disposal checklist to ensure critical elements are verified.
7. **Use of non-retrievable methods:** Physical destruction or overwriting techniques, with specific or generic patterns, should be used to perform disposal of highly sensitive information.
8. **Evaluation of damaged equipment:** Sometimes damaged devices need to be sent to external parties to be repaired. In these situations, the

device should be assessed for sensitive data to determine whether the items should be physically destroyed rather than sent for repair or discarded. ISO 31010 presents a good list of risk assessment techniques which can be used.

Sometimes the volume of items, or the technical requirements for disposal, makes the use of specialized organizations a good option, but care should be taken in selecting a suitable organization. Criteria you should consider are how it manages its security, disposal methods used and experience with your industry. Be sure to include all this in the service contracts. There are many reputable service providers available to perform shredding and destruction services on-site at your organization's location. While there is a cost associated with these services, this service is their core competency. You may find that their secure handling, on-site destruction, and delivery of Certificates of Destruction to the organization is worth the investment after a quick cost-benefit analysis.

5 tips for Media Disposal

1. **Physically destroy the media**: You can do this, for example, by incineration or shredding, etc. This physical destruction is also applicable to damaged devices. But, be careful, because a damaged media device can also have sensitive information that could be restored, so to avoid this, you should destroy it physically.
2. **Securely delete the information**: There are software tools that you can use to overwrite the information, or to delete it in a secure way.
3. **Select an external party**: There are a lot of companies providing the service of destruction of your media, but here you need to take care with the selection of the provider by defining a non-disclosure agreement.
4. **Avoid the aggregation effect**: It is better if you avoid having a lot of media containing non-sensitive information, because something within the group could become sensitive information.
5. **Register the disposal**: Registering the disposal provides you with useful information for audit trails.

Tips for Hard Drive Disposal

1. Encrypt the entire hard disk, using a strong algorithm and using a lengthy password;
2. Delete all the information in a secure way, using software solutions;
3. Physically destroy the media device;
4. In reality, this method would only be applicable to the most critical and sensitive data, and for data with less criticality, only one of these methods will be enough.

Technological Controls

A.8.1 User Endpoint Device

As per definition in ISO 27002, user endpoint device is a endpoint device used by users to access information processing services. According to ISO 27001, endpoint device is a network connected information and communication technology (ICT) hardware device. Endpoint device can refer to desktop computers, laptops, smart phones, tablets, thin clients, printers or other specialized hardware including smart meters and Internet of things (IoT) devices.

An endpoint device is a LAN- or WAN-connected hardware device that communicates across a network. Broadly speaking, the term can refer to any network connected device: desktop computers, laptops, smartphones, tablets, printers, or other specialized hardware like POS terminals or retail kiosks, that act as a user endpoint in a distributed network. One of the biggest issues with endpoint devices involves comprehensive security for a network or enterprise system. Security managers must determine whether various endpoint devices could be security gaps for a network, that is, whether unauthorized users can access an endpoint device and use it to pull off important sensitive data.

The most common examples are laptops, mobile phones, and desktop computers. However, the list keeps growing and now includes many non-traditional gadgets that protect your network resources and limit access such as, but not limited to Laptops, Mobile phones, Desktop computers, Printers, Appliances, Cameras, Health trackers, Smartwatches, Navigation systems, Point of sale systems, Servers.

If a device can connect to the internet, it can be a fully functional part of organizational endpoint protection. Intruders lurk behind every corner, hoping to catch the organization off-guard and steal data. Data loss isn't the only consequence of endpoint breaches. Intruders can also overwhelm servers with unwanted web traffic to prevent other users from regaining access. The only way to capitalize on endpoint devices is to limit access. This means organization should only allow administrators to adjust security controls and not all employees. Endpoint devices can help organization set up a bulletproof network. They detect suspicious traffic according to specific criteria. Once they alert about unusual behavior, IT/ Security Operations Center team can react on time and keep organization unharmed.

A.8.1 User Endpoint Device – A linkage with Ancient Era

Guards Guarding Lanka:

- **User Endpoint Devices as Guards:** In the context of a network or digital ecosystem, user endpoint devices can be metaphorically linked to the guards stationed around Lanka. Just as the guards protect the kingdom from external threats and intruders, user endpoint devices serve as the frontline defense against cyber threats and unauthorized access to the network.
- **Security Measures as Guarding Tactics:** Various security measures implemented in user endpoint devices, such as firewalls, antivirus software, encryption protocols, and multi-factor authentication, can be compared to the tactics employed by the guards to protect Lanka. These security measures act as barriers and deterrents, preventing malicious actors from infiltrating the network and compromising sensitive information.
- **Vigilance and Surveillance:** Similar to how guards maintain vigilance and surveillance to detect potential threats to Lanka, user endpoint devices constantly monitor network traffic and system activities to identify suspicious behavior or anomalies. Intrusion Detection Systems and Security Monitoring tools serve as the "eyes and ears" of the digital guardians, alerting users to potential security breaches.
- **Response to Threats:** When faced with threats or breaches, guards in Lanka must respond swiftly and decisively to neutralize the danger

and protect the kingdom. Similarly, user endpoint devices equipped with incident response mechanisms and security protocols must take immediate action to contain and mitigate cyber threats, minimizing the impact on the network and its users.

- **Collaboration and Coordination:** Just as guards stationed around Lanka collaborate and coordinate their efforts to ensure comprehensive security coverage, user endpoint devices work in tandem with network security infrastructure to establish a unified defense against cyber threats. This collaborative approach enhances the effectiveness of security measures and strengthens the overall resilience of the network.

Control

Information stored on, processed by or accessible via user endpoint devices should be protected.

Purpose

To protect information against the risks introduced by using user endpoint devices.

Guidance

General

The organization should establish a topic-specific policy on secure configuration and handling of user endpoint devices. The topic-specific policy should be communicated to all relevant personnel and consider the following:

- The type of information and the classification level that the user endpoint devices can handle, process, store or support;
- Registration of user endpoint devices;
- Requirements for physical protection;
- Restriction of software installation;
- Requirements for user endpoint device software and for applying updates;
- Rules for connection to information services, public networks or any other network off premises;

- Access Controls;
- Storage Device Encryption;
- Protection Against Malware;
- Remote Disabling, Deletion or Lockout;
- Backups;
- Usage of Web Services and Web Applications;
- End User Behavior Analytics
- The use of removable devices, including removable memory devices, and the possibility of disabling physical ports;
- The use of partitioning capabilities, if supported by the user endpoint device, which can securely separate the organization's information and other associated assets from other information and other associated assets on the device.

Consideration should be given as to whether certain information is so sensitive that it can only be accessed via user endpoint devices, but not stored on such devices. In such cases, additional technical safeguards can be required on the device. As far as possible, the recommendations on this control should be enforced through configuration management or automated tools.

User Responsibility

All users should be made aware of the security requirements and procedures for protecting user endpoint devices, as well as of their responsibilities for implementing such security measures. Users should be advised to:

- Log-off active sessions and terminate services when no longer needed;
- Protect user endpoint devices from unauthorized use with a physical control and logical control when not in use; not leave devices carrying important, sensitive or critical business information unattended;
- Use devices with special care in public places, open offices, meeting places and other unprotected areas;
- Physically protect user endpoint devices against theft.

A specific procedure taking into account legal, statutory, regulatory, contractual and other security requirements of the organization should be established for cases of theft or loss of user endpoint devices.

Use of Personal Devices

Where the organization allows the use of personal devices (BYOD), in addition to the guidance given in this control, the following should be considered:

- Separation of personal and business use of the devices, including using software to support such separation and protect business data on a private device;
- Providing access to business information only after users have acknowledged their duties, waiving ownership of business data, allowing remote wiping of data by the organization in case of theft or loss of the device or when no longer authorized to use the service. In such cases, PII protection legislation should be considered;
- Topic-specific policies and procedures to prevent disputes concerning rights to intellectual property developed on privately owned equipment;
- Access to privately owned equipment, which can be prevented by legislation;
- Software licensing agreements that are such that organizations can become liable for licensing for client software on user endpoint devices owned privately by personnel or external party users.

Wireless Connections

The organization should establish procedures for:

- The configuration of wireless connections on devices;
- Using wireless or wired connections with appropriate bandwidth in accordance with relevant topic-specific policies.

Other Information

Controls to protect information on user endpoint devices depend on whether the user endpoint device is used only inside of the organization's secured premises and network connections, or whether it is exposed to increased physical and network related threats outside of the organization.

The wireless connections for user endpoint devices are similar to other types of network connections but have important differences that should be considered when identifying controls. In particular, back-up of information stored on user endpoint devices can sometimes fail because of limited network bandwidth or because user endpoint devices are not connected at the times when backups are scheduled. For some USB ports, such as USB-C, disabling the USB port is not possible because it is used for other purposes (e.g., power delivery and display output).

Endpoint devices are an integral part of endpoint security. Endpoint security refers to protecting mobile device, desktop computer, or other endpoints from cyber security attacks. Endpoints often provide perfect gateways to the organizational network, which can be exploited by intruders. Endpoint security minimizes this risk by shielding the points from criminals. It examines the network or enterprise system, processes, and files, for malicious and suspicious activity. If it notices anything fishy, it can alert security managers so they can react on time and protect data. One of the most impressive features of endpoint security is that it can be installed on numerous devices. Whether the employee use smart phones, tablets, laptops, or servers, this strategy helps keep malicious users from infiltrating organizational network with malware. It can also be deployed alongside other monitoring and detection tactics to mark suspicious actions and prevent data breaches. There are three ways of organizing endpoint protection:

- **On-Location:** The on-premise or on-location approach typically involves data on host computers that function as hubs for management consoles. These devices communicate with the endpoints via different channels to help patch up security gaps. This strategy can work great, but it has a few drawbacks. Primarily, it's a legacy system. It's not as advanced as modern solutions since network owners can only manage it within a limited perimeter.
- **Cloud:** If you want to ensure comprehensive security, consider setting up cloud-based endpoint devices. They allow you to manage and monitor nearly all network types in the cloud. Under this arrangement, endpoints are connected to the network remotely. Cloud-based solutions are superior to on-location endpoint security due to their

greater scope. You can look past traditional perimeters and enhance your administrator reach.

- **Hybrid:** Another way to safeguard your data assets through endpoints is to set up a hybrid network. It combines cloud and on-location technologies. The strategy has become more prevalent in recent years due to an uptick in remote workers. Organizations have streamlined their legacy systems and integrated with cloud-based endpoints to keep sensitive data intact.

Optimized endpoint security has emerged as a result of such combinations and contains the following software to combat unauthorized access:

- Machine learning that detects threats;
- Firewall to safeguard against hostiles;
- Email gateways to reduce the risk of phishing;
- Insider protection to neutralize threats from within your network;
- Advanced anti-malware and antivirus to remove malware on your operating systems and endpoint devices;
- Proactive security for safe internet browsing;
- Disk encryption to shield organization data.

Establishing a User Endpoint Device:

The organization must be able to demonstrate policy and supporting security controls to reduce the risk posed by user end point devices. As a result of this, it is the organization's responsibility to issue a user end point devices policy that should cover the registration/de-registration of devices, physical security requirements, technical security requirements including remote connections, software control, access control and encryption at rest/in transit. The user end point devices. policy should state the businesses requirements for use of devices and when they are appropriate. It is in this policy that the organization should specify its expectations for topics such as Bring Your Own Device (BYOD). BYOD is a hot topic for information security, with many practitioners agreeing that the risks posed by unmanaged, personally owned devices are too high. ISO 27001 requires that the organization determines this, issues a policy stating their intentions and monitors compliance with this policy through an audit or technical controls. For example, a user end point device policy may state that "only corporately issued and managed devices can be used to process organization data" and that "unauthorized devices must not be used to access store or process organization data". If this is the policy, the organization must monitor for the use of unauthorized devices and specify what the consequences of not adhering to the policy may be e.g., disciplinary procedures. As well as BYOD, the policy should address technical subjects such as access control, secure configuration and remote access methods. For example, the organization may require its employees to utilize secure authentication methods such as two-factor authentication and only connect over encrypted channels such as VPN's. If these methods of connection are specified, as above, compliance with the policy should be enforced technically, monitored for compliance and reported on. In most cases, if the technical capability is not there to support the policy users will not adhere with it so making device builds include VPN clients and reminding users of the need for secure authentication goes a long way. Other considerations should include physical security of devices in public areas, shoulder surfing and other physical security issues.

Employees should be aware of the need to protect their device from unauthorized access at all times, especially when in public places such as on trains and coffee shops. The policy should include a section addressing these requirements. Once the policy has been issued, signed-off by management and communicated to all employees, the organization should continue to monitor compliance through auditing and technical controls. For example, Mobile device management (MDM) tools may be used to enforce policy and monitor for policy violations. Furthermore, logs may be reviewed periodically to identify unauthorized access attempts.

A policy-based approach to network security is paramount when safeguarding a network. The policy should require endpoint devices to meet specific criteria before being granted access to network resources. Security architecture is designed to handle endpoint devices in order to safeguard the data assets accessed through these systems. Companies that allow employees to bring their own device, as in laptops or smartphones, frequently face endpoint device security issues. Without a well-considered bring your own device (BYOD) policy, employee-owned devices may compromise the security of organization information, or of the network.

Organizations believe that close to 45% of corporate data is held on endpoint devices. These laptops, tablets and smartphones pose a huge risk to data security. The industrywide growth of endpoint device exposure means that it's easier than ever for data to be put at risk. Each time an employee connects over public Wi-Fi, downloads a suspicious app, or is targeted by a phishing scam, the risk is amplified. This is especially important because endpoint devices not only expose their data to possible seizure, they also serve as a potential conduit for a network wide breach of security.

Security policies, especially as they relate to BYOD protections, are an essential part of protecting endpoint devices from being exposed to attack. But the largest contributor to vulnerability is the quality of training and awareness given to employees. Bad habits can have a serious effect on the integrity of a secure network:

- **Lost or improperly decommissioned devices**: Employees who lose devices that are connected to the organization network may expose that network to attacks.
- **Poor adoption of security updates**: Out-of-date operating systems and applications can lead to any number of vulnerabilities within a device that has been given access to sensitive organization information.
- **Employees switching encryption off/on**: Employees are more likely to adjust the security controls on devices they own, and will rework settings to suit their needs. This can lead to unwanted access points.

With a proactive, always on' technology, IT can avoid these types of issues, while maintaining compliance and mitigating risk.

Traditionally, endpoint security systems are built on the framework of a client-server model. The security program is managed by a central server that controls the client program installed on all network drives. More recently, with the increasing adoption of software as a service platform (SaaS), the program and host server are both managed remotely by the SaaS provider. This business model gives organizations a chance to lower costs while ensuring constant updates to security parameters.

A.8.2 Privileged Access Rights

Privileged access allows organizations to secure their infrastructure and applications, run business efficiently and maintain the confidentiality of sensitive data and critical infrastructure. Privilege can be defined as the authority a given account or process has within a computing system or network. Privilege provides the authorization to override, or bypass, certain security restraints, and may include permissions to perform such actions as shutting down systems, loading device drivers, configuring networks or systems, provisioning and configuring accounts and cloud instances, etc. Privileges serve an important operational purpose by enabling users, applications, and other system processes elevated rights to access certain resources and complete work-related tasks.

Privileged access can be associated with human users as well as non-human users such as applications and machine identities. Privileges for various user accounts and processes are built into operating systems, file systems, applications, databases, hypervisors, cloud management platforms, etc. Privileges can be also assigned by certain types of privileged users, such as by a system or network administrator. Depending on the system, some privilege assignment, or delegation, to people may be based on attributes that are role-based, such as business unit, as well as a variety of other parameters. Malicious or incorrect use of elevated system administrator privileges is one of the major causes of ICT disruption across commercial networks all over the world. Privileged access rights allow organizations to control access to their infrastructure, applications, assets and maintain the integrity of all stored data and systems. Special access to data and systems requires strict controls on who gets it and how it's used because of the additional power it gives the person who has it. System by system clarity on privileged access permissions could fall under this category, as well as allocation based on actual usage rather than a blanket policy. All privileges issued to users should be documented, and the competency of those users granted the permissions must be constantly evaluated to ensure that they are able to perform their assigned responsibilities. It's also a good idea to keep separate identities for system administrators and regular users, especially if they're doing various jobs on the same platform.

A.8.2 Privileged Access Rights – A linkage with Ancient Era

The Ayodhya Kingdom

- **King Dashrath as the Administrator with Privileged Access:** In the Ayodhya kingdom, King Dashrath holds privileged access to resources, authority, and decision-making powers. As the ruler, He governs the kingdom and manages its affairs, similar to how administrators with privileged access rights oversee and control critical assets, systems, and data within a digital environment.
- **Royal Court and Councilors as Authorized Users:** Just as the Royal Court and Councilors in Ayodhya are granted access to the king's presence and participate in decision-making processes, authorized users in a digital environment may include trusted personnel, such as system administrators or IT managers, who are granted privileged access rights to perform specific tasks and responsibilities within the network.
- **Access Control and Hierarchy:** In the Ayodhya kingdom, access to certain areas or resources may be restricted based on hierarchical roles and responsibilities. Similarly, in a digital environment, access control mechanisms and privilege escalation policies regulate the allocation of privileged access rights, ensuring that only authorized individuals with a legitimate need can access sensitive information and critical systems.
- **Responsibility and Accountability:** King Dashrath, like administrators with privileged access rights, bears the responsibility of ensuring the well-being, security, and prosperity of the Ayodhya kingdom. He is held accountable for his actions and decisions, subject to oversight by his subjects and advisors. Similarly, administrators with privileged access rights are accountable for their activities within the digital domain, subject to monitoring, auditing, and oversight by security teams, compliance officers, or regulatory bodies to ensure compliance with policies and regulations.
- **Risk of Betrayal and Intrigue:** While privileged access rights are essential for efficient governance and administration, they also pose a risk of betrayal or misuse if wielded irresponsibly or maliciously. Just as power struggles, intrigue, and betrayals may threaten the stability of the Ayodhya kingdom, unauthorized or inappropriate use of privileged access rights can undermine the security and integrity

of digital assets, leading to data breaches, insider threats, or system compromises.

- **Guardianship and Protection:** Ultimately, both King Dashrath and administrators with privileged access rights serve as guardians and protectors of their domains, entrusted with the duty of preserving order, defending against external threats, and ensuring the welfare and prosperity of their subjects or stakeholders.

Control

The allocation and use of privileged access rights should be restricted and managed.

Purpose

To ensure only authorized users, software components and services are provided with privileged access rights.

Guidance

The allocation of privileged access rights should be controlled through an authorization process in accordance with the relevant topic-specific policy on access control. The following should be considered:

- Identifying users who need privileged access rights for each system or process;
- Allocating privileged access rights to users as needed and, on an event,-by-event basis in line with the topic-specific policy on access control;
- Maintaining an authorization process and a record of all privileges allocated;
- Defining and implementing requirements for expiry of privileged access rights;
- Taking measures to ensure that users are aware of their privileged access rights and when they are in privileged access mode. Possible measures include using specific user identities, user interface settings or even specific equipment;
- Authentication requirements for privileged access rights can be higher than the requirements for normal access rights. Re-authentication

or authentication step-up can be necessary before doing work with privileged access rights;

- Regularly, and after any organizational change, reviewing users working with privileged access rights in order to verify if their duties, roles, responsibilities and competence still qualify them for working with privileged access rights;
- Establishing specific rules in order to avoid the use of generic administration user IDs (root), depending on systems' configuration capabilities. Managing and protecting authentication information of such identities;
- Granting temporary privileged access just for the time window necessary to implement approved changes or activities, rather than permanently granting privileged access rights. This is often referred as break glass procedure, and often automated by privilege access management technologies;
- Logging all privileged access to systems for audit purposes;
- Not sharing or linking identities with privileged access rights to multiple persons, assigning each person a separate identity which allows assigning specific privileged access rights. Identities can be grouped in order to simplify the management of privileged access rights;
- Only using identities with privileged access rights for undertaking administrative tasks and not for day-to-day general tasks.

Other Information

Privileged access rights are access rights provided to an identity, a role or a process that allows the performance of activities that typical users or processes cannot perform. System administrator roles typically require privileged access rights. Inappropriate use of system administrator privileges is a major contributory factor to failures or breaches of systems. More information related to access management and the secure management of access to information and information and communications technologies resources can be found in ISO 29146.

The allocation and use of privileged access rights has to be tightly controlled given the extra rights usually conveyed over information assets and the systems controlling them. For example, the ability to delete work or fundamentally affect the integrity of the information. It should align with the formal authorization processes alongside the access control policy. That could include: system by system clarity on privileged access rights; allocation on a need-to-use basis not a blanket approach; a process and record of all privileges allocated should be maintained and the competence of employee granted the rights must be reviewed regularly to align with their duties. This is another good area to include in the internal audit to demonstrate control. One of the biggest contributory factors to failures or breaches of systems is inappropriate and blanket use of system administration privileges with human error leading to more damage or loss than if a 'least access' approach was taken. Other good practice relating to this area includes the separation of the systems administrator role from the day-to-day user role and having a user with two accounts if they perform different jobs on the same platform.

Management of privileged access right involves a combination of tools and technology used to secure, control and monitor access to an organization's critical information and resources. It is one of the best ways for an organization to protect against external threats by preventing malicious parties from accessing sensitive corporate data through internal accounts. It helps organizations effectively monitor the entire network and provides insight into which users have access to what data? This is critical because privileged accounts can pose major security risks to businesses. For example, a cybercriminal who compromises a standard user account will only have access to that specific user's information. But a hacker who compromises a privileged user account will have far greater access and possibly the power to destroy systems. In addition to combating external attacks, it can help companies combat threats, either malicious or inadvertent, originating from employees and other internal people with access to corporate data. It is also key to achieve compliance with industry and government regulations. As a part of a complete security program, enterprises can record and log every activity related to their critical information technology (IT) infrastructures and sensitive corporate data, helping to simplify audit and compliance requirements.

Some of the top privilege-related risks and challenges include:

1. **Lack of visibility and awareness of privileged users, accounts, assets,**

and credentials: Long-forgotten privileged accounts are commonly sprawled across organizations. These may number in the millions, and provide dangerous backdoors for attackers, including, former employees who have left the organization but retain access.

2. **Over-provisioning of privileges**: If privileged access controls are overly restrictive, they can disrupt user workflows, causing frustration and hindering productivity. Since end users rarely complain about possessing too many privileges, IT admins traditionally provision end users with broad sets of privileges. Additionally, an employee's role is often fluid and can evolve such that they accumulate new responsibilities and corresponding privileges, while still retaining privileges that they no longer use or require. All this privilege excess adds up to a bloated attack surface. Routine computing for employees on personal PC users might entail internet browsing, watching streaming video, use of MS Office and other basic applications, including SaaS. In the case of Windows PCs, users often log in with administrative account privileges and these excessive privileges massively increase the risk that malware or hackers may steal passwords or install malicious code that could be delivered via web surfing or email attachments. The malware or hacker could then leverage the entire set of privileges of the account, accessing data of the infected computer, and even launching an attack against other networked computers or servers.
3. **Shared accounts and passwords**: IT teams commonly share root, Windows Administrator, and many other privileged credentials for convenience so workloads and duties can be seamlessly shared as needed. However, with multiple people sharing an account password, it may be impossible to tie actions performed with an account to a single individual. This creates security, audit, and compliance issues.
4. **Hard-coded/Embedded Credentials**: Privileged credentials are needed to facilitate authentication for app-to-app (A2A) and application-to-database (A2D) communications and access. Applications, systems, network devices, and IoT devices may be shipped and deployed with embedded, default credentials that are easily guessable and pose substantial risk. Additionally, employees will often hardcode secrets in plain text, such as within a script, code, or a file, so it is easily accessible when they need it.

5. **Manual and/or decentralized credential management**: Privilege security controls are often immature. Privileged accounts and credentials may be managed differently across various organizational silos, leading to inconsistent enforcement of best practices. Human privilege management processes cannot possibly scale in most IT environments where thousands or even millions of privileged accounts, credentials, and assets can exist. With so many systems and accounts to manage, humans invariably take shortcuts, such as re-using credentials across multiple accounts and assets. One compromised account can therefore jeopardize the security of other accounts sharing the same credentials.
6. **Lack of visibility into application and service account privileges:** Applications and service accounts often automatically execute privileged processes to perform actions, as well as to communicate with other applications, services, resources, etc. Applications and service accounts frequently possess excessive privileged access rights by default, and also suffer from other serious security deficiencies.
7. **Multiple identity management tools and processes**: Modern IT environments typically run across multiple platforms (Windows, Mac, Unix, Linux) and environments (On-premises, Azure, AWS, Google Cloud), each separately maintained and managed. This practice equates to inconsistent administration for IT, added complexity for end users, and increased cyber risk.

Privileged Access Right Best Practices

1. **Establish and enforce a comprehensive privilege management policy**: The policy should govern how privileged access and accounts are provisioned/de-provisioned; address the inventory and classification of privileged identities and accounts; and enforce best practices for security and management.
2. **Identify and bring under management all privileged accounts and credentials**: Privileged account discovery should include all user and local accounts; application and service accounts database accounts; cloud and social media accounts; SSH keys; default and hard-coded passwords; and other privileged credentials – including those used by third parties/vendors. Discovery should also include platforms,

directories, hardware devices, applications, services/daemons, firewalls, routers, etc. The privilege discovery process should illuminate where and how privileged passwords are being used, and help reveal security blind spots and malpractice.

3. **Enforce least privilege over end users, endpoints, accounts, applications, services, systems, etc.:** A key piece of a successful least privilege implementation involves wholesale elimination of privileges everywhere they exist across your environment. Then, apply rules-based technology to elevate privileges as needed to perform specific actions, revoking privileges upon completion of the privileged activity. Ensuring true least privilege is not just about enforcing constraints on the breadth of access, but also on the duration of access. In IT security terms, this means implementing controls that provide just enough access (JEA) and just-in-time (JIT) access.

A.8.3 Information Access Restriction

Access to information and application system functions shall be restricted in accordance with the access control policy. There should be a complete description of the restriction applied to certain authorities under control access policies. Control on access should be applied complying to the stated access control policy and based on business application requirements. The organization can be controlling access to application system functionalities through menus and by limiting the data that a specific user has access to.

User access privileges, such as read, write, delete, and execute control needs to be applied and also controlling other applications' access rights. It must reduce the amount of data in outputs and there must be physical or logical access control to isolate sensitive applications, application data, and systems from the rest of the network.

A.8.3 Information Access Restriction – A linkage with Ancient Era

The Ayodhya Kingdom

- **Kingdom's Governance as Information Access Control**: In the Ayodhya Kingdom, King Dashrath and his advisors controlled the flow of information within the realm. They determined what information was disseminated to the citizens and what was kept confidential. Similarly, information access restriction in modern contexts involves controlling access to sensitive data and resources within an organization, ensuring that only authorized individuals can access certain information.
- **Royal Court and Trusted Advisors as Authorized Users:** Just as the Royal Court and Trusted Advisors in Ayodhya were granted access to privileged information, authorized users in an organization are granted access to specific data based on their roles and responsibilities. These individuals may include senior executives, department heads, or other trusted personnel who require access to sensitive information to perform their duties effectively.
- **Access Control Measures and Security Protocols:** In Ayodhya, access to certain chambers or information was restricted through physical security measures, such as guards or locked doors. Similarly, modern

organizations implement access control measures and security protocols, such as user authentication, encryption, and role-based access control (RBAC), to restrict access to sensitive data and prevent unauthorized users from accessing it.

- **Need-to-Know Basis and Principle of Least Privilege:** In both contexts, the principle of least privilege applies, wherein individuals are granted access only to the information necessary for their job functions. This minimizes the risk of data breaches or leaks and ensures that sensitive information is accessed only by those who require it to perform their duties.
- **Security Clearance and Confidentiality Oaths:** Just as individuals in Ayodhya may have been required to swear oaths of confidentiality or loyalty to access certain information, employees in modern organizations may be required to undergo security clearance processes or sign confidentiality agreements to access sensitive data.
- **Protection of State Secrets and Strategic Information:** In Ayodhya, certain information may have been classified as state secrets or strategic intelligence, requiring heightened levels of protection. Similarly, organizations classify sensitive data based on its importance and implement additional security measures to protect it from unauthorized access, disclosure, or tampering.

Control

Access to information and other associated assets should be restricted in accordance with the established topic-specific policy on access control.

Purpose

To ensure only authorized access and to prevent unauthorized access to information and other associated assets.

Guidance

In order to maintain effective control over information and ICT assets, and in support of access restriction measures, organizations should ensure the following in line with a topic-specific approach to information access:

- Not allowing access to sensitive information by unknown user identities or anonymously. Public or anonymous access should only be granted to storage locations that do not contain any sensitive information;

- Providing configuration mechanisms to control access to information in systems, applications and services;
- Controlling which data can be accessed by a particular user;
- Controlling which identities or group of identities have which access, such as read, write, delete and execute;
- Providing physical or logical access controls for the isolation of sensitive applications, application data, or systems.

Further, dynamic access management techniques and processes to protect sensitive information that has high value to the organization should be considered when the organization:

- Needs granular control over who can access such information during what period and in what way;
- Wants to share such information with people outside the organization and maintain control over who can access it;
- Wants to dynamically manage, in real-time, the use and distribution of such information;
- Wants to protect such information against unauthorized changes, copying and distribution (including printing);
- Wants to monitor the use of the information;
- Wants to record any changes to such information that take place in case a future investigation is required.

Dynamic access management techniques should protect information throughout its life cycle (i.e., creation, processing, storage, transmission and disposal), including:

- Establishing rules on the management of dynamic access based on specific use cases considering:
    - Granting access permissions based on identity, device, location or application;
    - Leveraging the classification scheme in order to determine

what information needs to be protected with dynamic access management techniques;

- Establishing operational, monitoring and reporting processes and supporting technical infrastructure.

Dynamic access management systems should protect information by:

- Requiring authentication, appropriate credentials or a certificate to access information;
- Restricting access, for example, to a specified time frame;
- Using encryption to protect information;
- Defining the printing permissions for the information;
- Recording who accesses the information and how the information is used;
- Raising alerts if attempts to misuse the information are detected.

Other Information

Dynamic access management techniques and other dynamic information protection technologies can support the protection of information even when data is shared beyond the originating organization, where traditional access controls cannot be enforced. It can be applied to documents, emails or other files containing information to limit who can access the content and in what way. It can be at a granular level and be adapted over the life cycle of the information. Dynamic access management techniques do not replace classical access management, but can add more factors for conditionality, real-time evaluation, just-in-time data reduction and other enhancements that can be useful for the most sensitive information. It offers a way to control access outside the organization's environment. Incident response can be supported by dynamic access management techniques as permissions can be modified or revoked at any time. Additional information on a framework for access management is provided in ISO 29146.

Dynamic Access Control enables administrators to apply access-control permissions and restrictions based on well-defined rules that can include the sensitivity of the resources, the job or role of the user, and the configuration of the device that is used to access these resources.

For example, a user might have different permissions when they access a resource from their office computer versus when they are using a portable computer over a virtual private network. Or access may be allowed only if a device meets the security requirements that are defined by the network administrators. When Dynamic Access Control is used, a user's permissions change dynamically without additional administrator intervention if the user's job or role changes.

Dynamic access management has numerous residual benefits for organizational processes that feature the need to share or use internal data with external users, including faster incident resolution times. Dynamic access management techniques protect a broad range of information types, from standard documents to emails and database information, and have the ability to be applied on a granular file-by-file basis, enabling tight control of data on an organizational level. Organizations should consider such an approach when:

- Requiring granular control over what human and non-human users are able to access such information at any given time;
- The need arises to share information with external parties;
- Considering a "real-time" approach to data management and distribution that involves monitoring and managing data use as it occurs;
- Safeguarding information against unauthorized amendments, sharing or output;
- Monitoring the access to and changing of information, particularly when the information in question is of a sensitive nature.

Dynamic access management is of particular use for organizations that need to monitor and protect data from creation through to deletion, including:

- Outlining a use case or series of use cases that apply data access rules based on the following variables: Identity, Device, Location, Application;
- Outlining a process that covers off the operation and monitoring of data, and establishing a thorough reporting process which is in turn informed by a sound technical infrastructure.

All efforts to formulate a dynamic access management approach should result in data being protected as mentioned in the Guidance section.

Features and concepts associated with Dynamic Access Management include:

- **Central Access Rules:** A central access rule is an expression of authorization rules that can include one or more conditions involving user groups, user claims, device claims, and resource properties. Multiple central access rules can be combined into a central access policy. If one or more central access rules have been defined, administrators can match specific rules to specific resources and business requirements.
- **Central Access Policies:** Central access policies are authorization policies that include conditional expressions. For example, let's say an organization has a business requirement to restrict access to PII in files to only the file owner and members of the HR department who are allowed to view PII information. This represents an organization-wide policy that applies to PII files wherever they are located on file servers across the organization. To implement this policy, an organization needs to be able to:
    - Identify and mark the files that contain the PII;
    - Identify the group of HR members who are allowed to view the PII information;
    - Add the central access policy to a central access rule, and apply the central access rule to all files that contain the PII, wherever they are located amongst the file servers across the organization.

  Central access policies act as security umbrella that an organization applies across its servers. These policies are in addition to (but do not replace) the local access policies or Discretionary Access Control Lists (DACLs) that are applied to files and folders.
- **Claims:** A claim is a unique piece of information about a user, device, or resource that has been published by a domain controller. The user's title, the department classification of a file, or the health state of a computer are valid examples of a claim. An entity can involve more than one claim, and any combination of claims can be used to authorize

access to resources. Claims make it possible for administrators to make precise organization- or enterprise-wide statements about users, devices, and resources that can be incorporated in expressions, rules, and policies.

- **Expressions:** Conditional expressions are an enhancement to access control management that allow or deny access to resources only when certain conditions are met. Expressions help administrators manage access to sensitive resources with flexible conditions in increasingly complex business environments.
- **Proposed Permissions:** Proposed permissions enable an administrator to more accurately model the impact of potential changes to access control settings without actually changing them. Predicting the effective access to a resource helps you plan and configure permissions for those resources before implementing those changes.

A.8.4 Access to Source Code

Restrictions must be placed on access to the program's source code. Access to program source code and associated items (such as designs, specifications, verification plans and validation plans) should be strictly controlled. There should be strong controls on who has access to program source code and related associated items. If a program's source code is not appropriately safeguarded, an attacker has a strong opportunity to gain access to the system in a covert manner. This is especially true if the source code is critical to the organization's success. Program source code can be vulnerable to attack if not adequately protected and can provide an attacker with a good means to compromise systems in an often-covert manner. If the source code is central to the business success it's loss can also destroy the business value quickly too.

A.8.4 Access to Source Code – A linkage with Ancient Era

Kurukshetra War

- **Source Code as the Blueprints of Technology:** In modern software development, source code serves as the blueprint or foundation upon which software applications are built. Similarly, the secrets of the Kurukshetra War, including military strategies, tactics, and divine weapons, can be linked to the blueprints of warfare, providing insights into the techniques and methodologies employed by ancient warriors.
- **Access to Source Code as Insider Knowledge:** Access to source code grants individual's insider knowledge about the inner workings of a software application, enabling them to understand its functionality, identify vulnerabilities, and potentially exploit or enhance its capabilities. Similarly, access to the secrets of the Kurukshetra War would provide individuals with insider knowledge about military strategies, battlefield tactics, and the use of celestial weapons, empowering them to gain a strategic advantage in warfare.
- **Control and Distribution of Source Code:** In software development, control over access to source code is tightly regulated to protect intellectual property rights, maintain security, and prevent unauthorized modifications or distribution. Similarly, in the Mahabharata, the secrets of the Kurukshetra War were closely guarded by military

commanders, strategic advisors, and divine beings to prevent their misuse or dissemination to enemies.

- **Security Risks and Vulnerabilities:** Unauthorized access to source code poses security risks and vulnerabilities, as malicious actors may exploit weaknesses or introduce malicious code to compromise the integrity or functionality of the software application. Similarly, unauthorized disclosure of the secrets of the Kurukshetra War could jeopardize military operations, compromise strategic positions, and undermine the morale of allied forces.
- **Ethical Considerations and Responsibilities:** Individuals with access to source code bear ethical responsibilities to use their knowledge responsibly, adhere to legal and ethical guidelines, and protect the interests of stakeholders. Similarly, individuals entrusted with the secrets of the Kurukshetra War had ethical obligations to uphold dharma, honor their allegiances, and safeguard the welfare of their allies and subjects.
- **Innovation and Advancement:** Access to source code enables software developers to innovate, refine, and enhance existing applications, driving technological advancement and progress. Similarly, the secrets of the Kurukshetra War, when understood and applied judiciously, could inspire military innovation, strategic thinking, and the development of new tactics and weaponry.

Control

Read and write access to source code, development tools and software libraries should be appropriately managed.

Purpose

To prevent the introduction of unauthorized functionality, avoid unintentional or malicious changes and to maintain the confidentiality of valuable intellectual property.

Guidance

Access to source code and associated items and development tools should be strictly controlled. For source code, this can be achieved by controlling central storage of such code, preferably in source code management system. Read access and write access to source code can differ based on the personnel's role. For example, read access to source code can be broadly provided inside the organization, but write access to source code is only made available to privileged personnel or designated owners. Where code components are used by several developers within an organization, read access to a centralized code repository should be implemented. Furthermore, if open-source code or third-party code components are used inside an organization, read access to such external code repositories can be broadly provided. However, write access should still be restricted. The following guidelines should be considered to control access to program source libraries in order to reduce the potential for corruption of computer programs:

- Managing the access to program source code and the program source libraries according to established procedures;
- Granting read and write access to source code based on business needs and managed to address risks of alteration or misuse and according to established procedures;
- Updating of source code and associated items and granting of access to source code in accordance with change control procedures and only performing it after appropriate authorization has been received;
- Not granting developers direct access to the source code repository, but through developer tools that control activities and authorizations on the source code;
- Holding program listings in a secure environment, where read and write access should be appropriately managed and assigned;
- Maintaining an audit log of all accesses and of all changes to source code.

If the program source code is intended to be published, additional controls to provide assurance on its integrity should be considered.

Other Information

If access to source code is not properly controlled, source code can be modified or some data in the development environment can be retrieved by unauthorized persons.

Organizations must confirm that there is appropriate segregation of duties between the employees responsible for moving a program into production and the staff responsible for developing a program. In addition, organizations must consider whether or not changes are performed in a segregated and controlled environment. To fulfill this requirement, administrators must ensure that logins to source code repositories and the permissions assigned to these users are appropriate for the tasks that they are allowed to perform. Users with overlapping permission sets should indicate a compromise in the segregation of duties control consideration. Administrators should also review the process to request and grant access to systems and data and confirm that the same person does not perform these functions. To prevent the introduction of unauthorized functionality and to avoid unintended changes, and to maintain the confidentiality of valuable intellectual property, it is necessary to strictly control access to source code and related associated items. For program source code, this can be achieved by controlling the central storage of such code, preferably in program source libraries. In order to minimize the potential for misuse of computer applications, the following guidelines will then be considered to control access to these source libraries:

- Where appropriate, software source libraries should not be kept in operating systems;
- The source code of the program and the source library of the program should be administered according to procedures;
- Support staff should have restricted access to program source libraries;
- The updating of program source libraries and related objects, and therefore the issuing of software sources to programmers, should be carried out only after sufficient authorization has been received;
- The program listings should be stored in a safe environment;
- The audit log of all accesses to program source libraries should be maintained;
- Strict change control procedures may refer to the management and copying of software source libraries.

A source code management system that allows organizations to centrally administer access to and their amendment of source code across its ICT estate. It asks organizations to consider access to source code along a set of strict read and/or write privileges, based on the nature of the source code, where it's being accessed from, and who is accessing it. When seeking to control access to source code, organizations should:

- Control access to source code in line with published procedures;
- Provide read and/or write access to source code in conjunction with a set of clearly defined business requirements on a case-by-case or user-by-user basis;
- Adhere to a clear set of change management procedures when administering access to source code, including proper authorization based on a range of access variables;
- Prevent the direct access of source code by developers, and instead provision access through a series of development tools that provide a top-down view of access rights and read/write privileges;
- Provision a secure space to store program listings and read/write privileges;
- Maintain a concurrent audit trail of all source code related activities;
- Ensure that digital signatures are used for any piece of code that is to be published outside of the organization.

Securing Source Code

- **Create a source code protection policy:** Set up a source code protection policy by defining a set of rules, requirements, and procedures for handling and protecting code. This policy will help safeguard software and devices from threats such as reverse engineering and code tampering. It should also cover source code development processes and personnel involved in code development. Include secure access and use of source code repositories. Your source code protection policy should also involve documentation and training on secure coding practices and the incorporation of secure development methodologies into the Software Development Lifecycle (SDLC).
- **Prevent the use of insecure source code:** Use source code security analysis tools, such as Static Application Security Testing (SAST), to detect security flaws and other issues during development.
- **Access control:** Define who's allowed to access source code, code base and source code repositories. There's little to no reason that

anyone other than hands-on employees work with the source code, but even for those that do, set up two-factor authentication. In this way, organization can ensure that no suspicious characters find their way into the source code. Through authentication and authorization, access control policies ensure that users are who they say they are and that they have appropriate access to organization data.

- **Use encryption and monitoring:** Make sure organization have the ability to encrypt sensitive data both in transit and at rest. It's also important to monitor the data at all times and be alerted when any suspicious activity comes to light. In this way, organization can be ready to act swiftly, whether it is about tracking, limiting, or reversing the damage and also preventing it before any acual harm happens.
- **Deploy network security tools:** Implementing network security solutions count as basic protection and these solutions safeguard the source code from external exploits of hackers and ensure secure data sharing between employees and data sources.
- **Don't forget about endpoint security:** Secure endpoints or entry points of end-user devices from risky activities and malicious attacks with endpoint security software. Data Loss Prevention (DLP) solutions can efficiently prevent the source code from leaving the endpoint and stop source code exfiltration. These tools can protect sensitive information both in physical and virtual environments, regardless of the endpoint's physical location and whether it's connected to the internet or not.
- **Pay attention to patents and copyright:** Make sure that all the concepts and inventions related to software are protected by copyright law and necessary patents. A major difference between these two is that while patents protect the idea, copyright safeguards the written code. As software-related inventions are increasingly popular, organization should treat this proprietary information just like other intellectual property.

A.8.5 Secure Authentication

Access to systems and applications must be controlled by a secure authentication technologies and procedure to prove the identity of the user. This can go beyond the typical password approach into multi-factor authentication, biometrics, smart cards, and other means of encryption based on the risk being considered. Secure authentication should be designed so it cannot be easily circumvented and that any authentication information is transmitted and stored encrypted to prevent interception and misuse. Secure authentication is the primary method which human and non-human users engage with when attempting to utilize an organization's ICT assets. Over the past decade, authentication technology has undergone a fundamental shift from traditional username/password-based validations into a variety of complementing techniques involving biometric information, logical and physical access controls, external device authentications, SMS codes and one-time passwords (OTP). The organizations should be controlling access to their ICT systems and assets via a secure login gateway. It is a preventative control that maintains risk by implementing technology and establishing topic-specific secure authentication procedures that ensure human and non-human users and identities undergo a robust and secure authentication procedure when attempting to access ICT resources.

A.8.5 Secure Authentication – A linkage with Ancient Era

Ashoka Vatika

While Lord Hanuman visits Mata Sita in the Ashoka Vatika, she requests that He describes the characteristics of Lord Ram. Further, she also inspects the ring that Lord Hanuman presents. This shows the importance of authentication. Multi-factor authentication is highly essential to ensure the identity of every user. This will help organizations keep malicious actors at bay. The zero-trust framework highly recommends organizations enforce MFA for authentication purposes.

Control

Secure authentication technologies and procedures should be implemented based on information access restrictions and the topic-specific policy on access control.

Purpose

To ensure a user or an entity is securely authenticated, when access to systems, applications and services is granted.

Guidance

A suitable authentication technique should be chosen to substantiate the claimed identity of a user, software, messages and other entities. The strength of authentication should be appropriate for the classification of the information to be accessed. Where strong authentication and identity verification is required, authentication methods alternative to passwords, should be used. Authentication information should be accompanied by additional authentication factors for accessing critical information systems (also known as MFA). Using a combination of MFA, such as what you know, what you have and what you are, reduces the possibilities for unauthorized accesses. MFA can be combined with other techniques to require additional factors under specific circumstances, based on predefined rules and patterns, such as access from an unusual location, from an unusual device or at an unusual time. Biometric authentication information should be invalidated if it is ever compromised. Biometric authentication can be unavailable depending on the conditions of use. To prepare for these issues, biometric authentication should be accompanied with at least one alternative authentication technique. The procedure for logging into a system or application should be designed to minimize the risk of unauthorized access. Log-on procedures and technologies should be implemented considering the following:

- Not displaying sensitive system or application information until the log-on process has been successfully completed in order to avoid providing an unauthorized user with any unnecessary assistance;
- Displaying a general notice warning that the system or the application or the service should only be accessed by authorized users;
- Not providing help messages during the log-on procedure that would aid an unauthorized user (e.g., if an error condition arises, the system should not indicate which part of the data is correct or incorrect);
- Validating the log-on information only on completion of all input data;
- Protecting against brute force log-on attempts on usernames and passwords;

- Logging unsuccessful and successful attempts;
- Raising a security event if a potential attempted or successful breach of log-on controls is detected;
- Displaying or sending the following information on a separate channel on completion of a successful log-on:
    - Date and time of the previous successful log-on;
    - Details of any unsuccessful log-on attempts since the last successful log-on;
- Not displaying a password in clear text when it is being entered; in some cases, it can be required to de-activate this functionality in order to facilitate user log-on;
- Not transmitting passwords in clear text over a network to avoid being captured by a network "sniffer" program;
- Terminating inactive sessions after a defined period of inactivity, especially in high-risk locations such as public or external areas outside the organization's security management or on user endpoint devices;
- Restricting connection duration times to provide additional security for high-risk applications and reduce the window of opportunity for unauthorized access.

Other Information

Additional information on entity authentication assurance can be found is ISO/IEC 29115.

Organizations should consider authentication controls that are relevant to the type and sensitivity of the data and network that's being accessed, including:

- Multi-Factor Authentication (MFA)
- Digital Certificates
- Smart Access Controls (smart cards)
- Biometric Logins
- Secure Tokens

To prevent and/or minimize the risk of unauthorized access to its protected systems, the organization should follow the steps mentioned in the Guidance section.

To control privileged access to systems and applications, the organization must implement secure authentication technologies and procedures. To log-on to systems and applications, users must access privileged credentials. Organizations can configure the log-on to display a general notice warning that access to the system or application is limited to authorized users. The log-on process can also display information upon completion of a successful log-on, such as number of previous failed log-on attempts since the last successful login. Organizations can protect against brute-force log-on attacks by limiting repeated access attempts. Users who fail authentication to the vault should be locked out until enabled by an administrator, preventing access to privileged credentials. Reauthentication for users or applications can be required based on inactivity or time-limits. Privileged session connection times can be restricted to certain times of day and sessions can be disconnected when a threshold (i.e., 15 minutes) is reached.

Application access can also be protected against brute-force log-on attacks. To perform designated tasks like processing information in a database and/or applications employees must be granted use of privileged accounts. Credentials are typically hardcoded and in clear text within applications, making them susceptible to brute-force attacks. For example, to access a database, an application must first have authorized access to the privileged credential in the vault. To gain access to the credential, an application is authenticated using advanced authentication methods, based not only on ID and password but also on specific application characteristics including the server it resides on, the operating system it uses, and a crypto "fingerprint." Organizations can ensure only authorized applications with the appropriate ID and characteristics can access the database. The system can record and monitor all access attempts to privileged credentials. All valid and invalid access attempts by privileged credentials can also be logged, such as an application attempting to connect to a database. For raising security events such as a potential attack on log-on controls, it can integrate with Security Information and Event Management (SIEM) and Event Log Systems.

Single Sign-On

The central authentication service can be used to securely integrate Web authentication in addition to providing single sign-on capabilities where appropriate. Although having a central authentication system makes account management easier, the exposure of one stolen account is greater when it gives the thief access to multiple systems on the network. Therefore, single sign-on is not necessarily desirable in higher education environments where password theft is a common risk. Less sign-on is ideal, using centralized authentication for most systems but maintaining separate accounts on computer systems that contain particularly sensitive data and require added protection.

Authentication

Authentication is the mechanism to confirm the identity of an entity requesting access to an information resource. Authentication is often a prerequisite to allow access to an information resource. To be properly authenticated, the entity is required to provide credentials, a unique identifier and a password, passphrase or token. The credentials are compared to the identifying information previously stored on the entity and if the credentials match the stored information, the entity is authenticated. Most organizations require all employees to have their own unique usernames and password to access certain IT resources. In addition, organizations authenticate these individuals before allowing them to connect to the network or the internet. This approach not only enables the organization to attribute network activities to individual accounts, but it also gives the opportunity to scan systems for vulnerabilities before they connect to the network.

- **Are a Username and Password Enough for Authentication?**

  Information security practitioners are increasingly making the case that passwords and password practices are bad and getting worse. Specifically, that usernames and passwords are no longer sufficient to authenticate to information resources containing confidential information. Two-Factor Authentication is the use of an additional factor to minimize the probability of fraudulent authentication.

- **What Is Two-Factor Authentication?**

  It is the use of two independent means of evidence (factors) to assert the identity of a user requesting access to some application or service to the organization that provides the application or service. The objective of two-factor authentication, as a method of electronic computer authentication, is to decrease the probability that the requester is not who he/she claims to be (providing false evidence of his/her identity). Two-factor authentication is achieved by a combination of any two of the three "Somethings" below:

  - **Something you know:** Personal Identification Number (PIN), Password
  - **Something you have:** Smartphone, Token, ID Badge/Smartcard
  - **Something you are:** Fingerprint, Retinal Scan, Voice Pattern, Typing Cadence

  Note that the use of a password in combination with a PIN, for example, is NOT considered two-factor authentication because both pieces of information involve a single factor, something you know. The use of two-factor authentication has been pervasive and ubiquitous for quite a long time already. Any person who has used an ATM machine to withdraw cash for a bank account has used two-factor authentication, you had to provide something you had (a card) and had to provide something you know (a PIN) in order to complete the transaction.

- **Difference Between Two-Factor and Multi-Factor Authentication (MFA)**

  The subtle difference is that, while two-factor authentication uses exactly two factors to assert the identity of a user, MFA uses two or more factors to assert identity. In essence, two-factor authentication is a subset of multi-factor authentication. An example of multi-factor authentication would be the requirement to insert a smart-card (something you have) into a smart-card reader, enter a PIN (something you know), and provide a valid fingerprint (something you are) provided via a biometric fingerprint reader. This example uses three factors to assert the identity of a user.

- **Business Reasons to Consider Two-Factor Authentication**

  Privacy and the threat of identity theft is increasingly a concern as more personal information finds its way to online applications. In addition, passwords alone can frequently be easily guessed or compromised through phishing or hacking, consequently, no longer providing adequate protection for mission-critical information systems and applications containing PII, Personal Health Information (PHI), and other confidential information. Some specific concerns:

  - As passwords become easier to guess or compromise, password complexity requirements are quickly coming to exceed what users can reasonably remember;
  - Password proliferation has increased the time and effort spent on user support because of forgotten passwords and the need to reset them;
  - Many passwords reset mechanisms are insecure, even if the passwords themselves are not;
  - The increased use of single sign-on increases the value of passwords and the number of ways by which those passwords can be potentially attacked;
  - Passwords are all-too-often cached in applications, stored off-site, and reused for multiple services, some highly sensitive.

Application and Information Access Control

- **Information Access Restriction:** The organization's access control page can contain publications, presentations, policies, podcasts, and blogs regarding mechanisms by which a system grants or revokes the right to access some data or perform some action.
- **Sensitive System Isolation:** Segregation can be defined as the action or state of setting someone or something apart from other people or things or being set apart. Information resources that are critical to the performance of the organization's mission, contain confidential information, or is otherwise considered sensitive should be segregated based on sensitivity and risk. The segregation of information resources can be accomplished by, but not limited to:

- Creating network domains: the collection of devices and subjects that share a common security policy and trusts a security bridge between domains to enable users of one domain to access resources from another are common practices in decentralized access implementations. Domains are defined based on risk and the specific security requirements of the domain.
- Implementing virtual local area networks (VLAN) and/or virtual private networks (VPN) for specific user/application groups.
- Controlling network data flows using network equipment routing/ switching capabilities.

- **Federation**

  A Federation is an association of organizations that come together to exchange information, as appropriate, about their users and resources in order to enable collaborations and transactions.

  - Increasingly, people must easily and securely exchange information in cyberspace among known individuals and be trusted to access restricted resources without having to struggle with numerous and onerous security processes;
  - Ideally, individuals would each like a single digital credential that can be securely used to authenticate his or her identity anytime authentication of identity is required to secure any transaction;
  - Traditional forms of authentication and authorization are no longer sufficient or the level of assurance needed by modern internet-based applications
    - Increase security
    - Compliance with Federal and State rules
  - Application security is becoming increasingly onerous (multiple applications, multiple enterprises, and multiple user roles in multiple contexts)
    - Inter-organizational collaboration
    - Operational efficiencies and cost control

- Examples:
    - The organization wants to offer services to their constituents but doesn't want to host them.
    - The vendor wants to offer a service to an organization but doesn't want the burden of managing user credentials and authentication.
    - The user wants seamless access to services, "Single-Sign-On".
    - The security officer wants to protect organization assets, user identity information, and passwords

- **Traditional Approach: Federated Approach:**
    - **First Steps:**

      Technically speaking, it involves:
        - New Policies;
        - New Processes;
        - New Trust Relationships;
        - New Authentication and Authorization Mechanisms;
        - New Enterprise Directories;
        - New Applications and much more;

      The participating organization must agree on:
        - Technical specifications: data attributes to exchange, the software to interoperate with;
        - Policy specifications: privacy, establish trust and trustworthy data.

      Must provide two sets of services:
        - Metadata management: aggregate, distribute, and maintain members' attribute data, syntax, and semantics;
        - Trust management: federation and member operation practices and control privacy and security policies.

Things to Think About:

- Policy work is very slow, but critical, start early
  - Identifiers
  - Privacy
  - Content copyright
- Do not underestimate the difficulty of application integration with new or legacy infrastructure;
- Authorization can be quite a challenge;
- Consider new support models;
- Communication and coordination are key;
- Keeping all stakeholders motivated and involved can be quite a challenge.

Policy Issues:

- Which services reside where?
- How is vetting/credentialing performed?
- How do application owners determine the required Level of Assurance (LOA) for their applications?
- How do identity providers comply with applications' LOA requirements?
- Who supports the end users and applications?
- Who audits identity providers' practices and what standards are used?
- What is the role of Information Security Governance?

Federation Technology Standards:

- Security Assertion Markup Language (SAML):
  - Standard developed and ratified by OASIS, an international non-profit standards organization, and managed by the OASIS Security Services Technical Committee
  - Has broad vendor and industry acceptance

- WS-Federation: a specification developed by IBM, Microsoft, BEA, and others.
- OASIS now has a technical committee tasked with standardizing WS-Fed.
- Liberty Identity Federation Framework (ID-FF): now integrated into the SAML 2.0 standard.
- Open ID: a user-centric distributed web-SSO technology perceived as being lighter weight and less focused on communities of trust than SAML

Benefits of Federation:

- Sharing of Resources;
- Collaboration;
- Increase security;
- Lower support costs;
- Improved user experience.

Challenges of Federation:

- Deploying new infrastructure is hard:
    - The infrastructure must be there before gains can be realized, which makes it just a challenge.
- Policy development can take considerable time.
- Trust can be difficult to achieve:
    - Good policy and governance help ("trust but verify")
- Making it ubiquitous across entities of varying sizes is a challenge:
    - Many times, it is the smaller organizations that can benefit the most.

Good security and identity practices help ensure that an individual using an electronic credential is the person you think it is. For Service Providers in an identity federation, having Identity Provider Operators support a standard practice set (or profile) can mitigate the risk of a service compromise. For Identity Providers, it is a way to provide single sign-on access to applications requiring an increased level of confidence in a credential.

- **Cloud Computing and Software as a Service (SaaS)**

  Cloud Computing describes the use of a collection of distributed services, applications, information and infrastructure comprised of pools of compute, network, information and storage resources. These components can be rapidly orchestrated, provisioned, implemented and decommissioned using an on-demand utility-like model of allocation and consumption. Software as a Service (SaaS) is the capability provided to the consumer to use a provider's applications running on a cloud infrastructure and accessible from various client devices through a thin client interface such as a Web browser.

- **Challenges:**
  - The decision to procure cloud computing services or SaaS may be driven mostly by individual departments instead of organizational IT strategy.
  - Integrating separately developed applications into an integrated approach.
    - How to manage access?
    - How to manage to provision?
    - How to integrate these applications into organizational web services?
    - How to reduce the number of credentials?
- **An Alternative Solution:**
  - Focus on four activities:
    - Develop an organizational Identity Management System;
    - Create a standard set of attributes for each person;
    - Use a federation to enable external access;
    - Require organizational developers and in RFPs that service providers support SAML and InCommon.
- **Mobile Computing and Teleworking**

  Teleworking (i.e., telecommuting), e-commerce, use of intranets, online education, and the increasing use of portable computing devices are driving the need for access to information resources from any place at any time. Today's mobile workforce or users are no longer just employees trying to check e-mail from home but part and full-time employees, telecommuters, business partners, vendors and customers who rely on access to organizational networks to accomplish day-to-day business functions. Information security controls specifically targeting mobile computing and remote access to information resources are becoming an increasingly critical component of any information security program ensuring the protection of the integrity of the organizational networks while allowing remote access to it.

- **Challenges of Mobile Computing:**
    - User Authentication;
    - Protection of Transmitted Data;
    - Protection of the Organizational Network.

To enable remote access to organizational information resources, organizations are implementing Virtual Private Networks (VPN) technology to provide a secure connection to the organizational network. VPNs send data securely through a shared network. VPNs can be established between remote users and a network or between two or more networks thus using the Internet as the medium for transmitting information securely over and between networks via a process called tunneling.

A.8.6 Capacity Management

Capacity Management is the broad term describing a variety of IT monitoring, administration and planning actions that are taken to ensure that a computing infrastructure has adequate resources to handle current data processing requirements as well as the capacity to accommodate future loads. The primary goal of capacity management is to ensure that IT resources are rightsized to meet current and future business requirements in a cost-effective manner. Capacity management, in the context of ICT, isn't limited to ensuring that organisations have adequate space on servers and associated storage media for data access and Backup and Disaster Recovery (BUDR) purposes. Organizations need to ensure that they have the ability to operate with a set of resources that cater to a broad range of business functions, including HR, information processing, the management of physical office locations and attached facilities. All of these functions have the ability to adversely affect an organization's information management controls. The use of resources must be monitored, tuned and projections made of future capacity requirements to ensure the required system performance to meet the business objectives. Capacity management typically looks at three primary types: Data Storage Capacity, Processing Power Capacity, and Communications Capacity. Capacity management also needs to be: Proactive, for example, using capacity considerations as part of change management; Reactive, for example, triggers and alerts for when capacity usage is reaching a critical point so that timely increases, temporary or permanent can be made.

A.8.6 Capacity Management – A linkage with Ancient Era

Ram Setu – Adam's Bridge

- **Planning and Resource Allocation:** Just as Capacity Management involves planning and allocating resources to meet demand efficiently, the construction of Ram Setu required meticulous planning and allocation of resources such as manpower, materials, and time. Lord Ram, along with his army of Vanar's (monkey warriors), strategically planned and allocated resources to build the bridge to Lanka to rescue Mata Sita.
- **Optimizing Utilization:** Capacity Management focuses on optimizing the utilization of resources to ensure optimal performance and

efficiency. Similarly, in the construction of Ram Setu, resources were utilized effectively to maximize the progress of the project. The Vanar's under the leadership of Lord Hanuman and other commanders efficiently utilized available materials and labor to build the bridge within the stipulated time frame.

- **Forecasting and Demand Prediction:** Capacity Management involves forecasting demand and predicting resource requirements to meet future needs. Similarly, in the construction of Ram Setu, Lord Ram and His advisors anticipated the demand for resources and planned accordingly to ensure a smooth construction process. They assessed the challenges posed by the ocean and the distance to be covered, making strategic decisions to overcome obstacles.
- **Adaptability and Flexibility:** Capacity Management requires adaptability and flexibility to adjust resource allocation in response to changing demand or circumstances. Similarly, during the construction of Ram Setu, the Vanar's encountered various challenges such as rough seas, adverse weather conditions, and attacks from demons. They demonstrated adaptability and flexibility by adjusting their strategies and utilizing available resources creatively to overcome obstacles.
- **Quality Assurance and Performance Monitoring:** Capacity Management involves monitoring performance and ensuring quality standards are met to deliver satisfactory outcomes. Similarly, in the construction of Ram Setu, Lord Ram and His advisors monitored the progress of the bridge-building project closely, ensuring that quality standards were maintained and that the bridge met the necessary specifications to support the army's passage to Lanka.
- **Risk Management:** Capacity Management includes identifying and mitigating risks that may impact resource availability or project timelines. Similarly, during the construction of Ram Setu, Lord Ram and His advisors assessed potential risks such as attacks from demons or natural calamities and implemented measures to mitigate these risks, ensuring the successful completion of the project.

Control

The use of resources should be monitored and adjusted in line with current and expected capacity requirements.

Purpose

To ensure the required capacity of information processing facilities, human resources, offices and other facilities.

Guidance

Capacity requirements for information processing facilities, human resources, offices and other facilities should be identified, taking into account the business criticality of the concerned systems and processes. System tuning and monitoring should be applied to ensure and, where necessary, improve the availability and efficiency of systems. The organization should perform stress-tests of systems and services to confirm that sufficient system capacity is available to meet peak performance requirements. Detective controls should be put in place to indicate problems in due time. Projections of future capacity requirements should take account of new business and system requirements and current and projected trends in the organization's information processing capabilities. Particular attention should be paid to any resources with long procurement lead times or high costs. Therefore, managers, service or product owners should monitor the utilization of key system resources. Managers should use capacity information to identify and avoid potential resource limitations and dependency on key personnel which can present a threat to system security or services and plan appropriate action. Providing sufficient capacity can be achieved by increasing capacity or by reducing demand. The following should be considered to increase capacity:

- Hiring new personnel;
- Obtaining new facilities or space;
- Acquiring more powerful processing systems, memory and storage;
- Making use of cloud computing, which has inherent characteristics that directly address issues of capacity.

Cloud computing has elasticity and scalability which enable on-demand rapid expansion and reduction in resources available to particular applications and services.

The following should be considered to reduce demand on the organization's resources:

- Deletion of obsolete data;
- Disposal of hardcopy records that have met their retention period;
- Decommissioning of applications, systems, databases or environments;
- Optimizing batch processes and schedules;
- Optimizing application code or database queries;
- Denying or restricting bandwidth for resource-consuming services if these are not critical.

A documented capacity management plan should be considered for mission critical systems.

The methodologies and processes used for IT capacity management may vary, it requires the ability to monitor IT resources closely enough to be able to gather and measure basic performance metrics. With that data in hand, IT managers and administrators can set baselines for operations to meet a organization's processing needs. The baselines or benchmarks represent average performance over a specific period of time and can be used to detect deviations from those established levels. Capacity management tools measure the volumes, speeds, latencies and efficiency of the movement of data as it is processed by an organization's applications. All facets of data's journey through the IT infrastructure must be monitored, so capacity management must be able to examine the operations of all the hardware and software in an environment and capture critical information about data flow. Capacity planning is typically based on the results and analysis of the data gathered during capacity management activities. By examining performance variances over time, IT management can use those performance statistics to help develop models describing anticipated processing which can be used for short- and long-term planning. By noting which particular resources are being stressed, current configurations can be appropriately revised and IT planners can assemble purchasing plans for hardware and software that will help meet future demands. Measurement and analysis tools must be able to observe the individual performances of IT assets, as well as how these assets interact. A comprehensive capacity management process should be able to monitor and measure the following IT elements, but not limited to:

- Servers;

- End-User Devices;
- Networks and Related Communications Devices;
- Storage Systems and Storage Network Devices;
- Cloud Services.

Organization's ability to operate as a business on an ongoing basis depends upon the following:

- Organizations should consider business continuity as a top priority when implementing capacity management controls, including the wholesale implementation of detective controls that flag up potential issues before they occur.
- Capacity management should be based upon the proactive functions of tuning and monitoring. Both of these elements should work in harmony to ensure that systems and business functions are not compromised.
- In operational terms, organizations should perform regular stress tests that interrogate a system's ability to cater to overall business needs. Such tests should be formulated on a case-by-case basis and be relevant to the area of operation that they are targeted at.
- Capacity management controls should not be limited to an organization's current data or operational needs, and should include any plans for commercial and technical expansion (both from a physical and digital perspective) in order to remain as future-proof as is realistically possible.
- Expanding organizational resources is subject to varying lead times and costs, depending on the system or business function in question. Resources that are more expensive and more difficult to expand should be subject to a higher degree of scrutiny, in order to safeguard business continuity.
- Senior Management should be mindful of single points of failure relating to a dependency on key personnel or individual resources. Should any difficulties arise with either of these factors, it can often lead to complications that are markedly more difficult to rectify.
- Formulate a capacity management plan that deals specifically with business-critical systems and business functions.

A dual-fronted approach to capacity management that either increases capacity, reduces demand upon a resource, or set of resources. When attempting to increase capacity and/or reduce demand, organizations should consider the steps mentioned in the Guidance section.

Formal capacity management processes involve conducting system tuning, monitoring the use of present resources and, with the support of user planning input, projecting future requirements. Controls in place to detect and respond to capacity problems can help lead to a timely reaction. This is often especially important for communications networks and shared resource environments (virtual infrastructure) where sudden changes in utilization can lead to poor performance and dissatisfied users. To address this, regular monitoring processes should be employed to collect, measure, analyze and predict capacity metrics including disk capacity, transmission throughput, service/application utilization. Also, periodic testing of capacity management plans and assumptions (whether tabletop exercises or direct simulations) can help proactively identify issues that may need to be addressed to preserve a high level of availability of services for critical services.

Whether capacity management is achieved via software, hardware or manual means or a combination of any of those it relies on the interception of data movement metrics and the internal processes of individual components. Capacity management could have a fairly narrow scope, providing high-level information on a variety of infrastructure components or, perhaps, providing detail metrics related to one segment of the computing environment. The trend, however, is to gather as much information as possible and then to attempt to correlate those measurements into an application-centric picture that focuses on the performance and requirements of mission-critical applications across the environment, rather than how individual components are performing. Still, to achieve that application-centric view of capacity management, virtually all elements of the IT infrastructure must be monitored and the definition of capacity must be broad enough to consider the impact an application will have on processing power, memory, storage capacity and speed for all physical and software components comprising an infrastructure.

- **Performance:** is a key metric in capacity management as it may point to processing bottlenecks that affect overall application processing performance. The Central Processor Unit (CPU) in servers and other connected devices, such as routers, storage and controllers, should be monitored to ensure that their processing capabilities are not frequently "pinning" at or near 100%. An overtaxed processor would be a candidate for upgrading.

- **Memory:** is also a factor in capacity management. Servers and other devices use their installed memory to run applications and process data if too little memory is installed, processing will slow down. It's relatively easy to determine if a server has adequate memory resources, but it's also important to monitor other devices in the environment to ensure that insufficient memory doesn't turn them into processing bottlenecks.
- **Physical space:** is what is most commonly associated with capacity management, with the focus generally on storage space for applications and data. Storage systems that are near capacity will have longer response times, as it takes longer to locate specific data when drives hard disk or solid-state are full or nearly full. As with processor and memory measurements, it's important to monitor space usage in devices other than servers and end-user PCs that may have installed storage that's used for caching data.

Capacity Management in Networking

Managing the capacity of IT networks can be a complex process given the number of different networking elements that can be found in an enterprise environment. The number and type of networks being monitored is likely to vary as well. In addition to the wired and wireless Ethernet-based network infrastructure that connects servers to storage, end-user devices, networking gear, etc., comprehensive network capacity management must also consider dedicated storage networks based on Fibre Channel (FC) technologies; the FC networks are likely to be physically isolated from other data networks and will require different tools for monitoring and management. External networking should also be monitored. Again, different tools will be required to track traffic and performance for network connections to remote offices and users, the internet and to cloud services. The networking devices that should be monitored include network interface cards (NICs), network switches, network routers, storage network interfaces, storage network switches and optical network devices. Although capacity management for networks doesn't directly address security, it can be a good method of keeping track of network access, which can help inform security procedures.

Benefits of Capacity Management

Capacity Management provides many benefits to an IT organization and is a factor in overall management of a computing infrastructure. In addition to ensuring that systems are performing at adequate levels to achieve a organization's goals, capacity management can often realize cost savings by avoiding over-provisioning of hardware and software resources. It can also help save money and time by identifying extraneous activities like backing up unused data or maintaining idle servers. Good capacity management can also result in more-effective purchasing to accommodate future growth by being able to more accurately anticipate needs and, thus, make purchases when prices may be lower. By constantly monitoring equipment and processing, problems that might have hindered production may be avoided, such as bottlenecks or imminent equipment failures.

Components of Capacity Management

The activities that support the capacity management process are crucial to the success and maturity of the process. Some of these are done on an ongoing basis, some daily, some weekly, and some at a longer, regular interval. Some are ad-hoc, based on current (or future) needs or requirements. Let's look at those:

- **Monitoring**: Keeping an eye on the performance and throughput or load on a server, cluster, or data center is extremely important. Not having enough headroom can cause performance issues. Having too much headroom can create larger-than necessary bills for hardware, software, power, etc.
- **Analysis**: Taking that measurement and monitoring data and drilling down to see the potential impact of changes in demand. As more and more data become available, having the tools needed to find the right data and make sense of it is very important.
- **Tuning:** Determining the most efficient use of existing infrastructure

should not be taken lightly. A lot of organizations have over-configured significant parts of the environment while under-configuring others. Simply reallocating resources could improve performance while keeping spend at current levels.

- **Demand Management**: Understanding the relationship of current and future demand and how the existing or new infrastructure can handle this is incredibly important. Predictive analytics can provide decision support to IT management. Also, moving non-critical workloads to quieter periods can delay purchase of additional hardware (and all the licenses and other costs that go with it).
- **Capacity Planning**: Determining the requirements for resources required over some future time. This can be done by predictive analysis, modeling, benchmarking, or other techniques, all of which have varying costs and levels of effectiveness.

A.8.7 Protection Against Malware

Malware, short for Malicious Software, is software that infects your computer so that cyber criminals can infiltrate or damage your system or device. A cybercriminal may use malware to steal information or carry out malicious activities. Malware represents the single largest threat to business continuity and information security faced by businesses in the digital age. The global commercial community faces innumerable daily threats from a broad range of attack vectors that seek to gain unauthorized access to sensitive systems and data, extract information and money, dupe unassuming employees and leverage ransomed data for extortionate sums of money. An organization's approach to malware protection should be front and centre of any information security policy. An array of measures that helps organizations to educate their employees as to the dangers of malicious software, and implement meaningful practical measures that stop internal and external attacks before they have a chance to cause disruption and data loss. Downloading programs is the most common way to infect your device with malware. But direct downloads while browsing websites aren't the only way you can get malware. You might infect your computer or device by opening or downloading attachments or clicking on links in emails or text messages.

A.8.7 Protection Against Malware – A linkage with Ancient Era

Various Types of Weapons in Warfare

- **Malware as Stealthy Attackers:** Malware, like stealthy attackers in warfare, infiltrates systems undetected and wreaks havoc from within. It can be linked to covert operatives or assassins who use stealth and deception to bypass defenses and inflict damage on targets. Just as soldiers must be vigilant and prepared to defend against unseen adversaries, organizations need robust cybersecurity measures to detect and thwart malware attacks before they cause harm.
- **Firearms as Rapidly Deployed Threats:** Firearms in warfare represent threats that can cause widespread damage quickly and indiscriminately. Similarly, certain types of malwares, such as ransomware or worms, can spread rapidly across networks, infecting multiple systems and disrupting operations on a large scale. Defending against such threats requires proactive measures, including network segmentation,

intrusion detection systems, and endpoint protection, to contain and neutralize malware before it spreads.

- **Close Combat Weapons as Targeted Attacks:** Close combat weapons, such as swords or spears, were used in warfare for targeted attacks against specific adversaries. Similarly, targeted malware attacks, such as spear-phishing or Advanced Persistent Threats (APTs), are tailored to exploit vulnerabilities in specific organizations or individuals. Defending against targeted attacks requires a combination of user awareness training, email filtering, and endpoint security solutions to identify and block malicious payloads before they can infiltrate systems.
- **Siege Weapons as Persistent Threats:** Siege Weapons, like catapults or trebuchets, were employed in warfare to breach fortified defenses through sustained bombardment. Similarly, certain types of malwares, such as Distributed Denial-of-Service (DDoS) attacks or botnets, launch persistent assaults on networks, overwhelming defenses and disrupting services. Defending against siege-like malware attacks requires robust perimeter defenses, traffic analysis, and response mechanisms to mitigate the impact and restore normal operations.
- **Chemical and Biological Weapons as Disruptive Agents:** Chemical and Biological Weapons in warfare cause disruption and chaos by poisoning or incapacitating adversaries. Similarly, malware variants designed to disrupt critical infrastructure or steal sensitive information can have devastating effects on organizations and societies. Defending against such disruptive malware requires threat intelligence, incident response planning, and continuous monitoring to identify and neutralize threats before they cause irreparable damage.

Control

Protection against malware should be implemented and supported by appropriate user awareness.

Purpose

To ensure information and other associated assets are protected against malware.

Guidance

Protection against malware should be based on malware detection and repair software, information security awareness, appropriate system access and change management controls. Use of malware detection and repair software alone is not usually adequate. The following guidance should be considered:

- Implementing rules and controls that prevent or detect the use of unauthorized software;
- Implementing controls that prevent or detect the use of known or suspected malicious websites;
- Reducing vulnerabilities that can be exploited by malware;
- Conducting regular automated validation of the software and data content of systems, especially for systems supporting critical business processes;
- Investigating the presence of any unapproved files or unauthorized amendments;
- Establishing protective measures against risks associated with obtaining files and software either from or via external networks or on any other medium;
- Installing and regularly updating malware detection and repair software to scan computers and electronic storage media. Carrying out regular scans that include:
    - Scanning any data received over networks or via any form of electronic storage media, for malware before use;
    - Scanning email and instant messaging attachments and downloads for malware before use. Carrying out this scan at different places and when entering the network of the organization;
    - Scanning web pages for malware when accessed;
- Determining the placement and configuration of malware detection and repair tools based on risk assessment outcomes and considering:
    - Defense in depth principles where they would be most effective. For example, this can lead to malware detection in a network gateway as well as user endpoint devices and servers;

  - The evasive techniques of attackers to deliver malware or the use of encryption protocols to transmit malware;

- Taking care to protect against the introduction of malware during maintenance and emergency procedures, which can bypass normal controls against malware;
- Implementing a process to authorize temporarily or permanently disable some or all measures against malware. This can be necessary when the protection against malware causes disruption to normal operations;
- Preparing appropriate business continuity plans for recovering from malware attacks, including all necessary data and software backup and recovery measures;
- Isolating environments where catastrophic consequences can occur;
- Defining procedures and responsibilities to deal with protection against malware on systems, including training in their use, reporting and recovering from malware attacks;
- Providing awareness or training to all users on how to identify and potentially mitigate the receipt, sending or installation of malware infected emails, files or programs;
- Implementing procedures to regularly collect information about new malware, such as subscribing to mailing lists or reviewing relevant websites;
- Verifying that information relating to malware, such as warning bulletins, comes from qualified and reputable sources and is accurate and informative.

Other Information

It is not always possible to install software that protects against malware on some systems (e.g., some industrial control systems). Some forms of malware infect computer operating systems and computer firmware such that common malware controls cannot clean the system and a full re-imaging of the operating system software and sometimes the computer firmware is necessary to return to a secure state.

It's rare for modern hackers to physically enter building premises because they may be caught or apprehended. Physical facility controls have a limited purpose in information security, to simply provide a local barrier for the physical intrusion. These localized barriers protect against common crimes by persons entering and leaving the facility. With the advent of the Internet, a smaller percentage of criminals will chance the risks of committing a physical crime. The new persistent threat is through electronic attacks. A hacker can commit the crime at a safe distance without fear of being physically caught. Attacks may originate from anywhere in the world or even be sponsored by a foreign government to gather intelligence data. Technical controls to protect against electronic attacks are usually spotty and inconsistent because of a lack of awareness for specific threats or lopsided implementations. It is very easy for the technical staff to inadvertently focus on only a few areas, thereby neglecting serious threats that still exist in others. Technical threats against software are usually difficult for lay-persons to visualize in the physical world. The adage out of sight, out of mind also means outside of the budget. Let's take a moment to understand how the electronic threat will manifest in the environment.

- **Malware:** This title refers to every malicious software program ever created, whether it exploits a known vulnerability or creates its own. There are so many different ones, it's easier to just call the entire group by the title of malware. The king of the malware threat is known as the Trojan Horse.
- **Trojan Horse**: A revised concept of the historical Trojan Horse has been adapted to attack computers. In a tale from the Trojan war, soldiers hid inside a bogus gift known as the Trojan Horse. The unassuming recipients accepted the horse and brought it inside their fortress, only to be attacked by enemy soldiers hiding within. Malicious programs frequently use the Trojan Horse concept to deliver viruses, worms, logic bombs, and other rootkits through downloaded files.
- **Virus:** The goal of a virus is to disrupt operations. Users inadvertently download a program built like a Trojan Horse containing the virus. The attacker's goal is usually to damage the programs or data files. Viruses append themselves to the end-of-file (EOF) marker on computerized files.
- **Internet Worm:** An Internet worm operates in a similar manner to

the Trojan or virus, with one major exception. Worm programs can freely travel between computers because they exploit unprotected data transfer ports to access other systems. Internet worms started by trying to access the automatic update function through software ports with poor authentication or no authentication mechanism.

- **Logic Bomb:** The concept of the logic bomb is designed around a dormant program code that is waiting for a trigger event to cause detonation. Unlike a virus or worm, logic bombs do not travel. The logic bomb remains in one location, awaiting detonation. Logic bombs are difficult to detect. Some logic bombs are intentional, and others are the unintentional result of poor programming. Intentional logic bombs can be set to detonate after the perpetrator is gone.
- **Time Bomb:** Programmers can install Time Bombs in their program to disable the software upon a predetermined date. Time bombs might be used to kill programs on symbolic dates such as April Fools' Day or the anniversary of a historic event. Free trial evaluation versions of software use the Time Bomb mechanism to disable their program after 30–60 days with the intention of forcing the user to purchase a license. Time Bombs can be installed by the vendor to eliminate perpetual customer support issues by forcing upgrades after a few years. The software installation utility will no longer run or install, because the programmer's Time Bomb setting disabled the program. Now when trying to run the software, a message directs the user to contact customer support to purchase an upgrade. Hackers use the same technique to disrupt operations.
- **Trapdoor:** Computer programmers frequently install a shortcut, also known as a trapdoor, for use during software testing. The trapdoor is a hidden access point within the computer software. A competent programmer will remove the majority of trapdoors before releasing a production version of the program. However, several vendors routinely leave a trapdoor in a computer program to facilitate user support. Commercial encryption software began to change in 1996 with the addition of "key recovery" features. This is basically a trap door feature to recover lost encryption keys and to allow the government to read encrypted files, if necessary.
- **Rootkit:** One of the most threatening attacks is the secret compromise

of the operating system kernel. Attackers embed a rootkit into the downloadable software. This malicious software will subvert security settings by linking itself directly into the kernel processes, system memory, address registers, and swap space. Rootkits operate in stealth to hide their presence. Hackers designed rootkits to never display their execution as running applications. The system resource monitor does not show any activity related to the presence of the rootkit. After the rootkit is installed, the hacker has control over the system. The computer is completely compromised. Automatic update features use the same techniques as malicious rootkits to allow the software vendor to bypass your security settings. Vendors know that using the term rootkit may alarm users. The software agent is just another name for a rootkit.

- **Brute Force Attack**: Brute force is the use of extreme effort to overcome an obstacle. Brute force attacks are frequently used against user login IDs and passwords. In one particular attack, all of the encrypted computer passwords are compared against a list of all the words encrypted from a language dictionary. After the match is identified, the attacker will use the unencrypted word that created the password match. This is why it is important to use passwords that do not appear in any language dictionary.
- **Denial of Service (DoS):** Attackers can disable a computer by rendering legitimate use impossible. The objective is to remotely shut down service by overloading the system or disable the user environment (shell) and thereby prevent the normal user from processing anything on the computer. Denial-of-Service (DoS) attacks may look similar to the loss of service while your system is downloading and installing vendor updates.
- **Distributed Denial of Service (DDoS):** The Denial of Service has evolved to use multiple systems for targeted attacks against another computer, to force its crash. This type of attack, Distributed Denial of Service (DDoS), is also known as the reflector attack. Your own computer is being used by the hacker to launch remote attacks against someone else. Hackers start the attack from unrelated systems that the hacker has already compromised. The attacking computers and target are drawn into the battle, similar in concept to starting a vicious

rumor between two strangers, which leads them to fight each other. The hackers sit safely out of the way while this battle wages.

Organizations to adopt an approach to malware protection that encompasses four key areas:

- Anti-Malware Software;
- Organizational Information Security User Awareness Training;
- Controlled Systems and Account Access;
- Change Management.

ISO categorically points out that it is a mistake to assume that anti-malware software alone represents an adequate set of measures. This control instead asks organizations to take an end-to-end approach to malware protection that begins with user education and ends with a tightly-controlled network that minimizes the risk of intrusion across a variety of attack vectors. To achieve this goal, organizations should implement controls that are mentioned in the Guidance section.

There are numerous ways to protect and remove malware from our computers. No one method is enough to ensure the computer is secure. The more layers of defense, the harder for hackers to use the computer.

- **Install a Firewall:** A firewall enacts the role of a security guard. There are two types of firewalls: a software firewall and a hardware firewall. Each serves similar, but different purposes. A firewall is the first step to provide security to the computer. It creates a barrier between the computer and any unauthorized program trying to come in through the Internet. If you are using a system at home, turn on the firewall permanently. It makes you aware if there are any unauthorized efforts to use your system.
- **Install Antivirus Software:** Antivirus is one other means to protect the computer. It is software that helps to protect the computer from any unauthorized code or software that creates a threat to the system. Unauthorized software includes viruses, keyloggers, trojans, etc. This might slow down the processing speed of the computer, delete important files and access personal information. Even if the system is virus-free, employee must install antivirus software to prevent the system from the further attack of the virus. Antivirus software plays

a major role in real-time protection, its added advantage of detecting threats helps computers and the information in it to be safe. Some advanced antivirus programs provide automatic updates, this further helps to protect the PC from newly created viruses.

- **Install Anti-Spyware Software:** Spyware is a software program that collects personal information or information about an organization without its approval. This information is redirected to a third-party website. Spyware is designed in such a way that they are not easy to be removed. Anti-Spyware software is solely dedicated to combat spyware. Similar to antivirus software, the anti-spyware software offers real-time protection. It scans all the incoming information and helps in blocking the threat once detected.
- **Check on the Security Settings of the Browser:** Browsers have various security and privacy settings that you should review and set to the level you desire. Recent browsers give you the ability to tell websites that do not track your movements, increasing your privacy and security.
- **Use Secure Authentication Methods:** The following best practices help keep accounts safe:
    - Require strong passwords with at least eight characters, including an uppercase letter, a lowercase letter, a number and a symbol in each password;
    - Enable MFA, such as a PIN or security questions in addition to a password;
    - Use biometric tools like fingerprints, voiceprints, facial recognition and iris scans;
    - Never save passwords on a computer or network. Use a secure password manager if needed.
- **Use administrator accounts only when absolutely necessary:** Malware often has the same privileges as the active user. Non-administrator accounts are usually blocked from accessing the most sensitive parts of a computer or network system. Therefore:
    - Avoid using administrative privileges to browse the web or check email;

  - Log in as an administrator only to perform administrative tasks;
  - Install software using administrator credentials only after it has been validated that the software is legitimate and secure.

- **Keep software updated:** No software package is completely safe against malware. However, software vendors regularly provide patches and updates to close whatever new vulnerabilities show up. As a best practice, validate and install all new software patches:
  - Regularly update operating systems, software tools, browsers and plugins;
  - Implement routine maintenance to ensure all software is current and check for signs of malware in log reports.
- **Control access to systems:** There are multiple ways to regulate the networks to protect against data breaches:
  - Install or implement a firewall, Intrusion Detection System (IDS) and Intrusion Prevention System (IPS).
  - Never use unfamiliar remote drives or media that was used on a publicly accessible device;
  - Close unused ports and disable unused protocols;
  - Remove inactive user accounts;
  - Carefully read all licensing agreements before installing software.
- **Adhere to the least-privilege model:** Adopt and enforce the principle of least-privilege; Grant users in the organization the minimum access to system capabilities, services and data they need to complete their work.
- **Limit Application Privileges:** A hacker only needs an open door to infiltrate the business. Limit the number of possible entryways by restricting application privileges on the devices. Allow only the application features and functions that are absolutely necessary to get work done.
- **Implement email security and spam protection:** Email is an essential business communication tool, but it's also a common malware channel. To reduce the risk of infection:

  - Scan all incoming email messages, including attachments, for malware;
  - Set spam filters to reduce unwanted emails;
  - Limit user access to only organization-approved links, messages and email addresses.
- **Monitor for suspicious activity:** Monitor all user accounts for suspicious activity. This includes:
  - Logging all incoming and outgoing traffic;
  - Baselining normal user activity and proactively looking for aberrations;
  - Investigating unusual actions promptly.
- **Educate your users:** At the end of the day, people are the best line of defense. By continually educating users, organization can help reduce the risk that they will be tricked by phishing or other tactics and accidentally introduce malware into the network. In particular:
  - Build awareness of common malware attacks;
  - Keep users up to date on basic cybersecurity trends and best practices;
  - Teach users how to recognize credible sites and what to do if they stumble onto a suspicious one;
  - Encourage users to report unusual system behavior;
  - Advise users to only join secure networks and to use VPNs when working outside the office.

A.8.8 Management of Technical Vulnerabilities

A vulnerability is defined in the ISO 27002 standard as "A weakness of an asset or group of assets that can be exploited by one or more threats". Vulnerability management is the process in which vulnerabilities in IT are identified and the risks of these vulnerabilities are evaluated. This evaluation leads to correcting the vulnerabilities and removing the risk or a formal risk acceptance by the management of an organization. The term vulnerability management is often confused with vulnerability scanning. Despite the fact both are related, there is an important difference between the two. Vulnerability scanning consists of using a computer program to identify vulnerabilities in networks, computer infrastructure or applications.

Vulnerability management is the process surrounding vulnerability scanning, also taking into account other aspects such as risk acceptance, remediation, etc. Depending on the size and structure of the organization, the approach to vulnerability scanning might differ. Small organizations that have a good understanding of IT resources throughout the enterprise might centralize vulnerability scanning. Larger organizations are more likely to have some degree of decentralization, so vulnerability scanning might be the responsibility of individual units. Some organizations might have a blend of both centralized and decentralized vulnerability assessment. Regardless, before starting a vulnerability scanning program, it is important to have the authority to conduct the scans and to understand the targets that will be scanned. Vulnerability scanning tools and methods are often somewhat tailored to varied types of information resources and vulnerability classes. The table below shows several important vulnerability classes and some relevant tools.

Common Types of Technical Vulnerabilities	**Relevant Assessment Tools**
Application Vulnerabilities	• Web Application Scanners (static and dynamic), • Web Application Firewalls

Network Layer Vulnerabilities	• Network Vulnerability Scanners, • Port Scanners, • Traffic Profilers
Host/System Layer Vulnerabilities	• Authenticated Vulnerability Scans, • Asset and Patch Management Tools, • Host Assessment and Scoring Tools

Information systems should be regularly reviewed for compliance with the organization's information security policies and standards. Automated tools are normally used to check systems and networks for technical compliance and these should be identified and implemented as appropriate. Where tools such as these are used, it is necessary to restrict their use to a few authorized personnel as possible and to carefully control and coordinate when they are used to prevent compromise of system availability and integrity.

A.8.8 Management of Technical Vulnerabilities – A linkage with Ancient Era

Lord Hanuman's Leap and Penetration Testing

Lord Hanuman's remarkable leap across the ocean to reach Lanka is a significant feat in the Ramayana. This can be associated with penetration testing in cybersecurity. Penetration testing, also known as ethical hacking, involves simulating real-world cyberattacks to identify vulnerabilities in systems or networks. Lord Hanuman's leap signifies the need for skilled professionals who possess the ability to explore and assess systems' security weaknesses, helping organizations strengthen their defenses against potential cyberattacks.

Control

Information about technical vulnerabilities of information systems in use should be obtained, the organization's exposure to such vulnerabilities should be evaluated and appropriate measures should be taken.

Purpose

To prevent exploitation of technical vulnerabilities.

Guidance

Identifying Technical Vulnerabilities

The organization should have an accurate inventory of assets as a prerequisite for effective technical vulnerability management; the inventory should include the software vendor, software name, version numbers, current state of deployment and the person within the organization responsible for the software. To identify technical vulnerabilities, the organization should consider:

- Defining and establishing the roles and responsibilities associated with technical vulnerability management, including vulnerability monitoring, vulnerability risk assessment, updating, asset tracking and any coordination responsibilities required;
- For software and other technologies, identifying information resources that will be used for identifying relevant technical vulnerabilities and maintaining awareness about them. Updating the list of information resources based on changes in the inventory or when other new or useful resources are found;
- Requiring suppliers of information system to ensure vulnerability reporting, handling and disclosure, including the requirements in applicable contracts;
- Using vulnerability scanning tools suitable for the technologies in use to identify vulnerabilities and to verify whether the patching of vulnerabilities was successful;
- Conducting planned, documented and repeatable penetration tests or vulnerability assessments by competent and authorized persons to support the identification of vulnerabilities. Exercising caution as such activities can lead to a compromise of the security of the system;
- Tracking the usage of third-party libraries and source code for vulnerabilities. This should be included in secure coding.

The organization should develop procedures and capabilities to:

- Detect the existence of vulnerabilities in its products and services including any external component used in these;
- Receive vulnerability reports from internal or external sources.

The organization should provide a public point of contact as part of a topic-specific policy on vulnerability disclosure so that researchers and others are able to report issues. The organization should establish vulnerability reporting procedures, online reporting forms and making use of appropriate threat intelligence or information sharing forums. The organization should also consider bug bounty programs where rewards are offered as an incentive to assist organizations in identifying vulnerabilities in order to appropriately remediate them. The organization should also share information with competent industry bodies or other interested parties.

Evaluating Technical Vulnerabilities

To evaluate identified technical vulnerabilities, the following guidance should be considered:

- Analyze and verify reports to determine what response and remediation activity is needed;
- Once a potential technical vulnerability has been identified, identifying the associated risks and the actions to be taken. Such actions can involve updating vulnerable systems or applying other controls.

Taking appropriate measures to address technical vulnerabilities

A software update management process should be implemented to ensure the most up-to-date approved patches and application updates are installed for all authorized software. If changes are necessary, the original software should be retained and the changes applied to a designated copy. All changes should be fully tested and documented, so that they can be reapplied, if necessary, to future software upgrades.

If required, the modifications should be tested and validated by an independent evaluation body. The following guidance should be considered to address technical vulnerabilities:

- Taking appropriate and timely action in response to the identification of potential technical vulnerabilities; defining a timeline to react to notifications of potentially relevant technical vulnerabilities;

- Depending on how urgently a technical vulnerability needs to be addressed, carrying out the action according to the controls related to change management or by following information security incident response procedures;
- Only using updates from legitimate sources;
- Testing and evaluating updates before they are installed to ensure they are effective and do not result in side effects that cannot be tolerated;
- Addressing systems at high risk first;
- Develop remediation, typically software updates or patches;
- Test to confirm if the remediation or mitigation is effective;
- Provide mechanisms to verify the authenticity of remediation;
- If no update is available or the update cannot be installed, considering other controls, such as:
    - Applying any workaround suggested by the software vendor or other relevant sources;
    - Turning off services or capabilities related to the vulnerability;
    - Adapting or adding access controls at network borders;
    - Shielding vulnerable systems, devices or applications from attack through deployment of suitable traffic filters;
    - Increasing monitoring to detect actual attacks;
    - Raising awareness of the vulnerability.

For acquired software, if the vendors regularly release information about security updates for their software and provide a facility to install such updates automatically, the organization should decide whether to use the automatic update or not.

Other Considerations

An audit log should be kept for all steps undertaken in technical vulnerability management. The technical vulnerability management process should be regularly monitored and evaluated in order to ensure its effectiveness and efficiency. An effective technical vulnerability management process should be aligned with incident management activities, to communicate data on vulnerabilities to the incident response function and provide technical procedures to be carried out in case an incident occurs. Where the organization uses a cloud service supplied by a third-party cloud service provider, technical vulnerability management of cloud service provider resources should be ensured by the cloud service provider. The cloud service provider's responsibilities for technical vulnerability management should be part of the cloud service agreement and this should include processes for reporting the cloud service provider's actions relating to technical vulnerabilities. For some cloud services, there are respective responsibilities for the cloud service provider and the cloud service customer. For example, the cloud service customer is responsible for vulnerability management of its own assets used for the cloud services.

Other Information

Technical vulnerability management can be viewed as a sub-function of change management and as such can take advantage of the change management processes and procedures. There is a possibility that an update does not address the problem adequately and has negative side effects. Also, in some cases, uninstalling an update cannot be easily achieved once the update has been applied. If adequate testing of the updates is not possible a delay in updating can be considered to evaluate the associated risks, based on the experience reported by other users. Where software patches or updates are produced, the organization can consider providing an automated update process where these updates are installed on affected systems or products without the need for intervention by the customer or the user. If an automated update process is offered, it can allow the customer or user to choose an option to turn off the automatic update or control the timing of the installation of the update. Where the vendor provides an automated update process and the updates can be installed on affected systems or products without the need for intervention, the organization determines if it applies the automated process or not.

One reason for not electing for automated update is to retain control over when the update is performed. For example, a software used for a business operation cannot be updated until the operation has completed.

A weakness with vulnerability scanning is that it is possible it does not fully account for defense in depth: two countermeasures that are always invoked in sequence can have vulnerabilities that are masked by strengths in the other. The composite countermeasure is not vulnerable, whereas a vulnerability scanner can report that both components are vulnerable. The organization should therefore take care in reviewing and acting on vulnerability reports. Many organizations supply software, systems, products and services not only within the organization but also to interested parties such as customers, partners or other users. These software, systems, products and services can have information security vulnerabilities that affect the security of users. Organizations can release remediation and disclose information about vulnerabilities to users and provide appropriate information for software vulnerability database services.

Prior to implementing and vulnerability controls, it's essential to obtain a complete and up-to-date list of physical and digital assets that are owned and operated by the organization. Software asset information should include, but not limited to:

- Vendor name;
- Application name;
- Version numbers currently in operation;
- Where the software is deployed.

When attempting to pinpoint technical vulnerabilities, organizations should:

- Clearly outline who (within the organization) is responsible for vulnerability management from a technical perspective, in accordance with its various functions, including (but not limited to):
    - Asset Management;
    - Risk Assessment;
    - Monitoring;
    - Updating.
- Who is responsible for the software within the organization?

- Maintain an inventory of applications and resources that will be used to identify technical vulnerabilities;
- Ask suppliers and vendors to disclose vulnerabilities upon the supply of new systems and hardware, and specify as such in all relevant contracts and service agreements;
- Make use of vulnerability scanning tools, including patching facilities;
- Carry out regular, documented penetration tests, either internally or via a certified third-party;
- Be mindful of the use of third-party code libraries and/or source code for underlying programmatic vulnerabilities.

In addition to internal systems, organizations should develop policies and procedures that detect vulnerabilities across all its products and services, and receive vulnerability assessments relating to the supply of said products and services. Organizations are to make a public effort to track down any vulnerabilities, and encourage third-parties to engage in vulnerability management efforts through the use of bounty programs. Organizations should make themselves available to the general public through forums, public email addresses and research activity so that the collective knowledge of the wider public can be used to safeguard products and services at source. Where remedial action has been taken that affects users or customers, organizations should consider releasing relevant information to the affected individuals or organizations, and engage with specialist security organizations to disseminate information about vulnerabilities and attack vectors. In addition, organizations should consider offering an automatic update procedure that customers are able to opt in or out of, based on their business needs. Adequate reporting is key to ensuring swift and effective remedial action when vulnerabilities are discovered. When evaluating vulnerabilities, organizations should:

- Carefully analyze any reports and decide what action needs to be taken, including (but not limited to) the amendment, updating or removal of affected systems and/or hardware.
- Agree upon a resolution that takes into account other ISO controls (particularly those related to ISO 27002:2022) and acknowledges the level of risks involved.

Software vulnerabilities are best combated with a proactive approach to software updates and patch management. Prior to any amendments being implemented, organizations should ensure that incumbent software versions are retained, all changes are fully tested and applied to a designated copy of the software. When directly addressing vulnerabilities after they have been identified, organizations should:

1. Seek to resolve all vulnerabilities in a timely and efficient manner;
2. Where possible, follow the organizational procedures on change management and incident response;
3. Only apply updates and patches that emanate from trusted and/ or certified sources, particularly in the vase of third-party vendor software and equipment;
4. Where vendor software is concerned, organizations should make a judgement call based on the information available as to whether it is necessary to apply automatic updates to acquired software and hardware;
5. Test any updates that are required prior to installation, to avoid any unforeseen incidents in an operational environment;
6. Seek to address high risk and business-critical systems as a priority;
7. Ensure that any remedial actions are effective and authentic.

In the event of an update not being available, or any issues that prevent an update being installed, organizations should consider other measures, such as:

1. Asking the vendor for advice on a workaround or "sticking plaster" solution whilst remedial efforts are ramped up;
2. Disabling or stopping any network services that are affected by the vulnerability;
3. Implementing network security controls at critical gateway points, including traffic rules and filters;
4. Increasing the overall level of monitoring in line with the associated risk;
5. Ensure that all affected parties are aware of the vulnerability, including suppliers and customers;

6. Delaying the update to better evaluate the associated risks, especially where operational cost may be an issue.

Organizations should keep an audit log of all relevant vulnerability management activities, in order to aid remedial efforts and improve procedures in the event of a security incident. The entire vulnerability management process should be periodically reviewed and evaluated, in order to improve performance and identify more vulnerabilities at source. If the organization used software hosted by a cloud service provider, the organization should ensure that the service provider's stance towards vulnerability management is aligned with its own, and should form a key part of any binding service agreement between the two parties, including any reporting procedures.

Steps in the Vulnerability Management Life cycle

- **Asset Discovery:** First, you must create or maintain asset directory. In this step, you take inventory of the organization's assets, including software, hardware, operating systems, and services, taking note of the current versions and applied patches. Establish a baseline of identified vulnerabilities to serve as a reference when detecting new vulnerabilities. Periodically revisit the inventory and update it when new assets is added.
- **Prioritization:** Classify assets based on their risk level and importance to business operations. Assign business values to every asset class to determine which assets should be first for vulnerability assessment. Core business software and hardware should be the priority.
- **Vulnerability Assessment:** Once baseline risk profiles has been established and determined the priority level of the assets, arrange them according to the degree of exposure to specific vulnerabilities. The vulnerability assessment should consider each asset's classification, criticality, and vulnerabilities. Research publicly available vulnerability lists and risk rankings to identify the exposure level of each asset to specific vulnerabilities.
- **Reporting:** Build an asset security strategy based on the identified risks and priority levels. Document the required remediation steps for each known vulnerability and continuously monitor suspicious behavior to lower the system's overall risk.

- **Remediation:** Implement the security strategy to remediate the prioritized vulnerabilities, addressing high-risk and critical assets first. This step typically involves updating software and hardware, applying vulnerability patches, modifying security configurations, and identifying vulnerable areas to protect critical assets and infrastructure. The organization might have to deactivate specific user accounts, provide additional security awareness training, or introduce new technologies to handle certain tasks that the IT team used to perform manually.
- **Evaluation and Verification:** The final step in the vulnerability management life cycle involves evaluating security strategy and verifying that the security measures have successfully reduced or eliminated the prioritized threats. This process will likely include several steps and should be a continuous effort with regular scans and assessments to ensure that vulnerability management policies are effective.

Vulnerability Assessment:

Vulnerability management and vulnerability assessment help address and resolve security vulnerabilities. Vulnerability assessment offers visibility into the current state of the situation, while vulnerability management provides continuous, real-time intelligence, reporting, and remediation guidance. A vulnerability assessment is typically the first step in a vulnerability management process. It involves using scanners to gather information from devices and systems on the corporate network and comparing the information to known vulnerabilities disclosed by software vendors. The organization's IT staff runs scans at regular intervals and schedules upgrades and patching. Vulnerability management is a continuous process rather than a scheduled process performed ad-hoc. It involves running an ongoing program that cycles through vulnerability assessments, prioritization, and remediation. The process employs multiple data sources to continually assess the situation and reassess the existing state of services and software. Vulnerability assessments aim to discover vulnerabilities as quickly as possible and are more effective for detecting known vulnerabilities, penetration tests provide an in-depth assessment to identify unknown vulnerabilities. Vulnerability assessment typically involves automated, repeatable scans, which are useful for evaluating remediation attempts. Vulnerability assessments identify outdated applications or operating systems and device configuration issues. They are best suited to detecting common vulnerabilities and exposures, or CVEs, listed on public databases. Vulnerability assessments involve automated tools that scan the network for known CVEs. There are many vulnerability scanning tools ranging from open source to commercial solutions. When choosing a tool, organizations should consider various factors, including the infrastructure to be tested and configuration and support options. Vulnerability management tools scan corporate networks for vulnerabilities that potential intruders could exploit. If the scan finds weaknesses, the software suggests or initiates corrective action. In this way, vulnerability management software reduces the likelihood of a cyber-attack. The most important features an organization should expect from a vulnerability assessment tool are:

1. **Quality and Speed:** Vulnerability scanning can take a long time in large networks, and can result in false positives. Test a prospective tool on organization network, see how long it takes to run, and compare selected findings with a manual assessment of vulnerabilities.
2. **User Experience**: The product should be easy to navigate and use, and vulnerability reports should be easy to understand by all relevant stakeholders.
3. **Compatibility**: The product's signature database should support all major operating systems, applications, and infrastructure components used by the organization.
4. **Cloud Support**: Most organizations are running workloads in the cloud, and the tool should be able to detect vulnerabilities in IaaS, PaaS and SaaS environments.
5. **Compliance**: The product must support all relevant compliance standards applicable to the organization, and should provide reports in the format required by auditors.
6. **Prioritization**: The product should offer both manual review of vulnerabilities and automated prioritization.
7. **Remediation Instructions**: The tool must provide actionable remediation instructions that can be easily followed by IT staff and developers.

Best Practices for an effective Vulnerability Management Program

- **Account for all IT Assets and Networks:** All organizations have hardware or software that are not in common use, or were deployed without the knowledge of IT staff. They may seem harmless, but these outdated programs and systems are often the most vulnerable parts of the security infrastructure, just waiting to be exploited by potential attackers. This makes it critical to perform a comprehensive inventory of all hardware and software in the organization, and scanning all assets for vulnerabilities.
- **Establish a Vulnerability Management Policy:** The purpose of a vulnerability management policy is to define rules for reviewing and evaluating vulnerabilities, applying system updates to mitigate them, and validating that the risk is no longer present. Vulnerability management policies typically cover network infrastructure, but policy scope can vary by organization size, type, and industry. They can extend to vulnerabilities affecting servers, operating systems, cloud environments, database servers, and more.
- **Use High Quality Threat Intelligence Feeds:** High quality data about threats can be a game changer in keeping your network secure. It allows IT and security teams to stay one step ahead of attackers, by being aware of the latest attack patterns and known vulnerabilities. Threat intelligence feeds can uncover newly discovered vulnerabilities and exploits. These feeds are maintained by experts who track potential threats. Continuous access to updated information is critical for augmenting automated vulnerability scanners.
- **Perform Regular Penetration Testing:** Penetration testing is conducted by ethical hackers working on behalf of an organization, and aims to identify exploitable vulnerabilities in networks or computing systems. It helps businesses find and fix high priority vulnerabilities that attackers can actually exploit.
- **Penetration testing** can help protect the network from external attacks, and also provides unbiased and expert insight into weaknesses in security infrastructure. When combined with other threat management processes, such as vulnerability assessments, regular penetration testing is a highly effective way to identify and remediate vulnerabilities.

Common Challenges

- **Scanning Can Cause Disruptions:** IT operations teams are quite reasonably very sensitive about how vulnerability scans are conducted and keen to understand any potential for operational disruptions. Often legacy systems and older equipment can have issues even with simple network port scans. To help with this issue, it can often be useful to build confidence in the scanning process by partnering with these teams to conduct risk evaluations before initiating or expanding a scanning program. It is also often important to discuss the "scan windows" when these vulnerability assessments will occur to ensure that they do not conflict with regular maintenance schedules.
- **Drowning in Vulnerability Data and False Positives:** Technical vulnerability management practices can produce very large data-sets. It is important to realize that just because a tool indicates that a vulnerability is present that there are frequently follow-up evaluations needed to validate these findings. Reviewing all of these vulnerabilities is usually infeasible for many teams. For this reason, it is very important to develop a vulnerability prioritization plan before initiating a large number of scans. These priority plans should be risk-driven to ensure that teams are spending their time dealing with the most important vulnerabilities in terms of both likelihoods of exploitation and impact.

A.8.9 Configuration Management

Configuration Management is the process of maintaining systems, such as computer hardware and software, in a desired state. Configuration Management is also a method of ensuring that systems perform in a manner consistent with expectations over time a governance and systems engineering process used to track and control IT resources and services across an enterprise. Configuration Management helps prevent undocumented changes from working their way into the environment. By doing so, Configuration Management can help prevent performance issues, system inconsistencies, or compliance issues that can lead to regulatory fines and penalties. Over time, these undocumented changes can lead to system downtime, instability, or failure. When properly implemented, configuration management ensures that an organization knows how its technology assets are configured and how those items relate to one another. Configuration Management ensure hardware, software, services, and networks function correctly with required security settings, and configuration is not altered by unauthorized or incorrect changes. The control is regarding configurations, including security configurations, of hardware, software, services and networks should be established, documented, implemented, monitored and reviewed. The organization should define and implement processes and tools to enforce the defined configurations for hardware, software, services and networks, for newly installed systems as well as for operational systems over their lifetime. Roles, responsibilities, and procedures should be in place to ensure satisfactory control of all configuration changes.

Utilizing a Configuration Management system helps avoid problems that occur when hardware and software systems are improperly configured. Simply tracking changes can help avoid expensive remediation projects down the road. Configuration Management is insurance you pay for today so you can prevent issues tomorrow. For example, Configuration Management helps ensure the development, test, and production environments are the same, so that deployed applications will behave in the manner that is expected of them. When problems do occur, Configuration Management can re-create the environment where an error occurred, or can replicate an environment to ease scaling and migration of workloads either on-premises or between clouds. Configuration Management tools use scripting to automate these administrative tasks, and enable rapid provisioning of servers, VMs and containers to the desired state in minutes, rather than days or weeks. A Configuration Management system allows the enterprise to define settings in a consistent manner, then to build and maintain them according to the established baselines. A configuration management plan should include a number of tools that:

1. Enable classification and management of systems in groups;
2. Make centralized modifications to baseline configurations;
3. Push changes automatically to all affected systems to automate updates and patching;
4. Identify problem configurations that are underperforming or non-compliant;
5. Automate prioritization of actions needed to remediate issues;
6. Apply remediation when needed.

The Configuration Management process begins with gathering information including configuration data from each application and the network topology. Secrets such as encryption keys and passwords should be identified so, they can be encrypted and stored safely. Once collected, configuration data should be loaded into files that become the central repository of the desired state, the single version of the truth. Once data has been collected the organization can establish a baseline configuration, which should be a known good configuration that can perform its intended operations without bugs or errors. Typically, this baseline is established by noting the configuration of the working production environment and storing those configuration settings as the baseline. When the baseline has been established, the organization should adopt a version control system. Many organizations utilize Git to create a repository of configuration data for this purpose. Auditing and accounting help to ensure that any changes that are applied to the configuration are reviewed by stakeholders and accepted, ensuring accountability and visibility into configuration changes.

A.8.9 Configuration Management – A linkage with Ancient Era

Lord Ram's Exile from Ayodhya

- **Adaptation to New Configurations:** Lord Ram's exile from Ayodhya represents a significant change in the configuration of power and resources within the kingdom. Despite being stripped of His princely status and exiled to the forest, Lord Ram demonstrates adaptability and resilience, adjusting to the new configuration of His life and responsibilities.

- **Resource Allocation and Planning:** During His exile, Lord Ram effectively manages resources such as manpower, knowledge, and alliances to navigate the challenges He faces. This can be linked to configuration management, where resources are allocated and plans are formulated to address evolving circumstances and achieve specific objectives.
- **Strategic Alliances and Resource Integration:** Throughout His exile, Lord Ram forms strategic alliances with various characters, including Sugriv, Lord Hanuman, and the Vanar army. These alliances involve integrating diverse resources, capabilities, and perspectives to overcome obstacles and fulfill His destiny, highlighting the importance of resource integration in configuration management.
- **Management of Relationships and Communication:** During His exile, Lord Ram maintains strong relationships and communication with His allies, advisors, and loved ones. Effective communication and relationship management are crucial aspects of configuration management, ensuring alignment, collaboration, and coordination among stakeholders to achieve common goals.
- **Adherence to Principles and Governance:** Despite the challenges He faces during His exile, Lord Ram adheres steadfastly to His principles of righteousness and governance. This commitment to moral and ethical values provides a guiding framework for decision-making and resource management, ensuring alignment with the broader objectives of His journey.
- **Preparation for Return and Restoration:** Throughout His exile, Lord Ram prepares diligently for His eventual return to Ayodhya and the restoration of order and justice in the kingdom. This involves careful planning, organization, and coordination of resources to reclaim His rightful place as king, underscoring the importance of strategic preparation and configuration management in achieving successful outcomes.

Control

Configurations, including security configurations, of hardware, software, services and networks should be established, documented, implemented, monitored and reviewed.

Purpose

To ensure hardware, software, services and networks function correctly with required security settings, and configuration is not altered by unauthorized or incorrect changes.

Guidance

General

The organization should define and implement processes and tools to enforce the defined configurations for hardware, software, services and networks, for newly installed systems as well as for operational systems over their lifetime. Roles, responsibilities and procedures should be in place to ensure satisfactory control of all configuration changes.

Standard Templates

Standard templates for the secure configuration of hardware, software, services and networks should be defined:

- Using publicly available guidance;
- Considering the level of protection needed in order to determine a sufficient level of security;
- Supporting the organization's information security policy, topic-specific policies, standards and other security requirements;
- Considering the feasibility and applicability of security configurations in the organization's context.

The templates should be reviewed periodically and updated when new threats or vulnerabilities need to be addressed, or when new software or hardware versions are introduced. The following should be considered for establishing standard templates for the secure configuration of hardware, software, services and networks:

- Minimizing the number of identities with privileged or administrator level access rights;

- Disabling unnecessary, unused or insecure identities;
- Disabling or restricting unnecessary functions and services;
- Restricting access to powerful utility programs and host parameter settings;
- Synchronizing clocks;
- Changing vendor default authentication information immediately after installation and reviewing other important default security related parameters;
- Invoking time-out facilities that automatically log off computing devices after a predetermined period of inactivity;
- Verifying that license requirements have been met.

Managing Configurations

Established configurations of hardware, software, services and networks should be recorded and a log should be maintained of all configuration changes. These records should be securely stored. This can be achieved in various ways, such as configuration databases or configuration templates. Changes to configurations should follow the change management process. Configuration records can contain as relevant:

- Up-to-date owner or point of contact information for the asset;
- Date of the last change of configuration;
- Version of configuration template;
- Relation to configurations of other assets.

Monitoring Configurations

Configurations should be monitored with a comprehensive set of system management tools and should be reviewed on a regular basis to verify configuration settings, evaluate password strengths and assess activities performed. Actual configurations can be compared with the defined target templates. Any deviations should be addressed, either by automatic enforcement of the defined target configuration or by manual analysis of the deviation followed by corrective actions.

Other Information

Documentation for systems often records details about the configuration of both hardware and software. System hardening is a typical part of configuration management. Configuration management can be integrated with asset management processes and associated tooling. Automation is usually more effective to manage security configuration. Configuration templates and targets can be confidential information and should be protected from unauthorized access accordingly.

Configurations, whether acting as a single config file, or a group of configurations linked together, are the underlying parameters that govern how hardware, software and even entire networks are managed. Configuration Management is an integral part of an organization's broader asset management operation. Configurations are key in ensuring that a network is not only operating as it should be, but also in securing devices against unauthorized changes or incorrect amendments on the part of maintenance staff and/or vendors. Established configurations of hardware, software, services, and networks should be recorded, and a log should be maintained of all configuration changes. These records should be securely stored. This can be achieved in various ways, such as through configuration databases or configuration templates. Configurations should be monitored with a comprehensive set of system management tools and should be reviewed on a regular basis to verify configuration settings, evaluate password strengths, and assess activities performed. This control maintains risk by establishing a series of policies that govern how an organization documents, implements, monitors and reviews the use of configurations across its entire network.

On the whole, organization's need to draft and implement configuration management policies for both new systems and hardware, and any that are already in use. Internal controls should include business critical elements such as security configurations, all hardware that holds a configuration file and any relevant software applications or systems. Organizations to consider all relevant roles and responsibilities when implementing a configuration policy, including the delegated ownership of configurations on a device-by-device, or application-by-application basis. Where possible, organizations should use standardized templates to secure all hardware, software and systems. Security is paramount when applying configuration templates, or amending existing templates in line with the above guidance.

An organization has a responsibility to maintain and store configurations, including keeping an audit trail of any amendments or new installations, in line with a published change management process. Logs should contain information that outlines:

- Who owns the asset?
- A timestamp for the latest configuration change;
- The current version of the configuration template;
- Any relevant information that explains the assets relationship with configurations held on other devices or systems.

Organizations should deploy a wide range of techniques to monitor the operation of configuration files across their network, including:

- Automation;
- Specialized configuration maintenance programs;
- Remote support tools that auto-populate configuration information on a device-by-device basis;
- Enterprise device and software management utilities that are designed to monitor large amounts of configuration data at once;
- BUDR software that automatically backs up configurations to a secure location, and restores templates either remotely or onsite to compromised and/or malfunctioning devices.

Organizations should configure specialized software to track any changes in a device's configuration, and take appropriate action to address the amendment as soon as possible, either by validating the change or reverting the configuration back to its original state.

Whether intentional or unintentional, changes are commonplace in IT infrastructures. Managers deploy and install software updates, end users or administrators change configuration settings intentionally or unintentionally, managers introduce new applications and systems with vigor, etc. When such decisions are made in haste, security considerations are often "left out of the equation." As a result, implementations are made quickly and without regard to change/release processes in order to meet deadlines and schedules. Even if IT systems have defined settings during the initial installation, deviations occur over time. It is usually difficult to keep track of the changes that lead to a configuration deviation via standard measures such as the widely used group policies. As a result, a management tool that provides a comprehensive and transparent overview becomes necessary. This allows an IT department to effectively monitor the situation and also take appropriate action if necessary. The best way to deal with configuration deviations is to strictly organize configuration management. In addition to this organizational measure, it is also imperative to technically monitor the actual, implemented configuration. The combination of regular and effective monitoring at the technical and process levels helps to create comprehensive security awareness and to keep the IT infrastructure under control. Another plus point is that evidence for internal and external audits is generated almost as a side effect. The best way to detect and, in the best case, prevent configuration deviations of IT systems consists of a multi-stage process.

- **Identify:** The initial configuration must be clear. Often, compliance departments and/or information security officers know existing internal and external security requirements. Existing industry standards and vendor recommendations also help in the evaluation.
- **Evaluate, develop and adapt:** Are existing IT systems configured to meet the specifications of internal and external recommendations and requirements? What differences exist? Which systems deviate regularly, if necessary, from the specifications? On the basis of stringent reporting, it is possible to develop and also implement a standardized, proprietary/hardening configuration.
- **Control:** During the lifetime of IT systems, which can be several years, continuous, ideally automated, monitoring is necessary. This enables deviations in the configuration to be detected. Questions to be asked here could be the following:
    - Does monitoring of all IT systems take place after implementation?
    - Are configuration deviations visualized transparently so that a rapid response is possible?
    - Does "automated self-healing" take place under certain circumstances?

- **Establish processes:** If deviations are detected, appropriate measures must be taken as quickly as possible. While this usually works on demand in small companies, larger companies with a strong separation of responsibilities need established and tested processes! For example, these things need to be clarified:
    - How can a configuration deviation be detected?
    - How quickly is the configuration deviation corrected?
    - To which person or persons do you report the deviations?
    - What do the regular reports look like?

Configuration Management is not an end in itself, but an important IT measure. One that ensures that a stringent and standardized hardening of IT systems is performed and controlled. System hardening is known to configure operating systems, applications, cloud solutions and more to better protect them. Data espionage, ransomware attempts and other cyber-attacks can be averted in this way or, optimally, fizzle out because the typical attack surfaces have been reduced in size. In order to carry out a system hardening efficiently, a check is required first. This determines the status quo of the system hardening.

The configuration of an IT asset is a representation of the system's components, how each component is configured, and how the components are connected or arranged to implement the asset. A misconfiguration may affect the security posture of the asset and infrastructure. The activities involved in managing the configuration process include planning, identification, establishment of the baseline configuration, change control, configuration monitoring and reporting. IT asset custodians must inventory, document, monitor and manage IT assets for which they are responsible. For each asset, the susceptibility to risk or exploit and the required level of protection required to comply with policies and standards must be determined. IT asset documentation and risk assessment information shall be made available to the CISO upon request.

Configuration Management Requirements in Information Security

IT asset custodians must ensure that data is properly protected, and

IT assets are properly hardened, monitored, and managed from initial installation, through configuration, maintenance, and support, to end-of-life decommissioning according to Configuration Management controls.

- **Configuration Management Policy and Procedures:** The CISO is responsible for establishing Configuration Management policies and standards that apply to enterprise and distributed IT Assets. Information Security Manager is responsible for ensuring appropriate configuration management within the organization to ensure the infrastructure is secure and resilient.
- **Configuration Management Plan:** Each IT asset custodian must develop, document, and implement a Configuration Management Plan for IT Assets that:
    - Addresses Configuration Management roles, responsibilities, standards, processes, and procedures.
    - Establishes a process for identifying configuration items throughout the System Development Life Cycle (SDLC), and ensures they align with established policies, standards, processes, and procedures.
    - Protects the Configuration Management Plan from unauthorized disclosure and modification.
- **IT Asset Inventory:** IT asset owners are responsible for establishing and maintaining an accurate, detailed, and up-to-date inventory of all IT assets and asset components connected to the infrastructure. This includes relevant hardware/software/system specific component information such as unit, IT asset owners, location, manufacturer, device type, model, serial number, version number, machine name, hardware address and specifications, software license information, software version numbers, etc. IT asset owners must maintain an inventory of IT assets and IT asset components:
    - Develop and document an inventory of IT asset components that:
        - Accurately reflects the current IT assets for which the IT asset owner is responsible;
        - Includes information necessary to achieve effective

infrastructure component accountability and proper management;

  - Is at the level of granularity deemed necessary for tracking and reporting.

- Review and update the component inventory as an integral part of installation, removal, and updates.
- Ensure that only currently supported and authorized IT assets are connected to the infrastructure unless an exception is approved according to the Request for Exception to IT Policy.
- Employ mechanisms to detect the presence of unauthorized hardware, software, and firmware. The IT asset owners must take action when unauthorized components are detected, such as disabling network access for such components, isolating the components, or notifying authorized points of contact.

- **Baseline Configurations:** Baselines are documented, formally reviewed and agreed-upon sets of specifications that ensure that IT Assets are properly configured and hardened to reduce vulnerabilities. Hardening includes removing superfluous programs, account functions, applications, ports, permissions, access, or other configuration changes to reduce attackers' ability to gain unauthorized access to the IT environment. Types of hardening activities include application hardening, operating system hardening, server hardening, database hardening and network hardening. Baseline configurations may also be used to create master configuration images, with required configuration settings already in place. Baseline configurations serve as a basis for future builds, releases, and changes to organization systems, system components, and networks. IT asset owners are responsible for selecting and tailoring appropriate security control baselines for all IT assets, based on the criticality and sensitivity of the information to be processed, stored, or transmitted by the system. Baseline configurations must be updated as needed to ensure system upgrades, patches or other significant changes are addressed according to compliance requirements identified by the IT Vulnerability Management Standard. Existing baseline configurations must be reviewed at least annually to ensure they are still applicable.

- **Configuration Change Control:** Configuration change control is the documented process for managing and controlling changes to the configuration of a system. Configuration change control includes, but is not limited to:
  - Changes to Baseline configurations for components and configuration items of IT assets;
  - Changes to configuration settings for information technology products;
  - Unscheduled/unauthorized changes;
  - Changes to remediate vulnerabilities.

  IT asset owners must ensure proper configuration change control:
  - Determine the types of changes to an information system or IT asset that impact configuration.
  - Review proposed configuration changes and approve or disapprove with explicit consideration for security impact analysis and document change decisions.
  - Properly test, validate, and document planned changes prior to implementation of approved changes.
  - Coordinate and provide oversight for change control activities through a change control entity that convenes regularly.
  - Retain previous configurations and records of changes for the life of the system or IT Asset to support audit, incident response and historical information.
  - Audit and review activities associated with configuration changes to the information system or IT Asset, including audit logs and rollback procedures.
- **Security Impact Analysis:** Each IT asset owners must analyze planned changes to an information system or IT asset to determine potential security impact prior to change implementation. Security impact analysis may include reviewing security plans to understand security control requirements and reviewing system design documentation to understand control implementation and how specific changes might affect the controls. Security impact analysis may also include

assessments of risk to better understand the impact of the changes and to determine if additional security controls are required. Analysis are scaled in accordance with the security requirements of the IT Asset. IT asset owners must ensure proper testing of configuration changes. Whenever possible, changes should be tested in a separate environment which is physically or logically isolated from the operational environment. After implementation, implemented changes must be verified to ensure that functions are implemented correctly, operating as intended, and producing the desired outcome to meet the security requirements of the system.

- **Access Restrictions for Change:** IT asset owners must define, document, approve, and enforce physical and logical access restrictions associated with changes to an information system or IT Asset. Only qualified and authorized individuals are provided access to information system components for purposes of initiating changes, including upgrades and modifications. Audit trails or change logs must be maintained to ensure that configuration change control is being implemented as intended and to support periodic audits.
- **Configuration Settings:** Configuration settings are the set of parameters that can be changed in hardware, software, or firmware components of the information system that affect the security posture and/or functionality of the system. Information technology products for which security-related configuration settings can be defined include mainframe computers, servers, workstations, input/output devices, network components, operating systems, middleware, and applications. Security-related parameters include registry settings; account, file, and directory permission settings; and settings for functions, ports, protocols, services, and remote connections. Organizations establish organization-wide configuration settings and subsequently derive specific settings for IT Assets. The established settings become part of the configuration baseline. Each IT Asset Custodian must maintain appropriate configuration settings:
    - Establish, document, and implement configuration settings for information technology products employed within the information system, that reflect the most restrictive mode consistent with operational requirements.

- Identify, document, and approve any deviations from established configuration settings.
- Monitor and control changes to configuration settings in accordance with policies.

- **Least Functionality:** The principle of least functionality provides that information systems and IT assets are configured to provide only essential capabilities and to prohibit or restrict the use of non-essential functions that are not integral to the operation of that asset. IT asset owners must ensure IT assets are configured to restrict access through least functionality:
  - Configure IT assets to provide only essential capabilities with respect to their relative security. At least annually, review the use of functions, ports, protocols, and services. Identify and disable or eliminate those deemed unnecessary, unused or detrimental to the system or business.
  - Identify and remove/disable unauthorized and/or non-secure functions, ports, protocols, services, and applications.
  - Limit component functionality to a single function per device, where feasible.
  - When a device with elevated security controls is used to access IT assets in locations deemed to be high risk, predefined security safeguards should be applied prior to joining it to the production network.

- **Software Usage Restrictions:** Each IT Asset Custodian must ensure proper management of software:
  - Use software in accordance with contractual agreements and copyright laws; and track the use of software protected for quantity licenses;
  - Strictly prohibit the use of peer-to-peer file sharing technology;
  - Establish, monitor, and enforce policies, standards and compliance governing the installation of software by end users;
  - Establish restrictions on the use of open-source software.

- **User-installed Software:** To maintain control over the types of software installed, IT asset owners must identify permitted and prohibited actions regarding software installation. Permitted software installations may include updates and security patches to existing software and downloading applications from organization-approved "App Stores." Prohibited software installations may include software with unknown or suspect pedigrees or software that organizations consider potentially malicious. User-installed software must require privileged status.
- **Incident Reporting:** It is the responsibility of each staff, contractor, or visitor to immediately report suspected or confirmed Information Security and Privacy Incidents to the Chief Information Security Officer (CISO).

A.8.10 Information Deletion

A fundamental principle of information security is that information that is not necessary for the business should not be kept. This principle is known as data minimization, and it is meant to protect against unnecessary and disproportionate harm in the event of a security breach. The most common method is to enact and enforce information retention and deletion policies across an organization This addresses deletion of information when no longer needed or when storage times exceed documented retention periods. The intent is to control the potential for leakage of sensitive data and to comply with any relevant privacy and other requirements.

Deletions could include data in IT systems, removable media, or cloud services. Information should be deleted when it is no longer needed for authorized purposes. The period of time that information remains necessary for authorized purposes, however, is not standardized across organizations, industries, or operations. Determining the appropriate time period requires an underlying knowledge of the information the organization has, how that is classified, how that information is used in the business, and any laws applicable to its retention.

The most common means of determining this time period is through the process of developing and documenting information retention policies and schedules. An information retention policy is a corporate policy that goes beyond statutory, legal requirements, and directs operations about which information the organization should retain, delete, or retain for a period and then delete. For information that is permitted under policy to be retained for a given period of time and then must be deleted, the retention period is generally documented in a retention schedule. Both the policy and the schedule should reflect the types of information the organization has, the laws applicable to its retention, and the risk position of the organization.

A.8.10 Information Deletion – A linkage with Ancient Era

The Kurukshetra War

- **Strategic Decisions and Information Management:** In the Kurukshetra War, strategic decisions played a crucial role in determining the outcome of battles. Similarly, in information deletion, strategic decisions about what data to remove or retain are significant. Just as Generals in the Mahabharata made calculated moves to gain an advantage, organizations must carefully manage information deletion to optimize storage space, maintain compliance, and protect sensitive data.

- **Erasures of History and Memory:** The Kurukshetra War involved erasures of history through the deaths of warriors, destruction of kingdoms, and the end of dynasties. Similarly, information deletion can lead to the loss of historical records, memories, and valuable insights. Both contexts highlight the potential consequences of erasing information, whether intentionally or inadvertently, and the impact it can have on collective knowledge and understanding.
- **Selective Retention and Preservation:** Just as certain characters and events in the Mahabharata were selectively retained in memory and literature, organizations must prioritize which data to retain and preserve. This includes critical information for legal, regulatory, or historical purposes, ensuring that valuable insights and lessons learned from past experiences are not lost through indiscriminate deletion.
- **Consequences of Information Deletion:** The consequences of information deletion in the Kurukshetra War were profound, leading to the loss of lives, the collapse of kingdoms, and the perpetuation of cycles of violence. Similarly, in modern contexts, the consequences of information deletion can include legal liabilities, data breaches, loss of trust, and damage to reputation. Organizations must weigh the potential risks and benefits of information deletion carefully to mitigate adverse outcomes.
- **Ethical Considerations:** The Mahabharata raises ethical dilemmas surrounding the use of violence and the consequences of war. Similarly, information deletion raises ethical considerations regarding privacy, transparency, and accountability. Organizations must consider the ethical implications of deleting information, ensuring that decisions align with principles of fairness, responsibility, and respect for individuals' rights.
- **Legacy and Collective Memory:** Despite the destruction and loss caused by the Kurukshetra War, the Mahabharata endures as a timeless epic, preserving the memory of its characters and events for future generations. Similarly, organizations must consider the

long-term implications of information deletion on their legacy and collective memory, recognizing the importance of preserving valuable insights and knowledge for posterity.

Control

Information stored in information systems, devices or in any other storage media should be deleted when no longer required.

Purpose

To prevent unnecessary exposure of sensitive information and to comply with legal, statutory, regulatory and contractual requirements for information deletion.

Guidance

General

Sensitive information should not be kept for longer than it is required to reduce the risk of undesirable disclosure. When deleting information on systems, applications and services, the following should be considered:

- Selecting a deletion method in accordance with business requirements and taking into consideration relevant laws and regulations;
- Recording the results of deletion as evidence;
- When using service suppliers of information deletion, obtaining evidence of information deletion from them.

Where third parties store the organization's information on its behalf, the organization should consider the inclusion of requirements on information deletion into the third-party agreements to enforce it during and upon termination of such services.

Deletion Methods

In accordance with the organization's topic-specific policy on data retention and taking into consideration relevant legislation and regulations, sensitive information should be deleted when no longer required, by:

- Configuring systems to securely destroy information when no longer required;

- Deleting obsolete versions, copies and temporary files wherever they are located;
- Using approved, secure deletion software to permanently delete information to help ensure information cannot be recovered by using specialist recovery or forensic tools;
- Using approved, certified providers of secure disposal services;
- Using disposal mechanisms appropriate for the type of storage media being disposed of.

Where cloud services are used, the organization should verify if the deletion method provided by the cloud service provider is acceptable, and if it is the case, the organization should use it, or request that the cloud service provider delete the information. These deletion processes should be automated in accordance with topic-specific policies, when available and applicable. Depending on the sensitivity of information deleted, logs can track or verify that these deletion processes have happened. To avoid the unintentional exposure of sensitive information when equipment is being sent back to vendors, sensitive information should be protected by removing auxiliary storage and memory before equipment leaves the organization's premises. Considering that the secure deletion of some devices can only be achieved through destruction or using the functions embedded in these devices, the organization should choose the appropriate method according to the classification of information handled by such devices. Control measures described in clause for Secure Disposal or Re-Use of Equipment should be applied to physically destroy the storage device and simultaneously delete the information it contains. An official record of information deletion is useful when analyzing the cause of a possible information leakage event.

There are a variety of methods for deleting data. These methods vary in effectiveness, from simply pressing the Delete button on a personal computer to manual destruction of the media on which the data is stored. The best method of data deletion can be determined based on the type and nature of the data and the risk associated with its exposure. As well as managing the ongoing use of data and information on internal servers and storage devices, organization's need to be acutely aware of their obligations towards removing and deleting any data held on employees, users, customers or organizations when it is reasonably necessary to do so. It can sometimes be difficult to ascertain when data should be deleted. As a general rule, organizations are to delete data when it is no longer required, in order to minimize what is referred to as undesirable disclosure, i.e., data being viewed by, or passed on to, individuals and organizations that are not authorized to access it. In accordance with this guideline, when the time comes to delete data, organization should follow the recommendations mentioned in the Guidance (General) section.

When formulating a deletion process, organization should follow the recommendation mentioned in the Deletion Methods under Guidance section.

When shipping equipment to vendors, organization should remove any internal or external storage devices before doing so. There should be full traceability and record keeping to evidence which information assets have been destroyed and how. For physical drives this may include recording the serial numbers of the hard drives, however it should be considered that serial numbers alone may not be enough to maintain a complete audit trail of the data. When using service suppliers for information deletion it is important to obtain evidence of information deletion from them, and conduct enough due diligence to be satisfied that the process has been completed effectively. An official record of information deletion is useful when analyzing the cause of a possible information leakage event.

Businesses must only keep personal data as long as necessary and only for the purposes they have specified. To manage this legal obligation successfully, organization'll need to start with an up-to-date data retention policy and schedule. These should clearly identify which types of personal data the business processes, for what purposes, how long each should typically be kept and under what circumstances organization might need to hold it for longer. These are the 5 key steps when an agreed retention period is reached.

1. Identify the relevant records which have reached their retention period;
2. Notify the relevant business owner to confirm they are no longer needed;

3. Consider any changes in circumstances which may require longer retention of the data;
4. Make a decision on what happens to the data;
5. Document the decision and keep evidence of the action.

There are different approaches an organization can take when the data retention period is reached, such as:

- Delete it – usually the default option;
- Anonymize it;
- Securely destroy it;

Deletion of records might seem the obvious choice, and it's often the best one too.

But take care how you delete data. Sometimes deleting whole records can affect key processes on your systems such as reporting, algorithms and other programs. There are software methods of deleting data, which may involve removing whole records from a dataset or overwriting them. For example, using of zeros and ones to overwrite the personal identifiers in the data. Once the personal identifiers are overwritten, that data will be rendered unrecoverable, and therefore it's no longer classed as personal data. This deletion process should include backup copies of data. Whilst personal data may be instantly deleted from live systems, personal data may still remain within the backup environment, until it is overwritten. If the backup data cannot be immediately overwritten it must be put 'beyond use', i.e., you must make sure the data is not used for any other purpose and is simply held on your systems until it's replaced, in line with an established schedule. Destruction is the final action for about 95% of most organizations' physical records. Physical destruction may include shredding, pulping or burning paper records. Destruction is likely to be the best course of action for physical records when the organization no longer needs to keep the data, and when it does not need to hold data in an anonymized format. Controllers are accountable for the way personal data is processed and consequently, the disposal decision should be documented in a disposal schedule. Many organizations use other organizations to manage their disposal or destruction of physical records. There are benefits of using third parties, such as reducing in-house storage costs. Remember, third parties providing this kind of service will be regarded as a data processor, therefore you'll need to make sure an appropriate contract is in place which includes the usual data protection clauses. Destruction may be carried out remotely following an agreed process. For instance, a processor might provide regular notifications of batches due to be destroyed in line with documented retention periods. Retention periods will also apply to unstructured data which contains personal identifiers. The most common being electronic communications records such as emails, instant messages, call recordings and so on. As you can imagine, unstructured data records present some real challenges. You'll need to be able to review the records to find any personal data stored there, so it can be deleted in line with the retention schedules, or for an erasure request. Depending on the size of your organization, you may need to use specialist software tools to perform content analysis of unstructured data.

A.8.11 Data Masking

Data Masking is a technique used to protect sensitive data, usually any data that could be deemed PII, over and above an organization standard information security protocols. Data masking, also known as data obfuscation, hides the actual data using modified content like character or numbers. The main objective of data masking is creating an alternate version of data that cannot be easily identifiable or reverse engineered, protecting data classified as sensitive. Importantly, the data will be consistent across multiple databases, and the usability will remain unchanged. It is a method of creating a structurally similar but inauthentic version of an organization's data that can be used for purposes such as software testing and user training. The purpose is to protect the actual data while having a functional substitute for occasions when the real data is not required. Data masking is often mentioned in legal, statutory and regulatory guidelines and laws governing the storage and access of employee, customer, user and vendor information. Data masking generally, applies to non-production environments, such as software development and testing, user training, etc., areas that do not need actual data.

Although most organizations have stringent security controls in place to protect production data in storage and in business use, sometimes that same data element has been used for operations that are less secure. The issue is often compounded if these operations are outsourced and the organization has less control over the environment. In the wake of compliance legislation, most organizations are no longer comfortable exposing real data unnecessarily. Data masking substitutes original values in a data set with randomized data using various data shuffling and manipulation techniques. The obfuscated data maintains the unique characteristics of the original data so that it yields the same results as the original data set. Data masking is a complex technical process that involves altering sensitive information, and preventing users from identifying data subjects through a variety of measures. Whilst this is itself an administrative task, the nature of data masking is directly related to an organisation's ability to remain compliant with laws, regulations and statutory guidelines concerning the storage, access and processing of data. As such, ownership should reside with the Chief Information Security Officer, or organizational equivalent.

A.8.11 Data Masking – A linkage with Ancient Era

Suparnakha

- **Concealing Identity:** In Data Masking, sensitive information is disguised or obfuscated to protect privacy and confidentiality. Similarly, Suparnakha, a character in the Ramayana, conceals her true identity as a demoness to interact with Lord Ram and His companions, disguising herself in various forms to deceive them.
- **Protecting Confidentiality:** Data Masking techniques such as substitution, shuffling, and encryption are employed to safeguard confidential data from unauthorized access or disclosure. Similarly, Suparnakha's deceptive behavior and disguises serve to protect her own interests and conceal her true intentions from others, maintaining a veil of secrecy around her actions.
- **Preventing Unintended Exposure:** Data Masking helps prevent unintended exposure of sensitive information to unauthorized individuals or entities. Similarly, Suparnakha's disguises and deceptive tactics prevent her true nature and intentions from being exposed to Rama and His allies, allowing her to manipulate situations to her advantage without arousing suspicion.
- **Maintaining Data Integrity:** While Data Masking obscures sensitive information, it preserves the integrity and usability of the underlying data for legitimate purposes. Similarly, Suparnakha's deceptive tactics and disguises do not fundamentally alter her identity or intentions but rather obscure them from others while allowing her to interact with them for her own ends.
- **Adaptability and Flexibility:** Data Masking techniques can be adapted to different data types and environments, ensuring consistent protection across various contexts. Similarly, Suparnakha demonstrates adaptability and flexibility in her deceptive schemes, altering her appearance and behavior as needed to achieve her goals and manipulate those around her.
- **Unmasking and Revelation:** Just as Data Masking can be reversed or overridden by authorized users with the appropriate permissions, Suparnakha's true identity and intentions are eventually revealed through the actions of Lord Ram and His companions. This unmasking

leads to consequences for Suparnakha, highlighting the risks of deception and manipulation when the truth is ultimately revealed.

Control

Data masking should be used in accordance with the organization's topic-specific policy on access control and other related topic-specific policies, and business requirements, taking applicable legislation into consideration.

Purpose

To limit the exposure of sensitive data including PII, and to comply with legal, statutory, regulatory and contractual requirements.

Guidance

Where the protection of sensitive data is a concern, the organization should consider hiding such data by using techniques such as data masking, pseudonymization or anonymization. Pseudonymization or anonymization techniques can hide PII, disguise the true identity of PII principals or other sensitive information, and disconnect the link between PII and the identity of the PII principal or the link between other sensitive information. When using pseudonymization or anonymization techniques, it should be verified that data has been adequately pseudonymized or anonymized. Data anonymization should consider all the elements of the sensitive information to be effective. As an example, if not considered properly, a person can be identified even if the data that can directly identify that person is anonymized, by the presence of further data which allows the person to be identified indirectly. Additional techniques for data masking include:

- Encryption;
- Nulling or Deleting Characters;
- Varying Numbers and Dates;
- Substitution;
- Replacing Values with their Hash.

The following should be considered when implementing data masking techniques:

- Not granting all users access to all data, therefore designing queries and masks in order to show only the minimum required data to the user;

- There are cases where some data should not be visible to the user for some records out of a set of data; in this case, designing and implementing a mechanism for obfuscation of data;
- When data are obfuscated, giving the PII principal the possibility to require that users cannot see if the data are obfuscated;
- Any legal or regulatory requirements.

The following should be considered when using data masking, pseudonymization or anonymization:

- Level of strength of data masking, pseudonymization or anonymization according to the usage of the processed data;
- Access controls to the processed data;
- Agreements or restrictions on usage of the processed data;
- Prohibiting collating the processed data with other information in order to identify the PII principal;
- Keeping track of providing and receiving the processed data.

Other Information

Anonymization irreversibly alters PII in such a way that the PII principal can no longer be identified directly or indirectly. Pseudonymization replaces the identifying information with an alias. Knowledge of the algorithm ("additional information") used to perform the pseudonymization allows for at least some form of identification of the PII principal. Such "additional information" should therefore be kept separate and protected. While pseudonymization is therefore weaker than anonymization, pseudonymized datasets can be more useful in statistical research. Data masking is a set of techniques to conceal, substitute or obfuscate sensitive data items. Data masking can be static, dynamic or on-the-fly. Hash functions can be used in order to anonymize PII. In order to prevent enumeration attacks, they should always be combined with a salt function. PII in resource identifiers and their attributes should be either avoided or appropriately anonymized. Additional controls concerning the protection of PII in public clouds are given in ISO/IEC 27018. Additional information on de-identification techniques is available in ISO/IEC 20889.

Data masking, which is also called data sanitization, keeps sensitive information private by making it unrecognizable but still usable. This lets developers, researchers and analysts use a data set without exposing the data to any risk. Data masking is different from encryption. Encrypted data can be decrypted and returned to its original state with the correct encryption key. With masked data, there is no algorithm to recover the original values. Masking generates a characteristically accurate but fictitious version of a data set that has zero value to hackers. It also cannot be reverse engineered, and statistical outputs cannot be used to identify individuals. Like data encryption, not every data field needs to be masked, although some fields must be completely hidden.

The organizations can consider data masking through the scope of two main techniques: pseudonymization and/or anonymization. Anonymization is the process of removing personal identifiers, both direct and indirect, that may lead to an individual being identified. An individual may be directly identified from their name, address, postcode, telephone number, photograph or image, or some other unique personal characteristic. An individual may be indirectly identifiable when certain information is linked together with other sources of information, including, their place of work, job title, salary, their postcode or even the fact that they have a particular diagnosis or condition. Once data is truly anonymized and individuals are no longer identifiable. Pseudonymization is the processing of personal data in such a way that the data can no longer be attributed to a specific data subject without the use of additional information, as long as such additional information is kept separately and subject to technical and organizational measures to ensure non-attribution to an identified or identifiable individual. Both of these methods are designed to disguise the true purpose of PII through disassociation – i.e. hiding the link between the raw data, and the subject.

Organizations should take great care to ensure that no single piece of data compromises the subject's identity. When using either of these techniques, organizations should consider: The level of pseudonymization and/or anonymization required, relative to the nature of the data.

- How the masked data is being accessed?

- Any binding agreements that restrict use of the data to be masked?
- Keeping the masked data separate from any other data types, in order to prevent the data subject being easily identified.
- Logging when the data was received, and how it has been provided to any internal or external sources.

Pseudonymization and anonymization aren't the only methods available to organizations looking to mask PII or sensitive data. The other methods that can be used to bolster data security:

- Key-Based Encryption;
- Voiding or deleting characters within the dataset;
- Varying numbers and dates;
- Replacing values across the data;
- Hash-based value masking.

Data masking is an important part of an organization's policy towards protecting PII and safeguarding the identity of the individuals whom it holds data on. As well as the above techniques, organizations should consider the below suggestions when strategizing their approach to data masking:

- Implement masking techniques that only reveal the minimum amount of data to anyone who uses it;
- 'Obfuscating' certain pieces of data at the request of the subject, and only allowing certain members of staff to access the sections that are relevant to them;
- Building their data masking operation around specific legal and regulatory guidelines;
- Where pseudonymization is implemented, the algorithm that is used to 'de-mask' the data is kept safe and secure.

Types of Data Masking

There are several types of data masking types you can use depending on your use-case. Of the many, static and on-the-fly data masking are the most common.

- **Static Data Masking (SDM)**: SDM generally works on a copy of a production database. SDM changes data to look accurate in order to develop, test, and train accurately, without revealing the actual data.
- **Dynamic Data Masking (DDM):** DDM happens dynamically at run time and streams data directly from a production system so that masked data will not need to be saved in another database. It is primarily used for processing role-based security for applications, such as processing customer inquiries and handling medical records. Thus, DDM applies to read-only scenarios to prevent writing the masked data back to the production system.
- **Deterministic Data Masking:** Deterministic data masking involves replacing column data with the same value.
- **On-the-fly Data Masking:** On-the-fly data masking occurs when data transfers from production environments to another environment, like test or development. On-the-fly data masking is ideal for organizations that: deploy software continuously, have heavy integrations. Because it is challenging to keep a backup copy of masked data continuously, this process will send only a subset of masked data when needed.
- **Statistical Data Obfuscation:** The production data can hold different statistical information, which statistical data obscuration techniques can masquerade. Differential privacy is one technique where you can share information about patterns in a data set without revealing information about the actual individuals in the data set.

Data Masking Techniques

A variety of data management techniques can be used to mask or anonymize PII and other private and sensitive data depending on the data type. These masking methods include the following:

- **Scrambling:** Scrambling randomly reorders alphanumeric characters to obscure the original content. Although scrambling is easy to implement, it only works on certain types of data. Data obfuscated this way is not as secure as other techniques.
- **Substitution:** This technique replaces the original data with another value from a supply of credible values. Lookup tables are often used to provide alternative values to the original, sensitive data. The values

must pass rule constraints and preserve the original characteristics of the data. It is harder to apply substitution than scrambling, but it can be applied to several data types and provides good security.

- **Shuffling:** Values within a column, such as user surnames, are shuffled to randomly reorder them. However, it is essential that the shuffling masking algorithm is kept secure so it cannot be used to reverse-engineer the data masking process.
- **Date Aging:** This method increases or decreases a date field by a specific date range. Again, the range value used must be kept secure.
- **Variance:** A variance is applied to a number or date field. This approach is often used for masking financial and transaction value and date information.
- **Masking Out:** Masking out only scrambles part of a value and is commonly applied to credit card numbers where only the last four digits remain visible.
- **Nullifying:** Nullifying replaces the real values in a data column with a null value, completely removing the data from view. Although this sort of deletion is simple to implement, the nullified column cannot be used in queries or analysis. As a result, it can degrade the integrity and quality of the data set for development and testing environments.

Data Masking Best Practices

- **Identify the sensitive data:** Before masking, any data, identify and catalog the:
    - Sensitive data location(s);
    - Authorized person(s) who can view them;
    - Their usage.

  Every single data element of a organization does not need masking. Instead, thoroughly identify the existing sensitive data in both production and non-production environments. Depending on the complexity of data and the organizational structure, this may require a significant amount of time.
- **Define your stack of data masking techniques:** It is not practical for large organizations to use only a single masking tool across the entire

enterprise since data varies greatly. Plus, the technique you choose may require you to comply with specific internal security policies or meet budgetary requirements. In some cases, you may have to develop your masking technique. So, consider all these necessary factors to choose the right set of techniques. Keep them in sync to ensure the same type of data uses the same technique to preserve referential integrity.

- **Secure your data masking techniques:** Masking techniques and associated data are as critical as sensitive data. Organizations should establish the required guidelines to allow only authorized persons to access the masking algorithms.
- **Make masking repeatable:** Over time, changes to an organization or a particular project or product can result in changes to the data. Instead, make masking a process that is repeatable, quick, and automatic, so you can implement them when changes to the sensitive data occur.
- **Define an end-to-end data masking process:** Organizations must have an end-to-end process that includes:
    - Identifying sensitive information
    - Applying the appropriate data masking technique;
    - Continuously auditing to ensure data masking is working as expected.

A.8.12 Data Leakage Prevention

Data Leakage Prevention has been added to ensure organizations have measures to detect and prevent the unauthorized disclosure and extraction of information by both individuals or systems. Data leakage can broadly be described as any information that is accessed, transferred or extracted by unauthorized internal and external personnel and systems, or malicious sources that target an organization's information operation. A data leak is an overlooked exposure of sensitive data, either electronically or physically. Data leaks could occur internally or via physical devices such as external hard drives or laptops. If a cybercriminal locates a data leak, they can use the information to arm themselves for a data breach attack. Data leaks are an easy attack vector for cyber criminals. A data leak is the accidental exposure of sensitive information. These events are not initiated by an external impetus. They're caused by vulnerabilities in the security controls protecting confidential data. Data leaks can also be caused by cyber criminals publishing stolen data on their official dark web noticeboards, also known as ransomware blogs. Exposed data allows unauthorized access to an organization's systems. This direct access enables hackers to carry out a range of cyber-attacks with less effort, such as:

- Ransomware and other types of malware injections;
- Social engineering, including phishing;
- Data exfiltration/data theft.

A.8.12 Data Leakage Prevention – A linkage with Ancient Era

Trust and Verification

The Ramayana teaches us to question appearances and verify before trusting. Similarly, in the digital world, we must exercise caution and practice critical thinking. Phishing attacks, social engineering and malicious websites often disguise themselves as trustworthy entities. By adopting a skeptical mindset and verifying the authenticity of online entities, we can avoid falling victim to cybercrimes.

When Lord Hanuman, arrives in Lanka in search of Mata Sita, He is cautious about revealing His identity and mission. He carefully assesses the situation and employs discretion to gather information about Mata Sita's whereabouts without arousing suspicion from King Ravan's forces.

In this episode, Lord Hanuman exercises caution and secrecy, emphasizing the importance of confidentiality and discretion when handling sensitive information. While the context is different from modern data security concerns, the principles of safeguarding information and preventing unauthorized access resonate across domains. Lord Hanuman's discretion in approaching Mata Sita and His cautious behavior in enemy territory highlight the importance of confidentiality, discretion, and strategic communication in safeguarding valuable information and preventing its unauthorized disclosure or exploitation.

Controls

Data leakage prevention measures should be applied to systems, networks and any other devices that process, store or transmit sensitive information.

Purpose

To detect and prevent the unauthorized disclosure and extraction of information by individuals or systems.

Guidance

The organization should consider the following to reduce the risk of data leakage:

- Identifying and classifying information to protect against leakage;
- Monitoring channels of data leakage;
- Acting to prevent information from leaking.

Data leakage prevention tools should be used to:

- Identify and monitor sensitive information at risk of unauthorized disclosure;
- Detect the disclosure of sensitive information;
- Block user actions or network transmissions that expose sensitive information.

The organization should determine if it is necessary to restrict a user's ability to copy and paste or upload data to services, devices and storage media outside of the organization. If that is the case, the organization should implement technology such as Data Leakage Prevention tools or the configuration of existing tools that allow users to view and manipulate data held remotely but prevent copy and paste outside of the organization's control. If data export is required, the data owner should be allowed to approve the export and hold users accountable for their actions. Taking screenshots or photographs of the screen should be addressed through terms and conditions of use, training and auditing. Where data is backed up, care should be taken to ensure sensitive information is protected using measures such as encryption, access control and physical protection of the storage media holding the backup. Data Leakage Prevention should also be considered to protect against the intelligence actions of an adversary from obtaining confidential or secret information which can be of interest for espionage or can be critical for the community. The Data Leakage Prevention actions should be oriented to confuse the adversary's decisions for example by replacing authentic information with false information, either as an independent action or as response to the adversary's intelligence actions. Examples of these kinds of actions are reverse social engineering or the use of honeypots to attract attackers.

Other Information

Data Leakage Prevention tools are designed to identify data, monitor data usage and movement, and take actions to prevent data from leaking. Data Leakage Prevention inherently involves monitoring personnel's communications and online activities, and by extension external party messages, which raises legal concerns that should be considered prior to deploying Data Leakage Prevention tools.

There is a variety of legislation relating to privacy, data protection, employment, interception of data and telecommunications that is applicable to monitoring and data processing in the context of Data Leakage Prevention. Data Leakage Prevention can be supported by standard security controls, such as topic-specific policies on access control and secure document management.

Data leakage is a common problem within organizations that deal with large amounts of data, of different classifications, across multiple standalone and linked ICT systems, applications and file servers. Data Leakage Prevention is a cyber security practice that involves implementing secure data practices to reduce accidental exposure. The control is regarding Data Leakage Prevention measures which should be applied to systems, networks and any other devices that process, store, or transmit information. While it can be difficult to detect data leakage within the organization, it is recommend starting with a detailed risk assessment of the data you handle. This will help organization to identify any weaknesses in their current data processing procedures that could lead to an unauthorized disclosure of data. Although prevention is better than cure, many organizations take an "assumed breach" approach and on that basis, they may also consider "seeding" datasets with uniquely identifiable information that they can easily detect via scans of 'dark web' or 'pasted' data. Organizations can apply the defined classification scheme to information, having techniques to monitor for data leakage, such as email scanning, file transfers and control of mobile storage devices and tools to block user actions that could expose sensitive information. Data leakage is difficult to eradicate entirely. That being said, to minimize the risks that are unique to their operation, organizations should:

- Classify data in line with recognized industry standards, in order to assign varying risk levels across the board;
- Closely monitor known data channels that are heavily utilized and prone to leakage;
- Take proactive measures to prevent data from being leaked;
- Restrict a user's ability to copy and paste data (where applicable) to and from specific platforms and systems;
- Require authorization from the data owner prior to any mass exports being carried out;
- Consider managing or preventing users from taking screenshots or photographing monitors that display protected data types;
- Encrypt backups that contain sensitive information;
- Formulate gateway security measures and leakage prevention measures that safeguard against external factors.

Data Leakage Prevention is linked to numerous other ISO security guidelines that seek to safeguard information and data across an organization's network, including access control measures and secure document management. Organizations should consider using dedicated data leakage tools and utility programs that:

- Work in tandem with the organization's approach to data classification, and identify the potential for leakage within high-risk data types;
- Detect and proactively alert upon the transfer and/or disclosure of data, especially to unauthorized systems, file sharing platforms or applications;
- Recognize the risks inherent within certain data transfer methods;
- Data Leakage Prevention tools are intrusive by their very nature, and should be implemented and managed in accordance with any regulatory requirements or legislation that deals with user privacy.

Data leaks occur when sensitive data is accidentally exposed publicly, either physical or digitally. Common causes of data leaks include:

- Misconfigured Software Settings;
- Social Engineering;
- Recycled or Weak Passwords;
- Physical Theft/Loss of Sensitive Devices;
- Software Vulnerabilities;
- Insider Threats.

There are four major categories of data leaks:

- **Customer Information:** Some of the biggest data breaches included customer data leaks that involved PII. Customer data is unique to each organization. Customer confidential information could include any of the following:
  - Customer names;
  - Addresses;
  - Phone number;
  - Email addresses;
  - Usernames;
  - Passwords;
  - Social Security numbers;
  - Payment's histories;

    - Product browsing habits;
    - Credit card numbers.

- **Organization Information:** Leaked organization information exposes sensitive internal activity. Such data leaks tend to be in the cross hairs of unscrupulous businesses pursuing the marketing plans of their competitors. Organization data leaks could include the following:

    - Internal Communications;
    - Performance Metrics;
    - Marketing Strategies.

- **Trade Secrets:** This is the most dangerous form of data leak to a business. Intellectual property theft destroys a business's growth potential, running it to the ground. Trade secret leakage could include the following types of data:

    - Upcoming Product Plans;
    - Software Coding;
    - Proprietary Technology Information.

- **Analytics:** Large data sets feed analytics dashboards, and cyber criminals are drawn to any sizable pool of data. Analytics software is, therefore, an attack vector that needs to be monitored. Analytics data leaks could include the following:

    - Customer Behavior Data;
    - Psychographic Data;
    - Modeled Data.

The following data security practices could prevent data leaks and minimize the chances of data breaches.

- **Evaluate the Risk of Third Parties:** Unfortunately, vendors may not take cybersecurity as seriously as the organization does. It's important to keep evaluating the security posture of all vendors to ensure they're not at risk of suffering data leaks through critical security vulnerabilities. Vendor risk assessments are a common method of identifying third-party security risks and ensuring compliance with regulatory standards.

- **Monitor all Network Access:** The more corporate network traffic being monitored, the higher the chances of identifying suspicious activity. Cyber-attacks are usually preceded by reconnaissance campaigns, cyber criminals need to identify the specific defenses that need circumventing during an attack. Data Leakage Prevention solutions empower organizations to identify and strengthen security vulnerabilities to prevent the possibility of reconnaissance campaigns. Information security policies may need to be revised to enforce privileged access to highly sensitive data.
- **Identify all Sensitive Data:** Data Leakage Prevention should be front of mind for organizations looking to enhance their information security strategies. Before Data Leakage Prevention policies can be initiated, businesses need to identify all of the sensitive data that needs to be secured. This data then needs to be correctly classified in line with strict security policies. With correct sensitive data discovery and classification, a business can tailor the most efficient Data Leakage Prevention defenses for each data category.
- **Secure all Endpoints:** An endpoint is any remote access point that communicates with a business network via end-users or autonomously. This includes Internet of Things (IoT) devices, desktop computers, and mobile devices. With most organizations now adopting some form of a remote working model, endpoints have become dispersed, making them harder to secure. Organizations must extend their coverage to cloud-based endpoint security. Organizations need to train their staff to recognize the trickery of cyberattacks, particularly email phishing and social engineering attacks.
- **Implement Data Loss Prevention (DLP) Software:** Data loss prevention is an overarching data protection strategy that should include data leak prevention as a core component. An effective DLP system combines processes and technology to ensure sensitive data is not lost, misused, or exposed to unauthorized users. Below are the six components of a DLP program requiring DLP solutions:

- **Data identification:** Many organizations leverage automation techniques, to streamline the data identification process.
- **Securing data in motion:** Deploy DLP software at the network edge to detect sensitive data transfers violating data loss prevention policies.
- **Securing endpoints:** Endpoint DLP agents can monitor user behavior in real-time and control data transfers between specified parties.
- **Securing data at rest:** DLP products can enforce access control, regulatory compliance requirements, encryption algorithms, and data storage policies to protect archived data.
- **Secure data in use:** Comprehensive DLP tools can monitor and flag unauthorized user behavior.
- **Data leak detection:** If data leak prevention strategies fall through, fast remediation is crucial to avoiding a data breach. Effective data leak detection tools can scan the open and deep web for data exposures, enabling faster removal of potential breach vectors.

- **Encrypt all Data:** Cyber criminals may find it difficult to exploit data leaks if the data is encrypted. There are two main categories of data encryption, Symmetric-Key Encryption and Public-Key Encryption. While encrypted data may stump amateur hackers, capable cyber attackers could decrypt the data without a decryption key. For this reason, data encryption shouldn't be the sole Data Leakage Prevention tactic but should be used alongside all the methods listed.
- **Evaluate all Permissions:** Organization confidential data could currently be accessed by users that don't require it. As an initial response, all permissions should be evaluated to ensure access isn't being granted to authorized parties. Once this has been verified, all critical data should be categorized into different levels of sensitivity to control access to different pools of data. Only trustworthy staff with essential requirements should have access to highly sensitive data. This privileged access assignment process may also identify malicious insiders facilitating sensitive data exfiltration.

A.8.13 Information Backup

One of the best ways to protect the computer and data from malware attacks is to make regular backups. An organization's backup operation should encompass a broad range of efforts that improve resilience and protect against loss of business by establishing a robust and tightly managed set of backup jobs, using dedicated software and utilities, with adequate retention levels and agreed upon recovery times. Organization should always create at least two backups: one to keep offline and another to keep in the cloud. They can create a full back up using the System Image Backup tool to make a copy of the entire machine, including files, settings, apps, and OS installation. Alternatively, if they don't have a lot of files, they could just make regular copies of the documents on a USB flash drive. If they're a light user and files don't change very often, they should at least be making a backup once a week. On the other hand, if they're dealing with business files, they should be making backups at least once or twice a day.

- **Online backup:** There are many ways to make backups online. OneDrive is a common example of online backup, but this solution should only be considered to protect the data against hardware failure, theft, or natural accidents. If the device gets infected with ransomware or another type of malware, OneDrive is likely to sync the changes making those files stored in the cloud unusable. A better solution includes subscribing to a third-party online backup service, that allows you to schedule or trigger backups on demand to prevent syncing infected or encrypted files. The only caveat is that most cloud storage services don't offer bare metal recovery. If that's something organization need, they could create a full back up as you would normally do and then upload the package to a paid cloud storage service.
- **Offline backup:** Organization recovery plan must include a full backup of the system and data to keep offline using an external hard drive or in a local network location. This is the kind of backup that will ensure organization can recover from any malware, hardware failure, errors, and natural accidents. Remember that there is no such thing as enough backup. If organization can make a backup of the backup that they can store offsite, do it. After creating a backup, always disconnect

the external drive and store it in a safe location, or disconnect the network location where organization can store the backup because if the drive stays online and accessible from your computer, malware can still infect those files.

A.8.13 Information Backup – A linkage with Ancient Era

- **Preservation of Knowledge:** In the Ramayana, the epic tale of Lord Ram's journey and the events surrounding it serve as invaluable knowledge and cultural heritage for future generations. Similarly, information backup in modern contexts involves preserving critical data and knowledge to ensure its availability for reference, analysis, and continuity.
- **Redundancy for Resilience:** Just as Lord Ram's story is retold through various versions and interpretations across different cultures and mediums, information backup involves creating redundant copies of data stored in different locations or formats to mitigate the risk of loss due to hardware failure, disasters, or other unforeseen events.
- **Recovery from Loss:** In the Ramayana, the story of Lord Ram's exile, trials, and eventual triumph over adversity symbolizes resilience and the ability to overcome loss and setbacks. Similarly, information backup serves as a mechanism for recovering lost or corrupted data, enabling organizations to restore operations and continuity in the face of disruptions.
- **Transmission Across Generations:** The transmission of the Ramayana through oral traditions, written texts, and cultural practices exemplifies the importance of passing down knowledge and stories across generations. Similarly, information backup ensures the continuity of organizational knowledge and institutional memory, enabling future generations to build upon the achievements and experiences of their predecessors.
- **Security and Protection:** In the Ramayana, Lord Ram's allies, such as Lord Hanuman and Sugriv, play crucial roles in protecting Him and preserving His legacy. Similarly, information backup involves implementing security measures and access controls to safeguard data from unauthorized access, corruption, or tampering, ensuring its integrity and confidentiality.

- **Adaptation and Evolution:** Over time, the story of the Ramayana has evolved and adapted to different cultural contexts and interpretations, reflecting changing societal values and beliefs. Similarly, information backup strategies must evolve to keep pace with technological advancements, regulatory requirements, and organizational needs, ensuring the continued relevance and effectiveness of data preservation practices.

Control

Backup copies of information, software and systems should be maintained and regularly tested in accordance with the agreed topic-specific policy on backup.

Purpose

To enable recovery from loss of data or systems.

Guidance

A topic-specific policy on backup should be established to address the organization's data retention and information security requirements. Adequate backup facilities should be provided to ensure that all essential information and software can be recovered following an incident or failure or loss of storage media. Plans should be developed and implemented for how the organization will back up information, software and systems, to address the topic-specific policy on backup. When designing a backup plan, the following items should be taken into consideration:

- Producing accurate and complete records of the backup copies and documented restoration procedures;
- Reflecting the business requirements of the organization, the security requirements of the information involved and the criticality of the information to the continued operation of the organization in the extent and frequency of backups;
- Storing the backups in a safe and secure remote location, at a sufficient distance to escape any damage from a disaster at the main site;
- Giving backup information an appropriate level of physical and environmental protection consistent with the standards applied at the main site;

- Regularly testing backup media to ensure that they can be relied on for emergency use when necessary. Testing the ability to restore backed-up data onto a test system, not by overwriting the original storage media in case the backup or restoration process fails and causes irreparable data damage or loss;
- Protecting backups by means of encryption according to the identified risks;
- Taking care to ensure that inadvertent data loss is detected before backup is taken.

Operational procedures should monitor the execution of backups and address failure of scheduled backups to ensure completeness of backups according to the topic-specific policy on backups. Backup measures for individual systems and services should be regularly tested to ensure that they meet the objectives of incident response and business continuity plans. This should be combined with a test of the restoration procedures and checked against the restoration time required by the business continuity plan. In the case of critical systems and services, backup measures should cover all systems information, applications and data necessary to recover the complete system in the event of a disaster. When the organization uses a cloud service, backup copies of the organization's information, applications and systems in the cloud service environment should be taken. The organization should determine if and how requirements for backup are fulfilled when using the information backup service provided as part of the cloud service. The retention period for essential business information should be determined, taking into account any requirement for retention of archive copies. The organization should consider the deletion of information in storage media used for backup once the information's retention period expires and should take into consideration legislation and regulations.

Organization should take a topic-specific approach to backups that includes bespoke processes for each individual topic, and takes into account the different types of data (and associated risk levels) that organization's process and access throughout their operation.

Organizations should draft topic-specific policies that directly address how the organization backs up the relevant areas of its network. Backup facilities should be implemented with the primary aim of ensuring that all business-critical data, software and systems are able to be recovered following the below events, but not limited to:

- Data Loss;
- Intrusion;
- Business Interruption;
- Failure of Systems, Applications or Storage Media.

Any backup plan created should aim to:

- Outline clear and concise restoration procedures that cover all relevant critical systems and services;
- Produce workable copies of any systems, data or applications that are covered under a backup job;
- Meet the unique commercial and operational requirements of the organization;
- Store backups in an appropriate location that is environmentally protected, physically distinct from the source data in order to prevent total data loss, and securely accessed for maintenance purposes;
- Mandate for regular testing of backup jobs, in order to guarantee data availability should the need arise to restore files, systems or applications at a moment's notice;
- Backup tests should be measured against the organization's agreed recovery times to ensure adherence in the event of data loss or system interruption;
- Encrypt data that has been backed up, in accordance with its risk level;
- Check for data loss before running any backup jobs;
- Implement a reporting system that alerts maintenance staff to the status of backup jobs, including complete or partial failures, so that remedial action can be taken;
- Include data from cloud-based platforms that are not directly managed by the organization;
- Store backup data in line with a topic-specific retention policy that takes into account the underlying nature and purpose of the data

that's been backed up, including transfer and/or archiving to storage media.

Organizations that implement Information Backup properly, will experience minimum downtime and smooth recovery in the event of a failure.

Backup types defined

- **Full back up** captures a copy of an entire data set. Although considered to be the most reliable backup method, performing a full backup is time-consuming and requires many disks or tapes. Most organizations run full backups only periodically.
- **Incremental back up** offers an alternative to full backups by backing up only the data that has changed since the last full backup. The drawback is that a full restore takes longer if an incremental-based data backup copy is used for recovery.
- **Differential backup** copies data changed since the last full backup. This enables a full restore to occur more quickly by requiring only the last full backup and the last differential backup. The downside is that progressive growth of differential backups tends to adversely affect the backup window.
- **Synthetic full backup** is a variation of differential backup. In a synthetic full backup, the backup server produces an additional full copy, which is based on the original full backup and data gleaned from incremental copies.
- **Incremental-forever backups** minimize the backup window while providing faster recovery access to data. An incremental-forever backup captures the full data set and then supplements it with incremental backups from that point forward. Backing up only changed blocks is also known as delta differencing. Full backups of data sets are typically stored on the backup server, which automates the restoration.
- **Reverse-Incremental backups** are changes made between two instances of a mirror. Once an initial full backup is taken, each successive incremental backup applies any changes to the existing full backup. This essentially generates a novel synthetic full backup

copy each time an incremental change is applied, while also providing reversion to previous full backups.

- **Hot Backup, or Dynamic Backup**, is applied to data that remains available to users as the update is in process. This method sidesteps user downtime and productivity loss. The risk with hot backup is that, if the data is amended while the backup is underway, the resulting backup copy might not match the final state of the data.

Techniques and technologies to complement data backup

- **Continuous Data Protection (CDP)** refers to layers of associated technologies designed to enhance data protection. A CDP-based storage system backs up all enterprise data whenever a change is made. CDP tools enable multiple copies of data to be created. Many CDP systems contain a built-in engine that replicates data from a primary to a secondary backup server and/or tape-based storage. Disk-to-disk- to-tape backup is a popular architecture for CDP systems.
- **Near-Continuous CDP** takes backup snapshots at set intervals, which are different from array-based vendor snapshots that are taken each time new data is written to storage.
- **Data reduction** lessens your storage footprint. There are two primary methods: data compression and data deduplication. These methods can be used singly, but vendors often combine the approaches. Reducing the size of data has implications on backup windows and restoration times.
- **Disk cloning** involves copying the contents of a computer's hard drive, saving it as an image file and transferring it to storage media. Disk cloning can be used for provisioning, system provisioning, system recovery and rebooting or returning a system to its original configuration.
- **Erasure coding, or forward error correction**, evolved as a scalable alternative to traditional RAID systems. Erasure coding most often is associated with object storage. RAID stripes data writes across multiple drives, using a parity drive to ensure redundancy and resilience. The technology breaks data into fragments and encodes it with other bits of redundant data. These encoded fragments are stored across different storage media, nodes or geographic locations.

The associated fragments are used to reconstruct corrupted data using a technique known as oversampling.

- **Flat Backup** is a data protection scheme in which a direct copy of a snapshot is moved to low-cost storage without the use of traditional backup software. The original snapshot retains its native format and location; the flat backup replica gets mounted should the original become unavailable or unusable.
- **Mirroring** places data files on more than one computer server to ensure it remains accessible to users. In synchronous mirroring, data is written to local and remote disk simultaneously. Writes from local storage are not acknowledged until a confirmation is sent from remote storage, thus ensuring the two sites have an identical data copy. Conversely, asynchronous local writes are complete before confirmation is sent from the remote server.
- **Replication** enables users to select the required number of replicas, or copies, of data needed to sustain or resume business operations. Data replication copies data from one location to another, providing an up-to-date copy to hasten DR.
- **Recovery-in-place, or instant recovery**, enables users to temporarily run a production application directly from a backup VM instance, thus maintaining data availability while the primary VM is being restored. Mounting a physical or VM instance directly on a backup or media server can hasten system-level recovery to within minutes. Recovery from a mounted image does result in degraded performance, since backup servers are not sized for production workloads.
- **Storage snapshots** capture a set of reference markers on disk for a given database, file or storage volume. Users refer to the markers, or pointers, to restore data from a selected point in time. Because it derives from an underlying source volume, an individual storage snapshot is an instance, not a full backup. As such, snapshots do not protect data against hardware failure.

Implementing Information Backup

- **What should be backed up?:** The organization should decide "what" should be backed up, and up to what level. A priority list of important information should be classified and levels assigned, based on the importance of the information.

- **Define Levels of Back-up information:** Define what backup procedures need to be maintained for each of these levels. Mock recoveries are conducted to make sure that the restoration process works well, in the event of an actual failure. The extent and frequency of backups should reflect the business requirements of the organization. Also consider the criticality of the information to the continued operation of the organization. Maybe the information doesn't change a lot during the week, but it has to be restored with Zero Downtime, in the event of a failure. In such conditions, a Fail-over solution would be ideal. In case of critical systems, the backup should cover all systems information, applications and data necessary to recover the complete system in the event of a disaster.
- **Log the Backups and Restoration:** Accurate and complete records should be maintained of the backup process and the backup copies. This helps to track who did the last backup and when. Logs should also be maintained for the mock restorations, in order to track that the restorations were successful or not. Mock restorations help discover flaws in the backup process.
- **Backups should be stored in a remote location:** Backups should be stored in a remote location, at a sufficient distance to escape any damage from a disaster at the main site. What remains to be decided, is the mode of such storage. Whether it has to be a fail-over server, or whether the information can simply be stored in tape drives. Consider the security requirements of the information involved. Is it safe to replicate the information in another off-location site? Maybe, the agreement with clients, doesn't allow you to transfer the information to another location.
- **Secure your Backups:** Backup information should be given appropriate level of physical and environmental protection. What this means is whatever controls that organization applies to media at the main site, should be extended to cover the back-up site. In certain cases, where confidentiality is of importance, the backups should be protected by means of encryption.
- **Test your Backups:** Make sure that the backup media is regularly

tested to ensure that they can be relied upon for emergency use when necessary. Use mock restoration procedures, so that you are sure that the backups are effective. Also ensure that backups can restore in the time allocated for recovery. Of course, it goes without saying that the mock restoration procedures "should" be logged.

- **How long should Backups be retained:** The backups should be retained for as long as the organization determines that the information is useful. The organization needs to decide the retention period, and also any requirement for archive copies to be permanently retained based on contractual, regulatory, statutory and organization's own requirements.

A.8.14 Redundancy of Information Processing Facilities

Any organization needs a system architecture that is sufficient to satisfy the business availability requirements. Redundancy ensures availability by having spare capacity in case of system failure, and often requires duplicate systems such as power supplies. An 'information processing facility' (IPF) is a broad term used to describe any piece of ICT infrastructure that's involved in processing data, such as IT equipment, software and physical facilities and locations. IPFs play a key role in maintaining business continuity and ensuring the smooth operation of an organization's ICT network(s). To increase resilience, organization's need to implement measures that increase the redundancy of their IPFs i.e., fail safe methodologies and processes that mitigate risk to systems and data in the event of failure, misuse or intrusion. Redundancy helps organization stored copies to maintain the availability of the information systems. Organization should conduct regular tests to confirm the viability of the redundancies as it would be a major disappointment if the backup also failed. Since redundant items are of such great value to organization system continuity, they must be stored either at the same level or better than the originals. Most companies these days use cloud storage to preserve their redundancies, if organization has a supplier relationship, you should discuss the status of your redundancies in the cloud. Suppliers should be well informed of the risks you face related to data security.

Adequate redundancy that can be spun up when necessary, forms an important part of business continuity planning and should be tested regularly. The overriding goal is to increase the availability of business services and information systems, which can be interpreted as any aspect of a network that allows the organization to conduct business. It advocates for duplication as the primary methods of achieving redundancy across its various IPFs, primarily through maintaining an inventory of spare parts, duplicate components and additional peripheral devices. A redundant system is only as good as its alerting facility. As such, organizations should ensure that failed IPFs are detected quickly, and remedial action is taken to either fail over to standby hardware, or to repair the malfunctioning IPF in as quick a time as possible.

A.8.14 Redundancy of Information Processing Facilities – A linkage with Ancient Era

The Ram Setu – emphasizing Resilience, Backup and Continuity

- **Building Redundant Structures:** In the Ramayana, Lord Ram constructs a bridge, known as Ram Setu or Adam's Bridge, to cross the ocean and reach Lanka. This bridge serves as a redundant structure, providing an alternate path for Lord Ram and His allies to navigate challenging terrain. Similarly, redundancy in information processing facilities involves building backup systems, networks, and infrastructure to ensure continuity of operations and mitigate the risk of failure or disruption.
- **Preparation for Contingencies:** Just as Lord Ram anticipates the possibility of obstacles during His journey and prepares contingencies like building the bridge, organizations plan for contingencies by implementing redundant information processing facilities. These redundant systems act as failovers, ensuring that critical operations can continue seamlessly in the event of hardware failures, natural disasters, or other disruptions.
- **Ensuring Continuity:** The construction of Ram Setu enables Lord Ram and His army to maintain continuity in their mission, ensuring that they can overcome obstacles and reach their destination despite challenges. Similarly, redundancy in information processing facilities ensures continuity of services, applications, and data access, enabling organizations to operate without interruption and fulfill their objectives effectively.
- **Diversification of Resources:** Lord Ram leverages the skills and resources of diverse allies, including the Vanar army, Sugriv, and Lord Hanuman, to construct Ram Setu and overcome obstacles. Similarly, redundancy in information processing facilities involves diversifying resources across multiple locations, data centers, and cloud environments to distribute risk and enhance resilience against potential failures or threats.
- **Adaptation to Changing Conditions:** Throughout the Ramayana, Lord Ram and His allies adapt to changing conditions and challenges, demonstrating flexibility and resourcefulness in overcoming obstacles. Similarly, organizations must adapt their redundancy strategies to evolving technological advancements, regulatory requirements, and

business needs to ensure optimal performance and effectiveness of information processing facilities.

- **Strategic Planning and Execution:** The construction of Ram Setu requires strategic planning, coordination, and execution to ensure its success. Similarly, implementing redundancy in information processing facilities involves strategic decision-making, investment in infrastructure, and ongoing maintenance to maintain operational readiness and resilience.

Control

Information processing facilities should be implemented with redundancy sufficient to meet availability requirements.

Purpose

To ensure the continuous operation of information processing facilities.

Guidance

The organization should identify requirements for the availability of business services and information systems. The organization should design and implement systems architecture with appropriate redundancy to meet these requirements. Redundancy can be introduced by duplicating information processing facilities in part or in their entirety. The organization should plan and implement procedures for the activation of the redundant components and processing facilities. The procedures should establish if the redundant components and processing activities are always activated, or in case of emergency, automatically or manually activated. The redundant components and information processing facilities should ensure the same security level as the primary ones. Mechanisms should be in place to alert the organization to any failure in the information processing facilities, enable executing the planned procedure and allow continued availability while the information processing facilities are repaired or replaced. The organization should consider the following when implementing redundant systems:

- Contracting with two or more suppliers of network and critical information processing facilities;
- Using redundant networks;

- Using two geographically separate data centers with mirrored systems;
- Using physically redundant power supplies or sources;
- Using multiple parallel instances of software components, with automatic load balancing between them;
- Having duplicated components in systems or in networks.

Where applicable, preferably in production mode, redundant information systems should be tested to ensure the failover from one component to another component works as intended.

Other Information

There is a strong relationship between redundancy and ICT readiness for business continuity especially if short recovery times are required. Many of the redundancy measures can be part of the ICT continuity strategies and solutions. The implementation of redundancies can introduce risks to the integrity or confidentiality of information and information systems, which need to be considered when designing information systems. Redundancy in information processing facilities does not usually address application unavailability due to faults within an application. With the use of public cloud computing, it is possible to have multiple live versions of information processing facilities, existing in multiple separate physical locations with automatic fail over and load balancing between them. Some of the technologies and techniques for providing redundancy and automatic fail-over in the context of cloud services are discussed in ISO/IEC TS 23167.

The objective of this control is to ensure availability of information processing facilities. Information processing facilities should be implemented with redundancy sufficient to meet availability requirements.

A good control describes how information processing facilities are implemented with redundancy sufficiency to meet availability requirements. Redundancy refers to implementing, typically, duplicate hardware to ensure the availability of information processing systems. The principle is that if one or more items fail, then there are redundant items that will take over. Critical to this is the testing of redundant components and systems periodically to ensure that fail-over will be achieved in a reasonable time-frame. Redundant components must be protected at the same level or greater than the primary components. Many organizations use cloud-based providers so they will want to ensure redundancy is addressed effectively in their contracts with suppliers and as part of the policy in A.15. The auditor will expect to see that testing is carried out on a periodic basis, where redundant components & systems are in place and in the control of the organization. When designing and installing redundancy measures, organizations should consider and adopt the guidelines as mentioned in the Guidance section.

As a critical element of maintaining continuity of services, there needs to be adequate redundancy of facilities, people, communications, documentation, training, and services. Redundancy Plans must anticipate a multitude of failures, causes, loss of data or facilities, unavailability of trained personnel, communications losses, powers losses, and more. Plans must assess the risks associated with each critical component and identify redundant/alternative means for providing for continuity of services under all conditions. Due to the nature of business continuity management, it is essential that all elements of a plan have adequate redundancies available, knowing that some elements may be compromised by the nature of the disruption. Redundancies include cross-training of personnel, alternate facilities at locations that do not share vulnerabilities, redundant communications methods and providers, power sources, physical access, and more.

Redundancy Plan – Avoid Potential Single Points of Failure

Location/ Geography	Metro Area, Flood Plain/River Bank, Avalanche, Hurricane or Tornado-Prone, Unreliable Power Source, Poor Transportation/Communication Systems, etc.
Facilities and Infrastructure	Power, Generators/Fuel Supplies/Suppliers, Air Conditioning, Communications Lines-Data, Voice, Multiple High-Speed Networks Connect, Network Topology, Environmental Conditions/Hazards, Central Organization, Schools, or Admin Units
Systems	Lost, Damaged, can't be "Touched" or "Reached"
Data	Lost, not accessible

People	Not 24x7 Staffing; off hours not on campus, no/limited transportation, not reachable via communications-voice, Internet, cell, text, etc., facilities disabled, unsafe conditions, evacuated, can't leave campus - government-enforced, not cross-trained, insufficient backup of skills
Documentation	Must document critical/emergency procedures and recovery procedures, must assume that "usual" trained people are unavailable, need for depth of cross-training, docs must be available to all potential users - not just on one, local system or in one place, vendor contacts - office, cell, text, social networking, IM, etc.

Key Considerations

Data is Essential and Must Be Replicated:

Data is more important than hardware. Data should be replicated by a variety of means and should be retrievable as needed. Hardware can always be replaced. Be aware of the dependencies between software and data. Cloud services may provide viable options for replication as long as security and privacy are maintained.

Alternate Sites for Web Hosting:

Consider the impact of a hurricane on physical facilities, life-safety issues, electrical power/network infrastructures, and an extended prognosis for the restoration of "normal operating conditions." A redundancy plan should identify alternative means to be used to provide essential services under such unthinkable circumstances. Services should include means for communicating information on the status and safety of the organization and its people to the rest of the world. Consider contracting for an alternate service for communicating key information with on and off-campus people while normal organizational web services cannot be provided.

Availability of Information Processing Facilities:

Despite the emergency or disruptive circumstances, information processing facilities must continue to function, be accessible for critical processing, and maintaining the security, integrity, and privacy of information. In creating plans, many variables need to be considered when choosing alternative sites, services, personnel, vendors, power/ communication means, and accessibility.

Choosing the right locations for locating emergency equipment and locations to serve as Continuity Centers:

First and foremost, consider all types of factors when evaluating locations to house emergency equipment. As learned from Super Storm Sandy, never locate generators in basements, locations below 100-year flood lines, or locations likely to be inaccessible for fuel deliveries. NYU Medical Center lost the use of all of its power generators when the East River overflowed its banks. Patients had to be evacuated to other hospitals because all power sources were down and all its generators were underwater. Restoration of power took weeks. Physical damage and lost revenues were beyond any expectations as no one expected the water level to rise to the extent it did. Only now are plans being made that consider rising water levels that are likely to recur more frequently.

A plan should include the identification of physical locations that will be used to coordinate during and immediately after an incident. Ideally, several locations should be chosen at increasingly distant locations from the organization. This allows for disruption in a key building, a metropolitan area, and a significant geographic designation while minimizing the impact on a continuity effort. Be cautious and exercise due diligence when considering locations and technologies for potential sites to serve as continuity centers. While some locations and facilities may be seen to have some very positive attributes that would seem to make them cost-effective choices, there are many critical issues that should be explored. Categories of considerations include:

- Physical locations;
- Virtual locations;
- Cloud resources;
- Availability of sufficient communications excellent/redundant/multi-vendor cell capacity, landlines, internet bandwidth from more than one vendor and physical supply and satellite access.

- Availability of alternative power sources;
- Multiple suppliers should be contracted for other types of fuel supply. Remember that generators need routine maintenance and testing;
- Sufficient physical access during emergency situations;
- Proximity to locations that contain hazardous material, or are near river banks/flood plains, avalanche zones, mudslide zones, frequent forest fires, or earthquake-prone locations.;
- Security and support for personnel staffing the continuity effort.

It is not critical that hot sites (physical, virtual, or cloud) be as extensive or as fast as normal resources. They are for emergency use, not daily operations. Communication facilities and contact information must be as accurate and complete as those used for daily operations. They provide the lifeline for all coordination of communication.

Good Vendor Relationships are Important:

Establishing a good, working relationship with key vendors can help in times of crisis. Resources may need to be replaced. Good relationships may help move organizational needs to the head of the queue of waiting orders. While there may be many others facing similar problems related to the same or other crisis, vendors are sensitive to the problems and will try to assist however and whenever possible when there is an existing relationship.

After the Resumption of Normalcy:

While everyone may be tired and anxious to get back to business as usual, bringing all the key individuals to a session to discuss how the plan worked or failed is important. This is a unique opportunity to get direct feedback on the usefulness of the plan. Scheduling a "postmortem" is invaluable in getting constructive feedback as well as complaints that need addressing. Drills are helpful, but a postmortem shares real experiences and feedback.

A.8.15 Logging

A log, in a computing context, is the automatically produced and time-stamped documentation of events relevant to a particular system. Virtually all software applications and systems produce log files. On a Web server, an access log lists all the individual files that people have requested from a website. These files will include the HTML files and their imbedded graphic images and any other associated files that get transmitted. From the server's log files, an administrator can identify numbers of visitors, the domains from which they're visiting, the number of requests for each page and usage patterns according to variables such as times of the day, week, month or year. In Microsoft Exchange, a transaction log records all changes made to an Exchange database. Information to be added to a mailbox database is first written to an Exchange transaction log. Afterwards, the contents of the transaction log are written to the Exchange Server database. An audit log (also known as an audit trail) records chronological documentation of any activities that could have affected a particular operation or event. Details typically include the resources that were accessed, destination and source addresses, a timestamp and user login information for the person who accessed the resources.

A.8.15 Logging - A linkage with Ancient Era

Jatayu - emphasizing Observation, Vigilance and Insight

- **Observation of Events:** In the Ramayana, characters like Lord Hanuman and Jatayu serve as vigilant observers, monitoring events and reporting back to Lord Ram with valuable information. Similarly, Log Monitoring involves observing system activities, events, and transactions recorded in logs to detect anomalies, identify patterns, and gain insights into the health and security of IT systems.
- **Vigilance against Threats:** Lord Hanuman's surveillance of Lanka and Jatayu's confrontation with King Ravan exemplify the vigilance against threats in the Ramayana. Similarly, Log Monitoring helps organizations detect and respond to security threats, such as unauthorized access attempts, malware infections, or suspicious behavior, by analyzing patterns and anomalies in log data.
- **Insight into Actions and Consequences:** Throughout the Ramayana, characters' actions have far-reaching consequences, influencing the

course of events and shaping the outcome of the story. Similarly, Log Monitoring provides insight into the actions and behaviors of users, applications, and systems, enabling organizations to understand the impact of these actions and make informed decisions to optimize performance, security, and compliance.

- **Forensics and Investigation:** When Mata Sita is abducted by King Ravan, Lord Ram and His allies conduct investigations and gather evidence to determine Her whereabouts and plan a rescue mission. Similarly, Log Monitoring supports forensic analysis and incident response by providing a trail of audit logs and system events, facilitating investigations into security incidents, data breaches, or compliance violations.
- **Real-time Alerting and Response:** In the Ramayana, Lord Hanuman's reconnaissance of Lanka alerts Lord Ram to Mata Sita's presence, prompting Him to devise a plan to rescue Her. Similarly, Log Monitoring systems can generate real-time alerts and notifications based on predefined thresholds or detection rules, enabling organizations to respond promptly to security incidents or performance issues and mitigate potential risks.
- **Continuous Improvement and Learning:** As Lord Ram and His allies learn from their experiences and adapt their strategies throughout the Ramayana, Log Monitoring enables organizations to continuously improve their security posture and operational efficiency by analyzing historical log data, identifying trends, and implementing preventive measures to address recurring issues or vulnerabilities.

Control

Logs that record activities, exceptions, faults and other relevant events should be produced, stored, protected and analyzed.

Purpose

To record events, generate evidence, ensure the integrity of log information, prevent against unauthorized access, identify information security events that can lead to an information security incident and to support investigations.

Guidance

General

The organization should determine the purpose for which logs are created, what data is collected and logged, and any log-specific requirements for protecting and handling the log data. This should be documented in a topic-specific policy on logging. Event logs should include for each event, as applicable:

- User IDs;
- System Activities;
- Dates, Times and Details of Relevant Events;
- Device Identity, System Identifier and Location;
- Network Addresses and Protocols.

The following events should be considered for logging:

- Successful and rejected system access attempts;
- Successful and rejected data and other resource access attempts;
- Changes to system configuration;
- Use of privileges;
- Use of utility programs and applications;
- Files accessed and the type of access, including deletion of important data files;
- Alarms raised by the access control system;
- Activation and de-activation of security systems, such as anti-virus systems and intrusion detection systems;
- Creation, modification or deletion of identities;
- Transactions executed by users in applications. In some cases, the applications are a service or product provided or run by a third party.

It is important for all systems to have synchronized time sources as this allows for correlation of logs between systems for analysis, alerting and investigation of an incident.

Protection of logs

Users, including those with privileged access rights, should not have permission to delete or de-activate logs of their own activities. They can potentially manipulate the logs on information processing facilities under their direct control. Therefore, it is necessary to protect and review the logs to maintain accountability for the privileged users. Controls should aim to protect against unauthorized changes to log information and operational problems with the logging facility including:

- Alterations to the message types that are recorded;
- Log files being edited or deleted;
- Failure to record events or over-writing of past recorded events if the storage media holding a log file is exceeded.

For protection of logs, the use of the following techniques should be considered: cryptographic hashing, recording in an append-only and read-only file, recording in a public transparency file. Some audit logs can be required to be archived because of requirements on data retention or requirements to collect and retain evidence and where the organization needs to send system or application logs to a vendor to assist with debugging or troubleshooting errors; logs should be de-identified where possible using data masking techniques for information such as usernames, internet protocol (IP) addresses, hostnames or organization name, before sending to the vendor. Event logs can contain sensitive data and personally identifiable information. Appropriate privacy protection measures should be taken.

Log Analysis

Log Analysis should cover the analysis and interpretation of information security events, to help identify unusual activity or anomalous behavior, which can represent indicators of compromise. Analysis of events should be performed by taking into account:

- The necessary skills for the experts performing the analysis;
- Determining the procedure of log analysis;
- The required attributes of each security-related event;
- Exceptions identified through the use of predetermined rules;

- Known behavior patterns and standard network traffic compared to anomalous activity and behavior [user and entity behavior analytics (UEBA)];
- Results of trend or pattern analysis;
- Available threat intelligence.

Log analysis should be supported by specific monitoring activities to help identify and analyze anomalous behavior, which includes:

- Reviewing successful and unsuccessful attempts to access protected resources;
- Checking DNS logs to identify outbound network connections to malicious servers;
- Examining usage reports from service providers for unusual activity within systems and networks;
- Including event logs of physical monitoring to ensure more accurate detection and incident analysis;
- Correlating logs to enable efficient and highly accurate analysis.

Suspected and actual information security incidents should be identified and be subject to further investigation.

Other Information

System logs often contain a large volume of information, much of which is extraneous to information security monitoring. To help identify significant events for information security monitoring purposes, the use of suitable utility programs or audit tools to perform file interrogation can be considered. Event logging sets the foundation for automated monitoring systems which are capable of generating consolidated reports and alerts on system security. A SIEM tool or equivalent service can be used to store, correlate, normalize and analyze log information, and to generate alerts. SIEMs tend to require careful configuration to optimize their benefits. Configurations to consider include identification and selection of appropriate log sources, tuning and testing of rules and development of use cases. Public transparency files for the recording of logs are used, for example, in certificate transparency systems. Such files can provide an additional detection mechanism useful for guarding against log tampering.

In cloud environments, log management responsibilities can be shared between the cloud service customer and the cloud service provider. Responsibilities vary depending on the type of cloud service being used.

Log files are automatically computer-generated whenever an event with a specific classification takes place on the network. The reason log files exist is that software and hardware, developers find it easier to troubleshoot and debug their creations when they access a textual record of the events that the system is producing. Each of the leading operating systems is uniquely configured to generate and categorize event logs in response to specific types of events. Log management systems centralize all log files, to gather, sort and analyze log data, and make it easy to understand, trace, and address key issues related to application performance.

Large IT organizations depend on an extensive network of IT infrastructure and applications to power key business services. Logfile monitoring and analysis increase the observability of this network, creating transparency and allowing visibility into the cloud computing environment. While observability should not be treated as an ultimate goal, it should always be seen as a mechanism for achieving real business objectives:

- **Improving the reliability of systems for the end-user:** Log files include information about system performance that can be used to determine when additional capacity is needed to optimize the user experience. Log files can help analysts identify slow queries, errors that are causing transactions to take too long or bugs that impact website or application performance.
- **Maintain the security posture of cloud computing environments and prevent data breaches:** Log files capture things like unsuccessful log-in attempts, failed user authentication, or unexpected server overloads, all of which can signal to an analyst that a cyber-attack might be in progress. The best security monitoring tools can send alerts and automate responses as soon as these events are detected on the network.
- **Improve business decision-making:** Log files capture the behavior of users within an application, giving rise to an area of inquiry known as user behavior analytics. By analyzing the actions of users within an application, developers can optimize the application to get users to

their goals more quickly, improving customer satisfaction and driving revenue in the process.

It is vitally important that all logs are linked to the same synchronized time source, and in the case of third-party application logs, any time discrepancies catered to and recorded.

Logs are the lowest common denominator for establishing user, system and application behavior on a given network, especially when faced with an investigation. It is therefore vitally important for organisations to ensure that users, regardless of their permission levels do not retain the ability to delete or amend their own event logs. Individual logs should be complete, accurate and protected against any unauthorized changes or operational problems.

Logs should be protected using the following methods:

- Cryptographic Hashing;
- Append-Only Recording;
- Read-Only Recording;
- Use of Public Transparency Files.

Organizations may need to send logs to vendors to resolve incidents and faults. Should this need arise, logs should be 'de-identified' and the following information should be masked:

- Usernames;
- IP addresses;
- Hostnames.

In addition to this, measures should be taken to safeguard PII in line with the organization's own data privacy protocols, and any prevailing legislation.

When analyzing logs for the purposes of identifying, resolving and analyzing information security events, with the end goal of preventing future occurrences, the factors mentioned in the Log Analysis section mentioned above to be performed.

Log analysis should not be carried out in isolation, and should be done in tandem with rigorous monitoring activities that pinpoint key patterns and anomalous behavior.

Organizations should consider using specialized utility programs that help them search through the vast amounts of information that system logs generate, in order to save time and resources when investigating security incidents, such as a SIEM tool. If an organization uses a cloud-based platform to carry out any part of their operation, log management should be considered as a shared responsibility between the service provider and the organization themselves.

System logs generated by servers and other various network apparatus can create data in vast quantities, and sooner or later, attempts at managing such information in an off-the-cuff fashion are no longer viable. Consequently, information systems managers are tasked with devising strategies for taming these volumes of log data to remain compliant with organization IT policy and also to gain holistic visibility across all IT systems deployed throughout the organization. Log management is defining what you need to log, how to log it, and how long to retain the information. This ultimately translates into requirements for hardware, software, and of course, policies. These are as follows:

- **Collection:** The organization needs to collect logs over encrypted channels. Their log management solution should ideally come equipped with multiple means to collect logs, but it should recommend the most reliable means of doing so. In general, organizations should use agent-based collection whenever possible, as this method is generally more secure and reliable than its agentless counterparts.
- **Storage:** Once they have collected them, organizations need to preserve, compress, encrypt, store, and archive their logs. Companies can look for additional functionality in their log management solution such as the ability to specify where they can store their logs geographically. This type of feature can help meet their compliance requirements and ensure scalability.
- **Search:** Organizations need to make sure they can find their logs once they've stored them, so they should index their records in such a way that they are discoverable. A comprehensive log management solution should enable companies to optimize each log search with filters and

classification tags. It should also allow them to view raw logs, conduct broad and detailed queries, and compare multiple queries at once.

- **Correlation:** Organizations need to create rules that they can use to detect interesting events and perform automated actions. Of course, most events don't occur on a single host in a single log. For that reason, companies should look for a log management solution that lets them create correlation rules according to the unique threats and requirements their environments face. They should also seek out a tool that allows them to import other data sources such as vulnerability scans and asset inventories.

Effective logging allows us to reach back in time to identify events, interactions, and changes that may have relevance to the security of information resources. A lack of logs often means that we lose the ability to investigate events and perform root cause analysis to determine causation. In the context of this control area, logs can be interpreted very broadly to include automated and handwritten logs of administrator and operator activities taken to ensure the integrity of operations in information processing facilities.

How do organization protect the value of log information?

Effective logging strategies must also consider how to log data that can be protected against tampering, sabotage, or deletion that devalues the integrity of log information This usually involves consideration of role-based access controls that partition the ability to read and modify log data based on business needs and position responsibilities. In addition, timestamp information is extremely critical when performing correlation analysis between log sources. One essential control needed to assist with this is ensuring that organizational systems all have their clocks synchronized to a common source (often achieve via NTP server) so that the timelining of events can be performed with high confidence.

What should be logged?

The question of what types of events to log must take into consideration a number of factors including relevant compliance obligations, organizational privacy policies, data storage costs, access control needs, and the ability to monitor and search large data sets in an appropriate time frame. When considering overall logging strategy, it can very often be helpful to "work backward". Rather than initially attempting to catalog all event types, it can be useful to frame investigatory questions beginning with those issues that occur on regular basis or have the potential to be associated with significant risk events. These questions can then lead to a focused review of the security event data that has the most relevance to these particular questions and issues. Ideally, events logs should include key information including:

- User IDs;
- System activities;
- Dates, Times and Details of key events;
- Device identity or location;
- Records of successful and rejected system access attempts;
- Records of successful and rejected resource access attempts;
- Changes to system configurations;
- Use of Privileges;
- Use of system utilities and applications;
- Files accessed and the kind of access;
- Network Addresses and Protocols;
- Alarms raised by the access control system;
- Activation and De-activation of protection system.

Output

Finally, companies need to be able to distribute log information to different users and groups using dashboards, reports, and email. Their log management solution should facilitate the exchange of data with other systems and the security team.

A.8.16 Monitoring Activities

Monitoring of network, systems and application is the cornerstone of any successful IT support and information security operation. It involves collecting and analyzing information to detect suspicious behavior or unauthorized system changes on the network, defining which types of behavior should trigger alerts, and taking action on alerts as needed. It is vitally important for organizations to promote a proactive approach to monitoring that seeks to prevent incidents before they happen, and works in tandem with reactive efforts to form an end-to-end information security and incident resolution strategy that ticks every last box. From hackers and malware, to disgruntled or careless employees, to outdated or otherwise vulnerable devices and operating systems, to mobile and public cloud computing, to third-party service providers, most companies are routinely exposed to security threats of varying severity in the normal course of conducting business. Given the ubiquitous, unavoidable nature of security risks, quick response time is essential to maintaining system security, and automated, continuous security monitoring is key to quick threat detection and response. This requires the management and monitoring of systems to identify unusual activity and to instigate appropriate incident responses. The control is regarding networks, systems and applications which should be monitored for anomalous behavior and appropriate actions taken to evaluate potential information security incidents.

A.8.16 Monitoring Activities – A linkage with Ancient Era

- **King Ravan's Spies and Intrusion Detection Systems**: In the Ramayana, King Ravan deploys spies in the form of his followers to gather intelligence and monitor the activities of Lord Ram's army. This can be associated with the use of Intrusion Detection Systems (IDS) in cybersecurity. King Ravan's spies highlight the need for proactive detection and monitoring of potential intrusions in the digital realm.
- **Vali and False Positives**: Vali, is mistakenly shot by Lord Ram due to a case of mistaken identity. This can be compared to the occurrence of false positives in cybersecurity. False positives are instances where a security system mistakenly identifies legitimate activities as malicious or unauthorized. Vali's story reminds us of the importance of refining security systems to minimize false positives and avoid unnecessary disruptions or harm to legitimate users of systems.

- **Vigilance and Surveillance**: The character of Krishna in the Mahabharata was known for His vigilance and ability to anticipate threats. Similarly, maintaining constant vigilance and employing robust surveillance mechanisms are key to identifying and mitigating cyber threats. Advanced monitoring systems, intrusion detection tools, and threat intelligence platforms can help organizations detect and respond to potential breaches in real-time.
- **The Consequences of Negligence**: The Ramayana teaches lessons about the consequences of negligence and taking security lightly. For example, the episode of Lord Hanuman burning the city of Lanka highlights the vulnerability of a seemingly impenetrable fortress. In cybersecurity, neglecting security measures or understanding the potential risks can lead to significant breaches and damage. The Ramayana serves as a reminder to remain vigilant and proactive in ensuring the security of digital systems and data.

Control

Networks, systems and applications should be monitored for anomalous behavior and appropriate actions taken to evaluate potential information security incidents.

Purpose

To detect anomalous behavior and potential information security incidents.

Guidance

The monitoring scope and level should be determined in accordance with business and information security requirements and taking into consideration relevant laws and regulations. Monitoring records should be maintained for defined retention periods. The following should be considered for inclusion within the monitoring system:

- Outbound and inbound network, system and application traffic;
- Access to systems, servers, networking equipment, monitoring system, critical applications, etc.;
- Critical or admin level system and network configuration files;
- Logs from security tools;

- Event logs relating to system and network activity;
- Checking that the code being executed is authorized to run in the system and that it has not been tampered with;
- Use of the resources and their performance.

The organization should establish a baseline of normal behavior and monitor against this baseline for anomalies. When establishing a baseline, the following should be considered:

- Reviewing utilization of systems at normal and peak periods;
- Usual time of access, location of access, frequency of access for each user or group of users.

The monitoring system should be configured against the established baseline to identify anomalous behavior, such as:

- Unplanned termination of processes or applications;
- Activity typically associated with malware or traffic originating from known malicious IP addresses or network domains;
- Known attack characteristics;
- Unusual system behavior;
- Bottlenecks and overloads;
- Unauthorized access to systems or information;
- Unauthorized scanning of business applications, systems and networks;
- Successful and unsuccessful attempts to access protected resources;
- Unusual user and system behavior in relation to expected behavior.

Continuous monitoring via a monitoring tool should be used. Monitoring should be done in real time or in periodic intervals, subject to organizational need and capabilities. Monitoring tools should include the ability to handle large amounts of data, adapt to a constantly changing threat landscape, and allow for real-time notification. The tools should also be able to recognize specific signatures and data or network or application behavior patterns. Automated monitoring software should be configured to generate alerts based on predefined thresholds. The alerting system should be tuned and trained on the organization's baseline to minimize false positives. Personnel should be dedicated to respond to alerts and should be properly trained to accurately interpret potential incidents. There should be redundant systems and processes in place to receive and respond to alert notifications. Abnormal events should be communicated to relevant parties in order to improve the following activities: auditing, security evaluation, vulnerability scanning and monitoring. Procedures should be in place to respond to positive indicators from the monitoring system in a timely manner, in order to minimize the effect of adverse events on information security. Procedures should also be established to identify and address false positives including tuning the monitoring software to reduce the number of future false positives.

Other Information

Security monitoring can be enhanced by:

- Leveraging threat intelligence systems;
- Leveraging machine learning and artificial intelligence capabilities;
- Using block lists or allow lists;
- Undertaking a range of technical security assessments, and using the results of these assessments to help determine baselines or acceptable behavior;
- Using performance monitoring systems to help establish and detect anomalous behavior;
- Leveraging logs in combination with monitoring systems.

Monitoring activities are often conducted using specialist software, such as IDS. These can be configured to a baseline of normal, acceptable and expected system and network activities. Monitoring for anomalous communications helps in the identification of botnets. If the computer is being controlled by an external device, there is a communication between the infected device and the controller. The organization should therefore employ technologies to monitor for anomalous communications and take such action as necessary.

Security Monitoring is a process of continuously observing the behavior on an organization's network or we can say keeping an eye on the traffic of an organization's network which are intended to harm its data (data breach) and making cyber threats, if this happens it will send the alert to the security incident. The main importance of security monitoring is to preserve the following aspects:

- Reputation;
- Privacy of User Data;
- Availability;
- Misuse of Organization Service.

The extent to which organization carry out monitoring activities should be determined in accordance with the security requirements from the risk assessment, and take into consideration relevant laws and regulations. Monitoring records should be retained for auditing purposes for a defined retention period. Monitoring should be first and foremost carried out in line with any regulatory requirements or prevailing legislation, and any records retained in accordance with organization retention policy. Suspect events should be reported to all relevant personnel in order to maintain network integrity and improve business continuity alongside the following processes:

- Auditing;
- Security and risk evaluation;
- Vulnerability scanning;
- Monitoring.

Organizations should gain a firm understanding of normal user activity and network behavior, and use this as a baseline to identify anomalous behavior across the network. The organizations should optimize its monitoring efforts using specialized monitoring tools that are suited to the type of network and traffic that they deal with on a daily basis. Monitoring tools should be able to:

- Handle large amounts of monitoring data;
- React to suspect data, traffic and user behavior patterns and one-off activities;
- Amend any monitoring activities to react to different risk level;
- Notify organizations of anomalous activity in real time, through a series of proactive alerts that contain a minimal amount of false positives;

- Rely on an adequate level of application redundancy in order to maintain a continuous monitoring operation;

There are many methods used by an attacker to make the website or application unavailable to the user by using method like DDoS attacks, injecting malicious code or commands, etc.

- **DDoS:** DDos stands for Distributed Denial of Service. In this attack, an attacker sent large number of packets or we can say a request which is made continuously until an error occurs which also results in unavailability of resources provided by the organization.
- **Injecting Malicious Code or Command:** When an attacker is injecting malicious code or command on different input field or URL endpoint then it can harm the privacy of user's data. By identifying these kinds of commands or code and block them is suggested. So, to prevent these types of malicious attack security monitoring is configured and done to prevent, block or reject these types of requests.
- **Cyber Security Threat Monitoring** gives the ability of real-time spectating on the network and helps to identify unusual or malicious behavior on the network. This will help the cyber security or IT team to take prevention steps before the occurrence of the attack incident. Consider two main types of monitoring:
    - **Endpoint Monitoring:** Endpoint monitoring consist of analyzing the behavior of the devices connected to a specific network and analyze their behavior. It will help IT team to detect threat and they can take prevention measures when the behavior malicious, unusual or suspicious.
    - **Network Monitoring:** Network Monitoring entails tracking and analyzing the network from which it will respond on the basis of the result network monitoring gets during monitoring. If the network components are not properly working means like component being overloaded, keeps crashing, slow etc. all that can lead to certain cyber threats and makes the system vulnerable.

There are many diagnostic tools which will keep diagnosing the components and keeps the logs of the result and if there is any disturbance or threat it will automatically notify the IT team instantly via many medium. From this the IT team can fix the error or problem. To prevent the organization from these kinds of cyber-attacks the organization have to monitor the network and packets which are being thrown toward the network and prevent any casualty from happening.

- **Minimize Data Breach:** Continuously monitoring of the network will help to detect any threat before the occurrence of the event and the organization can prevent these kinds of attacks from affecting the information that the organization holds of their users and employees. So, doing continuous security monitoring will help effectively.

- **Improve your Time to Respond to Attacks:** Most organizations take security measures to prevent cyber threats and attacks, but what if the bad guys somehow successfully attacked the organization, then the organization must be ready to respond to the attack and fix it as soon as it is detected. Because the assets of the organization must be available to its user 24x7.

- **Address Security Vulnerability:** Every system has loop holes (vulnerability). Address security vulnerability means to address or find the vulnerability the network has. Vulnerability is hunted and fix before any bad guy can find and exploit it. This category also includes keeping all the protocols and firewalls up-to-date. Even many organizations organize bug hunting program. In bug hunting program the organization invites ethical hackers to ethically hack the system and make a report of the vulnerability so the organization can confirm the vulnerability and fix it, they also provide bounties, swags or hall of fame according to the severity of the vulnerability.

- **Compliance with Standards and Regulations:** The most basic and fundamental term of cyber security is Confidentiality, Integrity and Availability. An organization is required to meet these set of rules for the possession of data. If even a single requirement is not met then it will increase the chances of vulnerability existence in the network which will also harm the reputation of the organization. So, continuous cyber security monitoring will help to fix these kinds of problems.

- **Reduce Downtime:** Reduce down time means being ensured that organization's network is fully functional and handles all operations, because networks downtime can harm the organization's reputation. And if organization face any threats they should respond and fix it as soon as possible. So, continuous cyber security monitoring will decrease the chances of getting the sever or the network down.

- **Nature of Threats has Changed:** Cyber criminals are getting smarter and sharper day by day. They are always trying to get through the defense which any organization sets up for their network. Day by day cyber criminals are bringing up new attack, trick and tactics to perform their malicious activity. Best way to tackle these kinds of problems is by continuously monitoring the network.
- **Rise in Remote Work:** Organization have started using cloud services to provide the essentials to their employees who are working from home. But this causes a problem that is to do the access control so that an unauthorized person cannot get access to the data even if he tries. But then also this can lead to unauthorized access because there is always a way. So, it's a good move to monitor the traffic and detect the threat or any unauthorized user trying to access should be blacklisted or blocked.
- **Increase Productivity of the Employee:** Employee plays an important role in any organization. Making the employee productive, that is the thing every organization wants. Focusing on the IT infrastructure will boost the productivity of the employee, because well-structured and secured network will help employees to focus on their core skills and job even can do their work faster. This can be done by keeping a security expert who will handle all the technical responsibilities will be great. So, this will boost the productivity of all the employees

Effective Steps for Cyber Security Monitoring

An organization should always be careful about the traffic which is going through their network because if it comes out to be a malicious packet then it will cost the organization its reputation and its money. An organization should focus on its networks traffic by taking some effective and efficient steps.

- **Security Information and Event Management (SIEM) Tools and Software Solutions:** SIEM platform plays an important role in any organization for security monitoring. SIEM is field where software and services are combined with security information management and security event management. The work of SIEM is to monitor and analyze log data efficiently then combine all the monitoring logs in one place to make the analyzing or further assessment easy. This will help the IT team to revise the logs and fix or even they can be prepared for further possible cyber threats.

- **Trained Experts:** All the tools discussed before will do their work properly but this is not enough. A trained expert is important in the team. The person who understands the infrastructure will be much easier for them because the expert will know where to look and for what to look. But an experienced expert is much means those who have knowledge, understanding and ability to identify the threat and fix it as soon as possible. The expert will also know how to make the system much faster for the response to the attack means improving the speed when a cyber threat occurs.
- **Trained Employees:** Trained employees play a vital role as same a trained expert plays in an organization for its security. It is important factor to educate or train the employee or the staff about that how to protect the organization from malicious and abrupt attack, the attacker might try to perform on the organization. A well-trained employee will know the symptoms, effects or precautions that should be taken against some cyber-attacks. They will also understand the importance of cyber security in the organization.
- **Managed Services:** Managed services are the most important factor because an attacker can exploit the services which are not required. By setting the strong protocols and metric will help in improving security. An organization should use or enable only the required services because it will reduce the risks effectively. Some services can help the organization manage or monitor the services running on their network and system. A small mistake in managing the services can lead to a huge reputation or financial loss of a organization.
- **Identify Assets and Events which needed to be Logged and Monitored:** The strange events should be logged (recorded) and monitored. It gives two advantages. First is that if any data compromise occurs, the investigation team can find the attacker. Second is, the security team will analyze the event which is recorded to find the vulnerability and fix it.
- **Establish Active Monitoring, Alerting and Incident Response Plan:** So,

here all organization cannot put team for blocking for rejecting every single, same type of event which can harm system so to fix this, three steps are followed.

- **Active Monitoring:** Active monitoring is continuously monitoring the traffic using a SIEM tool. The work of SIEM is to automate the process of monitoring. There are many SIEM tools available in the market which can be used.
- **Incident Response:** In incident response, the organization will preconfigure the SIEM tool, that which packet (request) should be accepted, rejected or blocked (blacklist) and it is decided on the basis of the structure or pattern of packet (request). Incident response is also done manually. If any big incident happens then the security professional creates a plan and takes instant decision to overcome the incident, this whole scenario is known as incident response.
- **Alerting:** Alerting is used to send alert notifications to the user or admin whose ID is configured. Basically, alerting is used when certain actions are made like if someone is trying to upload any malicious file, trying to brute force admin panel password, etc. Define the need for log and monitoring by using log, security team can improve the security as per the log content. By using monitoring, the best advantage is automation means even if there is no interaction of any security professional monitoring can block, reject or blacklist any request.

- **Keep Monitoring Plan, Firewall and Protocols up-to-date:** It is extremely essential to keep monitoring plan, firewall and protocols up-to-date because if any attacker gets the version of any service and if it is not at the latest version then the attacker can exploit that service and harm the organization. The update contains the latest bug fixes which makes system more secure.

A.8.17 Clock Synchronization

The clocks of all relevant information processing systems within an organization or security domain must be synchronized to a single reference time source. System clock synchronization is important, especially when evidencing events as part of an investigation or legal proceeding as it is often impossible or very difficult to prove "cause & effect" if clocks are not synchronized correctly. Being able to rely upon a pinpoint accurate synchronize time across an organization's information systems is of paramount importance not only for the ongoing operation of a organization's commercial systems, but also in the event of an ICT-related incident. Accurate time representation gives an organization the ability to provide itself and any law enforcement or regulatory bodies with a reliable account of how information has been managed, along with the actions of its employees and vendors. All systems should be configured with the same time and date; otherwise, if an incident occurs and we want to carry out a traceability test of what has happened in the different systems involved, it can be difficult if each one has a different configuration. Therefore, the ideal scenario would be that systems have a synchronized time, and this can be achieved in an automated manner with time servers (technically known as NTP servers, where "NTP" stands for an internet protocol for the synchronization of systems clocks).

A.8.17 Clock Synchronization – A linkage with Ancient Era

End of War before Sunset – emphasizing Coordination, Timing and Alignment

- **Coordination of Actions:** Just as Clock Synchronization involves coordinating the time across multiple devices or systems to ensure consistency, the end of the war before sunset in the Mahabharata requires coordination of actions among the warriors on both sides. This coordination ensures that the conflict concludes at the designated time, in accordance with the agreed-upon terms and conditions.

- **Precision Timing:** Clock Synchronization aims to achieve precise timing across different components or locations to ensure accurate data processing and communication. Similarly, the end of the war before sunset in the Mahabharata requires precise timing to adhere to the conditions set forth in the ceasefire agreement or battlefield protocol.

- **Alignment of Objectives:** In Clock Synchronization, all devices or systems must align their timekeeping objectives to ensure uniformity and coherence. Similarly, in the Mahabharata, both sides of the conflict must align their objectives to conclude the war before sunset, reflecting a shared commitment to honor the terms of the ceasefire or peace agreement.
- **Prevention of Discrepancies:** Clock Synchronization prevents discrepancies and inconsistencies in timekeeping, ensuring smooth operation and coordination across systems. Similarly, ending the war before sunset in the Mahabharata prevents discrepancies in the execution of the ceasefire terms, avoiding confusion or disputes regarding the timing of the cessation of hostilities.
- **Mitigation of Risks:** Clock Synchronization mitigates the risk of errors or failures that may occur when systems operate with disparate time references. Similarly, ending the war before sunset in the Mahabharata mitigates the risk of continued bloodshed, casualties, and destruction beyond the agreed-upon timeframe, minimizing the potential for further conflict or escalation.
- **Facilitation of Transition:** Clock Synchronization facilitates seamless transitions between different phases of operation or communication by ensuring that all systems are aligned in time. Similarly, ending the war before sunset in the Mahabharata facilitates a smooth transition from conflict to peace, allowing both sides to honor their commitments and begin the process of reconciliation and reconstruction.

Control

The clocks of information processing systems used by the organization should be synchronized to approved time sources.

Purpose

To enable the correlation and analysis of security-related events and other recorded data, and to support investigations into information security incidents.

Guidance

External and internal requirements for time representation, reliable synchronization and accuracy should be documented and implemented. Such requirements can be from legal, statutory, regulatory, contractual, standards and internal monitoring needs. A standard reference time for use within the organization should be defined and considered for all systems, including building management systems, entry and exit systems and others that can be used to aid investigations. A clock linked to a radio time broadcast from a national atomic clock or global positioning system (GPS) should be used as the reference clock for logging systems; a consistent, trusted date and time source to ensure accurate time-stamps. Protocols such as network time protocol (NTP) or precision time protocol (PTP) should be used to keep all networked systems in synchronization with a reference clock. The organization can use two external time sources at the same time in order to improve the reliability of external clocks, and appropriately manage any variance. Clock synchronization can be difficult when using multiple cloud services or when using both cloud and on-premises services. In this case, the clock of each service should be monitored and the difference recorded in order to mitigate risks arising from discrepancies.

Other Information

The correct setting of computer clocks is important to ensure the accuracy of event logs, which can be required for investigations or as evidence in legal and disciplinary cases. Inaccurate audit logs can hinder such investigations and damage the credibility of such evidence.

Organizations is to establish a standard reference time that can be used across all commercial, logistical and maintenance-based systems as a trusted date and time source for all the organization's needs. Organizations should:

- Draft internal and external requirements for three aspects of clock synchronization:
    - Time representation;
    - Reliable synchronization;
    - Accuracy.

When addressing said requirements, organizations should address their needs from 6 separate angles:

1. Legal;
2. Statutory;
3. Regulatory;
4. Contractual;
5. Standards;
6. Internal Monitoring.

Make use of a radio time broadcast linked to an atomic clock as a singular reference point, alongside the implementation of key protocols (NTP, PTP) to ensure adherence across the network. Consider managing two separate time sources to improve redundancy.

Distributed System is a collection of computers connected via the high-speed communication network. In the distributed system, the hardware and software components communicate and coordinate their actions by message passing. Each node in distributed systems can share their resources with other nodes. So, there is need of proper allocation of resources to preserve the state of resources and help coordinate between the several processes. To resolve such conflicts, synchronization is used.

Synchronization in distributed systems is achieved via clocks. The physical clocks are used to adjust the time of nodes. Each node in the system can share its local time with other nodes in the system. The time is set based on Universal Time Coordination (UTC). UTC is used as a reference time clock for the nodes in the system. The clock synchronization can be achieved by 2 ways: External and Internal Clock Synchronization.

- **External clock synchronization** is the one in which an external reference clock is present. It is used as a reference and the nodes in the system can set and adjust their time accordingly.
- **Internal clock synchronization** is the one in which each node shares its time with other nodes and all the nodes set and adjust their times accordingly.

There are 2 types of clock synchronization algorithms: Centralized and Distributed.

- **Centralized** is the one in which a time server is used as a reference. The single time server propagates it's time to the nodes and all the nodes adjust the time accordingly. It is dependent on single time server so if that node fails, the whole system will lose synchronization. Examples of centralized are: Berkeley Algorithm, Passive Time Server, Active Time Server etc.
- **Distributed** is the one in which there is no centralized time server present. Instead the nodes adjust their time by using their local time and then, taking the average of the differences of time with other nodes. Distributed algorithms overcome the issue of centralized algorithms like the scalability and single point failure. Examples of Distributed algorithms are: Global Averaging Algorithm, Localized Averaging Algorithm, NTP etc.

Network Time Protocol (NTP) is an internet protocol used to synchronize with computer clock time sources in a network. NTP was developed to co-ordinate the time of the Internet and networked computers. It belongs to and is one of the parts of the TCP/IP suite. The term NTP applies to both the protocol and the client-server programs that run on computers. NTP implements a hierarchical system of time references. The hierarchy level, referred to as stratum, represents the distance of a time synchronization server from a source reference clock. The lower the stratum, the closer the reference clock. Stratum 1 devices are connected directly to a hardware clock, such as a GPS or radio time source.

Once synchronized, the client updates the clock about once every 10 minutes, usually requiring only a single message exchange, in addition to client-server synchronization.

Precision Time Protocol (PTP) is a protocol that promotes the synchronization of clocks throughout a computer network. This protocol is used to synchronize clocks of different types of devices. PTP is a protocol that works for seamless communication between different devices. It uses a master-slave system of time resources and provides synchronization. This system consists of one or more communication devices and a single network connection provided by a grand master device. This grand master is responsible for the root timing reference. The grand master transmits synchronized information to the devices residing in the communication medium.

A.8.18 Use of Privileged Utility Programs

This control establishes guidelines that govern the use of any utility program that has the potential to override business critical system and application controls. The use of utility programs that might be capable of overriding system and application controls shall be restricted and tightly controlled. None out of the organization shall be sharing any sort of confidential details. Use of utility programs (an application that performs computer management tasks such as virus protection, password management, file compression, etc.), or other software that might be capable of overriding system and application controls or altering system configurations must be restricted. Management approval is required prior to the installation or use of any adhoc or third-party system utilities. A utility program is any piece of software that is designed to analyze or maintain a computer system or network. Examples of utility programs includes, but not limited to:

- Diagnostic Tools;
- Patching Assistants;
- Antivirus Programs;
- Disk Defragmenters;
- Backup Software;
- Networking Tools.

Utility programs are essential to the smooth running of any given LAN or WAN, and help network administrators to improve up time and increase resilience across a broad range of commercial functions. Given their intrusive nature, utility programs also have the potential to cause a significant amount of damage on a given network, unless their use is properly monitored. The Internet is bombarded with different utility programs, all seeking to help organization stay organized. Yet many of these software programs are viruses and malware that hacker's prey on to get into your system and even target your antivirus software and before you know it, they have access to confidential files. ISO 27001 warns against downloading random utility programs to your system. Those you used must be verified by competent staff and checked for any possible spyware, malware or insecure code. If the program is required, then only a small group of personnel should have privileged access rights to the software and its use monitored.

A.8.18 Use of Privileged Utility Programs – A linkage with Ancient Era

Lord Hanuman and Vanar Sena – emphasizing the role of specialized tools or resources in achieving specific objectives

- **Lord Hanuman's Special Abilities:** In the Ramayana, Lord Hanuman possesses extraordinary abilities granted by the Gods, such as the power to change His size at will, fly across great distances, and lift massive objects. These abilities can be linked to privileged utility programs in modern technology, which provide specialized functionalities or access rights beyond standard capabilities.
- **Vanar Army's Unique Skills:** The Vanar army, led by Lord Hanuman and Sugriv, comprises warriors with diverse abilities, including agility, strength, and intelligence. Each Vanar possesses unique skills and attributes that contribute to the collective strength of the army, similar to how privileged utility programs complement standard software applications by providing enhanced functionalities or access privileges.
- **Strategic Use of Resources:** Lord Ram and His allies strategically deploy Lord Hanuman and the Vanar army's unique abilities to overcome various challenges and obstacles during their quest to rescue Mata Sita. Similarly, organizations strategically deploy privileged utility programs to perform specialized tasks, such as system administration, network monitoring, or data analysis, that are beyond the capabilities of standard software applications.
- **Access to Restricted Areas:** Lord Hanuman's ability to infiltrate Lanka, the stronghold of King Ravan, and gather intelligence on behalf of Lord Ram demonstrates his access to restricted areas and information. Similarly, privileged utility programs often have access to restricted system resources or sensitive data, enabling administrators to perform tasks that require elevated permissions while maintaining security and control.
- **Responsibility and Trust:** Lord Ram entrusts Lord Hanuman and the Vanar army with critical missions, relying on their abilities and

loyalty to accomplish their objectives. Similarly, organizations entrust administrators with access to privileged utility programs, expecting them to exercise responsibility and discretion in performing their duties while adhering to security policies and best practices.

- **Collaboration and Integration:** Lord Hanuman and the Vanar army collaborate with Lord Ram and His allies, integrating their unique abilities and resources to achieve common goals. Similarly, privileged utility programs often integrate with other software applications and systems, enabling seamless collaboration and interoperability to enhance productivity and efficiency.

Control

The use of utility programs that can be capable of overriding system and application controls should be restricted and tightly controlled.

Purpose

To ensure the use of utility programs does not harm system and application controls for information security.

Guidance

The following guidelines for the use of utility programs that can be capable of overriding system and application controls should be considered:

- Limitation of the use of utility programs to the minimum practical number of trusted, authorized users;
- Use of identification, authentication and authorization procedures for utility programs, including unique identification of the person who uses the utility program;
- Defining and documenting of authorization levels for utility programs;
- Authorization for adhoc use of utility programs;
- Not making utility programs available to users who have access to applications on systems where segregation of duties is required;
- Removing or disabling all unnecessary utility programs;
- At a minimum, logical segregation of utility programs from application software. Where practical, segregating network communications for such programs from application traffic;

- Limitation of the availability of utility programs;
- Logging of all use of utility programs.

Other Information

Most information systems have one or more utility programs that can be capable of overriding system and application controls, for example diagnostics, patching, antivirus, disk defragmenters, debuggers, backup and network tools.

Utility computer programmes that might be capable of overriding system and application controls need to be carefully managed. Powerful system and network utility programs can create an attractive target for malicious attackers and access to them must be restricted to the smallest number of people. As such utility programs can be easily located and downloaded from the internet it is also important that users are restricted in their ability to install any software as much as possible weighed against business requirements and risk assessment. Use of utility programs should be logged and monitored/reviewed periodically to satisfy auditor requests. In order to maintain network integrity and bolster business continuity, organizations should follow the guidance as mentioned above.

A utility program is usually smaller than a standard application and refers to a program that is responsible for managing system resources and adding functionality to your computer. This can include screen savers, icon tools and other desktop enhancement features. A privileged utility program is an application that requires elevated (administrative) privileges to perform the specific task. This can include endpoint security tools, such as anti-virus software, software updates, device/process managers, disk encryption and software firewalls. Allowing employees access to privileged utilities from their standard user account introduces security risks into the network. This allows malware to cause much more damage as it can run with the privileges of the utility program. Therefore, it is advised to ensure that administrative accounts are not utilized to conduct daily business functions such as sending e-mails and browsing the web.

These accounts must only be utilized when conducting tasks that require admin privileges. Equally, standard users should not be given administrative rights over specific utilities/programs. If a standard user account is used and a privileged utility program is executed, it will prompt the User Access Control (UAC) and administrative credentials will need to be entered. Access to privileged utility programs should be heavily restricted to employees except those who require it to perform their daily tasks. If the user requests access to a privileged utility, justification should be provided, and it should be reviewed by a person with authority within the organization. Additionally, it is advised to identify and disable all unnecessary utility programs on the machines as well as monitor and review the event logs on a regular basis in order to identify any suspicious behavior or misassignment of correct account privileges within the organization.

The organization must restrict access to privileged utility programs and control utility program access to systems and applications, by controlling access to the privileged account credentials stored securely in the digital vault. Access can be restricted to a certain time period and can be disabled when not in use. "Dual Control" can specify that access to highly sensitive credentials requires confirmation by one or more authorized users. As well, administrators can be granted authorized access to resources but never see the privileged account password in clear text. Many utility programs involve the use of service accounts; services such as back-up or vulnerability scanning require privileged access to systems. To perform their designated tasks such as retrieve, process, transmit and store sensitive data, these programs require high levels of access to running processes. Service accounts are difficult to secure since the credentials are typically hard-coded and in clear text within the programs. The solution must eliminate hard-coded passwords from utility programs and uses an advanced means to authenticate the programs that are requesting credentials. Access to be granted only to trusted programs, with no impact to performance or downtime. The solution must provide a tamper-proof audit record to track all privileged account access to utility programs and all utility program service account access to systems.

A.8.19 Installation of Software on Operational Systems

Operational software can broadly be described as any piece of software that the business actively uses to conduct its operation, as distinct from test software or development projects. It is vitally important to ensure that software is installed and managed on a given network in accordance with a strict set of rules and requirements that minimize risk, improve efficiency and maintain security within internal and external networks and services.

A.8.19 Installation of Software on Operational Systems – A linkage with Ancient Era

Lord Ram and Vanar Sena – emphasizing implementation, integration and optimization

- **Deployment of Resources:** Just as the installation of software involves deploying resources such as code, configurations, and dependencies onto operational systems, the events in the Ramayana involve the deployment of resources like armies, alliances, and strategies to achieve specific objectives, such as rescuing Mata Sita or defeating King Ravan.
- **Integration with Existing Infrastructure:** When installing software on operational systems, compatibility and integration with existing infrastructure are crucial for seamless operation. Similarly, in the Ramayana, Lord Ram and His allies must integrate their forces, strategies, and alliances with existing structures such as kingdoms, alliances, and social systems to effectively confront challenges and achieve their goals.
- **Optimization of Performance:** After software installation, optimization measures are often taken to enhance performance and efficiency. Similarly, in the Ramayana, Lord Ram and His allies continually optimize their strategies, tactics, and alliances to adapt to changing circumstances and maximize their effectiveness in accomplishing their mission.
- **Risk Assessment and Mitigation:** Before installing software on operational systems, organizations conduct risk assessments and implement mitigation measures to address potential vulnerabilities or compatibility issues. Similarly, in the Ramayana, Lord Rama and His

advisors assess risks associated with various courses of action and take proactive measures to mitigate threats, anticipate challenges, and minimize adverse outcomes.

- **Monitoring and Maintenance:** After software installation, ongoing monitoring and maintenance are essential to ensure continued performance and security. Similarly, in the Ramayana, Rama and His allies must continually monitor developments, assess the effectiveness of their strategies, and make adjustments as needed to maintain momentum and address emerging threats.
- **Adaptation to Changing Conditions:** Both software installation and the events in the Ramayana require adaptation to changing conditions and unforeseen challenges. Flexibility, agility, and resilience are critical for successfully navigating uncertainties and achieving desired outcomes in both contexts.

Control

Procedures and measures should be implemented to securely manage software installation on operational systems.

Purpose

To ensure the integrity of operational systems and prevent exploitation of technical vulnerabilities.

Guidance

The following guidelines should be considered to securely manage changes and installation of software on operational systems:

- Performing updates of operational software only by trained administrators upon appropriate management authorization;
- Ensuring that only approved executable code and no development code or compilers is installed on operational systems;
- Only installing and updating software after extensive and successful testing;
- Updating all corresponding program source libraries;
- Using a configuration control system to keep control of all operational software as well as the system documentation;

- Defining a rollback strategy before changes are implemented;
- Maintaining an audit log of all updates to operational software;
- Archiving old versions of software, together with all required information and parameters, procedures, configuration details and supporting software as a contingency measure, and for as long as the software is required to read or process archived data.

Any decision to upgrade to a new release should take into account the business requirements for the change and the security of the release. Software patches should be applied when they can help to remove or reduce information security vulnerabilities.

Computer software can rely on externally supplied software and packages, which should be monitored and controlled to avoid unauthorized changes, because they can introduce information security vulnerabilities. Vendor supplied software used in operational systems should be maintained at a level supported by the supplier. Over time, software vendors will cease to support older versions of software. The organization should consider the risks of relying on unsupported software. Open-source software used in operational systems should be maintained to the latest appropriate release of the software. Over time, open-source code can cease to be maintained but is still available in an open-source software repository. The organization should also consider the risks of relying on unmaintained open-source software when used in operational systems.

When suppliers are involved in installing or updating software, physical or logical access should only be given when necessary and with appropriate authorization. The supplier's activities should be monitored. The organization should define and enforce strict rules on which types of software users can install. The principle of least privilege should be applied to software installation on operational systems. The organization should identify what types of software installations are permitted and what types of installations are prohibited. These privileges should be granted based on the roles of the users concerned.

In order to securely manage change and installations on their network, organizations should follow the recommendations as mentioned under the Guidance section.

Where vendor-supplied software is concerned such software should always be kept in good working order by referring to the vendor's guidelines for safe and secure operation. It's important to note that even where software or software modules are externally supplied and managed, steps should be taken to ensure that third party updates do not compromise on the integrity of the organization's network. Organizations should avoid using unsupported vendor software unless absolutely necessary, and consider the associated security risks of utilizing redundant applications as opposed to an upgrade to newer and more secure systems. If a vendor requires access to an organization's network to perform an installation or update, activity should be monitored and validated in line with all relevant authorization procedures.

Vendor supplied software used in operational systems should be maintained at a level supported by the supplier. Over time, software vendors will cease to support older versions of the software. The organization should consider the risks of relying on unsupported software. Any decision to upgrade to a new release should take into account the business requirements for the change and the security of the release. Software patches should be applied when they can help to remove or reduce information security weaknesses. Physical or logical access should only be given to suppliers for support purposes when necessary and with management approval. The supplier's activities should be monitored. Computer software may rely on externally supplied software and modules, which should be monitored and controlled to avoid unauthorized changes, which could introduce security weaknesses. Make sure to establish and maintain documented procedures to manage the installation of software on operational systems. Operational system software installations should only be performed by qualified, trained administrators. Updates to operating system software should utilize only approved and tested executable code. It is ideal to utilize a configuration control system and have a rollback strategy prior to any updates. Audit logs of updates and previous versions of updated software should be maintained. Third parties that require access to perform software updates should be monitored and access removed once updates are installed and tested.

Software should be upgraded, installed and/or patched in accordance with the organization's published change management procedures, to ensure uniformity with other areas of the business. Whenever a patch is identified that either totally eliminates a vulnerability, or helps in any way to improve the organization's information security operation, such changes should almost always be applied. Where the need arises to use open-source software, this should always be of the latest publicly available version that is actively maintained. Accordingly, organizations should consider the inherent risks of using unmaintained software within all business functions.

As a basic principle, the recommendation is that the software should be installed only by authorized personnel. This can be applied with the help of the information security policy, or any other rules or best practices established in the organization. To verify this, the organization could make periodic checks to analyze the software installed in the equipment of an employee selected at random. Another way to apply it is to limit user privileges to a minimum, although this will not always be possible, because there are profiles that need to have administrator privileges in the systems to manage them. These privileges also must be checked periodically, since an employee can change area, department, etc., which can mean that you have to enable new privileges, and/or disable others. The organizations must establish a rule that the software installed on the corporate equipment is only for professional use, because the software always consumes resources. Furthermore, all type of software is affected by threats, so the use of non-professional software in your organization could unnecessarily increase the risks. For the installation of new software, the following control may be established:

- Employees cannot download software from the Internet, or bring software from home without authorization;
- When an employee detects the need for use of a particular software, a request needs to be transmitted to the IT department. The request can be stored as a record or as evidence;
- The IT department shall determine if the organization has license of the software requested;
- If there is license, the IT department notifies the employee and will proceed to install the software on the computer of the user who requested it;
- If there is no license, a responsible party must assess whether the

requested software is really necessary for the performance of the duties of the employee. For the evaluation, the financial feasibility of the software purchase must also be analyzed, when the software costs money;

- If the software costs money, an analysis should be made as to whether there is another similar tool on the market that is cheaper or even free (Total Cost of Ownership must be calculated);
- Top management should participate in the decision on the acquisition of new software;
- Once the decision has been made, the IT department will proceed to include the software in their inventory and will install the software.

The IT department can define a repository, only for internal use, to store all corporative and definitive versions of applications used by the organization. This repository should be accessed only by authorized personnel. The main idea is that this repository is accessible by authorized personnel only from the internal network of the organization, which will be easier for the installation of the software on the equipment of employees when needed. It is also important to identify all software that is installed inside the organization.

A.8.20 Networks Security, A.8.21 Security of Network Services

The objective of this control is to ensure the protection of information in networks and its supporting information processing facilities. Communications encompass the breadth of digital data flows both within an organization and between external entities across network infrastructures. These flows now include data, voice, video, and all of their associated signaling protocols. Securing this information flows as they traverse Intranets, Extranets, and the Internet requires effective network infrastructure management as well as controls, policies, and procedures. This control provides guidance in planning, developing, and implementing the most essential elements of a Communications Security strategy.

Networks must be managed and controlled in order to protect information within systems and applications. Put in simple terms, the organization should use appropriate methods in order to ensure it is protecting any information within its systems and applications. These network controls should consider all operations of the business carefully, be adequately and proportionately designed, and implemented according to business requirements, risk assessment, classifications, and segregation requirements as appropriate. It is also important to enforce the fact that when connecting to public networks or those of other organizations outside organizational control, consider the increased risk levels and manage these risks with additional controls as appropriate.

The auditor will be looking to see these implemented controls are effective and managed appropriately, including the use of formal change management procedures. Security of network services in information security refers to the set of practices and technologies that are used to protect the various services that run on a network, such as email, web, file transfer, and database services. These services are often targeted by attackers because they are critical to the functioning of an organization and are typically the entry point for attackers to gain access to the network.

A.8.20 Network Security and A.8.21 Security of Network Services – A linkage with Ancient Era

- **The Bridge to Lanka and Network Security:** In the Ramayana, Lord

Ram and His army construct a bridge, known as Rama Setu or Adam's Bridge, to reach Lanka and confront King Ravan. This can be related to the concept of network security in cybersecurity. The bridge symbolizes the importance of establishing secure connections and controlling access points to protect a network from unauthorized entry. Similarly, in cybersecurity, network security measures such as firewalls, IDS, and secure access controls are essential to safeguard networks from potential threats.

- **Vulnerabilities in Trusted Networks: The story of the Yaksha's Questions:** In the Mahabharata, Yudhishthira, encountered a Yaksha who presented him with a series of challenging questions. Despite being warned not to drink water from a nearby lake, Yudhishthira's brothers ignored the advice and drank the water, leading to their demise. The story highlights the significance of vulnerabilities in trusted networks. Just as the lake appeared harmless but contained a hidden danger, networks and systems that are considered trustworthy can still harbor vulnerabilities. It is essential for cybersecurity professionals to conduct thorough network assessments, penetration testing, and vulnerability scans to identify potential weaknesses within trusted networks.
- **Defense in Depth and Layered Security: The Defense of Upaplavya:** When the Pandav and their allies established their camp at Upaplavya, they implemented a multi-layered defense strategy. They fortified the camp with trenches, moats, and a strong defensive perimeter. This made it difficult for the enemy to penetrate their defenses. The incident demonstrates the significance of defense in depth and layered security in cybersecurity. Organizations should implement multiple layers of security controls, such as firewalls, intrusion detection systems, antivirus software, and access controls to protect their assets. A multi-layered defense approach minimizes the likelihood of successful cyberattacks.
- **Jatayu and the importance of Perimeter Device Logs:** While King Ravan was abducting Mata Sita, Jatayu, tried to fight King Ravan. However, King Ravan emerges victorious in the battle and injures Jatayu. During their search for Mata Sita, Lord Ram and Lakshman meet Jatayu, who provides information on the whereabouts of King Ravan. Jatayu signifies the importance of monitoring perimeter logs in

the event of a cyberattack. Routers, Firewalls, IDS/IPS, etc. are some of the perimeter devices found in an organization. These devices keep track of the incoming and outgoing traffic on an organization's network. By checking logs from these devices, security administrators can get critical information about threat actors.

- **Lord Hanuman and Lateral Movement:** When Lord Hanuman visits the palace of King Ravan, the guards set Lord Hanuman's tail ablaze. However, Lord Hanuman ran amok and burned down the entire city. This incident shows the impact of lateral movement on an organization. Post the initial access, one of the things that attackers do is to move lateral across the network and create as much havoc as possible within the network.
- **King Ravan's Ten Heads and Multi-Layered Security:** King Ravan, the antagonist in the Ramayana, is depicted with ten heads, symbolizing his immense power and knowledge. This can be related to the concept of multilayered security in cybersecurity. Just as King Ravan's multiple heads represent his ability to strategize and plan, a multilayered security approach involves implementing various security measures at different levels to protect against different types of cyber threats. These layers may include firewalls, antivirus, software, encryption, intrusion detection systems and regular security updates, among others.

A.8.20 Networks security

Control

Networks and network devices should be secured, managed and controlled to protect information in systems and applications.

Purpose

To protect information in networks and its supporting information processing facilities from compromise via the network.

Guidance

Controls should be implemented to ensure the security of information in networks and to protect connected services from unauthorized access. In particular, the following items should be considered:

- The type and classification level of information that the network can support;
- Establishing responsibilities and procedures for the management of networking equipment and devices;
- Maintaining up to date documentation including network diagrams and configuration files of devices;
- Separating operational responsibility for networks from ICT system operations where appropriate;
- Establishing controls to safeguard the confidentiality and integrity of data passing over public networks, third-party networks or over wireless networks and to protect the connected systems and application. Additional controls can also be required to maintain the availability of the network services and computers connected to the network;
- Appropriately logging and monitoring to enable recording and detection of actions that can affect, or are relevant to, information security;
- Closely coordinating network management activities both to optimize the service to the organization and to ensure that controls are consistently applied across the information processing infrastructure;
- Authenticating systems on the network;

- Restricting and filtering systems connection to the network;
- Detecting, restricting and authenticating the connection of equipment and devices to the network;
- Hardening of network devices;
- Segregating network administration channels from other network traffic;
- Temporarily isolating critical sub networks if the network is under attack;
- Disabling vulnerable network protocols.

The organization should ensure that appropriate security controls are applied to the use of virtualized networks. Virtualized networks also cover software-defined networking (SDN, SD-WAN). Virtualized networks can be desirable from a security viewpoint, since they can permit logical separation of communication taking place over physical networks, particularly for systems and applications that are implemented using distributed computing.

Network security is a key component of an organization's broader information security policy. Whilst several controls deal with individual elements of an organization's LAN and WAN setup, it is a series of broad protocols that deal with the concept of network security as a governing principle in all its various forms. It is focused on two key aspects of network security across all its general guidance points information security and protection from unauthorized access. To achieve these two goals, organization must implement the steps mentioned in the Guidance section above.

Network security management includes the following controls:

- Network controls that will ensure information communicated through the networks will be protected. Annex A doesn't require documenting this control; however, in order to ensure effective network controls, responsibilities and procedures for managing network equipment can be documented.
- Security of network services will be managed by defining network service agreements with relevant security parameters and requirements such as the implementation of firewall and intrusion

detection systems and monitoring the performance of the network providers. This control should be documented by signing the network service agreements.

- Segregation in networks is one of the methods to manage the security of networks. This means dividing the network into smaller separate networks that are easier to manage and protect. This division can be made based on the criticality of the domain, based on the organizational departments, or some other combination suitable for the organization. ISO 27001 doesn't require documenting this control.

Establishing Responsibility and Procedures for Network Management and Operations

Information flowing across networks cannot be secured without effective management of the physical and logical network infrastructure, including physical cabling, logical topologies, network devices, and network services. A centralized entity with appropriate responsibility and authority are generally the most effective way to ensure consistency and manageability across the organization's Intranet and Extranets. In many organizations achieving a single point of responsibility and authority for all network infrastructure can be challenging. Management of network infrastructure includes network operations, which is a separate function from the data center or information processing operations. Network security operations are often another distinct function but must coordinate closely with network operations.

Network Controls

The large scale and high complexity of modern networks in the modern organization contribute to a challenging environment for security professionals and network administrators. The fundamental aspects of network services and protocols were not designed with information confidentiality in mind. Network Controls have been designed and implemented to compensate for this lack of security and continue to evolve as threat actors and their attack methods become more sophisticated.

Methods of Attack

Before determining which controls should be implemented and in which order, it is helpful to understand the common methods of attack. Note that a risk management approach is recommended to fully analyze all threats and responses. The ultimate goal of attackers is to gain access to or modify data of value. Their targets are typically servers, workstations, or other computers connected to the organization's networks, but they will make use of networks, other computers, people, or any other tool to achieve their objectives. Their attack strategies typically involve some form of reconnaissance, followed by exploitation, attempts to bypass or disable network or host security controls by exploiting vulnerabilities, and finally data modification or exfiltration. A Denial of Service (DoS) is a specific type of attack designed to disrupt operations or make networks and systems unavailable.

Control Types

Like other types of security controls, network controls can be categorized into various types, depending on their primary function.

- **Preventive Controls** seek to stop or prevent attacks or intrusions before they occur.
- **Detective Controls** seek to detect attacks or intrusions in progress or after they have already taken place.
- **Administrative Controls** direct users, employees, contractors, and partners, to follow specific procedures.
- **Technical Controls** often enforce administrative controls, but can also limit or prevent network activity/traffic, or isolate network segments or users to increase overall security.

Defense In-Depth

A sound network control strategy employs the concept of Defense In-Depth to provide optimal security. Firewalls at the network perimeter limit the traffic that is allowed in and out of the network. IDS/IPS devices detect and prevent traffic that is suspicious or known to be malicious. Internal network isolation limits the visibility of network traffic to devices and users by department or role. Access to wireless and wired networks is restricted to authenticated users only. Strong passwords are enforced for all network computers. Computers run host-based firewalls and antivirus software. Certain sensitive network traffic is encrypted so that it cannot be intercepted. All of these controls are combined together to provide a layered or In-Depth defensive strategy.

Network Design and Architecture

Centralized management of networks allows for strategic network design and architecture that can be more readily optimized for performance, availability, and security. All endpoints should terminate to network switches to remove the possibility of internal network traffic sniffing by computers and users. Highly sensitive data and traffic such as for data centers or communications facilities should be isolated through virtual LAN (VLAN) technology and/or firewalls. Highly unregulated traffic should also be isolated. The architecture of the network should allow for the strategic placement of firewalls, demilitarized zones (DMZ's), and IDS/IPS devices such that all network traffic between the organization Intranet and the Internet can be adequately controlled and monitored.

Perimeter Controls

Perimeter Controls must be strategically placed such that all network traffic flowing in and out of the organization's internal networks, can be controlled and monitored. These controls are critical to network functionality and security and therefore must be fault-tolerant and have redundant backups available. In addition, they must be capable of processing the anticipated peak volume of network traffic. This is especially important for larger organizations with extremely high aggregate Internet bandwidth. Typical perimeter controls include:

- **Routers:** The border router is typically capable of allowing or denying connections, but its primary purpose is to route traffic at the network border or DMZ.
- **Firewalls**: Firewalls block or limit traffic, typically by TCP/UDP port.
- **IDS/IPS**: An IDS and/or IPS adds an extra layer of protection, examining, limiting, or blocking traffic that was allowed through the border firewall, but is highly suspicious or known to be malicious.
- **Data Loss Prevention (DLP)**: Some DLP solutions inspect all network traffic to detect or block confidential data from leaving the Intranet.
- **"Next Generation" Firewalls**: The term "NextGen" is a marketing term used by some vendors to imply a higher level of sophistication and thus a higher level of protection. While many of these products do perform as advertised, they are essentially serving the same or combined functions like firewall and IDS/IPS technology.

- **Web Gateway**: A secure web gateway does not necessarily sit at the perimeter, but does filter web-based traffic, providing more granular IDS/IPS functionality for web-based traffic or content.
- **Network Address Translation (NAT)**: Not strictly a security control, NAT limits the visibility of endpoints within the organization intranet from potential attackers on the Internet.

Note on encryption, while encryption is an effective control for data in transit, security administrators should also be aware that too much encryption of network traffic can severely limit many perimeter controls such as IDS/IPS, DLP, and Secure Web Gateways. Many vendors are now providing cloud-based network protection, which can supplement or replace many of the on-premise perimeter or interior controls network and security administrators have used.

Interior/Endpoint Controls

- **Isolation:** Network segments or subnets within the organization intranet should be appropriately isolated according to the security requirements of the users and endpoints. Virtual LAN (VLAN) technology is the primary control used to isolate users and endpoints.
- **Endpoint Hardening**: All network devices and endpoints should be hardened to reduce their attack surface. Hardening involves maintaining current patch levels, antivirus, host-based firewalls, host-based IDS/IPS, disabling unnecessary services, using strong passwords, and other protections as appropriate. Software whitelisting can also provide additional endpoint protection. Network and security administrators should not neglect printers, multi-function devices, and other network-attached devices which often have insecure services opened up, such as FTP, Telnet, or SNMP.
- **Vulnerability Management**: A Vulnerability Management System can help ensure that all endpoints on the network are adequately hardened. Vulnerability Management should ideally include web-based applications to reduce vulnerability to SQL-Injection, Cross-Site Scripting, and other web-based exploits.
- **Network Access Control (NAC)**: Registering all endpoints before allowing connection to the network can prevent unauthorized devices from connecting as well as enforce security baselines.

- **Wi-Fi Security Controls** – The Wi-Fi should be protected and, in most cases, isolated from all other internal networks, particularly when the organization has chosen to make Wi-Fi open-access. Open-access Wi-Fi allows any computer within range to connect and therefore should be provided limited services such as Internet access only. Wi-Fi that connects to more sensitive portions of the network should be limited to authorized users only. All Wi-Fi should use WPA2 or stronger encryption. Note that enabling these levels of control across a large campus can be costly and require sophisticated equipment.
- **Remote Access**: Remote access to internal or intranet networks can be a high security risk if not properly planned and secured. While a Virtual Private Network (VPN) service is an excellent way to allow remote users to securely connect to the internal networks or intranet, it provides no assurance that the connecting endpoint computer is itself secure. Security administrators should strongly consider enforcing Network Access Control for VPN connections or strictly limiting the use of VPN to selected trusted users. Outbound VPN can also introduce the risk of opening up internal networks to potentially unsecured external networks. Many organizations chose to block outbound VPN at the firewall for this reason. Other remote access tools and protocols need to be carefully controlled or limited. Remote Desktop Protocol (RDP) and Secure Shell (SSH) can introduce additional risks. RDP is best blocked at the firewall on provided through an RDP Gateway. While SSH is a secure protocol, the Linux and Unix systems that typically use SSH are often administered outside of the organization directory service and can thus have weak passwords. External attackers routinely look for open SSH ports and attempt to use Rainbow tables or Brute Force to crack passwords. Web based services such as LogMeIn, VNC, GoToMyPC, etc. can also introduce the risk of unauthorized remote access. Security administrators should carefully assess the risks associated with these services.
- **Back Doors**: Remote access protocols and services can create “back doors” of access to internal networks and should be carefully administered. Other back doors include analog modems, cellular services on smartphones and tablets, Bluetooth personal area networks, and removable media such as USB and CD/CDRW drives.

- **Encryption**: Encryption of certain network traffic is an essential network control. All confidential or sensitive information leaving the network should be encrypted with proven strong encryption algorithms. Authentication protocols that transmit passwords or encryption keys over the network should also be encrypted. Secure Sockets Layer (SSL) is a common encryption protocol used for web traffic.

Network Security Policies

A strong set of network security policies complements technical controls. While policies cannot always be technically enforced, users need to be aware of behaviors that are unacceptable by the policy. Examples include:

- Use of strong passwords;
- No sharing of user account credentials;
- Users are not allowed to install and run illegal software;
- All user accounts must be centrally managed and issued;
- Prohibition of rogue switches, routers, hubs;
- All network cabling and outlets must be installed by central network services;
- The limited expectation of privacy.

Security policies provide a means of enforcement in the event of known violations.

Log Management and Auditing

Routers, switches, IDS/IPS, firewalls, Directory Services controllers, and other network devices have a wealth of information about activity on the network. However, the massive amount of data they produce makes it difficult to adequately correlate and review for possible intrusions or perform forensic investigations. A SIEM solution can greatly reduce the effort and expense involved and provide a much higher level of visibility for security - Network Access Control.

Penetration Testing

All network controls should be routinely validated by an authorized external third party. The process is typically referred to as Penetration Testing (Pen

Tests). A qualified pentester can help ensure that the controls you have carefully implemented are working effectively. Many organizations are required to perform such testing on an annual or biennial basis.

8.21 Security of Network Services

Control

Security mechanisms, service levels and service requirements of network services should be identified, implemented and monitored.

Purpose

To ensure security in the use of network services.

Guidance

The security measures necessary for particular services, such as security features, service levels and service requirements, should be identified and implemented. The organization should ensure that network service providers implement these measures. The ability of the network service provider to manage agreed services in a secure way should be determined and regularly monitored. The right to audit should be agreed between the organization and the provider. The organization should also consider third-party attestations provided by service providers to demonstrate they maintain appropriate security measures. Rules on the use of networks and network services should be formulated and implemented to cover:

- The networks and network services which are allowed to be accessed;
- Authentication requirements for accessing various network services;
- Authorization procedures for determining who is allowed to access which networks and networked services;
- Network management and technological controls and procedures to protect access to network connections and network services;
- The means used to access networks and network services;
- Time, location and other attributes of the user at the time of the access;
- Monitoring of the use of network services.

The following security features of network services should be considered:

- Technology applied for security of network services, such as authentication, encryption and network connection controls;
- Technical parameters required for secured connection with the

network services in accordance with the security and network connection rules;

- Caching and its parameters that allow users to choose the use of caching in accordance with performance, availability and confidentiality requirements;
- Procedures for the network service usage to restrict access to network services or applications, where necessary.

Other Information

Network services include the provision of connections, private network services and managed network security solutions such as firewalls and IDS. These services can range from simple unmanaged bandwidth to complex value-added offerings.

A 'network service' can broadly be described as a system running on the 'network application layer', such as e-mail, printing, or a file server. Network services also include managed applications and security solutions. Network services often represent the most important functional parts of a network, and are critical to the day-to-day operation of a modern commercial ICT network. Security is therefore paramount, and the use of network services needs to be closely monitored and directly managed to minimize the associated risk of failure, intrusion and business disruption. The three main security types, when addressing the broader concept of network service security:

- Security Features;
- Service Levels;
- Service Requirements.

These three measures should be taken into account by all internal and external network service providers, and the organization should take steps to ensure that providers are fulfilling their obligations at all times. Organizations should judge a network service provider on their ability to manage services as dictated by an unambiguous set of SLAs, and monitor adherence to the best of their ability. Part of this operational assessment should include references obtained from trusted sources that attest to a network service provider's ability to manage services in a secure and efficient manner. Network security rules should be implemented in accordance with the guidelines mentioned in the Guidance section.

To increase security across all network services, including back-end functionality and user operation.

- Organizations should consider security features such as authentication, encryption and connection controls.
- Rigid parameters should be established that dictate the connection to network services.
- Users should be able to choose the amount of data cached by a network service to both increase overall performance and ensure that data isn't excessively stored to the point of it being a tangible security risk.
- Restricting access to network services.

Security Features of Network Services

Network services are basically the provision of connections, private network services, firewalls, and IDS. Security features of the network services could also include:

- **Network Security Technology**: This can be implemented through the segregation of networks, for example configuring VLANs with routers/switches, or also if remote access is used, secure channels (encrypted) are necessary for the access, etc.
- **Configuring of Technical Parameters**: This can be implemented through Virtual Private Networks (VPN), using strong encryption algorithms, and establishing a secure procedure for the authentication.
- **Mechanisms to Restrict Access**: This can be implemented with firewalls, which can filter internal/external connections, and also can filter access to applications. IDS can also be used here, Basically, IDS are devices that can be based on hardware or software, and they constantly monitor connections to detect possible intrusions to the network of the organization. They can also help firewalls to accept or reject connections, depending on the defined rules. Here it is important to note that an IDS is a passive system, because it can only detect; but, there are also IPS, which can prevent intrusions. The IPS

are not specified by the standard, but are very useful and can also help firewalls.

Network Services Agreements

Network services should be included in network services agreements (or SLA, Service Level Agreements), being applicable to internal services provided in-house, and also to services provided from outside (outsourced). So, for the development of a network service agreement, basically you need to consider what network services are established, how they are offered, service levels, and other key components. If the network service is outsourced, it is also important to consider periodic meetings with the external organization, and in these meetings, it is important to review the SLAs. For the security mechanisms included in the SLA, the selection could be based on the results of the risk assessment, or even using the organization's contacts with special interest groups for specific environments, where the implementation of specific regulations could be needed.

Network services include Directory services, Domain Name Service (DNS), Dynamic Host Configuration Protocol (DHCP), authentication services, messaging/email, remote access, and others. These services have traditionally been provided on-premise by network and/or security administrators. Today, many organizations are turning to outsourced cloud providers for many of these services. Security mechanisms, service levels, and management requirements of all network services need to be identified and included in the network services agreements, whether these services are provided in-house or outsourced. The auditor will want to see that the design and implementation of networks take into account both the business requirements and security requirements, achieving a balance that is adequate and proportionate to both. They will be looking for evidence of this, along with evidence of a risk assessment.

On-Premise Services

Most organizations utilize some form of Directory Service. Other essential services include DHCP, DNS, and remote access services such as VPN. Because these services operate at the network and IP layers of the OSI stack, and they perform essential functions for all network hosts, they must be well-managed and secured. Only a very small number of network administrators should have administrative access to the underlying servers. These servers must also be hardened and kept up to date with security patches. Logging to an external aggregator or SIEM is also strongly recommended.

External Network Services

Highly available Internet connectivity has opened the door for organizations to shift network and other application services to external cloud providers. While there are many reputable and very capable providers, it is nonetheless more difficult to hold an external entity accountable at the same levels possible with internal staff. Organizations entering into agreements with cloud providers need to carefully review and negotiate the specific terms and conditions of these agreements. Service Level Agreements, Confidentiality Statements, and Privacy Policies are among the types of documents that must be carefully reviewed and updated. The default versions of these documents will typically be written in favor of the external provider rather than their customers. External service providers should be held to the same level of security controls as those that apply to internal services. Organizations should write into their agreements language that specifies required security controls, limitation of access by provider's employees, confidentiality statements, the right of the organizations to audit security controls, and any other provisions that reduce risks of data disclosure, alteration, or loss.

A.8.22 Segregation of Networks

When cyber criminals compromise computing networks, services, or devices, they do not limit themselves to the compromised assets. They leverage the initial intrusion to infiltrate an organization's entire network, gain access to sensitive information assets, or to carry out ransomware attacks. Organizations can implement and maintain appropriate network segregation techniques to eliminate risks to the availability, integrity, and confidentiality of information assets. Network segregation is a process that separates critical network elements from the internet and other less sensitive networks.

It allows IT teams to control traffic flow between various subnets based on granular policies. Organizations can leverage network segregation to improve network monitoring, performance, and security. Network segregation is the tool used for dividing a network into smaller parts which are called subnetworks or network segments. You can think of it as the division of rooms when constructing a new house. The most important thing to spend time thinking about in this case are the spacing and positioning as well as purposes.

A.8.22 Segregation of Networks – A linkage with Ancient Era

Construction of Ram Setu – emphasizing Isolation, Connectivity and Security

- **Isolation of Resources:** Segregation of Networks involves isolating different parts of a system or organization to prevent unauthorized access and limit the impact of security breaches. Similarly, the construction of Ram Setu isolates the mainland from the island of Lanka, creating a physical barrier that restricts movement and access between the two landmasses.
- **Connectivity for Strategic Purposes:** While Segregation of Networks limits direct communication between segments, it may also facilitate controlled connectivity for specific purpose. Similarly, Ram Setu serves as a strategic link between the mainland and Lanka, enabling Lord Ram and His allies to traverse the ocean and access the enemy stronghold for their mission to rescue Mata Sita.

- **Protection Against Threats:** Segregation of Networks helps protect sensitive or critical resources from external threats. Similarly, Ram Setu acts as a protective barrier against external threats, such as invading armies or hostile forces, providing a line of defense for the mainland against incursions from the island of Lanka.
- **Controlled Access and Permissions:** Segregation of Networks allows organizations to control access and permissions based on user roles, responsibilities, and security policies. Similarly, Ram Setu controls access between the mainland and Lanka, enabling Lord Ram and His allies to regulate the flow of troops, supplies, and intelligence across the bridge to support their mission objectives.
- **Maintenance of Sovereignty and Autonomy:** Segregation of Networks helps maintain sovereignty and autonomy over resources and operations within distinct segments. Similarly, Ram Setu symbolizes the sovereignty and autonomy of the mainland and Lanka, with each landmass governed by its own laws, customs, and rulers, despite the physical connection provided by the bridge.
- **Facilitation of Exchange and Collaboration:** While Segregation of Networks emphasizes isolation and control, it may also facilitate exchange and collaboration between interconnected segments for mutual benefit. Similarly, while Ram Setu physically separates the mainland and Lanka, it also serves as a conduit for exchange, communication, and collaboration between Rama's forces and allies across the ocean.

Control

Groups of information services, users and information systems should be segregated in the organization's networks.

Purpose

To split the network in security boundaries and to control traffic between them based on business needs.

Guidance

The organization should consider managing the security of large networks by dividing them into separate network domains and separating them from the public network. The domains can be chosen based on levels of trust, criticality and sensitivity, along organizational units or some combination. The segregation can be done using either physically different networks or by using different logical networks. The perimeter of each domain should be well-defined. If access between network domains is allowed, it should be controlled at the perimeter using a gateway. The criteria for segregation of networks into domains, and the access allowed through the gateways, should be based on an assessment of the security requirements of each domain. The assessment should be in accordance with the topic-specific policy on access control, access requirements, value and classification of information processed and take account of the relative cost and performance impact of incorporating suitable gateway technology. Wireless networks require special treatment due to the poorly-defined network perimeter. Radio coverage adjustment should be considered for segregation of wireless networks. For sensitive environments, consideration should be made to treat all wireless access as external connections and to segregate this access from internal networks until the access has passed through a gateway in accordance with network controls before granting access to internal systems. Wireless access network for guests should be segregated from those for personnel if personnel only use controlled user endpoint devices compliant to the organization's topic-specific policies. Wi-Fi for guests should have at least the same restrictions as Wi-Fi for personnel, in order to discourage the use of guest Wi-Fi by personnel.

Other Information

Networks often extend beyond organizational boundaries, as business partnerships are formed that require the interconnection or sharing of information processing and networking facilities. Such extensions can increase the risk of unauthorized access to the organization's information systems that use the network, some of which require protection from other network users because of their sensitivity or criticality.

Groups of information services, users, and information systems should be segregated on networks. Wherever possible consider segregating duties of network operations and computer/system operations. The network design and control must align to and support information classification policies and segregation requirements. One way to protect the confidential and/or critical systems is to segregate the networks along physical or logical lines. Using VLANs to separate the systems creates an additional layer of security between the regular network and the most sensitive systems. In order to properly control access to the segregated networks, organization should place a firewall or router at the perimeter of each network. That way, different networks can have different access control policies based on the sensitivity classification of the data that is created, transmitted, and/or stored. Special consideration should be given to wireless networks that allow anyone to connect for Internet access, if organization offer an unsecured connection to the wireless network, they should take steps to ensure that wireless traffic is kept separate from the rest of the network(s). Wireless users should not be able to access domain resources on the wired network without authenticating first, at least; most organizations now offer a secure wireless option to help maintain the confidentiality and integrity of their wired network. The Segregation of Networks is important, because organization will not want anyone to reach their system and have access to their files, hostile or accidental. To minimize the impact of such network intrusion, it should be difficult for the intruder to move undetected around the network and to access your information. Segregation is about identifying which systems you use and determining which networks need isolating.

Network segregation according to ISO 27001 also helps information security personnel with their jobs. With the rules determined, a segregated environment will allow them to establish better auditing and alerting strategies for attacks. They could identify a network intrusion and timely response to incidents.

When implementing network segregation measures, organizations should try to strike a balance between operational needs and security concerns. When segregating the network into smaller network sub-domains, organizations should consider the level of sensitivity and criticality of each network domain. Depending on this analysis, network sub-domains may be assigned to 'public domains', 'desktop domains', 'server domains', or 'high-risk systems. Furthermore, organizations can also consider the business departments such as HR, marketing, and finance when segregating the network. It is also noted that organizations can combine these two criteria and assign network subdomains into categories such as 'server domain connecting to sales department'. Organizations should define the perimeter of each network sub-domain clearly. If there will be access between two different network domains, this access should be restricted at the perimeter level via the gateway such as firewalls or filtering routers. Organizations should assess the security requirements for each specific domain when implementing network segregation and when authorizing access via the gateways. This assessment should be carried out in compliance with the access control policy as required and should also consider the following:

- Level of classification assigned to information assets;
- Criticality of information;
- Cost, and practical considerations for use of a particular gateway technology.

Considering that defining network security parameters for wireless networks is challenging, organizations can adhere to the following practices:

- The use of radio coverage adjustment techniques to segregate wireless networks should be assessed;
- For sensitive networks, organizations can assume all wireless access attempts as external connections and prevent access to internal networks until the gateway control approves access;
- If personnel only use their own devices in accordance with the organization's policy, the wireless network access provided for personnel and for guests should be segregated;
- Use of Wi-fi by guests should be subject to the same restrictions and controls imposed on the personnel.

Organizations often enter into various business partnerships with other businesses and share their network, IT devices, and other information facilities, therefore, sensitive networks may be exposed to a heightened risk of unauthorized access by other users and organizations should take appropriate measures to prevent this risk.

Benefits of Network Segregation

Segregated networks, require an extra amount of effort to set up. Once implemented, organizations can derive numerous benefits such as:

- **Enhancing operational performance**. Network segregation allows IT teams to reduce network congestion.
- **Limiting the damage from cyberattacks**. Network segregation enhances the organization's overall security posture by restricting how far an attack spreads within the organization.
- **Protecting vulnerable endpoints**. Segregating a network can prevent harmful traffic from reaching vulnerable devices. A segregated network isolates these endpoints, restricting the risk of exposure in an organization.
- **Minimizing the scope of compliance**. A segregated network can help you reduce the expenses associated with regulatory compliance because it limits the number of in-scope systems.

Best Practices of Network Segregation Implementation

- **Network Layers:** It is highly recommended that organization apply technologies at more than just the network layer. Each host and network has to be segregated and segmented. This type of strategy applies mostly to the data link layer up to the application layer. However, there are cases of sensitive information when physical isolation is suitable as well. Also, it should be noted that these types of protective network measures should be centrally monitored continuously.
- **Always use the principle of Least Privilege**. Implementing the principle of least privilege helps organization complement the minimization of privileges and attack surfaces within the organization.
- **Ensure organization isolate the hosts from the network**. Separating networks from hosts based on the criticality of business operations is a wise move because it improves the overall network visibility. Depending on various security domains and classifications for particular networks or hosts, organization can isolate different platforms to enhance visibility into the network infrastructure.
- **Refine the authorization process**. A well-defined authorization

process is essential because it allows to safeguard critical enterprise resources by permitting only authenticated and authorized users to the network. By restricting access to authorized users via rulesets, organization can monitor those who bypass the network easily and disable them if necessary.

- **Implement a network traffic whitelisting solution**. Organization should allow only legitimate users to access specific enterprise resources rather than denying access to threat actors or blocking specific services. Such a framework is an effective security policy can leverage to blacklist malicious actors because it enhances the organization's overall capacity to detect breaches while also improving productivity.

To fulfill the recommendations for network segregation, organization can consider the following models for network segmentation:

- **Criteria-based segmentation:** Pre-defined rules to establish perimeters and create new segments can reduce future administration efforts.
- **Use of physical and logical segmentation**: Depending upon the risk level indicated in the risk assessment, it may be necessary to use physically separated infrastructures to protect the organization's information and assets, or organization may use solutions based on logical segmentation.
- **Access rules for traffic flowing:** Traffic between segments, including those of allowed external parties, should be controlled according to the need to transmit/receive information. Gateways, like firewalls and routers, should be configured based on information classification and risk assessment. A specific case of access control applies to wireless networks, since they have poor perimeter definition.

A.8.23 Web Filtering

The control is regarding access to external websites which should be managed to reduce exposure to malicious content. Web filtering is a technique that monitors and manages the locations where users are browsing on the Internet, enabling an organization to either allow or block web traffic in order to protect against potential threats and enforce corporate policy. There is a risk of malware attacks on corporate networks and information systems if employees visit websites with malicious content. Therefore, organizations must implement appropriate web filtering controls to restrict and control access to external websites and prevent security threats. The organization must establish policies for the use of online resources which may include restricting access to undesirable or inappropriate websites and web-based applications, which may include an allow-list of acceptable websites or domains or a prohibited-list of websites or domains. A web filter, analyzes the web applications accessed by users and restricts access to block listed websites, content, and domains deemed malicious or inappropriate by admins.

Organizations employ web filtering software to block potential cyber risks, limit user interactions on websites, and prevent unsafe or explicit content from being accessed by users. Internet filtering is one of the layers of network security that thwarts cyber risks and maintain productivity. Admins might use web filters to:

- Block known dangerous websites or harmful URLs that may contain, for example, malware, or spyware;
- Restrict access to potential emails containing phishing links;
- Prevent users or students from accessing explicit content, gaming websites, or video streaming sites;
- Block access to personal data storage applications;
- Allow only websites or cloud applications authorized by the organization.

A.8.23 Web Filtering – A linkage with Ancient Era

The Golden Deer and Social Engineering

In the Ramayan, King Ravan disguises himself as a Golden Deer to lure Lord Ram and Lakshman away from their heritage, creating an opportunity for him to abduct Mata Sita. This can be compared to social engineering tactics used by the cyber attackers who often send deception emails or messages to trick individuals into revealing sensitive information or clicking on malicious links. Just as Lord Ram and Lakshman fell victim to the deception of the Golden Deer, individuals can unknowingly fall prey to social engineering attacks, emphasizing the need for awareness and caution in the digital world

Control

Access to external websites should be managed to reduce exposure to malicious content.

Purpose

To protect systems from being compromised by malware and to prevent access to unauthorized web resources.

Guidance

The organization should reduce the risks of its personnel accessing websites that contain illegal information or are known to contain viruses or phishing material. A technique for achieving this works by blocking the IP address or domain of the website(s) concerned. Some browsers and anti-malware technologies do this automatically or can be configured to do so. The organization should identify the types of websites to which personnel should or should not have access. The organization should consider blocking access to the following types of websites:

- Websites that have an information upload function unless permitted for valid business reasons;
- Known or suspected malicious websites;
- Command and control servers;
- Malicious website acquired from threat intelligence;
- Websites sharing illegal content.

Prior to deploying this control, the organization should establish rules for safe and appropriate use of online resources, including any restriction to undesirable or inappropriate websites and web-based applications. The rules should be kept up-to-date. Training should be given to personnel on the secure and appropriate use of online resources including access to the web. The training should include the organization's rules, contact point for raising security concerns, and exception process when restricted web resources need to be accessed for legitimate business reasons. Training should also be given to personnel to ensure that they do not overrule any browser advisory that reports that a website is not secure but allows the user to proceed.

Other Information

Web filtering can include a range of techniques including signatures, heuristics, list of acceptable websites or domains, list of prohibited websites or domains and bespoke configuration to help prevent malicious software and other malicious activity from attacking the organization's network and systems.

This control requires organization to manage which websites users are accessing, in order to protect IT systems. This way, organization can prevent their systems from being compromised by malicious code, and also prevent users from using illegal materials from the Internet. Organization could use tools that block access to particular IP addresses, which could include the usage of anti-malware software and could also use non-tech methods like developing a list of forbidden websites and asking users not to visit them. Organization should set up processes that determine which types of websites are not allowed, and how the web filtering tools are maintained. Make employees aware of the dangers of using the Internet and where to find guidelines for safe use, and train their system administrators on how to perform web filtering. Organizations should establish and implement necessary controls to prevent employees from accessing external websites that may contain viruses, phishing materials, or other types of illegal information. One effective technique to prevent access to dangerous external websites is blocking the IP address or domain of websites identified as dangerous. Organizations should determine which types of websites should not be accessed by employees.

Before designing and implementing this control, organizations are advised to put in place rules for safe and appropriate access to and use of online resources. This should also include imposing restrictions on websites that contain inappropriate materials. These rules should be reviewed and updated at regular intervals.

All employees should be provided with training on how to access and use online resources safely. This training should cover the organization's own rules and should address how employees can raise his/her security concerns by contacting the relevant individual within the organization. Furthermore, training should also address how staff can access restricted websites for valid business reasons and how this exception process works for such access. The training should also address browser advisory that warns users that a website is not secure but that permits users to proceed. Staff should be instructed not to ignore such warnings.

Web filtering provides an organization with the ability to control the locations where users are browsing, which is important for a number of reasons:

- **Malware Protection:** Phishing and other malicious sites can be used to deliver malware and other malicious content to users' computers. Web filtering makes it possible for an organization to block access to websites that pose a threat to organization and user security.
- **Data Security:** Phishing sites are commonly intended to steal user credentials and other sensitive data. By blocking access to these pages, an organization limits the risk that such data will be leaked or breached.
- **Regulatory Compliance:** Companies are responsible for complying with a growing number of data protection regulations, which mandate that they protect certain types of data from unauthorized access. With web filtering, an organization can manage access to sites that are likely to try to steal protected data and ones that may be used intentionally or unintentionally to leak data.
- **Policy Enforcement:** Web filtering enables an organization to enforce corporate policies for web usage. All types of web filtering can be used to block inappropriate use of corporate resources.

Types of Web Filtering

A web filtering service can work in a variety of ways. One of the ways by which web filtering solutions can be differentiated is by how they define acceptable content. Web filters can be defined in a few ways, including:

- **Allow Listing:** Allow lists are designed to specify the sites that a user, computer, or application is permitted to visit. All web traffic is compared to this list, and any requests with a destination not included on the list are dropped. This provides very strict control over the sites that can be visited.
- **Block Listing:** Block lists are the exact opposite of allow lists. Instead of specifying the sites that a user can visit, they list sites that should not be visited. With a blocklist, all traffic is inspected and any traffic to a destination on the list is dropped. This approach is commonly used to protect against known-bad locations.
- **Content Filtering:** Content and keyword filtering makes decisions whether to allow or block traffic based upon the content of a webpage. This filtering approach enables an organization to block malicious or inappropriate sites that they don't know exist.

In addition to filter types, different web filtering solutions can differ in terms of where they look to apply their rules. Filters can be applied in a few different ways, such as:

- **DNS Filtering:** The Domain Name Service (DNS) is the phone book of the Internet, translating domains to the IP addresses used by computers to route traffic. DNS filtering monitors requests for DNS lookups and allows or blocks the traffic based upon policy.
- **URL Filtering:** A URL is the address of a webpage. URL filtering inspects the URLs contained within web requests and determines whether or not to allow a request to go through based on policy.
- **Content Filtering:** Content filtering looks at the contents of a requested webpage. If a response violates policy, then it is blocked.

Finally, web filtering solutions can be classified by where the filter is applied. The options for this include:

- **Client-Side Filtering:** Client-side web filtering is performed by software installed on a user's computer. It inspects all outbound and inbound traffic and allows or blocks it based upon policy.

- **Server-Side Filtering:** Server-side filtering is performed via a solution located either on-premises or in the cloud. All web traffic is routed through this solution, providing it with visibility and control.

A.8.24 Use of Cryptography

Cryptography is a science that applies complex mathematics and logic to design strong encryption methods. Cryptography is used in information security to protect information from unauthorized or accidental disclosure while the information is in transit and while information is in storage. It is the practice of hiding information so that unauthorized persons can't read it. When information is transmitted between networks, and devices, cyber attackers may use various techniques to steal sensitive information during transit, tamper with the content of the information, impersonate the sender/recipient to gain unauthorized access to information or intercept the transfer of information. The use of cryptography such as encryption can be effective to protect the confidentiality, integrity, and availability of information assets when they are in transit. Furthermore, cryptographic techniques can also maintain the security of information assets when they are at rest. This control addresses how organizations can establish and implement rules and procedures for the use of cryptography.

Cryptography can be used to achieve several goals for information security, including Confidentiality, Integrity, and Authentication.

- **Confidentiality:** First, cryptography protects the confidentiality of information. Even when the transmission or storage medium has been compromised, the encrypted information is practically useless to unauthorized persons without the proper keys for decryption.
- **Integrity:** Cryptography can also be used to ensure integrity of information through the use of hashing algorithms and message digests.
- **Authentication:** Cryptography can be used for authentication services through digital signatures, digital certificates, or a Public Key Infrastructure (PKI).

The core principles of information security are confidentiality, integrity, authentication and non-repudiation, availability.

- **Authentication:** Authentication is any process by which you verify that someone is who he claims he is. This usually involves a username and a password but can include any other method of demonstrating identities.

- **Confidentiality:** Confidentiality means that only people with the right permission can access and use information. It also means protecting it from unauthorized access at all stages of its life cycle. Confidentiality is necessary for maintaining the privacy of the people whose personal information a system holds. Encryption is one way to make sure that information remains confidential while it's stored and transmitted.
- **Integrity:** Integrity means that information systems and their data are accurate. Integrity ensures that changes can't be made to data without appropriate permission. If a system has integrity, it means that the data in the system is moved and processed in predictable ways. The data doesn't change when it's processed.
- **Non-Repudiation:** Non repudiation means to ensure that a transferred message has been sent and received by the parties claiming to have sent and received the message. Non-repudiation is a way to guarantee that the sender of a message cannot later deny having sent the message and that the recipient cannot deny having received the message.
- **Availability:** Availability is the security goal of making sure information systems are reliable. It makes sure data is accessible. It also helps to ensure that individuals with proper permission can use systems and retrieve data in a dependable and timely manner.

Public Key Encryption

Public key encryption refers to a type of cipher architecture known as public-key cryptography that utilizes two keys, or a key pair, to encrypt and decrypt data. One of the two keys is a public key, which anyone can use to encrypt a message for the owner of that key. The encrypted message is sent and the recipient uses the private key to decrypt it. Public key cryptography was invented in 1976 by Whitfield Diffie and Martin Hellman. For this reason, it is sometimes called Diffie-Hellman encryption. It is also called asymmetric encryption because it uses two keys instead of one key (symmetric encryption). The latest research focus is on the cryptographic primitive named Signcryption. This represents the combination of the digital signature and the public key encryption in a single logical step. The most important advantage of this new method is the cost which is less than the sum for the cost of digital signature and the cost for encryption. This new encryption schema has been invented by

Yuliang Zheng. Public key cryptography is used to solve various problems that symmetric key algorithms cannot. In particular, it can be used to provide privacy and non-repudiation. Privacy is usually provided through key distribution and a symmetric key cipher. This is known as hybrid encryption. Nonrepudiation is usually provided through digital signatures and a hash function.

A.8.24 Use of Cryptography – A linkage with Ancient Era

Encoding and Decoding of Messages

- **Secret Codes and Symbolism:** Characters in the Ramayana often use symbolism and secret codes to communicate discreetly or convey hidden messages. For example, when Lord Hanuman ventures into Lanka to search for Mata Sita, He uses subtle gestures and signals to convey his identity as Lord Ram's messenger without arousing suspicion. This can be interpreted as a form of cryptography, where messages are encoded using symbolic gestures or subtle cues to protect their meaning from interception by adversaries.
- **Encoded Messages and Secret Signs:** Throughout the Ramayana, characters exchange encoded messages or secret signs to communicate securely and protect sensitive information from falling into the wrong hands. For instance, Lord Ram and His allies may use predetermined signals or gestures to convey tactical information or coordinate their movements during battles or covert operations. This practice can be seen as a form of message encryption, where information is encoded using predefined symbols or gestures to prevent interception or decipherment by adversaries.
- **Protection of Sensitive Information:** In the Ramayana, characters often take precautions to protect sensitive information from interception or eavesdropping by adversaries. For example, when devising strategies or making plans, Lord Ram and His allies may gather in secluded locations or speak in low voices to prevent their conversations from being overheard. This can be interpreted as a form of cryptography, where communication is conducted discreetly to safeguard the confidentiality of sensitive information.
- **Divine Assistance and Concealment:** In certain instances, in the Ramayana, divine beings or mystical powers are invoked to conceal

or protect sensitive information from interception by adversaries. For example, Lord Hanuman's ability to change His size at will or assume different forms allows him to evade detection while gathering intelligence in Lanka. This divine assistance can be linked to cryptographic techniques that provide concealment or protection of messages from unauthorized access or interception.

- **Subtle Messaging and Misdirection:** Characters in the Ramayana often employ subtle messaging and misdirection to deceive or confuse adversaries. For instance, when communicating with King Ravan, Mata Sita may convey hidden messages or subtle hints to Lord Ram's allies, signaling her true feelings or intentions without explicitly revealing them to her captor. This can be interpreted as a form of cryptography, where messages are encoded or disguised to convey hidden meanings or intentions to intended recipients while misleading adversaries.

Control

Rules for the effective use of cryptography, including cryptographic key management, should be defined and implemented.

Purpose

To ensure proper and effective use of cryptography to protect the confidentiality, authenticity or integrity of information according to business and information security requirements, and taking into consideration legal, statutory, regulatory and contractual requirements related to cryptography.

Guidance

General

When using cryptography, the following should be considered:

- The topic-specific policy on cryptography defined by the organization, including the general principles for the protection of information. A topic-specific policy on the use of cryptography is necessary to maximize the benefits and minimize the risks of using cryptographic techniques and to avoid inappropriate or incorrect use;
- Identifying the required level of protection and the classification of

the information and consequently establishing the type, strength and quality of the cryptographic algorithms required;

- The use of cryptography for protection of information held on mobile user endpoint devices or storage media and transmitted over networks to such devices or storage media;
- The approach to key management, including methods to deal with the generation and protection of cryptographic keys and the recovery of encrypted information in the case of lost, compromised or damaged keys;
- Roles and responsibilities for:
    - The implementation of the rules for the effective use of cryptography;
    - The key management, including key generation;
- The standards to be adopted, as well as cryptographic algorithms, cipher strength, cryptographic solutions and usage practices that are approved or required for use in the organization;
- The impact of using encrypted information on controls that rely on content inspection.

When implementing the organization's rules for effective use of cryptography, the regulations and national restrictions that can apply to the use of cryptographic techniques in different parts of the world should be taken into consideration as well as the issues of trans-border flow of encrypted information. The contents of service level agreements or contracts with external suppliers of cryptographic services should cover issues of liability, reliability of services and response times for the provision of services.

Key Management

Appropriate key management requires secure processes for generating, storing, archiving, retrieving, distributing, retiring and destroying cryptographic keys. A key management system should be based on an agreed set of standards, procedures and secure methods for:

- Generating keys for different cryptographic systems and different applications;

- Issuing and obtaining public key certificates;
- Distributing keys to intended entities, including how to activate keys when received;
- Storing keys, including how authorized users obtain access to keys;
- Changing or updating keys including rules on when to change keys and how this will be done;
- Dealing with compromised keys;
- Revoking keys including how to withdraw or deactivate keys;
- Recovering keys that are lost or corrupted;
- Backing up or archiving keys;
- Destroying keys;
- Logging and auditing of key management related activities;
- Setting activation and deactivation dates for keys so that the keys can only be used for the period of time according to the organization's rules on key management;
- Handling legal requests for access to cryptographic keys.

All cryptographic keys should be protected against modification and loss. In addition, secret and private keys need protection against unauthorized use as well as disclosure. Equipment used to generate, store and archive keys should be physically protected. In addition to integrity, for many use cases, the authenticity of public keys should also be considered.

Other Information

The authenticity of public keys is usually addressed by public key management processes using certificate authorities and public key certificates, but it is also possible to address it by using technologies such as applying manual processes for small number keys. Cryptography can be used to achieve different information security objectives, such as Confidentiality, Integrity or Authenticity, Non-Repudiation, Authentication.

When implementing the organization's cryptographic policy consideration should be given to the regulations and national restrictions that might apply to the use of cryptographic techniques in different parts of the world and to the issues of the transborder flow of encrypted information.

Making a decision as to whether a cryptographic solution is appropriate should be seen as part of the wider process of risk assessment and selection of controls. This assessment can then be used to determine whether a cryptographic control is appropriate, what type of control should be applied and for what purpose and business processes. A policy on the use of cryptographic controls is necessary to maximize the benefits and minimize the risks of using cryptographic techniques and to avoid inappropriate or incorrect use. Specialist advice should be sought in selecting appropriate cryptographic controls to meet the information security policy objectives.

In order to implement encryption effectively throughout the organization, start by developing a strategy that incorporates risk management, compliance requirements, data protection, policies, and standards.

- **Develop Requirement**
    - **Asset Management:** discusses the need to identify and categorize/classify all your information assets. Understanding/knowing where confidential information resides is a critical component in establishing an encryption strategy.
    - **Access Control**: addresses the need to ensure authorized access to information resources. Confidential information needs to be protected throughout its lifecycle.
    - **Compliance:** provides information in relation to various legal and information security requirements that stipulate the need to protect specific types of information. These types of requirements discuss the need to encrypt specific types of data.
    - **Risk Management:** emphasizes the importance of analyzing risks to information. Risk treatment activities may include deploying encryption solutions to protect confidential information.
    - **Information Security Policies**: stresses that policies provide the direction organizational leadership wants to take in regards to information security goals and objectives. In order to develop an organizational strategy for encryption that will be widely

supported and adopted, it's necessary to gain the support of organizational leadership.

- **Seek** to protect data at rest and in motion using Full Disk Encryption (FDE) solutions and transport layer encryption protocols.
- **Ensure** that your encryption keys are sufficiently strong and well protected using professional and open-source vetted encryption products.
- **Use** encryption algorithms that are up-to-date and strong. AES 256-bit encryption is the gold standard for FDE. TLS 1.2 or greater is the current gold standard for transport layer security.
- **Provide** a means for organizational staff to process confidential data while it is encrypted. Ensure secure data transfer environments in internal and external communication channels.
- **Protect** encryption keys by using long, complex passwords with proper access rights to the keys. Maintain audit logs of access to encryption keys.
- **Develop** a key management process that automates the process of verifying identity and access rights. Active Directory ensures that only active organizational users can access and authenticate secure resources.

Encryption is often a computationally-intensive process and may degrade the performance of IT applications or infrastructure if not implemented in an optimal way. Be sure to calculate the performance requirements of enterprise services and end-users before implementing encryption methods. Develop an implementation strategy, gather requirements, complete test plans, deploy the following best practices of products, and effectively manage ongoing encryption solutions. When considering cryptographic controls, it is often helpful to first consider your organization's data. This data exists in one of three states: at rest, in transit, or undergoing processing. Data are particularly vulnerable to unauthorized access when in transit or at rest. Portable computers (storing data at rest) are a common target for physical theft, while attackers may intercept data in transit over a network through man-in-the-middle attacks or packet capturing and analysis. Unauthorized access may also occur while data processes, but here security systems may rely on the processing application to control and report on such access attempts. When used appropriately, encryption is a powerful tool to prevent unauthorized access to data.

Key Management

The processes underlying all widely accepted ciphers are and should be known, allowing extensive testing by all interested parties: not just the originating cryptographer. A good encryption solution follows Auguste Kerckhoffs' principle:

Managing keys requires three considerations:

- Where will you store them?
- How will you ensure they are protected but available when needed?
- What key strength is adequate for the data protected?

Key Storage

Many organizations store key files on the same system, and often the same drive, as the encrypted database or files. While this might seem like a good idea if your key is encrypted, it is bad security. What happens if the system fails and the key is not recoverable? Having usable backups helps, but backup restores do not always work as planned. Regardless of where you keep your key, encrypt it. Of course, now you have to decide where to store the encryption key for the encrypted encryption key. None of this confusion is necessary if you store all keys in a secure, central location. Further, do not rely solely on backups. Consider storing keys in escrow, allowing access by a limited number of employees ("key escrow,"). Escrow storage can be a safe deposit box, a trusted third party, etc. Under no circumstances allow any one employee to privately encrypt your keys.

Key Protection

Encrypted keys protecting encrypted production data cannot be locked away and only brought out by trusted employees as needed. Rather, keep the keys available but safe. Key access security is, at its most basic level, a function of the strength of your authentication methods. Regardless of how well protected your keys are when not used, authenticated users must gain access. Ensure identity verification is strong and aggressively enforce separation of duties, least privilege, and need-to-know.

Key Strength

Most, if not all, attacks against your encryption will try to acquire one or more of your keys. Use of weak keys or untested/questionable ciphers might achieve compliance, but it provides your organization, its customers, and its investors with a false sense of security. So, what is considered a strong key for a cipher like AES? AES can use 128-, 192-, or 256-bit keys. 128-bit keys are strong enough for most business data if you make them as random as possible. The key strength is measured by key size and an attacker's ability to step through possible combinations until the right key is found. However, you choose your keys, ensure you get as close as possible to a key selection process in which all bit combinations are equally likely to appear in the keyspace (all possible keys).

Key Sharing and Digital Signatures

It is obvious from the sections on keys and algorithms that secrecy of the key is critical to the success of any encryption solution. However, it is often necessary to share encrypted information with outside organizations or individuals. For them to decrypt the ciphertext, they need our key. Transferring a symmetric cipher key is problematic. We have to make sure all recipients have the key and properly secure it. Further, if the key is compromised in some way, it must be quickly retired from use by anyone who has it. Finally, the distribution of the key must be secure.

When to Encrypt

- **Encrypt data that moves**: Data moving from one trust zone to another, whether within the organization or between organization and an external network, is at high risk of interception. Encrypt it. Data moving from trusted portions of the network to end-user devices over wireless LANs almost always at high risk. Encrypt it.
- **Encrypt for separation of duties when access controls are not granular enough:** For flat file storage, encrypting a spreadsheet file in a department share provides an additional layer of separation. Only employees with the right authorization have access. Application access controls protecting databases often do not provide granular control to strictly enforce need-to-know or least privilege. Using database solutions with the field- and row-level encryption capabilities can help strengthen weak application-level access controls.

- **Encrypt when someone tells you to:** And then there are local, state, and federal regulations. Couple regulatory constraints with auditor insistence and you often find yourself encrypting because you have to. This type of encryption is often based on generalizations instead of the existing security context.
- **Encrypt when it is a reasonable and appropriate method of reducing risk in a given situation:** This law is actually a summary of the previous three. After performing a risk assessment, if you believe the risk is too high because existing controls do not adequately protect sensitive information, encrypt. This applies to risk from attacks or non-compliance.

How to Encrypt?

Implementing secure and operationally efficient encryption solutions is not easy, and maintaining them adds to the total cost of ownership (TCO). Further, data is often spread between internal and cloud-based storage. Any solution you select must support all current and future data storage and transport characteristics. One approach is to purchase a system, install it in your data center, and assign in-house staff to manage it. While this might seem like a good idea, the opportunity costs are high. Consequently, consider outsourcing encryption and key management. Encryption-as-a-Service (EaaS) vendors provide all the services and protection, including key management and encryption according to business policy. In addition to encrypting the data center, they can also serve as a third-party that ensures all data housed by other cloud service providers are managed by encryption policies as if it were in organization own data center. The EaaS provider does not house organization data, only organization keys. Organization in-house administrator, via a Web interface, performs configuration of encryption policies and subject access. Software as a service (SaaS) or storage as service providers has no access to data while at rest. Finally, the "cloud" can also mean organization own data center. Whether in-house or outsourced, make sure the centralized encryption solution meets the following requirements:

- Enforcement of organization data encryption policies across all relevant data, wherever it is in the network or in the cloud;

- Granular access to policy and key management functions based on the separation of duties and least privilege;
- Publicly known, tested, and unbroken ciphers used for all encryption.

A.8.25 Secure Development Life Cycle

Rules for the development of software and systems should be established and applied to developments within the organization. Secure development lifecycle is used to ensure that development environments are themselves secure and that the processes for developing and implementing systems and system changes encourage the use of secure coding and development practices. It will include showing how security needs to be considered at all stages of the development lifecycle from design through to live implementation. Specific coding languages and development tools have different vulnerabilities and require different "hardening" techniques accordingly and it is important that these are identified and agreed upon and developers are made aware of their responsibilities to follow them. Compliant policies will address security checkpoints during development; secure repositories; security in version control; application security knowledge; and developers' ability to avoid vulnerabilities, then find and fix them when they occur. The auditor will be looking here to see that security considerations are appropriate to the level of risk for the systems being developed or changed and that those doing the development understand the need to include security considerations throughout the development lifecycle. Strong initial screening in hiring for these skills, in-life management, and training of resources is essential and practices like pair programming, peer reviews and independent quality assurance, code reviews, and testing are all positive attributes.

A.8.25 Secure Development Life Cycle – A linkage with Ancient Era

Rescue of Mata Sita

- **Requirements Gathering and Analysis:** In the Ramayana, before embarking on His journey to rescue Mata Sita, Lord Ram analyzes the situation carefully, gathering information about the enemy's strength, Mata Sita's whereabouts, and the challenges He will face. Similarly, in the SDLC, gathering and analyzing requirements involves understanding the goals, constraints, and risks associated with the software project.
- **Threat Modeling:** Just as software developers conduct threat modeling to identify potential security threats and vulnerabilities in

their applications, Lord Ram and His allies in the Ramayana assess the threats posed by demons, hostile forces, and environmental obstacles they encounter during their journey. They devise strategies to mitigate these threats and protect themselves and their mission.

- **Design and Architecture:** During the design phase of the SDLC, developers create the architectural blueprint for the software, considering factors such as scalability, reliability, and security. Similarly, Lord Ram and His allies carefully plan their strategies and tactics, considering factors such as terrain, enemy strengths and weaknesses, and logistical considerations to ensure the success of their mission.
- **Implementation and Coding:** In the implementation phase of the SDLC, developers write the code for the software, following best practices and security guidelines to minimize vulnerabilities. Similarly, Lord Ram and His allies execute their plans with precision and skill, employing various tactics and techniques to overcome obstacles and adversaries while minimizing risks to themselves and their mission.
- **Testing and Validation:** In the testing phase of the SDLC, developers conduct various tests to ensure that the software functions correctly and securely under different conditions. Similarly, Lord Ram and His allies face trials and tests of their courage, skill, and determination throughout the Ramayana, validating their readiness and resilience for the challenges ahead.
- **Deployment and Maintenance:** After completing development, software is deployed to production environments, where it requires ongoing maintenance and updates to address bugs, vulnerabilities, and evolving threats. Similarly, in the Ramayana, Lord Ram's victory in rescuing Mata Sita marks the successful deployment of His mission, but the story doesn't end there. Lord Ram continues to govern Ayodhya, facing new challenges and responsibilities that require ongoing vigilance and adaptation.

Control

Rules for the secure development of software and systems should be established and applied.

Purpose

To ensure information security is designed and implemented within the secure development life cycle of software and systems.

Guidance

Secure development is a requirement to build up a secure service, architecture, software and system. To achieve this, the following aspects should be considered:

- Separation of development, test and production environments;
- Guidance on the security in the software development life cycle:
- Security in the software development methodology;
- Secure coding guidelines for each programming language used;
- Security requirements in the specification and design phase;
- Security checkpoints in projects;
- System and security testing, such as regression testing, code scan and penetration tests;
- Secure repositories for source code and configuration;
- Security in the version control;
- Required application security knowledge and training;
- Developers' capability for preventing, finding and fixing vulnerabilities;
- Licensing requirements and alternatives to ensure cost-effective solutions while avoiding future licensing issues.

If development is outsourced, the organization should obtain assurance that the supplier complies with the organization's rules for secure development.

Other Information

Development can also take place inside applications, such as office applications, scripting, browsers and databases. The SDLC is a process that standardizes security best practices across a range of products and/or applications. It captures industry-standard security activities, packaging them so they may be easily implemented. The lack of a standard approach to securing products causes problems. For one thing, vulnerabilities run rampant in shipped products. The second problem is that developers tend to repeat the same security mistakes, each time expecting a different response. The standard approach to SDLC includes requirements, design, implementation, test, and release/response.

- **The requirements phase:** In the requirements phase, best practices for security are integrated into a product. These practices may come from industry standards or be based on responses to problems that have occurred in the past. Requirements exist to define the functional security requirements implemented in the product, and include all the activities of the SDLC.
- **The design phase:** The design phase of the SDLC consists of activities that occur prior to writing code. Secure design is about quantifying an architecture and then searching for problems.
- **Implementation or coding:** The next phase is implementation, or writing secure code. The SDLC contains a few things programmers must do to ensure that their code has the best chance of being secure. The process involves a mixture of standards and automated tools. Implementation tools include Static Application Security Testing (SAST) and Dynamic Application Security Testing (DAST) software.
- **The test phase:** Formal test activities include security functional test plans, vulnerability scanning, and penetration testing. Vulnerability scanning uses industry-standard tools to determine if any system-level vulnerabilities exist with the application or product.
- **The final phase - Release/Response**: Release occurs when all the security activities are confirmed against the final build and the software is sent to customers. Response is the interface for external customers and security researchers to report security problems in products. Part of the response should include a product security-incident response team that focuses on training and communicating product vulnerabilities, both individual bugs and those that will require industry-wide collaboration.

To build secure software products, systems, and architecture, the organizations should comply with the aspects mentioned in the Guidance section.

Furthermore, if an organization outsources certain development tasks to external parties, it must ensure that the external party adheres to the organization's rules and procedures for the secure development of software and system.

Security is a requirement that must be included within every phase of a system development lifecycle. A system development lifecycle that includes formally defined security activities within its phases is known as a secure SDLC. Per the Information Security Policy, a secure SDLC must be utilized in the development of all applications and systems. At a minimum, an SDLC must contain the following security activities. These activities must be documented or referenced within an associated information security plan.

Documentation must be sufficiently detailed to demonstrate the extent to which each security activity is applied.

1. **Define Security Roles and Responsibilities:** Security roles must be defined and each security activity within the SDLC must be clearly assigned to one or more security roles. These roles must be documented and include the persons responsible for the security activities assigned to each role.
2. **Orient Staff to the SDLC Security Tasks:** All parties involved in the execution of a project's SDLC security activities must understand the purpose, objectives and deliverables of each security activity in which they are involved or for which they are responsible.
3. **Establish System Criticality Level:** When initiating an application or system, the criticality of the system must be established. The criticality level must reflect the business value of the function provided by the system and the potential business damage that might result from a loss of access to this functionality.
4. **Classify Information:** As per the Information Security Policy, all information contained within, manipulated by or passing through a system or application must be classified. Classification must reflect the importance of the information's confidentiality, integrity and availability.
5. **Establish Identity Credential Requirements:** All applications or systems which require authentication must establish a user identity credential. The identity credential must reflect the required confidence level that

the person seeking to access the system is who they claim to and the potential impact to the security and integrity of the system if the person is not who they claim to be.

6. **Establish Security Profile Objectives:** When initiating an application or system, the security profile objectives must be identified and documented. These objectives must state the importance and relevance of identified security concepts to the system and indicate the extent and rigor with which each security concept is to be built in or reflected in the system and software. Each security concept must be considered throughout each life cycle phase and any special considerations or needs documented. The purpose behind establishing system security profiles and monitoring them throughout the lifecycle is to be actively aware of the relative priority, weight and relevance of each security concept at each phase of the system's life cycle. Entities must verify that the security profile objectives adequately consider all federal, state and external security mandates for which the system must be compliant.
7. **Profile the System:** The system or application being developed must be iteratively profiled by technical teams within the SDLC. A system profile is a high-level overview of the application that identifies the application's attributes such as the physical topology, the logical tiers, components, services, actors, technologies, external dependencies and access rights. This profile must be updated throughout the various phases of the SDLC.
8. **Decompose the System:** The system or application must be decomposed into finer components and its mechanics must be documented. This activity is to be iteratively performed within the SDLC. Decomposition includes identifying trust boundaries, information entry and exit points, data flows and privileged code.
9. **Assess Vulnerabilities and Threats:** Vulnerability assessments must be iteratively performed within the SDLC process. Threat assessments must consider not only technical threats, but also administrative and physical threats that could have a potential negative impact on the confidentiality, availability and integrity of the system. Threat assessments must consider and document the threat sources, threat source motivations and attack methods that could potentially pose

threats to the security of the system. Threat assessments must adhere to all relevant state and federal mandates to which the entity must comply and follow industry best practices including the documentation of the assessment processes. Threat assessments and the underlying threat modeling deliverables that support the assessment must also be fully documented.

10. **Assess Risk:** Risk assessments must be iteratively performed within the SDLC process. These begin as an informal, high-level process early in the SDLC and become a formal, comprehensive process prior to placing a system or software into production. All realistic threats and vulnerabilities identified in the threat assessments must be addressed in the risk assessments. The risk assessments must be based on the value of the information in the system, the classification of the information, the value of the business function provided by the system, the potential threats to the system, the likelihood of occurrence, the impact of the failure of the system and the consequences of the failure of security controls. All identified risks are to be appropriately managed by avoiding, transferring, accepting or mitigating the risk. Ignoring risk is prohibited. Risk assessments must adhere to all relevant state and federal mandates that the entity must document and be compliant. The risk assessments must be periodically reviewed and updated as necessary whenever the underlying threat assessment is modified or whenever significant changes are made to the system.

11. **Select and Document Security Controls:** Appropriate security controls must be implemented to mitigate risks that are not avoided, transferred or accepted. Security controls must be justified and documented based on the risk assessments, threat assessments and analysis of the cost of implementing a potential security control relative to the decrease in risk afforded by implementing the control. Documentation of controls must be sufficiently detailed to enable verification that all systems and applications adhere to all relevant security policies and to respond efficiently to new threats that may require modifications to existing controls. Residual risk must be documented and maintained at acceptable levels. A formal risk acceptance, with executive management sign-off, must be performed for medium and high risks that remain after mitigating controls have been implemented. Security

control requirements must be periodically reviewed and updated as necessary whenever the system or the underlying risk assessment is modified.

12. **Create Test Data:** A process for the development of significant test data must be created for all applications. A test process must be available for applications to perform security and regression testing. Confidential production data should not be used for testing purposes. If production data is used, entities must comply with all applicable federal, state and external policies and standards regarding the protection and disposal of production data.

13. **Test Security Controls:** All controls are to be thoroughly tested in pre-production environments that are identical, in as much as feasibly possible, to the corresponding production environment. This includes the hardware, software, system configurations, controls and any other customization. The testing process, including regression testing, must demonstrate that all security controls have been applied appropriately, implemented correctly and are functioning properly and actually countering the threats and vulnerabilities for which they are intended. The testing process must also include vulnerability testing and demonstrate the remediation of critical vulnerabilities prior to placing the system into production. Appropriate separation of duties must be observed throughout the testing processes such as ensuring that different individuals are responsible for development, quality assurance and accreditation.

14. **Perform Accreditation:** The system security plan must be analyzed, updated, and accepted by executive management.

15. **Manage and Control Change:** A formal change management process must be followed whenever a system or application is modified in order to avoid direct or indirect negative impacts that the change might impose. The change management process must ensure that all SDLC security activities are considered and performed, if relevant, and that all SDLC security controls and documentation that are impacted by the change are updated.

16. **Measure Security Compliance:** All applications and systems are required to undergo periodic security compliance assessments to ensure they reflect a security posture commensurate with the

definition of acceptable risk. Security compliance assessments must include assessments for compliance with all federal, state and external compliance standards for which the entity is required to comply. Security compliance assessments must be performed after all system and application changes and periodically as part of continuous system compliance monitoring.

17. **Perform System Disposal:** The information contained in applications and systems must be protected once a system has reached end of life. Information must be retained according to applicable federal and state mandates or other retention requirements. Information without retention requirements must be discarded or destroyed and all disposed media must be sanitized in accordance with applicable federal and state standards to remove residual information.

Responsibility for each security activity within the SDLC must be assigned to one or more security roles. To accomplish this, the default definition of an SDLC role may be expanded to include security responsibilities and/or new security roles may be defined to encompass security activities. In all cases, the assignment of security activities to roles, and the identification of persons given responsibility for these roles, must be clearly documented.

Secure Development Lifecycle best practice

- **Think security from the beginning:** Before creating a single line of code, begin planning how organization will integrate security into every phase of the SDLC. Engage the power of automation in testing and monitoring vulnerabilities from day one. Security needs to be baked into the culture and code, and there's no better place to start than in the earliest development phase.
- **Create a secure software development policy:** This will provide a guideline for preparing the people, processes, and technology to perform secure software development. This formal policy supplies specific instructions for approaching and instrumenting security in each phase of the SDLC. In addition, it provides the governing rules and defines roles to help people, processes, and tools minimize the vulnerability risk in software production.
- **Employ a secure software development framework:** A proven framework will add structure and consistency to the team's effort

in adhering to secure software best practices. Frameworks can help answer the "What do we do next?" question and benefit all new software developers.

- **Design software with best practices to meet security requirements:** Clearly define all security requirements, then train developers to write code in alignment with these parameters using only secure coding practices. Ensure all the third-party vendors are aware of organization security requirements and demonstrate compliance, as they can provide an easy pathway for an attack.
- **Protect code integrity:** Keep all code in secure repositories allowing only authorized access to prevent tampering. Strictly regulate all contact with the code, monitor changes, and closely oversee the code signing process to preserve integrity.
- **Review and test code early and often:** Breakaway from the traditional development pattern of testing code toward the end of the SDLC. Instead, use both developer reviews and automated testing to continually examine code for flaws. Catching vulnerabilities early in the life cycle saves money and time while preventing developer frustration later on.
- **Be prepared to mitigate vulnerabilities quickly:** Vulnerabilities are a fact of life in software development. It's not if they occur, but when, so be ready with a team, plan, and processes in place to address incidents in real-time. Remember, the faster you can identify and respond to vulnerabilities the better, shortening the window of opportunity for exploitation.
- **Configure secure default settings:** Many customers remain vulnerable simply for lack of knowledge of their new software's functions. This added customer service touch ensures the consumer will be protected in the early stages of adoption.
- **Use checklists:** There are many moving parts to track and monitor during secure software development. Help your team by using action checklists at periodic intervals such as weekly or monthly meetings to ensure all necessary security policies and procedures are current and functional.
- **Remain agile and proactive:** Wise software developers study

vulnerabilities - learning their root causes, spotting patterns, preventing repeat occurrences, and updating their SDLC with improved knowledge. They also watch trends and stay up-to-date on best practices.

A.8.26 Application Security Requirements

Application security is the practice of using security software, hardware, techniques, best practices and procedures to protect computer applications from external security threats. Application software programs are vital to many critical business operations. However, these applications are often exposed to security vulnerabilities that may result in the compromise of sensitive information. Organizations can establish and apply information security requirements for the development, use, and acquisition of applications. Application security describes security measures at the application level that aim to prevent data or code within the app from being stolen or hijacked. It encompasses the security considerations that happen during application development and design, but it also involves systems and approaches to protect apps after they get deployed. Application security may include hardware, software, and procedures that identify or minimize security vulnerabilities. A router that prevents anyone from viewing a computer's IP address from the Internet is a form of hardware application security. But security measures at the application level are also typically built into the software, such as an application firewall that strictly defines what activities are allowed and prohibited. Procedures can entail things like an application security routine that includes protocols such as regular testing.

A.8.26 Application Security Requirements – A linkage with Ancient Era

Ramayana – emphasizing Protection, Integrity and Resilience

- **Identification of Threats:** In the Ramayana, characters face various threats, including demon attacks, deceitful schemes, and supernatural obstacles. Similarly, in application security, identifying potential threats involves analyzing the risks posed by vulnerabilities, malicious actors, and external factors that may compromise the integrity or functionality of the software.
- **Authentication and Access Control:** Throughout the Ramayana, characters must verify the identities of allies and adversaries to prevent infiltration or unauthorized access to sensitive information. Similarly, in application security, implementing authentication mechanisms

and access controls ensures that only authorized users can interact with the software, protecting against unauthorized access and data breaches.

- **Data Protection and Encryption:** Sensitive Information in the Ramayana, such as battle plans, strategic alliances, and secret communications, must be protected from interception or tampering by adversaries. Similarly, in application security, encrypting data and communications helps safeguard confidentiality and integrity, preventing unauthorized parties from accessing or altering sensitive information.
- **Secure Communication Channels:** Characters in the Ramayana often use secure communication channels, such as encrypted messages or secret codes, to convey sensitive information without risking interception by adversaries. Similarly, in application security, securing communication channels using protocols like HTTPS or SSL/TLS helps prevent eavesdropping and man-in-the-middle attacks, ensuring the confidentiality and integrity of data transmission.
- **Authorization and Privilege Management:** In the Ramayana, characters must manage privileges and permissions carefully to prevent misuse or abuse of power within their kingdoms or alliances. Similarly, in application security, implementing authorization mechanisms and privilege management controls restricts access to sensitive features or functionalities based on user roles and responsibilities, reducing the risk of unauthorized actions or data breaches.
- **Resilience and Continuity:** Throughout the Ramayana, characters demonstrate resilience and adaptability in the face of adversity, overcoming challenges and setbacks to achieve their objectives. Similarly, in application security, building resilience and continuity measures, such as backups, disaster recovery plans, and redundancy, helps mitigate the impact of security incidents or system failures, ensuring the continued operation and availability of the software.

Control

Information security requirements should be identified, specified and approved when developing or acquiring applications.

Purpose

To ensure all information security requirements are identified and addressed when developing or acquiring applications.

Guidance

General

Application security requirements should be identified and specified. These requirements are usually determined through a risk assessment. The requirements should be developed with the support of information security specialists. Application security requirements can cover a wide range of topics, depending on the purpose of the application.

Application security requirements should include, as applicable:

- Level of trust in identity of entities;
- Identifying the type of information and classification level to be processed by the application;
- Need for segregation of access and level of access to data and functions in the application;
- Resilience against malicious attacks or unintentional disruptions;
- Legal, statutory and regulatory requirements in the jurisdiction where the transaction is generated, processed, completed or stored;
- Need for privacy associated with all parties involved;
- The protection requirements of any confidential information;
- Protection of data while being processed, in transit and at rest;
- Need to securely encrypt communications between all involved parties;
- Input controls, including integrity checks and input validation;
- Automated controls;
- Output controls, also considering who can access outputs and its authorization;
- Restrictions around content of "free-text" fields, as these can lead to uncontrolled storage of confidential data;

- Requirements derived from the business process, such as transaction logging and monitoring, non-repudiation requirements;
- Requirements mandated by other security controls;
- Error message handling.

Transactional Services

Additionally, for applications offering transactional services between the organization and a partner, the following should be considered when identifying information security requirements:

- The level of trust each party requires in each other's claimed identity;
- The level of trust required in the integrity of information exchanged or processed and the mechanisms for identification of lack of integrity;
- Authorization processes associated with who can approve contents of, issue or sign key transactional documents;
- Confidentiality, integrity, proof of dispatch and receipt of key documents and the non-repudiation;
- The confidentiality and integrity of any transactions;
- Requirements on how long to maintain a transaction confidential;
- Insurance and other contractual requirements.

Electronic Ordering and Payment Applications

Additionally, for applications involving electronic ordering and payment, the following should be considered:

- Requirements for maintaining the confidentiality and integrity of order information;
- The degree of verification appropriate to verify payment information supplied by a customer;
- Avoidance of loss or duplication of transaction information;
- Storing transaction details outside of any publicly accessible environment;
- Where a trusted authority is used security is integrated and embedded throughout the entire end- to-end certificate or signature management process.

Several of the above considerations can be addressed by the application of cryptography, taking into consideration legal requirements

Other Information

Applications accessible via networks are subject to a range of network related threats, such as fraudulent activities, contract disputes or disclosure of information to the public; incomplete transmission, mis-routing, unauthorized message alteration, duplication or replay. Therefore, detailed risk assessments and careful determination of controls are indispensable. Controls required often include cryptographic methods for authentication and securing data transfer.

Application security is the process of developing, adding, and testing security features within applications to prevent security vulnerabilities against threats. Application security is important because today's applications are often available over various networks and connected to the cloud, increasing vulnerabilities to security threats and breaches. There is increasing pressure and incentive to not only ensure security at the network level but also within applications themselves. One reason for this is because hackers are going after apps with their attacks more today than in the past. Application security testing can reveal weaknesses at the application level, helping to prevent these attacks. Security measures include improving security practices in the software development lifecycle and throughout the application lifecycle. All application security activities should minimize the likelihood that malicious actors can gain unauthorized access to systems, applications or data. The ultimate goal of application security is to prevent attackers from accessing, modifying or deleting sensitive or proprietary data. Any action taken to ensure application security is a countermeasure or security control. Security control can be defined as a safeguard or countermeasure prescribed for an information system or an organization designed to protect the confidentiality, integrity, and availability of its information and to meet a set of defined security requirements.

Countermeasures include the following:

- Firewalls;
- Encryption and decryption programs;
- Antivirus programs;

- Spyware detection and removal programs;
- Biometric authentication systems.

Types of Application Security

Different types of application security features include authentication, authorization, encryption, logging, and application security testing. Developers can also code applications to reduce security vulnerabilities.

- **Authentication:** When software developers build procedures into an application to ensure that only authorized users gain access to it. Authentication procedures ensure that a user is who they say they are. This can be accomplished by requiring the user to provide a user name and password when logging in to an application. Multi-factor authentication requires more than one form of authentication, the factors might include something you know (a password), something you have (a mobile device), and something you are (a thumb print or facial recognition).
- **Authorization:** After a user has been authenticated, the user may be authorized to access and use the application. The system can validate that a user has permission to access the application by comparing the user's identity with a list of authorized users. Authentication must happen before authorization so that the application matches only validated user credentials to the authorized user list.
- **Encryption:** After a user has been authenticated and is using the application, other security measures can protect sensitive data from being seen or even used by a cybercriminal. In cloud-based applications, where traffic containing sensitive data travels between the end user and the cloud, that traffic can be encrypted to keep the data safe.
- **Logging:** If there is a security breach in an application, logging can help identify who got access to the data and how. Application log files provide a time-stamped record of which aspects of the application were accessed and by whom.
- **Application Security Testing:** A necessary process to ensure that all of these security controls work properly.

Organizations should carry out a risk assessment to determine the type of information security requirements appropriate to a particular application. While the content and types of information security requirements may vary depending on the nature of the application, the requirements should address and include the recommendations as mentioned in General section under Guidance.

Organizations to take into account the seven recommendations when an application offers transactional services between the organization and a partner as mentioned in the Transactional Services section under Guidance.

When applications include payment and electronic ordering functionality, organizations should take into account the following recommedaions as mentioned in Electronic Ordering and Payment Applications section under Guidance.

Application security controls are techniques to enhance the security of an application at the coding level, making it less vulnerable to threats. Many of these controls deal with how the application responds to unexpected inputs that a cybercriminal might use to exploit a weakness. A programmer can write code for an application in such a way that the programmer has more control over the outcome of these unexpected inputs. Fuzzing is a type of application security testing where developers test the results of unexpected values or inputs to discover which ones cause the application to act in an unexpected way that might open a security hole. When applications are accessed through networks, they are vulnerable to threats such as contract disputes, fraudulent activities, misrouting, unauthorized changes to the content of communications, or loss of confidentiality of sensitive information. Organizations to perform comprehensive risk assessments to identify appropriate controls such as the use of cryptography to ensure the security of information transfers.

The information involved in application service transactions must be protected to prevent incomplete transmission, misrouting, unauthorized message alteration, unauthorized disclosure, unauthorized message duplication, or replay. Additional protection is likely to secure application service transaction, which may include; use of electronic signatures, encryption; and secure protocols. The ongoing monitoring of such transactions in a near to real-time manner is also likely to be required.

Application developers perform application security testing as part of the software development process to ensure there are no security vulnerabilities in a new or updated version of a software application. A security audit can make sure the application is in compliance with a specific set of security criteria. After the application passes the audit, developers must ensure that only authorized users can access it. In penetration testing, a developer thinks like a cybercriminal and looks for ways to break into the application. Penetration testing may include social engineering or trying to fool users into allowing unauthorized access. Testers commonly administer both unauthenticated security scans and authenticated security scans to detect security vulnerabilities that may not show up in both states.

A.8.27 Secure System Architecture and Engineering Principles

Principles for engineering secure systems must be established, documented, maintained, and applied to any information system implementation efforts. Secure software engineering principles exist at both general levels and specific to development platforms and coding languages. Wherever development is being carried out, consideration for the selection and application of such principles should be considered, assessed, formally documented, and mandated. The auditor will want to see that as with many controls, the use of system engineering principles is considered against the risk levels identified and will be looking for evidence to support the choices made.

Organizations apply security engineering principles primarily to new development information systems or systems undergoing major upgrades. For legacy systems, organizations apply security engineering principles to system upgrades and modifications to the extent feasible, given the current state of hardware, software, and firmware within those systems. Security engineering principles include, for example: (i) developing layered protections; (ii) establishing sound security policy, architecture, and controls as the foundation for design; (iii) incorporating security requirements into the system development life cycle; (iv) delineating physical and logical security boundaries; (v) ensuring that system developers are trained on how to build secure software; (vi) tailoring security controls to meet organizational and operational needs; (vii) performing threat modeling to identify use cases, threat agents, attack vectors, and attack patterns as well as compensating controls and design patterns needed to mitigate risk; and (viii) reducing risk to acceptable levels, thus enabling informed risk management decisions.

A.8.27 Secure System Architecture and Engineering Principles – A linkage with Ancient Era

Ram Setu – Emphasizing Strategic Planning, Resilience and Protection

- **Strategic Planning and Design:** Just as architects and engineers meticulously plan and design secure systems to withstand threats and vulnerabilities, Lord Ram and His allies strategically plan their actions and defenses against adversaries in the Ramayana. This involves considering factors such as terrain, resources, and enemy capabilities to develop robust strategies and architectures for achieving their objectives and protecting their interests.

- **Layered Defense Mechanisms**: Secure System Architecture often incorporates layered defense mechanisms to provide multiple lines of protection against potential threats. Similarly, in the Ramayana, Lord Ram and His allies deploy various layers of defense, including physical barriers, fortifications, and strategic alliances, to safeguard their kingdoms and territories from external threats and invasions.
- **Resilience and Redundancy:** Secure System Engineering emphasizes resilience and redundancy to ensure continued operation and availability in the face of disruptions or failures. Similarly, Lord Ram and His allies build resilience by establishing backup plans, alternative routes, and fallback positions to adapt to changing circumstances and overcome obstacles encountered during their journey.
- **Access Control and Authorization:** Secure System Architecture includes access control and authorization mechanisms to restrict privileges and permissions based on user roles and responsibilities. Similarly, in the Ramayana, characters employ access control measures to protect sensitive information, strategic resources, and critical infrastructure from unauthorized access or misuse by adversaries.
- **Encryption and Data Protection:** Secure System Engineering involves encrypting data and communications to protect confidentiality and integrity against eavesdropping or tampering. Similarly, in the Ramayana, characters use encryption techniques such as secret codes, ciphers, and symbolic gestures to convey sensitive information securely and prevent interception by adversaries.
- **Continuous Monitoring and Adaptation:** Secure System Architecture requires continuous monitoring and adaptation to detect and respond to evolving threats and vulnerabilities. Similarly, in the Ramayana, Lord Ram and His allies remain vigilant, constantly monitoring the environment for signs of danger and adapting their strategies and defenses to counter new threats and challenges encountered during their quest.

Control

Principles for engineering secure systems should be established, documented, maintained and applied to any information system development activities.

Purpose

To ensure information systems are securely designed, implemented and operated within the development life cycle.

Guidance

Security engineering principles should be established, documented and applied to information system engineering activities. Security should be designed into all architecture layers. New technology should be analyzed for security risks and the design should be reviewed against known attack patterns. Secure engineering principles provide guidance on user authentication techniques, secure session control and data validation and sanitation. Secure system engineering principles should include analysis of:

- The full range of security controls required to protect information and systems against identified threats;
- The capabilities of security controls to prevent, detect or respond to security events;
- Specific security controls required by particular business processes;
- Where and how security controls are to be applied;
- How individual security controls work together to produce an integrated set of controls.

Security engineering principles should take account of:

- The need to integrate with a security architecture;
- Technical security infrastructure;
- Capability of the organization to develop and support the chosen technology;
- Cost, time and complexity of meeting security requirements;
- Current good practices.

Secure system engineering should involve:

- The use of security architecture principles, such as "security by design", "defense in depth", "security by default", "default deny", "fail securely", "distrust input from external applications", "security in deployment", "assume breach", "least privilege", "usability and manageability" and "least functionality";
- A security-oriented design review to help identify information security vulnerabilities, ensure security controls are specified and meet security requirements;
- Documentation and formal acknowledgement of security controls that do not fully meet requirements;
- Hardening of systems.

The organization should consider "zero trust" principles such as:

- Assuming the organization's information systems are already breached and thus not be reliant on network perimeter security alone;
- Employing a "never trust and always verify" approach for access to information systems;
- Ensuring that requests to information systems are encrypted end-to-end;
- Verifying each request to an information system as if it originated from an open, external network, even if these requests originated internal to the organization;
- Using "least privilege" and dynamic access control techniques. This includes authenticating and authorizing requests for information or to systems based on contextual information such as authentication information, user identities, data about the user endpoint device, and data classification;
- Always authenticating requester and always validating authorization requests to information systems based on information including authentication information and user identities, data about the user endpoint device, and data classification.

The established security engineering principles should be applied, where applicable, to outsourced development of information systems through the contracts and other binding agreements between the organization and the supplier to whom the organization outsources. The organization should ensure that suppliers' security engineering practices align with the organization's needs. The security engineering principles and the established engineering procedures should be regularly reviewed to ensure that they are effectively contributing to enhanced standards of security within the engineering process. They should also be regularly reviewed to ensure that they remain up-to-date in terms of combating any new potential threats and in remaining applicable to advances in the technologies and solutions being applied.

Other Information

Secure engineering principles can be applied to the design or configuration of a range of techniques, such as:

- Fault Tolerance and Other Resilience Techniques;
- Segregation;
- Tamper Resistance.

Use of secure virtualization technology can help eliminate the risk of interception between two applications running on the same device. Use of tamper resistance systems can help identify both the logical and physical tampering with information systems and prevent unauthorized extraction of information.

Secure virtualization techniques can be used to prevent interference between applications running on the same physical device. If a virtual instance of an application is compromised by an attacker, only that instance is affected. The attack has no effect on any other application or data. Tamper resistance techniques can be used to detect tampering of information containers, whether physical or logical. A characteristic of such techniques is that there is a record of the attempt to tamper with the container. In addition, the control can prevent the successful extraction of data through its destruction.

Organizations can eliminate security threats to information systems by creating secure system engineering principles that are applied to all phases of the information system lifecycle. Organizations are to maintain the security of information systems during the design, deployment, operation stages by establishing and implementing secure system engineering principles that system engineers comply with. Secure engineering is actually how you will apply security while developing your IT projects. In order to do that, you should take into account threats from natural disasters and humans, which may include: earthquakes, tornadoes, floods, misuse, and malicious human behavior. To assure management of those threats, high-level rules are defined to apply security. These are the secure engineering principles. It is important that secure IT engineering procedures based on security engineering principles be defined, documented, and applied in the IT engineering department of the organization. It is important to balance data security and accessibility across every architecture layer. There is a need to evaluate new technology for security threats and review the design of documented attack patterns. To make certain that these principles and developed engineering processes contribute effectively toward improved safety standards, the processes should be reviewed periodically. As well as being reviewed regularly, they should also be updated as needed to keep up with changes in technology and to make certain that they remain applicable to any new threats. Developing agreements and other binding agreements between outsourced organizations and their suppliers should apply the established principles of security engineering to outsourced information systems as appropriate. Suppliers must adhere to the same rigorous security engineering standards as the organization does. A secure engineering approach should be applied during the development of applications with input/output interfaces. Using secure engineering techniques you can prevent unauthorized access to accounts, control secure access to accounts, validate data, perform sanitation, and remove debugging codes from the system. Organizations should embed security into all layers of information systems, including business processes, applications, and data architecture. Secure engineering principles should apply to all activities related to information systems and should be subject to regular review and updates taking into account emerging threats and attack patterns. In addition to information systems developed and operated internally, it also applies to information systems created by external service providers. Therefore, organisations should ensure that service providers' practices and standards comply with their own secure engineering principles.

- Guidance on user authentication methods;

- Guidance on secure session control;
- Guidance on data sanitization and validation procedures;
- Comprehensive analysis of all security measures needed to protect information assets and systems against known threats;
- Comprehensive analysis on capabilities of security measures to identify, eliminate and respond to security threats;
- Analyzing security measures applied to specific business activities;
- How security measures will be implemented and where. This may include the integration of a specific security control within technical infrastructure;
- How different security measures work together and operate as a combined set of controls?

To aid in designing secure information systems, the National Institute of Standards and Technology (NIST) compiled a set of engineering principles for system security. These principles provide a foundation upon which a more consistent and structured approach to the design, development, and implementation of IT security capabilities can be constructed. While the primary focus of these principles is the implementation of technical controls, these principles highlight the fact that, to be effective, a system security design should also consider non-technical issues. Ideally, the principles presented here would be used from the onset of a program then employed throughout the system's lifecycle. However, these principles are also helpful in affirming or confirming the security posture of already deployed information systems. The principles are short and concise and can be used by all organizations to develop their system lifecycle policies. The principles presented herein can be used by:

- Users when developing and evaluating functional requirements, or when operating information systems within their organizations;
- System Engineers and Architects when designing, implementing, or modifying an information system;
- IT Specialists during all phases of the system lifecycle;
- Program Managers and Information Security Officers to ensure adequate security measures have been considered for all phases of the system life-cycle.

The application of security engineering principles is primarily targeted at new information systems under development or systems undergoing major upgrades and should be integrated into the system development lifecycle. For legacy information systems, organizations should apply security engineering principles to system upgrades and modifications, to the extent feasible, given the current state of the hardware, software, and firmware components within the system.

A.8.28 Secure Coding

Code is the core of a computer program. If there are any vulnerabilities in it, then the whole program may be compromised by cyber-attacks. Secure coding is the practice in which any software is developed in a way that protects accidental security vulnerabilities. It governs the coding techniques, practices, and decisions that developers make during the development. Secure coding's core aim is to ensure that the written code can minimize any vulnerabilities. It involves writing code in a high-level language that adheres to strict principles of security. Secure coding is much more than just writing, compiling, running, and releasing code into the production environment. To completely embrace secure coding, you must also create a secure development environment that is built on secure and reliable infrastructure using secured software, services, and providers. Besides, the code must not have any logic flaws, bugs, errors, and defects that can form security risks. Poor coding practices such as improper input validation and weak key generation can expose information systems to security vulnerabilities and result in cyber attacks and compromise of sensitive information assets. Organizations should ensure that secure coding principles are followed so that poor coding practices do not lead to security vulnerabilities. The goal of software security is to maintain the integrity, confidentiality, and availability of information resources to establish successful business operations that can only be achieved by integrating security practices. Flaws in security can happen at any stage of the development life cycle, like:

- Failure to identify requirements of security upfront;
- Errors in conceptual designs;
- Technical vulnerabilities are introduced due to poor coding practices;
- Implementing the software improperly or introducing errors during maintenance or updates.

However, secure coding techniques make it easier for developers to remove common vulnerabilities by following security standards for coding. It also helps in weeding out exploited risks, preventing cyber-attacks and leaks of sensitive information.

A.8.28 Secure Coding – A linkage with Ancient Era

Rescue of Mata Sita from Lanka – Emphasizing Attention to Detail, Robustness and Reliability

- **Input Validation and Sanitization:** Secure Coding involves validating and sanitizing input to prevent vulnerabilities such as injection attacks. In the Ramayana, when Lord Hanuman searches for Mata Sita in Lanka, He carefully validates information gathered from various sources to ensure its accuracy and reliability, preventing the infiltration of deceptive or misleading data that could compromise the rescue mission.
- **Error Handling and Exception Management:** Secure Coding includes robust error handling and exception management to prevent exploitation of unexpected conditions. Similarly, when Lord Ram and His allies encounter unexpected obstacles or setbacks during the rescue mission, they adapt quickly, employing contingency plans and alternative strategies to overcome challenges and maintain progress toward their objective.
- **Authentication and Authorization:** Secure Coding incorporates strong authentication and authorization mechanisms to control access to sensitive functionality or data. Lord Ram and His allies use authentication techniques such as secret signs, tokens, or passwords to verify the identities of allies and confirm their allegiance before entrusting them with critical tasks or information related to the rescue of Mata Sita.
- **Data Encryption and Confidentiality:** Secure Coding involves encrypting sensitive data to protect its confidentiality and integrity. Similarly, in the Ramayana, characters may use encryption techniques to communicate securely and protect sensitive information related to the rescue mission from interception or decipherment by adversaries.
- **Code Reviews and Testing:** Secure Coding practices include code reviews and testing to identify and address vulnerabilities before deployment. Similarly, Lord Ram and His allies meticulously review their plans and strategies, anticipating potential weaknesses or vulnerabilities that could jeopardize the success of the rescue mission. They conduct tests and simulations to validate their approaches and ensure readiness for the challenges ahead.

- **Continuous Improvement and Adaptation:** Secure Coding emphasizes continuous improvement and adaptation to evolving threats and challenges. Similarly, Lord Ram and His allies continuously assess their progress, learn from their experiences, and adapt their strategies and tactics in real-time to overcome obstacles and achieve their ultimate goal of rescuing Sita from captivity.

Control

Secure coding principles should be applied to software development.

Purpose

To ensure software is written securely thereby reducing the number of potential information security vulnerabilities in the software.

Guidance

General

The organization should establish organization-wide processes to provide good governance for secure coding. A minimum secure baseline should be established and applied. Additionally, such processes and governance should be extended to cover software components from third parties and open-source software. The organization should monitor real world threats and up-to-date advice and information on software vulnerabilities to guide the organization's secure coding principles through continual improvement and learning. This can help with ensuring effective secure coding practices are implemented to combat the fast-changing threat landscape.

Planning and Before Coding

Secure coding principles should be used both for new developments and in reuse scenarios. These principles should be applied to development activities both within the organization and for products and services supplied by the organization to others. Planning and prerequisites before coding should include:

- Organization-specific expectations and approved principles for secure coding to be used for both in-house and outsourced code developments;

- Common and historical coding practices and defects that lead to information security vulnerabilities;
- Configuring development tools, such as integrated development environments (IDE), to help enforce the creation of secure code;
- Following guidance issued by the providers of development tools and execution environments as applicable;
- Maintenance and use of updated development tools;
- Qualification of developers in writing secure code;
- Secure design and architecture, including threat modelling;
- Secure coding standards and where relevant mandating their use;
- Use of controlled environments for development.

During Coding

Considerations during coding should include:

- Secure coding practices specific to the programming languages and techniques being used;
- Using secure programming techniques;
- Using structured programming techniques;
- Documenting code and removing programming defects, which can allow information security vulnerabilities to be exploited;
- Prohibiting the use of insecure design techniques;
- Security testing should be performed both during and after the development.

Testing should be conducted during and after development. Static Application Security Testing (SAST) processes can identify security vulnerabilities in software. Before software is made operational, the following should be evaluated:

- Attack surface and the principle of least privilege;
- Conducting an analysis of the most common programming errors and documenting that these have been mitigated.

Review and Maintenance

After code has been made operational:

- Updates should be securely packaged and deployed;
- Reported information security vulnerabilities should be handled;
- Errors and suspected attacks should be logged and logs regularly reviewed to make adjustments to the code as necessary;
- Source code should be protected against unauthorized access and tampering.

If using external tools and libraries, the organization should consider:

- Ensuring that external libraries are managed and regularly updated with release cycles;
- Selection, authorization and reuse of well-vetted components, particularly authentication and cryptographic components;
- The license, security and history of external components;
- Ensuring that software is maintainable, tracked and originates from proven, reputable sources;
- Sufficiently long-term availability of development resources and artifacts.

Where a software package needs to be modified the following points should be considered:

- The risk of built-in controls and integrity processes being compromised;
- Whether to obtain the consent of the vendor;
- The possibility of obtaining the required changes from the vendor as standard program updates;
- The impact if the organization becomes responsible for the future maintenance of the software as a result of changes;
- Compatibility with other software in use.

Other Information

A guiding principle is to ensure security-relevant code is invoked when necessary and is tamper-resistant. Programs installed from compiled binary code also have these properties but only for data held within the application. For interpreted languages, the concept only works when the code is executed on a server that is otherwise inaccessible by the users and processes that use it, and that its data is held in a similarly protected database. For example, the interpreted code can be run on a cloud service where access to the code itself requires administrator privileges. Such administrator access should be protected by security mechanisms such as just-in-time administration principles and strong authentication. If the application owner can access scripts by direct remote access to the server, so in principle can an attacker? Web servers should be configured to prevent directory browsing in such cases. Application code is best designed on the assumption that it is always subject to attack, through error or malicious action. In addition, critical applications can be designed to be tolerant of internal faults. For example, the output from a complex algorithm can be checked to ensure that it lies within safe bounds before the data is used in an application such as a safety or financial critical application. The code that performs the boundary checks is simple and therefore much easier to prove correctness. Some web applications are susceptible to a variety of vulnerabilities that are introduced by poor design and coding, such as database injection and cross-site scripting attacks. In these attacks, requests can be manipulated to abuse the web server functionality.

Organizations are to establish and implement organization-wide processes for secure coding that applies to both software products obtained from external parties and to open-source software components. Organizations should keep up-to-date with evolving real-world security threats and with the most recent information on known or potential software security vulnerabilities. This will enable organizations to improve, and implement robust secure software coding principles that are effective against evolving cyber threats. Secure software coding principles should be followed both for new coding projects and for software reuse operations. These principles should be adhered to both for in-house software development activities and for the transfer of the organization's software products or services to third parties.

Planning and Precoding

Both new code development and code reuse require the application of secure coding principles, regardless of whether the code is written for internal software or for external products and services. This requires the evaluation of the organization-specific expectations and definition of recognized principles in advance. In addition, recommended actions for planning and precoding take into account known common and historical coding practices and errors that could lead to vulnerabilities. The configuration of development tools, such as rule-based in integrated development environments (IDE), should enforce the creation of secure code. Quite critical is the qualification of developers and their familiarity with secure architectures and programming standards. The inclusion of information security expertise in the development team goes without saying. When establishing a plan for secure coding principles and determining the prerequisites for secure coding, organizations should comply with the following recommendations mentioned under Planning and Before Coding section in Guidance.

During the Coding Process

During the coding process, coding practices and structured programming techniques play a primary role, taking into account the specific use case and its security needs. Insecure design techniques should be consistently prohibited. Code should be adequately documented and reviewed to best eliminate security-related bugs. Code review should take place both during and after development, via Static Application Security Testing (SAST) or similar. Static testing methods support the shift left approach ("test early and often") by shifting left in the lifecycle by testing visible code for rule conformance early. This allows early identification of tainted code, connections to files or specific object classes, or application-level gaps that can be abused for unnoticed interaction with third-party programs as exploitable vulnerabilities. Before the software is put into operation, this control requires an evaluation of attack surfaces and the implementation of the least privilege principle. The analysis performed of the most common programming errors and documentation of their correction should be evaluated. Secure coding practices and procedures should take into account the coding process as recommended in the section During Coding in Gudiance.

Before putting the software into actual use in the live application environment, organizations should consider the following:

- What is the attack surface?

- Is the principle of least privilege followed?

Carrying out an analysis of the most prevalent programming mistakes and documenting that these risks have been eliminated.

Review and Maintenance

Even after the software has gone live, the topic of secure coding remains relevant. This includes secure updates as well as checks for known vulnerabilities in one's code. In addition, errors and suspected attacks must be documented so that necessary adjustments can be made promptly. In any case, unauthorized access to the source code must be reliably prevented by suitable tools. After the code is put into use in the production environment, updates should be applied in a secure manner. Security vulnerabilities reported should be addressed. Suspected attacks on information systems and errors should be recorded and these records should be reviewed on regular intervals so that appropriate changes to code can be made. Unauthorized access to, use of, or changes to source code should be prevented via mechanisms such as management tools. When organizations use external tools, they should take into account the recommendations mentioned in the section Review and Maintenance under Gudiance.

When making changes to a software package, the points as mentioned in the section Review and Maintenance under Guidance should be considered

In the area of verification and maintenance, it additionally lists explicit instructions for the use of external tools and libraries, such as open-source software. These code components should be managed, updated and maintained in inventories. This can be done, for example, via a Software Bill of Material (SBOM). An SBOM is a formal, structured record of a software's packages and libraries and their relationships to each other and within the supply chain, in particular to keep track of reused code and open-source components. The SBOM supports software maintainability and targeted security updates. Organizations should ensure that security-relevant code is used when it is necessary and is resistant to tampering:

- While programs installed via binary code include security-relevant code, this is limited to the data stored within the application itself

- Concept of security-relevant code is only useful when code is run on a server that is not accessible to the user and it is segregated from the processes that use it and its data is kept securely in another database. It is recommended that the organization protect these access rights via methods such as just-in-time administrator privileges and robust authentication mechanisms;
- Appropriate configurations on web servers should be implemented to prevent unauthorized access to and browsing of the directory;
- When designing application code, you should start with the assumption that the code is vulnerable to attacks due to coding errors and actions by malicious actors. You should design critical applications in a way that they are not vulnerable to internal faults;
- Certain web applications are highly vulnerable to security threats due to poor coding practice.

Top Secure Coding Checklist

1. **Input Validation:** For input validation, organization need to conduct data validation on the authenticated server, determine trusted and untrustworthy data sources, specify accurate character sets and encode data into common characters before validating. In case of input rejection, there must be a validation failure.
2. **Authentication:** Another important factor to maintain the security of the code is authentication. It is crucial to authenticate all the pages as well as resources and enforce the authentication system on a trusted system. After that, organization can easily establish and use standard authentication services. Another important thing to consider while authenticating is to segregate authentication logic from the resource that is being requested.
3. **Password Management:** When it comes to passwords, they should be concealed on the user's screen, and if someone is trying to access the account with the wrong credentials the account should be disabled for a certain time period to discourage brute force of password guessing. Temporary passwords should have a short expiration time and users must be verified in case of password reset. You can also add multi-factor authentication for highly sensitive or transactional accounts.

4. **Access Control:** While developing an app you should restrict access to protected URLs, functions, services, object references, application data, user and data attributes, and security configurations to authorized users only. Moreover, the app should deny all access if the security configuration information cannot be accessed.

5. **Error Handling:** Most software errors are caused by bugs, which can lead to vulnerabilities. Keeping a log of errors and handling them accordingly are two of the best ways to minimize their impact. Error handling attempts to prevent catastrophic failures by identifying errors in the code before they occur. Using error logging, developers can diagnose errors and mitigate their effects. To comply with secure coding standards, it is necessary to document and log all errors, exceptions, and failures.

6. **Data Protection:** To improve data protection, you should encrypt highly sensitive information on the server-side by using cryptographic hashes and protect server-side code from being downloaded by the user. Disabling the auto-complete feature on forms containing sensitive information can also help in enhancing security.

7. **Communication Security:** Implement encryption for sensitive data transmission by incorporating Transport Layer Security (TLS) certificates.

8. **System Configuration:** System configuration can be secured if you are using the latest versions of frameworks, servers, and other system components, or removing unnecessary files, functionalities, test codes, etc., from HTTP response headers. Provide access to only authorized development and test groups and isolate development environments from the production network. Development environments are seldom as secure as production environments, which enables attackers to identify shared vulnerabilities or exploit them. It is thus imperative that you implement a software change control system to manage and track changes in both production and development environments.

9. **Database Security:** For database security, use strongly typed queries, use input and output validation and use secure credentials to access the database. You should also change or remove the default passwords of the database with strong passwords or multi-factor authentication.

General Coding Practices

Now that we have gone through the checklist of secure coding, it is time to have a look at general coding practices that any developer should follow:

- Always use tested and approved codes rather than unmanageable code;
- Do not allow the app to directly issue commands to the operating system using initiated command shells instead use task specified APIs that conduct tasks related to the OS;
- To verify the integrity of libraries, interpreted codes, configuration files, and executables use hashes or checksums;
- Protect shared resources and variables from ill-suited intersecting access;
- Don't pass user-provided data to a dynamic function;
- Users should not be able to alter existing code or develop new ones;
- Review all third-party code, applications, and libraries to ensure safe functionality and business necessity;
- Use cryptographic signatures for code in case of automatic updates and determine signature verification by clients.

A.8.29 Security Testing in Development and Acceptance

Security testing is a type of Software Testing that uncovers vulnerabilities, threats, risks in a software application and prevents malicious attacks from intruders. The purpose of security tests is to identify all possible loopholes and weaknesses of the software system which might result in a loss of information, revenue, repute at the hands of the employees or outsiders of the organization. Cyber criminals are constantly inventing new ways and are improving their strategies to infiltrate corporate networks and gain access to sensitive information assets. If an application, software, or IT system is deployed in the real world with vulnerabilities, this would expose sensitive information assets to the risk of compromise. Therefore, organizations should establish and implement an appropriate security testing procedure to identify and remedy all vulnerabilities in IT systems before they are deployed to the real world. Organizations to verify that all information security requirements are satisfied when new applications, databases, software, or code are put into operation by establishing and applying a robust security testing procedure. This helps organisations to detect and eliminate vulnerabilities in the code, networks, servers, applications, or other IT systems before they are used in the real world.

A.8.29 Security Testing in Development and Acceptance – A linkage with Ancient Era

Ram Setu – Emphasizing Preparation, Validation and Resilience

- **Preparation and Planning:** Before embarking on the construction of Ram Setu, Lord Ram and His allies conduct thorough preparation and planning. Similarly, in security testing during development and acceptance, teams prepare comprehensive test plans and strategies to identify and mitigate potential vulnerabilities and risks in the system.
- **Construction and Implementation:** The construction of Ram Setu involves careful execution of engineering techniques and coordination among the Vanar army. Similarly, during security testing in development, developers implement security controls and measures in the software code, while in acceptance testing, stakeholders ensure that these measures align with security requirements and standards.
- **Validation and Verification:** As Ram Setu nears completion, Lord Ram and His allies validate its structural integrity through testing

and inspection. Similarly, in security testing, developers validate the effectiveness of security controls through techniques such as penetration testing, code review, and vulnerability scanning to ensure that the system can withstand potential threats and attacks.

- **Resilience and Endurance:** Ram Setu demonstrates resilience and endurance when faced with natural forces and environmental challenges. Similarly, during security testing, the system is evaluated for resilience against various security threats, including malicious attacks, data breaches, and system failures, to ensure that it can maintain functionality and integrity under adverse conditions.
- **Acceptance and Certification:** Once Ram Setu is deemed structurally sound and capable of serving its purpose, it gains acceptance and certification from Lord Ram and His allies. Similarly, in security testing, stakeholders review the results of testing and validation to determine whether the system meets security requirements and standards for acceptance and deployment.
- **Continuous Monitoring and Improvement:** Even after the construction of Ram Setu, Lord Ram and His allies continue to monitor its condition and make improvements as needed. Similarly, in security testing, organizations implement continuous monitoring and improvement processes to detect and respond to new security threats and vulnerabilities that may arise over time.

Control

Security testing processes should be defined and implemented in the development life cycle.

Purpose

To validate if information security requirements are met when applications or code are deployed to the production environment.

Guidance

New information systems, upgrades and new versions should be thoroughly tested and verified during the development processes. Security testing should be an integral part of the testing for systems or components. Security testing should be conducted against a set of requirements, which can be expressed as functional or non-functional. Security testing should include testing of:

- Security Functions;
- Secure Coding;
- Secure Configurations.

Test plans should be determined using a set of criteria. The extent of testing should be in proportion to the importance, nature of the system and the potential impact of the change being introduced. The test plan should include:

- Detailed schedule of activities and tests;
- Inputs and expected outputs under a range of conditions;
- Criteria to evaluate the results;
- Decision for further actions as necessary.

The organization can leverage automated tools, such as code analysis tools or vulnerability scanners, and should verify the remediation of security related defects. For in-house developments, such tests should initially be performed by the development team. Independent acceptance testing should then be undertaken to ensure that the system works as expected and only as expected. The following should be considered:

- Performing code review activities as a relevant element for testing for security flaws, including unanticipated inputs and conditions;
- Performing vulnerability scanning to identify insecure configurations and system vulnerabilities;
- Performing penetration testing to identify insecure code and design.

For outsourced development and purchasing components, an acquisition process should be followed. Contracts with the supplier should address the identified security requirements. Products and services should be evaluated against these criteria before acquisition. Testing should be performed in a test environment that matches the target production environment as closely as possible to ensure that the system does not introduce vulnerabilities to the organization's environment and that the tests are reliable.

Other Information

Multiple test environments can be established, which can be used for different kinds of testing. These different environments can be virtual, with individual configurations to simulate a variety of operating environments. Testing and monitoring of test environments, tools and technologies also needs to be considered to ensure effective testing. The same considerations apply to monitoring of the monitoring systems deployed in development, test and production settings. Judgement is needed, guided by the sensitivity of the systems and data, to determine how many layers of meta-testing are useful.

Security Testing ensures that the software system and application are free from any threats or risks that can cause a loss. The goal of security testing is to:

- To identify the threats in the system;
- To measure the potential vulnerabilities of the system;
- To help in detecting every possible security risk in the system;
- To help developers in fixing the security problems through coding;
- The main objectives of security testing are to:
    - **Identify vulnerabilities:** Security testing helps identify vulnerabilities in the system that could be exploited by attackers.
    - **Evaluate the system's ability to withstand an attack:** Security testing evaluates the system's ability to withstand different types of attacks.
    - **Ensure compliance:** Security testing helps ensure that the system meets relevant security standards and regulations
    - **Provide a comprehensive security assessment:** Security testing provides a comprehensive assessment of the system's security posture, including the identification of vulnerabilities, the evaluation of the system's ability to withstand an attack, and compliance with relevant security standards.
    - **Help organizations prepare for potential security incidents:** Security testing helps organizations understand the potential

risks and vulnerabilities that they face, enabling them to prepare for and respond to potential security incidents.

- **Identify and fix potential security issues before deployment to production:** Security testing helps identify and fix security issues before the system is deployed to production. This helps reduce the risk of a security incident occurring in a production environment.

Major focus areas in Security Testing:

1. Network Security
2. System Software Security
3. Client-Side Application Security
4. Server-Side Application Security
5. Authentication and Authorization
6. Network and Infrastructure Security
7. Database Security
8. Application Security
9. Data Security
10. Compliance
11. Cloud Security

Testing of security functionality needs to be carried out during development. Specific testing of security functionality for any development must be carried out and signed-off by an appropriate authority with security competency and responsibility. Security testing expected outcomes should be documented before testing commences and should be based on business requirements for security. The auditor will want to see that there is evidence that security-specific testing has been carried out in any development that is security-relevant. Acceptance testing programs and related criteria must be established for new information systems, upgrades and new versions. For acceptance testing, the tests and the criteria for demonstrating a successful test should be designed and developed based on business requirements prior to tests being carried out. Acceptance testing should also include security testing. The auditor will be looking for evidence that shows acceptance testing criteria and methods were designed according to business requirements and include provisions for security acceptance testing. Basic principles of security testing: Confidentiality, Integrity, Authentication, Authorization, Availability, Non-Repudiation.

Organizations should incorporate security testing into the testing process for all systems and they must ensure that all new information systems and their new/updated versions satisfy the information security requirements when they are in the production environment. When designing security testing plans, organizations should take into account the level of criticality and nature of the information system at hand. If appropriate, decisions to take actions based upon the results. When IT systems are developed by the in-house development team, this team should carry out the initial security testing to ensure the IT system satisfies security requirements. This initial testing should then be followed by an independence acceptance testing.

Types of Security Testing:

1. **Vulnerability Scanning:** Vulnerability scanning is performed with the help of automated software to scan a system to detect the known vulnerability patterns.
2. **Security Scanning:** Security scanning is the identification of network and system weaknesses. Later on it provides solutions for reducing these defects or risks. Security scanning can be carried out in both manual and automated ways.
3. **Penetration Testing:** Penetration testing is the simulation of the attack from a malicious hacker. It includes an analysis of a particular system to examine for potential vulnerabilities from a malicious hacker that attempts to hack the system.
4. **Risk Assessment:** In risk assessment testing security risks observed in the organization are analyzed. This testing endorses controls and measures to minimize the risk.
5. **Security Auditing:** Security auditing is an internal inspection of applications and operating systems for security defects. An audit can also be carried out via line-by-line checking of code.
6. **Ethical Hacking:** Ethical hacking is different from malicious hacking. The purpose of ethical hacking is to expose security flaws in the organization's system.

7. **Posture Assessment:** It combines security scanning, ethical hacking and risk assessments to provide an overall security posture of an application.
8. **Application security testing:** Application security testing is a type of testing that focuses on identifying vulnerabilities in the application itself, which includes testing the application's code, configuration, and dependencies to identify any potential vulnerabilities.
9. **Network security testing:** Network security testing is a type of testing that focuses on identifying vulnerabilities in the network infrastructure, which includes testing firewalls, routers, and other network devices to identify potential vulnerabilities.
10. **Social engineering testing:** Social engineering testing is a type of testing that simulates phishing, baiting, and other types of social engineering attacks to identify vulnerabilities in the system's human element.
11. **Tools** can be used to automate and simplify the process of security testing. It's important to ensure that security testing is done regularly and that any vulnerabilities or threats identified during testing are fixed immediately to protect the system from potential attacks organization.

Organizations should follow a strict acquisition process when they outsource development or when they purchase IT components from external parties. Organizations should enter into an agreement with their suppliers and this agreement should address the information security requirements. Furthermore, organizations should ensure that the products and services they purchase are in compliance with the information security standards. Organizations can create multiple test environments to carry out various testing such as functional, non-functional, and performance testing. Furthermore, they can create virtual test environments and then configure these environments to test the IT systems in various operational settings. Effective security testing requires organizations to test and monitor the testing environments, tools, and technologies. Organizations should take into account the level of sensitivity and criticality of data when determining the number of layers of meta-testing.

A.8.30 Outsourced Development

Outsourcing and offshoring are common in software development and testing, but pose two information security risks. First, the sourcing partners obtain sensitive data they should not have. Second, their software development and testing processes might not address the information security needs properly. It requires the supervision of outsourced development and testing. The work can be outsourced but the responsibility stays with the organization. In general, ISO 27001 requires suppliers also to be managed with regard to information security. Any supplier management can enforce this. The controls are not specific to software development and testing, though the checks might differ slightly. It requires organizations to supervise and monitor all outsourcing activities and to ensure that the outsourced development process satisfies information security requirements. The organization must supervise and monitor the activity of outsourced system development. Where system and software development is outsourced either wholly or partly to external parties the security requirements must be specified in a contract or attached agreement. This is where it is important to have correct nondisclosure and confidentiality. It is also important to supervise and monitor development to gain assurance that organizational standards and requirements for security within systems are achieved. Depending on how embedded outsourced partners are within the organization, especially if staff is located on organizational premises, it is important to include their staff in security awareness training and awareness programme and communications. It is critical to ensure that the internal security practices of the outsourced partner, at least meet assurance requirements relevant to the risk levels related to the developments they will be working on. The auditor will be looking to see that where outsourcing is used, there is evidence of due diligence before, during, and after the engagement of the outsourced partner has been conducted and includes consideration for information security provisions.

A.8.30 Outsourced Development – A linkage with Ancient Era

Ram Setu – Emphasizing Delegation, Collaboration and Expertise Utilization

- **Delegation of Tasks:** Lord Ram delegates the task of building Ram Setu to the Vanar army, led by Lord Hanuman and other skilled engineers.

Similarly, outsourced development involves delegating specific tasks or components of a project to external vendors or contractors with specialized expertise in those areas.

- **Utilization of Specialized Skills:** The construction of Ram Setu requires specialized skills in engineering, architecture, and construction techniques. Similarly, outsourced development leverages the specialized skills and capabilities of external partners to complement and enhance the capabilities of the core development team, ensuring the successful completion of the project.
- **Collaboration and Communication:** Collaboration and Communication are essential during the construction of Ram Setu to ensure coordination among different teams and alignment with Lord Ram's vision. Similarly, outsourced development requires effective collaboration and communication between the internal development team and external vendors to clarify requirements, address issues, and ensure that deliverables meet quality standards and timelines.
- **Risk Management:** Delegating tasks to external partners involve inherent risks, such as delays, quality issues, or misalignment with project goals. Similarly, outsourced development requires careful risk management and mitigation strategies to minimize the impact of potential issues and ensure the successful delivery of the project.
- **Quality Assurance and Oversight:** Lord Ram oversees the construction of Ram Setu to ensure that it meets quality standards and fulfills its intended purpose. Similarly, in outsourced development, organizations maintain oversight and quality assurance processes to monitor the progress of external vendors, review deliverables, and ensure that they meet the required specifications and standards.
- **Integration and Deployment:** Once Ram Setu is constructed, it is integrated into the overall infrastructure and deployed to serve its purpose of facilitating Lord Ram's journey to Lanka. Similarly, in outsourced development, external deliverables are integrated into the overall project and deployed according to the project plan, ensuring seamless functionality and alignment with business objectives.

Control

The organization should direct, monitor and review the activities related to outsourced system development.

Purpose

To ensure information security measures required by the organization are implemented in outsourced system development.

Guidance

Where system development is outsourced, the organization should communicate and agree requirements and expectations, and continually monitor and review whether the delivery of outsourced work meets these expectations. The following points should be considered across the organization's entire external supply chain:

- Licensing agreements, code ownership and intellectual property rights related to the outsourced content;
- Contractual requirements for secure design, coding and testing practices provision of the threat model to consider by external developers;
- Acceptance testing for the quality and accuracy of the deliverables;
- Provision of evidence that minimum acceptable levels of security and privacy capabilities are established;
- Provision of evidence that sufficient testing has been applied to guard against the presence of malicious content upon delivery;
- Provision of evidence that sufficient testing has been applied to guard against the presence of known vulnerabilities;
- Escrow agreements for the software source code;
- Contractual right to audit development processes and controls;
- Security requirements for the development environment;
- Taking consideration of applicable legislation.

The organizations should continuously monitor and verify that the delivery of outsourced development work satisfies the information security requirements imposed on the external service provider.

While outsourcing the organization should conduct suitable due diligence processes in selecting an appropriate service provider and in monitoring its ongoing performance. It is important to entities exercise due care, skill, and diligence in the selection of service providers. The organization should be satisfied that the service provider has the ability and capacity to undertake the provision of the outsourced task effectively at all times. The organization should also establish appropriate processes and procedures for monitoring the performance of the service provider on an ongoing basis to ensure that it retains the ability and capacity to continue to provide the outsourced task. In determining the appropriate level of monitoring, it should consider the criticality of the outsourced task to the ongoing business and to its regulatory obligations. The organization should enter into a legally binding written contract with each service provider, the nature and detail of which should be appropriate to the criticality of the outsourced task to the business. A legally binding written contract between the organization and a service provider is the critical element underpinning the relationship between the organization and the service provider. Contractual provisions can reduce the risks of non-performance or aid the resolution of disagreements about the scope, nature, and quality of the service to be provided. A written contract will assist the monitoring of the outsourced tasks by the organization and/ or by regulators. The level of detail of the written contract should reflect the level of monitoring, assessment, inspection and auditing required, as well as the risks, size and complexity of the outsourced services involved. Where different regulatory requirements may apply for the organization and the service provider due to the cross-border nature of the service, the service provider should recognize and accommodate the requirements of each jurisdiction in which it operates, as appropriate, and ensure it acts in a manner that is consistent with the organization's regulatory obligations. The organization should include written provisions relating to the termination of outsourced tasks in its contract with service providers and ensure that it maintains appropriate exit strategies.

Step to take when Outsourcing Development

- **Do your due diligence:** It is important to conduct due diligence on a vendor before entering into an agreement with the vendor. The scope of such due diligence should include the vendor's reputation and any past breaches.Organization should also investigate the vendor's internal risk measures, their ability to safeguard their IP and what its response would be to a data breach within their organization. If organization is hiring a vendor overseas, they should also consider how the IP will be protected by the laws of that country and the legal remedies available to them for the breach of the IP rights.

- **Sign Non-Disclosure Agreement (NDA):** Before hiring a vendor, or after hiring a vendor but before sharing any confidential information, organization should enter into a NDA with the vendor. As the name implies, NDAs place an obligation on a party or parties not to disclose certain information, including software development or technical data, to third parties. The NDA should be wide enough to cover the scope of the vendor's services, but also narrow enough to define confidential information and what amounts to a breach. The NDA should also bind the vendor's employees or subcontractors who would be working on the task. The non-disclosure obligations in NDAs would typically outlive organization business relationship with the vendor. This may be in perpetuity, if possible, or for a number of years after the completion of the project. Therefore, at the end of the project, organization should reiterate the vendor's obligations to not disclose confidential information.
- **Use the legal framework applicable:** The legal framework and available measures to protect organization rights differ from country to country. It is advisable to seek legal counsel before executing an outsourcing agreement.
- **Draft a comprehensive Master Service Agreement (MSA):** A MSA is an agreement that documents the terms of future contracts between the parties. Also known as a Framework Agreement, it states the terms of service delivery, work standards, payment terms, rights and liabilities, confidentiality, ownership of intellectual property rights to the final product, and data protection mechanisms. It is important to pay attention to ownership of the IP rights to the work product. Vendors would usually prefer to retain ownership to use the deliverables in future projects. The contract should clearly state the creators, authors, and owners of the work product. It should identify the organization as the owner of the work product and preserve the right to use, assign, and modify the work product. The MSA should also include dispute

resolution mechanisms, in case a party breaches the agreement. The organization should anticipate how they would enforce their IPR under the agreement and identify intellectual property offices they may contact where there is a violation of their IP rights. Preferably, they should state their jurisdiction as the applicable governing law and venue for resolution of the agreement, to ensure that disputes that arise from the agreement are resolved within their jurisdiction.

- **Inquire about the processes of a potential partner:** Verify you are working with a firm that follows correct procedures. The correct practices are ultimately what will safeguard your work, rights and information. The questions below provide an excellent starting point.
    - What contracts do they have in place with their staff and consultants?
    - Is any of their work subcontracted? If so, how do they safeguard their intellectual property?
    - Are they utilizing appropriate project management tools?
    - Where do they keep their servers and source code? Is there a backup support mechanism in place if something occurs at a local office?
    - How does their team interact and exchange documents?
    - How do they ensure that data and documents are removed from the possession of departing or dismissed employees?
    - Allow employees to utilize personal tools and email, or do they require employees to use just organization-authorized resources?
    - What is their laptop and internet access security policy?
    - Do they have procedures in place for remote employees?
- **Limit Server and Data Access:** Limiting server and data access is also another means of ensuring protection of organization intellectual property when outsourcing to third parties. Organization should ensure that data is stored on their servers. At no point should organization data reside in any place other than on their cloud. Allow the vendors to work remotely via their cloud services, where organization can closely watch everything, they do and have documented proof in the security

or data breach. Access to organization server, API and data should also be limited to only what is necessary to complete the outsourced task. If the task requires access to all or a core part of organization intellectual property, then they may consider executing some of the task inhouse or asking the in-house team to integrate the developer's work product into the software. Transition protocols should also be discussed before the project commences. There have been cases of vendors' refusal to transfer the source codes to their clients when disputes arise or the vendor is moving to another firm. To forestall such occurrences, all applications should be built on organization's servers right from the start of the project. Source code should also be stored within organization's account.

A.8.31 Separation of Development, Test and Production Environments

Separation of development, test and production environments are important to achieve segregation of functions involved. It is appropriate that the rules for the development to transfer to production environments are well defined and documented. Failure to properly segregate development, test, and production environments may result in loss of availability, confidentiality, and integrity of information assets. Production computing environments shall be either logically or physically separate from development and test environments. Developer access to production environments shall be prohibited or limited to troubleshooting and all activity recorded and monitored. Logon procedures and passwords shall be different for production and development/test environments. Procedures shall exist for transferring software or hardware from development and test to production. Where physical separation for development/test is not feasible, security measures shall be equal to or higher than that required for the production environment. Therefore, organizations should implement appropriate procedures and controls to securely segregate development, test, and production environments to eliminate security risk. When developing and testing staff have access to the production environment, they can introduce untested or unauthorized code, or even change the actual data of the system. In some systems, this capability can be hardly used to implement fraud or introduction of malicious code or not tested. This type of code can cause serious operational problems. The development of staff and in charge of the tests also pose a threat to confidentiality of production information. The development and testing activities may cause unintended changes to software and information if they share the same computing environment. The separation of resource development, test and operational is this very desirable way to reduce the risk of accidental modification or unauthorized access to operational software and business data.

A.8.31 Separation of Development, Test and Production Environments – A linkage with Ancient Era

Ram Setu – Emphasizing Preparation, Validation and Resilience

- **Development Environment - Planning and Preparation:** The construction of Ram Setu begins with planning and preparation, akin to a development environment where ideas are conceptualized, designs are drafted, and initial groundwork is laid. Just as the Vanar army meticulously plans the construction of the bridge, developers in a development environment lay the groundwork for building software, experimenting with different ideas and solutions.

- **Test Environment - Validation and Evaluation:** As the construction progresses, the structural integrity of Ram Setu is evaluated through testing, similar to a test environment in software development. Testing ensures that the bridge can withstand the intended load and environmental conditions. Likewise, in a test environment, software undergoes rigorous testing to validate its functionality, performance, and security before deployment to production.
- **Production Environment - Deployment and Utilization:** Once Ram Setu is deemed structurally sound and capable of serving its purpose, it is deployed for practical use, similar to a production environment in software development. In the production environment, the completed software is deployed for real-world use, serving its intended purpose while adhering to strict security and performance standards.
- **Isolation and Protection:** Separating development, test, and production environments ensures the isolation and protection of each stage from the others, minimizing the risk of unintended consequences. Similarly, during the construction of Ram Setu, each phase is carefully managed and isolated to prevent disruptions or delays in the overall project.
- **Validation and Quality Assurance:** In both the construction of Ram Setu and software development, validation and quality assurance are critical at each stage of the process. Through rigorous testing and evaluation, any defects or weaknesses are identified and addressed before moving to the next stage, ensuring the overall integrity and reliability of the final product.
- **Continual Improvement and Iteration:** Just as the construction of Ram Setu may require adjustments and refinements based on feedback and experience, software development involves continual improvement and iteration based on user feedback and changing requirements. This iterative process allows for the refinement of features and

functionality over time, enhancing the overall quality and usability of the product.

Control

Development, testing and production environments should be separated and secured.

Purpose

To protect the production environment and data from compromise by development and test activities.

Guidance

The level of separation between production, testing and development environments that is necessary to prevent production problems should be identified and implemented. The following items should be considered:

- Adequately separating development and production systems and operating them in different domains;
- Defining, documenting and implementing rules and authorization for the deployment of software from development to production status;
- Testing changes to production systems and applications in a testing or staging environment prior to being applied to production systems;
- Not testing in production environments except in circumstances that have been defined and approved;
- Compilers, editors and other development tools or utility programs not being accessible from production systems when not required;
- Displaying appropriate environment identification labels in menus to reduce the risk of error;
- Not copying sensitive information into the development and testing system environments unless equivalent controls are provided for the development and testing systems.

In all cases, development and testing environments should be protected considering:

- Patching and updating of all the development, integration and testing tools;

- Secure configuration of systems and software;
- Control of access to the environments;
- Monitoring of change to the environment and code stored therein;
- Secure monitoring of the environments;
- Taking backups of the environments.

A single person should not have the ability to make changes to both development and production without prior review and approval. This can be achieved for example through segregation of access rights or through rules that are monitored. In exceptional situations, should be implemented in order to detect and act on unauthorized changes.

Other Information

Without adequate measures and procedures, developers and testers having access to production systems can introduce significant risks. There is a need to maintain a known and stable environment in which to perform meaningful testing and to prevent inappropriate developer access to the production environment. Measures and procedures include carefully designed roles in conjunction with implementing segregation of duty requirements and having adequate monitoring processes in place. Development and testing personnel also pose a threat to the confidentiality of production information. Development and testing activities can cause unintended changes to software or information if they share the same computing environment. Separating development, testing and production environments is therefore desirable to reduce the risk of accidental change or unauthorized access to production software and business data. In some cases, the distinction between development, test and production environments can be deliberately blurred and testing can be carried out in a development environment or through controlled roll outs to live users or servers. In some cases, product testing can occur through live use of the product inside the organization. Furthermore, to reduce downtime of live deployments, two identical production environments can be supported where only one is live at any one time.

Supporting processes for the use of production data in development and testing environments are necessary. Organizations can also consider the guidance provided in this section for training environments when conducting end user training. In the software development life cycle, three environments are commonly used: development, testing, and production environment. These environments differ in their level of control, access, and stability. The organizations are to maintain the confidentiality, integrity, and availability of sensitive information assets by segregating developing, testing, and production environments through appropriate procedures, controls, and policies.

- **Development Environment:** A development environment allows developers to write code and make changes or updates without breaking anything in a live environment. New features and updates can be tried and your end users aren't affected. This environment is great in reducing potential errors and maintaining a streamlined workflow. Additionally, at this stage, a lot of preliminary testing happens before moving on to the testing environment.
- **Testing Environment:** A test environment is a setup where software undergoes a series of experimental tests. These environments allow you to test individual components of app, eliminate bugs, provide accurate feedback about the quality and behavior of the app, and encourage improvement and innovation, among others.
- **Production Environment:** The production environment is the stage where all apps, software, or product are live for their intended use and its users. Any bugs, issues, or versions are tested and fixed prior to this stage, so the product or update should work perfectly. The production environment contains only the final version of the product or app in order to avoid any confusion or security vulnerabilities.

This type of infrastructure allows teams to ensure high-quality products for their users, while encouraging fast innovation and improvements.

In all three environments, developers and other stakeholders have varying degrees of control and access. To minimize disruptions to end users, changes to the application or service in a production environment are usually restricted to a few authorized users. Access is typically more open in the testing environment to test different scenarios and configurations, and changes can be made more quickly and easily. Typically, developers have even greater access to the code base in a development environment and can experiment and make changes as needed to explore different approaches and ideas. Organizations should take into account the potential production problems that should be prevented when determining the required level of separation between the three environments;

- Segregation and operation of development and production systems to an adequate degree;
- Appropriate rules and authorization procedures should be established, documented, and applied for the use of software in the production environment after going through the development environment;
- Organizations should review and test changes made to applications and production systems in a test environment separate from the production environment before these changes are used in the production environment;
- Testing in production environments should not be allowed unless such testing is defined and approved prior to testing;
- Development tools such as compilers and editors should not be accessible from the production environments unless this access is absolutely necessary;
- To minimize errors, proper environment identification labels should be prominently displayed in menus;
- Sensitive information assets should not be transferred into development and testing environments unless equivalent security measures are applied in the development and testing systems;

Environment	Purpose	Control and Access	Stability and Reliability
Development Environment	Development and building environments for software applications and services.	Developers are free to experiment with the codebase and make changes as necessary to explore different ideas.	Application or service is still being built and refined. Therefore, stability and reliability are less than in a testing environment.
Testing Environment	An environment that simulates the production environment so developers and QA professionals can test the application's performance, functionality, and reliability.	The environment is more open for testing different scenarios and configurations, and changes can be made more quickly and easily.	Due to stress tests and scenarios, the application or service is less stable and reliable than in production.
Production Environment	The application or service is deployed and made available to end users in this live environment.	The service is limited to a limited number of authorized users, and any changes must be carefully planned and coordinated, so that end users are not disrupted.	Minimal downtime and disruption, with stable and reliable performance.

There is also an important difference in each environment's stability and reliability levels. Due to the fact that the application is yet in the process of being created and refined, it may need to be more stable and reliable in the development environment. As the application or service undergoes different stress tests and scenarios in the testing environment, it might be less stable and reliable. Application or service stability and availability are expected in the production environment, with very little downtime or disruption. In addition, organizations can also consider extra technical controls such as logging of all access activities and real-time monitoring of all access to these environments.

If organizations fail to implement necessary measures, their information systems can face significant security risks. Therefore, organizations need a stable environment to perform robust testing on the code and to prevent developers from accessing the production environments where sensitive real-world data is hosted and processed. Organizations should also apply measures such as designated roles together with separation of duty requirements. Another threat to the confidentiality of production data is the development and testing personnel. When the development and testing teams perform their activities using the same computing devices, they may accidentally make changes to sensitive information or software programs. Organizations are advised to establish supporting processes for the use of the production data in testing and development systems in compliance. Moreover, organizations should take into account the measures addressed in this control when they perform end-user training in training environments. Organizations need to establish and appropriately protect secure development environments for system development and integration efforts that cover the entire system development lifecycle.

Development environments need to be protected to ensure the malicious or accidental development and update of code that may create vulnerabilities or compromise confidentiality, integrity, and availability. Protection requirements should be determined from risk assessment, business requirements, and other internal and external requirements including legislation, regulation, contractual agreement, or policies. In particular, if any form of live data is used in development environments it needs to be specially protected and controlled.

A.8.32 Change Management

Changes to information systems such as replacing a network device, creating a new database instance, or upgrading software are often necessary for improved performance, reduced costs, and higher efficiencies. However, those changes to information processing facilities and systems, if not implemented properly, may lead to the compromise of information assets stored in or processed by these facilities. Risks arise when changes are performed in an uncontrolled way. Organizations can establish and apply change management procedures to monitor, review and control changes made to the information processing facilities and systems. Change management which requires that changes to the organization, business processes, information processing facilities, and systems that affect information security are controlled. Change management is a structured process for reviewing proposed IT system or service changes. This process occurs prior to implementing the requested change on an organization's network, thus minimizing or eliminating network outages. IT change management is necessary to ensure any changes to the network will not degrade the performance of the network. Any changes to the network should be a defined, purposeful action to eliminate a found vulnerability, upgrade a component on the network for improved performance, or replace a currently obsolete or faulty network component. Changes can be categorized into three types:

- **Standard Changes:** Standard changes are routine, and follow a pre-established process regarding risk analysis and pre-approvals. These changes are vetted processes that have been pre-approved for execution.
- **Normal Changes:** Normal changes do not have a pre-established process. A risk analysis and deployment plan must be submitted for approval prior to implementing these changes on the IT network.
- **Emergency Changes:** Emergency changes are when an unplanned outage has occurred, or is likely to occur, due to a discovered vulnerability that possesses a significant threat to the network.

Changes in technology are very frequent, and so are changes that affect the ISMS (not only for the sake of improvements, but also in daily business). But if we don't manage them according to a procedure, we might find surprises that can (often) involve an information security incident or an interruption of the business, which can also affect the customers.

A.8.32 Change Management – A linkage with Ancient Era

Ram Setu – Emphasizing Adaptation, Communication and Stakeholder Management

- **Adaptation to Evolving Conditions:** During the construction of Ram Setu, the Vanar army must adapt to evolving conditions, such as changes in the terrain, weather, or resource availability. Similarly, in Change Management, organizations must adapt to evolving business needs, market conditions, and technological advancements by implementing changes to processes, systems, and strategies.
- **Communication and Stakeholder Engagement:** Effective communication and stakeholder engagement are essential during the construction of Ram Setu to ensure alignment with Lord Ram's vision and gain support from allies and stakeholders. Similarly, in Change Management, organizations must communicate changes effectively to stakeholders, address concerns, and obtain buy-in to facilitate successful implementation and adoption.
- **Risk Assessment and Mitigation:** Throughout the construction of Ram Setu, Lord Ram and His allies assess risks and uncertainties, such as potential attacks from adversaries or logistical challenges, and implement mitigation measures to minimize their impact. Similarly, in Change Management, organizations identify potential risks and obstacles to change, such as resistance from employees or disruptions to operations, and develop strategies to mitigate these risks and ensure smooth implementation.
- **Contingency Planning:** In the event of unforeseen challenges or setbacks during the construction of Ram Setu, Lord Ram and his allies develop contingency plans to adapt and overcome obstacles while staying aligned with their ultimate goal. Similarly, in Change Management, organizations develop contingency plans to address unexpected issues or resistance to change, allowing them to respond effectively and minimize disruption to business operations.
- **Feedback and Continuous Improvement:** As construction progresses,

Lord Ram and His allies gather feedback from the Vanar army and make adjustments to their plans and strategies based on lessons learned and emerging challenges. Similarly, in Change Management, organizations gather feedback from stakeholders and users to assess the impact of changes and identify opportunities for improvement, facilitating continuous learning and adaptation.

- **Celebrating Success and Milestones:** Upon completion of Ram Setu, Lord Ram and His allies celebrate their success and the achievement of a significant milestone in their journey. Similarly, in Change Management, organizations celebrate successful change initiatives and milestones to recognize the efforts of individuals and teams involved, build morale, and reinforce a culture of innovation and adaptability.

Control

Changes to information processing facilities and information systems should be subject to change management procedures.

Purpose

To preserve information security when executing changes.

Guidance

Introduction of new systems and major changes to existing systems should follow agreed rules and a formal process of documentation, specification, testing, quality control and managed implementation. Management responsibilities and procedures should be in place to ensure satisfactory control of all changes. Change control procedures should be documented and enforced to ensure the confidentiality, integrity and availability of information in information processing facilities and information systems, for the entire system development lifecycle from the early design stages through all subsequent maintenance efforts. Wherever practicable, change control procedures for ICT infrastructure and software should be integrated. The change control procedures should include:

- Planning and assessing the potential impact of changes considering all dependencies;
- Authorization of changes;

- Communicating changes to relevant interested parties;
- Tests and acceptance of tests for the changes;
- Implementation of changes including deployment plans;
- Emergency and contingency considerations including fallback procedures;
- Maintaining records of changes that include all of the above;
- Ensuring that operating documentation and user procedures are changed as necessary to remain appropriate;
- Ensuring that ICT continuity plans and response and recovery procedures are changed as necessary to remain appropriate.

Other Information

Inadequate control of changes to information processing facilities and information systems is a common cause of system or security failures. Changes to the production environment, especially when transferring software from development to operational environment, can impact on the integrity and availability of applications. Changing software can impact the production environment and vice versa. Good practice includes the testing of ICT components in an environment segregated from both the production and development environments. This provides a means of having control over new software and allowing additional protection of operational information that is used for testing purposes. This should include patches, service packs and other updates. Production environment includes operating systems, databases and middle ware platforms. The control should be applied for changes of applications and infrastructures.

Change management processes are essential for ensuring that risks associated with significant revisions to software, systems, and key processes are identified, assessed, and weighed in the context of an approval process. It is critical that information security considerations be included as part of a change review and approval process alongside other objectives such as support and service level management. Change management is a broad subject matter, however, some important considerations from an information security perspective include:

- Helping to ensure that changes are identified and recorded;

- Assessing and reporting on information security risks relevant to proposed changes;
- Helping classify changes according to the overall significance of the change in terms of risk;
- Helping establish or evaluate planning, testing, and "back out" steps for significant changes;
- Helping ensure that change communications is handled in a structured manner;
- Ensure that emergency change processes are well defined, communicated and that security evaluation of these changes is also performed post-change.

All major changes to information systems and the introduction of new systems should be subject to an agreed set of rules and procedures. These changes should be formally specified and documented. Furthermore, they should go through the testing and quality control processes. To ensure that all changes comply with the change control rules and standards, organizations should assign management responsibilities to appropriate management and should set out the necessary procedures.

Changes to the production environments such as operating systems, and databases may compromise the integrity and availability of applications, particularly the transfer of software from development to production environment. Another risk that organizations should be cautious against is changing software in the production environment may have unintended consequences. To prevent these risks, organizations should perform tests on ICT components in an environment isolated from the development and production environments. This will enable organisations to have greater control over new software and will provide an extra layer of protection for real-world data used for testing purposes. This extra protection can be achieved via patches and service packs.

Steps to manage change includes:

- **Request for Change:** Each change can be initiated as a Request – better known as a "Request for Change" or "RFC." This request will also serve as a record and as evidence that a particular change has been requested. The change can be initiated internally (by an employee) or externally (by a customer), and will be registered in a specific form. Changes may affect assets of the organization, but can also affect processes, services, agreements, etc. Therefore, it is important that detailed information about the type of change is recorded in the RFC. It is also important to record more information, such as the person requesting the change, the date, the department (or interested party) affected, etc.

- **Approval Process:** The RFC is received by a person who is responsible for analyzing it, so this person is the first filter. This person is only responsible for studying the details of the request and identifying the potential impact to the business, including economic impacts and impacts related to the information security. Further on, another person (typically the person responsible for changes), based on the information generated previously, will decide if the change is approved or rejected. For that decision, it is important to consider all the implications that the change may have, including internal ones as well as external ones. Finally, if the change is approved, another person (typically appointed for change implementation) is responsible for planning the change and its implementation. That same person will also plan tests that allow for checking that changes are performed in the correct way. These three persons can be the same person, although it is recommended that they are different for bigger companies, because in such way it will be possible to separate roles/functions. Finally, not all the changes are equally important, so it is necessary to classify them. This classification can be based on the impacts to the business and to the ISMS.
- **Communication:** It is also important that the organization keeps in contact with the person who initiated the change, or interested parties involved in the change, because they must be informed of every decision or action that is carried out in relation to the change that is being managed. These communications can be via phone or email, meetings, etc.
- **Fallback and Emergency Changes:** Another important issue to consider is when an error takes place during the implementation of the change. In this case, it is important to have a fallback procedure to return to the previous state. The person responsible for executing the fallback procedure can be the same person responsible for the change

implementation. Finally, this fallback procedure can be defined during the planning-for-implementation step, establishing what needs to be done to return to the previous stage.

Changes to systems within the development lifecycle must be controlled by the use of formal change control procedures. System change control procedures should integrate with, be aligned to and support operational change control. Formal change management procedures are designed to reduce the risk of accidental or deliberate development of vulnerabilities that may allow systems to be compromised once the changes are put live. For system change control, it is important that the system owner understands what changes are being made to their system, why and by whom. It is their responsibility to ensure that their systems are not compromised through poor or malicious development. They should therefore be involved in setting the rules for authorization and pre-live testing and checking. Audit logs are required to provide evidence of the correct use of change procedures. Many aspects of change control that should be included, ranging from simple documentation of the changes through to consideration of the time for deployment to avoid negative business impact. When operating platforms are changed, business-critical applications need to be reviewed and tested to ensure there is no adverse impact on organizational operations or security. When operating system platforms are changed it is commonplace that some applications may have compatibility problems. It is important therefore to test operating system changes in a development or test environment where critical business applications can be checked for compatibility with the changed OS. Procedures for control and testing of operating system changes should follow standard change management control. Modifications to software packages need to be discouraged, limited to necessary changes and all changes should be strictly controlled. Vendor supplied software packages are designed for the mass-market and are not really designed for organizations making their own changes to them. In fact, most of the time the ability to make such changes is locked out by the vendor and customization limited to within the package. Where open-source software is used, it is far more likely that changes can be made by the organization, however, this should be restricted and controlled to ensure that the changes made do not have an adverse impact on the internal integrity or security of the software.

Common Challenges

Change management processes are susceptible to becoming overly complex. Employees who conduct changes are more likely to attempt to bypass change management processes they feel are too burdensome by intentionally classifying their changes at low levels or even not reporting them. If you are starting a Change Management program it is often helpful to first focus on modelling large-scale changes and then working to find the right change level definitions which help balance risk reduction with operational agility and efficiency.

A.8.33 Test Information

Test information must be selected carefully, protected and controlled. It should ideally be created in a generic form with no relation to live system information. However, it is recognized that often live data must be used to perform accurate testing. Where live data is used for testing it should be; anonymized as far as possible; carefully selected and secured for the period of testing; securely deleted when testing is complete. Use of live data must be pre-authorized, logged and monitored. The auditor will expect to see robust procedures in place to protect data being used in test environments, especially if this is wholly or partly live data. While non-production test environments are essential to building high-quality software products and applications free of bugs or errors, the use of real data and lack of security measures in these environments expose information assets to heightened risks. Therefore, organizations should put in place appropriate controls and procedures to protect real-world data used for testing.

- To protect and maintain the confidentiality of information used in the testing environment;
- Selection and use of test information that will yield reliable results.

A.8.33 Test Information – A linkage with Ancient Era

Ram Setu – Emphasizing Validation, Quality Assurance, and Risk Mitigation

- **Structural Integrity Testing:** During the construction of Ram Setu, the Vanar army likely conducted tests to ensure the structural integrity of the bridge. Similarly, in software development, testing is conducted to verify that the system meets functional requirements and performs reliably under various conditions.
- **Load Testing:** Just as Ram Setu needed to support the weight of Lord Ram's army and equipment, software undergoes load testing to assess its performance under expected and peak usage conditions. This ensures that the system can handle the anticipated workload without degradation or failure.
- **Environmental Testing:** Ram Setu was built in a challenging environment, with factors such as water currents and weather

conditions impacting its construction. Similarly, software undergoes environmental testing to assess its performance in different operating environments.

- **Security Testing:** Given the strategic importance of Ram Setu, security would have been a concern. Similarly, software undergoes security testing to identify vulnerabilities and ensure that sensitive data is protected from unauthorized access or malicious attacks.
- **User Acceptance Testing:** Before Lord Ram's army crossed Ram Setu, it's likely that the bridge underwent user acceptance testing to ensure it met their requirements and expectations. Similarly, software undergoes user acceptance testing to verify that it meets the needs and preferences of end-users.
- **Risk Assessment and Mitigation:** Throughout the construction of Ram Setu, risks such as structural failure or attacks from adversaries would have been assessed and mitigated. Similarly, in software development, risk assessment and mitigation strategies are employed to identify and address potential threats to the success of the project.

Control

Test information should be appropriately selected, protected and managed.

Purpose

To ensure relevance of testing and protection of operational information used for testing.

Guidance

Test information should be selected to ensure the reliability of tests results and the confidentiality of the relevant operational information. Sensitive information should not be copied into the development and testing environments. The following guidelines should be applied to protect the copies of operational information, when used for testing purposes, whether the test environment is built in-house or on a cloud service:

- Applying the same access control procedures to test environments as those applied to operational environments;
- Having a separate authorization each time operational information is copied to a test environment;

- Logging the copying and use of operational information to provide an audit trail;
- Protecting sensitive information by removal or masking if used for testing;
- Properly deleting operational information from a test environment immediately after the testing is complete to prevent unauthorized use of test information.

Test information should be securely stored and only used for testing purposes.

Other Information

System and acceptance testing can require substantial volumes of test information that are as close as possible to operational information. Data used in testing environments must be protected against unauthorized access. Accounts may be disabled so that only a subset of accounts can be used for testing. Copying data between production and test environment should be approved where possible data used for testing should not contain PII. Generating non-meaningful test data for performance testing is not a difficult exercise, but generating meaningful data that looks and behaves like real production data for functional testing is the challenge. Meaningful data contains all the characteristics of production data, but is anonymized for data privacy compliance. While developing an application, developers need to make sure they are testing it under conditions that closely simulate a production environment. Most tests rely on sample data for testing. If the data is manually entered into a test environment, it cannot match the volume and variety of data that the application normally would accumulate in production. Behavior may differ because data inserted into the test database will not match real-world usage, possibly leaving significant bugs. Development/test managers, application owners, and others know that simulated data fails to effectively support development, and manual scripting cannot keep up with the demand for fast timelines between application development and production. Building a test database with meaningful, protected test data allows the application owner to see and assess how the application will perform once it released. Without meaningful test data in the test environment, it is impossible to predict the way the application will behave after the release. Organizations testing non-production data want to see data that looks real to understand how real data would perform in their application.

- **Choosing the right data set type:** Choosing your test data is a huge decision. In any testing environment, production data would be the best choice but this is no longer acceptable. Using production data is too great a risk for your business and you could be held liable for fines and penalties if that data was lost or landed in the wrong hands. With that in mind, it's important instead to use test data that is as close to production as possible, resulting in a realistic testing environment. Test data management is key here to ensure a process of obfuscating or generating synthetic data.
- **Creating obfuscated or synthetic data:** Managed test data can help to create test environments on demand, with synthetic data able to deliver a highly repeatable solution. In turn, this can enhance the speed of your business' testing turnaround time.
- **Obfuscated or synthetic test data** can allow you to test on demand to achieve faster and cost-efficient delivery, without risking the integrity of any sensitive data. Having an automated method to support your test data management can help you take this to the next level.

Guidelines for data de-identification or anonymization should be followed to remove sensitive information or to modify it beyond recognition when used for testing purposes. If production data is used unchanged for testing, the data should be protected with the same level of controls used for the production system. Test data must be selected carefully, protected, and controlled. Test data should ideally be created in a generic form with no relation to living system data. However, it is recognized that often live data must be used to perform accurate testing. Where live data is used for testing it should be; anonymized as far as possible; carefully selected and secured for the period of testing; securely deleted when testing is complete. Use of live data must be pre-authorized, logged, and monitored. The auditor will expect to see robust procedures in place to protect data being used in test environments, especially if this is wholly or partly live data. Organizations should not use sensitive information, including personal data, in the development and testing environments. It is noted that system and acceptance testing may require an enormous amount of test information, equivalent to operational information. To protect the test information against loss of confidentiality and integrity, organizations should comply with the recommendations maintained in the Guidance section.

When it comes to testing, there are many factors that require consideration to ensure the correct use and protection of data. Compliance standards like the Privacy Act, set out requirements for companies to ensure different types of data are carefully managed and protected. Test data should ideally be created in a generic form with no relation to live system data. However, often data needs to reflect actual real data to ensure accurate testing. If you must use "real" data for testing purposes consider implementing a robust data masking technique to protect the data.

Technique to Mask Data

- **Data Encryption**: An encryption algorithm is used to lock the data from anyone being able to see it other than the person who has the key. For testing purposes, it is often not helpful as it requires the system to continually lock and unlock the data and processes need to be in place manage and share encryption keys.
- **Data Scrambling**: Reorganize characters in the data set in a random order, replacing the original content. Easy to do to but can be less secure if someone figures out the process and can reverse engineer the changes.
- **Nulling Out**: Data is replaced with "null" or is deleted. Not helpful during testing if you need the data to perform certain functions or test outputs appear on a page correctly.
- **Value Variance**: Replace original data values by using a function, such as the difference between the lowest and highest value in a series. This can help protect anyone getting access to the original dataset.
- **Data Substitution**: Data values are substituted with fake, but realistic, alternative values.
- **Data Shuffling:** Similar to substitution, except data values are switched within the same dataset.

A.8.34 Protection of Information Systems during Audit Testing

Audit tests play a critical role in detecting and eliminating security risks and vulnerabilities in the information systems. However, the audit process, whether performed in operational, testing, or development environments, can expose sensitive information to the risks of unauthorized disclosure, or loss of integrity and availability. It is important to ensure that all IT controls and information security audits are planned events, rather than reactive 'on-the-spot' challenges. Audit requirements and activities involving verification of operational systems need to be carefully planned and agreed on to minimize disruptions to the business processes. Whenever carrying out tests and audit activities on operational systems, consideration needs to be given to ensure that operations are not negatively impacted. Additionally, the scope and depth of testing must be defined. Any such auditing or testing of operational systems must be through a formal and appropriately authorized process. It is highly important that audit standards for access to systems and data should be negotiated with appropriate management. A technical audit team must update and control the information if there is any changes to the technical networks.

A.8.34 Protection of Information Systems During Audit Testing – A linkage with Ancient Era

Ram Setu – Emphasizing Confidentiality, Integrity and Security

- **Confidentiality of Plans and Strategies:** Just as Lord Ram and His allies kept their plans to construct Ram Setu confidential to prevent adversaries from intercepting or sabotaging them, organizations protect sensitive information related to their information systems during audit testing to prevent unauthorized access or exploitation by external parties.
- **Integrity of Construction Processes:** During the construction of Ram Setu, maintaining the integrity of the construction processes was crucial to ensure the stability and reliability of the bridge. Similarly, organizations ensure the integrity of their information systems during audit testing by verifying that processes and controls are operating as intended and that data integrity is preserved.

- **Security of Access Controls:** Access to the construction site of Ram Setu was likely restricted to authorized personnel to prevent sabotage or espionage by adversaries. Similarly, organizations enforce strict access controls during audit testing to limit access to sensitive systems and data, reducing the risk of unauthorized manipulation or disclosure.
- **Protection Against Interference:** Lord Ram and His allies likely implemented security measures to protect Ram Setu from interference or disruption by adversaries during its construction. Similarly, organizations protect their information systems from interference or disruption during audit testing by implementing safeguards such as intrusion detection systems, firewalls, and encryption.
- **Monitoring and Surveillance:** Lord Ram and His allies may have employed surveillance and monitoring techniques to oversee the construction progress of Ram Setu and detect any suspicious activities or deviations from the plan. Similarly, organizations monitor their information systems during audit testing to identify anomalies or security incidents that may indicate unauthorized access or malicious activity.
- **Documentation and Evidence Preservation:** Throughout the construction of Ram Setu, detailed documentation and records were likely maintained to track progress, expenses, and materials used. Similarly, organizations maintain comprehensive documentation and evidence of audit testing activities to demonstrate compliance with regulatory requirements and provide assurance of the security and integrity of their information systems.

Control

Audit tests and other assurance activities involving assessment of operational systems should be planned and agreed between the tester and appropriate management.

Purpose

To minimize the impact of audit and other assurance activities on operational systems and business processes.

Guidance

The following guidelines should be observed:

- Agreeing audit requests for access to systems and data with appropriate management;
- Agreeing and controlling the scope of technical audit tests;
- Limiting audit tests to read-only access to software and data. If read-only access is not available to obtain the necessary information, executing the test by an experienced administrator who has the necessary access rights on behalf of the auditor;
- If access is granted, establishing and verifying the security requirements of the devices used for accessing the systems before allowing the access;
- Only allowing access other than read-only for isolated copies of system files, deleting them when the audit is completed, or giving them appropriate protection if there is an obligation to keep such files under audit documentation requirements;
- Identifying and agreeing on requests for special or additional processing;
- Running audit tests that can affect system availability outside business hours;
- Monitoring and logging all access for audit and test purposes.

Other Information

Most organization undergo a series of security audits each year ranging from financial IT controls reviews to targeted assessments of critical systems. A security audit is a systematic evaluation of the security of a organization's information system by measuring how well it conforms to an established set of criteria. Steps involved in a security audit. These five steps are generally part of a security audit:

- **Agree on Goals**: include all stakeholders in discussions of what should be achieved with the audit.
- **Define the Scope of the Audit**: list all assets to be audited, including computer equipment, internal documentation and processed data.
- **Conduct the Audit and Identify Threats**: list potential threats related

to each threats can include the loss of data, equipment or records through natural disasters, malware or unauthorized users.

- **Evaluate Security and Risks**: assess the risk of each of the identified threats happening, and how well the organization can defend against them.
- **Determine the Needed Controls**: identify what security measures must be implemented or improved to minimize risks.

A thorough audit typically assesses the security of the system's physical configuration and environment, software, information handling processes and user practices. Auditors should take privacy regulations and risks into account when planning, performing, and reporting assurance and consulting assignments. Due to the increasing risk of reputation damage and litigation, Auditor/System tester has to take a significant spectrum of privacy issues and ramifications into account when managing the audit function. Key areas of concern are the staff management process; audit planning; collecting, handling, and storing information when performing and reporting audit results; and potential data leaks. When hiring auditors, there is even a greater need for due diligence to ensure that newly hired auditors act in accordance with relevant laws and policies when using personal information during assurance or consulting engagements. Internal auditors must understand that it may be inappropriate, and in some cases illegal, to access, retrieve, review, manipulate, or use personal information when conducting internal audit engagements. Audit trails maintain a record of system activity both by system and application processes and by user activity of systems and applications. In conjunction with appropriate tools and procedures, audit trails can assist in detecting security violations, performance problems, and flaws in applications. The auditor can obtain valuable information about activity on a computer system from the audit trail. Audit trails improve the auditability of the computer system. Organizations must maintain a complete and accurate audit trail for network devices, servers and applications as this enables organizations to address how businesses identify root causes of issues that might introduce inaccuracy in reporting. Also, problem management system must provide for adequate audit trail facilities that allow tracing from incident to underlying cause. IT security administration must monitor and log security activity, and identify security violations to report to senior management. This control directly addresses the control for audit controls over information systems and networks. To fulfil this control objective, administrators must ensure all network devices, servers, and applications are properly configured to log to a centralized server. Administrators must also periodically review logging status to ensure that these devices, servers and applications are logging correctly. Finally, internal auditors should consider related privacy regulations, regulatory requirements, and legal considerations when reporting information outside the organization.

Audits that include testing activities can prove disruptive to users if any unforeseen outages occur as a result of testing or assessments. Through working with leadership, it should be possible to determine when audits will occur and obtain relevant information in advance about the specific IT controls that will be examined or tested. Develop an 'audit plan' for each audit that provides information relevant to each system and area to be assessed. These audit plans should take into consideration:

- Asset Inventory with contact information for system administrators/ owners;
- Requirements for testing/maintenance windows;
- Information about backups (if applicable) in case systems later need to be restored due to unplanned outages;
- Checklists or other materials provided in advance by auditors, etc.

If applicable, work with IT and other departments to provide audit preparation services to ensure that everyone understands their roles in the audit and how to respond to auditors' questions, issues, and concerns. Protecting sensitive information during audits is critical, and documents provided to auditors should be recovered, if possible, shortly before audits are completed. Any and all audit activity, to assess an operational system, should always be managed to minimize any impact on the system during required hours of operation. Any testing of operating systems that could pose an adverse effect on the system should be conducted during off-hours.

When audits are performed on testing or development environments, organizations should be cautious against the following risks: compromise of the integrity of code and loss of confidentiality of sensitive information.

Foreword - About the Book

"ISO/IEC 27001:2022 – Control A Ologies" is a comprehensive resource for organizations seeking to enhance their information security practices. This book provides practical insights into implementing ISO 27001 controls effectively. The book is a valuable companion for anyone involved in information security management. Whether you're a CISO, IT Manager, or Consultant, this book equips you with the knowledge needed to navigate ISO 27001 successfully.

-Nishid Shivdas
Co Founder & Executive Director
ISOQAR India Pvt. Ltd.

Made in United States
Orlando, FL
05 November 2026

90241894R10423